Hoopla:

A Century of College Basketball

by
Peter C. Bjarkman

A Division of Howard W. Sams & Company
A Bell Atlantic Company

Masters Press (A Division of Howard W. Sams & Co.)
2647 Waterfront Parkway, East Drive, Suite 300
Indianapolis, IN 46214

96 97 98 99 00 01   10 9 8 7 6 5 4 3 2 1

Library of Congress Cataloging-in-Publication Data

Bjarkman, Peter C., 1941.
    Hoopla: a century of college basketball / by Peter C. Bjarkman.
        p. cm.
    ISBN: 1-57028-039-8: $19.95
    1. Basketball--United States--History. 2. College Sports--United States--
History.
    I. Title

GV885.7.B53   1995
796.323'63'0973--dc20   95-43174
                                                              CIP

Dedication

Art Quimby

For Art Quimby, Worthy Patterson and Jimmie Ahearn — my first hoops heroes — wherever they may be.

Credits:

Cover design by Phil Velikan

Cover Photos © Brian Spurlock; Photo of author by Ronnie B. Wilbur

Edited by Kim Heusel

Photographic reproduction assistance by Terry Varvel

Text layout by Kim Heusel

Table of Contents

Celebrating America's Game

Basketball is contemporary America's most native and best-loved sport. The popular mythology, of course, does not support such a bold claim. But then there is altogether little surrounding our American spectator sports - in terms of either popular opinions or the historical record — where acknowledged fact stands up very well against fanciful legend.

A popular notion remains intact that baseball is the unchallenged national pastime and thus has primacy of tradition as well as primacy of rooting passions. Even the devastating players' strike of 1994 was insufficient in the eyes of most sports fanatics to knock baseball from its inherited place of preference. And as pure television spectacle, football has reportedly largely taken over as the spectator game of choice during the electronic-video age. Although basketball is usually admitted to be fast gaining ground on its two major rivals, the reigning belief is still that the indoor winter sport stands a distant third in line.

And yet by almost every reasonable measure it is indeed basketball, and not any of its competitors, that holds the most legitimate claim to the current title of America's national pastime. When it comes to stadium (or gymnasium) attendance there is no contest. More people attend live basketball games at the high school, college and professional levels than any other single team sport; and the smaller gymnasiums and arenas in which the cage game is normally played have always resulted in basketball also turning away more potential spectators than any of its sisters. This has unquestionably been the case since the mid-1930s, and the spectator gap has only widened with each subsequent decade. With basketball there are also more players of all ages, more teams, more leagues and conferences, and more informal five-on-five, three-on-three, or one-on-one pickup contests in driveways, schoolyards, playgrounds and school gyms than in all other sports combined.

With the nation's youth, especially, basketball is a clear hands-down winner. This is certainly the case when it comes to national folk heroes and cultural icons adopted wholesale by our MTV-generation American youth. Michael Jordan — with a huge boost from the "global village mentality" of television — has long since replaced Babe Ruth or Joe DiMaggio as the most popular and recognizable sports hero of American history.

It is also basketball heroes who are now our most popular commercial pitchmen as well; the airwaves are crammed with household names from the NBA ranks who endorse soft drinks, athletic shoes, breakfast cereals and all manner of other baubles and trinkets. Any list of the most recognized pro athletes or the best-paid sports-celebrity-endorsers contains seven or eight cage stars in the top 10 (Jordan has remained atop such lists for a decade, while Larry Bird and Magic Johnson have now been supplanted by the likes of Shaquille O'Neal, Grant Hill and David Robinson); baseball and football are fortunate to have even one or two entries on the same list.

Gary Bradds of Ohio State skies for a rebound against West Virginia. A year earlier, the 1964 Player of the Year was an understudy to Jerry Lucas on one of the most memorable title teams in college basketball history. (Naismith Basketball Hall of Fame)

Other measures of basketball's primacy with the American sporting public are not difficult to locate. Start with the annual ritual which is the NCAA college basketball championship tournament. It is today a reasonable argument that March Madness, with its three-week hold on the nation's heartstrings, has outstripped even the World Series and the Super Bowl. From the tensions of "Selection Sunday" through three drama-filled weekends of first- and second-round sudden-death eliminations, regional title matches and Final Four magic, an entire nation of fans is gripped and held captive in a manner impossible with any single-day event like football's Super Bowl or the two-team face-off of baseball's World Series. Schooldays loyalties, regional pride, the diverse pull of 64 different teams and dozens upon dozens of superstar players, the unbearable pressure of a single-loss elimination format — all combine to make the march (as well as the entire March) to the Final Four the most enticing spectacle found anywhere on the American sporting scene.

On the world stage of course there is simply no argument about primacy. Basketball, of the three major American games and perhaps of all the world's ball-throwing or ball-kicking games, reigns supreme. Both Europe and Latin America have adopted the cage sport as second in popularity only to home-grown soccer.

European stars like Detlef Schrempf, Rik Smits, Dino Radja and Drazen Petrovic, plus African-born super athletes like Hakeem Olajuwon, Dikembe Mutombo and Manute Bol, or Caribbean island natives like Patrick Ewing and Mychal Thompson, have today internationalized both the NBA and the American collegiate game in equal measure. American-style basketball grips audiences in Greece, Italy, Spain, the former Yugoslavia and the former Soviet Union, almost to the same degree that it captivates fans throughout Kentuckiana, California's Gold Coast or the North American inner city.

Author Neil Isaacs had already recognized these facts in his excellent (if now dated) history of college basketball (*All the Moves*, Lippincott, 1975) first published more than two full decades ago. For Isaacs, it was only the electronic television media which still seemed to ignore basketball's pre-eminence during the early 1970s. Writing in *All the Moves*, Isaacs would lament that television ratings alone failed to support his own claim for basketball's unrivaled popularity. This was due, Isaacs speculated, to the then-arguable fact that basketball lacked the elaborate spectacle and ritual elements of football and baseball, and also to the less debatable claim that the cage sport with its continuous action and difficult camera angles was simply less conducive to successful TV coverage.

This is also no longer the case, of course. If it is still true that the brief-action-then-pause-for-analysis format of baseball and football seem to work hand and glove with on-air analysis of play-by-play action (complete with commercial breaks which do not seemingly interrupt the flow of game action), it is also true that it is now basketball more than the other two which is altogether in synch with a heightened drama, instantaneous and continuous action, and swirling controlled violence now demanded by youthful MTV-generation viewers. Isaacs indeed has proven quite prophetic with his 1975 speculations about a perfect future synergistic relationship between basketball and the flickering television image, a relationship he believed would blossom once video directors finally learned the proper camera angles and the proper exploitation of the game's essential actions.

What, then, are the bottom-line reasons for this overriding popularity of Dr. James Naismith's simple yet glorious sport of dribbling, passing, shot-blocking and jump shooting? The explanations are of course in the end quite numerous. Foremost in raw appeal for today's audiences is the rapid-fire end-to-end movement of the court game, that frenetic element of nonstop dribbling and passing which is most in tune with a television-bred generation itself oriented toward instant gratification and non-stop stimulation. And basketball is also our most beautiful game to watch in terms of its physical actions, ballet-like poses and airborne athleticism.

It is also the one game in which the intellectual or cerebral elements and the physical elements of play are truly merged as one. Here is a game of split-second mental and physical recognition, response, analysis, invention and creativity. As Isaacs has so deftly phrased it, this game, above all others, is one in which "the smarts are never quite separable from the moves." An Air Jordan solo above the rim or a Julius Erving gravity-defying flight to the hoop, or even a power-packed Shaquille O'Neal or Derrick Coleman bone-crunching and rim-rattling slam dunk; basketball's best "moves" are always two parts artistic instinct and two parts pure muscle-memory.

Basketball heroes also lend themselves more readily to spectator identification (and thus spectator idolization) than do athletes of the other major team sports. A football player is always hidden from our view by impenetrable armor (face-hiding helmet and physique-hiding shoulder pads) and is also usually lost during game action within a sea of distant midfield collisions. The baseball slugger or pitcher stands squarely on center stage during only a small percentage of diamond play. Barry Bonds or Ken Griffey Jr. strides to the plate at most four or five times in an afternoon's play. But Air Jordan and Shaq O'Neal and Grant Hill and David Robinson twirl their magic out in plain view, from end to end of the court, and throughout most of a game's ongoing competition.

A third factor would seem to be basketball's clear-cut urban ethos. Here is the ideal "city game" for an increasingly city-oriented culture. Baseball long drew its popularity from a pastoral myth grounded in the nation's 19th-century rural roots; football thrived in the Vietnam-era '60s when a more heroic myth glorified mock warfare and stressed idealization of committee-driven corporate America. While once ubiquitous baseball diamonds and extensive rural sandlots have disappeared from the national scene, the driveway iron hoop and the schoolyard backboard now become a distinctive part of our increasingly urban and suburban American landscape.

Basketball is also thoroughly urban in its game-pace, spacial arrangements, playing rules (and their enforcement), and black-culture ethos. The cage sport has been frequently and appropriately identified with the extemporized and free-flowing rhythms of the black man's music — blues and jazz. It is played with the largest ball, and yet its actions are confined within the most cramped and crowded physical spaces. In no other sport, in fact, is awareness of spatial boundaries quite so crucial to success. And like the inner city environment itself (the land of towering skyscrapers and elevated working and living spaces), basketball play always expands upward into thin space and not outward (as with baseball or football) toward the sprawling horizon. Baseball is circular in its essential movements around the basepaths; football is starkly horizontal. Basketball — with its shooting, rebounding, leaping and dunking — is strictly vertical.

Here also is the sport whose game officials act as urban traffic cops, arbiters whose primary role is to insure that the flow of action on the court continues largely unimpeded. Basketball referees intervene in this action only to enforce open violations of law (of "the rules") which prohibit violence within crowds or between rival gangs — that is, between the opposing teams.

By contrast, baseball umpires are merely impartial judges (their calls of balls and strikes and "safe" or "out" interpret and thus create reality) and football referees are essentially engineers who function mainly to set each individual play in motion (they also time the action and penalize erratic play). The very language of basketball, by contrast, is itself full of mass-transit metaphors — *moves, walking, traveling, driving,* foul *lanes* — and of urban crime lingo as well — *stealing, picking* a rival's pocket (stealing the ball), *dealing out* or *delivering* passes, and the like. If the inner city thug or drug user often "scores to get high" then the modern basketball hero (with his soaring dunks and leaping jump shots) also "gets high to score" — a not entirely accidental and most perfectly appropriate turn of phrase.

Dr. J, Julius Erving, revolutionized the professional style of play in the 1970s and 1980s. He utilized the same style of airborne game to become one of only a half-dozen college players to average both 20 points and 20 rebounds per game during their collegiate careers. (Frank P. McGrath Jr. photo)

Rick Mount of Purdue was among a legion of '60s-era sharpshooters whose prodigious scoring feats would capture the fancy of droves of collegiate hoops fans. (Purdue University photo)

Even more central to contemporary basketball is its city-based economic structure and its firm roots in the "success ethos" of an urban (and thus essentially black) street culture. The game has evolved — since the '60s at least — as an idealized athletic expression of "urban cool" based upon individual one-on-one "in-the-face" moves, trash-talking challenges and deceptive feints and fakes, and hard-won playground "reputation" which is always a badge of survival. If black stars like Erving, McAdoo, Walt Frazier or Earl Monroe display little outward emotion when they dominate a defensive opponent they are only reflecting the "coolness" and self-confidence which is an expected calling card of inner-city street leadership.

Game action is thus comprised largely of bold individual displays of deception ("fakes" and "feints") and style ("the moves" of the black street game) which have largely supplanted earlier group expressions of team patterns and team harmony (staples of the white man's rural barnyard game). Gone are the slow-moving precision passing attacks, rigid zone defenses and long-range set shooting; popular instead are slam dunks, one-on-one solos, and "shake-and-bake" moves to the hoop. It is this last factor of "urban cool" that accounts for the popularity of formal slam dunk exhibitions and also of one-on-one or three-on-three playground tussles.

A final element contributing to the game's magnetic late-century appeal is the high-scoring nature of the sport. All team ball games are of course based upon outscoring an opponent in a set amount of time (baseball alone eliminates the time restriction). But it is only basketball among major sports in which both teams regularly score more frequently than once a minute. It is the cage game that thus extends both controlling elements of team contests (point scoring and a limiting time-clock framework) to their ultimate extremes. There is not only the pressure of the game clock, which marks quarters and halves, but also that of the shot clock as well, which divides competition into even smaller segments. Here then is not only the most action-packed sport but also the game most sensitive to the pressure of pace, just as it is the inner city that is also our most fast-paced and pressurized living environment. Just as in inner-city life, on the basketball court one must "hustle" and "score" repeatedly to get ahead; points are wealth and time is money to an unrivalled degree when it comes to basketball play.

The inherent pressures of basketball play are therefore as much those of *pace* as of *space*. In baseball it is *suspense* (between outs, between pitches, between batter and pitcher) which provides the game's motivating tension or pressure. In football this is supplied by the *physical force* of hand-to-hand combat. In basketball it is also the game's rapid-fire *pace* which holds our attention: more points are scored more frequently and by fewer players, and in the game of shortest time-clock duration. By this essential measure it is basketball and not low-scoring and long-duration hockey (with its three 20-minute periods) that is the fastest-paced game.

All this explains why true fans of basketball resent the "freeze" or stalling techniques in the same way that baseball partisans find distasteful the role of the designated hitter. "Letting the air out of the ball" protects the wealth of a team in the lead, and always at the expense of the poor (the trailing team). Any such strategy is hardly expected to find popularity within most inner-city environments.

If such artistic symbols and metaphors surrounding all sports are at all compelling, then economic-based parallels and images are always even more so. With its profuse point-a-minute scoring, its larger-than-life made-for-TV athlete-heroes, its cramped and teeming urban settings, its reflections of a brash urban "coolness" in action and its soaring space-age "above-the-rim" movement, Dr. Naismith's century-old game of basketball has now come fully of age as contemporary America's unchallenged spectator game of choice.

Over the past fifteen years or so it has admittedly been the NBA game which seems to hold the greatest sway with an American rooting public. This has been true at least since the dramatic 1979 debut of Larry Bird and Earvin "Magic" Johnson upon the televised NBA stage. And professional basketball's apparent pre-eminence as "America's Game" has only been further enhanced by the colorful career, magical personality, and megamarketing promotional successes of an unparalleled Chicago Bulls star named Michael Jordan.

And yet the college version of the game has steadfastly maintained its own devoted following as well. The postseason NCAA tournament has reached an equal zenith of its own over the past two decades. New college stars emerge with each and every season, and the recent phenomenon of college frontliners like Glenn Robinson and Chris Webber departing for the pro ranks after only two undergraduate seasons has only seemed to increase the rapidity with which new undergraduate sensations like Corliss Williamson (Arkansas), Felipe Lopez (St. John's), Joe Smith (Maryland), Tim Duncan (Wake Forest), and Shawn Respert (Michigan State) annually explode upon the scene. Even the women's Final Four April shootout is now suddenly a year-end prime-time television event.

Before the sudden emergence of the NBA in its fourth decade (the 1980s), however, it was the college hoops game that had held fullest sway for nearly half a century. College basketball's tradition, legacy, history and living legends are as rich as those found in any corner of the American sporting scene.

First came the great coaching paragons who shaped the infant game and its evolving strategies of play. Doc Meanwell at Wisconsin invented set patterns of offensive attack; Ward "Piggy" Lambert of Purdue pioneered a fast-breaking style which eventually thwarted Meanwell's controlled style; CCNY's Nat Holman, Manhattan's Honey Russell, NYU's Howard Cann and disciple Joe Lapchick at St. John's, all pioneered a "city-game" style born of tough-minded defense and deadly set-shooting accuracy. Phog Allen (James Naismith's successor at Kansas) and Adolph "Baron" Rupp (a player under Allen and then a visionary coach at Kentucky) fashioned the first true "dynasty teams" deep in America's heartland, while Duke's Vic Bubas and North Carolina State's Everett Case hammered out the fast-breaking styles that would soon foster roundball fanaticism everywhere along Carolina's Tobacco Road. And many others as well — Clair Bee (LIU), Frank Keaney (Rhode Island), Doc Carlson (Pittsburgh), John Castellani (Seattle), Howie Dallmar (Stanford), Howard Hobson (Oregon and Yale), Hank Iba (Oklahoma A&M), Ken Loeffler (La Salle), Branch McCracken (Indiana), Bones McKinney (Wake Forest), Pete Newell and Phil Woolpert (both at San Francisco) — all of whom shaped the game, nurtured it and even drastically reinvented it along the way.

Yet college basketball took its largest leaps forward on the national stage only when East Coast entrepreneurial promoters first entered the scene. Two developments of the 1930s would combine to hike a fast-growing sport to truly national dimensions. The first was a brainchild of two budding New York sportswriters, Dan Daniel and Ned Irish, the latter a Penn grad who witnessed firsthand the early successes of inter-city college games in Philadelphia's recently opened Palestra in the late '20s. Together Daniel and Irish organized basketball doubleheaders and even tripleheaders as prime attractions in New York City's own new showcase arena, Madison Square Garden. (Madison Square Garden III had opened its doors in 1925.) The phenomenon was launched in the dark shadows of the 1929 stock market crash when Daniel (at the urging of Mayor Jimmy Walker) staged a January 1931 extravaganza featuring the nation's best team, the St. John's University "Wonder Five" alongside local teams from Columbia, Manhattan, New York University, Fordham and City College of New York.

St. John's extended its record unbeaten streak to 22 games that night, but it was the fans and city that proved the big winners. Better than 16,000 turned out for an event which raised thousands of dollars for Mayor Walker's Unemployment Relief Fund and at the same time served to launch the cage sport's modern era of marquee

Small college gyms have often hosted budding cage legends. Here Bob McAdoo of Vincennes Junior College in Indiana displays the leaping abilities that would later make him a major college (North Carolina) and NBA phenomenon. (Frank P. McGrath Jr. photo)

attractions. In December 1934 Ned Irish would place New York City basketball as well as the college game even more squarely on the map with the first major double-header to match intersectional rivals — St. John's versus Westminster (Pennsylvania) and NYU versus Notre Dame.

A second landmark of the '30s was this mid-decade debut of intersectional contests which also constituted the first true interregional rivalries. No single game was more crucial to this latter development than the December 30, 1936, clash between Clair Bee's Eastern powerhouse LIU, with its 43-game winning streak, and West Coast front-runner Stanford, with its poster boy one-hand shooting star Hank Luisetti. Stanford stormed out of Madison Square Garden with a surprise 45-31 victory before 18,000, a win which legitimized not only Luisetti's flashy one-handed shooting style but all of West Coast basketball to boot. One immediate outgrowth of these two pioneering developments — Madison Square Garden doubleheaders and attractive intersectional competitions — were the year-end festivals soon known as the National Invitation Tournament (NIT) and National Collegiate Athletic Association Tourney (NCAA) which were simultaneously born at the tail end of the '30s.

Such sudden growth soon predictably led to new pressures and even proved to contain the seeds of hidden disaster. Before the next decade was out the immensely popular collegiate game would be rent asunder by its first taste of foul-smelling scandal. Just as baseball's showcase World Series had fallen prey to the manipulations of gamblers and game-fixers 30 years earlier, widespread betting in the postwar era would nearly scuttle the hoops game as well. A nation of sports enthusiasts was shocked in the early weeks of 1951 when news broke that star players for national champion CCNY (winner of both the NIT and NCAA playdowns during the spring of 1950) had been guilty of fixing games for underhanded cash payments.

The ink was hardly dry on the CCNY story when the exploding scandal spread to players from most of the other New York City colleges as well, and also to Rupp's powerhouse Kentucky team and Everett Case's North Carolina State ballclub which ruled the Deep South. The widening scandal effectively ruined Madison Square Garden attractions, undercut the long-standing center stage role of New York City basketball, and sabotaged budding pro careers for potential stars like Kentucky's Alex Groza, Columbia's Jack Molinas, CCNY's Ed Warner and LIU's Sherm White. In all, 32 players and seven schools were directly implicated, and the fallout even claimed coaching legend Clair Bee (the very same Bee who penned the popular "Chip Hilton" sports novels), who ended his 21-year college career (with a 412-87 record) once scandal-plagued LIU decided to drop the roundball sport. Thus college basketball and basketball as a whole almost didn't survive past the end of its fifth decade.

In the '50s and '60s the college game would be miraculously reborn from the near death knell of these horrendous scandals, and salvation would be provided by a colorful contingent of larger-than-life jump-shooting heroes whose incredible scoring feats overnight propped up the game in the same way that Babe Ruth's home run exploits had salvaged baseball from a similar tint of scandal. Dick Groat (Duke), the O'Brien twins (Johnny and Eddie at Seattle), Bevo Francis (Rio Grande of Ohio), Frank Selvy (Furman), Wilt Chamberlain (Kansas), Jerry West (West Virginia), and Oscar "The Big O" Robertson (Cincinnati) would all author scoring feats that stretched the imaginations of fans as well as the outer borders of basketball popularity. Bevo Francis of tiny Rio Grande (pronounced "Rye-O Grand") and Frank Selvy at Furman would perform the near-impossible by each tossing in more than 100 points in a single game, a feat which has never since been duplicated in major college play. Selvy would also become the nation's first 40-points-per-game man and by decade's end Robertson and West would elevate prolific long-range shooting to an unrivaled art form.

The Golden Era of Naismith's game, however, may well have been the decade-plus stretch which witnessed the birth and life span of one of the most remarkable dynasties in all of American sporting history. The late '60s and early '70s were years which belonged almost exclusively to Westwood Wizard John Wooden and the remarkable winning program he fashioned as head coach of the UCLA Bruins. Wooden's streak of seven straight NCAA championships and 10 national titles in 12 years is indisputably the greatest such unblemished string in sports history. Neither the Casey Stengel New York Yankees in baseball nor the Red Auerbach Boston Celtics in pro basketball can reasonably compare. And out of this same dozen-year era also arose some of the game's greatest individual legends — Wooden's own two dominating centers, Lew Alcindor (the choice of many as college basketball's greatest player ever) and Bill Walton; Princeton's phenomenal Bill Bradley; Pete Maravich and Calvin Murphy, the greatest all-around scorer and greatest pure shooter, respectively, that basketball has ever known.

College basketball has grown and prospered as never before since the close of the UCLA dynasty years. Competition has sharpened to such a level that nearly two decades would pass before another back-to-back champion would emerge in NCAA tournament play. The era of the great college conferences has reached full flower as well during the past two decades with teams from the ACC, Big Ten, Southeastern Conference and Big Eight dominating top 20 rankings and postseason NCAA selections on an annual basis. The NCAA Tournament has gained full eminence as the annual showpiece of the college sport. Even the subsequent explosion of NBA popularity has only thrust new emphasis on the college sport — now as an inexhaustible talent font and glamorous "minor-league" farm system for development of future professional stars. And yet at the same time, the college game has continued to be anything but "minor-league" in stature.

New stars and new memorable championship teams have emerged with nearly every new season. While there have been no true dynasties emerging in the shadows of Wooden's Bruins, nonetheless there have been some most memorable outfits, like Michigan's Fab Five all-freshman lineup in 1992, the 1975-76 Indiana teams of Bob Knight that fell a mere game and a single injury short of UCLA-like back-to-back undefeated campaigns, and near-dynasty Duke teams under coach Mike Krzyzewski that closed out the '80s and launched the '90s with five straight NCAA Final Four visits. And there are also the perennial powerhouses — Duke, North Carolina, Indiana, Kentucky, Georgetown, Kansas — as well as the year-in and year-out list of endless Cinderellas (Jim Valvano's North Carolina State Wolfpack in 1983, Villanova in 1985, the resurgent 1992 Cincinnati Bearcats and the miracle 1995 UCLA Bruins) that spice annual post-season play.

The past two decades have also brought new coaching legends to erase the elongated shadows of the legendary John Wooden and the mythical Adolph Rupp. There is Bobby Knight at Indiana who now owns three national titles and a spot high on the all-time victory list which can nevertheless barely dim his reputation for outrageous and sometimes distasteful behavior. There is Dean Smith at North Carolina (second only to Rupp in career victories with 830), who has often been accused of failing to "win it all" at the Big Dance and yet whose 35-year program has been arguably the most consistently excellent since the departure of John Wooden from the championship scene. There is "Coach K" at Duke who has somehow found a magic ticket straight into Final Four competition. And there are others of only slightly lesser reputation — Purdue's Gene Keady, Kentucky's Rick Pitino, Arizona's Lute Olsen, Roy Williams of Kansas, Texas-El Paso's Don Haskins, Louisville's Denny Crum and a host of others almost too numerous to detail.

With the 1995-96 season, college basketball celebrates an unofficial close to its first complete century of spirited competitions. Unlike baseball, with its outrageous Doubleday-Cooperstown myth, or football, with its lengthy heritage of European leather ball games, basketball is the one sport able to pinpoint its origin at a single moment of time — in Springfield, Massachusetts, in the winter of 1891. Some debate does, however, surround the issue of what should be recognized as the first true collegiate contest and there are actually several legitimate candidates for the honor. Should we settle perhaps on the informal February 9, 1895, contest between Hamline College and the Minnesota State School of Agriculture, or perhaps on the March 23, 1895, match between Haverford and Temple? Or is a better choice the first contest known to employ five-man squads — a January 16, 1896, affair between the University of Chicago and an Iowa City YMCA squad which was made up exclusively of University of Iowa athletes?

Some careful historians would contend that the former two contests, both played with nine-man squads (the number also used in Naismith's very first game at the Springfield YMCA), were not yet basketball in its true modern format; the latter Chicago-Iowa game is often also dismissed as the actual landmark contest since the Iowa club was not truly a sanctioned university team. For these more precise chroniclers of the sport the true birthright falls perhaps upon the March 20, 1897, exhibition in which Yale drubbed Penn 32-10 in a game featuring five-man teams wearing legitimate school colors. Whatever the choice, the fact remains that the cage sport has now completed a full century since the first scholar-athletes faced off in pioneering primitive attempts at intercollegiate competition.

The true birth of the sport unquestionably lies somewhere in the 1895, 1896 or 1897 winter months. It was indeed a dizzyingly rapid evolution from that point forward. Iron rims with chord nets replaced peach baskets in 1893, soccer balls gave way to larger specially designed rubber spheres in 1894, backboards were first introduced in 1895 (to keep balcony spectators from interfering with tosses at the hoop), the Yale College team began employing the "dribble" as an offensive strategy in 1896, five-man teams were settled upon as the standard by 1897, and male and female college squads competed quite regularly everywhere in the country by the end of the decade.

The color and excitement of college basketball are captured fully in this 1966 action as Billy Keller of Purdue drives through traffic to the basket in a game against the University of Washington. (Purdue University photo)

All that seemed lacking during this first decade of runaway popularity for the new winter sport was a formalized organizational structure governing intercollegiate competition. The first colleges to form both men's teams and women's teams played mostly against local YMCA squads, informal club teams or touring professional outfits. The three pioneering college leagues that had organized around the turn of the century for football competition — the Western Conference (later dubbed the Big Ten), the Intercollegiate League (forerunner of the Ivy League) and the New England League (Amherst, Holy Cross, Williams, Dartmouth and Trinity College) — did not pursue formalized basketball play until around 1905. It is thus the later date, then, which might best serve as a true jumping off point for a formalized history of college basketball play.

Whatever the agreed-upon origins, once launched, college basketball gripped an entire nation by firestorm. While professional leagues would not thrive until the post-World War II "boom era" for spectator sports, colleges were already building huge field houses to accommodate cage fans before the end of the first World War; drastic rules changes and coaching innovations such as zone defenses and fast-break offenses sped up and enlivened the spectacle during the 1920s; the decade of the 1930s brought sold-out intersectional doubleheaders in New York's Madison Square Garden as well as the cage sport's first glamorous national hero in Stanford's Hank Luisetti; with the war-era 1940s came the first big men (á la George Mikan and Bob Kurland) as well as the popular year-end national championship tournaments (NIT and NCAA) which more than any other single innovation inflamed basketball passions everywhere across the nation. As the full century slowly unfolded, college basketball grew by leaps and bounds and embellished into its present position as a favored — perhaps even *the favored* — American sporting pastime.

In the pages which follow, college basketball's glorious history is concisely and colorfully recounted in all its most glorious detail. These chapters will explore the hidden corners as well as the front-page headlines that have embellished the game for 10 full decades. Familiar on-court and sideline heroes like Bill Russell, Wilt Chamberlain, Oscar Robertson, Jerry Lucas, Adolph Rupp, Dean Smith, Bobby Knight, Magic Johnson and Larry Bird here reenact their fleeting moments of most memorable victory and most numbing defeat. The great power teams of Kentucky, CCNY, La Salle, San Francisco, Duke, North Carolina, Indiana, Ohio State and UCLA are celebrated and analyzed. Lesser-known but equally vital figures like Clarence "Bevo" Francis, Tom Gola, Frank Selvy, Walter "Doc" Meanwell, Carol Blazejowski, George Mikan and Bob Kurland are also lionized for their landmark contributions to the sport's meteoric rise to pre-eminence.

The reader will uncover in these chapters precisely why it is that the college edition of Dr. Naismith's beloved game has never for a moment had to relinquish pride of place to its professional competitor. Here are the immortal cage heroes of yesteryear, legendary scorers and magical ball handlers, ground-breaking promoters and strategy-shaping coaches, landmark rules changes and evolutions in playing style, unforgettable on-court events, dramatic championship showdowns — all that has made up the colorful history of the remarkable and engaging game of college basketball. Here is page upon page of evidence for precisely why it is that basketball — especially college basketball — today remains the most exhilarating and breathtakingly beautiful of all our major sports.

1

Opening Decades

The Era of Dr. Naismith's Peach Baskets

"Naismith's game is nothing more than the silly business of throwing an inflated bag through a hoop."
— Dan Parker, New York Sportswriter

Unlike baseball's mythic past, basketball's birthright is largely a matter of public record. Certainly the exact place, time and circumstances of the game's "immaculate conception" can be fixed with absolute assurance. There are no competing legends here anything like the Cooperstown, Hoboken or Ontario "creation myths" which confuse the issue of baseball's true parentage. In fact, there are few if any corners of the story about basketball's sudden appearance where myth and legend of any kind have squeezed out the more reliable (and more desirable) factual accounts.

The bare facts surrounding basketball's miraculous and indeed spontaneous birth — and its even more miraculous early growth — have often been told, and even told in great and loving detail. Still these facts are not part of the public's shared knowledge, as is the fuzzier and largely fictionalized early history of baseball's emergence. One irony here is that baseball as an institution has long fostered a "creation myth" account of its origins when there was none — Abner Doubleday did not invent the game on the spur of the moment in a pasture outside of Cooperstown. Indeed, no one "invented" baseball at any give moment; the sport evolved over many decades, in many competing versions, and from a variety of popular primitive European bat and ball games. It is basketball's roots, by contrast, that are far more consistent with the notion of a creation myth. James Naismith did indeed dream up the game on the spur of the moment and then try it out in a basement gym inside of Springfield, Massachusetts. Or at least it was nearly that way.

America has an ongoing love affair with creation myths, especially when it comes to accounting for our popular institutions drawn from the world of sports or entertainment or politics. Evolutionist Stephen Jay Gould has eloquently and often described this preference for creation stories over the facts of evolutionary history. As Gould tells us, all stories about beginnings come in but two basic forms — one that claims an explicit point of origin and a fixed time and place for creation, and one that suggests that an object, event or phenomenon has no definable point of entry

1

into the world. It seems that Americans in particular — and humans in general — in Gould's words "seem to prefer the alternative model of origin by a moment of creation — for then we can have heroes and sacred places." It appears that heroes and sacred places are a basic requirement for our psychic survival as a nation.

Baseball thus had to invent Doubleday and Cooperstown to meet such a need in explaining the enduring grip of the nation's earliest "national pastime." The game which now seems poised to supplant baseball as the nation's top passion is faced with no such dilemma, however. The details of Naismith's miraculous invention of the game in Springfield are a well-worn corner of American sports history. The story has been told many times and the facts are quite consistent in most of the tellings. Two things are rather remarkable, of course, about the story of Naismith's invention. Foremost and perhaps in true American spirit, here was a game which sprang up overnight to meet only the

Canadian Dr. James Naismith laid down 13 rules for the game of basketball in December 1891, and some of those original rules still form the basis for the modern game a full century later. (Naismith Basketball Hall of Fame photo)

most pragmatic of needs. And secondly, the game as Naismith envisioned it and then shaped it was almost nothing like the game we know today, except in the barest of essentials — those of shooting a ball through an elevated hoop.

Jim Naismith had enrolled at the International YMCA Training School (later Springfield College) as a student early in 1891 after a varied religious and athletic training at McGill University in his native Canada. His goal was to combine dual interests in religious education and sport (he was a talented rugby player and dabbled in American-style football, even later inventing the football helmet) by becoming an instructor in the American YMCA system.

By fall he had completed an initial course of study and had signed on under Dr. Luther Gulick as an instructor in the school's physical education department. Gulick was at the time facing a considerable administrative challenge involving his own curriculum: students had for some time been rebelling against a winter semester regimen of repeated marching, gymnastics and calisthenics. What could be done to entertain and at the same time educate the uncooperative classes during the indoor months between fall football matches and springtime baseball play? In one of the truly fortuitous moments of sports history Gulick next recalled an idle boast by one of his charges (Naismith) earlier that year that a new sport could indeed be invented for such purposes. The frustrated physical education director quickly turned to his former student with the assignment, and destiny and Jim Naismith were about to collide.

Young Naismith from all reports accepted his assignment with enthusiasm and good spirit, although he would soon meet some setbacks along the way. The first few weeks of December were filled with a half-dozen failed experiments: he would later report that "drop the handkerchief" had no appeal for the young men in the class and efforts at indoor rugby, soccer and lacrosse provided the expected disasters of broken windows and bruised knees. Naismith knew after those ill-fated attempts that his game (which he thought could best be derived by combining elements of existing sports) must have at least three requirements: interest would require a ball, since all successful team games were ball games; violence and injury could only be prevented if there was no running or tackling allowed and therefore the game would have to progress by passing the ball and not by kicking or carrying it; emphasis should be on skill and not size or brute strength and therefore a goal as target for the ball would be best placed above the players heads, so that shooters would have to loop the ball and not fire it at point-blank range.

Once the basic principles were settled on there was only the remaining need for some method of putting the ball into play. This would come with the ingenious concept of the center jump in which the referee tossed the ball between only two players (and not entire teams as with more violent rugby scrimmages). The final set of deliberations resulted in a list of 13 rules that were neatly typed and posted on the wall of the school's basement gym on December 21, 1891. Once a loose soccer ball and a set of peach baskets had been obtained (the building janitor supplied the later when he couldn't come up with the square 18-inch boxes Naismith requested) the first experimental game was held. Baskets were nailed to the 10-foot-high balconies at both ends (thus this seemingly perfect height was another mere accident) and the 18-man class was divided into two competing teams. Less than a month later the same set of rules was published in the school newspaper and thus spread to Y's throughout the United States, Canada and beyond.

What Naismith had invented was of course a game that did not look much at all like the contest of constant movement and athleticism which we enjoy and celebrate a full century later. The true nature of Naismith's game is nonetheless found crystallized within his original rules. Add to these a few early innovations that befell the sport almost immediately — dribbling, smaller teams and foul shots — and we have a fair notion of what the early game was like.

Naismith's Original 13 Rules for Basketball

Naismith's original rules were printed in the Springfield YMCA School for Christian Workers newspaper (*The Triangle*) on January 15, 1892. Rules (or parts of rules) appearing here in boldface are those still largely or wholly in effect today. Wording has been condensed and modernized where appropriate.

1) **The ball may be thrown in any direction with one or both hands.**

2) **The ball may be batted in any direction with one or both hands, but never with the fist.**

3) **A player can not run with the ball but must throw it from the spot where he catches it.** Allowance is made for a man who catches the ball when running at a good speed.

4) The ball must be held in or between the hands; the arms or the body must not be used for holding the ball.

5) **No shouldering, holding, pushing, tripping or striking of an opponent shall be allowed.** The first infringement of this rule by any person shall count as a foul, the second shall disqualify him until the next goal is made. If there is evident intent to injure an opponent to put him out of the game, no substitute shall be allowed for the disqualified player.

6) A foul is striking at the ball with the fist, violations of Rules 3 and 4, and such violations as are described in Rule 5.

7) If either side makes three consecutive fouls, this shall count as a goal for the opponents. Consecutive means without the opponents in the meantime making a foul.

8) **A goal shall be made when the ball is thrown or batted from the ground into the basket and stays there, providing those defending the goal do not touch or disturb the goal.** If the ball rests on the edge and the opponent moves the basket, it shall count as a goal.

9) When the ball goes out of bounds, it shall be thrown into the field (onto the court) and played by the person first touching it. In case of a dispute, the umpire shall throw it straight into the field (court). **The thrower-in is allowed five seconds. If he holds it longer, it shall go to the opponent. If any side persists in delaying the game, the umpire shall call a foul on them.**

10) **The umpire shall be the judge of the men and shall note the fouls** and notify the referee when three consecutive fouls are made. He has power to disqualify men according to Rule 5.

11) **The referee shall be the judge of the ball and shall decide when the ball is in play, in bounds, to which side it belongs, and shall keep the time. He shall decide when a goal has been made, and keep account of the goals, with any other duties that are usually performed by a referee.**

12) The time shall be two 15-minute halves, with five minutes rest time between.

13) **The side making the most goals in that time shall be declared the winners.** In case of a draw, the game may, by agreement of the captains, be continued until another goal is made.

It was from these few rules that the game would rapidly evolve through a couple of winters of play and early experimentation. From the first months that the game was played the emphasis was clearly on experimentation and almost constant change. It would be an orientation, of course, that would remain basketball's defining element down through its history. The number of players was the first feature to be modified; Naismith's notion of as many as possible participating for recreational benefit simply was not practical given the tiny indoor facilities that the winter game was forced to accept. In 1893 five-man (or woman) teams were recommended for small gyms but nine preferred for league action; a year later the number was set at five, seven or nine depending on the floor available; by 1897 printed rules required five men without exception. The invention of backboards was a happy accident of the 1895 season when they were first deemed necessary to prevent crowd interference (from balconies) with shots at the basket. Backboards to a degree also worked against Naismith's original intentions for the horizontal goal, but they nonetheless added a new dimension of skill to the game. Since the early wire versions didn't allow for consistent caroms, wood was quickly substituted.

It was the addition of backboards that more than anything changed the original Naismith conception of the game after 1895. Shooting now became far more a practiced art rather than a rare hit-and-miss affair and specialization entered the sport. And along with new backboards there was within the first decade or two a rapid movement to open baskets with nets, balls made specially for the game (soccer balls had first been used) and the unique notion of "dribbling" the ball.

Perhaps the most interesting series of early refinements in the game were those that had to do with the ongoing debate over the status of dribbling. The strategy had entered the game almost immediately as part and parcel of efforts during the first few winters of play to relax Naismith's original strictures against running with the ball (Rule 3). Pivoting (moving one foot) was first ruled not to be a traveling violation but soon it was discovered that action picked up if a man with the ball being tightly guarded could be allowed to escape by tossing the ball into the air and recapturing it (the "air dribble"). Yale's team reportedly expanded the strategy as a serious weapon by also bouncing the sphere while moving toward the goal. Such methods of escaping the defense seemed to many to be a vast improvement, yet soon the early basketball establishment was radically divided over both the advisability and appropriateness of dribbling the ball. Several new dribbling legislations would go in and out of favor during the next several decades (one of them being that the dribbler could not also shoot the ball).

So heated was this battle that the National Association of Basketball Coaches was finally created specifically to protect the sport against the encroachments of the anti-dribbling forces. There is a most delightful story surrounding the meeting of coaches to resolve the dribbling issue one last time in the late '20s. Wisconsin's Doc Meanwell had led a final onslaught by conservatives in 1929 to kill the dribble by limiting players to a single legal bounce. Meanwell, who believed that the pro-style game of continuous passing made dribbles unnecessary and even unaesthetic, would present one side to the annual NABC meeting and receive a 9-8 vote in his favor. The coaches' group then adjourned to watch a pro game featuring Cleveland's Rosenblums and the Original Celtics, a match which seemed to argue for Meanwell's version of a game that might be played with passing and shooting alone. Then Nat Holman, who was already coaching the CCNY team while still himself playing for these same Celtics, asked for a reconvening of the group. In an impassioned speech he pointed out that college youngsters were not prepared to play like pros and needed the dribble as a strategy. The vote was retaken and this time the forces loyal to Holman and the other dribble supporters finally held sway.

What was truly remarkable was the speed with which the new game spread. Even the missionary zeal of the YMCA trainees as they took to their new posts throughout the country and lugged the invention with them can hardly account for such wildfire acceptance. But unlike baseball the venue for competition would not be in the form of immediate pro leagues. There were early barnstorming professionals to be sure, once local clubs found that admissions were needed to cover the cost of renting dance halls for their exhibitions (there were few if any gyms as we now know them since these were a later product of the game itself). But from the outset the game was largely a school game and a collegiate game, and it remained so right up until the end of World War II.

From the outset the new recreational sport proved especially popular on the nation's college campuses, and within a year or two of Naismith's experiment in Springfield college students had taken up the game from coast to coast. The spread was chaotic but it was also rapid and highly contagious. The nine trainees who gathered for Naismith's first experimental game might qualify as well as any others for the title of "first college team." Naismith had his nine-man club on the road for educational exhibitions of the sport in 1892 and they played what could be considered the first "public game" against their own instructors (including Naismith, Gulick and Stagg) on March 11 of that same year. The winter of 1892-93 also saw college teams spring up at Geneva College (Pennsylvania), Yale, the University of Toronto (making the game already international) and Vanderbilt. There is little record, however, of what games, if any, these loose-knit clubs played against outside competition. What then qualifies as the first formal collegiate game? Here the matter is more murky. And here evolution rather than spontaneous and instant creation seems to take over.

The first few winters witnessed informal play that was still oriented toward exercise and recreation, as Naismith originally had envisioned. But it was not long before the idea of friendly intercollegiate competitions took furtive hold. What is not so clear from the maze of sketchy printed reports and surviving anecdotal records is quite where the true honor belongs for the very first contests between competing college fives.

There are actually several legitimate contenders for what might be today honored as the very first among legitimate college games. (As evolutionist Gould has deftly pointed out, our overwhelming and deep-seated desire for cultural heroes and sacred places — especially in our sports and other cultural institutions — fuels our endemic American need to uncover such moments of spontaneous creation.) Each candidate boasts solid arguments for recognition and at the same time each seems also to own a feature or two that would convince many to set it aside as a mere historical curiosity and not the sought-after landmark event at all. Perhaps the most reasonable choice is the January 16, 1896, game matching students from the universities of Iowa and Chicago. Alonzo Stagg had come to Chicago from Springfield College in 1893 as the Midwest school's first athletic director and had immediately set up a varsity team which for more than two years had nothing better to do than play the new game amongst themselves. Their first game against outside competition was played in Iowa City and Stagg's Chicago team prevailed 15-12, but in true

Naismith's original conception of basketball assumed players less than six feet tall who would pass with accuracy and shoot at a goal well above their heads. One modern-era college player Naismith might have most admired would have been Niagara's uncanny 5-9 sharpshooter Calvin Murphy. (Niagara University photo)

Naismith spirit the contingent of Iowa athletes (all enrolled at the state university in that city) were official representatives of the Iowa City YMCA and not of the university at all. This was likely the first five-on-five contest — even the true beginnings of five-man basketball — but likely should be dismissed as representing a true "intercollegiate" competition.

The Chicago-Iowa contest may indeed not have been the pioneer at all when it comes to five-man contests, as another match on April 26, 1893, featured a combined team representing the Iowa City Y and Iowa University (organized by Naismith disciple Henry Kallenberg) defeating the Cedar Rapids Y 12-2 during another reported five-man game. This, of course, was clearly not a college competition and details of this game also remain somewhat less well-documented than the one between Kallenberg's and Stagg's teams almost three years later.

There were other slightly earlier if not as justified competitors for the honor of primacy. At Hamline University in St. Paul, Minnesota, another 1891-92 Naismith colleague from Springfield named Ray Kaighn (a player in the historic original game in Springfield) had also set up a team in 1893 and even played a game against opponents from the Minneapolis Y in the basement of a science building where the ceilings were only nine feet high. What was likely an odd-appearing contest at best ended in a 13-12 victory for the YMCA club. Then Hamline took the floor again on February 9, 1895 (eleven months before the Iowa-Chicago match) in a match that holds perhaps the strongest claim as the first between two full-fledged college teams. Hamline again lost, to the Minnesota State School of Agriculture, this time by a 9-3 count. (It is not recorded what the height of the baskets might have been in this second match but the lower score suggests higher rims.) The Hamline game loses some of its status for historians simply because it was a nine-to-a-side game and not five-man basketball as we would soon know it. In another such oversized early competition recorded on March 23, 1895, Haverford (Pennsylvania) defeated Temple, 6-4. The Temple team had also been organized by a former Naismith student, Charles Williams.

Another qualifier for the sought-after "first game" distinction might even be found on the women's side of the ledger. There is much evidence, indeed, that the game was equally popular in the earliest years with the female players and numerous teams were overnight established on campuses of women's colleges. Within 12 months of the game's invention in Springfield a Lithuanian-born physical education instructor named Sendra Berenson was recasting Naismith's original rules to fit with Victorian attitudes about needs for gentler competitions among women. Berenson organized games among the coeds at nearby Smith College while neighboring Mount Holyoke College was also holding women's contests with 11-a-side that same winter. And there are at least one or two qualifiers for "first college game" on the distaff side that can be pinpointed during the first three winters — women's teams from Stanford and California universities reputedly met sometime in 1896, as did clubs representing Smith and Vassar colleges. One existing hand-drawn illustration of the Stanford-Cal match suggests that the number of players on each team may have well surpassed a dozen or more.

There were still other early noteworthy pioneering contests in the first five-plus years of the game's existence. It is a March 1897 game between Yale and Penn, for example, that in the end owns perhaps the strongest claim on the honor of launching the college side of competition more or less in the form we know today. Yale won this five-man contest handily, 32-10, over the school that would come to dominate Eastern play once the Ivy League was tacked together. But the Eli of Yale had even stronger claims than this single game for their prominence as a most significant pioneer of the college sport: Yale teams of the first decade popularized the five-man team game and they did so by also initiating intersectional play with a primitive road trip consisting of a Western tour held in the turn-of-the-century year of 1899-1900. That Christmas season the eight-man Yale squad billed its westward junket as "the longest trip ever taken by a United States college team" but the trip turned out to be more hype than headlines. There were a couple of victories on the way out to Chicago and back but several games were also canceled, and there were three embarrassing losses in last-minute makeshift games against the non-college Company E team in Fond du Lac, Wisconsin. But most lasting in its effect, to be sure, was Yale's early experimentation with a new method of offensive attack know as the dribble.

Yet despite the earliest intercollegiate games in 1895, 1896 and 1897, college teams where they existed continued for the first decade and more to play YMCA clubs and touring semipro outfits far more frequently than they played each other. It is only in 1905 with the first organized attempts at conference play — with the coalescence of the New England League (Amherst, Holy Cross, Williams, Dartmouth and Trinity) and the Intercollegiate League (soon the Eastern League) in 1901-1902 and the Western Conference four years later — that the true history of college basketball substantially begins.

Early play within New England arose from the development of a league involving college teams that would eventually be known as the Ivy League but was first called the Intercollegiate League and then the Eastern League. The founding members were Yale, Harvard, Princeton, Columbia and Cornell. Pennsylvania joined up in 1904 and Dartmouth College in 1912. It would not be a perfectly stable venture, however, and there would be some early seasons (1909, 1910) with only informal competition. Yale and Harvard had opened in the New England League in 1901 but abandoned that affiliation for the future Ivy group the following winter. Harvard would drop its conference affiliation in 1909 but resume competition in the circuit after 1934.

The Midwestern part of the country did not lag far behind and within a few seasons of the birth of the Ivy-Eastern League a new western affiliation was also taking up the game in earnest. The Western Conference had been formed for football competitions back in 1895 and now the future "Big Ten" also took up basketball play in 1905 with the seven gridiron schools (Minnesota, the first year's winner, plus Wisconsin, Indiana, Chicago, Illinois, Purdue and Iowa) competing in the first winter's round robin cage play. And the result of these new "conferences" was that there were soon timid boasts and claims of individual teams for national championship status. There would be several seasons when intersectional games between some of the nation's best teams did allow at least a tentative cry for No. 1. Columbia, for one, made such a boast in 1905 after beating both Wisconsin and Minnesota when they came East to challenge the Lions; the two Western League clubs had both in turn beaten league rival Chicago, and this formed the basis for Columbia's claim. There was even one attempt at an "official" postseason playoff for "No. 1" between the Western ("Big Ten") and Eastern ("Ivy") Leagues. And another by-product of these exciting but limited hookups of teams from different parts of the country was that regional playing styles could now be put on center stage and evaluated. And while such games were showcasing regional differences they also did much to level out even the most obvious features of regionalism. The game was already entering its great melting pot era.

It would be the Western Conference that would soon prove to be home to the game's greatest early innovators. First there were Pat Page (the pioneer of guard play) and John Schommer (the first prototype center) at Chicago, leading one of the early great teams to a string of conference titles and then continued to influence the game's development long after their playing days had ended. Page distinguished himself in undergraduate days as a stellar defender and accurate left-handed shooter on the hardwood and a versatile defensive end and southpaw passer for Alonzo Stagg's football club. Despite player-of-the-year recognition in 1910, however, Page would make his biggest mark with a highly successful three-decade coaching career which started at his alma mater and later took him to Butler, Indiana and the College of Idaho. Schommer (a football star as well) would also stay on as the Maroons'

James Naismith could hardly have imagined the high-flying and graceful athletes of modern basketball such as 1960s Syracuse star Dave Bing (22). (Syracuse University photo)

coach for a single season after his playing days and then enter a prominent non-basketball career as a college chemistry professor. But he was never far from the game (for years he coached and served as athletic director at the Illinois Institute of Technology) and would earn a special place with his design of the modern-style backboard. In the immediate aftermath of these Chicago innovators of the 1900s there would also be Meanwell at Wisconsin in the Teens and '20s and then Lambert at Purdue in the '20s and '30s — two titans whose influences on playing styles would quickly reach far and wide beyond their Midwest stronghold. As a whole the Western Conference (it truly became "The Big Ten" after Ohio State's entry in fall 1917) would set the early standard for consistency and uninterrupted league play and today remains the oldest conference as well as perhaps the most influential.

Solidification of conference play (and therefore of regional characteristics) was one of the two foremost — even crucial — innovations that thus came to the emerging sport in the two decades after 1905. By the First World War the Big Ten in the West and Ivy Leaguers in the East were providing the excitement and the headlines

10

and most of the star players. As the popularity of the game grew and spread, new leagues continued to spring up elsewhere. The Southern Intercollegiate Athletic Association was formed with Auburn (the first champion), Howard College (District of Columbia), Mercer College (Georgia), Tulane, Vanderbilt, Georgia and Georgia Tech. The Pacific Coast Conference debuted in 1916 and included California, Oregon, Oregon State and Washington in its first lineup. But many of the colleges that now had teams were still not affiliated with conferences and many thus played against non-college teams for the bulk of their annual dozen or more games.

A second important innovation was the recognition of the significance of professional coaching. For it is basketball with its complexities of team play, of course, in which the entire sport is most obviously dependent on the role of the mastermind coach. Early teams had perhaps a playing captain, or a non-playing former captain from the previous year's squad, who signalled substitutions and shouted encouragements but did little else to regulate the rough and disorganized flow of oncourt action. It was only the appearance of "scientific" coaches who figured out offensive and defensive schemes and instituted designed methods of attacking the defense and the basket (or stopping such attacks) that ultimately brought the first signs of discipline to an otherwise truly chaotic event. Soon enough, styles and systems of play were being labelled not by the college or region in which they originated, but instead by the coach who pioneered and perfected them.

One early pioneer in the concept of a super team matched with a coaching genius was the University of Chicago squad which merits top ranking as the dominant team of the opening two decades. Chicago was among the first programs to employ a coach who received a salary for his services. Dr. Joseph Raycroft earned his small stipend for the Western Conference school by abandoning altogether the prevailing concept of three moving players teamed with a basket defender at one end of the court and a basket-hanger at the other; Raycroft instead molded a five-man moving offense that exploited the contrasting talents of a mobile big man in Schommer and a quick mobile guard in Page. Chicago under the tutelage of Raycroft and Wisconsin guided by former player Emmett Angell were thus the early bullies of the Western Conference and tied for league honors in both 1907 and 1908. But Raycroft's team was the true pride of the Midwest during this stretch and between 1900 and 1909 the Maroons would boast an overall 78-12 record that left little doubt of their year-in and year-out dominance. The 6-3 Schommer (a true giant in his day) paced the Western League in scoring three straight years (after Angell at Wisconsin had won the league's very first scoring title in 1906) and he did so in the age of plodding play with an average barely above 10 points per game.

Chicago's victories in the league in 1908 would set up a memorable battle for national bragging rights between the Maroons and the Eastern League team from Penn. It would be the first national championship playoff series of a sort, though indeed it was an informal playoff and one that excluded any open competition with the rest of the nation's best (like the teams from the New England League or the far West Coast). Penn, with star forward Charles Keinath ("an electrifying dribbler" according to the *Spalding Guide*), did seem, however, to be the undisputed best in the Eastern sector, winning 23 straight after losing two of its opening three and

11

capturing all eight Ivy League games. Chicago had earned an invitation to challenge the Quakers by besting rival Western Conference power Wisconsin in a league tie-breaker at Madison, 18-16, on a last-minute shot by Pat Page.

When Penn came to Chicago for the East-West playoff opener it was Raycroft's team that survived again, 21-18, as Schommer provided clutch scoring with four buckets and Page again made a memorable goal by this time shooting from his knees when tied up by a couple of defenders. The Philadelphia rematch was also Chicago's game, by a narrow 16-15 count, and the "Big Ten" club claimed national bragging rights with its 21-2 record. When Raycroft's club posted a perfect 12-0 Western Conference mark a season later (Schommer's fourth and final season as an All-American) it would have to settle for a hollower claim for a national championship when an attempt to renew the East-West postseason series with Ivy champ Columbia fell through. It would be almost three decades before the idea would be resurrected in the form of a true year-end playoff system.

Of the many pioneers who brought something of themselves to the game, perhaps the two most important organizers and innovators were two Docs — Meanwell (a native of Leeds, England, with a medical degree from the University of Maryland) at Wisconsin, and Carlson (who played professional football to finance his own medical studies) at Pittsburgh. Walter Meanwell took over the basketball program at Wisconsin in 1912 (winning 35 of his first 36 games and the league title his first three seasons) and immediately began molding successful teams around such strategies as the short passing game, blocks and screens, and crisscrossing offensive weaves. The short-pass strategy that became his trademark was supposedly devised when his first teams at Baltimore's Loyola University played in an exceptionally tiny basement gym. Carlson pioneered what might be legitimately seen as the first true patterned offensive scheme, a system he called the "Figure Eight" or the "continuity" offense.

With such planned tactical maneuvers the two Docs contributed mightily to infusing much-needed structure into what had previously been a helter-skelter game (sometimes almost a violent free-for-all), and thus together they provided our best pioneer models for picturing the basketball mentor as skilled choreographer. The head football coach might well be viewed as military commander marshalling forces and planning battlefield sieges. The basketball coach — especially when cut in the mold of Meanwell and Carlson — would increasingly be recognized as an orchestrator of free-lancing yet always controlled patterns, as the man who choreographed each step and surge and swirl and then set the whole marvelous dance in full motion.

Doc Meanwell was the ingenious innovator of the patterned style of play that he himself often called "scientific basketball" and that proved most popular (and also most effective) during the game's first several decades. One measure of Meanwell's successes were his conference titles (four of them along with four runner-up finishes) and his winning percentage of better than 70 percent at both Wisconsin (246-99) and over a full 22-year career (290-101). Another was the impressive list of future mentors who trained under him — Bud Foster (Wisconsin), Rollie Williams, Bill Chandler, Harold Olsen (Ohio State) and Gus Tebell. Few coaches have started out with a bigger bang than Meanwell's first two teams which established a Western

Wisconsin coach Walter "Doc" Meanwell was a pioneer of patterned passing offenses and one of the game's arch-conservative voices. In the late '20s Meanwell led a nearly successful drive to ban dribbling entirely from the college game. (University of Wisconsin photo)

Conference record with 23 uninterrupted victories. And if he is remembered best for his disciplined offensive systems he was a skilled teacher of defensive tactics as well, established by the fact that his 1923 Badgers stood as the best-yet Western Conference defensive squad when it restricted opponents to only 161 points in 12 league games (less than 14 per contest).

While one Doc was advancing the game in Wisconsin another was having similar impact farther to the East. Doc Carlson would also leave an important mark on the science of basketball play from his base in Pittsburgh, once he put aside his medical practice as a physician for U.S. Steel Corporation and devoted himself full-time to the cage fortunes of the University of Pittsburgh team for which he had once played. Carlson would eventually be a legend in the Steel City and his status would depend as much on colorful sideline behavior and powerhouse Pitt teams as it would on the new directions he thrust upon the sport.

Carlson established his niche early as an innovator, pioneering intersectional competition in 1931 and 1932 when he took his Pitt Panthers westward to face Phog Allen's Kansas club and then extend the road trip to Colorado, Stanford and Southern Cal. But perhaps he would be best remembered for his early experiments with the fundamentals of the stall; this Doc hated the zone defense and on several occasions had his team hold the ball for much of the game in order to counter zone play. He also fostered a plan for "continuity" of attack on offense which was basically a three-man weaving Figure Eight with two other players remaining stationary and setting picks. Ken Loeffler at La Salle would later employ a similar concept with his own brilliant five-man weave, Rupp would work a variation with his "guard-through" rotation system, and numerous others would also copy the offense in one version or another down through the years.

Carlson was as much a showman as he was a chalkboard innovator and his colorful style would often bring memorable responses from opposition arena crowds that witnessed his teams on the road. He was known to throw peanuts into the stands to hostile home crowds when his visiting Panthers slowed down their offense on the road against zone defenses. On one occasion he was struck on the head with an umbrella wielded by a matronly patron at Washington and Jefferson, and on still another he had a bucket of ice water poured on his head from the stands behind the Pittsburgh bench by West Virginia fans (he had been shouting "This burns me up" at the game officials just before his unexpected shower).

If both Meanwell and Carlson had their many disciples among their own ex-players in the years between the two world wars, there were many more disciples as well who never played under either (or even against either) but nonetheless adopted wholesale or piecemeal their numerous proven ideas. Joe Lapchick, the Hall of Fame coach and ex-star of the Original Celtics and himself a major innovator, would eventually boldly claim that every modern offensive scheme in some way or another comes out of the inventions of Pittsburgh's Doc Carlson.

While the first four decades (1890s through 1920s) are best known for pioneer coaches who shaped the contours of the game, there were also some star players and memorable teams during this earliest era. Christian Steinmetz staked an early claim as "Father of Wisconsin Basketball" when he starred in 1904 and 1905 for coach Emmett Angell in Madison as perhaps the sport's first great scorer. Steinmetz reached the 1,000-point plateau before his career was over, a remarkable feat given the low-scoring pace of the early game. And he gained notoriety with a 44-point single-game outburst during an 80-10 thrashing of rival Beloit College, then topped 50 points in another game later that same season. Remarkably his top two single-game totals remain school records at the Big Ten institution even today, as do his marks for field goals (20) and free throws (26) made in a single game; his one-season point total of 462 stood well into the second half of the century.

But Steinmetz would have at least one rival for the honor of basketball's earliest scoring phenom, and that rival would be found down in South Carolina where a scoring record that still stands was set in one school's very first game ever. J.O. Erwin bagged 58 points (on 29 baskets without a free-throw attempt) when the 1912 Clemson team took the floor for its inaugural match against a non-college five known as the Butler Guards. Erwin's surprising total has never been equalled at the basketball-rich institution that now performs out of the Atlantic Coast Conference. A more shadowy figure, John Anderson, reportedly also pumped in an incredible 80 points in 1903 when Bucknell University embarrassed the Philadelphia College of Pharmacy 159-5 (one can only imagine the spectacle of endless trips back to midcourt for center jumps that must have been controlled time after time by a dominant Bucknell center). And when it came to remarkable shooting performances of the first three decades still another was turned in by Forrest DeBernardi who logged an even 50 for Westminster in 1920 during the first of his three All-American seasons (one as a guard, one as a forward and one as a center). Other individual players like Chicago's tandem of John Schommer and H.O. "Pat" Page and Penn's Charles Keinath also built memorable reputations, but these like all the rest were soon buried by the stars that began to emerge in the '20s and '30s when the game opened up to better athletes and also to more wide-open styles of offensive play.

If the first noteworthy teams were those at Yale in the East and Chicago in the West, there were also others who carved their special page in the game's history. Tiny Hiram College out of Ohio would win the first tournament that claimed to crown a national college champion — in this case even a world's champion — however inflated that claim might have actually been at the time. The event took place at the Louisiana Purchase Exposition and World's Fair staged in St. Louis and also host to a largely USA-oriented Olympic Games competition. Part of the bill of fare were two outdoor basketball tournaments designed to show off the new sport and crown Olympic and collegiate champions. The Buffalo German YMCA club would capture the gold medal in the five-team Olympic event, while Hiram joined Wheaton College and Latter Day Saints University (now Brigham Young) in the small group willing to contest the college trophy. It would of course be another three-plus decades before this pioneering concept of a national college championship tournament would bear fruition.

Beginning with the 1913 season the University of Texas fielded a crack team that played the bulk of its games outdoors (often in freezing conditions) and blitzed all opponents during a 44-game unbeaten streak that eventually stretched through three undefeated campaigns and also the end and beginning of two other seasons. Star players for the Longhorns were All-American Clyde Littlefield, Pete Edmond and Gus "Pig" Dittmar, and during the 1916 season this contingent and their teammates would outscore the opposition 560-185 and claim one victory over San Marcos Baptist by a remarkable 102-1 tally. Texas coach R.B. Henderson not only inspired heavy scoring from his talented athletes but also pioneered with defensive strategies, introducing a scheme that had guard Pig Dittmar stationed as a permanent defender beneath the opponent's basket while the remainder of the team concentrated on scoring at the other end. When the Texas unbeaten streak reached 40 school officials decided to build the team a new indoor facility, one of the first in the region. By the time they moved onto "the best floor in the Southwest" the stars had graduated, however, and the Texas team had sunk back into mediocrity.

But the best known of the early college clubs (outside of its own region that is) was a 1922 and 1923 Kansas team later to be recognized by the Helms Foundation as retroactive winners of consecutive national championship honors. Despite its 33-3 two-year mark (two of the losses came at the hands of the Kansas City AC and the third was to Missouri early in 1922), this was a team that would etch its mark for future historians more than anything else because of several famous squad members. Phog Allen was the 37-year-old mentor, freshly returned to Lawrence after a seven-year furlough at Central Missouri State and about to now embark on a four-decade stint that would earn his reputation as one of the great strategists and most colorful coaching personalities of the first half-century. (Allen like Meanwell and Carlson was also a "Doc" with a degree in osteopathic medicine, and he also doubled as the school's football coach for a spell.) Naismith himself played a minor role as Allen's coaching assistant. And one of the team's less-heralded players was none other than Adolph Rupp, the man who would one day surpass even Allen's considerable coaching legacy.

Rupp never played much at Kansas since he had the ill fortune to sit on the bench behind the truest Jayhawk star, Paul Endacott. Endacott was the school's first All-American and would one day become president of the Phillips Petroleum Company, where he had signed on after undergraduate days as a star player for its famed

Phillips 66ers championship AAU cage team. As a 5-10 guard Endacott was only a modest scorer but nonetheless one of the first defensive greats who also used his leaping ability to control the center jumps (a crucial factor in games of the era) against often much taller opponents. For all the glory that fell to Endacott, however, it was the coach, Phog Allen, who with his rigid conditioning programs and his meticulous training of his players (many like Rupp, Dutch Lonborg, Johnny Bunn, Ralph Miller, Dick Harp and Dean Smith became legendary coaches themselves) remained the heart and soul of Jayhawks basketball. It was still very much a coach's era, in Kansas and throughout the land.

While giants among the coaches' ranks like Allen in Kansas, Meanwell in Wisconsin and Carlson at Pittsburgh were staking out the nature of the game and evolving its lasting patterns, strategies and styles of play, there was also another ongoing revolution simultaneously taking place in the years before, during and after the First World War. It was a revolution that was often anything but silent in its nature or subtle in its impact. For this was one that involved the shifting rules and playing conditions that sustained the game and from time to time even reoriented the best-laid coaching strategies.

Most central to the "appearance" of basketball as a spectacle was the issue of the center jump. In fact most of the heated debate over rules during the first two decades of the present century involved the issue of the center jump. And it was the eventual beheading of the center jump after each and every basket that gave us the broad shape of cage play as we know it today. Many if not most early coaches had held firmly to the belief that college athletes simply could not cope with the strain of constant running that would be required without the breaks after each basket in which teams regrouped and met at center court for another toss. An extensive camp of traditionalists supported the old system for decades for the same reasons that all traditions are sustained — it had been designed that way by Jim Naismith and it had always been done that way and that was good enough for most tastes.

In reality, the disputes about center jumping were part of a larger issue concerning workable methods for putting the basketball in play. When wire cages or net enclosures were used in the first few decades of the century to protect players from ornery crowds of spectators (hence the origin of the term "cagers") there was no issue of "out-of-bounds" legislation since a ball hitting the surrounding cage remained in play. The competing "sideline" version of the game created more difficulties in this area, which were first addressed with a rule which awarded the ball to the first team to touch it over the line. The violent scrambles which resulted (and early basketball was a most chaotic and violent game) caused a rule adjust in 1913 which awarded the ball to the last team not to touch it in play. After each goal, however, the center jump was still the method to put the ball back into play and it was a method which gave an obvious advantage to height.

Naismith himself had argued that finesse should count for more than physical endowment in his new sport (this was the original idea behind having elevated goals to shoot at) but wanted to solve the problem by simply having officials make better and higher tosses of the ball in jumping situations. West Coast coaches like Sam Barry (Southern Cal) and Nibs Price (California) eventually held sway in the late

George Mikan was the most famous of the new breed of World War II-era giants who changed the original conceptions of Dr. Naismith's peach basket game. The 1944 restriction against defensive goaltending would soon become known as "The Mikan Rule." (Naimsith Basketball Hall of Fame photo)

'30s, however, and the center jump was first dropped after free throws in 1937 and after all buckets a year later. If this improved the game a small degree by taking a bit of the edge away from teams benefitting from a behemoth in the lineup it also nudged it forward a much greater distance by speeding up action and rewarding the new fast-break offenses that pushed the ball rapidly up the floor and put the numbers up rapidly on the scoreboard.

By the late 1920s the foundations for the modern game of college basketball were firmly in place. A decade later the game had already taken on the precise appearance of the running, shooting, jumping and brilliantly orchestrated athletic spectacle that we have come to recognize as Naismith's (largely unintended) legacy. It had been a wild, sometimes chaotic, first three or four decades. But it was a productive stretch as well, one filled with experiments, controversies, competing traditions and bold evolutions necessary to fashion the perfect by-product of Naismith's original inspiration.

No other American game has evolved so rapidly and shaped itself so perfectly in so short a time. Baseball was nearly perfect in its conception from the start and has been little altered in its essential methods of play — at least since Candy Cummings began tossing curveballs in 1867 (thus making the moundsman a "hurler" and not a "server") and the pitcher's distance was fixed at 60 feet 6 inches (1893, two years after Naismith's experiment). Football seems to have never had much that was artistic about it and is in the end the very contest of brute strength Naismith sought to avoid; despite great advances in protective equipment (the only true innovation in rules or play being the forward pass) football remains what it was at the start, 11 men in one uniform seizing chunks of territory by brutally overpowering 11 men in a different uniform. But basketball, by contrast, evolved in a handful of years from a flawed game with great potential into a near perfect instrument for the most challenging and entertaining kind of athletic competition.

Chronology of 35 Major Rule Changes and Innovations

1890s

1893 — Pivot play (shifting one foot while anchoring the other) ruled not to be traveling violation.

1895 — Backboards introduced to eliminate crowd interference (from balcony) with shots at goal.

1897 — Yale University team introduces dribbling as offensive strategy (since no rule bans this).

1897 — Number of players fixed at five on side. Previously seven- and nine-man (woman) teams were commonplace.

1898 — Overhead dribble and double dribble are banned.

1900s - 1910s

1901-1915 — Dribbler not allowed to shoot ball at the basket or to score points.

1910 — Glass backboards introduced as improvement on screens and wooden backboards, both of which blocked spectators' views of the court.

1914 — Rough scrambles for out-of-bounds balls eliminated by rule awarding ball to team opposite the one that last touched ball inbounds.

1916 — Glass backboards are temporarily banned by requirement of white paint for all backboards.

1920s - 30s

1924 — Free throws no longer awarded for non-contact violations like traveling (those that are not personal fouls).

1929 — Collegiate Joint Rules Committee outlaws dribbling (under the influence of Wisconsin's Walter Meanwell), then immediately reverses the decision (under influence of CCNY's Nat Holman)

1930 — Five-second backcourt held-ball rule adopted to discourage stalling by offense.

1933 — Ten-second backcourt violation adopted to prevent stalling by offense.

1936 — Three-second lane violation established (offensive player can't remain between foul lines for more than three seconds at a time).

1937 — Center jump eliminated after free throws.

1938 — Center jump eliminated after field goals.

1940s

1944 — Defensive goaltending (blocking shots on their downward flight) outlawed ("The Mikan Rule").

1944 — Five personal fouls disqualify a player (instead of the four in effect since 1910). One extra foul still allowed for overtime periods.

1948 — Glass backboards sanctioned for all games.

1949 — Pacific Coast Conference experiments with discouraging deliberate free-throw misses by giving defensive men both inside rebounding positions.

1949 — Coaches now allowed to talk with players during time-out.

1950s

1952 — Game changed from 20-minute halves to four 10-minute periods.

1953 — Teams can no longer waive free throws in favor of taking ball out of bounds.

1955 — Game changed from 10-minute quarters back to 20-minute halves.

1956 — Twelve-foot foul lane replaces six-foot lane.

1958 — Offensive goaltending (touching the ball inside the cylinder) outlawed ("The Chamberlain Rule").

1960s-70s

1968 — Dunk shot (or dunking in pregame practice) is banned ("The Alcindor Rule").

1969 — Women's games are restructured to include five players on each side, full-court action and a 30-second shot clock. (Women collegians begin playing by men's rules.)

1977 — Dunk shot is once again made legal.

1980s-90s

1982 — Jump ball now employed only to start games and begin all overtimes. Alternate possession arrow now indicates possessions throughout game on all previous jump-ball situations.

1983 — Jump ball eliminated in five-second "closely guarded" situations. Five-second held ball now a violation and defensive team is awarded possession.

1986 — Colleges introduce 45-second shot clock.

1987 — Colleges adopt three-point field goal with line set at 19 feet 9 inches.

1988 — Intentional fouls now result in two-shot penalty plus possession of ball.

1994 — Shot clock reduced from 45 seconds to 35 seconds for men's games.

2

The Twenties and Early Thirties

Piggy and Phog and the Boys of the Big Apple

===============

"The team that makes the most mistakes will most likely win the game."
— Ward "Piggy" Lambert, Purdue head coach

With the boom-era of college basketball in the late '40s and early '50s came also the dawning of an age of individual star players. The game would always maintain its high-profile head coaches, especially at the collegiate level. But with the advent of a running and gunning one-handed jump-shooting spectacle — and thus of the age of free-lancing high scorers — a dramatic change took place almost overnight. It would now be the dancer himself, rather than the choreographer, who would own center stage.

Often teams were molded to fit the star at hand and thus no longer reflected, season after season, a single coach's ongoing philosophy. Wooden would eventually be the supreme example of such perfect plasticity as he bent his own hard-line views to accommodate the personalities and talents of first Alcindor and then Walton. But even Rupp and Iba in the '40s and Loeffler and Newell in the '50s adjusted to the personnel at hand. And fans of course now turned out to see individual one-on-one action as much as patterned team play. Newt Oliver at tiny Rio Grande was not the only coach who caught on quickly that while hundreds might appreciate a well-drilled unit scoring 50 as a team, thousands would pour in to witness a single hot-handed marksman do the same on his own. Thus while the sport's biggest names in the '20s and '30s had been Lambert, Meanwell, Carlson and Freeman, in the '40s and early '50s the headliners would be Kurland, Mikan, Arizin, Sailors, Selvy and even the rough-cut Bevo Francis.

Yet in 20-plus years that would separate the country's two world wars, basketball was still very much a patterned game and college contests were — at their most simplistic — most often supreme tests of different coaching styles. Often these styles reflected regions of the country — patient, methodical "weave and pass" in the East, run-and-shoot (usually one-handed style) on the Plains and in the Far West. But just as often they reflected the strong personalities and unbendable theories of the individual mentors who had established and maintained these regional preferences in the first place.

Nat Holman's CCNY teams carried on the tightly patterned play ("Holman's Wheel") of the Original Celtics for whom Holman himself had once played a starring role. Walter Meanwell at Wisconsin and Doc Carlson at Pittsburgh taught controlled and patterned styles of offense which depended heavily on exacting passing skills. Carlson's slow and deliberate Figure Eight scheme which produced a 21-0 ledger in 1928 was only marginally different from Holman's Celtics-style approach. Buck Freeman's even more cautious "give-and-go" scheme — repeated endlessly in search of the perfect open shot — was often less than popular even with crowds of the day (Freeman's Redmen were booed mercilessly for their boring performance during a 17-9 defeat of CCNY in the first heavily promoted Madison Square Garden tripleheader in 1931), even if it had generated an 86-8 record between 1927 and 1930. Ward Lambert at Purdue pioneered the "racehorse" fast-breaking style that had earlier been employed by Ed Wachter's Troy (New York) Trojans on the pro barnstorming circuit. And Forrest "Phog" Allen arduously developed the science of defense, drilling his teams on a new method of "zones" which would guard against the fast-breaking style suddenly so popular throughout his own Midwestern sector of the nation.

When it came to regional preferences in playing styles there were indeed definable differences during the pioneering era of the 1920s and 1930s. The game was still slow and plodding by modern standards — with its mandatory center jumps after baskets and the emphasis on two-handed stationary shooting. The conditions of court (dark and drafty) and ball (misshapen and full of laces) also worked against a more wide-open scoring game. But in the Midwest, nonetheless, Lambert's style edged out Meanwell's by the early '30s and that section of the country thus became the favorite home of racehorse and free-shooting offenses. It was known as Western-style play and nowhere was it better exemplified than in Lambert's best Purdue teams at the end of the '20s and start of the '30s. It took a special player like Johnny Wooden at Purdue to make it work well. And Piggy Lambert eventually had that player, and a bunch more to go with him.

And there were other schools farther west, like Montana State (36-2 in 1929), that also specialized in this new-style running game. The Bobcats had been noticed as early as 1917 (19-1) and 1920 (13-0) yet only reached true national prominence in the '20s. This came with an ambitious schedule that matched them against a number of Big Ten teams and other Eastern rivals, and with a running system of their own under coach Ott Romney that manufactured a 144-31 six-year record. The zenith was reached in 1929 and 1930 under the guidance of Romney's successor Schubert Dyche and behind the offensive prowess of All-Americans John "Cat" Thompson (1929, 1930) and Frank Ward (1930). In his debut season of 1929 Dyche not only matched Romney's previous-season record of 36-2 but also gained the Helms national title as well.

Eastern-style cage play, by contrast, followed the model established by Doc Carlson at Pittsburgh and Buck Freeman with his "Wonder Five" at New York's St. John's. This was the patient and methodical style that Nat Holman had played with the Original Celtics in the mid-20s and then instituted with his own college teams at City College when he took up coaching as well as playing. Holman started coaching the CCNY team on a volunteer basis in 1919, two years before he joined the Original Celtics as a barnstorming pro, and would stay on as head coach for 37 seasons. For the first third of that time he would maintain dual hats as barnstorming pro and dedicated college mentor. But if Holman first popularized the patterned style, Carlson and Freeman seemed to have the most satisfying early successes. It was the style of Figure Eight weaves run by two or three players around their stationary teammates, confusing the defense and opening up high-percentage shots. It was a proven method

Purdue coach Ward "Piggy" Lambert introduced "racehorse basketball" to the Big Ten Conference. (Purdue University photo)

that would make Pittsburgh an acknowledged national champion in 1928 and again in 1930 and would also make St. John's perhaps the most famous New York-area team of all time.

A few of the best-known pioneering coaching personalties thus now loomed above the history of the game. A handful who reached their peak in the two decades between the two world wars left the largest individual marks on playing style. Perhaps the most influential of all was Ward "Piggy" Lambert at Purdue. It was Lambert more than anyone who first moved the game dramatically away from the style of Meanwell and Carlson that had so dominated the early years of tightly choreographed coaching systems.

Lambert was father of the fast break, if only in the sense that he was first to build a crack team on this system that could legitimately call itself a national champion. His three decades in West Lafayette would account for 371 victories (228 in the conference, which remains second only to Bob Knight) and 11 league trophies, and he tutored 10 consensus All-Americans and nine league scoring champs. At first his teams didn't look all that different from competitors anywhere else in the Big Ten — Illinois and Indiana featured teams that scored every bit as much, and Illinois speedster Chuck Carney provided the big scoring shows of the late '20s — yet by the early '30s Lambert was leading a series of clubs that would garner six league titles during the decade by simply beating opponents up and down the floor on a regular basis. If Frank Keaney at Rhode Island and Bill Reinhart at George Washington would later get the bulk of the credit for perfecting the running style, it was Lambert who first conceived its potential.

Purdue's system took off running (quite literally) once Piggy had the proverbial horses. Those "horses" arrived at the end of the '20s with two stellar players named John Wooden and Charles Murphy. One was appropriately dubbed "Stretch" and the other was the "India Rubber Man," and the clever sobriquets give an important clue to their roles and contributions to the Boilermakers' upscale game.

Lambert's notion of a fast-break style — like just about every version that has followed — was based on the necessary concept of a big man to complement and kick-start a handful of thoroughbreds. It is the rebounder-cum-shot blocker who must remain anchored to the opposition goal, clearing the boards of misses and arching long lead passes downcourt to three or four teammates who are free to break for the other end each time an enemy missile is launched. The 6-foot-6 string bean Murphy provided this role as a senior during Wooden's sophomore season (with the team finishing 13-2 and undefeated atop the Big Ten); the next two seasons the role was filled admirably by 6-4 "back guard" Ralph Parmenter. With Parmenter launching the break, Wooden galloped to his national player of the year honors during a stellar senior season and at 17-1 (the only loss was to Illinois by seven points) Purdue was crowned the consensus national champion.

Still another Midwestern pioneer of enormous influence was Forrest "Phog" Allen out in Kansas. Allen inherited the game from the most original of possible sources, Jim Naismith himself. But the game that Allen soon taught his young Jayhawk recruits was far different from the one James Naismith originally conceived. Naismith as a one-time chaplain, staid faculty member and paragon advocate of amateurism had been a reluctant coach at best. He had come to Kansas in the first decade of the new century as a professor of physical education and chapel director, after first earning a doctor of medicine degree in Denver. Reluctantly he had agreed to coach the new college team for the sole purpose of fostering needed recreational activity (that was, after all, the purpose for which he had shaped his new game in the first place). For Naismith basketball always remained a social event to be played and enjoyed for comradeship and healthful exercise aimed at stretching both body and soul. Winning was not so important (not impor-

All-American center Charles "Stretch" Murphy teamed with John Wooden to provide Piggy Lambert with the horses necessary to carry Purdue's running-style offense. (Purdue University photo)

tant at all for that matter) and entertaining spectators less so. When he would later see large crowds of 10,000 or more witness games by professionals like the Original Celtics Naismith would be appalled, claiming it should be the other way around, with 10 watching and 10,000 playing.

It is not surprising then that Naismith would be the school's only long-term coach with a losing record. It was not until he turned over the program in 1908 to one of his former players, Forrest Allen who had played on his 1906 team, that Kansas basketball began moving toward organized and skilled teams focused more on winning than on having a grand time. Despite their philosophical differences, the two co-existed in harmony on the Lawrence campus for years and Naismith stayed on as a complaint assistant while Allen began forging winners in the '20s. Naismith would himself acknowledge the difference between them years later when he inscribed a photo to Allen (one of Phog's dearest possessions) with these revealing words: "From the father of basketball to the father of basketball coaching."

Forrest Allen would quickly make his mark both in Kansas and around the rest of the nation. His first badge was the booming voice that he directed at players and referees alike, thus earning his most unusual nickname. His second badge was a reputation for undiluted excellence, for innovation and even for a bit of an eccentric streak. Allen's methods were indeed unorthodox for his own time or for any time. This was especially the case when he is contrasted with his famous predecessor. Allen quickly saw the potential for strategy in the game and he soon took up a role as champion of innovation that would last until his retirement at mid-century.

Allen's sense of innovation was first reflected in the teams he coached. Perhaps the best of those teams came in the '20s with five straight Missouri Valley Conference championships (1923-28) and '30s with seven Big Six titles over eight seasons (1931-38). He specialized in complex shifting zone defenses designed to slow other teams' running games, and if it was hard to crack the labels attached to some of these (he called one the "Stratified Transitional Man-for-Man Defense with a Zone Principle") it was harder still to overcome them on the hardwood floor. He was also a fanatic about training and athletic conditioning and a bit of an eccentric to boot: he demanded his players pour down gallons of water during the season as an appropriate training method and often chose his starters simply because he could detect a special "victory light" shining in their eyes.

And the man best suited perhaps to be called "Father of Basketball Coaching" also remained an important and influential innovator in his role as conscience of the coaches' rules committee. In this capacity Allen pioneered several important changes in the game over the years. He long campaigned vocally against dunking as the game's bane (although he did ironically recruit Chamberlain), he invented fan-shaped backboards, championed the 10-second backcourt rule as a forward thinker (although he also called for the return of the center jump as a reactionary), and vehemently (in a losing cause) opposed introduction of a bonus foul-shooting rule.

However unorthodox Allen was, he was also highly successful at every turn. His teams would earn two mythical national titles in the '20s, being tabbed retroactively by the Helms Foundation for a 16-2 record against top-flight competition in 1922 and a 17-1 standard a year later. The 1923 Jayhawk outfit featured Paul Endacott, the best player of the Midwest, and lost only to a non-collegiate Kansas City AC ballclub; a little-used sub that year was Kansas native Adolph Rupp. Decades later when tournament play was finally part of the landscape, Allen would also earn two trips into the Final Four of NCAA competition. He would even capture a national title in 1952 with his one stellar big man, Indiana recruit Clyde Lovellette, only four seasons before his 48-year sojourn (39 seasons at Kansas) finally closed

One of college basketball's first great teams was this undefeated 1923 Kansas club featuring four of the game's greatest names: James Naismith, assistant coach (middle row, center), Phog Allen, head coach (left of Naismith), Adolph Rupp, substitute player (top row, far left) and Paul Endacott, early playing great (front row center with ball). (University of Kansas photo)

down to mandatory retirement. And in the end Allen would also be remembered as the man who brought Wilt Chamberlain to Kansas, even if the legendary mentor never got to coach his most prized recruit. The most impressive record of all, of course, was that when it was all over his career victory total (746) stood second only to Rupp's. And in future years only Dean Smith, Ed Diddle and old rival Henry Iba would ever catch him.

But if Lambert and Allen first pioneered running basketball as a viable method of attack, it would be a coach back east who would first unlock the true potential in the concept and then show off that potential to the game's growing fandom. Frank Keaney at Rhode Island State was the man who first excited the ticket-buying public to the true possibilities of fast-break basketball.

Keaney was not only a superb innovator but also a great showman. He was the originator of dumping towels and jackets and anything he could put his hands on out onto the court as a show of his dismay with distasteful officiating when it didn't go his way. The flamboyant mentor was apparently something of an early Bob Knight during the game's horse and buggy age. He also reportedly inspired his charges by treating them to poetry readings rather than "X" and "O" chalk sessions in the pre-game locker room. But he brought more than sideline antics to his new brand of hardwood entertainment. Hating zone defenses which slowed the game and ruined its aesthetic appeal, Keaney developed high-powered offenses trained to shoot rapidly and accurately whenever the opportunity allowed. The first Rhode Island team he coached after arriving from Putnam College ran up 80 points in a single game (this was with center jumps after each basket, recall); he had his first point-a-minute team (averaging 40 ppg for the season) in 1927; and by 1937 his offenses were registering 1,000 points for a 21-game season.

It was in the years immediately before the outbreak of the second world war that Keaney had his greatest teams and greatest successes, however, and this is not surprising in light of the change in the center jump rule which further unfettered his team's running game after 1937. But rule adjustments aside, it was also then that he had his fastest horses which came in a swift succession of great players beginning with his own son Warner, a 6-6 giant who was employed (under rules of the day) as a goaltending defender and rebounder while four teammates harassed and gambled as additional defenders and then broke for the enemy basket after each shot against them. With Warner Keaney rebounding and firing court-length passes, Rhode Island was able to implement Ward Lambert's theory of numerous gambling mistakes resulting in numerous scoring opportunities and thus numerous victories. Keaney's teams often, if not always, now led opponents in turnovers, but they were also pacesetters in points, victories and fan excitement.

The system reached its zenith in the decade between 1938 and 1948 when Keaney was able to recruit athletes best suited to his running system like Chet Jaworski, Stan Stutz Modzelewski and finally Ernie Calverley (eventually his coaching successor as well as his most talented player). Jaworski followed Stanford's Hank Luisetti as the nation's scoring leader in 1938 and 1939 with 20-plus averages; Modzelewski did the same in 1940 (23.1), 1941 (18.5) and 1942 (21.4) before changing his name to Stan Stutz and enjoying a proficient pro career. And in Ernie Calverley Keaney found a player whom Red Auerbach would later call "the finest passer coming down the middle of the fast break anywhere in college basketball" and the near-equal of his own Bob Cousy in Boston. Ernie Calverley indeed became something of the Hank Luisetti of the Eastern Seaboard.

The game which had moved forward only by fits and starts in the years before World War I — essentially owing its distinctive regional flavors more to various interpretations of the rules and the intended methods of play than to any structured innovations by coaches or players — began to find its direction in the third and fourth decades of the century. Emerging philosophies of play would evolve mainly in the Midwest and along the Eastern Seaboard during the two subsequent decades that separated the great wars. But for all the innovation in Indiana, Kentucky, Kansas and New England there was yet another locale where the game was also establishing a firm stronghold. The roots of Naismith's game had been planted on campuses all over the country. But the greatest flowering in the aftermath of World War I was about the take place in the city of New York.

The New York basketball tradition was already rich from the earliest days of the game. Columbia sat atop the Ivy League in the first two decades of the century and provided some of the country's best teams of the era. The Eastern Intercollegiate

League (Ivy League) championship belonged to Columbia on seven different occasions before 1914 (the Lions had back-to-back undefeated seasons in 1904, 1905) and Pennsylvania would not make its mark as the big winner in the pioneering conference until 1921. Ivy League powerhouse teams of the Teens and '20s would soon have plenty of company from the city's half-dozen or so other institutions that also took willingly to the game. NYU would beat both Princeton and Yale in 1910 and by 1918 Columbia would fall to teams from CCNY, NYU and even Brooklyn Polytechnic all in the same season.

Basketball by the decade of the 1920s was largely a matter of shifting rules and experimental styles of play. Most of those styles, as already noted, continued to take on a regional hue, but now more through organized effort than chaotic happenstance. Many were also variations on a few simple and related themes such as the ones preached by Holman at CCNY, Cann at NYU or Carlson over at Pittsburgh. And there was, of course, a reason why local styles and even local stars remained so long dominant in one region and at the same time almost unknown in other sectors. In the end that reason was as much economic as it was anything else.

By the '20s and certainly by the '30s college football stars boasted nationwide reputations. "Galloping Ghost" Red Grange of Illinois was a national hero and not just a Midwest idol and was imitated on schoolyards from Trenton to Culver City and back. The college gridiron teams played their games in large stadiums — sometimes seating 80,000 or even 100,000 — and if there was no television there was often coast-to-coast radio coverage of the major games. Huge revenues from sold-out stadiums also generated funds that allowed top teams to travel to other sectors, where as a top draw they would both be welcomed and also able to extract still another huge payday. There were year-end Bowl games, as well, to focus attention on the best teams and best players at season's end.

College basketball had no such year-end playoff system and no such mass exposure. The games were played in tiny gyms which often allowed no more than several hundred fans. Most of the students at a basketball hotbed like Kansas or Kentucky or Purdue were therefore likely never to have seen the school's home five in action. This also meant no media exposure beyond a most limited local one for top college cagers; and it also meant that lengthy road trips for intersectional games were simply not feasible. This would only begin to change once daring East Coast promoters chanced twin bills in massive and centrally located arenas like New York's Madison Square Garden or Philadelphia's Palestra. There alone would large turnouts make featured intersectional matches both profitable and thus also highly desirable. And there alone would bigger audiences justify more extensive press coverage of both the games and the athletes. In the meantime, regional competitions remained the order of the day, playing styles and coaching philosophies developed in relative isolation, All-Americans like John Wooden at Purdue or Paul Endacott at Kansas earned fame that rarely stretched beyond state borders, and what was already a popular participant's game still languished as a minor spectator sport.

There were of course some early signs of the economic potential of the game as a crowd-pleasing event. The first of these came as early as 1920 when a landmark game was staged in New York City between New York University and City College, teams that had already become fierce rivals in the dozen or more years during which they had seriously practiced the winter sport. When they met again in the late winter of 1920 the two rivals were both experiencing especially good seasons, NYU at 11-1 and CCNY in the first year under Holman at 13-2. Without its own gymnasium NYU had played some of its games on the deck of a local barge in the Hudson River and others in available dance halls. Since a large turnout was anticipated for the pitched year-end battle it was decided by both schools to rent the 168th Street Regiment Armory for the affair, a wise decision in light of the nearly 10,000 spectators who showed up on the night of the match. NYU ran off to a 39-21 victory in a particularly high-scoring affair for the era, but the true winners were of course those who totalled up the ticket receipts at both colleges. It might well have been the largest crowd ever to witness a basketball contest up to that time, though records are sketchy on such matters. Would-be promoters could not help but begin taking at least some notice, however.

NYU had established its early dominance over the New York scene with a 15-1 finish in 1920, the sound thrashing of Holman's first CCNY club, and an impressive victory in Atlanta that would earn a national AAU title. The AAU championship win would come over another metropolitan-area team from Rutgers and was keyed by the stellar play of forward Howard Cann, the man who would take over the coaching reins upon completion of undergraduate days. Georgia sportswriters called Cann "the greatest basketball player in the world" in the wake of his obviously impressive Atlanta tournament outing. But Nat Holman would have some impressive teams of his own before the decade was out, even if his own coaching was sandwiched in between extensive barnstorming tours with a seemingly endless list of pro teams to which he continued to sell his services. And if Holman began to win consistently in the mid-20s he also exerted even greater influence with his scientific approaches to the game. It was the Holman system if not always the Holman teams that soon ruled the New York roundball scene.

Nat Holman would himself star with the world's most famous professional outfit, the team known as the Original Celtics that dominated pro play in the decade after World War I. Nat had jumped to the Celtics from the rival New York Whirlwinds in 1921, a year after he had already begun coaching the college boys on a part-time basis. Manhattan businessman Jim Furey would collect the finest basketballers of the day in Celtics uniforms and Holman would be the high scorer and also the highest-paid player; it was there that he teamed with burly Dutch Dehnert and gangly Joe Lapchick and was thus part of such innovations as the pivot play, defensive switching, the give-and-go pass and the weaving style offense that worked like the precision wheels inside a clock. It was this system that he now simultaneously brought to the college team he coached. His own particular version — the "Holman Wheel" — was a patient offense in which all five players cut and swerved through endless loops around the basket until the uncontested shot could be found. It was soon a favorite of coaches throughout the northeast quadrant of the country and would thus have its many imitators and its equally many variants. And it was eventually turned into the methodical play of the next great New York college squad, the St. John's Wonder Five that would arrive at decade's end.

There were some other memorable college fives in the area, like the Fordham club of the late '20s. While Pittsburgh and Montana State were grabbing the bulk of the headlines on the national scene as the Roaring '20s took their last curtain call, it was Ed Kelleher's team, paced by John Zakszewski, that may in reality have been the best in the land in 1927 with an unbeaten ledger. Fordham again remained unscathed the following year, at least until suffering a late-season 26-25 upset loss to Holman and CCNY when normally reliable Bo Adams missed a technical foul shot at game's end that might have clinched another unblemished season. NYU and Howard Cann would also topple the Rams unexpectedly in 1929, but nonetheless Fordham stood 48-4 over the final three campaigns of the decade.

But in the end the best team of the period was not one fielded by Holman or Bee or Howard Cann or even Ed Kelleher. At the close of the '20s a group of exceptional athletes would cluster on the campus of St. John's University. Matty Begovich (an import from Hoboken) was a giant in his day at 6-5 and would soon specialize in controlling the center jumps that were still the deciding factor of most games. Max Posnack (a forward) and Jack "Rip" Gerson (a guard) were excellent defenders and some would also call Posnack the best passer anywhere outside of the seasoned pros. But the two true center pieces would prove to be guard Allie Schuckman, whose quick-release set shot became the team's top offensive weapon, and pint-sized 5-8 guard Mac Kinsbrunner, a magician at ballhandling branded by no lesser figures than Holman and Red Auerbach as the best dribbler either had ever seen.

Thus in 1928 the biggest New York basketball story was destined to be the debut of this first among legendary New York clubs. The St. John's "Wonder Five" was James "Buck" Freeman's proudest creation in a coaching career that would only last until 1936 (when he gave way to another legend named Lapchick); it was also the outfit that truly put New York (and thus East Coast) cage play back on the map at the end of the '20s and dawn of the '30s. With its four Jewish starters (Gerson, Posnack, Schuckman and Kinsbrunner) and a fifth teammate (Begovich) the Roman Catholic college would make plenty of news on the hardwoods over the next several seasons.

In their very first game as a unit the "Wonder Five" would pull off an upset over a heavily favored CCNY club that would draw immediate notice. They would win eight straight, in fact, before losing to above-mentioned Fordham by an even dozen. At the end of the year they stood 18-4. The three additional loses came against St. Joseph's and Scranton in Pennsylvania (both of whom they defeated in rematches) and also a talented semipro outfit (not a rare occurrence for the day) known as the Crescent AC. Basketball had now arrived at St. John's with a youthful team that had surprised by averaging better than 36 a game while at the same time holding opponents to 10 points less than that per contest.

But this was just the start. As sophomores, the Wonder Five unit would continue to jell and thus to capture even larger notice. A loss in the third game of the season at Providence by a single bucket was followed by 18 victories without defeat. The streak collapsed with another loss at the hands of Fordham. The final record this time would stand at 23-2 and their almost error-free ball-control game had become a marvel of the region. Furthermore, Freeman's perfectly schooled team would remain

30

one of the most potent offensive units and stingy defensive contingents in the land. While the scoring now seems modest by modern standards (it had tailed off to 32 a game), the 10-point average margin of victory was truly marvelous for an era when most teams only scored around 30 in a contest.

As juniors, the unbreakable pattern continued — domination of the New York scene, patient offense and air-tight defense both based on a strategy of keeping the ball away from the opponents, and a 24-1 ledger at season's end. The one slip came in a rematch with Providence on the road (they had already beaten the Friars early in the year to revenge one of the two 1929 losses) in a game that would cause much local consternation over the fact that the underdog home team received 26 trips to the free-throw line and the New Yorkers only six. But perhaps the year's highlight was a hard-earned victory over Trenton's Rider College, then coached by a young upstart named Clair Bee. (Bee would transfer to LIU two seasons later.) It was a game that demonstrated clearly the frustrating successes (for fans and opponents alike) of the Redmen's methods. The high-scoring Rider club (with over 1,000 points for the season) owned the halftime lead and scored again on the first possession after intermission. But St. John's then turned the tide by controlling the next tap and holding the ball for 11 minutes before earning an easy shot and bucket. Such relentless patience soon wilted the Rider attack.

The senior year would prove even better for Freeman's soon-legendary outfit. That season the team would pile up 21 more victories against stiffer opposition, run its winning streak to 27 before being tripped for the only time all winter by NYU and set still new standards for defensive stinginess. In the last game of the year the Redmen would actually hold Manhattan scoreless from the floor. And in the famed Madison Square Garden tripleheader match with CCNY (a 17-9 victory) they would even hold the talented Beavers scoreless for more than 38 minutes of running clock time. Their four-year record would ultimately stand at 86-8, and at 68-4 for the final three campaigns. They had maintained an iron grip over New York City cage play which was arguably the strongest brand of basketball in the country. They had also given St. John's a top billing from which the school would never slip very far (under coaches Joe Lapchick and Lou Carnesecca) throughout most of the next several decades. And then the wonderful quintet would move directly onto the barnstorming pro circuit and enjoy further successes there as well.

But the Wonder Five would also leave an even more lasting legacy and one that stretched beyond their mere victory totals and on-court prowess. For it was this special team — more than any of the other five involved — that was most responsible for drawing a huge crowd into Madison Square Garden in January 1931 to witness the single event that would mark the beginning of big-time basketball in New York City (and in another sense the nation as well). Freeman's Wonder Five thus had truly launched an era with their talented brand of winning play. And they would, at the very same time, also end an era with that same relentless brand of cautious patterned offense which had made them so successful. It was in that same January 1931 game — one that packed in 16,138 paying customers for the first Garden tripleheader — that the Redmen's method of play revealed itself to be quite ill-suited for satisfying the mass audiences which college basketball now hoped to draw. It was a plodding and boring style that would soon have to change and the rules makers quickly saw to it that it did. With its very successes, the Freeman-coached team had taken one aspect of the sport to an ultimate dead end. In direct response to the strategies employed by Buck Freeman's team the rules makers would now be forced to introduce an important piece of novel legislation.

The relentless winning of the Wonder Five had of course been built on the famed passing-style game of the professional Celtics which numerous other college fives also imitated, though never with quite the same degree of perfection. Freeman's disciplined passing game was combined with a tough switching defense to make it doubly effective. With the original center jump rule still in effect, after each scored basket the Redmen would rely on Matty Begovich to control the ensuing tap. They would then slowly work the ball into position for the perfect set shot, usually by Schuckman. If the shot didn't emerge as planned they would move to the far end of the court and launch a new painstaking passing attack. There was no center court line and backcourt violations thus did not exist. Max Posnack as the unparalleled ball handler and Mac Kinsbrunner as superb dribbler would maintain control of the ball for as much as 10 minutes at a time with a shot rarely if ever taken. It was a ploy effective enough in generating frustration and usually collapse by the opposition, but hardly a crowd-pleasing spectacle.

The handwriting was on the wall for promoters; large throngs could be enticed by the college competitions, provided there was enough action to lace the competition. Thus pressure was now put on rules makers to change the nature of the spectacle. The following year (with the St. John's Wonder Five themselves now moved on as a unit to an awaiting pro career as the Brooklyn Jewels) the midcourt line and 10-second rules were introduced. A team now had to advance the ball past halfcourt within 10 seconds or lose possession. While deliberate play was not entirely ruled out (for a team could still stall as long as it wished in the forecourt and often still did), at least the offense now had to promptly get the ball into the offensive zone and then keep it there.

Between them Cann's NYU, Holman's CCNY and Freeman's St. John's had in the decade and a half after the first great war made New York City basketball a showcase event. Up the road a piece, Syracuse had also boosted the region's reputation with its own All-American star Vic Hanson (Helms national player of the year for 1927) and innovative coach Lew Andreas (whose second team in 1926 was selected national champion by the Helms Foundation). Clair Bee would soon bring tiny Brooklyn-based Long Island University into the picture as well with his arrival in 1931, the Blackbirds posting a remarkable 149-11 mark between 1934 and 1939. Perhaps the best early team for Holman at City College was his 1922 club which claimed an unofficial regional championship by beating Ivy League champion Princeton. But most notable in the region were the emerging series of long-term coaching assignments launched during this era. Holman took the reins at CCNY in 1919, though he continued to play pro ball on the side for more than a dozen years after that. Ed Kelleher was installed at Fordham in 1922 and remained until the middle of World War II; Howard Cann emerged at NYU in 1923 and was still guiding the Violet and White at the end of the '50s. At Syracuse, Lew Andreas served for a full quarter-century after 1924 and once Clair Bee was lodged at LIU he didn't budge until the scandals of the early '50s closed down his program and eliminated his job from under him.

But the man most responsible for lifting New York City basketball up by the bootstraps and making it front page news was neither a coach nor a player. He was instead an innovative young newspaper reporter named Edward "Ned" Irish. Natural collegiate rivalries, a souped-up game with more scoring and more uninterrupted action, talented star players and crack teams — all would soon inevitably conspire to reveal that basketball seemingly lacked only the proper larger venues to transform it into the big-time sporting spectacle which could rival fall gridiron contests and summertime baseball play. The discovery of those venues would constitute perhaps the most notable off-court innovation of cage play in the '30s. And the man behind that discovery was destined to be New York's Ned Irish.

As a student at the University of Pennsylvania in 1927 and 1928 Irish was already covering the region's sports events for most of the New York papers as well as for the *Philadelphia Record*; in these roles he had witnessed Philly's own successful experiments with college games in the new Palestra and the Philadelphia Arena. On his return to Manhattan in 1929 he took up a post reporting on college sports for the *World-Telegram* (moonlighting as a publicist for the New York Giants pro football team) and developed in the process a deep appreciation for the unexploited popularity of college cage games. Such events regularly turned away hundreds from cramped out-of-the-way campus gyms. One popular (and thus very likely apocryphal) story maintains that as a cub reporter Irish was once forced to crawl through an open window of the sold-out Manhattan College gym in order to gain access to a game he had been assigned to cover, tearing his new trousers in the process and also envisioning in a flash a huge marketing potential that was obviously falling by the wayside.

There had already been a few encouraging experiments around the city with basketball on a grander stage. Early in the 1930-31 season a record throng of 12,000 had turned out at the 106th Infantry Armory to see the Wonder Five do battle with CCNY and defeat their major rivals 26-21. But the grand breakthrough came on the night later that same winter when these two powerful ballclubs met for a much anticipated rematch.

The contest would be part of a rare triple bill scheduled for January 21, 1931, and booked into Madison Square Garden (the third edition of the showcase arena, which had opened in 1925 and stood 16 blocks north of its 1968 replacement, perched atop Pennsylvania Station). This was the height of the Great Depression and popular mayor James J. Walker had already sponsored a successful college football event earlier that same fall to raise funds for unemployment relief; buoyed by the successes of that first venture the mayor would now try again with a marquee basketball program. Appointed to promote and manage the big event was veteran *World-Telegram* sportswriter Dan Daniel, who in turn brought in Irish to assist him.

The key drawing card was of course Buck Freeman's Wonder Five. Also participating were CCNY, Columbia, Fordham, Manhattan and NYU. The multiple-game program was deemed a necessity since a single 40-minute competition would

With his immensely popular Madison Square Garden double and tripleheaders in the 1930s, promoter Ned Irish became the true father of modern-era intersectional college basketball. (Naismith Basketball Hall of Fame photo)

hardly provide a glamorous enough bill to draw the sellout throng hoped for. On the other hand, shortened 15-minute halves also seemed in order to prevent the evening from drawing on far too long. It all worked to a tee, as better than 16,000 (some sources say 15,000) twirled the turnstiles and $20,000 in handsome profits were realized on the venture.

Not the least important was the fact that the bulging audience was treated to three fine contests, each one keeping rooters in suspense right into the final moments. Columbia surprised Fordham in the opener 21-18, and then Manhattan edged NYU by the still narrower count of 16-14. In the featured match, Holman's challengers registered the game's very first bucket but were soon stymied completely by the blanketing St. John's defense, failing to log another bucket until the closing minute of play and thus falling to the favorites 17-9. Although there was widespread fan displeasure with the patented St. John's slowdown game during the nightcap, the whole affair had nonetheless been a rousing success, by any measure, and one that had surpassed even the promoters' wildest expectations.

Dan Daniels had apparently stumbled upon a potential gold mine yet one he was apparently either unprepared or unwilling to exploit further. By 1934 Irish was himself ready to duplicate the Garden card, however, and he aimed to seize upon precisely the right moment to insure further successes. Both NYU and CCNY were undefeated as their season-ending game loomed on the horizon. Irish planned to book the game into the Garden and apparently had full cooperation of both schools. But the plan fell through at the last minute when a fight card previously booked for the same date could not be rescheduled by Garden officials. The contest went on has originally scheduled in a local armory and the 5,000 who held tickets were nearly matched by several thousand more turned away in disappointment. One NYU starter almost missed the game, in fact, when he was arrested for scalping his complementary tickets to the highly attractive match.

More convinced about the scheme than ever as a result of the overflow crowds that had turned out at the armory for the game he had failed to relocate, Irish now moved back into action. In December 1934 he pulled off a doubleheader card that was every bit as significant as the 1931 tripleheader had already been. Irish's idea was now to expand the horizons and bring in intersectional rivals to compete with the local city schools. In his first great extravaganza it would therefore be St. John's facing Westminster of Pennsylvania. In the nightcap NYU would battle a Notre Dame team that was widely considered a champion of the Midwest. Westminster is all but forgotten today but the tiny Pennsylvania school at the time was a cage powerhouse that featured a stellar center, Wes Bennett, and sported an undefeated record on the season. With Bennett in the lineup the club would pay several New York visits and acquit itself well each time.

Irish worked around the clock to promote his event and his boss at the *World-Telegram* (senior editor Joe Williams) was soon prompted to warn the budding entrepreneur that he better decide once and for all whether he wanted to be a full-time promoter or a full-time sportswriter. Another 16,000-plus in the seats and $20,000 in the coffers (Irish had prayed for a turnout of 10,000) was soon enough to make that decision for him. When the big night arrived Westminster controlled the lidlifter 37-33 on the strength of Bennett's impressive 21-point performance. In the nightcap NYU rallied against the imported team from South Bend for a 25-18 win and thus stretched its two-year winning streak to 20.

A second twin bill had already been put in place for a week later and provided the same successes both at the turnstiles and on the hardwood. CCNY knocked off St. John's in the first half of this one in a rough-and-tumble contest that set the tone for a more pugnacious nightcap. The second feature was again an intersectional match, this time between the still-unbeaten Violet and White of NYU and a Southern power coached by Adolph Rupp that was visiting the big city on the first of numerous upcoming occasions. With a huge lift from local officiating that allowed Howard Cann's team to manhandle Kentucky center Leroy Edwards under the boards, NYU held on down to the wire. NYU then triumphed only when Edwards was once again victimized by the referees — this time with a disputed foul call against him for blocking that put Sid Gross on the charity stripe for the winning free throws. While the first Garden tripleheader back in 1931 had been instrumental in fostering the 10-second backcourt rule, it would now be this particular game that would prove instrumental in further rule adjustment the following season. This time it would be the introduction of a three-second lane violation (designed to remove pivotmen from under the bucket and thus cut down on brutal fouling within that zone).

It was with Irish and his Madison Square Garden bills of fare that basketball went big-time and that New York suddenly became a center-stage venue for the sport. With this handful of events a minor sport was almost overnight transformed into a prime-time spectacle. Basketball had opened the '30s still immersed in an age of barnstorming, dance halls and claustrophobic gymnasiums with often little or no

Players from Ohio State (white uniforms) and Oregon battle for a rebound during the finals of the first-ever NCAA Tournament staged in Evanston, Ill. It was with the introduction of postseason tournaments at the end of the 1930s that collegiate basketball finally became a national craze and not just a regional sensation. (Naismith Basketball Hall of Fame photo)

spectator space. Now, largely if not exclusively through Irish, basketball had come to the big city and on a major scale. Not that Madison Square Garden provided the first and only spacious arena, for there were already huge field houses on the campuses of several Midwestern universities that could seat almost as many. And not that the Garden's twin bills of 1931 and 1934 actually materialized overnight and out of thin air; indeed they were quite a long time in the making. But in sport, as in seemingly all other aspects of life, what happens in New York somehow always seems to shine a little brighter, to hold a little more luster, to demand just a little more attention and command a bit more respect.

Eight Garden doubleheaders staged by Ned Irish during the 1934-35 season drew a total of 99,995 patrons, a number reported to be half of the estimated total attendance for all college games in the metropolitan New York area that winter. But there were quality games being played and enjoyed elsewhere as well, and elsewhere was sometimes a bit off the beaten path. Long Island University, for example, had neither an established big-name coach, a fixed nickname (they were first the Red

Devils, then the Blue Devils and finally the Blackbirds), a winning tradition to compete with NYU or CCNY or St. John's, nor a campus gym of its own at the downtown Brooklyn campus it occupied when Irish began the feature Garden events. This would all change in a hurry after Clair Bee was brought over from Rider College to start the 1932 season. Or at least much of it would change. The tiny borrowed home floor at the neighboring Brooklyn College of Pharmacy (where the Blackbirds would eventually capture 139 straight home games during the '30s) long remained the most inadequate venue employed by of any of the city's schools.

Clair Bee would of necessity build his remarkable LIU cage program under the most unlikely circumstances. If the home court was marginal the practice facilities were also minimal. Such trappings and little reputation as a basketball school meant few star players to draw upon in the earliest years. But Bee was a master innovator who could get the most out of his limited talent in the early going; he posted 16 victories his first winter in Brooklyn and then turned in an unexpected 26-1 season in the year preceding the first big Ned Irish Garden promotions. But the very year that Irish launched his string of megasuccesses, Bee also launched his assault of the city hardwoods. And only a few years down the road it would be Bee's team that would be the biggest ticket item in some of Irish's grandest events.

The seasons of 1934-35 and 1935-36 were the coming-of-age period for the LIU Blackbirds under Clair Bee. The master innovator had already led his young team to a 26-1 mark in 1934 and during that season (his third in Brooklyn) he had duplicated the high-power offense and the 1,000-point scoring that had earlier brought him notice at Rider. A year later he had Arthur Kameros at center as his first quality player and the team won its final seven games to close out a campaign which showed only two losses overall. In 1936 Bee's Blackbirds completed their rapid climb to the top and were unbeaten in 25 games. And by the middle of the following season they were still winning relentlessly and now owned a record string of 43 straight. In a city full of such glamorous mentors as Holman, Cann, Kelleher and Freeman it was now also impossible to ignore the presence of Clair Bee.

The 1936 LIU team and the one that followed it were full of stars as Bee's early successors had begun to attract admirers who could dribble and run as well as root. Julie Bender was the school's first All-American at guard and could dribble almost as well as Kinsbrunner for the Redmen. Leo Merson was a perfect companion in the backcourt who could launch a deadly set shot but also hang back as a defender while Bender slashed and drove on offense. Art Hillhouse was the replacement for Kameros and at 6-6 was both the biggest star and also the tallest player Bee had ever had. Together they teamed with Marius Russo (later a big-league pitcher with the Yankees) and Ben Kramer at the forward slots to provide the best all-around team East Coast basketball had yet produced and a team truly worthy of challengers from anywhere else around the land.

And such challenges were not now long in coming. Ned Irish and his popular Garden promotions would see to that. For the stage was now set for a landmark game that would go a long way toward making college basketball a full-fledged national spectacle. There was also now a team out on the West Coast that was stirring plenty of notice with its own impressive victory strings (culminating in a Pacific

By the 1940s Madison Square Garden had become a grand stage for battles between local stars like NYU's Dolph Schayes (4) and Midwestern hotshots like "Easy Ed" Macauley (behind Schayes) of Saint Louis University. (Naismith Basketball Hall of Fame photo)

Coast Conference championship in 1936) and a hot-shot gunner who had scored more points in 1936 than anyone in the country (416, 20.3 ppg) and was winning raves with a revolutionary new shooting style. Irish knew a natural at the ticket gate when he saw one and soon had Stanford booked for an Eastern tour that would include games at the Philadelphia Arena (promoted by Irish, of course) and in the Garden with Bee's Blackbirds. This time history as well as profits were sure to be made.

The December 1936 clash in Madison Square Garden between Stanford and LIU was truly a classic struggle. It was more than a game between two of the nation's best teams; it was also a clash for supremacy between regional coaching and playing styles. And more importantly it was a clash between an outgoing age (one of controlled patterned offense) and an incoming age (featuring wide-open "shoot-and-run" free-lance basketball).

Hank Luisetti and his one-handed style triumphed in the Garden with a surprisingly easy victory over Bee's men and in the process he established a new direction for the sport of basketball. One-handed offense would soon reign supreme and a new wrinkle called the jump shot was only the next bold experiment away. The game was passing from dominate coaches who choreographed every preconceived play to individual superstars who created as they went during the heat of the action. The first of these stars was destined to be the handsome and daring Stanford gunner who arrived from the West Coast at the invitation of Ned Irish. But the stage on which Luisetti was launched was destined to be the true birthplace of modern basketball. Luisetti's fortuitous stage was Ned Irish's New York City game and it was one which would be alive and well for decades to come.

3

The Forties, Part 1

Luisetti and the Birth of the Jump Shot

The true birth of college basketball as we today know it came in the late 1930s. And it came in the form of three revolutionary events, all clustered around the memorable career of a single athlete of true mythic dimensions, and each destined to transform the cage game almost beyond recognition.

First there was the birth of the modern superstar player who came onto the scene in the guise of Stanford's one-hand shooting wonder Hank Luisetti. Simultaneously there was the game's most significant of all rule changes, the two-part adjustment which first eliminated a mandatory center jump after each successful free throw (this was introduced at the beginning of Luisetti's junior season) and then did away with the jump ball after all baskets (just in time for Luisetti's senior year). And finally there was the discovery of a grand new stage on which the college game could finally become the crowd-pleasing spectacle it always seemed capable of being. This exciting new forum was the heavily promoted college basketball doubleheader (sometimes tripleheader) featuring attractive intersectional rivals and drawing huge overflow crowds to New York's Madison Square Garden. Of these new headline events which marked the middle years of the '30s, none provided more impetus for the game's popular explosion than the one featuring Luisetti and his Pacific Coast Conference champion Stanford Indians (now Cardinals) versus Clair Bee's 1936 Long Island University squad, itself the undisputed best of the East and owner of a then-record 43-game unbeaten streak.

But in a society already devoted to personality worship the largest headlines were inevitably saved for the first larger-than-life basketball matinee idol. As a strikingly handsome athlete with movie-star "good looks" and irrepressible individual style, Stanford University's Angelo "Hank" Luisetti owned the perfect combination of natural talent and exploitable image necessary to become the cage sport's first noteworthy national star. But Luisetti was blessed as much as anything with a gift of impeccable timing off the court as well as on. His career would coincide perfectly with the much-needed stage (Ned Irish's Garden doubleheaders) and a much-needed shift in playing conditions (elimination of the center jump) that would provide precise conditions prerequisite for pioneering national stardom. When America's sportswriters were polled at the end of World War II in a campaign to select the greatest player of basketball's first half-century their easy first choice was George Mikan and their inevitable second choice was Hank Luisetti. These were fitting selections, indeed, since it was Mikan who had shaped the modern game and Luisetti who had originally launched it.

The first of basketball's transforming events was thus the advent of the glamorous college superstar. Other American entertainment spectacles all boasted this same "personality" feature and they all thrived upon it to an equal degree. There was the endless supply of matinee idols (from Errol Flynn to Clark Gable) and pinup girls (Betty Grable was only the end of a long line) who offered box office appeal for the American cinema. Baseball had its share of glamorous photogenic heroes also — from Cobb to Walter Johnson, and from Babe Ruth to Lou Gehrig, Jimmy Foxx and Hank Greenberg. And to a lesser degree so did college football with its year-in and year-out supply of Saturday afternoon collegiate pigskin heroes — Illinois' Red Grange, Yale's Albie Booth, TCU's Sammy Baugh, Army's Doc Blanchard and Glenn Davis, and countless other touchdown slingers and broken-field runners between the two world wars.

Now it was at long last basketball's turn. And the perfect box office attraction for the cage sport fittingly turned up in precisely the most expected location. Like the glamorous stars of stage and screen, he too came riding out of America's genuine Dreamland — Gold Coast California — toting a special frontier flair and combining the perfect elements of superb athletic talent with a dashing dark-eyed profile and winning personal charm. So attractive was Luisetti as a matinee idol that

Hank Luisetti earned a place in college basketball history as the game's pioneering one-handed shooter; but he also earned immense popularity in his own era as basketball's first legitimate matinee idol folk hero. (Stanford University photo)

his basketball playing days were predictably followed with an unabashed effort at exploiting his magnetism upon the Hollywood silver screen. Shortly after graduation the ex-cager was featured (along with several of his Stanford teammates playing bit roles) in an ill-fated film about college hoop action entitled *Campus Confessions*. It was a glitzy production which costarred no less a fellow matinee idol than Grable herself and which was clearly conceived to capitalize on nothing more than Hank's considerable reputation and dazzling good looks.

Hank Luisetti was as immediate a bust in the movies as he was a prodigy on the basketball court. Yet his three-year cage career at Stanford was, by contrast, one of the game's true early milestone events. Luisetti is today remembered largely for giving basketball the one-handed shot. But in reality he brought the sport considerably more, especially in the way of front-page recognition.

His biggest role in the end was to provide the nation's poor-cousin sport with its first object of both idolization and imitation, the kind of figure through whom the glamour of the emerging game could now be widely hyped and promoted. On the heels of Stanford's first visit to Madison Square Garden the sensational West Coast cager would be profiled and celebrated with a New York City media campaign unlike anything Naismith's sport had ever known. There were feature spreads not just on the sports pages but also in *Colliers* and *The Saturday Evening Post* and there were even photos in news magazines and tabloids from coast to coast. Nine thousand fans crammed into every available seat in the Philadelphia Arena to see the new phenom play against Temple on the eve of his first New York appearance. Before the start of his memorable 50-point game against Duquesne on a neutral court in Cleveland an unruly mob of adoring fans even attempted to rip the jacket and pants from the body of their newly beloved hero.

But it was his impact on the playing style of the game itself that was most dramatic in the long run. Once Luisetti's success was witnessed by wide audiences of fans on the East Coast and experienced by large numbers of opponents and rival coaches in intersectional play it was only inevitable that there would be hordes of admirers and imitators. That the Stanford whiz would grab so many headlines with this style — and his team at the same time could capture victory after victory with the versatile offensive weapon it provided — was enough to guarantee wholesale counterfeiting. Thus Luisetti's shooting style and all-around skilled play became an immediate model for players and coaches almost everywhere. After Hank Luisetti, the game would forevermore be played much differently.

Luisetti's career at Stanford was nothing short of spectacular in an era when teams and not individuals usually grabbed the headlines during cage play. The Stanford star of course had not actually invented the one-handed shooting style. Such a method of launching shots is well-documented long before his arrival on the scene. Famed broadcaster and All-American Curt Gowdy would later report that it was used years before by himself and his teammates at Wyoming. Cage historian Neil Isaacs has also documented references to this type of shooting appearing in print nearly 30 years earlier (an early *Spalding Guide* labels it the "Mississippi Valley" style in 1906). It was a method Luisetti himself had picked up on San Francisco playgrounds (he later claimed it was the only way he could reach the hoop when he took up the game as a four-foot youngster) and then perfected under coach Tommy DeNike at Galileo High School near Fisherman's Wharf.

What was special, of course, was the success which young Luisetti found with the new method of scoring. It was a success that depended in large part on his own special athletic gifts. He was fast and agile and strong, and in high school had been attractive to recruiters because he flashed hard-nosed defense, clever dribbling and pinpoint passing skills. As a senior at Galileo (the same school that had already

Like Kurland and Mikan with their defensive intimidation, and Russell and Gola with their rebounding, Hank Luisetti with his early one-handed shooting style would establish the future direction of modern basketball. (Stanford University photo)

produced Joe DiMaggio and would later also give the world O.J. Simpson) he would score only 54 points all season long. But the showcase piece was already the one-hander he could launch either when stationary or on the dead run (or while dribbling). And there would soon be many fellow cagers more than willing to try this style out, especially when the East Coast players saw what this West Coast hotshot could do with his unorthodox weapons. New York coaches like Nat Holman and Howard Cann (NYU) first ridiculed and derided the unparalleled method. Then they begrudgingly adopted it once all their own players showed up using it with almost equal deadly effectiveness.

Luisetti and his Stanford team highlighted the distinct regional styles which contrasted basketball played along the Eastern Seaboard with that practiced out in the frontier West. It was run and gun versus weave and pass. It was also Luisetti's sharpshooting and Stanford's sudden winning that indeed for the very first time lifted Western schools onto an equal footing with those back East. Coach Johnny Bunn had himself come from Kansas where he trained as a player under Jim Naismith and Phog Allen. He had known relatively little success (five straight losing seasons) out

42

on the coast, however, until he inherited Luisetti from the freshman team in 1936. During a surprising All-American sophomore campaign Hank Luisetti would provide Bunn and Stanford with their first highly successful impact team.

It didn't hurt, of course, that they had other talented athletes to go with the new sharpshooter and that the team benefitted as well from Bunn's new ingenious defensive schemes. Art Stoefen filled the center lane, and Jack Calderwood and H.B. Lee played on the wings. The team raced to a 22-7 record and eventually won the Pacific Coast Conference title when it avenged an earlier double loss to Washington's Huskies with pressure-packed back-to-back victories in late February. Luisetti made his own mark with 416 points (better than 20 per game) during his first varsity season, including some big outbursts against Oregon (20 points from the inside post) and Southern Cal (a game-winning 24 during the last 11 minutes when his coach urged him to start shooting and stop passing). As their reputation spread, an East Coast tour was hastily planned by the Stanford Indians for December 1936. It was a tour, of course, that would soon turn college basketball on its ear.

The birth of Luisetti as a national star, as well as the emergence of the West Coast game as rival to Eastern-style play, all unfolded on a single memorable evening at New York's Madison Square Garden during that first trip East. Luisetti would here prove himself once and for all to a doubting sporting press and a nay-saying Eastern coaching establishment. Others had already come into the spotlight of Madison Square Garden from outlying regions and wilted, and many more would do so in the future. But not the unflappable Luisetti.

The Stanford team that came east at the beginning of Luisetti's junior season was a tall outfit averaging better than 6 feet 4 inches per man. Stoefen, at 6-6, still provided beef under the bucket and Calderwood teamed with Captain Dinty Moore in the backcourt while senior Howell Turner complemented Luisetti up front. Best of all, they were masters of Johnny Bunn's collapsing 3-2 zone defense. They warmed up by beating Atlantic Coast power Temple in Philadelphia on their way into New York (on a night when Luisetti drew a turn-away throng of 9,000 admirers and curiosity seekers). But the Madison Square Garden game was the one the promoters had most eagerly awaited. It would draw double the Philly crowd — nearly 18,000 — and the contest that transpired didn't disappoint a single sole among them.

LIU under Clair Bee had emerged over the past three seasons as the best New York had to offer. Bee's squad had gone unbeaten for almost three seasons and the lineup of Art Hillhouse, Irving Torgoff, Danny Kaplowitz, John Bromberg and Dolly King boasted the balance and potency of an all-star squad. Now they carried the banner of the Eastern Region with their stationary game of rugged inside power play and long-range deadeye set shooting. That game was built particularly around All-American Art Hillhouse, a giant who controlled rebounds as well as the endless strings of center jumps.

But Luisetti wowed the LIU starters from the opening whistle with his one-handers and thus wowed the partisan crowd as well. And he wowed them as much with his tough defense and stellar passing to open teammates as he did with the shooting which had earlier made his reputation. The Stanford star did unleash some of his patented running one-handers and these left Hillhouse and other Blackbird defenders amazed and outmatched. But he and his companions also wrapped up the Blackbirds with a sticky pressing defense which soon revealed itself to be a disguised man-to-man and not the zone which Bee's scouting reports had cautioned him to expect. Luisetti would score 15 on the night and the visiting Indians would end the Blackbirds' streak, 45-31. It was a solid offensive show by the West Coasters for such a low-scoring era. This game was played, recall, in the final season of the jump ball after each basket.

With his first New York visit Luisetti irreversibly established the direction of basketball's future. And that future took the form of the one-handed running shot. But of equal importance was the fact that the Stanford ace had also established the legitimacy of Western teams and of the more wide-open Western style of play. The pioneering steps (and shots) he had taken in Madison Square Garden would soon enough be followed by other Western teams and their hot-shooting stars out of places like Oregon, Oklahoma, Wyoming and Utah. It would all begin to happen once postseason tournaments became the year-end rage only a few short seasons later. But Hank Luisetti had already been there first.

The foremost attraction with Hank Luisetti, of course, was his prodigious scoring. That scoring may not seem like much today. But in the era before World War II it was still almost unthinkable that individuals would score as many as 20 points per contest on a regular basis. This was still a time when teams usually won games by tallying 30 or 40 and holding opponents to 10 or 20. Yet folk legends like Hank Luisetti somehow seem quite capable of even the unthinkable.

That become clear to the nation's sports fans on New Year's Day of 1938 when Stanford stopped off in Cleveland on the return trip from its second East Coast junket just long enough to take on a Duquesne team from down the road in Pittsburgh. Inspired by the wide-open game now available during the first year of center jump-free basketball, Stanford's players decided to see just what their hot-shooting but selfless teammate might accomplish if he were forced to limber up his shooting arm all the way. With teammates feeding him every time down the court and also returning each of his own passes, Luisetti was now forced to bomb away shamelessly. Reluctantly he poured in a remarkable total of 50 points before the evening was out. It was this outing more than any other that now demonstrated just what might happen in college action without a center jump to constantly slow up the offensive show.

Such scoring would continue throughout Luisetti's final two seasons as he posted 410 points (17.1 ppg) as a junior and 465 more (17.2) as a senior. At career's end he not surprisingly owned the national scoring record, although many of the earlier histories incorrectly credit him with 1,596 career points by adding on the 305 he tallied for an undefeated 1935 freshman squad. The three-year varsity total of 1,291 was in its own day impressive enough, however.

In both his final two seasons the West Coast shooting wizard was also the acknowledged national player of the year (later sanctioned by the retroactive Helms Foundation Award). And in a return trip to the Garden as a senior he and his team were again twice victorious, edging Nat Holman's powerhouse CCNY team 45-42 in a draining contest and two nights later again flattening Clair Bee and LIU, this

Bob Kurland of Oklahoma A&M was the most dominating "big-man" force for the 1940s alongside George Mikan. When it came to winning NCAA titles, however, Kurland and his Aggies would hold a clear advantage over Mikan and his DePaul Blue Demons. (Naismith Basketball Hall of Fame photo)

time by 14. When the pesky 6-3 Luisetti uncorked his one-handed bombs against CCNY the conservative Holman was aghast at such unorthodox play. He would, of course, sing a far different tune only a decade later when his own star, Irwin Dambrot, would be winning games with an almost identical one-handed push.

Stanford would unfortunately lose a possible claim on the mythical national championship, however, when the travel-weary Indians next lost by four in a re-match at the Philadelphia Convention Hall against the Temple Owls, a James Usilton-coached team that would capture the first National Invitation Tournament at year's end. But the greatest triumph of those final two seasons was perhaps the fact that Stanford twice more walked off with the Pacific Coast Conference title, an honor it had only once earned (back in 1920) before Hank Luisetti had arrived on campus.

For all the successes that surrounded Luisetti's three years at Stanford there were also elements of disappointment attached to his fairy-tale career. If he benefitted by good timing in one sense, he was at the same time equal victim of fated coinci-

This wartime college all-star team posing before the annual East-West match in Madison Square Garden features Bob Kurland (17) of 1944 and 1945 NCAA champion Oklahoma A&M, and Milo Komenich (7) and Earl Ray (15) of 1943 NCAA champ Utah. Bulky kneepads, seamless balls and playground-style sneakers all indicate a less well-equipped game from a far different era. (John Parker photo)

dence. For one thing, the college game's greatest showcase event — the postseason national tournament — would only be launched with NIT and NCAA matches during the first two seasons immediately after his own graduation. Luisetti had been just a shade too early for postseason excitement and had thus lost out on both sanctioned national titles and further year-end individual glory. And of course there were no existing pro leagues in which he could star for years to come and earn a comfortable living in the process. Like Bob Kurland a few seasons down the road he would be forced to turn instead to the AAU circuit, where he starred in the early war years for both the San Francisco Olympic Club and the same Phillips 66ers outfit for which Kurland would also soon be suiting up.

The next (and final) stop in the postcollege gypsy basketball life that Luisetti had now inherited would be the Navy's St. Mary's Pre-Flight team, on which he starred for two years after his wartime enlistment. It was here that his overall game perhaps reached its greatest heights and on several occasions he clearly outplayed another ex-Stanford great named Jim Pollard. (Pollard, fresh off the 1942 NCAA title-winning Stanford club, would in a few more seasons be building an NBA Hall of Fame career of his own alongside George Mikan with the Minneapolis Lakers.) Yet it was also during his Navy service in 1944 that Luisetti tragically contracted a case of spinal meningitis which left him in a coma for a week and soon spelled an unfortunate end to his brilliant competitive athletic career. There would miraculously be a full recovery from the affliction, but also a stern warning from doctors that he must now give up the tough competitive AAU and pro-style levels of competition. Only in his early 30s at decade's end, a healthy Luisetti might well have still popped in his running one-handers with one of the talent-hungry teams in the newly formed Basketball Association of America. And had fate only treated him a bit more kindly in the end, the legend might well have loomed even larger than it already did.

Luisetti's scoring outbursts were of course made possible by the single most important rule change in the history of an ever-evolving sport. This had been the elimination of a center jump after each and every basket scored. It was this rule change, in fact, that stood right alongside the birth of the basketball superstar as the second important basketball innovation of the 1930s. And Luisetti's scoring itself played no small part in triggering the change. Coaches and promoters could not fail to envision a far more entertaining spectacle certain to grab headlines and thus also fill arena seats.

The center jump rule adjustment indeed had a most far-reaching effect on the pace and thus the nature of basketball play. Even before Luisetti's incredible 50-point outburst in Cleveland little more than a month into the new season, St. John's and Illinois had already availed themselves of the streamlined game with a record-setting scoring performance of their own in the first Madison Square Garden doubleheader of the year. Illinois won that one 60-45 with some aid from a hot-handed guard named Lou Boudreau, the eventual baseball Hall of Famer. Such scoring had previously been ruled out by dead time alone (while players walked repeatedly back and forth between center jumps with the scoreboard clock eating up potential minutes of play); now the sport could leap forward from the slow-paced game of position envisioned by Naismith himself to the spontaneous action-packed freelance type of action we have come to expect (and relish) today.

Another immediate result of the successes of Irish's Madison Square Garden promotions and of the showcasing of regional stars like Luisetti would now constitute yet a fourth major development of the 1930s. This would be the elaborate postseason tournaments involving numerous teams from throughout the country and staged in big-city venues from New York to Chicago to St. Louis and San Francisco. Again the important pioneering figure would be one Ned Irish, a man who today stands as worthy candidate for the mythical title of "father of the modern game."

The appeal of such tournaments would not only be the revenue guaranteed by such an event. It would also be the chance to foster regional competition and thus finally move toward a reasonable method for crowning a true national collegiate champion. Previous to this time there had been mythical champions, of course, teams claiming national pre-eminence on the basis of hefty self-promotion and perhaps a key midseason triumph or two over established winners from other sides of the country (like Columbia's claim in 1905 after home-floor victories over touring Wisconsin and Minnesota, the acknowledged best clubs of the West; or the stronger claims of Phog Allen's rarely beaten Kansas squads in 1922 and 1923). But there had never been anything formal or precise about the process. Now a new opportunity and mechanism happily presented itself.

The first national tournament to come on the scene would be the aptly named National Invitation Tournament, an invention of Irish and his New York backers at the close of the '30s. Ned Irish had long dreamed of such an affair that might decide a national college champion. Now with the Metropolitan Basketball Writers Association acting as a formal sponsor for an event that Irish could promote as the "Rose Bowl of Basketball" the wily promoter again sprang into action. The grand event would be set up on an East-West basis: NYU, LIU, Temple and Bradley would play in an opening round, with Oklahoma A&M and Colorado drawing automatic byes into the semifinals.

The debut NIT got off to a rousing start at the end of the 1937-38 season. The largely entertaining spectacle opened on a high note when NYU and LIU squared off for the first time ever and Howard Cann's NYU team gained local bragging rights with a 39-37 squeaker. Ultimate bragging privileges eventually fell to the team out of Philadelphia, however, as Temple's Owls made easy work of Colorado and its football All-American Whizzer White in the one-sided finals, pulling away down the stretch in a 60-36 laugher.

The first year of the NIT was followed with another rousing affair to close out the decade. This time Clair Bee's Long Island University team would race to the title by holding off Chicago's Loyola College when Mike Sewitch, despite his broken arm, put a tight blanket over the Ramblers' 6-8 scoring star Mike Novak and held him without a single bucket during the 12-point LIU victory. Bee would call this his greatest win ever and it capped an undefeated season which also left the Blackbirds with a sterling nine-year ledger of 216-99 and a current winning streak that would play out to 34 games before ending against Southern Cal on Christmas Eve of 1939. In stringing together perhaps its finest winter ever under Clair Bee the LIU team had also survived a brawl in the year's final game against La Salle, an embarrassing and dangerous riot which left Johnny Bromberg's nose broken, Irv Torgoff's head severely gashed, and Sewitch's arm disabled and in a cast. LIU, however, could now boast of being the first collegiate team to win a national crown under the new postseason playoff format while also maintaining a season-long untainted record. And the title affair between LIU and Loyola was also the very first that matched two teams still toting unblemished ledgers.

The idea seemed to work quite well. So well in fact that it immediately began to occur to collegiate athletic administrators around the country that they should perhaps have their own show to collect on some of the postseason revenue-generating action. Why let all the promotion and thus all of the profits of the colleges' athletic labors fall to the hands of Irish and a small group of New York promoters who themselves — for all their assistance to the sport — nonetheless fell clearly outside the close-knit and self-serving college athletic community.

The answer was of course for the colleges to launch their own postseason competitions. Such an event would at first be primarily the brainchild of Ohio State coach and athletic director Harold Olsen. Once sufficient support for Olsen's concept could be garnered it was decided that such competitions should first be staged on neutral grounds, perhaps even on a college campus or smack in the middle of the heartland. Such a location would assure less expensive travel for the participants

Long Island University's Hank Beenders recovers a rebound in 1941 NIT semifinal action against Seton Hall. Seton Hall's brilliant playmaker Bob Davies (11) is at the far right. (Naismith Basketball Hall of Fame photo)

and also distinguish the event from the one already being staged by profit-minded newspaper promoters back in New York. And the format would best be one that would truly match east and west sectors to crown a mythical national champion of the college leagues.

Thus the NCAA initiated its own late-winter tourney in March of 1939. While staged on a smaller scale than the Madison Square Garden affair, it was itself something of a modest success when 6,000 turned out for the Western playoffs and 3,500 entered the Palestra for two nights of action in the East. This meant a net loss of only about $2,500 for the collective NCAA coffers. The first title matchup (drawing several thousand more to the campus field house of Northwestern University in Evanston, Illinois) would fittingly involve Olsen's own Ohio State Buckeyes. But the first winner would be the West Coast entrant from Oregon coached by the influential Howard Hobson. Oregon's well-schooled Ducks with their "Tall Timbers" lineup featuring 6-8 Slim Wintermute overcame Jimmy Hull and the Buckeyes 46-33.

The early NCAA event looked very little like today's 64-school extravaganza. The small number of entrants (only eight until the field doubled in 1951) played in regional venues to determine the teams that would come together on neutral ground for the championship. Throughout the coming decade both tournaments would grow and prosper as the sport itself grew and prospered. One key to the side-by-side success of the competing March carnivals was the fact that there was virtually no competition for teams to fill up the programs of both venues. Throughout the first dozen years of the two postseason events the same powerhouse teams were magnanimously shared by both tourneys simultaneously.

There was an immediate and indirect bonus spinoff of the two postseason tournaments as they evolved throughout the 1940s. This was the birth of the college "big man" as heir to Luisetti's late-30s role of collegiate basketball superstar. While there would be many of these overgrown hulks showing up on U.S. campuses throughout the seasons preceding and surrounding the world war, there were only two who approximated the legendary stature that Luisetti had once known. And in their own ways each had just as great an impact as the Stanford hotshot on further transforming Naismith's concepts of basketball almost beyond recognition.

The first leviathan star would be a towheaded center off the plains of Oklahoma named Bob Kurland — basketball's first imposing 7-footer. While Kurland and his Oklahoma A&M teammates enjoyed several fine seasons for coach Hank Iba out in the Missouri Valley Conference (despite the fact that official league play was suspended for two seasons during the war), it would be in the postseason and in Madison Square Garden tourney play that they would hone their national reputation. A&M (today Oklahoma State) would first explode on the national scene in the mid-40s with a series of heralded performances in Madison Square Garden tournament play which included a semifinals loss in the NIT to DePaul and George Mikan in 1944, a pair of NCAA titles in '45 and '46, and a convincing post-tournament rematch victory in 1945 over Mikan and DePaul to close out Kurland's junior season on the highest possible note.

Kurland, for his own part, was a rare physical specimen and talented all-around player who brought a new dimension to the evolving cage game. And that dimension for the first time pointed straight up and over the rim. In the days when shot blocking was still legal, the giant center would make his reputation as a defender, setting up near the hoop and swatting away enemy bullets almost at will. But he was soon a talented performer at the offensive end as well. Phog Allen would be quick to refer to this unique performer as a mere "glandular goon" destined to cheapen the game; but Kurland was an inspired athlete who worked endlessly to develop his motor skills and build up his leg speed and stamina. By the time he was a senior, and then later an incomparable AAU and Olympic performer, Kurland could handle himself around the basket with the same facility as the more agile players who stood deep in his shadow.

Today Bob Kurland remains the forgotten figure of basketball's early modern era. That his reputation is not far bigger falls of course to the fact that he did not choose to follow his college cage career with a tour in the barnstorming leagues that then constituted professional basketball. Instead he would perform for a decade largely behind the scenes with the AAU champion Phillips 66ers team (also simultaneously earning a handsome salary with the firm as a front office executive). And in 1948 and 1952 he would be the towering force who would dominate international Olympic play, earning his nation's gratitude but little in the way of front-page personal glory. Had he chosen differently, of course, Kurland might well have been the Mikan and even the Russell of the first decade in the emerging NBA.

Mikan, his 6-10 rival out of Chicago, would of course occupy that very role by choosing a far different path — one which led in postcollegiate days through the NBL and BAA into the infant NBA, and eventually to a Hall of Fame slot alongside Kurland in Springfield. But first Mikan would also have to construct his own campus legend, one which would in the end fall only slightly short of that of Kurland's. Mikan was also an awkward behemoth who would have to transform clumsiness into athletic prowess with years of tedious and painstaking practice under the tutelage of coach Ray Meyer at DePaul. So tangle-footed was the bespectacled Mikan when he first arrived on the DePaul campus (after failing a tryout at Notre Dame) that Coach Meyer had to prescribe an ingenious regimen of ballroom dancing and rope skipping for his huge reclamation project. The noble experiment would soon pay off handsomely, however, with three seasons of first-team All-American status and two years of leading the nation in scoring. (Although "official" NCAA scoring titles were not awarded until 1948, Mikan nonetheless paced the nation with a 23.3 average in 1945 and a 23.1 mark during his following senior campaign.)

Perhaps the most memorable single image of collegiate basketball at the height of the war years was the handful of titanic head-to-head collisions between Mikan and Kurland. The highlight came in the spring of 1945. That year Oklahoma A&M would finish the season with a No. 2 ranking in most of the "unofficial" nose counts; DePaul was generally ranked third. Iowa out of the Big Ten had also made plenty of news of its own with a consensus No. 1 ranking and with the appearance of Dick Culberson, the first African-American to play in the Big Ten Conference. But Iowa, still sensitive to wartime pressures, would decline an NCAA invitation, despite its 17-1 overall record. This left the door to national prominence open for both A&M with one giant center and DePaul with the other.

The men of Hank Iba would run unfettered through the NCAAs, edging local favorite NYU and an up-and-coming youngster named Dolph Schayes in the finals when Kurland banged home 22 and himself held Schayes to only six. DePaul in the meantime manhandled the competition in the NIT, drubbing West Virginia and Rhode Island and coasting against Bowling Green. Mikan would set a school record with 53 points in the semifinal against Rhode Island State.

Then came the much-heralded showdown during a postseason extra session known as the American Red Cross War Fund Benefit Game. Oklahoma A&M would come out on top in the third and final of these matchups that had been yet another promotional brainchild of Ned Irish and featured a showcase affair between NCAA and NIT winners. The Blue Demons led early but Mikan fouled out after only 14 minutes with his team still up 21-14. Kurland would hang on to pace the win and collect 14 points in Mikan's absence. But the scoring star in this one turned out to be Cecil Hankins with 20 points on a variety of corner set shots and running hooks. Hankins, ironically, had also been the leading pass-catcher on A&M's Cotton Bowl winner in Dallas a few months earlier.

51

The boys from Oklahoma would become the first repeat champions a year later when the NCAA staged its title tilt in New York City for the fourth straight season. This time the Aggies would win a close one from North Carolina by a 43-40 count with Kurland alone now dominating the scene. The 7-footer would be the only one of Hank Iba's players to score in double figures in any of the Aggies' three tourney games and he would in fact become the only player in history to log more than half of a championship team's total points throughout an entire postseason's play. The giant this time around laid in and hooked in 72 points in the three matches to record 51.8 percent of the A&M point total. So one-dimensional indeed was the Aggies' attack that during semifinals and finals action only three of Iba's men could score more than five points in either contest. It was not surprising, then, that it was again also Kurland who walked off with the NCAA MVP trophy.

But there were other glorious stories to be culled from the wartime basketball seasons that were to play out as backdrop to Kurland and Mikan. There were other great teams and other great stars and some of these were just as instrumental in changing the game's course and image as were the two giants who had so revolutionized defensive styles. The bulk of the glory would continue to be earned during the new phenomena of postseason play and would thus continue to stem from New York City. Thus while most of the powerhouse teams and star players were now coming out of the Midwest and Far West, nonetheless the ever more glamorous postseason venue of Madison Square Garden indeed made this the true era of "The City Game" in college basketball.

It would be the nation's oldest conference, the Big Ten, that would dominate the first decade of

Bob Kurland would elect an AAU career with the Phillips 66 Oilers over a full-time professional career in the BAA or NBL. But wherever he played, the 7-foot giant continued to dominate rivals with his goaltending techniques. (Naismith Basketball Hall of Fame photo)

postseason play, at least in the NCAA tournament, since the NIT would not witness a Big Ten finalist until its fourth decade of play. First there were teams from Ohio State (finalist in the inaugural tourney, with Oregon), Indiana (winner in 1940 over Kansas) and Wisconsin (1941 champ by beating Washington State) who together made a clean sweep of championship game visits during the opening three seasons of the March event. And the Big Ten was now providing great individual stars as well as memorable powerhouse teams — Andy Phillip and Bill Hapac at Illinois, John

Kotz and Gene Englund of Wisconsin, Northwestern's Max Morris and Otto Graham (the future football immortal), Indiana's Curly Armstrong, and Jimmy Hull who paced the 1939 Ohio State NCAA finalists. The conference grip on NCAA championships might have been greater still when another Big Ten powerhouse came out of the University of Illinois during the 1943 campaign. But the Illini "Whiz Kids" outfit, which had found no parallel on the hardwood in January and February, would disband by March when a call to arms sounded far sweeter than the lure of meaningless athletic play.

The Big Ten teams would have to share glory in the Midwest sector of the country, however. For the noblest of heartland traditions year-in and year-out during the 1940s did not reside with Big Ten standard bearers at all but rather with Adolph Rupp's dynamo outfits at the University of Kentucky. Rupp's greatest pride was a team known as "The Fabulous Five" and it was a five-man wrecking crew that would make a huge mark on both NIT and NCAA tournament play. In top-billed NIT action the Wildcats would win a 1946 title over a Rhode Island team led by tiny sharpshooter Ernie Calverley and pioneering the popular fast-breaking style of play more often associated with schools from beyond the Great Divide. A year later they would finish as disappointed runners-up to Utah even though Groza was back from the war and only two teams had been able to slow them all season. In 1948 and 1949 Rupp's Fabulous Five would take back-to-back national titles behind maturing stars Groza and Ralph Beard.

This would be a Kentucky team soon tainted by scandal. But in the late '40s the contingent that starred Groza and Beard and also featured overshadowed players like Barker, Jones, Barnstable, Line and Rollins — all good enough for "top dog" status on any other campus in the land — sat astride the college basketball world with little challenge from any quarter. The entire starting 1948 team would form half the Olympic squad that same year and bring home an easy gold medal from London. Groza, Beard, Barker, Jones and 1947 starter Joe Holland would also enter the pros as a unit — renamed the Indianapolis Olympians — and play several seasons in the spanking new NBA before past sins scuttled the careers of the two brightest stars.

The West had its own set of super teams that stretched beyond Hank Iba's Kurland-led Aggies at Oklahoma A&M. First came a collection of wild and woolly straight-shooting Cowboys out of Wyoming who had their own agile post player anticipating Mikan and Kurland and their own all-around dazzling offensive genius recalling Luisetti. It was a combination deadly enough to rule the land (at least the NCAA half of it) in one giddy midwar season. Then followed the rags-to-riches bunch off the Salt Lake City campus of the University of Utah. Wyoming would capture one NCAA title by dazzling Georgetown with Kenny Sailors' dribbling and shooting sideshow and Utah another by shocking Dartmouth with a lineup built around six freshmen and a sophomore.

The two Mountain States teams would also do further double-barreled damage to the reputation of Eastern standard bearers with back-to-back victories over St. John's in the two inaugural sessions of the special Red Cross Charity game: the Cowboys climbed over Joe Lapchick's Redmen 52-47 in overtime in '43 and the Utes had an even easier time of it with the repeat NIT champs a season later. It was those first two showcase games of the short-lived charity event as much as anything that dramatically boosted prestige of the upstart NCAA tourney as equal to the loftier NIT. (Iba and Oklahoma A&M of course made it a complete sweep for the NCAA teams a season later.) And it didn't hurt the surging reputation of Western-style cage play either that the Utes (their fabulous freshmen now matured into battle-scarred senior veterans) would also return as NIT winners a few years later in 1947.

Teams from west of the Mississippi like Wyoming and Utah could have their dramatic impact on East Coast audiences in part because after an inaugural session in Evanston and three sessions in Kansas City the NCAA would move its own championship match into Manhattan for the first time in 1943. Wyoming, in particular, would take full advantage of the new exposure by trucking to the center stage in Madison Square Garden with another colorful innovator in the Western mold of play. His name was Kenny Sailors and he brought collegiate basketball a new and spectacular variation on the running style of one-handed shooting that had been all the rage in the half-dozen seasons since Luisetti. In reality, Sailors' brand of shooting wasn't all that different from the one that Luisetti and others had already exhibited. The Cowboys themselves already owned a tradition of one-hand shooters that stretched back a decade to Les Witte who had piled up 1,000 points between 1931 and 1934 with his unorthodox running missiles. But the new Wyoming star had a special flair that involved springing above defenders and not just hooking or tossing while on the dead run.

Sailors' forte was a strange looking wrinkle in rapid shooting now known as the jump shot. The 5-11 junior speedster had taken Luisetti's innovation one step farther and launched his own missiles by leaping above his opponents at the moment of release, a maneuver all but impossible to defend. His legacy would soon be followed at the end of the decade by pro players like Joe Fulks and Paul Arizin in Philadelphia, Bob Pettit in Milwaukee and St. Louis, and George Yardley in Fort Wayne, and before the next 10 years were out the new style had made a virtual dinosaur of the stationary two-handed release that had ruled the game for nearly 50 years. Once perfected by players everywhere the jump shot would signal the true birth of the high-scoring age in which teams gunning at all angles actually began hitting as frequently as they missed, even from long-distance. While one-handed shooting brought the fast break, jump shooting would elevate a running game into an airborne one. It was the biggest leap yet (quite literally) toward the sport we know today.

Wyoming with Sailors thus made its own unique mark on the annals of postseason play. The Cowboys' year was 1942-43, an unsettled season which fell smack in the midst of the full-scale overseas war effort. Some schools cancelled schedules, others lost star players to enlistment, freshmen became eligible to compensate for reduced rosters, many colleges played games against service teams, industrial league clubs and even YMCA outfits, and of course the games didn't seem to hold quite as much meaning as in the past. It was against this background that coach Everett Shelton's Cowboys fashioned a 31-2 record that left them better than anyone in the land save perhaps a crack Illinois team that owned the Big Ten at 12-0 (17-1 overall, with a meaningless early-season loss to a Camp Grant Military club when Doug Mills chose to play a lineup of his reserves.) But the Illinois "Whiz Kids" passed on

With a 17-1 record the "Whiz Kids" of Illinois may have been the nation's best outfit in 1943, yet they chose to bypass the wartime NCAA Tournament to enlist in the armed services. From left are Coach Doug Mills, Art Mathisen, Jack Smiley, Gene Vance, Ken Menke and future NBA star Andy Phillip. (University of Illinois photo)

postseason competition when the team broke up on March 1 and its stellar lineup of Andy Phillip, Ken Menke, Art Mathisen, Jack Smiley and Gene Vance jointly enlisted in the war effort. This left Wyoming a clear path in the NCAAs which was exploited fully with a gutsy opening-round victory over Oklahoma (53-50), an equally narrow semifinal triumph against Texas (58-54) and the championship duel versus a surprise Georgetown team featuring a 6-8 center named John Mahnken as its biggest offensive threat.

Milo Komenich, one of the best big men in the country and a native of Gary, Indiana, had actually paced the Wyoming team in scoring in the 30 regular season games with a 16.7 average, assisted ably by Sailors who hit his sensational jumpers often enough to average an even 15. In the semifinal match with Texas Komenich carried the scoring load but forward Jim Weir keyed a late rally that overcame a 29-point performance from Longhorns forward John Hargis. When Mahnken neutralized Komenich in the finals it was Sailors who flashed his unparalleled ability to control a game down the stretch. The Cowboys scored the final nine points, Sailors was the game's only double-figure scorer with 16 and the jump-shooting specialist would also be the tourney's unanimous MVP.

Utah would also have a glorious four-year run in postseason play which would begin when the Utes followed Wyoming to the NCAA mountaintop with a freshman-studded lineup in 1944. The string would continue with a second short-lived NCAA visit in 1945 (as first-round losers to eventual champion Oklahoma A&M) and end with an NIT title, earned in 1947 when the same Cinderella crew finally played its swan song season as seniors.

Actually, the Utah entry in the 1944 NCAA Tourney was a bit of raw luck in the first place. The Utes were entered only after a terrible auto accident had wiped out the heart of the Southwestern Conference entry from Arkansas, crippling two of the team's starters and forcing a tragic withdrawal from postseason play. Coach Vadal Peterson's team which reigned as champion of the now defunct Mountain States Conference (also Wyoming's nesting place) had first nixed a bid to play in the NCAA Western Regional in favor of a trip to the Big Apple for NIT competition; but after a disappointing opening night loss to Kentucky and a second invite in the wake of the Arkansas tragedy the Utes were finally back on the path that fate had carefully selected for them.

It was quickly enough apparent that Peterson's team was indeed a worthy postseason entrant despite the 46-38 bashing by Rupp's superior Wildcats. Like conference rival Wyoming a winter earlier they were a consensus choice as the best team out of the West though "official" wire service rankings were still five seasons away. And they were also a title-bound team that featured four freshmen in the starting lineup — something that would not again occur until Michigan's much-heralded "Fab Five" showed up in the NCAA championship game nearly a half-century later. They would also be the last club to get into the NCAA title round with a freshman as leading scorer (Arnie Ferrin), again until Michigan turned the trick with Jalen Rose as its leading marksman in 1992.

The finals of the 1944 NCAA Tourney would come down to Utah and East Coast powerhouse Dartmouth after the Utes ruled the West with a 40-31 cakewalk against Iowa State, and Dartmouth trimmed Big Ten entrant Ohio State by a nearly identical margin (60-53). The game in Madison Square Garden would turn out as one of the most dramatic to date and would go all the way to the wire, with the teams trading baskets down the home stretch and the crowd of 14,990 in a near frenzy. Arnie Ferrin carried the day when he scored 22, more than half of Utah's winning total. Ferrin was clearly the star player of the final contest and also of the tourney as a whole. But freshman Wat Misaka also contributed mightily with harassing defensive play. And another frosh, Herb Wilkinson, salted away the 42-40 overtime victory with a long, arching one-handed bucket from behind the key with but three seconds remaining on the clock.

Before the Cinderella youngsters boarded a train loaded down with trophies for the long trek home there would be one final victory to cap a phenomenal season for a bunch of crowd-pleasing 18-year-olds. In the last game of the long campaign, Peterson's overachieving club would also gain a small measure of revenge in the wake the team's NIT failure a week earlier. This came when Utah squared off with St. John's in the annual Red Cross Fund Raiser before better than 18,000 Garden patrons and trimmed the NIT victors as well, 43-36.

If Dartmouth failed in its bid for East Coast supremacy it was happily not the only club from this long dormant region to challenge the big boys from the Western and Midwest strongholds, although the full rebound of Atlantic Region basketball would not come until the next decade (first with Cinderella CCNY and later La Salle and other Philadelphia teams like Temple in 1956-58 and St. Joseph's in 1961). There was yet another New England team that also carried the East Coast banner immediately after the war. That team reared up overnight off the Massachusetts campus of Holy Cross College in 1946-47, and even though it didn't own a campus gym in which to play its own home games, Holy Cross did nonetheless feature a tandem of hot shooters and sharp ball handlers that were the toast of the first post-war winter. It was also a group of athletes good enough to bring prominence back to a region that had not ranked very high in basketball matters since Naismith himself had left the area at the turn of the century.

The first of these Holy Cross "whiz kids" was a spunky New Yorker named George Kaftan, a 6-3 sophomore forward (and sometimes center) with an extraordinary ability to leap far above the rim. The second was a dazzling, if scrawny, freshman, also out of New York and named Bob Cousy, who already displayed a special talent for passing and dribbling that must have seemed like little more than raw showboating to arch-conservative coaches of the day. Also on the Crusaders' roster was a 6-foot guard, a returning service veteran named Joe Mullaney, who would later establish considerable coaching credentials of his

All-Star Team for the Era (1938-1949)			
	Pos.	Pts. (Ppg)	Best Year
Hank Luisetti (Stanford)	F	1291 (16.1)	20.3 (So.)
Bob Kurland (Oklahoma A&M)	C	1669 (14.1)	19.5 (Sr.)
George Mikan (DePaul)	C	1870 (19.1)	23.3 (Jr.)
Alex Groza (Kentucky)	C	1744 (14.5)	20.5 (Sr.)
Bob Davies (Seton Hall)	G	661 (11.2)	11.8 (Sr.)

Honorable Mention: Bob Cousy (G, Holy Cross), Arnie Ferrin (G, Utah), Ralph Beard (G, Kentucky), Wah Wah Jones (F, Kentucky), Vince Boryla (F, Denver), Ed Macauley (F-C, St. Louis), Gerry Tucker (C, Oklahoma), George Kaftan (F, Holy Cross)
Coach of the Era: Adolph Rupp (Kentucky), NCAA Champion (1948, 1949), NIT Champion (1946)

own at neighboring Providence College. Together they led Doggie Julian's crew to an NCAA title, the first ever won by a school out of the Northeast and also the first ever captured by a non-conference team.

Holy Cross would tangle in the March title game with another postseason new-comer, Oklahoma's Big Six Conference champion Sooners, a 24-7 team under coach Bruce Drake that now provided the unlikely state of Oklahoma with its third straight trip into the NCAA finals. Kaftan and forward Dermie O'Connell would be the offensive stars for the Crusaders in the year's biggest match, racking up 18 and 16 points, respectively. The final would stand 58-47 in favor of Holy Cross, thanks mainly to a distinct edge in both speed and depth for the New Englanders. But it would be a title match that was destined to become legend, if only for a reported encounter between Kaftan and Oklahoma star Gerry Tucker just before the opening tip. Tucker was a 26-year-old returning service veteran who had led the Sooners all season at the center post; Kaftan was the 19-year-old "wonder boy" who had already done some impressive scoring in earlier tourney rounds. "So you're the young hotshot who scored 30 the other night," taunted Tucker as the teams lined up at center court. "Hang in there, Gerry," quipped the unfazed Kaftan, "they say it's a young man's game." Tucker would indeed hang in there and score 22 points before the final buzzer. But it was Kaftan who was soon sticking his finger into a championship ring.

Freshman Cousy would play only a minor role in the championship game, though he was already the team's third-leading scorer (7.6 ppg) throughout 27 regular-season contests. Relegated to a reserve's role in the postseason, "Cooz" would bag only 10 points for the entire three outings and go without a basket altogether in the championship match. But Cousy would have three brilliant collegiate seasons still stretching out before him (though he would never again get his team out of the second round of postseason play). And during that time he would evolve the magician-like passing and ballhandling skills (most especially a crowd-pleasing behind-the-back "blind" pass) that would make him an NBA legend during the next decade-and-a-half in Boston.

Not only was the NCAA Tourney gaining a full head of steam by the late 1940s. But also in the immediate post-war years the NIT was itself reaching a zenith of popularity and also of competitive balance. The argument might even be made that the 1948 NIT was the most competitive ever staged. Although there was no single accepted national ranking system at the time, nonetheless what appeared to be five of the nation's top seven or so teams (including Kentucky, Saint Louis, Western Kentucky and North Carolina State) would face off in the NIT that year. Future pro star Ed Macauley, an agile pivot player who shot like a forward and moved like a guard, would lead Saint Louis University to the 65-52 championship victory over local favorite NYU, winners of 19 straight entering the trophy game. A key was the 6-8 junior's handy victory in his personal matchup with another future NBA legend, NYU's stellar Dolph Schayes (Macauley easily outpointed Schayes 24 to 8). Macauley would later return to the city of St. Louis during his substantial pro career after being traded back there by the Boston Celtics in the very deal that brought Bill Russell to Auerbach's team. But the encore would never quite match the opening act since as a collegian it was "Easy Ed" Macauley who had already given the Missouri city its one shining moment in the collegiate basketball spotlight.

By the late 1940s, in the wake of the world war, basketball like everything else in America — certainly anything that smelled of fun and spectacle — was truly a boom industry. And the nationwide rush for new entertainment of almost any stimulating form now launched basketball straight into the main spectator arena alongside baseball and football. So strong, in fact, was the desire for expanded hoop play that even the often-failed experiment in professional basketball was once again ambitiously launched. This time even barnstorming professional action seemed to catch on with the entertainment-starved audiences. The National Basketball League (already operating for more than a decade as a rarely noticed industrial league circuit) began to thrive in the Midwest, especially after landing George Mikan from DePaul and Bob Davies from Seton Hall. And a new venture called the Basketball Association of America boldly moved into college basketball's own backyard in both Madison Square Garden and Boston Garden, and also in other large Eastern arenas (Washington, Philadelphia, Providence, Baltimore, Detroit, Cleveland, Pittsburgh).

But the college sport was still undisputed king. The game played during winter nights on the nation's campuses and in its big-city arenas was more popular than ever before. The past decade had seen the first wave of true stars in the persons of Luisetti, Mikan, Kurland, Davies, Sailors and others. Both postseason collegiate tournaments were now healthy adolescents and were also cooperatively sharing an ever-expanding wealth of both talented teams and enthusiastic fans. The future could not have seemed much brighter. But there were indeed huge storm clouds now also gathering along the horizon.

4

The Forties, Part 2

The Scandal and Its Aftermath

"I'm bringing in all these people and playing my heart out for them," the boys must have said to themselves. "Clair Bee is getting all the credit and Ned Irish and the college are getting all the gravy. Where do I come in?"

— Clair Bee, LIU Coach

Nowhere in the annals of college basketball — or American sports history at large — are there two glamorous Cinderella stories to compare with those surrounding Nat Holman's 1950 City College (New York) team or the 1948 powerhouse painstakingly built and then deftly guided by Baron Adolph Rupp down in Kentucky. In the post-war limelight of basketball's greatest "boom era" these were the true glory squads that fired a nation's imagination and launched a new era of invincible dynasty teams. And yet at the same time there are nowhere to be found two more tragic tales of scandal, deception and woeful self-destruction. Overnight the nation would discover that the two powerhouse basketball programs most responsible for explosive popularity in the cage sport were also the two that seemingly had rung out its death knell. In the end both these Cinderellas would be far better known for their pumpkin carriages than their storied glass slippers.

Rupp's Kentucky team by early 1949 seemed on the verge of owning the sport's post-war boom era. They first won the prestigious NIT affair in 1946 and then also posted the second-ever back-to-back NCAA sweep with 1948 and 1949 March titles. Rupp's 1948 starting unit was justifiably labelled the "Fabulous Five" and was widely acknowledged, then and for years to come, as the most talented quintet ever to suit up for a single season or more. Olympic glories followed next for this crack lineup of Alex Groza, Ralph Beard, Wallace Jones, Cliff Barker and Kenny Rollins when the Bluegrass five teamed with starters from the AAU champion Phillips Oilers (including Bob Kurland) to claim an automatic gold medal victory in London.

But there had also been a small handful of unaccountable upsets along the way and it was these rare stumbles more than all the victories that were destined to become the most gripping plot lines in the saga of Kentucky's greatest team ever. Surprise losses to St. Louis (twice — in 1949 and again with the 1951 team starring Bill Spivey) during the Christmas Week Sugar Bowl Tourney, and to unheralded Loyola-Chicago during the year-end NIT, found their shocking explanation when dramatic news broke in the early '50s that this Kentucky team had actually been so

59

The Baron and his Fabulous Five team of 1948. Front row, from left, Ralph Beard, Coach Adolph Rupp and Ken Rollins; back row, Wah Wah Jones, Alex Groza and Cliff Barker. (University of Kentucky photo)

talented that it (or at least a few of its brightest stars) had even controlled and manipulated the results of its games. Groza and company (and apparently Spivey and company as well) were so good they even tinkered with the precise margins by which they humiliated their hapless opponents.

But if Kentucky won relentlessly in 1948 and 1949 (and during the several seasons after that also) they had indeed always been just about the very best the Southland had to offer. Nat Holman's CCNY ballclub of 1949-50 thus provided an even more popular version of the true Cinderella, and one also found smack in the backyard of the sport's most thriving existing venue of New York City. Holman's Beavers had been big losers only a few seasons earlier, during the height of the war years (6-11 in 1944 and 12-14 in 1945). And they had not seemed all that exceptional in regular-season play even during what would eventually turn out as their most miraculous season of 1950. Down the stretch run of the current campaign they had surprisingly lost in close succession to rather average teams from Canisius, Niagara and also Syracuse.

Then during tournament action the boys coached by one of the city's most experienced and masterful tacticians seemed to catch fire and also catch everyone else napping. Holman, who had already posted a 359-127 lifetime mark, had early on predicted this new group of sophomores (Ed Roman, Ed Warner, Floyd Lane and Al Roth) would be his best group ever, and by March they were indeed overnight miraculously transformed into hardwood giants.

The season's final weeks belonged entirely to CCNY as the disciplined Beavers gunned down the nation's best challengers to achieve what had never been accomplished before and has never been duplicated since. The CCNY squad behind Roman (16.4 ppg) and Warner (14.8) would shock the nation's basketball observers by sweeping to easy victories in both the NIT and NCAAs and in the process would become the college sport's only double national champion ever. Such inconsistent performance — midseason slumping and late-season invincibility — from one of the greatest single-year teams in cage history was certainly beyond easy comprehension at the time.

But it was not long before the rather sordid explanation emerged for all to see. CCNY, it turned out, was not such an average ballclub after all, as at times it had appeared before postseason tournament time rolled around. Rather it was a team which harbored a handful of skilled athletes who were conspiring with gamblers to control fine details of their own game results. The Beavers starters had evidently dumped a number of regular-season contests and had "shaved points" in others to tip the betting odds in favor of those in the know. (The popular practice of the day was to wager on the point spread rather than the mere winners and losers of contests.) The favorite sport of millions had now received a huge black eye and it was a black eye from which, in the short run at least, it almost never recovered.

Rupp's post-war Kentucky team had been put together with a series of most fortunate breaks. It was as though world events were conspiring to give Rupp a huge assist that most of his rivals were sure he never needed. Cliff Barker was freed from a German prisoner-of-war camp by the actions of General Patton's European Army in time to return to campus in 1946 as the 27-year old veteran of the squad. During his confinement behind German lines Barker had actually improved his athletic skills with long hours of ballhandling drills using a volleyball, sufficient practice to turn him into Rupp's eventual "Super Magician" and "Basketball Banshee" in the frontcourt. Wallace Jones and Ralph Beard at the same time received benefit of a special ruling which allowed them four years of varsity competition, keeping the crack unit together long enough to enjoy Barker's and Groza's return from service. And Groza himself was nurtured and developed as an athlete during a service stint which transformed him from a skinny 1945 freshman into a rock-solid pivotman four seasons later.

The biggest of Rupp's breaks, however, would be the somewhat accidental recruitment of Alex Groza who had never intended to play for Rupp in the first place. The Martins Ferry, Ohio, youngster had long dreamed of following his football-playing brother (Lou Groza, the Cleveland Browns Hall of Famer) to Ohio State but had been spurned by the Buckeyes as a less-than-promising prospect. Harold Olsen's loss in Columbus was of course quickly to turn into one of Rupp's biggest victories in Lexington.

And another stroke of pure fortune would be the discovery of Wallace Jones from Harlan, Kentucky. Jones arrived on campus for the beginning of the 1946 season, along with Ralph Beard from Louisville and Joe Holland from Benton, and it was Jones who first emerged as a star among the fabled five. Already a Kentucky schoolboy legend who had taken his small-town Cinderella school to four state tournaments and established a national scholastic scoring record (2,398 points), Jones had hoped to play at Tennessee. But at the last minute his former high school sweetheart and future wife, already a student at Lexington, insisted that Wallace enroll at Kentucky as well. It seemed at the time that everyone was conspiring to help Rupp's dynasty-building efforts.

In 1946 — with freshmen Jones and Beard teaming up with juniors Jack Parkinson and Jack Tingle, and senior Wilbur Schu — the 28-2 Wildcats finally emerged as a first-rate national power. Earlier Kentucky teams had dominated their own region but sometimes struggled on their forays into other sections — especially the mecca of Madison Square Garden. Now the Wildcats would begin manhandling teams from New York or Philadelphia or the Midwest the same way they beat up on squads from Nashville or Knoxville. In their second-ever visit to the NIT the Ruppmen walked over Arizona and survived against West Virginia, the latter victory at 59-51 coming when the Cats scored eight straight in the final two minutes to break open a game that had been tied 14 times down the stretch. A victory over Rhode Island State for the tournament title, secured by Beard's game-ending free throws, was enough to put the Wildcats firmly on the national map. The next season the Kentucky club would also be back in the Madison Square Garden postseason event, this time as a defending champion and not a Southern interloper. This time, however, Kentucky would fall to Utah in the finals by four points, despite a lineup that now had Groza, Rollins and Holland alongside Beard, Jones and Barker. But it was only a temporary lull before the storm.

Two measures of the intensity of Kentucky basketball in the post-war years are the mere numbers who turned out both to play and to watch. So deep was the talent pool reporting to Rupp in the fall of 1946 — the first season after the NIT championship and the year Groza returned — that team candidates arriving for fall practice at Alumni Gym were divided into two squads, 19 players on the "A Team" and 23 more with the "B Team" roster; the squad included four returning All-Americans — Beard, Jordan, Parkinson and Brannum, and three of these were guards. And basketball fever combined with increased campus enrollments after the war to make the competition every bit as difficult for a fan hoping to see a game as it was for athletes hoping to make the team. Of the 12 home games only students were admitted into 11 (a far cry from today's collegiate audiences on most campuses which consist mainly of alumni and boosters who make large payments to scholarship funds to guarantee available seats). The 12th game was reserved for faculty and staff members only. There were no tickets for alumni or the general public and each student buying tickets was allowed a maximum of five games.

The zenith in Bluegrass fortunes came with the 1948 and 1949 campaigns. In those two seasons the Fabulous Five team (with Dale Barnstable replacing Ken Rollins the second year) rolled up records of 36-3 (1948) and 32-2 (1949). The only regular-season losses in the stretch were to Temple (1948), Notre Dame (1948) and St. Louis (1949 Sugar Bowl Tournament), and the postseason losses came in the 1948 year-end Olympic Trials (to Bob Kurland and the AAU Phillips Oilers) and the 1949 NIT (Loyola). Baylor would be crushed 77-59 in the Finals of the 1948 NCAA tourney at Madison Square Garden with hardly a sweat being broken. A year later the Rupp team would make in two in a row by rolling over Oklahoma A&M 46-36 out in Seattle. Not only had the Wildcats handily defeated the latest talented Hank Iba squad but they had now also equalled A&M's unique feat of back-to-back NCAA titles.

The four-year run at the peak of Rupp's career would also bring the Kentucky program an even more special distinction. It had now accomplished a feat that would never again be duplicated. First there had been consecutive trips to the NIT Finals in '46 and '47. This was followed directly with two visits to the NCAA final game. Only twice again would a school combine even a single visit to the NCAA championship finale with an adjacent trip to the NIT title match. First Dayton would be NCAA runner-up to UCLA in 1967 and NIT champ the following spring. Then Kentucky itself (under Rupp's successor Joe Hall) would again turn the trick with a runner-up slot behind the same Bruins in the 1975 NCAA, followed by an NIT title victory against UNC-Charlotte a year later.

But for all the glorious triumphs of the Fabulous Five in the four seasons immediately after the war, still Kentucky would fall somewhat short of expectations — theirs as well as just about everybody else's. In the end, Rupp's dream of tandem victories in the two postseason tournaments had proven a near-miss failure. This was one of the only setbacks that Rupp had so far received — along with the narrow championship licking at the hands of Utah in the 1947 NIT when the Baron's whirlwind attack was finally stalled by the Utes' deliberate offensive style. By the end of the decade Rupp's Fab Five was lost to graduation and he would seemingly have to take his lumps for a year or two. Those lumps would begin, of course, when Holman's surprising Beavers ran his Wildcats into the ground with an 89-50 pasting in the NCAA quarterfinals a mere year later. What would make that particular lopsided defeat an even more bitter pill than it might otherwise have been was, of course, the fact that CCNY was now itself well along the road toward accomplishing precisely what Rupp had coveted and then lost.

The Holman-coached team that rose so quickly to national prominence in March 1950 claimed a starting five displaying immense individual talents — a surprising set of events for a public school offering free tuition and open admissions and committed to academics far more than athletics. In his three decades at CCNY (the first 14 of which he also moonlighted as a pro player) Holman had amassed an impressive 359-127 record even though he rarely attracted top athletes. This sophomore-laced squad with which he launched the new decade, however, was talented enough and spirited enough to generate a special enthusiasm among Manhattan's legions of rooters. Several of the city's schools used Madison Square Garden as a regular or part-time home base, but as the city's "free" school CCNY enjoyed especially wide fan support. Floyd Layne would later recall that his team was to Manhattan and the Bronx what the baseball Dodgers were to Brooklyn. The popular cheer and battle cry of "allagaroo, allagaroo" (reportedly a distortion of the French *allez guerre* — "on to war") which rang out from City College boosters at every home game would thus eventually captivate the entire city throughout the first two winters of the '50s.

Holman had taken his lumps at CCNY in the late '30s and early '40s largely because he had refused to change with the times. His teams were still playing the old-style basketball he had mastered in his own playing days with the famed Original Celtics. He continued to run an offensive scheme known as the "Holman Wheel" and featuring four men weaving around the stationary post. But in an era that had adopted jump shooting and wide open run-and-gun offenses Holman's teams were usually outmanned and outsized, and the strategy simply didn't work like it once had. While CCNY had rarely been a loser in the '30s, now there would be a rare streak of three losing seasons at the height of the war years (1943-1945) and a slip from the city's top rung.

Without bigger and more agile players like those his rivals were now landing, Holman's teams still specialized in the long-range set shot; the clever, small ball handler; short crisp passing; and fancy dribbling to eat up the clock. It had become clear, however, that the game was now passing them by in this era of behemoths like Bob Kurland out on the Plains, Mikan in the Midwest, and even the tall, agile jump shooters now appearing right in their own backyard at LIU, Manhattan, St. John's, Seton Hall and elsewhere around the Northeast Corridor.

But by the end of the '40s Holman had finally been forced to change his strategy. And by the 1949-50 campaign he suddenly had the horses to provide something of a revival in fortunes. Personnel was no longer lacking and Holman was flexible enough, at long last, to take advantage. The only senior in the 1950 starting lineup would be 6-4 forward Irwin Dambrot who served as captain, provided rebounding strength and shown brightest on defense. A second important senior was top reserve Norm Mager who provided a lift with his exceptional outside shooting. Floyd Layne was the most talented among an exceptional bunch of sophomores and as an athletic shooting and rebounding guard seemed a perfect prototype for the modern pro-style player. Ed Roman at 6-6 was the agile center, anchor of the offense and the tallest player Holman had ever coached. Ed Warner (6-4 forward) could also play in the pivot and was eventually moved there; he was two inches shorter than Roman but nonetheless a natural pivot player who owned a great array of unguardable feints and fakes. "Fats" Roth was another tall guard at 6-3 who ran the offense with confidence. With this group Holman was able to construct the kind of fast-breaking attack that had over the past decade already proved so effective for a host of other similarly gifted teams.

At first he thought his sophomores were a year or more away from an impact statement. But Holman's young team breezed in the early going, winning 13 of 15 and climbing into the Associated Press weekly rankings, reaching as high as seventh. Then in late season they slumped with the three losses to upstate rivals and some less than spectacular wins over Manhattan (two points) and rival NYU (three points in the season's finale). By year's end a tourney berth in either postseason affair was not at all a sure matter. But the NIT was strapped for quality teams and leaned toward selecting a local entrant for the obvious gate support that it could bring. And Holman's team perhaps got the nod in the end only because it had the best record (17-5) among the city's half-dozen candidates to carry the local banner.

The Madison Square Garden gathering staged by the NIT at the end of the 1950 season was perhaps simultaneously both the high and low points for the pioneering year-end playoff which for its first dozen years remained truly the marquee postsea-

Ed Warner (4) was one of several stars of the 1950 Cinderella CCNY championship team whose careers would crash and burn with the revelations of the 1951 college betting scandal. (Naismith Basketball Hall of Fame photo)

son event. Certainly the field put together was arguably the strongest of NIT history. Forddy Anderson's Bradley club was a three-time loser that had sat atop the AP poll almost all season; Kentucky (third) and Duquesne (sixth) were also Top Ten clubs and three other entrants (Western Kentucky, La Salle and Arizona) had all won 20. San Francisco owned 19 victories and was the defending champion. Yet despite the stacked field and the series of dramatic games that were soon to follow, the results in the end would throw a shadow across the NIT from which it never quite recovered. Cinderella's moment at the dance was about to be followed by the inevitable pumpkin transformation.

Handed the break of a perhaps undeserved selection, Holman's team now came to life and ran over San Francisco and Kentucky with surprising ease. San Francisco, in Pete Newell's fourth and final season at the helm, was simply no match for

Former Duquense University star Chuck Cooper made basketball history in 1950 when the Boston Celtics tabbed him as the first African-American drafted by an NBA team. (Duquense University photo)

the Beavers in the opening round and crumbled 65-46; Holman had made the necessary adjustments to overcome the same kind of screening tactics that Oklahoma had used to beat him earlier in the year. Rupp's team was perhaps still stewing over a snub from the NCAA selection committee; but whatever the distraction, it was enough to open the door on another blowout. The whipping administered against the Wildcats (89-50) was the worst of Rupp's proud career and not one he took very lightly. It may indeed have been the Baron's most embarrassing moment in four decades of coaching. In the semis Duquesne would offer a much sterner test (62-52) as Chuck Cooper almost carried the day for Dudey Moore's Dukes with his clutch second-half shooting. (A few months down the road the 6-5 Cooper would become the first black player ever drafted by the NBA.) While CCNY was cutting a fairly easy path to the finals, Bradley (one of the four teams with first-round byes) was having it equally soft with comfortable victories over Syracuse (78-66) and St. John's (83-72).

The matchup in the finals would thus be against No. 1 Bradley with sensational 1950 All-American Paul Unruh (a 6-4 forward) and budding 1951 All-American Gene Melchiorre (a 5-8 guard). It was not an easy match — Bradley could also boast rugged 6-7 center Elmer Behnke — but the Beavers prevailed in the end by a margin of victory that was far closer than the score of 69-61 might reveal. CCNY dug itself a huge hole early with poor foul shooting (17-for-28 for the game); excellent overall floor play, especially from Dambrot and Roth, would rescue the Beavers in the later stages, however. Dambrot (with 23), Warner (16) and Roman (19) would carry the scoring load after intermission and Holman's big three were quite enough by themselves to outpoint the entire impressive Bradley roster (which got only 15 apiece from Unruh and Behnke).

The final stages of the hotly contested game would hinge on a memorable historical anachronism which proved a surprising boon for CCNY and a deadly bane for Bradley. A short-lived 38-plus-2 rule which provided jump balls after all free throws in the final two minutes offered Bradley a chance to catch up in the closing moments. But on seven occasions during those final two minutes of play the 6-3 Ed Warner would outjump 6-7 Behnke for crucial possessions and thus the margin of victory remained at eight by the final buzzer.

The last-minute invite to the NIT was now followed by a similar last-minute call to the NCAAs, which would also be staging its Eastern District play and its title matchup in New York's famed Garden. NCAA selection bigwigs had experienced difficulty deciding between City College, Duquesne and St. John's for an Eastern District invite and had ultimately settled on awaiting the outcome of the NIT — the team among these three which survived longest would also get the NCAA nod. Thus when the Beavers had outlasted Chuck Cooper and Duquesne in the NIT semis they had also earned the right to take on the NCAA field.

Bradley, on the strength of its own NIT performance and yearlong rankings, was a more automatic choice. And as fate would have it, the two NIT finalists were soon on a direct collision course toward an "instant-replay" rematch. These were the fifth and sixth teams to have competed in both the NCAAs and NIT in the same year. Kentucky had won one playoff series the previous year but stumbled in the other. Utah had similarly been one-for-two in 1944, as had Colorado in 1940. Duquesne (1940) had also logged such a back-to-back performance, losing in both the East Regional NCAA title game and the NIT final.

But first the New York contingent would have to get by a talented North Carolina State club coached by Everett Case in the regional finals which also served as tournament semifinals. State had been a surprise selection over Kentucky to represent the region (there were still only eight teams in the entire tournament back in 1950). Floyd Lane drew the assignment of covering ACC scoring ace Sam Ranzino (who nonetheless canned a game-high 24) while Ed Roman (with 21) provided most of the CCNY offense at the other end of the floor. It was barely enough to account for a 78-73 victory that would lift Holman's men into their second championship match of the month.

Meanwhile Bradley had earned an adjoining spot by climbing over Baylor out in Kansas City by a slim two points when balanced scoring from four starters was enough to offset a sensational 26-point effort by unheralded Baylor center Don Heathington. But of all the playdown games the toughest and most dramatic was probably the opener of the Eastern Regionals in which CCNY got by Ohio State by a single point (56-55) mainly on the strength of some sensational long-range set-shooting down the stretch by Layne (17 points) and Mager (15 points).

The finals were seen as an opportunity for revenge by the yearlong front-running Bradley Braves. But of course it didn't turn out that way. Unruh (8 points) and Behnke (9 points) were shut down this time but Melchiorre (16) and substitute guard Aaron Preece (12) picked up the Bradley scoring load. City had the balance, however, with four starters plus sixth-man Mager in double figures. With little more than a minute to play the score was identical to that of the NIT game — 69-61 — but Bradley did soon close to within a point. Gene Melchiorre was stopped on a final desperate drive, however, and the turnover which resulted next led to a pass from Dambrot to Mager and a final CCNY bucket to seal victory. Again Holman's team had enjoyed a dose of luck as well as the slight edge in talent. And it had again all come down to the closing seconds.

In the hindsight of history it was a game of great significance — the last NCAA title game ever played in Madison Square Garden and, as subsequent events would suggest, perhaps the only NCAA title match that may not have been entirely free of dishonest dealings. But none of this was known at the time, though perhaps some of it should have been. Instead it appeared as no more or less than the final cap on a rather remarkable dual-championship season. To post their unique double the Beavers had to climb over the 12th-, sixth-, fifth-, third- and second-ranked teams in the nation. Then they had also beaten the No. 1-ranked outfit not merely once but twice.

CCNY had now brought basketball euphoria back to Madison Square Garden, to New York City and to the entire Eastern region of the nation. Holy Cross had been the first Eastern NCAA champ only a few years earlier. Now a team from the original colonies had reigned supreme in both tourneys, something that would never again happen. But the Cinderella bunch that brought such euphoria would also be the same crew that would shortly deliver an even bigger dose of disaster. Holman himself had spoken in the wake of the NCAA triumph of perhaps needing a lifetime to ever forget his team's two incredible titles. His words would soon prove to be perhaps the most prophetic and sadly ironic in the entire history of the sport.

The storm clouds had long been forming on the horizon but had also been long ignored. For some time now there had been circulating rumors and suspicions surrounding the integrity of the collegiate game. Some losses by heavily favored teams in important intersectional matches and tournament playdowns had indeed seemed strange. Why had CCNY, for example, played so poorly right before the two 1950 tournaments and then played so well only a few weeks later with championship titles on the line? What had happened to Rupp's juggernaut a year earlier in the lidlifter of the NIT? And what of the many rumors that were floating around the New York scene in the wake of almost every big game?

There had indeed even been some earlier confirmed reports of fixes. One of these occurred in 1945 when five Brooklyn College players reportedly took $1,000 to dump a scheduled Madison Square Garden contest with Akron. When an uncooperative teammate named Bill Rosenblatt discovered and reported the plot the game was cancelled, two bookmakers were arrested and eventually sentenced to jail terms, and the five guilty players were hastily expelled from campus. Although this might have seemed like an isolated incident, Phog Allen out at Kansas already suspected wider connivances and contacted Ned Irish directly with the names of some players at Eastern schools he suspected of questionable double-dealings. Irish and the entire New York basketball establishment were still quite willing to glance the other way, however, and thus wish the whole matter onto the back burner.

There was also the case of a George Washington game two seasons later, in which four gamblers had approached co-captain and star Dave Shapiro with a reported offer of $1,000 to throw an upcoming Madison Square Garden tilt with Manhattan and $10,000 more to manipulate game scores throughout the remainder of the season. After reporting this contact to New York district attorney Frank Hogan, Shapiro was enlisted to go along with the scheme, setting up the arrest of all four game-fixers on the eve of the scheduled game. The Colonials actually won the contest 71-63 and gamblers who thought the fix was still on reportedly lost close to $5 million in wagers.

But the lid finally popped off altogether when a star player from Manhattan College, Junius Kellogg, approached the district attorney with knowledge of gamblers also infiltrating his own team. Kellogg was a talented sophomore and already the top player on the Manhattan team during the 1950-51 season. He was one of a group of emerging black stars that also included Warner and Layne at CCNY and Sherman White of LIU. The trim 6-8 center was the first black, in fact, ever to play for the Jaspers of coach Ken Norton. But when he was approached by ex-Manhattan player Henry Poppe, Kellogg would prove to be a star of another sort as well, one like Shapiro and Rosenblatt who was cut from a different and more honest mold than many of the city's other star players — both white and black. Kellogg was shocked by the planned deceit and went first to Coach Norton with the news and then on to DA Frank Hogan. The cat was now completely out of the bag.

The exploding revelations cut most quickly and deeply around the LIU program of legendary coach Clair Bee. The team Bee fielded in 1950 and 1951 promised to be his best since the great ballclubs of the late '30s that had starred Art Hillhouse, Irving Torgoff, Danny Kaplowitz and Dolly King, and had lost to Stanford and Luisetti in the Garden. Sherman White as a rangy 6-7 forward with a trunkload of moves may have been the best player in the entire city, perhaps the entire nation. But it would soon come to light that some of Bee's players had unknowingly been laying down on the job as far back as 1948.

It apparently had started with frontline Blackbird player Ed Gard, who had fallen under the influence of big-time gambler Salvatore (Tarto) Sollazzo and then had recruited teammate Adolph Burgos to aid him in making some easy spending cash by fixing games for Sollazzo and his cronies. The teammates were to receive $1,000 each for losing a game in 1950 to North Carolina State. When White smelled a plot and approached his crooked teammates (with an accusation that something was up, since they never passed him the ball) he was quickly taken into the fold. Then when Gard completed his own playing eligibility he remained enrolled at the school and also remained deeply involved with the fix. He simply signed up his on-court replacement, Leroy Smith, to carry on what he had already started.

When the news eventually broke that Gard and White and others had been dealing with gamblers it was indeed a stunning revelation for a veteran coach who had been such a consistent model of integrity. Now while the heartbroken Bee continued to preach morality and accept total responsibility for failing to properly educate his wayward boys, the university simply shut down the scandal-wracked basketball program altogether. Bee's career had unfortunately ended in the most wretched disappointment (he would never coach again) and cage play at the Brooklyn campus would not be resurrected for another seven long years.

Next to fall in disgrace were Holman's Cinderellas. The "toast-of-the-town" team that had won so handsomely in both tournaments in March of 1950 was still together a season later and off to another fast start early the following winter. But their world also crashed in like Bee's during a train ride from Philadelphia back to Manhattan in the aftermath of a solid victory over powerful Temple. Holman was informed somewhere in New Jersey that his players would be rounded up for questioning when the trained reached Penn Station. The shocked mentor hurriedly met with his charges and urged them to tell the truth and stoically accept the consequences. Upon arrival in Penn Station plainclothes officers took Warner, Roman and Roth — the three biggest stars — into immediate custody. All three were soon charged with accepting bribes ranging from $500 to $1,500 for throwing games during the previous year. The slump before the tournaments was now no longer quite such a deep mystery.

In subsequent hearings the gory details would all come to light. Former LIU star Eddie Gard had been the go-between in all dealings with both Holman's team and Bee's players. Sal Sollazzo had continued to be the mastermind behind the operation. Gard would eventually infiltrate the CCNY squad, but he had of course begun with his own former team at LIU; and LIU had been the biggest offender, at least in New York. The 1950-51 Blackbird team had opened with 16 straight wins but many were closer than they should have been. One game that they had won big over Duquesne (84-52) was now revealed to have been a game which conspiring team members had originally agreed to dump; but with rumors of a fix spreading the athletes had gotten cold feet and played up to snuff to cover their tracks. On this one game alone Sollazzo lost big money. But on others and with LIU players cooperating fully he had already scored large killings.

The scandal in New York seemed to grow like an ugly cancer once it was exposed and at each new turn there were shocking new developments. After the arrests and immediate confessions of Warner, Roth and Roman at CCNY the students and athletic officials at that school held a mass pep rally in support of remaining team members. No one was cheered louder than leftover star Floyd Layne, a player many contemporary observers contended would have been the best pro cager of the lot. Layne, a black star like Warner and like White at LIU, was an early prototype for the modern-era point guard. But a week later Layne himself was arrested when he admitted accepting $3,000 for his part in shaving points in two Madison Square Garden games. Three more CCNY players (star center Irwin Dambrot, Norm Mager and Herb Cohen) were arrested a month later, as were three former LIU players (Nathan Miller, Lou Lipmann and Dick Feurtado). They all eventually admitted fixes stretching back all the way to 1948.

Then news broke that Bradley was also involved. This was significant because for the first time it was clear that it was not Madison Square Garden alone where

It was this 1949 championship team that spurred Kentucky coach Adolph Rupp (first row, far left) to prematurely claim that "gamblers can't touch my boys with a 10-foot pole." Among the players on that team was future coach Joe B. Hall (31), as well as Dale Barnstable (18) and Jim Line (25). Barnstable and Line were later implicated with Alex Groza (15) and Ralph Beard (12) in the 1951 point-shaving scandal. (University of Kentucky photo)

such corruptions could be expected. It had been the hypocritical Bradley players who in an act of self-serving piousness that topped even Rupp's pronouncements of innocence had only weeks before unanimously voted never to play again in the "sin bin" that was now Madison Square Garden. Yet Bradley was fixing its own games all along, and right in the All-American heartland of Peoria, Illinois. Four of the five Bradley starters, including All-American star Gene Melchiorre, were arrested and later convicted of taking bribes to fix games and control scores.

Suddenly the double loss by the Braves in the dual 1950 title games against CCNY took on a whole new dimension. It was now apparent that both of those contests were staged with two teams (or at least members of both teams) possibly not playing entirely aboveboard. If CCNY's double championship had already been cheapened by the Beavers themselves, it was now blighted beyond all repair in light of these latest charges.

The biggest shock of all came when Baron Rupp's Kentucky team was also implicated. There must have been considerable glee among many rival coaches — despite their inevitable dismay at the huge black mark now cast against their own sport — when stories broke concerning the involvement of Rupp's boys down in Lexington. Rupp not only beat up on his neighbors and rivals season after season, but the pious mentor had been so quick to scatter all the blame elsewhere. Now it turned out that the biggest Wildcat stars had been controlling their own game results right along with the unsavory players elsewhere. And right there in Lexington, not just in that acknowledged den of iniquity out on the East Coast.

Barnstable, Beard and Groza would now admit to sharing $2,000 in cash to win by only the narrowest margin during the 1949 NIT match with Loyola (the game they had unaccountably lost), but they had also been accepting hefty payments from Brooklyn native Nick "The Greek" Englisis (a former Kentucky freshman football player) and his brother Tony to control point spreads of games played in Lexington, Knoxville and elsewhere around the SEC circuit. The breaking news about Kentucky's involvement was indeed bizarre testimony to just how good the Wildcats actually were over the past several seasons. Not only had the Fabulous Five and its successors won game after game, but they had often determined the precise margins of victory with consummate undetected skill. And the few times they did lose were apparently not upsets at all, but only botched scams of their own doing.

The fallout in Kentucky was indeed huge. The pro careers of Groza and Beard would of course be utterly ruined. So would that of Bill Spivey whose crimes were lesser and apparently involved only perjury. Spivey was called to testify and adamantly swore his innocence. He stood trial nonetheless and when his jury was hung it was reported that the majority had voted for acquittal. The university dropped the star player despite the skimpy evidence against him and the NBA backed away as well. With Groza and Beard the axe fell just as ruthlessly. Both had already completed two NBA seasons with Indianapolis and Groza especially was an emerging star who had trailed only Mikan in the league scoring race during both pro campaigns. On the eve of a preseason college all-star game the pair were arrested outside of Chicago Stadium. Before their own courtroom dramas were played out both were banned for life by a pro circuit that wanted no part of the growing smell of scandal that was now ripe throughout the rival college game.

The scandal was of course not restricted to players at CCNY, LIU, Bradley and Kentucky. The shocking news in fact was just how widespread the infiltration of gamblers had been. Game-fixing or at least score-fixing was a most regular occurrence, especially in big-venue high-interest competitions like those scheduled into Madison Square Garden. Although there were undoubtedly hundreds of honest college games going on every week of the winter in every corner of the country, cynics now had to wonder if any contest that didn't turn out just as anticipated might not be filled with the odor of foul play. Once the most exciting element of the game, the "upset" had suddenly become basketball's nightmare element and even the game's "dirtiest" word.

Other sports had their scandals as well. There was the infamous Black Sox fix in baseball that made Shoeless Joe Jackson a household name and brought Judge Kennesaw Mountain Landis to power as the national pastime's only unfettered czar; there were isolated incidents in football, at both the pro and college levels. Within a decade the NFL would suspend popular Green Bay Packers backfield star Paul Hornung for placing bets on the outcomes of his own team's games. But never had any major sport seen anything quite so widespread or blatantly corrupt, at least not in the United States. Partly it had to do with the fanatic interest the game had by now generated, especially in the New York City area and especially surrounding the local college teams. Wagering almost seemed the very rationale for big-time college games, and it wasn't at all unusual for thousands of fans to cheer wildly for or against the shrinking point spread in the closing moments of Madison Square Garden contests where the winner or loser might already have been determined long before game's end.

And then of course there was the nature of the game itself. Basketball, above all games was the easiest to control for wagering purposes. It doesn't take a genius or an expert to figure this out. Basketball is a fluid competition of endless ebb and flow movement, with constant action and with both teams scoring repeatedly and in rapid succession, with each basket made or missed depending on a fraction of an inch in shooting accuracy or a half step in defensive maneuvering. The difference between swisher or rim-clanger is impossible to appreciate or detect from any sideline vantage point (even from the bench or the floor itself). In a game of tempo and pace the individual player or group of players can easily control the action for positive or negative ends and without the slightest detection or appreciation from either closeup or afar. A missed layup at a crucial moment — or a misdirected pass or two — spells the difference between a five-point margin or a two-point margin, or even between victory and defeat. If gamblers control a single player or two on a talented team they control the entire game. And unlike baseball play, no perceptive sideline viewer (not even coach or teammates) can ever detect the decisive deceits of the skillful.

Much has been written about the causes and the meaning of the betting scandals of 1951. Much also remains totally murky more than four decades latter. At the time they occurred, the scandals were distorted by press, coaches, university officials and fans alike, as each brought his or her own special prejudices to interpretations of the heartbreaking events. In more recent decades historians have done much the same thing. But several points do nonetheless remain absolutely clear.

For one thing, it seems evident that only a small percentage of the guilty parties were ever caught. The grand jury which pursued the case between February 1951 and April 1953 eventually tabbed 32 guilty players from seven schools and concluded that 86 games had been fixed between 1947 and 1950. It was probably a mere fraction in terms of either guilty players or crooked contests. Major fixers among the gamblers did receive hefty prison terms with Sollazzo slapped with eight to 16 years.

It is also obvious that the country and the system remained in a complete state of denial during the immediate aftermath of the first disturbing revelations out of New York. While guilty players at Bradley first covered their tracks by righteously voting never to play another game in sin-bathed New York, soon-to-be-implicated Floyd Layne also delivered an inspirational speech to rallying CCNY students who had turned out in full support of those remaining innocent (it was wrongly presumed) Beavers players. Rupp's response down in Kentucky ("They couldn't touch our boys with a 10-foot pole!") was also most typical of feelings everywhere around the land. Typical as well were the provincial views that focused all the blame on the largely imaged corruptions of New York City as the single wicked source of all evils in both sport and society.

A third indisputable observation is that the whole matter was stuffed full with blatant hypocrisy. The corruption attributed to gamblers was after all based entirely on a morality system largely identical to the one on which the schools had long themselves been building their burgeoning basketball programs. Basketball had clearly become a for-profit business and the way that business was now conducted was dehumanizing to the athletes in every respect. Ballplayers were recruited to fill school coffers with victories and dollars; they were cast quickly aside when they could no longer produce or when they used up eligibility; every rule of legal recruitment and every academic standard was bent to get the best players needed for winning teams.

Although it also involved making money off these once innocent games, gambling certainly depended upon honest competition between teams for its own profits. It was always in the self-interest of the bookmaker to encourage as much betting as possible on each team (the bookmaker made his profit only by holding back a small percentage — a service charge — on all winnings) and thus accurate and honest point spreads were essential. Those who now corrupted the waging activities were doing so because they held the same corrupt value system as illegal recruiters and unscrupulous coaches and administrators who fixed academic records or paid players under the table to attend their schools. Both the schools and the corrupt gamblers were treating the players as commodities. One was now condemned for this while the other was glossed over and even encouraged by victory-starved alumni and college presidents. Over the years this hypocrisy has only increased exponentially.

Finally, it remains quite clear that those who were caught and punished in the aftermath of the scandal that broke full tilt in 1951 were largely scapegoats. Kentucky and CCNY became the focal points of the investigations beyond all else because these were the championship programs with the most smug and even sanctimonious coaches. The punishments that were eventually handed out, in turn, were designed to treat symptoms and not causes. Kentucky was banned for the 1953 season for infractions of rules governing payment to players, and they were tripped up in the end only on the most minor type of infractions (extras in meal money) at that. Never were either Rupp or the Wildcat program made to suffer any direct consequences for the dumping of games by the players that were their responsibility. Only the individual players themselves were punished (and likely only a small handful of these), and they were punished by the NBA and not the colleges themselves, once the pro league withheld contracts to the small contingent of offending stars.

Some of the guilty indeed served prison time for their roles. And yet when it was all over, there was still a lingering feeling that maybe the whole mess had not completely gone away. The college game was now severely tainted. Yet it would revive, of course, and one day not too far down the road a new generation of fans would hardly hear the whispers of what once had been. Sports fans have the nation's shortest memories. Besides, the business was now too successful for the investigative probes of district attorney Hogan to take much of a bite out of the profitable and entertaining sport. And yet it would be many years nonetheless before college basketball would shake quite such a dark shadow altogether.

Perhaps there was a silver lining yet to be found in the entire sordid mess that was the 1951 basketball scandal. Perhaps if the lessons were well-learned and well-remembered, then at least some profit could be derived from the sport's darkest hour. But even here there was little to suggest much hope or promise. Within a decade the festering mess would open up anew. This time the uncovered conspiring and point-shaving would be centered far from New York, mostly in the Southland. The biggest bombshell involved North Carolina State where four players were arrested in May of 1961; Mississippi State and Seton Hall were also soon implicated as major offenders. This time around a new grand jury probe would find 20 players guilty of accepting nearly $45,000 to affect the outcome of 44 games over a five-year span.

Mastermind of the new game-fixing ring would eventually prove to be Jack Molinas, a star forward at Columbia during the previous wave of scandal and a player who had apparently earlier slipped through the net with his own earlier point-shaving skills. As a promising pro rookie Molinas was thrown out of the NBA in 1954 (29 games into the season) when he refused to cease his known betting on games involving his own Fort Wayne Pistons team. Now Molinas would receive a 15-year prison term and in the mid-70s his life in the fast last would come to a tragic end when the compulsive gambler was shot to death over a money dispute at his California home. While the scandals of 1961 seemed to blow over more quickly than the trauma of a decade earlier, there was again little evidence that the guardians of the sport were taking steps to rid the game of such blight. By 1965 the taint of scandal had returned yet again when several players were expelled from campus for accepting bribes at Seattle University.

If today's college action seems free from any hint of game-fixing activities this may be due — for good or bad — only to an economic climate which has removed most of the motives for player cooperation with game-fixers, even if it has done nothing to discourage either honest of dishonest wagering on collegiate cage action. Players of the '50s had seemingly less to risk and far more reason to look cynically at their own roles within the game. They had little economic stake in their performances other than what they could perhaps squeeze from the sport's seamer side. But with talented players today dreaming of million-dollar pro signing bonuses from the NBA and likely already stuffed with numerous hidden perks from the schools themselves, there is less to be gained from consorting with gamblers and far, far more to lose. There is little evidence that today's sport is any cleaner or any less of a bottom-line profit-oriented business; but all signs do point to the fact that today's athletes already own a far larger stake in the game's ever-expanding wealth.

Chronology of the 1951 Scandal

1945 — Five Brooklyn College players admit accepting bribes to throw a game with Akron University that was later cancelled when suspicions arose that the game might be rigged.

1949 — George Washington University player reports that he had been approached by gamblers to "do business" with them concerning upcoming games. No arrests or suspensions of players are made, however.

1947-1950 — Subsequent investigation by the office of New York DA Frank Hogan reveals that during four-year span 86 games had been fixed in 23 cities and 17 states, with 32 players and seven colleges involved (CCNY, LIU, NYU, Manhattan, Kentucky, Bradley and Toledo). Many players and gamblers involved were probably never caught. Major result was that several top New York City and Midwest stars were banned from lucrative pro careers, including: Sherman White (LIU), Ed Warner (CCNY), Floyd Layne (CCNY), Gene Melchiorre (Bradley) and Ed Roman (CCNY).

March 1949 — Heavily favored Kentucky unexpectedly loses to Loyola-Chicago (61-56) in NIT quarterfinals and thus misses opportunity to become first double postseason tournament winner (Kentucky next won the NCAAs). Later revelations suggest that upset loss was result of bungled efforts by Kentucky players to keep the point spread close, a plan which backfired when Wildcat players couldn't catch up in game's closing moments.

March 1950 — CCNY suffers late-season slump before surging to win both postseason tourneys. Later investigations reveal that some late-season losses probably resulted from game-dumping or bungled point-spread fixing. It would also soon be questioned (though never proven) whether CCNY's NCAA and NIT victories over Bradley may both have been helped along by halfhearted play by some of Bradley's own dishonest stars.

January 1951 — Junius Kellogg, 6-8 star at Manhattan and perhaps country's best player, reports to DA's office that he has been offered $1,000 bribe to control point spreads. As a result, two teammates and three gamblers are arrested.

February 19, 1951 — DA's officials arrest several members of coach Nat Holman's CCNY team on train in Manhattan's Pennsylvania Station. CCNY's 1950 NCAA and NIT championships were at the time returning from an impressive late-season victory over Temple in Philadelphia.

March 1951 — Kentucky coach Rupp proclaims that New York gamblers "couldn't touch my boys with a 10-foot pole" and then discovers along with rest of nation that his "Fabulous Five" team of late '40s had controlled point spreads in numerous games. Alex Groza and Ralph Beard, both already NBA stars, are banned for life as result of breaking revelations. Kentucky's 1951 ace, 7-footer Bill Spivey, also accused of associating with gamblers yet never prosecuted or convicted; Spivey is nonetheless also banned from NBA play.

1952 — Additional fallout from 1951 scandal darkens sport as Clair Bee resigns from LIU coaching assignment, LIU drops basketball for remainder of decade and NCAA elects to move its championship tournament finals out of Madison Square Garden on permanent basis.

1961 — Second lesser scandal (also investigated by DA Frank Hogan) involves 37 players from 22 schools. Investigations also lead to banning of New York schoolboy stars Connie Hawkins (enrolled at Iowa) and Roger Brown (enrolled at Dayton) from future college and NBA play for alleged "associations" with gamblers on city's playgrounds. Hawkins later wins NBA reinstatement in legal courts, and both Hawkins and Brown also star in ABA.

1965 — Final dark chapter breaks when two Seattle University players are arrested and convicted of point-shaving in West Coast collegiate games.

5

The Fifties, Part 1

The Ballad of Bevo and a Tale of Two Titans

American sports history often reads like a litany of painfully familiar and oft-repeated cycles. Big league baseball, for starters, reached its initial zenith of national popularity on the eve of the First Great War, only then to be torn asunder by game-fixing scandals which shook fan confidence and undercut much of the integrity of the nation's favorite pastime. Then smack in the middle of its very darkest hour Abner Doubleday's wildly popular bat and ball game was somehow miraculously rescued, quite single-handedly, by a most unlikely savior. George Herman "Babe" Ruth arrived from Baltimore's back alleys as America's first larger-than-life sports icon — a fun-loving bumpkin of a ballplaying hero capable of slugging prodigious home run balls and thus elevating the game to a new level of fan frenzy.

Basketball — the popular college variety — would ironically repeat this pattern little more than three decades latter. At the close of a Second Great War the college cage game was approaching its own mountaintop of fan popularity, especially in urban centers all along the northeastern seaboard. College doubleheaders and even tripleheaders, especially in New York's Madison Square Garden and Philadelphia's Palestra, had proven themselves as huge moneymakers in the years immediately preceding global conflict. One-handed shooting á la Hank Luisetti (Stanford) and Kenny Sailors (Wyoming) and Paul Arizin (Villanova) had truly revolutionized the game — speeding it up, increasing scoring, adding new dimensions of artistry and unrivaled thrills. And there was also now a burgeoning new audience, created almost overnight by an economic "boom era" sweeping across post-war America. It was an audience lusting after novel sports entertainment and new athletic heroes of all imaginable types.

The pro version of Dr. Naismith's indoor game would be one by-product of this unslaked thirst for roundball action, as the midwest-based National Basketball League (featuring George Mikan's Minneapolis Lakers) leaped from semipro industrial league status to full-blown play-for-pay status. At the same time, out East, the infant Basketball Association of America (featuring Boston, New York, Philadelphia, Baltimore, Providence and Washington venues) provided pro hockey moguls with a new profitable spectacle for their "off-night" idle arenas. Yet professional basketball was nonetheless — despite Mikan's towering presence — painfully slow to take flight; the pro game was ragged and brutal and often resembled a street brawl rather than today's athletic ballet of shooting and leaping. Thus it was college basketball, primarily, that seemed ideally perched to become true king of the sporting scene as the "boom era" of American sports flung open upon the optimistic 1950s.

Then the dreaded death-knell sounded once more. Overnight, the game-fixing scandals breaking around the heads of Nat Holman's Cinderella CCNY national champions had seemed to wipe away almost everything that had been gained by four decades of steady growth. The New York "city game" rooted in Madison Square Garden seemed ruined beyond repair as a prime-time attraction, once noted Gotham stars like Junius Kellogg of Manhattan, Jack Molinas of Columbia, Sherman White at LIU, and Ed Roman and Irwin Dambrot at CCNY either admitted or reported their own teams' complicity in throwing games and controlling point spreads during some of the city's biggest headline contests of recent past seasons. A rancid smell identical to the one emanating from the 1919 and 1920 baseball seasons now filled the air throughout the 1950-51 basketball campaign and it seemed that any game that did not end as expected was subject to a skeptical eye. With its very survival firmly in mind, the NCAA governing committee was quick to relocate its year-end 1951 tournament finals to Minneapolis, as far away from scandal-rocked Madison Square Garden as possible.

Basketball's unfolding illness was, of course, soon enough discovered to reach nationwide. The victor in that relocated 1951 NCAA title game had already become something of a regular fixture of NCAA title play; Adolph Rupp's powerhouse Kentucky Wildcats had now taken three of the last four NCAA championship games. The "Fabulous Five" unit of All-Americans Groza, Beard, Jones, Rollins and Barker had departed two seasons earlier and was now performing intact as a successful NBA act under the banner of the Indianapolis Olympians. Kentucky this time around was led by a new towering force in 7-footer Bill Spivey. As Spivey and the Wildcats concluded yet another dream Kentucky season, however, news was already leaking out that Groza and Beard had themselves been deeply involved in game fixing and score fixing throughout their brilliant collegiate careers.

A shockingly unaccountable one-point upset loss by the Wildcats to Loyola-Chicago during the 1949 NIT — the only defeat of the season for a Rupp team which immediately bounced back to handily win the NCAA postseason festival — was now at last explained. Groza and Beard, along with Dale Barnstable, had reportedly divided $2,000 in gamblers payoffs for keeping the score close in that first-round contest; unfortunately the talented trio had also in the process accidently blown the game during the closing moments. Groza and Beard would now suddenly find their own professional careers terminated by NBA commissioner Maurice Podoloff. Bill Spivey himself would be indicted, but only on perjury charges stemming from his apparent coverup of knowledge about his teammates' misdeeds.

Spivey would nonetheless find his own senior season at Kentucky also quickly terminated (when the UK Athletic Board suspended his remaining eligibility) and would later have a reported NBA contract offer from the Rochester Royals rescinded as well against a backdrop of protests from other NBA clubs. The careers of some of the game's brightest stars (Sherm White, Jack Molinas, Ed Roman, Bradley's Gene Melchiorre and CCNY's Floyd Layne) from the half-dozen post-war seasons were overnight left in shambles. The heartland's strongest college team and reigning dynasty ballclub (Rupp's Kentucky) was now also completely sabotaged.

It was against this tragic backdrop that basketball would fortuitously discover its own small-scale version of the slugging Bambino. Just like baseball's Babe, this unsuspected man-child would emerge unheralded from altogether murky origins befitting a true mythic hero. His name — "Bevo" Francis — was also better suited to a comic book than a lineup card; his physical appearance — like the Babe's — was more roughcast and gangly than dashing; his athletic feats were equally prodigious and even legendary in their own right; his meteoric rise to fame was just as much the stuff of a Paul Bunyan-like fairy tale. He was indeed a most unlikely savior from an altogether unlikely place.

The parallels were almost uncanny since, like baseball's Babe, this basketball Bevo sported a catchy name, an unmatched talent for Herculean feats, and tons of charisma mixed with proper doses of intriguing mystery. While the Babe smacked long balls at twice or three times the rate of his forerunners, so did basketball's new backwater prodigy score baskets at a similar whirlwind clip. Francis was first sighted deep in the basketball hinterland, on a tiny southern Ohio campus that could hardly claim even a snippet of previous athletic legitimacy. But his prodigious shooting and adding-machine scoring totals would soon have an impact on the reeling world of college basketball not unlike

Clarence "Bevo" Francis became an instant folk hero in 1953-54. His scoring displays impacted the scandal-torn college basketball world much like the 1920s-era home run displays of Babe Ruth. (Rio Grande College photo)

those glamorous roundtrippers smacked by Ruth during baseball's own most dire hour of despair.

The 1953 college season was bumping along without mighty Kentucky — as Rupp's boys served out a one-year NCAA suspension — and without any reigning superstars — Duke's Dick Groat was graduated, Spivey was expelled, and three lesser lights named Frank Selvy (Furman), Larry Hennessey (Villanova) and Johnny O'Brien (Seattle) paced the nation in scoring. No other time in the sport's annals could have been more ripe for Bevo Francis and his equally strange-sounding school to first grab headlines on the nation's sports pages.

Bevo's jump shot was always sure to draw a gang of defenders like this three-man wall from Butler University. But more often than not, the shot found nothing but net. (Rio Grande College photo)

The institution, nestled in a sleepy mining region of southeastern Ohio, bore the label of Rio Grande College — pronounced "rye-oh grand" — and at the time it could boast but 92 students, 38 of them men and a dozen of these suited up as members of the basketball squad. It played its home games in a ramshackle and leaky auditorium popularly called "The Hog Pen" (officially Community Hall) which held an audience of barely 150 spectators crammed along the sidelines on makeshift rows of folding medal chairs. Its unlikely star player was a 6-9 farmboy from the tiny hamlet of Highlandtown who had arrived on campus in the fall of 1952 not only without many press clippings but also without his high school diploma. Yet if Francis was an unknown outside of his own home county, he came on the scene already toting full-blown credentials has one of the most phenomenal gunners in Ohio state schoolboy history.

This unlikely overnight star would literally burst on the scene amidst reports of truly mind-boggling scoring feats that were at first widely celebrated by the national press, later doubted and discounted by media and rival coaches alike, and finally even officially disqualified from the record books by the nation's basketball establishment. Yet record books are rarely sufficient to define lasting legends, and when the wire service reports of nightly 50-point scoring performances gradually reached East Coast and West Coast basketball hotbeds during the late 1953 season an instant folk-hero captured the imaginations of roundball fanatics everywhere across the North American landscape.

Backwater Basketball by Barnum

Bevo Francis was not only a rare basketball shooting machine but an ideal figure for instant folk-hero status. Son of a poor Ohio brickyard worker, Francis had reportedly picked up his unusual nickname from his laborer father. The senior Francis had been widely known among friends and even casual acquaintances as "Beve" — after the popular Anheuser-Busch "near-beer" soft drink which he guzzled regularly during Prohibition years. Thus a single male offspring was only naturally dubbed "Little Beve" by the locals, a nickname later simplified to Bevo.

From the outset Bevo Francis thus possessed the raw materials of colorful legend. Yet the legend was nonetheless somewhat slow in getting off the ground. A childhood bout with anemia had caused the lanky youngster to miss two years of elementary school and thus made him two years older (and, at well over 6 feet, considerably taller) than most of his high school classmates. Bevo's talents with a basketball were of course apparent early on and when he transferred into Wellsville High School from his hometown of Highlandtown he lost a sophomore season of basketball eligibility due to widespread suspicions about recruiting irregularities. A sensational junior year (1951-52) for the Wellsville team nonetheless brought sudden notoriety as Francis averaged 33.1 points for a 19-1 squad. On no less than eight different occasions Bevo outscored the entire opposing team by himself. Before his senior campaign could get underway, however, Francis turned 20 and was thus ruled ineligible for any further schoolboy competition.

One productive season seemingly was enough, however, to fuel a budding reputation. Francis' regular scoring outbursts had already proven nothing less than phenomenal at the high school level and included a state-record 57 points against neighboring Alliance High. At the end of his single campaign Bevo Francis already ranked second in the state behind another local schoolboy hotshot, Cincinnati's pint-sized Robin Freeman. Freeman would soon write a considerable legacy of his own as the Big Ten scoring champion at Ohio State. With his own eligibility lapsed and basketball scholarships suddenly pouring in from 60 or more schools around the country (including Kentucky, Wyoming and Cincinnati) the ill-starred high school gunner from Wellsville elected not to complete his final year of public education. He was, after all, already married and the father of a young child. And foremost in his mind now burned the universal dream of playing big-time college basketball.

It was at this point that Bevo Francis formed an unlikely partnership that would soon both fuel and cloud the remainder of his roller-coaster basketball career. Bevo's coach at Wellsville had been a dynamic self-promoter named Newt Oliver, himself once a record-breaking scorer at tiny Rio Grande College where he led the nation with 725 points in 1948. With Francis in tow and his alma mater suffering severe financial pressure due to a sagging enrollment of less than 100 students, Newt Oliver sensed a once-in-a-lifetime opportunity. Thus he approached Rio Grande officials with what seemed a sure-fire proposal. He would deliver Francis and his lofty scoring average to the tiny cash-starved campus in exchange for the head coaching slot. Oliver was convinced that a soft Division II schedule coupled with Bevo's amazing shooting prowess would be more than enough to put himself, his star and his alma mater squarely on the basketball map almost overnight.

Every Don Quixote has his Sancho Panza and every three-ring circus has its masterminding P.T. Barnum. In this case the second image is especially fitting, for despite his schoolboy heroics Bevo Francis seemed destined for basketball obscurity as a one-year high school wonder. That was until Newt Oliver recognized the marketing potential of his newfound prodigy. A few years down the road the Barnum-image attached to Oliver would be front and center when *Look* magazine printed a feature story entitled "Basketball by Barnum" and detailing the sudden miraculous rise of the nation's newest sportsworld phenomenon.

Oliver for his own part had to do some serious arm-twisting with his 6-9 meal ticket, and then some fast talking with both the college administration and with his other Rio Grande cage recruits as well. From Bevo he coerced a reluctant promise to go along with the scheme to attend Rio Grande, and also to enroll simultaneously in Rio Grande High School in order to pick up the needed credits for college eligibility. From the college he extracted a meager $3,500 annual salary and an all-important $25 to join the NCAA statistical service, guaranteeing that Bevo's expected scoring outbursts would appear in weekly national summaries and thus collect all-important media attention.

On the first day of fall practice with his other 1952-53 Rio Grande recruits he also made his new team a bold promise: that if they subordinated their own play to Bevo's scoring he could personally guarantee that within a year they would all be performing on the hallowed floor of basketball's one true national Mecca — Madison Square Garden.

It was clear from the start that Newt Oliver had an ambitious dream, a firm game-plan, and the endless drive to carry it all out. For his own part Bevo Francis received a modest scholarship consisting of free tuition and books, a $75 monthly stipend to feed his small family, and $35 a month to fund a furnished apartment. The game-plan consisted of some flawless logic. Few fans at Rio Grande or elsewhere would turn out to watch five unheralded athletes score 15 points each. But Oliver reas   quite rightly that hordes would spin the turnstiles to see one gunner score 50 c.   ore.

    liver's hypothesis was first proven with a single miraculous game in January 1953 that would provide the unofficial "coming-out party" for college basketball's first postscandal superstar. Recent games played before crowds that rarely topped

82

several dozen had quietly witnessed the Rio Grande center stuff home point totals of 58 (against Sue Bennett College) then 69 (versus Wilberforce) and finally 72 (California State) and 76 (at Lees College). These were astronomical numbers for this or any other era. Yet they hardly prepared anyone for what would next transpire on January 9, 1953.

Ashland (Kentucky) Junior College offered the opposition for undefeated Rio Grande in the season's 18th game and Community Hall was suddenly stuffed with a capacity throng of 150 locals. Never have so few patrons been treated to so much history, for it was on this special night that the fabulous freshman gunner simply couldn't miss a long-range hook or a medium-range jumper. Over the course of four 10-minute quarters Bevo poured in an unheard of 47 field goals (better than one per minute) from all angles and against a hapless "gang defense" powerless to contain him. The tiny gym echoed during the final quarter with screams from Oliver to his players to foul at every opportunity and thus return the ball to his unstoppable scoring machine. The strategy was flawless and the "unconscious" Francis would rack up 55 points, his entire team's total, in the final 10-minute session alone. In perhaps the finest piece of irony in all of college sports history, the 116 points tallied by Francis during this greatest scoring frenzy on record nearly matched the entire head count present in the bandbox arena that memorable night.

Instantaneously Oliver had won his desired national audience. When news of the 116-point performance spread across country in wire service reports, the world was transformed drastically and seemingly overnight for the tiny Ohio campus and for its unwitting "shooting star" ballplayer as well. Both the delighted coach and the reluctant record-breaker would soon pay a stiff price, however, for the newfound media attention which engulfed both Francis and Rio Grande in the weeks following the historic Ashland game.

For one thing, the master promoter now attracted more than his fair share of severe critics and caustic opponents. Perhaps prompted mostly by thinly veiled jealousy, many among the nation's coaching community demanded immediate investigation of such bogus scoring records as the ones being reported out of southern Ohio. Who and what was this Bevo Francis, went the hue and cry, and what manner of cheap opposition was he nightly facing?

Of course, whatever the integrity of such records it was all great theater indeed, and magazine reporters and photographers soon prowled the Ohio campus to document such a genuine rags-to-riches tale. Coming months would even feature New York television appearances with network stars like Ed Sullivan and Dave Garroway, while back home long lines of fans now formed for tickets to see the latest college phenom wherever he played. "The Hog Pen" had now also seen the last of Bevo Francis as all remaining Rio Grande home games were shifted out of Community Hall and into larger neighborhood arenas.

Further negatives soon arrived by the truckload as well. Francis would finish out the season with a continued scoring binge that included five additional games above 60 points, a 50-plus scoring average and 1,952 total points. Only a handful of players had ever registered that many during a full four-year career, let alone a single year's 39-game schedule. But the groundswell opposition against these records had already reached steamroller proportions among big-school coaches and officials. Any one-year point total approaching 2,000 simply had to be a sham; it was only a single season earlier, after all, that diminutive Johnny O'Brien of Seattle College (also a Division II school feeding on weak opposition) had become the first collegian to amass even 1,000 points in a single winter. Not surprisingly the august NCAA rules committee took quick action during the summer of 1953 and voted to remove retroactively any records from the books that were not made against legitimate four-year schools. Back on the Rio Grande campus coach Oliver could only scream foul play, condemn the system that had robbed him of his sudden notoriety, and immediately begin plotting his revenge against the big-school record-keeping system.

But all was not lost for Newt Oliver, who bristled at the "official" dismissal of Bevo's freshman records but also celebrated their economic impact as offers of big-time opponents in big-time moneymaking venues poured in from all around the country. The stream of incredulous inquiries in the wake of the Ashland game ("What is a Bevo Francis?") had turned in short order to an endless stream of invitations from East Coast promoters who now saw a chance to buoy sagging postscandal basketball attendance with the best traveling basketball circus act anywhere in the land.

"Basketball by Barnum" during Bevo's freshman season had not exactly been without its bizarre and even ludicrous moments. At times the circus even threatened to turn ugly. Astronomical scoring had made Francis a marked man and opponents now plotted ingenious ways to avoid embarrassment in the face of his accurate jump shots. Farcical heights were reached shortly after the Ashland game on a night when the Troy (Ohio) Arena hosted a matchup between Francis and Cedarville College. Cedarville's coach and players resorted to an old but always unpopular ploy when they held the opening tipoff and refused to shoot or even dribble the ball.

A throng of over 7,000 had turned out on this particular night to see the heralded "100-point man" burn the nets with his nonstop scoring; thus the scene now threatened to turn riotous as disgruntled patrons stamped their feet and pelted the floor with coins and paper cups. Play (such as it was) was halted in the face of the fans' outbursts, and while a group of his Rio Grande teammates sat on the bench and played cards, Francis himself conducted a radio interview by the scorer's table and then milled with the unhappy crowd to sign autographs. Fortunately for all involved, Cedarville's embarrassed athletic director soon calculated that his coach's tactics might cost both teams a share of the substantial gate receipts, since fans soon tired of the impromptu autograph session and began threatening to exit en masse. Cooler heads prevailed, Cedarville agreed to play at normal tempo, and Bevo pocketed 38 points in a lopsided 66-28 stomping of yet another outmanned opponent.

Act Two of the Oliver-Francis road show opened with a chance at evening the score against NCAA doubters and second-guessers who had so quickly belittled Bevo's freshman campaign. When Oliver learned that Yale coach Howard Hobson had led the legal onslaught against Bevo's freshman records he promptly challenged the Elis to a grudge game but was just as promptly rebuffed. But others were not so quick to turn aside this cash cow for the sake of face-saving, and thus the backwater school which merely a year earlier was often pocketing gate receipts of less than $100 was now delightfully in a position to turn aside five-figure guarantees.

Oliver had strung in place a 1953-54 schedule of 28 road contests which opened at Buffalo (NY) Auditorium with Bevo ringing up 63 in a 120-59 victory over Erie Tech, the game being played out before 5,000 delighted ticket holders. Game two was stiffer stuff, a match with Adelphi College before 13,000 in the very Mecca of Madison Square Garden itself. The paycheck was handsome (to say nothing of Oliver's earlier promise being fulfilled to his players) but the reviews were less than mixed. When Bevo's 32 points accompanied a losing effort against a weak-sister New York opponent, Gotham's press corps joined the bandwagon in freshly labelling Rio Grande's earlier 1953 successes as little more than "a travesty on the entire structure of intercollegiate athletics."

But soon narrow victories over Providence (89-87, 41 for Bevo) at Boston Garden and Wake Forest (67-65, 32 for Bevo) in Raleigh, plus close losses to Villanova (93-92, 39 for Bevo) in Philadelphia and North Carolina State (92-77, 34 for Bevo) at Raleigh, were enough to create some converted believers. And now the attention and the money rolled in just as Newt Oliver had once dreamed and schemed it eventually would. In a season of endless road trips, Rio Grande would play before more than 164,000 spectators and share enough gate receipts to put the staggering college squarely back on its financial feet. The point totals which Bevo racked up against these "legitimate" opponents (including 48 against Butler, 49 and 41 versus Creighton, and 28 while slowed by injury against Arizona State) were also sufficient to erase any doubts that he was a big-time player.

But the grandest show of all was saved for early February of 1954. Now playing all games including "home" contests on the road, Newt Oliver's Redmen were scheduled into nearby Jackson (Ohio) High School for a February 2nd match with the Hillsdale (Michigan) team. A makeshift court had been erected on a temporary stage and several hundred eager spectators were shoehorned into the remaining corners of the gym. Only moments into Rio Grande's 20th contest of the dwindling season something became obvious to even casual watchers among the cramped spectators: Bevo had his deadly jumpers and smooth hooks clicking with exceptional accuracy on this particular night, meaning that it was now redemption time for those banished scoring records from Bevo's freshman campaign.

Oliver quickly warmed to the scene, again inflamed about the records and recognition denied to his program by NCAA zealots (as he saw it) a season earlier. At halftime, Bevo's unconscious shooting rhythm had racked up 43 points and the score stood 68-38. In the locker room Oliver had one pleading message for his charges: "I want that record back tonight!" As the third quarter opened he paced the sidelines urging his players to feed Bevo each time the Redmen touched the ball. One writer would later dub the single-minded offense as "an uncomplicated food chain leading directly to Bevo." Thirty-one more Francis points drained the net in the third frame, and even with Hillsdale quadruple-teaming him the jump shots continued to fall in eerie succession during the final quarter as well.

Teammate Wayne Wiseman would recall in the pages of *Sports Illustrated* nearly four decades later a particularly surrealistic basket made by Francis in the closing moments, after he had already recrossed the century mark. As Bevo broke from a crowd of Hillsdale defenders Wiseman hit him with a pass along the baseline. Four

Hillsdale defenders chased Francis as he lunged to the ball, elevated with his back still to the basket, spun in midflight and drained yet another bucket from the baseline corner. "I didn't think it had a chance," recalled Wiseman, "but it hit nothing but chord and they fouled him and he made the free throw as well...It was just one of those nights."

The final ledger would read 134-91 for Rio Grande; 113 points for Francis on 38 field goals (the number of attempts was never accurately recorded) and 37 of 42 foul shot attempts. Ironically, the collegiate rule allowing a bonus toss when a one-shot foul is converted would not be adopted for yet another year; had such a rule already been in effect on February 2, 1954, Francis would have enjoyed at least 20 more charity tosses and likely would have scored 130 points or better.

The dizzying game against Hillsdale would also underscore a vital point about the incredible scoring skills of the improbable Rio Grande star. Francis was first and foremost a pure shooter. He was capable of drilling the ball repeatedly from anywhere on the court. Though a big man by standards of the day, his scoring was never a matter of dominating play under the boards against shorter and less physical opponents, after the fashion of a George Mikan or Bob Kurland or Wilt Chamberlain. While Chamberlain often scored less than he might have because of poor free-throw shooting skills, Francis would drill the ball from the free-throw line as easily as other 6-9 players would make layups. It was this ability that in large part accounts for his twin triple-digit games. A total of 59 out of 229 points (slightly over 25 percent) in those two games came from the charity stripe, 37 versus Hillsdale and 22 against Ashland. More responsible still was an uncanny jump-shooting eye from 10-12 feet out that was unerring even with three or four defenders draped on his arms or flailing hands flung in his face. Give Bevo Francis the ball and he was as unstoppable a dozen paces from the hoop — at least against average defenses — as any shooter anywhere ever has been.

Bevo Francis had now brought the nation's attention to profligate scoring on a single night in February 1954. It was the second time that Francis had topped 100 and while few may have taken notice or believed the first time around, the nation of basketball watchers was gripped by the event when it played as an encore. No one else would ever match the feat of twice scoring 100 points in a single collegiate game.

Indeed only high schoolers would outstrip the lofty Francis totals of 116 and 113. The first schoolboy gunner to reach the unthinkable milestone was another Ohioan, Dick Bogenrife who popped in 120 for Midway High in Sedalia only a month after Bevo's 1953 game against Ashland. Eventually the scholastic men's mark would soar to 135 when West Virginian Danny Heater (January 1960) crammed home bucket after bucket in Burnsville's undersized 30-by-50-foot gym, including 55 in the final 10 minutes to match Bevo's fourth quarter against Ashland. While Marie Boyd of Lonaconing, Maryland, once canned 156 in a 1924 women's high school match featuring six on a side and stationary shooters, only Cheryl Miller (later of Southern Cal fame) has yet to better the century mark (with 105 for Riverside Poly in January 1982) during a women's five-on-five game. No one save Pete Maravich would leave behind as impressive a legacy of career records, even if some

The "Basketball by Barnum" traveling cage circus at tiny Rio Grande College included far more tricks than this one by the fabulous Bevo Francis (32). Bevo's sense of balance also included an uncanny jump shot and unfailing eye for the hoop. (Rio Grande College photo)

of Bevo's standards would later be dismissed as a cheap result of scheduling unsanctioned opponents. Those records (largely from the Hillsdale game) include the following litany: single-game points (113), single-game field goals attempted (71), single-game field goals made (38), single-game free throws made (37), season's free throws attempted (510), season's per-game average (46.5), games over 50 points in a season (8), games over 50 points in a career (14). The latter three marks of course pale in comparison with Bevo's discounted freshman records of 50.1 points per game, 19 50-point games, and a full-career total (counting all 1953 games) of 27 such 50-point-plus contests. Official published Division II NCAA records would later include only 27 of Bevo's 39 freshman games (those against four-year schools), and would also list Bevo's sophomore figures as 1,255 points and 46.5 points per game, discounting the season-opening contest (63 points) with Erie Tech.

Then suddenly it was over after a mere two seasons; the comet had set as quickly as it had arrived. A sprained ankle six games from the end of the 1954 campaign (suffered ironically versus another school named Ashland, this one a four-year college in Ohio) would leave Francis hobbled for the final weeks of his sophomore season (although he still averaged 31 points per game over his final five injury-slowed games). But a bigger burden for Francis and his teammates and coach was a campus backlash against the celebrity squad which had raked in cash and publicity yet rudely disrupted quiet campus life. Faculty and administrators now regularly turned cold shoulders upon the basketball star when crossing his path anywhere on campus. A disgruntled Francis would thus drop out of Rio Grande at the end of the spring semester and wouldn't set foot back in town for more than a full decade.

In the end it was hard to get an accurate reading on the Bevo Francis legacy. His records were clearly doomed to permanent disregard once they were labelled "illegitimate" — at least in the eyes of NCAA record keepers and most of the nation's basketball press. After a two-year circus-wagon campaign which had totalled an amazing 67 games (Rio Grande was 59-8 over the span) against obscure opponents with names like Ashland, Alliance, Bluffton, Mayo State, Salem, Bliss, Cedarville,

Sue Bennett and Wilberforce, Bevo Francis was merely a blip on the screen of basketball history.

But even in 1954, notoriety and celebrity counted for as much as talent or true noteworthiness and Bevo's headlines would translate into NCAA selection as Midwest Regional Honorable Mention All-American and Associated Press Second Team All-American. First team laurels that year went to Frank Selvy (Furman), Tom Gola (La Salle), Don Schlundt (Indiana), Bob Pettit (LSU) and Cliff Hagan (Kentucky) — Division I stars all. More importantly, however, the gangly jump shooter with the uncanny eye had done as much with his high-powered offensive explosions as any of the big school All-Americans to rivet attention back upon the scandal-racked collegiate roundball sport.

The Two-Year Scoring Legacy of Clarence "Bevo" Francis

1952-53 (Freshman) 1,952 Pts (50.1 Ppg) Opponent (39-0) .... Score ...... Bevo's Points	1953-54 (Sophomore) .... 1,318 Pts (47.0* Ppg) Opponent (20-8) .... Score .... Bevo's Points
Rio Grande Alumni (H) 116-48 44	**Erie Tech (Buffalo) .... 120-59 .... 63**
Cumberland (H) 84-75 45	Adelphi (MSG, NY) 76-83 32
Sue Bennett (H) 121-99 58	Villanova (Philadelphia) 92-93 39
Waynesburg (H) 108-70 46	Providence (Boston) 89-87 41
Dayton Freshman (H) 93-89 35	**Bluffton (A) .... 116-71 .... 82**
Wilberforce (H) 111-71 69	Hillsdale (A) 82-45 43
Bluefield (A) 99-63 21	Miami (Florida) 98-88 48
Denison (A) 88-78 26	North Carolina State (A) 77-92 34
Marietta (A) 76-73 37	Wake Forest (A) 67-65 32
Beckley College (A) 90-71 46	Salem College (A) 96-99 38
California State, Pa. (H) .. 105-73 72	Butler (Indianapolis) 81-68 48
Sue Bennett (A) 114-68 59	Morris Harvey (A) 86-63 42
Steubenville (H) 107-58 50	Alliance (Erie, PA) 107-77 61
Pikeville (A) 72-52 25	**Alliance (A) .... 133-68 .... 84**
Lees College (A) 102-64 76	Ashland (A) 117-74 55
Cumberland (A) 78-49 34	Findlay (A) 74-71 32
Findlay (A) 91-88 44	Creighton (Troy, OH) 96-90 49
Ashland Jr. College (H) .. 150-85 116	Morris Harvey (A) 74-62 26
Mayo State (H) 119-91 63	Buffalo St. (Buffalo) 81-65 31
Wright-Patterson (A) 113-85 55	**Hillsdale (Jackson, OH) ... 134-91 .... 113**
Bliss College (A) 101-53 51	Anderson College (A) 101-85 59
Lockbourne Air Force (A) 84-50 36	Salem College (A) 115-76 58
Cedarville (A) 66-29 38	Ashland (A) 121-61 53
Cincinnati Seminary (A) ... 79-54 42	Arizona St. (Kansas City) ... 90-74 28
Mountain State (A) 133-83 63	SE Louisiana (Kan. City) ... 65-78 .... 27 (NAIA)
Beckley College (A) 102-69 46	Shurtleff (St. Louis) .... 72-77 .... 37 (NAIA)
Steubenville (A) 78-65 41	Rockhurst (Kansas City) ..... 50-56 .... 22 (NAIA)
Pikeville (A) 97-62 61	Creighton (Omaha) .... 75-93 .... 41 (NAIA)
Mayo State (A) 126-98 60	
Cedarville (A) 104-48 51	*NCAA recognized 1,255 (46.5) in 27 games for 1954
Mountain State (A) 116-65 37	
Bliss College (A) 105-69 49	**Boldface means Bevo totaled more than opposition**
Lockbourne Air Force (A) 95-80 47	
Lees College (A) 128-57 63	
Wilberforce (A) 100-51 52	
Bluefield (H) 128-73 53	
Ashland Jr. College (A) 70-63 25	
Cincinnati Seminary (A) ... 111-86 59	
Wilberforce (A) 109-55 54	**2 Year Totals .... 3270 Pts (48.8 Ppg)**

The scoring onslaughts by Bevo Francis soon proved to be anything but isolated backwater events. Instead, they were signs of an emerging trend and not at all mere aberrations. Almost overnight other hot-handed scorers were appearing everywhere upon the college scene. Six-foot-four forward Paul Arizin of Villanova featured a spectacular "low-trajectory" jumper and had already posted some phenomenal numbers, logging the first 25 points per game season average in winning the 1950 national scoring title. Behind Arizin, the Villanova team itself averaged 72-plus points per game and thus ended a 14-year run by Rhode Island State as the nation's most potent offensive team.

Uncanny Arizin tossed in 85 points in one 1950 contest for the major college "record" although his own effort came against an opponent (the Philadelphia Navy Air Materials Center) that was neither a four-year college nor a degree-issuing school. St. John's gunner Bob Zawoluk would earn temporary fame with a school-record 65-point outburst against St. Peter's during the same season. And there was also Bill Mlkvy at Temple who upped the single-season scoring record to 29.2 points per game in 1951 and also logged the "recognized" Division I single-game high of 73 against Wilkes College. Washington & Lee's Jay Handlan, who trailed Mlkvy in the national scoring race, anticipated Francis with 71 field-goal attempts against Furman in February 1951. Joe Fulks didn't make as much of a college splash at Murray State Teachers College (Kentucky) as his future Philadelphia Warriors teammate Paul Arizin had at Villanova, yet when unleashed on the pros Fulks and his unique two-handed jumper had already set the tone in the late '40s (with a record 63-point game against the Indianapolis Jets of the BAA) for the awesome scoring displays that were soon to come.

But perhaps the biggest point-making circus of them all was one now unfolding in the hinterlands of Greenville, South Carolina, in perfect tandem with the efforts of Bevo Francis and his own Rio Grande traveling sideshow. While Bevo was posting his astronomical and often questionable numbers in 1952-53, an even more remarkable shooter was warming up down south at yet another small-time school. Furman College's Frank Selvy was also ready to explode onto the hardwood scene.

Selvy held some weighty advantages in his own run at the national headlines. While largely uncelebrated in athletic circles, Furman College was nonetheless a full-fledged NCAA school, one that played a largely respectable schedule and belonged to the venerable Southern Conference, a 30-year-old circuit featuring the likes of West Virginia, Richmond and George Washington University (and formerly home to Kentucky, Mississippi and most of the Atlantic Coast Conference schools as well). Southern Conference play guaranteed larger venues for Selvy's act and his own home court, Textile Hall, could accommodate better than 4,000 fans to cheer on his exploits. And despite as own machine-gun accuracy Selvy was also not entirely a one-man show; he teamed with Darrell Floyd (himself a national scoring champion during the coming two seasons) for a combined 66 points per game average. Senior Selvy and sophomore Floyd were thus the highest scoring duo in major college basketball history.

There was also a universe of difference in style between the jump-shooting but largely stationary 6-9 Francis and the agile 6-3 Furman forward. Selvy owned a full

Furman's Frank Selvy set the college basketball world on its ear when he became the sport's second 100-point man within a month during February 1954. (Furman University photo)

arsenal of running shots and was an almost unguardable moving target for hapless defenders. The Furman star had himself already crossed the 50-point plateau in four separate games during the 1954 season (something Francis had done nine times that year and an incredible 19 times a season earlier) and it only seemed a matter of time and luck before he too would enjoy a night to be remembered for all ages.

Ironically, when that night finally did come, it was but 11 days after Bevo's own outburst against Hillsdale. Ink was barely dry on the press accounts of the Rio Grande-Hillsdale game when Frank Selvy also unloaded for a miraculous 100 points. Unleashing his potent jump shots and relentless driving layups upon an overmatched Newberry College team, Selvy poured in 41 of 66 field-goal tries, canned 18 of 22 charity tosses, rang up three buckets in the game's final half-minute, and finally reached the century mark on a half-court bomb uncorked mere seconds before the game-ending buzzer.

Selvy's one-game scoring onslaught was — like those of Bevo Francis — the culmination of a long string of truly prodigious point-making efforts. Selvy had in fact been burning the nets for three full seasons before his record-breaking curtain call of February 13, 1954. At the time, no player outside of Bevo a season earlier had ever averaged above 30 for a complete campaign, and Bevo's marks had already been stricken from the record books. Selvy would approach the lofty total as a junior (29.5 points per game) and thus barely hop over Bill Mlkvy's national mark of 29.2 set two winters earlier.

Then, as a senior, the Furman ace would suddenly lift scoring performance to a new level of proficiency. By midseason he was averaging close to 40, clearly on a record-shattering pace. (Francis was averaging above 45 that year but his totals were still not being sanctioned by the NCAA and would later be listed as NAIA small school marks.) As the season wore down in mid-February, Selvy was approaching the 1949 career scoring standard of 2,154 owned by Jim Lacy of Baltimore's Loyola College. With a huge assist from his fateful late-season encounter with Newberry College, Selvy (playing but three years) would soon stretch the four-year standard all the way to 2,538 points (a 32.5 points per game career average).

Selvy's 100-point game was even more remarkable than the two posted by Bevo Francis on at least three distinct counts. Foremost, it was accomplished by a relative "little man" who fired bombs of all types and from all over the court. Selvy's outing also came on a level of competition that could not so easily be dismissed as illegitimate due to "non-college" opponents. And finally, it all transpired with a far larger contingent of hometown fans and media providing disbelieving eyewitness. *Life* magazine had, in fact, chosen the very week of the Furman-Newberry game to post a staff reporter and cameraman on the Greenville campus; *Life* was already preparing a feature story on the Southern Conference sharpshooter who had just toppled the career NCAA scoring record. And most ironically fitting of all, the game was the very first sporting event ever to be televised live across the entire state of South Carolina. Selvy's timing was as perfect as his deadly running jump shot.

Selvy's unmatched night of individual glory was also one of unrelenting drama. This particular late-season game was not only a historic television event, but it was also a night when hometown fans had arrived all the way from Corbin, Kentucky, to cheer on their native son. More than 100 residents of tiny Corbin had formed a motorcade to make the 250-mile trek into Greenville for a special "Frank Selvy Night" affair. Thus, even Selvy's mother was there to see her son perform for the first time ever in a college uniform. And Furman's sensational scorer didn't disappoint family, friends, Furman boosters, or a nation of basketball fans suddenly caught up in the scoring frenzy launched by the small-college wonder up in Ohio less than two weeks earlier.

The first two minutes-plus incredibly saw the opposition's best defensive player, forward Bob Bailey, foul out in a futile effort to control the Furman whirling dervish shooter. By the time Bailey was whistled for his fifth personal with only 2:43 run off the clock Selvy was already in double figures; at the end of the first 10-minute quarter "The Furman Rifle" had already outscored Newberry single-handedly by a 24-19 count. At the end of another quarter the total for Selvy was 37, a new school record for first-half point production.

The pattern had been set early with the tall guard (Selvy's 6-3½ frame was indeed towering for a backcourt man in 1954) bringing the ball up the floor, then roaming the paint around the basket in search of easy jumpers and layins. With the score already standing at 77-44 and with their star burning the nets at a record pace, during intermission Selvy's teammates decided they would now feed him exclusively. Although the Furman ace was not himself at first in on this conspiracy, it quickly became clear what the new game plan was. "Every time I tried to pass the ball I got it right back," Selvy later mused about his most famous game. And there was another conspiracy in the works as well. With the game already firmly in their back pocket the Furman team simply let their Newberry opponents fire up uncontested shots each time down the floor, a strategy designed to put the ball right back in Selvy's hands as rapidly as possible.

Selvy was now on fire and he took total advantage. With the feeding frenzy building, the scene was near pandemonium in the stuffed 4,000-seat gym as the closing moments of the final quarter ticked down. A third-quarter total of 25 for Selvy (Newberry had 22) brought the count to 62, a point short of the hotshot's own single-game school record. The recognized NCAA single game standard of 73 set by Temple's Bill Mlkvy two seasons earlier went by the wayside only minutes into the fourth quarter. At the outset of the final frame, Selvy had still stood an unreachable 38 points away from the century mark, but with layups and jumpers falling like hail stones the impossible was suddenly but a handful of accurate shots away.

Fittingly for such a historic occasion the most spectacular moment of all was saved for the ultimate curtain closer. Two Selvy buckets in the final 30 seconds had raised his count to 98, and with a mere half-dozen ticks left on the clock Furman had one final inbounds play at the far end of the court. In the excitement of the moment Selvy mistakenly inbounded the ball himself in what seemed for a painful instant like a fatal flaw in strategy. But a teammate was able to return the pass and Selvy drove frantically to half-court and unleashed a desperation heave from four or five steps inside the midcourt circle. Like everything else he had thrown up all night this final shot somehow found its mark. When it did the charmed Furman Rifle had just as suddenly and unexpectedly found a truly indelible spot in basketball history.

The final ledger reads like a page from a Clair Bee fictional account of some superman Chip Hilton, perhaps boasting a pretentious title like "Scoreboard Explosion" or "Shooting Circus" or the like. Furman 149, Newberry 95; Selvy 41-for-66 from the field, 18-for-22 from the foul line. Miraculously, three other players had also topped 25 points in the game — Furman's Darrell Floyd (25) and Newberry's Blanko (35) and Davis (32) — and yet they didn't even merit a single line of praise in next-day game accounts. And in four decades that have followed, no other sharp-shooter has even come within 20 points of matching such a truly Herculean effort.

Selvy would later remember the incredible game from the vantage point of several decades. He today occasionally watches the video tape he still owns and always marvels anew at just how easily and how often he actually did score. He is also aware that the only way any player can reach such an unthinkable point total within the time frame of a collegiate game is with constant feeds from his willing teammates, as well as with a huge assist from Lady Luck. "It was one of those shots where more luck than skill was involved, but sometimes there has to be plenty of both," he muses about the final field goal. That final shot itself was indeed a "one-in-a-million" happenstance. Yet it came on a night when Frank Selvy was perhaps as unaccountably charmed as any single player ever has been.

Frank Selvy's scoring — like that of Bevo Francis — was not restricted to a single outburst or even a handful of such "unconscious" shooting nights. While he never again reached quite such single-game heights, Selvy would spend the entire

1954 season obliterating the national scoring standards. His century-mark game still stands in the NCAA record books as the top mark against "small-college" opposition; Kevin Bradshaw's 72 points for U.S. International (versus Loyola Marymount in January 1991) is today credited as the Division I record. The 41 field goals against Newberry have never since been topped in any NCAA game at any level. Selvy's career total of 2,538 (3 seasons) was quickly passed by Dickie Hemric's four-year total of 2,587 for Wake Forest a mere season later, yet the three-year mark stood intact until Oscar Robertson eventually upped the ante in 1960.

The surviving sophomore-season records of Bevo Francis today remain on the ledgers only as less prestigious small school marks. Bevo is thus remembered in the NCAA record book with only a handful of entries (several marked by an asterisk) under Division II scoring champions. The Division II season's record is today still Bevo's 1,255 points (46.5 points per game) in 1954; his 1953 total of 1,952 (50.1) has been long since washed away as illegitimate and unnoteworthy. But Frank Selvy would remain in the NCAA record books for all time and all ages as the first-ever 40-point producer for an entire college season. And Selvy's 100-point single-game mark is now perhaps the most unassailable record in all of American big-time sports.

When it came to postcollege heroics, the careers of Francis and Selvy would also pursue far different dates with destiny. Neither ever enjoyed quite the same limelight away from the college game, yet Selvy indeed experienced a far more luminous professional career.

Drafted in 1956 by the Philadelphia Warriors, Bevo Francis turned down an NBA contract he considered too skimpy and instead opted for a better-paying yet dead-end and short-lived career as a showpiece with the Globetrotters' touring companions, the Boston Whirlwinds. The stint paid $12,000 a year and lasted but a couple of winters. For his own part, Frank Selvy would a few seasons later be displaying his own wares in the newly popular professional league known as the National Basketball Association. A top pick of the Baltimore Bullets in the 1954 NBA draft, the Furman ace would be traded to the Milwaukee Hawks by midseason. There he teamed with stellar rookie center Bob Pettit for two seasons before a journeyman career took him on to the Minneapolis Lakers, New York Knicks, Syracuse Nationals, and then the Lakers once more, just in time for that team's westward move to Los Angeles and its reemergence as a true league powerhouse. Selvy's best offensive year would be his rookie season split between Baltimore and Milwaukee (19.0 points per game), but his very best all-around seasons were his first three in Los Angeles (1961-63) where he eventually replaced Hot Rod Hundley as Jerry West's backcourt running mate.

And it was with Los Angeles, ironically, that one of the truly great shooters of college hoops history fell victim to a single unfortunate career moment tinged with considerable infamy. The Lakers stood on the verge of dethroning the three-time champion Boston Celtics and capturing their own first-ever world title at the close of a crucial seventh game in the 1962 NBA finals. With the score knotted at 100 the Lakers owned the final possession and Selvy's short jumper rolled off the rim as the final buzzer sounded. Given a second life, Auerbach's Celtics prevailed in overtime and continued their march toward eight consecutive NBA titles. Thus Selvy, for all his shooting prowess, had failed to connect on what was unquestionably the most important shot of his entire career, and one of the most memorable in NBA history. Ironically, the man who could shoot perhaps better than almost anyone who ever launched a layup or popped a jumper would thus be forever remembered for the single errant shot he somehow unaccountably could not convert.

Bevo Francis and Frank Selvy would in the end be yoked by a single undeserved fate as perhaps the roundball game's most underrated and underappreciated early stars. Together they would remain isolated in history as unparalleled shooting wizards whose awesome talents were somehow still not quite enough to capture a larger measure of basketball immortality. Those who saw him play would always contend that Bevo Francis, especially, was far more than just a lumbering giant who simply rang up unrealistic point totals by dunking over unskilled opponents. Francis was — despite the small-time trappings surrounding him — one of the truly miraculous marksmen ever to step upon a hardwood court. Legendary pro talent sleuth Marty Blake saw him perform and called him a truly great shooter, one of the greatest shooters of all time. And Blake — although himself still a novice scout at the time — was even back then no mean judge of such true basketball talent.

If Selvy somewhat unfairly tarnished his image with his single "brick shot" in Boston Garden, Bevo Francis just as quickly lost any lasting luster when he turned a cold shoulder on the Warriors NBA contract offer. Francis was seemingly unwilling to leave his small-town trappings and test his mettle against the legitimate pros. Remaining with mentor Newt Oliver (who also signed on to coach the Boston Whirlwinds) and settling for a lofty paycheck from the Harlem Globetrotters to tour as an opposition sideshow was a safe living for the short haul; but it was also a guaranteed ticket to oblivion. The role of Globetrotter lackey would last 2½ years of endless one-night stands. Bevo Francis would thus fade from the consciousness of the basketball world even more quickly than had Furman's Frank Selvy. Almost overnight the two most remarkable shooters of the decade were already lost in the glow of a college basketball heaven suddenly crammed with other supernovas who could outstrip their flash and notoriety, even if none would ever again quite reach such astronomical scorebook numbers.

Other prodigious scorers also erected their personal monuments across the landscape during the early '50s. One — Bill Mlkvy at Temple (the famed "Owl Without a Vowel") — is remembered for his record-breaking single-game onslaughts (he registered the mind-bending total of 73 in one game against Wilkes College) and his nearly 30-point nation's best scoring average in 1951, as well as his strange vowelless name. Another — "Hot Rod" Hundley at West Virginia — didn't log anything like the point totals of Selvy or Mlkvy or even Paul Arizin at Villanova. Nonetheless, the entertaining gunner from the Mountaineer State was perhaps the most outrageously colorful athlete ever to come down the pipe, in this or any other decade.

If Rod Hundley didn't fill the nets at the same dizzying pace as some of the top gunners now turning up at hoop-crazed campuses, he indeed had no peer when it came to pleasing crowds who paid admissions to see him play. So sensational were his shooting and ballhandling skills in high school, in fact, that the Charleston native stirred an all-out recruiting war among more than 100 colleges coast to coast. An apparent born showman who delighted in turning on crowds with his dribbling and passing antics, Hundley at first leaned toward attending powerhouse North Carolina State, the dominant team in the just-formed Atlantic Coast Conference. Yet when the Wolfpack program was suddenly slapped with both NCAA and ACC sanctions for numerous recruiting violations, longtime NC State coach Everett Case nobly advised Hundley against casting his lot with a program which might now doom his promising career even before it got off the ground. Hundley wisely swallowed the advice, opted to stay closer to home, and signed up with coach Red Brown in Morgantown, just before Brown turned over the West Virginia program to ex-Mountaineer star Fred Schaus.

The decision was not only a boon to the West Virginia schoolboy star but to the state's leading institution as well. "Hot Rod" Hundley would overnight become a Mountaineer legend whose catchy nickname as fittingly captured his flaky personality as it did his deadeye basket-making. A proficient enough scorer, Hundley would average a shade under 25 a game during his three WVU seasons. But clowning on the court always seemed to take precedence over honing almost limitless offensive skills. In a few short seasons a pair of other sensational Mountaineer forwards, Jerry West and Rod Thorn, would win games, league titles and even postseason honors in droves for West Virginia's growing cage program. Rod Hundley instead expended most of his own energies on winning the crowd with his outrageous antics.

A cross between the Harlem Globetrotters and Houdini, this original "court jester" played seriously enough to pace his team to 19 wins and their first-ever Southern Conference title as a sophomore rookie, racking up 711 points in the process for a sophomore-season NCAA record. As a junior, he averaged 26.6 points per game, brought WVU a second league title and completely outgunned Frank Selvy's Furman successor Darrell Floyd in a head-to-head matchup (Hundley had 32 in the first half alone). As a senior he garnered All-American honors, a third conference team crown and the top spot in the first round of the NBA player draft.

And through all the glory, Hot Rod also, night after night, lived up to his growing reputation for pure show business on the hardwoods. With his team safely in the lead (which it frequently was) he would shoot with either hand, spin the ball on his fingertips Globetrotter-style, dribble with his knees and elbows, and punch layups into the hoop volleyball-style with a closed fist. Frequently, he offered the ball to a defender with one hand while dribbling downcourt, then flipped it over his shoulder and caught it behind his back with the opposite hand. He launched his "praying mantis" long-range set shots from his knees, hooked foul shots and refused to shoot at all if his team built too large a lead. Another crowd-pleasing feature of the Rod Hundley sideshow was to shoot free throws blindly over his shoulder with his back facing the basket.

College basketball had never before seen anything quite like the Rod Hundley Show and would never again quite find his equal. (Nor do the contemporary NBA antics of the modern anti-star, Dennis Rodman, rate for comparison; Rodman's act has always detracted from his court presence and never served to heighten or embellish it.) It was rare enough to have a court star who seemed to double as the team's public relations officer; it was rarer still to have a full-fledged oncourt clown tal-

Bill Russell of San Francisco demonstrates his inside dominance as teammate Carl Boldt (19) and La Salle's Bob Maples (14) watch during the 1955 NCAA championship game. (La Salle University photo)

ented enough to twice win All-America honors and even check in as the No. 1 overall draft pick (by the Cincinnati Royals) of the win-at-all-cost pro league.

Other areas of the country also boasted their high-scoring stars. Tommy Heinsohn of Holy Cross paced the Northeast, with an able assist from Chet Forte at Columbia and Rudy LaRusso of Dartmouth. Robin Freeman carried the Midwestern banner out of Ohio State with consecutive 30-plus scoring campaigns in the mid-50s. Dickie Hemric of Wake Forest was a gem in the Deep South and would soon be rewriting the legend and the records of his Dixie predecessor Frank Selvy. Darrell Floyd followed Selvy as a national scoring champ for two years at Furman College, while Grady Wallace (1957 scoring champ at 31.2) was another hot-shooting Southerner out of South Carolina. Out West there would be first Johnny O'Brien and then Elgin Baylor, both from tiny and unheralded Seattle University. O'Brien still remains the only player to toss in more than 40 points (42 versus Idaho State in 1953) in his first-ever NCAA postseason game; Baylor remains the only gunner to post 30-plus scoring averages with two different schools (Seattle and the College of Idaho) during his NCAA career. But none could ever quite reach the heights that Selvy had already mastered a few seasons earlier.

Seattle's Johnny O'Brien, in particular, drew instant attention to himself and his teammates when he poured home 43 points during a memorable 84-81 exhibition victory over Goose Tatum and the famed Harlem Globetrotters (who were at the time still playing serious basketball and thus generally ranked with the NBA champion Minneapolis Lakers as the world's best pro outfit). The January 1952 fundraiser (aiding the 1952 US Olympic Team) was at the time touted as one of the greatest upsets in both college and pro cage history. The contest drew a packed house into the University of Washington Pavilion and featured famed jazz musician Louie Armstrong as halftime entertainment. But the show in the end belonged entirely to the phenomenal Johnny O alone. Not only did the versatile O'Brien sink the Trotters with a hefty scoring barrage, but he did so by directly challenging the much taller Tatum at the big man's own pivot position. Goose Tatum had some choice words about his diminutive rival after the 5-8 New Jersey native dazzled him with an unstoppable scoring onslaught from directly under the bucket: "That Johnny O'Brien's no little man," grinned Tatum, "He's nothing but a big man!"

The Name of the Game is Still Defense

While emphasis remained focused on offense in the early and mid-50s, defensive basketball was not entirely relegated to the junk heap, either. Indeed, the greatest team of the era, as well as arguably the greatest all-around player, both made their marks with defensive prowess rather than mere offensive fireworks.

In fact, while Francis and Selvy and other gunners grabbed their share of headlines with explosive scoring during the first few years of the decade, the 1950s in the end would largely belong to two huge centers whose innate game was mostly basket-side intimidation and never long-range sharpshooting. One of these behemoths was destined to nurture the image of basketball's truest unsurpassed winner. Elongated Bill Russell would lead a small and previously unheralded West Coast Jesuit school, the University of San Francisco, to surprising back-to-back national titles plus a new record for uninterrupted winning.

And the undaunted winner's image was one that Russell would steadfastly maintain for more than another decade, once he took his unparalleled rebounding and shot-blocking act into the cutthroat pro game as the defensive pillar of Auerbach's Boston Celtics dynasty. In 13 seasons Russell's NBA teams won 70.5 percent of their regular-season games and 63.9 percent of their playoff games; in the NBA Finals he was 11-for-12. Only Magic Johnson, with a 74.2 regular-season winning ledger (one admittedly compiled against more watered-down competition), can boast comparable domination.

The other defensive monster who revolutionized '50s play was an even more spectacular all-around performer and even more imposing physical presence, both as pro and collegian. Yet unlike Bill Russell, Wilt Chamberlain would also be a player cursed with an unshakable reputation for losing in the clutch. Chamberlain would enter a Kansas program long controlled by Phog Allen and widely recognized as the most glamorous in the land. Few doubted that with the towering 7-foot Wilt in tow the Kansas Jayhawks would enjoy nothing less than the kind of relentless winning San Francisco had just relished behind Russell. It was also therefore a foregone conclusion that USF's record winning streak of 1955 and 1956 (60 games) would inevitably be overhauled by Chamberlain and his Kansas caddies before the 1957 and 1958 seasons were history.

But it never turned out that way and the Jayhawks had trouble enough just staying atop their own competitive conference. Wilt did carry his team all the way to the NCAA title game as a sophomore, but there he was beaten by a never-say-die North Carolina team, and beaten in a fashion that would quickly raise doubts about his missing killer's instinct. And this would be the unfortunate image that would dog Chamberlain throughout a subsequent and otherwise brilliant professional career. Russell and Chamberlain would never meet face-to-face on the college hardwoods since their careers failed to overlap by only a single season. But in the coming decade they would foster the greatest head-to-head rivalry in professional basketball history. And in the four college seasons that immediately preceded that Russell-Wilt NBA rivalry, the tone of that forthcoming decade-long battle of the titans was already being firmly set in stone.

The building of the basketball program at the University of San Francisco did not exactly begin with the fall 1953 arrival of Bill Russell. Nor did it quite begin with the debut of coach Phil Woolpert a few seasons earlier. It had all actually been launched under another defensive-minded coach in the late 1940s. That man was Pete Newell, an eventual Hall of Famer who would soon be building still another championship program across the bay at Berkeley. Both Newell and Woolpert (along with Scotty McDonald) had served playing apprenticeships at Los Angeles Loyola College under coach James Needles. Needles had pioneered a scheme of hard-nosed aggressive defense and disciplined patterned offense that soon become the prevailing West Coast style. Newell and Woolpert (both at San Francisco) and McDonald (at Loyola) were the leading disciples who fine-tuned and perfected what Needles had first conceived.

Newell would spend only four years (1947-1950) at San Francisco and log but two truly outstanding campaigns (25-5 in 1949, 19-7 in 1950). Yet in that brief tenure he would lay the solid foundations for Woolpert, who himself took the reins in the fall of 1950. And Newell would also give the school its first taste of big-time postseason success.

That initial success would come with a surprise visit to the NIT finals in Madison Square Garden during March of 1949, and with an even more surprising NIT victory celebration at the conclusion of that rare East Coast visit. It all transpired during the most topsy-turvy NIT event of the wartime and immediate post-war eras. Riding a 21-5 record into Madison Square Garden, the underappreciated USF Dons parlayed upsets of Manhattan, Utah and Bowling Green into a title contest with Loyola of Chicago. Paced by star Don Lofgran, who tallied nearly half the points, Newell's team then surprised the Chicago club in a 48-47 thriller. After such a victory on college basketball's prime center stage, even a slide back to losing seasons in Woolpert's first three campaigns would not be enough to thrust the USF Dons back into total obscurity.

Yet it would not be until several years down the road that Woolpert and USF would make further serious inroads on the national scene. Woolpert was only the

Bill Russell brought a new dimension to shot blocking skillfully guiding rejected shots into the hands of his waiting teammates. In the 1956 NCAA title game against Iowa, Russell demonstrates ballet-like moves as he swats away another Iowa shot. (University of Iowa photo)

latest in a long lineage of West Coast defensive-minded coaches to begin stirring up notice for himself and his program from distant corners of the basketball map. It was not the freewheeling offensive tactics of Hank Luisetti and coach Johnny Bunn (a disciple of Phog Allen at Kansas) over at Stanford that represented the true flavor of California-style play. That style was instead the one honed by Needles and McDonald at Loyola and later practiced successfully by Forrest Twogood and Bob Boyd at Southern Cal. Phil Woolpert (whose playing career under Needles ended in 1940) also fit directly into the mold of these Needles-trained defensive architects, coaches who methodically built their teams around ball control, defensive harassment and carefully crafted set offensive movements. It was this proven program that Woolpert worked hard to continue at San Francisco once he had supplanted Newell as the Dons head coach.

The linchpin would of course be Russell, a gangly San Francisco-area young-ster who would turn out to be one of the rarest finds in the history of big-time college recruiting. There were no headline-grabbing recruiting wars over Russell like the ones surrounding Chamberlain or Oscar Robertson or Rod Hundley out in West Virginia. Russell's family had moved frequently around the country, from his birth-place in Louisiana, to Detroit, then on to Oakland where his father finally found permanent work in the local shipyards. Bill enrolled at McClymonds High School (alma mater of '50s-era baseball stars Frank Robinson, Vada Pinson and Curt Flood) in order to avoid uncomfortable comparisons with his more talented older brother who was already starring in several sports at rival Oakland Tech.

The spindly and awkward converted left-hander showed little athletic promise in the first season or two at McClymonds. Russell was cut by the junior varsity football squad and later taken on only as a charity case by JV basketball coach George Powles. But along the way he had already acquired a sound piece of early coaching. An uncle who had once failed a Negro League baseball tryout had convinced young William Felton Russell to develop left-handed shooting for versatility, and also as a hedge against the athletic failures that he himself attributed to righthandedness during his own short-lived baseball-playing past. It soon proved a chunk of advice well-heeded.

Under the patient tutelage of Powles, Russell was able to mature quietly into a third-string backup as a junior and then a 6-6 unpolished starting center as a senior. Few colleges took notice, however, and only a lukewarm scouting report delivered to Woolpert over at the hometown Jesuit college induced even a modest scholarship offer. Russell would later be quoted as recalling that coach Woolpert didn't think much of his game at first because he had simply never seen anyone block shots before. To Woolpert's undying credit remains the fact that he didn't rush headlong into trying to convert his unorthodox recruit into just another oversized jump shooter.

When Russell first came on the college scene he was indeed the rarest of phenomena. The skinny 130-pound high schooler had emerged as a 6-9 200-pounder by the night of his sophomore-season college debut. He would also drill endless hours with Woolpert's assistant, Ross Guidice, perfecting a close-range hook shot that paid off in a 20-point average for a season of freshman competition. In his varsity debut against Cal-Berkeley's all-league center Bob McKeen the untried recruit proved he was largely ready when he outpointed the rugged veteran 23-14 and blocked eight of McKeen's close-range shots.

But it wouldn't be a one-man "Bill Russell Show" entirely that would catapult Woolpert's team straight to the top. For the Dons also owned a local recruit named K.C. Jones, another "sleeper" who had caused equally little stir upon the San Francisco schoolboy scene despite setting a local prep-league scoring record at Commerce High. Jones, like Russell, had been bypassed by collegiate recruiters, at least until a local reporter penned a helpful story which stretched the truth more than just a fair bit. The friendly writer had hinted falsely that cage powerhouses the likes of Stanford, UCLA and Cal-Berkeley were beating a hot path straight to Jones' door; this was enough bait for Woolpert to swallow hook, line and sinker. Jones had thus also been offered a USF grant-in-aid, one that made him only the second black player ever to suit up for the Dons' program when he first took the floor in December 1951.

And there was also the coaching skill of Woolpert himself. Here indeed was the perfect coach to exploit and unleash Russell's rare and novel talents. While defense was this coach's passion and his forte, he also drilled his charges for hour upon hour on precise set offensive plays fine-tuned to achieve perfection. More importantly, however, Woolpert recognized the unprecedented impact Russell might have if he were simply allowed to develop his native inclinations to camp near the bucket, ward off any and all rivals for missed shots and reject enemy missiles by the dozens.

Dormant since their brief taste of success in 1949, the Dons would suddenly begin to come of age early in 1954-55. But there was little reason at the outset of Russell's 1953 sophomore season to believe that this was yet a team of any special destiny. The cash-poor and thus facility-poor institution still shifted around its home games between 5,000-seat Kezar Stadium, the smaller San Francisco Cow Palace, and a third dingy court in nearby San Jose. The vagabond Dons also practiced at St. Ignacius High School since they lacked any campus gymnasium of their own. An improved 14-7 record during Russell's sophomore campaign left Woolpert's modest four-year ledger at only 44-48 since taking over from Newell. And at the outset of that same season junior backcourt star K.C. Jones had suffered an appendicitis attack which had benched him for the entire year after only a single December game.

Then an impossible dream began to take shape in the early winter of 1954. USF would at long last overtake the Southern California Trojans of coach Forrest Twogood, the Santa Clara Broncos of coach Bob Feerick, and the Washington Huskies of coach Tippy Dye as the best outfit on the West Coast. And Woolpert's charges would quickly spread their newfound reputation from coast to coast as well.

The Dons opened in December 1954 with two quick wins, and the season's lidlifter with Chico State almost proved ludicrous as a 6-1 opposing center tried to match up with towering 6-9 Russell. Then came a not unexpected loss to John Wooden's ever-improving UCLA team in the Westwood bandbox that preceded Pauley Pavilion, to the final count of 47-40. Russell did outplay Wooden's own first legitimate star, Willie Naulls, in that one. And no one could have predicted at the time that it would be the last loss that Bill Russell would ever suffer over the final two winters of his unfolding college career.

UCLA had been the turning point, even in defeat, and this was never clearer than when the now-inspired Dons captured a return match against the Bruins on their own home floor only a week later. With K.C. Jones and running mate Hal Perry now manning the backcourt posts with increased confidence, momentum built during a series of impressive victories in the All-College midseason tourney in Oklahoma City. Highly rated Wichita State, host Oklahoma City and East Coast contender George Washington all fell in rapid succession, while Bill Russell pocketed his first tournament MVP trophy and the surprising Dons quickly climbed toward the top of the weekly AP and UPI popularity polls.

Russell's airtight blanket in the lane and harassing backcourt defense from Jones and Perry combined for 16 straight additional victories down the stretch. The relaxed Dons thus swept into postseason play now wearing the clear favorite's hat in their pursuit of a first-ever NCAA title. The NCAA West Regionals hardly slowed the USF express train as one-sided victories were checked off against West Texas State (89-66) and fast-breaking Utah (78-59) thus setting the stage for a heart-stopping close call during the Regional title match with a formidable 22-8 team from Oregon State. Not only had the Pacific Coast Conference champion endured a tougher year-long schedule, but the squad coached by Slats Gill would also have the added advantage of playing the regional title game on its own home floor in Corvallis.

Bill Russell was the first leaper to control an entire game from the defensive end of the court. Here he rejects a shot by Iowa's Sharm Scheuerman during the 1956 NCAA championship game. (University of Iowa photo)

The Beavers were able to neutralize Russell for much of the hard-fought contest by double-teaming him with 7-3 giant Swede Halbrook and rugged 6-6 forward Tony Vlastelica. This strategy kept the contest even deep into the closing moments during which the now fortune-kissed Dons survived a technical foul call against Jones, a missed shot from the corner by Beaver hot-shot forward Ron Robins, and a mad-scramble for a loose ball at the buzzer. The final count of 57-56 put Woolpert's Cinderella team into the Final Four alongside Iowa, Colorado and the surviving 1954 defending champions, the Tom Gola-led La Salle Explorers.

The 1955 Final Four weekend was one seemingly orchestrated by a gifted Hollywood script writer. An easy Frisco semifinal triumph by a dozen points over Colorado combined with La Salle's narrow 76-73 win over the Iowa Hawkeyes to set up a seeming dream match between the nation's two premier rebounders and inside strongboys, Gola and Russell. The head-to-head collision of stars never quite materialized, however, due to the subtle coaching genius of Phil Woolpert.

In a stunning move, Woolpert would line up K.C. Jones and not Russell oppo-site Gola; it was a surprise ploy that almost sent Jones into shock when announced in the pregame locker room. It was also a ploy which paid huge immediate dividends once the teams took to the hardwood. The tenacious and much quicker USF back-court ace clamped down on Gola, holding him to 16 points, while firing in 24 points of his own. Free to roam the lane unmolested, Russell in turn also bagged 23 points as well as the tourney MVP prize. Outmanned La Salle fell behind by nine by inter-mission and slipped further arrears as the game wore down. The final tally was 77-63; the defending East Coast champ had been dethroned, and the West Coast had its first NCAA titlist since Everett Dean and Stanford had corralled a victory against Dartmouth a full 13 seasons earlier.

Russell and the Dons were no longer a secret after their NCAA title victory in Kansas City against Gola and the best the East Coast had to offer. Woolpert's fine-tuned machine now ruled the college scene and few experts expected them to be stalled or even seriously challenged during a 1956 campaign that would mark senior seasons for the trio of Russell, Jones and Perry. Fresh reinforcements had now been added in the persons of sophomore forward Mike Farmer, sophomore guard Gene Brown and junior forward Carl Boldt. This added firepower was enough to prove the experts right as Woolpert's team cakewalked through a second unblemished cam-paign. The narrowest margin of victory during 25 regular-season games was seven points. The victory streak that stood at 26 when the season opened would stretch out to 55 by the time the door had closed on another national title and on the first unde-feated record (29-0) in NCAA tourney history.

Rules makers did attempt to neutralize Woolpert's colossus at the outset of Russell's senior season with a new rule widening the foul lane from 6 to 12 feet. It was a change aimed directly at Russell himself and yet one that only seemed to give the imposing Dons center extra advantage in the end. Pro teammate Tom Heinsohn would observe a few winters later that Russell's athletic skills were so immense that the super-talented pivotman had an effective rebounding range of 18 feet - 9 feet on either side of the rim. "If he was 9 feet off to one side of the basket," Heinsohn observed, "he could race over to pull down a rebound 9 feet to the other side." (Quoted by Nelson George, *Elevating the Game*, 150)

The Dons next came East into prestigious Madison Square Garden during Christ-mas break of Big Bill's final winter and nobly defended their growing national press clippings in the process. By facing a loaded field during the Holiday Festival Tour-nament Woolpert's club was clearly placing their long unbeaten streak (standing at 33 at the time) in serious jeopardy. But it soon proved to be the case that there was little true challenge in the offering as Gola-less La Salle quickly fell 79-62 in a rematch of the NCAA title game. Three future Celtics greats next matched up as Jones and Russell tackled Tom Heinsohn and powerful Holy Cross, resulting in another USF romp, 67-51, with Russell doubling Heinsohn's output (24 points to 12) and capturing an even two dozen rebounds as well. The New York sojourn ended on an even higher note as California rival UCLA, with Willie Naulls still in the fold, collapsed 70-53, handing USF the midseason tourney crown and also handing Rus-sell yet another much-deserved MVP trophy.

The major college mark for consecutive wins was still held jointly by a pair of East Coast powers of yesteryear — LIU, which had posted 39 straight before falling to Stanford and Hank Luisetti in the Garden in December 1936, and Seton Hall, which had matched the Blackbirds' standard between 1939 and 1941. The night the Dons finally surpassed the record was also the night they faced the only all-out stall thrown at them during the three Russell seasons. Woolpert's predecessor, Pete Newell, had his California Bears primed to disrupt the normal rhythms of USF's juggernaut. Newell stationed his center, Joe Hagler, at midcourt to hold the ball unchallenged for minutes at a time in the futile effort to draw Russell outside of the lane. The Dons were content to sit back and wait, then press furiously for the final quarter of action and pull out a 33-24 record-setting win. The unblemished string then ran itself out with no other serious challenge until season's end.

Postseason play for the Dons would present a new and most daunting challenge, however. If the NCAA ruling regarding foul-lane dimensions had not slowed USF, another NCAA edict regarding player eligibility nearly would. Russell would again be ready for all comers during 1956 postseason play, but K.C. Jones would now be relegated to the sidelines. The junior-season appendicitis bout two years earlier had earned the team catalyst an extra year of varsity eligibility, but that grace period extended only through regular-season play. Russell would now have to defend his NCAA crown with no help from Jones. Most fortunately for USF players, coaches and boosters, Gene Brown — called "the best substitute in the country" by Duquesne coach Dudey Moore — would now step up very big, posting a team-high 23 points in the opening NCAA battle with old rivals UCLA and Willie Naulls.

The loss of Jones would thus prove nothing more than a bother. The Dons hardly broke a real sweat in blasting Utah 92-77 (with 27 from Russell and 18 more from Brown) to earn a West Regional title and a return trip to the Final Four. An 86-68 crushing of SMU with All-American center Jim Krebs was the final stepping stone to the repeat NCAA title match, this time with Big Ten champ Iowa and its "Fabulous Five" starting unit of Bill Logan, Carl Cain, Bill Seaberg, Bill Schoof and Sharm Scheuerman. Iowa, under coach Bucky O'Connor, had gamely battled Gola and La Salle during a three-point semifinal loss a year earlier; this time they provided only moderate resistance to Woolpert and company as they wilted down the stretch under the pressure of what was perhaps Russell's finest all-around game.

Never more agile on offense or intimidating on defense, Russell netted 26 points (Brown, Perry and Boldt also scored in double figures), collected 27 rebounds, and forced his opponent, Logan (who had 36 in the semifinals), into tentative shots from the distant corners of the forecourt. Logan scored a mere 12 points and was never a factor in the contest. The final score was 83-71 and the USF Dons were now only the third repeat titlist in tournament history. If there was any surprising element to the Final Four festivities staged in Evanston, Illinois, it was only that Bill Russell in his finest final hour of triumph was passed over for the prestigious individual MVP award. This honor went to diminutive Temple guard Hal Lear who lit up the nets with a record 48-point performance during the consolation-game shootout with SMU. Defense was indeed now winning championship banners, but spectacular offense was still enough to corner the market on headlines.

The Big Ten's original "Fab Five" was the Iowa contingent of, from left, Sharm Scheuerman, Bill Logan, Carl Cain, coach Bucky O'Connor, Bill Schoof and Bill Seaberg. The Hawkeyes failed in their bid to block San Francisco and Bill Russell's bid for a second straight NCAA title. (University of Iowa photo)

Two years with Russell in command had brought another subtle change on the college cage scene. With USF so clearly the cream of the collegiate crop for two seasons running, attention had now been focused squarely on the postseason NCAA event where the Dons continued to strut their magical game. For the first time, in 1955 and 1956, it seemed absolutely clear that the NCAA event was indeed the tourney that was providing the nation's undisputed national champion. Louisville, with its own inside force in the persona of Charlie Tyra, would defeat Dayton 93-80 for the NIT title. But it now did so in relative obscurity. And this state of decreasing prestige for the original Madison Square Garden year-end event would indeed remain the case from this point on.

When Bill Russell exploded upon the college cage scene he had indeed been a bird of a far different feather. Basketball had always been (and continues to be) far more a game of all-around athletic skill than one of narrow specialization. There are no parallels to designated hitters or place-kicking specialists in the cage game. Russell would never possess the fine-honed all-around skills of a Tom Gola or Clyde Lovellette or Dick Groat or other stars of the mid- and early-50s. He started out as a poor shooter and after three varsity seasons had become only a fair shooter. He was never an accomplished ball handler or very dangerous passer. What he did possess was an entirely new type of intimidating defensive game which he had perfected through hard work and natural talent far beyond any of his rivals. Never before or since had a one-dimensional player (perhaps a two-dimensional player, given his talents for shot-blocking and rebounding together) so dominated even the very best of the competition.

Sharpshooters of Russell's own era would nudge modern basketball toward becoming a wide-open offensive sideshow. But Russell now also brought a new formula for winning. It would never prove a very popular formula, especially once the black-inspired playground one-on-one style emerged over the next two decades. But as Auerbach and the Boston Celtics would soon join Russell in proving, it was nonetheless an unassailable one.

Russell and Jones would now depart, first for the summer Olympic festival in Melbourne, Australia, and then for the pro battlefields of the NBA in Boston. Bill Russell had vanished from the scene almost as quickly as he had arrived, leaving in his wake the longest uninterrupted victory skein in history and the NCAA's first undefeated champion. Yet the college game had undergone a most radical change during his tenure. Team basketball would now never be quite the same and the search for the perfect winning ingredient would from this time forward always seem to reduce itself to a search for the perfect shot-blocking and board-clearing big man.

The Stilt and a House Built of Sticks

It is one of the delicious ironies of the epoch that while Bill Russell was developing as the sport's premier defensive big man, he was also sharing the limelight with another arriving Goliath who would be his rival for years to come within the NBA ranks. And while the more offensive-minded Wilt Chamberlain would always play second fiddle to Russell in the pros, that pattern had already been seemingly set in iron a few years earlier at the level of collegiate competition.

Chamberlain entered a proud Kansas program the very year that Russell had departed the scene, and the universal expectation — from Yonkers to Yakima — was that he would almost effortlessly lift the Jayhawks to even greater heights than those achieved by Russell with the Dons. But the entire venture, before it was over at least, would be more filled with bitter disappointments and endless frustrations than anything else. Wilt would indeed carry the Kansas club of rookie coach Dick Harp into the national championship game in his very first year on the scene. But he would never win the national title that was everywhere expected from him and that other dominating giants like Russell and Alcindor and Walton were able to command so easily. And he would eventually even leave Kansas early (at the end of his junior season) and amid much personal and team exasperation.

Wilt from the start was dogged by the same hopeless curse in college that shadowed him in the pros. For all his individual talent he was never allowed by opposing defenses to play his own game on anything like a level court. Each new opponent had a new defensive scheme designed especially to thwart the big man: some teams stalled and slowed play to an absolute crawl; others used double- and triple-team gangs to surround and harass Wilt before he ever touched the ball; many used bench players as hockey-type "goons" willing to sacrifice themselves with fouls in order to keep Wilt stationed on the foul line rather than camped near the bucket.

And Wilt for his own part also failed to make his surrounding teammates better players in quite the same way Russell always did. (Cynics would always contend that while a Russell-led team was greater than the sum of its parts, a Wilt-led team was just the opposite.) His game, in contrast to Russell's, was narrowly oriented

Wilt Chamberlain came to the University of Kansas carrying the greatest set of expectations ever attached to a new recruit. He immediately lifted the Jayhawks into the NCAA Finals, and yet his collegiate career would be shadowed by huge disappointments. (University of Kansas photo)

toward attracting the ball and thus the defenses directly his own way; Russell instead provided a defensive safety valve geared toward deflecting countless rebounds and rejections deftly downcourt into the hands of his fast-breaking teammates.

Wilt also came to Kansas toting several impossible burdens. One was his unmatched high school successes and thus the overextended expectations that surrounded his forthcoming college debut. At Philadelphia's Overbrook High School the 6-11 teen-ager had dominated opponents a foot shorter with such ridiculous ease that he appeared a He-Man among helpless schoolboys. Here was a multitalented and truly agile giant who was apparently a breed apart from the lumbering hulks that Mikan or Kurland had been at a similar stage of development. When Mikan had arrived on the DePaul campus, remember, he was still so awkward and unathletic that a desperate coach Ray Meyer had prescribed a radical regimen of ballroom dancing lessons and rope skipping in order to successfully launch his reclamation project.

The recruiting frenzy set off by this most publicized high school player in history was something never previously witnessed, and if Chamberlain was destined to be "the ultimate prize" as a raw 18-year-old recruit he was also doomed to wear a label that bore a painfully heavy price. Russell clearly had benefitted from coming upon the scene as a complete unknown and thus an athlete unfettered by this terrible curse of unlimited and thus unreachable potential.

A second burden for Wilt was the legacy that Kansas University basketball already owned. Forrest "Phog" Allen, entrenched in the Jayhawks' head coaching slot since 1919, had been a genuine pioneer of the same stature as Adolph Rupp or Ward Lambert or Doc Meanwell. Over the years and the decades Allen and his Jayhawks had won Big Seven (Big Six) Conference championships by the armfuls (12 Big Seven titles since leaving the Missouri Valley Conference and joining up in 1928) and already owned a pair of mythical national championships (1922, 1923) from the decades before the postseason tournaments had been born. Kansas had also been adopted home to the game's inventor, James Naismith, who had coached there in the first two decades of the century and even owned the ironic distinction of being the school's only head coach with a lifetime losing ledger. During Allen's recent twilight seasons, the Jayhawks had once again risen to the top of the heap and had recently captured a first NCAA national title behind another hulking big man, All-American center Clyde Lovellette out of basketball-crazy Indiana.

Kansas already had all the championship pieces in place for the 1952 season, a full five years before Chamberlain ever came onto the collegiate scene. The bulky 230-pound Lovellette was the nation's top player that year and his dominance was sufficient to carry the Jayhawks all the way to the NCAA Finals once the season-long No. 1 team, Baron Rupp's 29-3 Kentucky Wildcats, were felled early in NCAA action by the upset-minded St. John's Redmen. Kansas made its own run to the top on the strength of a 28-3 overall record and Lovellette's unbeatable combination of rugged inside play and soft-touch medium-range shooting.

In the championship game the Jayhawks would topple surprising St. John's by a comfortable margin (80-63) as Lovellette tossed in 33 points and swept the boards for 17 rebounds. The 6-9 Terre Haute native also finished his final season as the nation's top scorer (28.4) after edging out future major-league baseball star Dick Groat (Duke) and future NBA great Bob Pettit (LSU) for the coveted honor. And when Lovellette was also named the NCAA tourney MVP, as well, he had achieved a rare triple (scoring champ, tourney MVP, national champion) that would soon take on even greater significance as subsequent seasons continued to peel off the calendar. Never before or since would a single player pace the nation's scorers and also walk off with an NCAA championship ring to crown the very same season.

A year later Lovellette was gone, but Kansas and Phog Allen were back nonetheless. Few had held out serious hope for a title defense, since Allen had been forced to replace not only his bulky center but three other starters as well. The revamped Kansas team stayed near the top of the national polls all season long, however, losing only five contests and trailing only Indiana and Seton Hall in the final Associated Press team rankings. The defending champions would again work their way into the NCAA trophy game, by first beating both Oklahoma City and Oklahoma State in regional play, and then also toppling Washington with Helms Foundation player-of-the-year Bob Houbregs in the national semifinal. This time the road to a championship would end a step short, however, as the defense-minded Jayhawks would lose their finale to Branch McCracken's Indiana Hoosiers in a game still widely referred to as perhaps the ugliest in NCAA championship history.

Controversy exploded late in the title game when Jayhawks star B.H. Born (Lovellette's replacement at center) committed what was first ruled to be his fifth personal foul, then acknowledged at the official scorer's table to be only his fourth. By midway through the fourth quarter, however, Born would indeed be disqualified, with the Hoosiers now nursing a slim 68-65 cushion. But down the stretch there were several more explosions of excessive temper and finally three rapid-fire technicals against the Indiana team almost handed the game back over to Kansas. Indiana would desperately hold on, however, capturing the nip-and-tuck affair on some clutch foul shooting in the waning seconds. The deciding charity toss would be registered by future ABA coaching legend Bob "Slick" Leonard with 27 seconds remaining and it would be just enough to keep the Kansas Jayhawks from becoming the NCAA's third-ever repeat champion.

The 1953 season now seems in hindsight to have been Phog Allen's unofficial swan song, though his actual retirement would not be forced upon him until after the 1955-56 campaign. For one thing, Allen would never again return to the NCAA tournament fray, and his final two ballclubs would finish far off the conference pace in fifth place. Yet Phog Allen would nonetheless enjoy one final triumph almost as important as any he had previously engineered over the years in Lawrence, and this victory would come in the intense recruiting wars to obtain the services of Wilt Chamberlain. College sport had never before witnessed quite the same level of furor as that surrounding the pursuit of this particular Philadelphia high schooler who seemed to spell instant success for any coach or program fortunate enough to corral him. Only with the frenzied chase after Lew Alcindor more than a decade later, would anything quite like it ever be seen again.

It was Allen in the end who signed Wilt on and then stepped aside immediately after the big guy's warmup season with the Kansas freshman team; Allen had now reached the mandatory retirement age of 70 and this meant that his eight-year assistant Dick Harp would not only inherit his mentor's program after 39 years (and 588 victories) but that he would also be handed Phog's greatest recruiting triumph and most sure-fire invincible team as well.

Wilt's first and greatest college season also turned out to be his most frustrating. The Kansas club did post a 21-2 regular-season mark and did climb over SMU (in overtime), Oklahoma City and San Francisco University to reach the season's prestigious final game in late March. Wilt had poured in a school-record 52 points in his debut outing against Northwestern and had continued to average a shade under 30 (29.6) for the entire winter. But the 1957 campaign was a constant uphill struggle for a team that was expected to win every game. And the man who had won the two-year recruiting battle to bring Chamberlain to Kansas also hadn't exactly made it easy on either his prize recruit or his former assistant once he had stepped aside. Phog Allen had been widely quoted in the national press on the eve of the 1957 postseason, saying that his former team could undoubtedly coast to a national title even with "Wilt, two sorority girls and two Phi Beta Kappas" in the starting lineup.

The 1957 title matchup between Wilt's Kansas team and the ACC champions from North Carolina was indeed a game for all ages. It may well even have been the greatest single college game ever played — at tournament time or any other time. Certainly it was the most exciting NCAA tourney final of all time; and indisputably it must also stand alongside a Phoenix Suns-Boston Celtics NBA title-round slugfest of 1976 as basketball's most drama-filled marathon contest. But unlike the Boston-Phoenix matchup, this one was sudden-death and for all the marbles. And as it dragged on through its three overtime sessions the struggle became truly titanic in every imaginable sense.

North Carolina's own draining back-to-back battles in the 1957 NCAA Final Four were something that has never been quite equalled before or since in postseason play. The Tar Heels would have to earn their first-ever NCAA banner by surviving not one but two consecutive triple-overtime nail-biters. On the evening of the semifinals, while Kansas was able to coast 80-56 against San Francisco with Wilt dropping in 32 and hardly breaking a sweat, Carolina had to sweat plenty while being extended through three extra sessions before pulling out a narrow 74-70 victory against overachieving Michigan State. Guard Bob Cunningham was the big hero with a 21-point effort that tripled his regular-season average.

Once in the Finals the Tar Heels of coach Frank McGuire had a seemingly foolproof plan to neutralize Chamberlain. They would simply let the unstoppable behemoth have his two or three dozen points while they concentrated all their attentions on the remaining Jayhawk shooters. Not that the North Carolina team was not an equal match to begin with. With a starting lineup recruited entirely from inner-city New York, McGuire's team had battled through a tough ACC schedule and survived a most challenging league qualifying tourney with an unblemished record, thus becoming only the second team in history to reach the NCAA Finals while still undefeated. But the Tar Heels had admittedly not seen a player quite like Wilt all year, and matters were only made worse by the fact that the game was being played in the Municipal Auditorium in Kansas City, smack in the Jayhawks' own backyard.

McGuire broke the tension in the Tar Heels' locker room before game time by telling his team only half seriously that Chamberlain was so good that they might be better off not even taking the floor. He carried the psychological warfare a step further by having 5-7 guard Tommy Kearns face off with Wilt for the game-opening center jump. While McGuire had decided to instruct his team to let Chamberlain have his points and to close down the remainder of the Jayhawk offense, Kansas coach Dick Harp opted for a quite different approach. Kansas seemed more concerned about Len Rosenbluth, the top Tar Heels scorer (28.0), than Carolina was about Wilt. The Jayhawks thus spent the full first half in a diamond-and-one defense with Chamberlain guarding the basket and another defender constantly shadowing Rosenbluth. It proved a huge mistake, however, since it opened up plenty of room for

At 5-foot-7, North Carolina's backcourt ace Tommy Kearns was a most surprising candidate to jump center against Wilt Chamberlain in the 1957 triple-overtime NCAA championship game. (University of North Carolina photo)

the Heels' outside shooting and North Carolina bombed away at a 64.7 percent clip throughout the opening stanza.

As the game wore on, the Tar Heels' strategy appeared to work to near perfection. And yet Chamberlain was still the equal of anything the North Carolina club had to offer. The opponents thus continued to pound each other into near exhaustion. As the second half evaporated the Jayhawks inched back from a 29-22 halftime deficit and eventually edged in front 46-43 with less than two minutes remaining. The tide seemed to turn, however, when Rosenbluth fouled out with only 1:45 remaining; then a free throw by Kearns was able to knot the contest again at 46-all and send the grueling affair into overtime.

Each team scored only once during a first extra session and the two exhausted opponents next played an even more cautious and scoreless second overtime session as well. At the outset of the third extra period the Tar Heels finally edged back into the lead on a basket and two free throws by the cool-headed Tommy Kearns. But the issue was not yet quite decided. A clutch three-point play (bucket and foul shot) by Wilt kept Kansas even. Carolina now played for a final game-deciding shot for the third time on the evening, but this strategy almost backfired on them when a deflected pass resulted in a rare turnover, a Carolina foul and two charity tosses by Jayhawk forward Gene Elstun. When Elstun missed the first but converted the second Kansas had its final lead with only 31 seconds now remaining.

The game would end with a wild flurry of action only fitting for such a tense shootout packed with heartstopping drama. Kearns drove the lane for a layup that was slapped aside by Chamberlain but grabbed by the trailing Joe Quigg. Quigg's desperate attempt at a final shot drew air but also drew a fatal Kansas foul. In a script befitting both Hollywood and every schoolyard fantasy ever dreamed the 6-9 junior center stepped straight into Carolina folklore by calmly sinking the two game-winning shots.

It might be concluded (and often has been) that the longest game in NCAA championship history provided a perfect capsule image of Chamberlain's entire college and pro cage career. Wilt was the true paragon of the tragic embattled warrior during that unforgettable game, as he often later was in similar NBA matches versus Boston's charmed Celtics. If he lost in the end he indeed lost nobly, and the defeat fell more at the hands of his team's inadequacies than his own. Tar Heels coach Frank

111

McGuire would later wryly observe that: "We played him not Kansas. We beat Kansas, not him."

But critics would later have an inevitable field day nonetheless. Chamberlain would be awarded the 1957 tourney MVP trophy, yet he had seemingly already traded personal glory for team achievement. This would soon also be the lasting image of his pro career, or at least the popular image which that career always reflected. Year after year Wilt would set all the records, win all the individual hosannas and capture all the statistical titles. Yet all his teams (Warriors, Sixers, Lakers) would seemingly come up short, especially against Russell and the Celtics. He was thus doomed to live over and over again what had already happened against North Carolina that one fateful night in Kansas City.

The 1957 title game was perhaps already enough to convince Chamberlain that his days on the college hardwoods were no longer worth the effort. It was clear that Wilt was no longer free to enjoy the game as it was meant to be played, and furthermore that the Jayhawks were doomed to an endless series of ruthless blockades thrown up by their rivals. As Wilt struggled through his junior season he was hacked and mauled by each new opponent. Although such tactics were not enough to steal away most games from the Jayhawks, they were nonetheless effective enough to make most games boring for both Wilt and the grandstand spectators.

All-Star Team for the Era (1950-1958)				
	Pos	Pts. (Ppg.)	Best Year	NPY
Tom Gola (La Salle)	F	2462 (20.9)	24.2 (Sr.)	1955
Bill Russell (San Francisco)	C	1636 (20.7)	21.4 (Jr..)	1956
Wilt Chamberlain (Kansas)	C	1433 (29.9)	30.1 (Jr.)	—
Elgin Baylor (Seattle)	F	2500 (31.3)	32.5 (Sr.)	1958
Dick Groat (Duke)	G	1886 (23.0)	26.0 (Sr.)	1951

NPY = National Player of the Year

Honorable Mention: Paul Arizin (F, Villanova), Walt Bellamy (C, Indiana), Ernie Beck (F, Pennsylvania), Clyde Lovellette (C, Kansas), Frank Selvy (G, Furman), Bevo Francis (C, Rio Grande), Gene Melchiorre (G, Bradley), Bill Mlkvy (F, Temple)

Coaches of the Era: Phil Woolpert (San Francisco), NCAA Champion (1955, 1956); and Frank McGuire (North Carolina), NCAA Champion (1957)

Kansas finished up with an 18-5 record, didn't even win the title in its own conference (Kansas State did that), and stayed home from postseason play. A victim of such ruthless defensive tactics, Chamberlain also lost out in the individual scoring race, trailing Oscar Robertson (35.1) and Seattle's Elgin Baylor (32.5); but the beleaguered Goliath did average better than 30 (30.1) and did establish a new conference single-game record with 36 rebounds against Iowa State.

If it was now clear that Kansas wouldn't win consistently simply by having a talented giant standing under the hoop, it was even more obvious that Chamberlain himself simply wasn't any longer having much fun with the game that now surrounded him. Wilt would soon decide he had indeed had enough and would leave the Lawrence campus on the heels of his junior season. There were no NBA hardship exemptions for collegians in the 1950s, of course. Thus Wilt would have to play out the coming summer and winter for hard cash with the touring Harlem Globetrotters and patiently wait for the more serious pro league to come calling once his own senior class had finally graduated.

But if he had been a disappointment in almost every quarter, Chamberlain had also left something of a large and looming legacy behind nonetheless. It was with that single memorable marathon between Frank McGuire's Tar Heels and Wilt Chamberlain's Jayhawks — perhaps more than with any other single game of the sport's first half-century — that postseason championship cage play had seemed to arrive overnight on the American sporting scene. No other NCAA championship match before or since was more fascinating in its pregame buildup or more bizarre in its eventual outcome; none contained a more compelling story line; none more vividly highlighted the titanic clash between the ultimate one-man show and the ultimate team concept.

March Madness would henceforth carry the same luster and prominence as the World Series, or the New Year's Day gridiron bowl matchups, or the NFL Super Bowl title game. There would still be decades of steady growth ahead before college basketball's biggest postseason extravaganza would inflate to the point where it demanded the frenzied following of more fans than any of the nation's other sporting events. But already college basketball had now entered a popular new era. The taint of past game-fixing scandals seemed altogether to have faded. Basketball was now ready for the full fan popularity it had almost grasped a decade or two earlier, then almost let slip hopelessly away. There would now seem to be too much momentum for any further slippage. The game of iron rims and slam dunks and towering giants was at long last apparently here to stay.

6

The Fifties, Part 2

Gola and the Philadelphia Story

════════════════════════

Tom Gola, at 6 feet 7 inches, had the strength and timing to rebound with the biggest centers, the ballhandling and passing and outside shooting to play back-court with the best, and the speed and inside moves to play All-American forward.....Gola was thus the perfect prototype of the modern playground player.
— Neil Isaacs

Cage historian and author Neil Isaacs once called them Philadelphia's best advertisement this side of W.C. Fields' tombstone. Gotham City might well own the showcase venue of Madison Square Garden; the American heartland has admittedly always brimmed over with barnyard phenoms and layers of playground tradition. But in Philadelphia they have the Big Five, and it is the Big Five as much as any league or circuit that has remained an unmatched magnet for basketball excitement across four full decades.

La Salle, Penn, St. Joseph's, Temple and Villanova — basketball powers all, down through the decades from as early as the '30s, and especially across the affluent '50s and turbulent '60s. Individually, these five schools boast some of the greatest stars of college basketball's middle years (1940s, 1950s, 1960s); collectively they have produced a head-to-head five-pronged rivalry not surpassed even by the venerable Big Ten, the hotbed ACC or the Johnny-Come-Lately Big East Conference. Hoosier Hysteria, Tobacco Road Madness and even Ned Irish's New York City Game all hold nothing on the ongoing basketball wars fought annually in the City of Brotherly Love.

While each of these schools can point to a rich basketball history in the century's first half, it was not until 1956 (two years after formation of the Atlantic Coast Conference and a full half-century after the birth of Big Ten competition) that a complete and regular competition was finally established between the full contingent. In the 40 years to follow, the intense internecine warfare (as Isaacs has termed it) between these five city cage rivals has always outstripped any excitement generated by the different conference races in which each might happen to be involved. Each of the five has also at one time or another risen to the top of the heap as the city's primary standard bearer during postseason play. But especially during the first decade and a half (1956-1970) of regular competitions between the five, the intracity basketball warfare in Philly would generate one of the college cage sport's most intense and most entertaining ongoing subplots.

Down through the years they have each boasted their own unforgettable moments and unforgettable stars. Villanova arose first in the late '40s and early '50s, with Paul Arizin in the limelight as the most productive scorer in the land and also one of the last postwar players to be "informally" acknowledged as national player of the year (the "official" wire service awards did not begin until 1955 with La Salle's Tom Gola). And when Arizin (25.3 ppg) shot his way to the national scoring title in 1950 it was another Philly sharpshooter that he comfortably outdistanced for the honor — George Senesky of St. Joseph's (22.4 ppg).

Pennsylvania had Ernie Beck at the same time, a rugged All-American who corralled rebounds after the same fashion that Arizin threw down points. During the first year that the NCAA bothered to keep official rebounding

Tom Gola rebounded with the biggest centers, handled the ball on a par with the most talented guards and shot like the most agile forward. In short, he was the perfect prototype of the modern playground player. (La Salle University photo)

statistics it was Penn's 6-4 sophomore forward who was crowned as the inaugural national rebounding champion (he was also third a year later, though his total 551 caroms were again the best in the land). Beck also proved almost as consistent a scorer as Arizin, averaging above 20 per game each of his three seasons and standing fifth in the nation with a 25.9 average as a senior (a year in which he also showed up in the top 10 in free-throw percentage).

Two additional prolific scorers of the early '50s also emerged from the Philadelphia scene: Temple's Bill Mlkvy followed immediately on Arizin's heels in the role of nation's leading pointmaker in 1951, while in '53 Villanova's Larry Hennessey (29.2) also stood proudly in second spot only a shade behind Furman's Frank Selvy (29.5). Between them, Villanova's Arizin and Hennessey, Penn's Beck, Temple's Mlkvy, and George Senesky of St. Joseph's combined to keep the offense-minded Philadelphia schools smack in the limelight with their stellar shooting and rebounding exploits.

But despite these individual accomplishments it was the team achievements of La Salle (under coach Ken Loeffler) and Temple (under coach Harry Litwack) that

116

truly put Ben Franklin's town on the national basketball map. When the National Invitation Tournament opened up shop at Madison Square Garden back in 1938 it had been the Temple squad of coach James Usilton that had run roughshod over Colorado and its famed All-American Byron "Whizzer" White, 60-36, to claim the very first national tournament title. La Salle would soon capture a second NIT crown for the area in 1952 behind the inspired freshman play of Gola, then ride Gola's growing talents to become the area's first NCAA winner two seasons later. Between them La Salle and Temple would visit the NCAA Final Four and NIT Final Four a collective six times during the decade of the 1950s alone. And Penn (1953 NCAA) and St. Joseph's (1956 NIT) would add to the city's boasting rights by making it there once apiece as well.

Over the years it has been the Temple Owls, however, who have managed to maintain the most impressive and consistent winning tradition. It began of course with the impressive victory in the inaugural NIT better than a half-century ago. Then with the arrival of Litwack in 1953 there were the three straight years of national third-place finishes (1956 NCAA, 1957 NIT, 1958 NCAA). Such tradition has continued in the more recent past — despite a few flat valleys along the way — with two top 10 finishes during the late '80s (8th in 1987, 1st in 1988) and also a slew of NCAA tournament appearances (10 in 12 years) under current coach John Chaney. The 1988 version of Chaney's Owls paced the wire service polls from November straight through to March before bowing to Duke in the Eastern Regional NCAA finals.

Villanova has also, in this recent era, again brought renewed glory to the Pennsylvania port city with its own entry into the prestigious Big East Conference, one of the elite powerpacked college circuits of the '80s and '90s. Villanova Wildcat basketball first peaked in the Big East under firebrand coach Rollie Massimino with a surprising run straight to an NCAA national championship in 1985, Massimino's 12th year on the job. Villanova's rise to the top came during a wild and wooly NCAA tourney conclusion which saw three members of the upstart Big East Conference (St. John's and Georgetown were the others) all survive into the season's final glamorous weekend. Villanova would indeed provide one of the most dramatic moments in NCAA history when a largely unheralded 25-10 team featuring Ed Pinckney, Dwayne McLain and Harold Pressley shocked fellow Big East competitor Georgetown 66-64 for the national title. In upending the defending NCAA champions Massimino's Wildcats also became the second team of the '80s to suffer 10 or more regular season defeats yet nonetheless jell just in time to capture a national postseason tournament crown.

Philadelphia has always been a steamy basketball hotbed. The city was of course one of the original cradles of the post-World War II play-for-pay circuit that eventually struggled to its feet in 1949-50 as the National Basketball Association. Eddie Gottlieb's Philadelphia Warriors had been original charter members of the NBA-ancestor Basketball Association of America back in '46, also owned the league's first scoring champ in Jumpin' Joe Fulks, and even captured the first official league championship (with a dramatic playoff victory over the Chicago Stags) in the spanking new circuit which only two years down the road would become the NBA. The

Paul Arizin of Villanova paced the nation in scoring in 1950. Here he is shown driving the lane in a 1949 college basketball all-star charity game at Madison Square Garden. (Villanova University photo)

very first NCAA tourney game, as well, was staged right there in the City of Broth-erly Love, with local representative Villanova opening up March 1939 postseason play by manhandling Ivy League representative Brown, 42-30, before an enthusias-tic overflow crowd tucked into the venerable Philadelphia Palestra.

The Philly tradition was extended still further when inner-city Overbrook High produced in rapid succession two of the most luminous stars of the '50s — fabulous Wilt Chamberlain and UCLA's Walt Hazzard. While Chamberlain earned immedi-ate notoriety as the most heavily recruited high school athlete ever (and many still maintain, the greatest total-package basketball talent ever as well), it was the less-touted Hazzard as much as anyone who would play the leading role in launching John Wooden's incomparable dynasty out at UCLA. Yet despite this impressive legacy of blockbuster events, noteworthy stars and truly memorable teams, nothing in Phila-delphia hoops history has ever been any bigger than Gola and Arizin, who together ruled the college basketball scene at the outset of the Fabulous Fifties.

Big-Time Gunners in the Cradle of Liberty

Philadelphia's basketball heyday largely begins with the sensational exploits of Villanova's Paul Arizin in the immediate shadows of the Second World War. Arizin was but one among a handful of local South Philly products from the post-war decade of the late '40s and early '50s who would enhance the city's growing basketball reputation by staying close to home and starring first with local college fives and later with the city's popular NBA team. A list that later featured Gola, Ernie Beck, Guy Rodgers and Ken Durrett was launched with this sensational jump-shooter whose unorthodox one-handed shooting style and relentless offensive energy would quickly earn him the apt moniker of "Pitchin' Paul" and status as one of the city's most popular athletic heroes.

Few Hall of Famers in any sport have enjoyed a more bizarre success story. For starters, Arizin would ironically attend the same small local Catholic high school that would a couple of years later produce Gola. Far more ironic, however, is the fact that he never performed on the basketball team there, instead honing his game while playing in several of the evening recreational leagues then active throughout the city. If Arizin as a youngster harbored any dreams of athletic glory, those dreams were strictly fantasies of one day pitching for the National League Phillies or starring on the gridiron for the NFL Eagles or perhaps even the Villanova Wildcats. Basketball simply didn't seem part of the plan. Thus when he finally did enroll at Villanova in the fall of 1946 as a commuter student majoring in chemistry, Arizin never considered for a moment trying out for coach Al Severance's varsity basketball squad. Instead he continued plying his talents (which by now were attracting some serious notice) on the city's evening recreational league circuit.

Diamonds, even in the rough, can not remain hidden for long, especially in a basketball hotbed like Philadelphia at the end of the 1940s. Arizin's 30-plus nightly scoring feats on the local amateur circuit had soon caught the attention of both Wildcats coach Severance (who was stunned to discover that the city's best "unknown" player was enrolled on his own campus) and Warriors owner Eddie Gottlieb (who was impressed enough to be ready to offer an immediate NBA contract). Gottlieb would indeed eventually own Arizin's talents, but he would have to wait while Severance enjoyed rightful first dibs on the local phenom.

Talked into joining the Wildcat varsity as a sophomore, Arizin quickly broke into the starting lineup and was the team's leading scorer by season's end. As a junior his scoring average would soar to 22 points (second best in the nation behind Yale's All-American Tony Lavelli), helped out considerably by an incredible 85-point effort in a ludicrous game versus an outclassed team representing the Philadelphia Navy Air Materials Center. It was one of those still popular affairs (with coaches and athletics directors of elite teams) which had been added as padding to the Villanova early-season schedule (and to the Wildcat won-lost record). Although no major school player had ever before scored that many points in a single outing, nevertheless the effort was not allowed as an official record since it had not come against a sanctioned four-year accredited college.

Arizin's nightly scoring outbursts were enough to pace the Wildcats to a 23-4 record and a berth in the NCAA tourney where they quickly fell as an opening-round

119

victim of the eventual national champions from Kentucky. Back for a final season in 1950, Arizin raised his per-game scoring mark to 25.3, good enough to outpace cross-city rival George Senesky of St. Joseph's for individual national honors. And again the Wildcats posted a brilliant record (25-4), though this time they were passed over when it came to selecting teams for postseason play. La Salle at 21-4 instead represented the city with a short-lived NIT visit.

Arizin's three-year career at Villanova not only put Al Severance's program squarely on the national map but helped revolutionize existing playing styles now long in vogue. It was an era still noted for standing set shots (usually of the two-handed variety) as the long-range scoring weapon of choice. Flying in the face of time-worn practice Arizin from his earliest days at Villanova pioneered a running one-handed jumper (similar to the two-handed leaper of late '40s Warriors star Joe Fulks) which he launched with uncanny speed and deadly accuracy. It was an unorthodox move for the era and one he later attributed to playing on slippery dance hall floors in the city's Catholic rec leagues; the excessively waxed gym floors made running hooks and drives to the basket quite difficult to execute and the enterprising Arizin thus learned a leaping shooting style to compensate. It was a style that — along with the puffing and wheezing that resulted from a permanent asthmatic condition — provided Arizin with a colorful reputation that would follow him throughout his decade-long NBA all-star career as well as during Philadelphia college days.

But the high scoring tradition at Villanova also spread beyond Paul Arizin himself. Alex Severance's team during Arizin's three-season stay was overall an exceptional high-scoring outfit for the era, averaging 70 points per contest across Arizin's junior and senior seasons. In 1950 the Wildcats in fact ran up the highest offensive numbers in the land with their then quite sensational 72.8 nightly scoring average.

Arizin also seemed to set the tone for other high-scoring acts in the City of Brotherly Love. The next quick-loading bombardier would appear down the road at Temple, the school that had been playing the game as long as anyone in the land. Temple had first dabbled in cage play long before any of its neighbors, as early in fact as 1895 when it took part in a pioneering game with Haverford College. And decades later the school would lay at least a weak claim to a national championship with its victory in the first major postseason tournament at the six-team 1938 NIT. But it would nonetheless be a full half-century plus a decade after James Naismith's Springfield experiment before Temple would ever make much of an impact in the way of national headlines.

Then Bill Mlkvy had changed all that with his own headline-hogging scoring outbursts that even surpassed those Arizin had been posting in immediately preceding years. The slim 6-4 forward with the strange-looking name (he was immediately dubbed "The Owl Without a Vowel" by a press still enamored of such catchy epithets) burst upon the scene with a single outing when he rang up a new one-game record, exploding for 73 against an outclassed team from tiny Wilkes College. This prodigious effort came smack in the middle of Mlkvy's single phenomenal season of 1950-51, a year in which he succeeded Arizin as the national scoring champ, pumped up a then-record 964 shots, registered the highest season-long average yet (29.2), and earned unanimous first-team All-America honors for his eye-popping efforts.

Temple's Bill Mlkvy earned fame for his unusual name ("The Owl Without a Vowel") and also for his phenomenal scoring during the 1950-51 season. (Temple University photo)

One measure of Mlkvy's "one-season-wonder" status during his junior year is the fact that he averaged but 16.3 points per game as a sophomore and then fell back again to 17.4 for his senior campaign. Yet if the Temple sensation was a single-season comet in the basketball heavens he was certainly anything but a one-dimensional athlete when it came to measuring the range of his considerable on-court skills. During his heady junior campaign, Mlkvy pulled off a rare "triple" reminiscent of the later Oscar Robertson when he also completed the year as the national runner-up in both rebounds (18.9) and assists (7.0). Perhaps only Oscar has ever been quite so productive in all facets of offense, especially for an entire season of play. Yet it was largely for naught as Mlkvy's shooting and playmaking did little to salvage a wasteland season for an otherwise punchless Temple team that despite his productiveness finished with an uninspired 12-13 losing ledger.

While Mlkvy was reaching new scoring standards at Temple, crosstown rival Pennsylvania had a star of its own in 6-4 forward Ernie Beck. Beck was a native inner-city Philadelphia product just like Arizin, and just like Arizin and Mlkvy he was a complete-package ballplayer who shot, rebounded and passed the ball with equal consummate skill. While Mlkvy was providing the city with its second straight national scoring leader in 1951, sophomore Beck was the same year providing a rare single-city double as the nation's top rebounder (edging none other than Mlkvy himself for the honor). Ernie Beck was in fact the first official NCAA rebounding champion, as his sophomore season was the very first during which national rankings were tabulated for this now standard category.

The trio of All-Americans at Villanova, Temple and Penn soon surprisingly proved to be little more than an exciting prologue and not quite the main event after all. For the very best player in the city would pop up but a year after Mlkvy's great season and thus but two years after Arizin's departure, and he would wear the uniform of tiny La Salle College. It would not be long before this third local product (Mlkvy was from outlying Palmerton and thus not strictly a Philadelphia native), Tom Gola, was singlehandedly putting previously unrecognized La Salle squarely on the college basketball map. And in fact Tom Gola would soon be putting the entire Philadelphia basketball hotbed smack in the center-stage glare of the nation's sporting scene.

David in a Nation of Goliaths

The argument is not unreasonable (then or now) that inch-for-inch Tom Gola was the greatest collegiate basketballer of all time. For those of us who saw him play he would always remain fixed in the permanence of youthful memory as the rarest of all players — a perfectly agile small man blessed with residence in a big man's overpowering body. Neil Isaacs, better than any other writer, has captured the essence of Gola's immense talents: "He had the strength and timing to rebound with the biggest centers, the ballhandling and passing and outside shooting to play backcourt with the best, and the speed and inside moves to play All-American forward."

In short, he indisputably owned the greatest all-around skills of any college hoopster before and probably since; clearly he possessed All-American talents at all three positions and it would be hard to think of another player for whom the same claim could be made (for example, just imagine Air Jordan or Oscar Robertson, for all their brilliance, as everyday low-post centers). Only Magic Johnson comes to mind when one searches for similar versatility — but only Earvin Johnson as a pro with the L.A. Lakers and not Johnson as a college sophomore with the Michigan State Spartans. Isaacs would rightly call Tom Gola the perfect prototype of the modern playground player.

One can search long and hard through the annals of college sport and never uncover a stranger recruiting story than the one that attaches to the signing of Tom Gola to play basketball for La Salle College. Certainly no school has ever found a greater superstar any closer to its own backyard — or in this case right in the middle of its own backyard. Gola, it turns out, attended high school classes and played high school games in the very same building that housed the basement gymnasium of the college team that would eventually recruit his services.

While starring at La Salle High (an extension of La Salle College) the athletically precocious youngster had often entertained thoughts of playing college ball for one of the nation's limelight teams or coaches — perhaps for Baron Rupp at Kentucky or Everett Case at North Carolina State. Gola did make recruiting visits to both Lexington and Raleigh. But in the end he quietly decided to cast his lot with the tiny college outfit across the street, the one that practiced every day in the same gym that housed his high school squad. In doing so he turned the first page on a key chapter of college basketball history.

That Gola would cast his lot with a backwater college rather than with an athletic factory like Kentucky or North Carolina State was not entirely surprising in light of family and personal circumstances. The combined college-high school urban campus run by the Catholic order of Christian Brothers offered a homey family atmosphere especially appealing to a shy youngster who was already personally acquainted with the La Salle College president during high school days; two of Gola's brothers would soon follow him into the college and would also enjoy scholarships that were a huge consideration for the middle class family struggling to survive with seven children and the salary of an underpaid city policeman.

The rest of Gola's La Salle teammates flashed talent as well. Guard Frank O'Hara at 5-11 was a superb ball handler and pinpoint passer whose inspired

122

There are those who still contend Tom Gola was not only the best Philadelphia player ever, but the best college basketball player ever — bar none. (La Salle University photo)

playmaking complemented Gola's inside shooting and solid rebounding game. Norm Grekin was around only for Gola's freshman year yet sparkled enough in the postseason of 1952 to share an NIT MVP trophy with the super-talented newcomer. And during the 1954 NCAA title win over Bradley two years later it was the entire rest of the starting lineup that came through in spades when Gola fell victim to overloaded defenses keyed on him alone. Forwards Charles Singley and Frank Blatcher (both 10 points per game scorers on the season) benefitted from their star teammate's generous dish-offs that night and came through mightily in the most important contest of the season with 23 points apiece.

And the flamboyant coach, Ken Loeffler, was a large piece of the puzzle as well. Owning academic training as a lawyer and already boasting a long previous pedigree as both college mentor (Geneva College, Yale, Denver) and pro coach (BAA St. Louis Bombers and Providence Steamrollers), Loeffler was the perfect architect of victory as he crafted Gola and the exceptional pieces that surrounded him into a winning outfit. Even before Gola's arrival in 1951-52 Loeffler had already lit a fire under a La Salle cage program that had floundered throughout the '30s and '40s, then took a brief upturn under Charles McGlone with 20-win seasons in '47, '48 and '49. Loeffler posted two 20-victory campaigns of his own and took the Explorers to the postseason NIT in both of his pre-Gola La Salle seasons.

But the main text of La Salle's improbable success story began in 1952, Gola's freshman season, and it came with an improbable run all the way to an NIT championship banner. Gola had been allowed onto the varsity roster that first year only because of a technicality then on the NCAA rule books: the tiny Philadelphia college enrolled less than 1,000 students and was therefore granted an exemption from the edict banning four years of college play (regular freshman eligibility was still two decades away). With the freshman hotshot already pacing his team in both scoring (17.2) and rebounding (16.5), the Explorers, playing out of the loosely knit Middle Atlantic Conference, built up a 20-5 season record and thus earned a third-straight bid under Loeffler to the still-prestigious March event in Madison Square Garden.

Somewhat surprising victories over Eastern powers Seton Hall (with 7-footer Walter Dukes), St. John's (upset winner over both No. 1 Kentucky and No. 2 Illinois earlier in the season), and Duquesne (the Associated Press' fourth-ranked team) put Loeffler's upstart Explorers into the championship game opposite Dayton, also a top-20 club. Before a packed arena of 18,845 enthusiastic fans Gola and fellow forward Norm Grekin (the tourney co-MVPs) inspired a 75-64 La Salle victory. It came despite an impressive offensive show by Dayton's Don Meineke (later an NBA rookie of the year) who even in defeat reigned as the top NIT scorer for the second year running.

Gola's sophomore season provided a heady encore, although there would be a stiff measure of disappointment in the year's surprising conclusion. The 1953 regular season witnessed an improved 25-2 ledger spoiled only by a pair of losses to Chicago's DePaul (one coming during the Madison Square Garden Holiday Festival Tourney); it was a record certainly worthy of reward with a return trip to Madison Square Garden for defense of the previous year's NIT crown. And for the second year in a row Gola and crew proved to be the tourney's biggest surprise, although this time under far less pleasant circumstances. The March Madness shocker came this time around in the form of a devastating one-point quarterfinal loss to St. John's, a defeat which blocked an anticipated rematch with Seton Hall and the towering Walter Dukes. Sophomore Gola was by now already a first-team All-America choice of both AP and UPI balloters, yet a late-season injury had unfortunately slowed him just in time for NIT play. And when graduation wiped out almost the entire La Salle squad, save Gola and 5-11 guard Frank O'Hara, prospects didn't seem especially bright for the upcoming 1954 campaign, either.

La Salle coach Ken Loeffler was one of the most cerebral and colorful coaches in the 1950s. He was also one of the luckiest when he signed Tom Gola from the high school across the street.(La Salle University photo)

But the best still lay ahead for both Gola and La Salle in the form of a brilliant and altogether surprising 1954 run at an unexpected national title. Since expectations had been lowered in the face of numerous lineup changes, two early-season losses to Niagara and another to Kentucky were not especially surprising; but only a one-point defeat at the hands of cross-town Temple prevented the rapidly improving team of Gola's junior year from running off 15 straight wins over the season's second half. It looked like another trip to the NIT was now in the offing, at least until a surprising NCAA invitation landed squarely in the Explorers' laps. Here was a new challenge and it came La Salle's way as a direct result of the newly expanded field (from 16 to 22) for the first time being offered by the NCAA-sponsored postseason event.

The 1954 enlarged NCAA tournament turned out to be unquestionably one of the most exciting postseason bonanzas to date. La Salle had ridden a solid 21-4 record and a second-place national ranking (behind undefeated Kentucky) into the opening round of postseason play while Rupp's unblemished Wildcats sat disappointed on the sidelines. Kentucky had decided to bypass tournament action once their three top stars (Hagan, Tsioropoulos, and Ramsey) had all been ruled ineligible for year-end competition. During their legitimate senior season (1952-53) the three had missed out altogether on intercollegiate competition while Kentucky served out a one-year suspension brought on by a raft of NCAA violations; a fourth year of eligibility was granted for 1954 but this extended only through regular-season action. Thus the trio had now used up four years of eligibility and had actually competed during their final year while enrolled as graduate students.

La Salle, meantime, faced its own toughest "second season" challenge in the NCAA opener against Fordham and Eddie Conlin, a contest which matched up the nation's two best rebounders (certainly for that season, and perhaps for any other season as well). La Salle had narrowly escaped, 61-56, when the two teams met in regular season action, and the NCAA lidlifter in the Buffalo Auditorium promised more of the same exciting brand of high-spirited play. With Conlin enjoying a slight edge over Gola on the boards, the Fordham Rams pressed the action and led into the final seconds of exactly the kind of barn burner contest that everyone had expected. Loeffler's well-drilled team only escaped when Gola fed a perfect pass to guard Frank O'Malley for a game-tying shot just ahead of the final buzzer. In the overtime period La Salle managed to eke out a narrow 76-74 victory.

If the postseason opener was the year's most dramatic contest, it was the final game of 1954, without doubt, that best displayed Gola's rare big-game adaptability. Longtime Missouri Valley kingpin Bradley University provided the opposition and even offered a stern challenge for the first half of play as the Braves nursed a 43-42 lead at intermission. But as the game roared down its homestretch it was again clear that Gola by himself was simply too much for the opposition to handle. Having accumulated four fouls early in the second half the La Salle ace moved out to a deep corner post and spent most of the stretch drive merely setting up his teammates for easy baskets; he would score 19 points (while teammates Charles Singley and Frank Blatcher each registered 23) but would also pull down 19 boards and ring up numerous timely assists. When the game ended with La Salle on the long end of a 92-76 count Tom Gola owned the Final Four MVP trophy to go along with his team's new set of championship rings.

Bradley star Paul Unruh would provide perhaps the best assessment ever of Gola and it came in the wake of that championship embarrassment at the hands of the incomparable La Salle All-American: "He makes plays a little man should make, and then turns around and does things only a big man usually does." It was concise praise, as understated and straight on target as Gola's relentless play itself.

When Associated Press post-tourney polls still had the Kentucky Wildcats ranked in the No. 1 slot above the NCAA champion La Salle Explorers few in the Blue Grass State at least thought the postseason vote anything but appropriate. After all, Rupp's team had soundly beaten Gola and the rest of the Explorers head-to-head (73-60) back in December, in their own Kentucky Invitational Tournament final. But a year-end snub by wire service pollsters did little to sour the taste of a national title for the Gola-led men of coach Ken Loeffler.

The 1954 collegiate season had produced the first truly memorable large-scale contingent of major stars. It was a season filled with names like Bob Pettit (LSU),

Frank Selvy (Furman), Cliff Hagan (Kentucky), Frank Ramsey (Kentucky), Don Schlundt (Indiana), Dick Ricketts (Duquesne) and Togo Palazzi (Holy Cross). But Gola rose above them all and was an easy choice for player of the year, although the UPI wire service award for "individual best" would not be launched until the following season (with Gola, of course, its first winner). The national recognition that came on the heels of 1953-54 successes placed La Salle's major attraction squarely in a Philly cage tradition already launched a few seasons earlier with the city's back-to-back national scoring champions. But Gola was already a star of far greater stature than either Arizin or Mlkvy had ever been.

And the story was far from over. Gola still had a final year remaining, his fourth, and it would be crammed with still further heroics. His senior-season totals would include career bests for points (750) and scoring average (24.2) and another 600-plus rebound campaign as well. And when United Press International announced its first national player-of-the-year at season's end, it was not surprisingly Tom Gola.

But there was now a new featured attraction vying for its equal share of the headlines as the college basketball world turned a corner at the middle of the decade. San Francisco's Dons, with their defensive-minded coach Phil Woolpert and their shot-blocking string bean center Bill Russell, shot to the top of the pack early in 1954-55 and retained a No. 1 wire service ranking right up to the eve of tournament action. The still-formidable defending champs from La Salle and the new kingpins out west clearly seemed on a collision course all winter long as they hurdled toward an inevitable Final Four showdown. This time around, La Salle would have no tense struggles in the early rounds of postseason play, squashing West Virginia (95-61), Princeton (73-46) and Canisius (99-64) before bumping and grinding to a 76-73 semifinal win over pesky Big Ten representative Iowa. But in San Francisco Loeffler's crew would finally meet a well-disciplined unit which not only had plenty of firepower but also owned the defensive tools sufficient to finally neutralize Gola.

With K.C. Jones sticking to the La Salle star like human crazy glue (limiting him to 16 points, most of those coming only after the affair was already decided) and with Bill Russell blocking countless shots, canning 23 points and climbing over Gola for a remarkable 25 rebounds, La Salle was altogether doomed. In the final game of his brilliant career Tom Gola was decidedly outplayed for the first and only time during his collegiate tenure. It was perhaps a small consolation to Gola and his legions of fans that in the end it admittedly had taken the greatest defensive team in college basketball history, playing at the very top of its game, to finally thwart him.

If Gola's final campaign unfortunately ended in defeat there would also be many memorable milestones before that last season had run its full course. His UPI plaudits as national player of the year came largely on the strength of another 600-plus rebounding season and his highest scoring average (24.2) in four brilliant years. A new system for ranking rebounders (in effect from 1956 through 1962, and based on highest percentage of individual recoveries out of the total rebounds by both teams in all games) saw Gola slip from third place in the national rankings as a junior to eighth during his senior season. But the four-year star who had never managed to lead the nation in any individual season nonetheless now became the first man ever to reach the 2,000 career rebound total. Only George Washington's Joe

126

Holup (the very next season) would ever join him in that most select circle in all the years that have subsequently passed.

Tom Gola thus left behind a mind-stretching four-year legacy. His career rebounding totals by themselves stand as perhaps the most secure record in all of sports. Rebound numbers simply can never be as high today as they were in the '50s or '60s — recall that Chamberlain (22.9) and Russell (22.5) completed their entire NBA careers with lifetime averages above 20 in this department, and even Bob Pettit logged a 10-year career average well above 15 (16.2). Today fans and writers are enthralled when Dennis Rodman leads a single NBA season with an average slightly above a dozen. Yet it must also be remembered that Gola was not a big man — he checked in at 6-6, played forward in most of his college games and was later assigned a guard position when he went to the NBA Warriors. What is truly amazing, however, is the actual percentage of loose shots that he corralled, no matter how many of those available errant shots there may or may not have been. Those who are today impressed by Dennis Rodman and even imagine that the controversial and one-dimensional Pistons/Spurs/Bulls star is a true rebounding paragon simply forget how spectacular the early generations of pro and college rebounders actually were. Could those now so enamored of Rodman have only seen Gola in action, perhaps but once, and a substantial reality check would most certainly have set in.

Yet Gola was not alone among voracious rebounders. An extraordinary set of athletes plus an era of low shooting percentages (usually hovering around the high 30 percent range) combined to convert the mid-1950s into a veritable rebounding sideshow. Seven of the top eight career rebounding totals still belong to players who graduated in either 1955 or

12 Most Prolific Double Threats

Players With 4,000 Career Points and Rebounds

Player (School)	Years	Pts	RB	Tot.
Tom Gola (La Salle)	1952-55	2462	2201	4663
L. Simmons (La Salle)	1987-90	3217	1429	4646
Elvin Hayes (Houston)	1966-68	2884	1602	4486
D. Hemric (Wake Forest)	1952-55	2587	1802	4389
Oscar Robertson (Cin.)	1958-60	2973	1338	4311
Joe Holup (Geo. Wash.)	1953-56	2226	2030	4256
Pete Maravich (LSU)	1968-70	3667	528	4195
Harry Kelly (Texas Sou.)	1980-83	3066	1085	4151
Danny Manning (Kansas)	1985-88	2951	1187	4138
Larry Bird (Indiana State)	1977-79	2850	1247	4097
E. Baylor (Idaho Col./Sea.)	1956-58	2500	1559	4059
M. Brooks (La Salle)	1977-80	2628	1372	4000

Philadelphia Area Players (from La Salle) in Boldface

1956. Joe Holup of George Washington, Charlie Slack of Marshall and Eddie Conlin of Fordham trail directly behind Gola on the all-time career list. Not far off the pace stand Dickie Hemric of Wake Forest and Art Quimby of Connecticut.

Perhaps the best rebounder of the era doesn't even appear in these NCAA listings, however. Tom Hart, a 6-4 center for Division II Middlebury College in Vermont, posted incredible rebound averages of 29.5 in both his junior (1955) and senior (1956) seasons and completed his 63-game career with a 27.6 average that remains unmatched in NCAA history. Twice Hart pulled down 46 caroms in a single contest (versus Trinity College and Clarkson, respectively) and, as incredible as it may seem, both these unmatched efforts came within the very same week late in the 1955 season. Tom Hart today remains as legendary among carom chasers as Bevo Francis and Frank Selvy do among the game's prodigious scorers.

Again, rebounders of the 1950s can not be realistically compared to those of later eras. Shooting percentages in the age of dimly lit gyms with irregular floors and often near-frigid temperatures were consistently a full 10 to 15 percent below those of the contemporary epoch; this factor of lowered shooting accuracy combined with an increase in run-and-gun one-handed shooting during the immediate post-war decade to increase rebounding opportunities far beyond those of any era before or since. Not only were more shots taken but far more shots were missed. And yet there was something special about the '50s breed of rebounders nonetheless. Because rebounding was a bigger part of the game in an era of sloppier shooting, some of the best athletes concentrated far more heavily on this important corner of the game. Thus these earlier specialists in retrieving errant missiles were themselves among the most exciting and dedicated athletes in the entire history of college basketball.

Birth of a Hometown Tradition

The loss of Tom Gola and the departure of Ken Loeffler (who moved to Texas A&M upon Gola's graduation in 1955) were certain to dull the luster at La Salle. The mid-50s would hardly sound the death knell for a brilliant Philadelphia hoops tradition, however. In some ways the departure of the city's biggest star (almost like Cincinnati's loss of Oscar Robertson at the end of the same decade) merely signalled the beginnings of some far better things to come. For the 1955-56 college campaign — the first in five years without Gola's towering presence — would mark the birth of formal Big Five competition between La Salle, Temple, Villanova, Penn and St. Joe's. And with the new inner-city warfare came what was soon to be a sufficiently glamorous tradition in its own right.

Penn had been the city's most consistent powerhouse during the first half of the century and had dominated Ivy League play by capturing 14 (of its eventual 24) league titles before 1956. The Quakers, now coached by Howie Dallmar, had enjoyed special prominence in recent years (1951-53) by averaging 20 victories in three seasons with Ernie Beck doing yeoman duty in the trenches. And the city's Ivy League representative had often played head-to-head with its other Philadelphia-area neighbors as well. But while schools like Muhlenberg, Lehigh, Susquehanna, Bucknell and Lafayette frequently dotted the Penn schedule, games with the four competing major city schools were far less frequent. Penn battled with Temple only once (1921) before the mid-50s, Villanova twice (1910, 1922) and La Salle on but seven occasions (twice in the '40s and once in the '50s). Only with St. Joseph's did the Ivy league power maintain an ongoing court relationship, engaging the Hawks in battle every season between 1923 and 1937, and also between 1944 and 1949.

Other city schools were even less quick to test each other. Temple in particular shunned a couple of its inner-city rivals (Villanova and Penn), yet did hold regular series with La Salle (after 1937) and with St. Joseph's (since 1932). St. Joe's was perhaps most committed to meeting other Philadelphia opponents and regularly did battle with both Temple and La Salle (after the early '30s), as well as holding a brief series with Villanova throughout the '20s and '30s. But after 1956 a regular series was finally in place between all five, with many (but not all) contests scheduled into the storied and spacious Palestra. The annual meetings on a round-robin basis quickly

Ken Durrett was only one in a long line of Philadelphia college sharpshooters to later take his game to the local NBA scene. (La Salle University photo)

became the staple of Philadelphia basketball, and before the end of the decade these new rivalries were even a rationale as well as a showcase for the city's finest cage competitions.

The revved-up intracity competition fortuitously coincided with a distinct upturn in fortunes for Philly schools in general. Villanova's stock had dipped a bit after the loss of Arizin in 1950 and after a seven-year stretch (1949-1955) which had never known fewer than 18 victories; and Penn (12-13 in '56 and 7-19 in '57) also withered in the wake of Ernie Beck. But Temple was clearly on the upsurge with the arrival of Guy Rodgers on the scene in the fall of 1955; and St. Joseph's the same fall would launch its own marvelous streak, a prosperous decade during which a 20-victory average would be maintained across the entire 11-year tenure of coach Jack Ramsay. If La Salle sagged somewhat in the immediate absence of Gola and Loeffler, even the Explorers were able to recapture something of their once noble tradition.

For one thing, La Salle would remain a nurturing place for individual stars. Eventually there would be Ken Durrett who averaged better than 23 a game at the end of the '60s, as well as Hubie Marshall (21.3 ppg), Larry Canon (19.1) and Frank Corace (19.3), all of whom were also '60s-vintage stars who topped the career 1,400-point plateau. And eventually, years down the road, Lionel Simmons and Michael Brooks would both overhaul even Gola's career scoring totals and thus carry on this La Salle star-making tradition. Of the mere dozen players with 4,000 or more career points and rebounds, the two at the top of the list both hail from La Salle — Tom Gola and Lionel Simmons. And a third player on this prestigious list, Michael Brooks, would boast La Salle as his college affiliation as well.

Over the next quarter century Big Five schools would especially excel in postseason tournament action. Across the 15-year stretch that began with the 1956 debut of Big Five intracity competitions and closed at the end of the '60s, the five major Philadelphia schools would enjoy a run of postseason successes never before or since duplicated by any substantial group of entrants from a single metropolitan area. Never during this entire stretch would Philadelphia be without at least one NCAA or NIT tourney representative at season's end. Only once over the same period would there be but one tourney entrant from the City of Brotherly Love (1957, with Temple as the lonely NIT visitor); on nine different occasions at least three from the Big Five were invited to enjoy March Madness; twice four of the five were around for postseason celebrations.

These postseason successes for Philly schools over the first decade and a half of Big Five competition bear detailed summary. La Salle returned to the NIT three times and the NCAA once during this stretch and also missed 1969 postseason play (despite a 23-1 record and No. 2 national ranking with Gola as coach) only because of a one-year NCAA sanction imposed for recruiting violations. Villanova enjoyed still greater successes with seven NIT visits (including second-, third- and fourth-place finishes) and six NCAA invitations (topped by a climb into the Finals against UCLA in 1971). Temple enjoyed an identical seven NIT trips, six NCAA invites, and reached the zenith with an NIT title in 1969 and the two third-place NCAA finishes during the Guy Rodgers-Hal Lear era. St. Joseph's recorded the most NCAA invitations of the group, nine, and experienced the semifinals in 1961 before bowing to Jerry Lucas, John Havlicek and runner-up Ohio State. And finally, Penn also tasted NCAA play thrice and survived long enough to appear in the Eastern Regional finals on two separate occasions.

During the same stretch St. Joseph's would launch an especially noteworthy tradition. In addition to their nine NCAA postseason trips the Jack Ramsay-coached Hawks would also climb into the NIT three times (1956, 1958, 1964) and garner 1956 third-place honors with a hard-fought 93-82 consolation victory over St. Francis of New York. Both the highlight and lowlight moment came near the end of the 1961 NCAA Final Four weekend, however, when Ramsay's Hawks (25-5 on the year and paced by the hefty scoring of 6-6 forward Jack Egan) lined up against Utah's Redmen (with their own scoring machine, Billy McGill) in a third-place consolation shootout that remains one of the oddest moments in all of collegiate postseason history.

Never has so much drama been packed into a pitched battle with nothing more at stake than the "bragging rights" of a consolation prize. The quirky spectacle would be recalled whimsically by future generations of NCAA historians as the memorable "longest game with the shortest score" and today it almost defies belief in the perspective of hindsight.

With future NBA coaches Jim Lynam (the starting point guard) and Paul Westhead (a second-line reserve) in their lineup, the Hawks locked horns in Kansas City with a Utah team featuring future national scoring champ Billy "The Hill" McGill, and the resulting marathon match would delay for nearly an hour the main card attraction scheduled for national television viewing by a prime-time audience. When network coverage kicked in at nine o'clock the nation was unexpectedly soon wrapped up in a sensational set of overtime periods attached to what was supposed to be a meaningless warmup event. Thus perhaps the most unforgettable preliminary contest in all of basketball history ultimately stole nearly all the thunder from a featured championship battle on tap later that evening between Cincinnati and Ohio State.

The contest stretched on for four overtime periods before Lynam ignited a desperate rally late in the fourth extra session which finally brought victory to St. Joseph's by the inflated score of 127-120. The game's length and the expanded two-team point totals were both playoff records which still remain on the NCAA books, if only with a tarnished "unofficial" status. For in the end the game and all its records were wiped away on a technicality and the final tally sheet would show Utah and not St. Joseph's at all as the "official" victor by the improbable forfeit score of 1-0.

The culprit here was the only case of dishonest dealing ever to taint the august NCAA postseason party. Hawks' star forward and leading scorer Jack Egan (who outpointed McGill 42-34 during the elongated consolation affair) had already been targeted for investigation by NCAA officials before postseason play even began; Egan had been suspected of possible point-shaving activities earlier in the season. It turned out that several of Ramsay's players had in fact agreed to control game scores, then later realized the folly of their actions and backed away from any further contact with game-fixers. The St. Joe's star had already met with NCAA investigators and admitted his own involvement in the early-season game-fixing. Yet when Egan's distasteful dealings with gamblers were eventually confirmed, only days after the NCAA Finals, an embarrassed St. Joseph's team was stripped of its tournament achievements and even of its hard-won third-place victory. The remarkable game which had refused to end was now relegated to the cheap stuff of barroom trivia.

But perhaps the most remarkable story in Philly during the remainder of the '50s would be the dynamite backcourt duo of Hal Lear and Guy Rodgers over at Temple. This dynamic pair of "Mighty Mites" would provide coach Harry Litwack's squad with a dazzling tandem of offensive weapons that overlapped for a single season in 1955-56. And that single year of the power-packed duo was enough to catapult the 27-4 Owls straight into the NCAA Final Four, where they fell ever so short in an 83-76 loss to Iowa in the semifinals. Two years later, during Guy Rodgers' senior season, Litwack's Owls would come even closer in the quest for a national title. This time they would again be upended in the semifinals by eventual champion Kentucky, and this time only by the narrowest of possible margins.

Of all the talented athletes to emerge from the playgrounds of South Philadelphia in the immediate post-war years only Gola and Arizin can match or surpass Guy Rodgers for a balanced array of superb basketball skills. Perhaps the flashiest (and certainly the fastest) ball handler the city has ever produced, the lightning-quick 6-footer emerged from an all-city high school career as a dynamo destined to lead Temple back down Glory Street. With Rodgers the Owls would achieve their greatest heights as immediate successor to La Salle in the destined role as the city's biggest cage boasting point.

In three years with Rodgers running the offense Litwack's Owls posted school-best records of 27-4 (1956), 20-9 (1957) and 27-3 (1958). Rodgers' sophomore campaign ended with the third-place NCAA finish sparked largely by Hal Lear's record scoring feats during a semifinal loss to Iowa and a consolation triumph over Southern Methodist University. His junior year brought another third-place postseason finish with a 67-50 consolation match triumph over St. Bonaventure, this time in the NIT. And his final season was capped with the heartbreaking semifinal 61-60 loss to eventual champion Kentucky during a return to NCAA action. For the third year in a row Rodgers and the Owls would capture a third-place national slot by edging Kansas State and All-American Bob Boozer in the consolation match.

131

Guy Rodgers was the fastest and flashiest backcourt ace ever to come off the playgrounds of South Philadelphia. In three seasons with the Temple Owls, Rodgers' teams posted a rare string of three national third-place finishes, two in the NCAA (1956, 1958) and one in the NIT (1957). (Temple University photo)

In no single game over this brilliant three-year run were the spectacular backcourt talents of Guy Rodgers any more evident than in the narrow 1958 semifinals loss to Adolph Rupp's vaunted Kentucky Wildcats. The two teams had met earlier in the season on Bluegrass turf in Lexington and the Wildcats had only narrowly survived on a half-court desperation shot by Vern Hatton at the end of a third overtime period. The NCAA semifinal rematch back in Kentucky stomping grounds (at Louisville) was every bit as close. Brilliant floor play and a game-high 22-point effort by Rodgers had left the Owls with a 60-59 lead with but 23 seconds remaining in the tense contest. After Kentucky snatched the lead on a crucial bucket by Hatton the Owls had one final chance to rescue victory. Only a misplay by sophomore Bill Kennedy of a brilliant pass from Rodgers as time elapsed prevented Temple from facing off with Elgin Baylor and Seattle for the 1958 national title.

Guy Rodgers' three years at Temple ended with an overall 74-16 winning mark (.822) and a brilliant 9-3 postseason ledger, as well as the three tourney third-place trophies. His career 19.6 scoring average was supplemented with a 23.3 scoring pace in three NIT postseason appearances and a 17.9 average over nine NCAA tournament games. The crowd-pleasing backcourt ace also finished his senior season with school records for career scoring, field goals and assists. During his final campaign he also chalked up a record 15 assists in a single game against Manhattan

College and led the Owls to a midseason Holiday Festival Tournament champion-ship in Madison Square Garden as an encore.

Immediately after graduation Rodgers toured briefly with a college all-star squad that competed nightly against the famed Harlem Globetrotters. The Trotters would make the sensational ball handler an attractive offer at tour's end, but Rodgers would instead opt to cast his lot with the hometown NBA Warriors who had selected him as their special territorial draft pick. Eddie Gottlieb's Warriors had already built their team around native Philadelphia products Arizin and Gola, and had also offered a brief (if unsuccessful) trial to Rodgers' sophomore Temple running mate Hal Lear. Penn's Ernie Beck also logged six unspectacular seasons (averaging double figures only once) with Gottlieb's team. At the end of the decade the local NBA club would now continue the tradition by bringing on board both Guy Rodgers (1959) and Philly high school product Wilt Chamberlain (1960), the latter representing clearly the biggest catch of all. For three years Rodgers would employ his backcourt skills to feed the high-scoring Chamberlain and in the process help convert the hometown Warriors into the single biggest nemesis challenging Red Auerbach's dynasty Bos-ton Celtics who ruled the NBA of the late '50s and early '60s.

Rodgers' sterling running mate during his rookie sophomore campaign was an even smaller dynamo who provided backcourt scoring power sufficient to lift the 1956 Owls to the very threshold of a coveted national championship. At 5-11 Hal Lear was another diminutive speedster who could regularly unleash truly prodigious scoring outbursts. Together sophomore Rodgers and senior Lear combined to score 73.5 percent of Temple's points in two Final Four games — a semifinal loss to Iowa and a consolation game victory over Southern Methodist.

Lear had been the Owls' leading scorer (24.0 ppg) throughout his senior sea-son, with Rodgers (18.5 ppg) a shade behind. Yet his greatest scoring feats would all be bunched tightly together at the very end of his collegiate career and thus his national fame would rest on his single unaccountable explosion during five NCAA tourney games. That incredible stretch would find Lear first erupting for 40 points (61.5 percent of the total Temple offense) during a 65-59 East Regional semifinal victory over Connecticut (a game in which Temple's Fred Cohen would also estab-lish a postseason mark by corralling 34 rebounds). Across five tournament games Lear would log 160 points, in the process smashing a previous tourney record of 141 owned by Clyde Lovellette of Kansas. And in the 90-81 Temple consolation game victory over SMU Lear would grab another postseason mark when he logged a sensational 48-point effort, enough to obliterate the 45-point record of Washington's Bob Houbregs set in 1953.

For his remarkable efforts Hal Lear would walk off with the tournament MVP trophy after clearly overshadowing outstanding Final Four players like Bill Russell of San Francisco and SMU's outstanding junior center Jim Krebs. Most amazing of all, however, was the fact that the Temple sharpshooter's five-game NCAA scoring average (32.0 ppg) was a full 25 percent higher than his season-long mark (24.0 ppg). Few players have ever stepped up quite as big under the pressures of March Madness competition as did Temple's Hal Lear during the memorable postseason of 1956.

There were other individual stars from the region as the next dozen seasons played out. St. Joseph's could boast Matt Guokas as the third member of a three-generation string of college and pro stars by that name. La Salle would eventually find another star in Ken Durrett, who previewed his own solid NBA career with three seasons (1969-71) as a 20-point scorer and the team's leading offensive threat. And Villanova soon had Howard Porter and then Chris Ford. Porter was a high-scoring All-American 6-8 forward (23.5 points per game as a senior) who teamed with junior center Hank Siemiontkowski and junior playmaker Ford (the future Boston Celtics coach) to provide John Wooden's dynasty UCLA Bruins with their toughest NCAA championship match ever.

Porter would even earn the tourney MVP trophy for his stellar performance during the 1971 Final Four. Yet this best among all Villanova teams would also provide a dose of the same kind of embarrassing scandal that had tarnished another city school exactly one decade earlier. The brilliant Final Four play of the Wildcats (they beat Western Kentucky 92-89 in the semis and fell to UCLA 68-62 in the finals) was all for naught as Villanova, like St. Joseph's before it, was quickly stripped of NCAA achievements in the wake of discovered rules violations. Disaster made a call when it was soon revealed that Howard Porter had hired an agent and also illegally signed a professional contract with the ABA Pittsburgh Condors while post-season tournament action was still in progress.

There was a tradition of marvelous coaches as well. In the afterglow of Ken Loeffler at La Salle, Dudey Moore would continue a fine winning tradition for the Explorers at the end of the '50s and across the first four seasons of the '60s, even getting back into the NIT in 1963. Across the same two decades the threesome of Howie Dallmar, Jack McCloskey and Dick Harter would keep Penn always near the top of the Ivy League standings and also assure that the Fighting Quakers remained a prominent player in annual Big Five

---

Philadelphia's All-Time All-Star Team

	Pos	Pts. (Ppg)	Best Year	NPY
Tom Gola (La Salle)	F-C	2462 (20.9)	24.2 (Sr.)	1954
Paul Arizin (Villanova)	F	1596 (20.0)	25.3 (Sr..)	1950
Bill Mlkvy (Temple)	F	1539 (21.1)	29.2 (Jr.)	—
L. Simmons (La Salle)	F	3217 (24.6)	28.4 (Jr.)	1990
Guy Rodgers (Temple)	G	1767 (19.6)	20.4 (Jr.)	—

NPY = National Player of the Year

Honorable Mention: Ken Durrett (F, La Salle), Jack Egan (F, St. Joseph's), Ernie Beck (F, Pennsylvania), Howard Porter (G, Villanova), Chris Ford (F, Villanova), Larry Foust (C, La Salle), George Senesky (F, St. Joseph's), Ed Pinckney (F, Villanova), Hal Lear (G, Temple), Michael Brooks (F, La Salle)

Coaches: Ken Loeffler (La Salle), NCAA Champion (1954), NCAA Runner-Up (1955) and Harry Litwack (Temple), NCAA 3rd-Place (1956, 1958), NIT 3rd-Place (1957)

---

struggles as well. Jack Ramsay and Jack McKinney would meantime build an outstanding program at St. Joseph's, one that would be the equal of anything else the Big Five had to offer during what proved to be its strongest era. And over at Villanova Jack Kraft continued to turn out winning teams and star players (Howard Porter was the truest prince among paupers) at the same remarkable pace, churning out four 20-win campaigns in the early '60s and four more to launch the 1970s.

But among the coaching geniuses none surpassed Loeffler at La Salle, Litwack at Temple and Alex Severance at Villanova. Loeffler was at one and the same time

UConn's Art Quimby was one of the most outstanding board sweepers in a tribe of relentless rebounders who invaded the college game of the early 1950s. (University of Connecticut photo)

one of the most intelligent yet most colorful coaches found anywhere on the national scene. He was also a winner on the court (thanks perhaps mainly to Gola) and thus all six of his seasons at La Salle were 20-win campaigns. And with the incomparable Gola in tow he would leave a landmark that still remains the most accomplished in the city's remarkable cage history. Litwack, for his part, revived a Temple tradition that had earlier peaked in the NIT and NCAA in 1938 and 1944. His twin jewels were Rodgers and Lear, and with those gems he came close to equaling (and given the more competitive modern era, perhaps even surpassing) the school's earlier heights in both championship tournaments.

Finally, Alex Severance guided Villanova through an entire quarter-century of cage play that stretched from the first NCAA tournament (in which the Wildcats lost the East Regional title game to eventual runner-up Ohio State) to the onset of the turbulent 1960s and thus established countless memorable milestones along the way. Villanova would remain a model of coaching stability as Jack Kraft would succeed Severance with nearly as long a tenure; the school that produced Arizin in the '50s, Howard Porter in the '60s and Keith Herron in the '70s, would in fact have only two coaches over the nearly four decades which separated the beginning of postseason tourney play and the onset of the modern-era '70s. In 25 memorable campaigns with the Wildcats, Severance himself would post 416 victories and suffer only five losing winters.

The Philadelphia "Big Five" of the 1950s would be best remembered by future decades for their outstanding play against teams from other sections of the country, especially when it came down to the showcase matches of March tournament time. But it was also the intense warfare within their own tight circle that provided perhaps the most lasting legacy of Philadelphia mid-century basketball. A memory-strewn Philadelphia Palestra during the era of Gola, Beck, Rodgers, Lear and their immediate successors soon became almost as storied and hallowed for its dramatic season-long shootouts as New York's venerable Madison Square Garden during two previous decades.

7

The Sixties, Part 1

Buckeye Sharpshooters in the Turbulent Sixties

When it comes to debates about naming the nation's premier college hoops conference there are only two legitimate candidates. Broaching the issue from any imaginable angle — historical or contemporary — it always seems to come down to the granddaddy Big Ten and the upstart Atlantic Coast Conference. There simply are no hefty outside contenders.

Star players (from Jerry Lucas, Walt Bellamy and Magic Johnson to Art Heyman, David Thompson and Michael "Air" Jordan), competitive year-in and year-out conference title chases, lofty year-end rankings in the popular national wire service polls, controversial and legendary coaches (from Doc Meanwell, Ward Lambert and Bobby Knight to Everett Case, Dean Smith and Mike Krzyzewski), even NCAA Tournament domination (Duke, North Carolina, North Carolina State, Indiana, Michigan). Choose your familiar yardstick; only the Big Ten and the ACC boast competitive credentials for the mythical title.

The Southeastern Conference has had "Pistol Pete" Maravich, Kentucky's Big Blue Machine and Baron Adolph Rupp to ennoble its past, yet remains strictly a football conference in the public perception; the "new-kid-on-the-block" Big East Conference has only emerged over the past several seasons (with back-to-back national titles for Georgetown and Villanova in the mid-80s) as a truly entertaining and competitive circuit crammed with heavyweights; UCLA alone (set aside the brief run by California's Golden Bears in the late '50s) remains the pride of the constantly reshuffling Pac-10. Thus history again falls squarely on the sides of the tradition-rich ACC and the century-old Big Ten.

To take the most obvious measure of conference dominance — the showcase NCAA sudden-death shootout which crowns each and every season — the case for pre-eminence in the Big Ten and ACC becomes all the more clear-cut. It is the nation's oldest sports conference, the Big Ten (first called the Western Conference after its inception in 1905), that fittingly boasted one of two first-ever NCAA finalists back in 1939 (Ohio State lost to Oregon in a game played on Big Ten home grounds at Evanston, Illinois). Indeed it was Ohio State head coach Harold Olsen who had most strenuously pushed the governing body of collegiate athletics into establishing their own postseason event as a rival to the NIT affair already run by New York City promoters.

Jerry Lucas jams home a rebound in St. John Arena against Wichita State. At 6-foot-8, Lucas was the most dominant post player of his era, leading the nation three straight years in field-goal accuracy and twice in rebounding. (Ohio State University photo)

Big Ten teams proceeded to cop the tourney title in two of the first three seasons, with Indiana, coached by Branch McCracken, winning in 1940 and Wisconsin under Bud Foster duplicating the feat in 1941. And this was only a sign of things to come. Indiana from the Big Ten remains the only school to own NCAA titles in four different decades; the conference as a whole boasts nine national titles — five for Indiana and one each for Wisconsin, Ohio State, Michigan and Michigan State.

Since its own forced birth out of the ruins of the once-powerful Southern Conference in the early '50s, the ACC has nearly kept pace with its graybeard Midwestern rival. Total up overall game victories and winning percentages in NCAA postseason play and the ACC ranks first (with the Big Ten not surprisingly standing second). Tabulate Final Four appearances, title game visits, or overall tournament appearances, and the two power conferences simply switch places, with the Big Ten emerging on top. No other conference (not even the Pac-10 with 11 titles from UCLA or the Southeastern with five from Kentucky) comes close to matching the ACC and Big Ten co-domination of postseason play.

In the end, the nod perhaps goes to the venerable Big Ten on historical grounds alone. It was, after all, the country's pioneer collegiate athletic confederation, formed way back in January 1895 by Illinois, Iowa, Chicago, Purdue, Minnesota, Wisconsin and Indiana. Two of the original Big Ten schools actually share credit for the first legitimate college cage game ever played: the University of Chicago defeated Iowa on January 16, 1896, in the first recorded collegiate game to feature five players on a side. It was Walter "Doc" Meanwell of Wisconsin (champion of controlled-pattern play) and Ward "Piggy" Lambert of Purdue (true inventor of the racehorse fast-break offense) that shaped the early evolutions of the game. Even UCLA's John Wooden, after all, first learned his trade as an All-American Big Ten player at Purdue under Lambert, then took his old mentor's odd notion of gambling offense ("The team that makes the most mistakes usually wins") with him as the foundation of his own dynasty in Westwood.

Of course, for nearly half the history of the college cage sport the ACC didn't even exist, though it has most certainly made up for lost time in the second half-century. Admittedly across the past quarter century at least — especially given the postseason brashness of both Duke and North Carolina — things stand pretty much at an even draw.

For all its glory and prestige, however, the Big Ten reached no greater peak than those three short seasons which came only a half-dozen winters after the ACC — formed from the wreckage of the old Southern Conference — had drawn its own first tentative breath. For it was during the 1960, 1961 and 1962 seasons that the league famed for Piggy Lambert, Bob Knight, Cazzie Russell, Magic Johnson and Glenn Robinson showcased its finest crown jewel — arguably the most dominant individual player and most talented single team in the entire history of college basketball.

Jerry Lucas and the Greatest Team Ever Invented

There are many who would give the nod to UCLA as basketball's greatest collegiate dynasty. But it must be remembered that the Bruins' dozen-year run under Wooden was achieved by several distinctly different teams — not by one changeless unit. Granted that Walton and Alcindor both led ballclubs that not only matched the Buckeyes' run of three straight NCAA title games, but also proved victorious in either all (Alcindor) or two-thirds (Walton) of their Final Four tours. Yet by other measures, the Buckeyes' squad of Lucas, Havlicek, Siegfried, Mel Nowell and Joe Roberts has somewhat the greater claim on unmatched hoop legend.

This Buckeye team of the early '60s was truly a team for all ages. For openers, no previous college starting five had ever graduated into the pro ranks *en toto* as did the contingent of Lucas, Havlicek, Nowell, Roberts and Siegfried from Ohio State. All five had surprisingly played at the center post in high school, though Siegfried stood only 6-foot-4 and Nowell was a mere 6-2. But when blended together in Columbus they would become the greatest shooting unit that college basketball had ever seen. No team before this Ohio State group had ever led the nation in offensive output (averaging better than 90 points a game) and then won a national championship as well. But it was the spectacular won-lost record and the ability to march through an entire schedule into championship showdowns three straight seasons that was in the end the true hallmark of this greatest of all Big Ten wonder teams.

The zenith season for Lucas and company was arguably their very first campaign out of the blocks. Kentucky (96-93) and Utah (97-92) provided high-scoring early-season road losses, but once the sophomore-studded club (Joe Roberts was a senior and Larry Siegfried a junior) reached its stride during conference play it would lose only a single time at Indiana (99-83) the rest of the way.

By the opening tip of postseason, coach Fred Taylor's crack unit had become not only the best team in OSU annals but likely the best in conference annals as well. And it may indeed have been the most dominant single team of all collegiate basketball history, a worthy rival for the best clubs ever fielded by John Wooden's dynasty-era Bruins. The Bucks had trailed Oscar Robertson's Cincinnati Bearcats and California's Golden Bears (with All-American center Darrall Imhoff) in the national polls entering the NCAA tournament fray; yet behind Lucas's nation-leading 63.7 shooting percentage, Taylor's outfit now seemed to improve dramatically with each outing, battering first Western Kentucky (98-79) and then Georgia Tech (86-69) to leap into the exclusive Final Four matches set for the San Francisco Cow Palace.

The top-ranked California Bears (1st UPI, 2nd AP) and Cincinnati Bearcats (1st AP, 2nd UPI) first locked horns in one national semifinal in which the defending national champs from California rudely eliminated Oscar's team from the tournament for the second year running. OSU in the meantime toyed with Satch Sanders and NYU, 76-54, as Lucas and Siegfried each logged 19 points. The Finals would thus pit the nation's leader in offense (Ohio State at 90.4 points per game) against the national pacesetter in defense (California had yielded but 49.5 points per game), and this time the old sports adage about the superiority of defense would simply fly out the window. The Buckeyes were superb at both ends of the court and quickly overwhelmed the California defenders by hitting 16 of 19 first-half shots while holding the Bears to only 30 percent shooting efficiency during the same stanza. With Lucas completely shackling Imhoff on the inside the Buckeyes rolled to the school's first-ever national title by a comfortable 20-point margin.

The next two years unfortunately fell short of repeat glory by only a single game in each campaign. The fatal blow of course was that this single game in both cases happened to be the most important contest of the entire year. Each time it was an NCAA title matchup against cross-state rival Cincinnati, now without Oscar Robertson but an even better team on balance; and each time it ruined a season that was by all other measures even superior to the title campaign of Lucas' sophomore year. It was indeed all a very bitter pill to swallow for Buckeye faithful, especially at the tail end of so much relentless winning.

It should also be noted that in both of their championship game losses over the course of the next two seasons the Buckeyes were deflated each time more by a cruel twist of fate than by their own flaws or any true superiority on the part of the rival Bearcats. The 1961 Finals witnessed one of the rare classics of NCAA tourney

Two-time national player of the year Jerry Lucas led the Ohio State Buckeyes to the national championship game in all three of his varsity seasons. (Ohio State University photo)

history, a thrilling overtime match in which a clutch game-tying bucket from reserve junior Bob Knight was eventually nullified by superb team defensive play on the part of the Ed Jucker-coached Bearcats. Benefiting from balanced scoring and tenacious man-to-man defense, Jucker's well-drilled team pulled away for good during the extra session. Cincinnati in the end had won on exceptional team play from a lineup of Paul Hogue, Tom Thacker and Tony Yates, but it was Jerry Lucas (29 points in the semifinals and 27 in the finals) who was for the second straight time judged to be the clear-cut tournament MVP selection.

If a rare upset had felled the Buckeyes in 1961 it would be an even more fateful twist — a crucial injury to Lucas in the semifinal contest with Wake Forest — that would do them in during one final attempt at recapturing those championship glories of 1960. The 27-0 record which the '61 club had carried into the tourney finale was nearly replicated by the 26-1 mark compiled during Lucas' senior season. Jucker's Bearcats (28-2) would now be back again as well, primed to prove that a first championship showdown a year earlier had been anything but an undeserved accident.

But the second shootout between the bitter state rivals would lose something of its glamour a day before the final night's tipoff. Full-blown disaster struck for the Buckeye supporters when their star 6-8 center was knocked out by a debilitating knee injury with less than seven minutes remaining in the lopsided OSU-Wake Forest semifinal.

There was no way that Lucas would not attempt to perform in the title game, but the scales had already been tipped hopelessly in Cincinnati's favor. Gangly sophomore sub Gary Bradds would now be forced to perform nobly as Lucas' replacement, but the untested Bradds would simply not be enough (despite 5-for-7 shooting and a team-best 15 points and 4 rebounds) to prevent a Bearcat runaway (71-59) and yet another disappointment to cap the OSU dynasty string. The spindly sophomore indeed battled quite gamely yet could not contain the experienced Paul Hogue, who collected 22 points and 19 boards. And Havlicek was rendered ineffective when his own man, Ron Bonham, successfully roamed the perimeter and thus kept the No. 2 Buckeye rebounder safely away from the glass.

141

The 1962 tournament defeat was indeed a rare crushing moment for Fred Taylor's three-season "Dream Team" ballclub. In the end, however, this had nonetheless been the greatest Big Ten Conference glory run of all-time, a three-year visit to the Final Four never replicated by a Midwest team before or since.

Lucas had been the centerpiece, but he was hardly the entire five-star act. For starters there was the incomparable Havlicek. The eventual greatest "sixth man" of NBA history was also the greatest understudy ever to lace up hightops for the collegiate game. Havlicek played smack in the shadow of Jerry Lucas, and the two together were the most unbeatable combo in conference history (78-6, three league titles, one NCAA crown, three Final Fours). Despite his role as "second banana" the youngster called "Hondo" was nonetheless a recognized franchise player from the start; twice he was tabbed All-Big Ten and once named a first team All-American. And for his stellar play in the first and third of his three national title games Havlicek was also twice honored on the NCAA all-tourney team.

One of college basketball's fiercest competitors, John Havlicek drives to the basket during a 1961 NCAA regional game against Kentucky. (Ohio State University photo)

But if Hondo Havlicek never quite emerged fully from Jerry Lucas' shadow during undergraduate days he would soon enough dwarf his teammate's own considerable stature once the two reached the pro ranks. Havlicek would opt for a near-miss tryout with the NFL Cleveland Browns (despite not playing any football in college) before finally settling on a career with Red Auerbach's Boston Celtics, a 16-season sojourn which brought eventual hosannas as one of the sport's true all-time immortals. Hondo's reputation was soon established as the greatest bench player and greatest hustler in all of pro cage history. The Naismith Hall of Famer would one day own eight NBA championship rings, stand sixth all time in career scoring (26,395 points), fourth in career games played (1,270), fourth in career minutes (46,471), and fifth in career field goals (10,513). No other Big Ten alumnus has ever posted pro cage numbers that have even come close to this.

Spindly Gary Bradds, left, seen guarding Minnesota's Lou Hudson, would understudy an injured Jerry Lucas in the 1962 NCAA championship game then become Ohio State's third national player of the year in 1964. (Ohio State University photo)

Lucas received support from another quarter as well — from a backup player unfortunately largely forgotten by all but the most avid college basketball history buffs. Gary Bradds was the basketball equivalent of Haley's Comet. He first appeared as a slight background glimmer during his sophomore season and was hardly noticed at all in the afterglow of All-Americans Lucas and Havlicek. That was until the devastating injury to Lucas in the year's penultimate game suddenly threw Bradds smack into the limelight during the 1962 NCAA Finals.

Then with Lucas and Havlicek departed for the pros, the lanky center who averaged but 4.4 points per game his first season literally exploded unannounced upon the collegiate basketball scene. First his scoring numbers zoomed to 28.0 in 1963, then to more than 30 points per game in 1964. In his senior season he was national player of the year, OSU's third such superstar in only four campaigns. Few in fact have ever enjoyed a single season any more spectacular (he also pulled down 13.4 rebounds per contest) than the one with which Bradds concluded his OSU career.

And then suddenly the brightest star in the heavens dimmed once more. Bradds plodded through a short-lived and mostly unproductive pro career. He hardly distinguished himself in 45 games spread over two seasons with the NBA Baltimore Bullets; next the OSU All-American escaped to the fledgling ABA where he fared little better for Oakland, Washington, Carolina and finally the laughingstock Texas Chaparrals. The numbers for a six-year pro sojourn were less than impressive (254 games, 3,106 points, 12.2 points per game); the legend was soon forgotten everywhere but in Columbus. But it was not just basketball skills that would prove fleeting for one-time cage superstar Gary Bradds. Life itself was a brief burst and then endless silence. In July 1983, at only 40 years of age, Bradds would prematurely succumb to the ravages of cancer. It was indeed a tragic and untimely death which also cut short a promising second career as a highly successful elementary school principal in rural Bowerville, Ohio.

Almost as completely lost in the dust bin of hoops history is the remarkable collegiate career of rock-steady understudy Larry Siegfried. Siegfried had launched his schoolboy and collegiate hoops career as a rising star of the brightest magnitude; then suddenly this can't-miss prime-time player was relegated to an unfamiliar and uncomfortable slot as backstage role player. Unlike most spoiled superstars of the modern era, however, Siegfried adjusted quite admirably to his new diminished stature. An immensely talented Ohio schoolboy star, Siegfried had averaged a thunderous 38 per game during his final high school season; as a Buckeye sophomore he maintained his spot as scoring front-runner pacing the 11-11 1958-59 OSU team with a 19.6 average. Then sophomores Lucas and Havlicek suddenly arrived on the scene, and while the OSU team soared, Siegfried was just as suddenly forced out of the limelight.

It was a far different era, of course, and there was no whining from Siegfried about lost scoring chances and also no threats of transfer to another program. He would later admit that the new role as caddy to Lucas and Havlicek did not suit him at all well. Yet through it all he would nonetheless quietly accept his fate and continue to contribute more than adequately to the endless (and undoubtedly consoling) team victories. Siegfried was the second leading pointmaker (13.3) in the balanced championship lineup of 1960; as a senior he again was the No. 2 scorer (15.2) behind Lucas. And down the road there would still be a credible pro career, though one that also extended Siegfried's destined role in the supporting cast (as a member of seven editions of the "dynasty" Boston Celtics teams of the 1960s) and deep in the shadow of teammate John Havlicek. Larry Siegfried was fated to be that type of semi-important player who always remains a key cog in the team wheel yet nonetheless never quite manages to emerge as the blustery hero who can enjoy center stage.

Behind the frontline forces of Lucas, Havlicek, Siegfried and Bradds stood the strong supporting cast of Nowell and Roberts, plus that dark horse of future hoops history — Robert Montgomery Knight. And what a supporting cast it was. Knight would one day become a coaching legend, of course, and earn his own brand of immortality with the rare double of NCAA tournament titles earned as both player and coach (ACC immortal Dean Smith holds the same distinction). Knight would remain a bit player at OSU, however, and score but 93 points in three seasons (merely a good three-night outing for Lucas); yet as a fierce competitor the 6-4 reserve forward would nonetheless play a key role in several tense NCAA tourney games.

Mel Nowell was a hometown product, a sharp-shooting all-state guard from Columbus East High School who maintained a double-figure average (13.1) over three varsity seasons. The muscle on the '59-'60 team was provided by a pair of 6-7 seniors named Joe Roberts and Dick Furry, and it was indeed the presence of Roberts and Furry that has caused many to opt for the 1960 OSU club as the greatest of Lucas' three championship teams. Both Roberts (three years with the NBA Syracuse Nats and one with the ABA Kentucky Colonels) and Nowell (two seasons split between the NBA Chicago Packers and ABA New Jersey Americans) would also enjoy limited successes in their later abbreviated professional careers.

But the true prize in the end was of course Hall of Famer Lucas. He may well have been the most dominant collegiate player of all time — at least outside of Oscar Robertson, Bill Walton, Tom Gola and Bill Russell. We are not here talking about huge offensive numbers á la Pete Maravich or Glenn Robinson; nor is future pro stardom a yardstick, as in the case of Magic Johnson or Isiah Thomas. At issue here is the rare combination of skilled, crowd-pleasing offensive and defensive play coupled with the ability to lift the team around him to true championship heights. For three seasons the Ohio State Buckeyes (despite their talented supporting cast of Havlicek, Siegfried and others) largely rode the shooting and rebounding of Jerry Lucas, and they rode it all the way to the season's final championship game. Only Walton and Alcindor carried their teams to equal championship glories in quite the same fashion.

Lucas' collegiate numbers are indeed solid enough, yet they are more moderate than outstanding. For three seasons he averaged better than 20 points per game; still he owns no school scoring records or conference point-making crowns. The latter fact can be attributed to the coincidence that Purdue's Terry Dischinger (a 30 points per game scorer as a senior) was in the league at exactly the same time. Rebounding was of course Lucas' true forte and he paced the entire nation in that department for two seasons running. For three seasons he was a unanimous first team All-American and for two years the nation's clear-cut player of the year. Only a handful of roundball's greatest stars share the first distinction; only Alcindor, Oscar Robertson (thrice), Bill Walton and David Thompson of North Carolina State divide the latter honor.

But perhaps the truest (and most costly) measure of Lucas' impact had to rest with the most disappointing game in Buckeye cage history. The national title won by OSU during Lucas' sophomore season had been rudely ripped away by an inspired Cincinnati club during a tense overtime match a year later. Some knowledgeable observers dismissed that first Buckeye failure as a mere fluke. Poised to regain their lost crown during Lucas' and Havlicek's senior season the Buckeyes first rode the scoring and rebounding prowess of the nation's top player through a 26-1 campaign, then climbed back into an expected NCAA Finals rematch with the same rival Bearcats. But disaster struck suddenly on the eve of that rematch when Lucas suffered his severe leg injury in the meaningless concluding moments of the fateful Wake Forest game.

A hobbled Lucas gamely tried to perform a single night later but had to be spelled for much of the contest by promising, though inexperienced, sophomore Gary Bradds. Without their workhorse at full strength the Big Ten champs were in the end simply no match for the national champion Bearcats. Cincinnati won for a second straight season — this time even more convincingly to the tune of 71-59. Thus Jerry Lucas would bow out in most uncharacteristic fashion, with only the sixth loss of his entire collegiate career, yet his second in the prestigious NCAA championship game.

Many would argue that the Ohio State team at the outset of the 1960s was the greatest college five-man unit ever assembled. To these Buckeye enthusiasts the argument seems only to be which of the three years of the Lucas-Havlicek tandem was truly the greatest. The 1960 outfit had won a national title and certainly gets the nod on that count. The 1961 club failed in the upset-marred finals, but it was nonetheless undefeated all the way until that point. And the 1962 team was neither a national champ nor an undefeated regular-season ballclub. Yet it was nonetheless perhaps the most spectacular combo of all — despite the loss of linchpin Siegfried. Only the injury to Lucas in the title rematch with Cincinnati had prevented this from being the acknowledged zenith of the Buckeye Golden Era.

In the Wake of the Incredible "Big O"

There was one inescapable irony enriching the titanic NCAA championship battles between Ohio State and cross-state Cincinnati. The title matchups of 1961 and 1962 not only showcased college basketball's new-found popularity at the outset of the 1960s, but they also made a statement about the seemingly inexhaustible supplies of renewed talent now enriching the big-time college scene.

Ohio State had finally emerged as a first-rate national power behind its greatest all-time individual superstar, Jerry Lucas, along with one of the most formidable supporting casts in the sport's century-long history. But Cincinnati, under new coach Ed Jucker, had made it to the top of the heap only in the wake of its own all-time greatest star, Oscar Robertson. With the "Big O" dominating the scene for the final three seasons of George Smith's tenure, the Bearcats indeed emerged as a powerhouse of the first rank. Yet with Oscar dominating the ball and the headlines, Smith's starting five could never quite mesh total team success with individual heroics from Oscar. The Missouri Valley kingpin was one of the best clubs around from December through February, yet always found an insurmountable roadblock lying in the way of Oscar and his teammates once the tournament pressures of March rolled in.

When Oscar Robertson first hit the collegiate scene he was a phenomenon the likes of which had never been seen before. The game of the early and mid-50s had known great scorers like Arizin and Selvy and Mlkvy and Baylor. Elgin Baylor had already set new standards for all-around flashy play. But never had there been a force quite as totally dominant as the one Oscar brought to the game the very first time he stepped on the court as a college sophomore.

Robertson's arrival was anything but unheralded. The Tennessee-born athlete (and younger brother of Bailey Robertson who would put in a stint with the Harlem Globetrotters) had been raised in semipoverty in inner-city Indianapolis, where he led the all-black Crispus Attucks High School team to two straight Indiana state championships and a 45-game win streak. Recruited by nearly every big-time program in the country, the shy if talented youngster had opted to remain close to his hometown roots and become the first-ever black player at the University of Cincinnati.

*"The Big O" may
have rivaled Jerry
Lucas for the title of
best college player of
all time, but unlike
Lucas, Oscar was
never able to lead his
University of
Cincinnati team to an
NCAA championship.
(University of
Cincinnati photo)*

Robertson ruled the 1957-58 campaign almost from the opening tip, posting prodigious point totals but also feeding his talented teammates with uncanny accuracy, and in the process he became the first sophomore ever to win the national scoring title. His 35.1 points per game average and the support of 6-9 teammate Connie Dierking were also enough to lead the emerging Bearcats to their very first Missouri Valley Conference title and a 25-3 overall record. Yet it was just in time for Oscar's maiden campaign that NCAA rules makers had decided to take a chunk out of scoring averages by altering the free-throw bonus rule. A extra shot would now be awarded only after six team fouls in a half and the diminished foul-shooting opportunities for the biggest gunners predictably brought a lowering in scoring averages throughout the land. Only Robertson, Baylor and Kansas giant Wilt Chamberlain were able to maintain year-long 30 points per game scoring averages.

As a junior, Oscar continued his individual onslaught, again scoring better than 30 (32.6) and again ranking as the nation's offensive pacesetter. And once again Cincinnati was able to stand atop the powerful Missouri Valley Conference, ahead of powerhouses like Bradley with Bobby Joe Mason and St. Louis with Bob Ferry. But this time the Cincinnati team which had failed a year earlier in the Midwest regional semifinals was primed to make a more serious run at a national title. With Oscar leading the charge, the Bearcats this time around climbed out of the regional playdowns by surviving an opening-round scare against Texas Christian and then bowling over the year-long No. 1-ranked ballclub, Kansas State. The nation's best player in his second year out of the gate was now close enough to a national championship to almost taste it.

It was another future pro backcourt whiz who would now enjoy an even closer near-miss at the national title than Oscar, however. Jerry West played in Robertson's shadow for most of the 1959 regular season. He posted the nation's sixth best scoring mark at 26.6 but if he didn't score more it was because the experienced and balanced team on which he played didn't need one-man shooting exhibitions. Behind West's phenomenal shooting and the ample support of Bob Smith, Bucky Bolyard and Willie Akers, the longtime bridesmaid team from West Virginia was finally able to make it out of the NCAA opening round. A year earlier, with West starting as a sophomore and supported by 6-10 Lloyd Sharrar, Fred Schaus' Mountaineers had stood No. 1 in the country for almost the entire year, finishing the season at 26-2 and still atop both the UPI and AP polls. But in the tournament an old jinx held up and the Mountaineers fell once again, this time to unranked and unheralded Manhattan College in the NCAA opening round.

But such a jinx could not last forever in the face of so much West Virginia talent and the offensive presence of a superstar net-filler like Jerry West. Owning momentum from a fifth consecutive Southern Conference title, the 1959 Mountaineers defeated Dartmouth, St. Joseph's and Boston University to claim an East Regional title and a trip to the Final Four festival in Louisville's Freedom Hall. West Virginia would hardly break a sweat in bombing the host Louisville Cardinals 94-79 behind West's 38-point sharpshooting. Yet in the finals neither West nor his supporting cast — like many fine teams before them — would be able to crack Pete Newell's iron-clad California defense.

The championship game nonetheless went right down to the wire, but only when the outclassed Mountaineers stormed back from a 57-44 deficit over the final 10 minutes. West had racked up four fouls and sat out the middle stretches of the second half, but eventually he returned to lead a charge that pulled West Virginia within a single point but no closer. Like Oscar, West too would fail to win the coveted national title. Nonetheless Jerry West did salvage a small measure of individual glory by at least reaching the title contest and also earning the handsome Final Four MVP trophy.

The 1959 campaign had thus been a year of considerable glory tinged with ultimate frustration for West Virginia's All-American gunner. It was exactly the same scenario for Jerry West's rival up the road in Cincinnati. Oscar Robertson's second memorable season also in the end brought only further heart-wrenching disappointments.

Oscar's Bearcats had themselves seemed bound for an expected national title as they raced through the Midwest Regional and straight into the Final Four. Most fans indeed expected a spotlight shootout between Robertson and West with a national title on the line. But then Cincinnati also ran smack into the same Pete Newell-engineered style of defense that was simply too stingy to bend or break against even the finest of freewheeling scorers.

Newell's teams were exceptionally well-conditioned and usually pressed their opponents from end-to-end of the court and from opening tap to closing bucket. Now the California master strategist designed a gang-style defense to frustrate Oscar by pushing the Bearcat star toward the middle of the floor and taking away his favored

One of the most remarkable long-range sharpshooters in collegiate annals, Jerry West seemingly lived in the shadows of Jerry Lucas at Ohio State and Oscar Robertson at Cincinnati. But West did experience one near-miss at a championship trophy during the NCAA finals against California. (West Virginia University photo)

"move" of backing toward the baseline. The ploy was a huge success and limited the Cincinnati star to a sub-par 19-point night during a relatively easy 64-58 Cal victory. The Bearcats had to settle for the third-place consolation prize against host Louisville and then a seat on the sidelines to watch another high-scoring one-man show — Jerry West — also fall victim to Pete Newell's "scientific basketball" and California's overpowering control style inside game.

Oscar's senior season in 1960 offered still more of the same. There was another scoring title (33.7 points per game), leaving Oscar with the very first three-year sweep of that honor. Only LSU's "Pistol Pete" Maravich would subsequently pull off a similar triple reign. There was also a third straight Missouri Valley title and even a year-long No. 1 AP ranking. And there was a second straight trip as well through the Midwest Regional and back into the NCAA Final Four. But here the good news would abruptly end, for there was also a second straight semifinal loss to Pete Newell and his stingy California Golden Bears. California had by now become something of a full-fledged nemesis for Eastern teams, having dispatched Cincinnati twice and West Virginia once on consecutive Final Four weekends before finally meeting their match in Ohio State and Jerry Lucas. There was of course very little consolation for coach Smith's ill-fated Cincinnati team (and especially for the graduating Oscar Robertson) in the fact that there was also a second straight Bearcat victory in the Final Four consolation game (this time 95-71 over NYU), as well as a third consecutive "National Player of the Year" award for the unparalleled Big O.

How good was "The Big O" in the final analysis? Writer Neil Isaacs perhaps already had the last and best word when he observed that in settling debates about the all-time best player the discussion always reduces itself to two choices only — Oscar Robertson or someone else. Older fans might champion Gola or Luisetti, but playing styles of the '30s, '40s and early '50s were different enough to make comparisons of those players with modern-era stars quite ludicrous. Champions of the "big man theory" will likely opt for Mikan, Russell, Chamberlain, Alcindor or even Walton. Other destined Hall of Famers like Bird and Julius Erving and David Thompson have all been spectacular for the short haul yet simply don't measure up over a three-year span. And if Jordan has now surpassed Oscar in most eyes on the pro stage, as a college player Jordan never accomplished the total domination that marked Oscar's remarkable three-year stint. Stars who faced Oscar and then went on to battle the best during lengthy "Golden Era" NBA careers have absolutely no doubt about the matter. Jerry West and Bob Cousy, among others, have been often quoted as saying that Robertson was simply the unrivalled best in all phases of the game of any they ever saw.

Purdue's Terry Dischinger enjoyed three high-octane seasons in the Big Ten (26.3, 28.2, 30.3) but was largely lost in the shadows of Jerry Lucas and Company. (Purdue University photo)

But individual brilliance does not translate directly into team invincibility and sometimes even works against it. It was only with Oscar's graduation that the Cincinnati Bearcats were ironically able to put together the balanced team that was capable of finally winning the big ones in late March and thus of also sustaining a drive all the way into the national title game.

Oscar had much to do with this ultimate success in a somewhat indirect fashion, of course, if only by putting the school squarely on the map and thus making recruitment of a national powerhouse team more possible for Bearcat coaches. Thus when Oscar left for even grander stardom in the NBA it was hardly the end of an era on the Cincinnati campus. A new coach was about to be handed all the tools necessary for a legitimate championship season. Forty-one-year-old Ed Jucker had by now been a valued assistant under George Smith for several winters. What he would inherit in Oscar's wake was a team that was even stronger than the one Oscar had been surrounded with. But in large part it can also be said that it was only stronger because of drastic changes introduced immediately by the new and daring Cincinnati mentor.

Despite the fabulous 79-9 record, the top national rankings, and the hordes of new fans attracted by Cincinnati's run-and-gun offense spearheaded by Oscar, the back-to-back losses in NCAA play to Pete Newell's California team had provided a valuable lesson. Jucker, from his own vantage point on the Cincinnati bench, had come to admire Newell's tightly controlled offensive and defensive schemes and was therefore quick to insert his own version of the system when practice opened without Oscar in the autumn of 1960. Fortunately he already had the necessary horses in the gym to carry out the new game plan. Junior center Paul Hogue at 6-9 and 235 pounds was a key player and proved to be a tower of strength directly beneath the glass. Bob Weisenhahn and Carl Bouldin, a crack 6-4 forward and a sure-handed 6-1 guard, were key holdovers from the Oscar era. And a 6-2 sophomore named Tom Thacker soon proved he could play several feet above the rim. But the biggest addition was perhaps another celebrated Indiana high school star, the 6-5 Ron Bonham. It was Bonham and Hogue who would now have to carry the sagging scoring load.

Jucker had several major obstacles to overcome and he faced them all bravely. Neither the fans or his own players were easily sold on the new system. Grandstand patrons had loved to see Robertson and his Bearcat teammates run wildly up and down the floor, but in the end such a strategy had been the team's death knell against the defensive pressures of an opponent like California. And there was also a considerable box office challenge from the city's new professional franchise which now featured hometown hero Oscar Robertson himself. Rochester's financially stressed NBA Royals had relocated to the Queen City in 1957 with the rather obvious intention of obtaining "The Big O" as a territorial draft pick.

The new coach had hoped at best to win regularly enough to keep fans from jumping ship altogether. His method was to downsize the offense, upgrade the defense, and physically condition his players after the proven methods of Pete Newell. Bonham would latter remember that the new coach demanded three weeks of pre-season defensive skull sessions and taxing conditioning drills before his starters were even allowed to shoot during inter-squad scrimmages. The strategy worked so well that even the cautiously optimistic coach was shocked by the mid-season results. Slow but sure progress through the early part of the 1960-61 campaign allowed the corner eventually to be turned. The only two losses of the year came early in December, by a single point and by two points in overtime. And by tournament time the revamped Bearcats would provide one of the biggest surprises of the entire decade.

The 1962 Ohio State and Cincinnati teams together provided a showcase year for Buckeye State hoops fanatics and college roundball fans everywhere around the country. It was indeed a year that mirrored even if never quite matching the incredible doings that same winter on the professional level. For it was in 1962 that the NBA ballplayers gave loud notice that a new era of explosive scoring and superstar heroics had now dawned and that the cage sport would therefore never be quite the same again.

The college game was still king, of course, and some of the NBA heroics admittedly went on almost in total obscurity. But it was quite a show in NBA arenas nonetheless, and it did steal some of the college thunder. Foremost were the almost surreal exploits of the new giant named Wilt Chamberlain. Chamberlain took individual scoring to a truly improbable realm when he averaged better than 50 a game, collected more than 4,000 points for the year, and even topped 100 in one game against the hapless Knicks. And then there was Oscar Robertson himself, back in familiar surroundings in Cincinnati. While Oscar's former collegiate teammates were charging to a second straight NCAA title without him, Oscar was hardly sitting on the sidelines bemoaning lost schoolday opportunities. He was instead himself enjoying unquestionably the greatest all-around individual season in pro basketball history — in this only his second pro season — by averaging a season-long triple-double (30.8 points, and 12.5 rebounds and 11.4 assists per game). And he was doing it right there on the scene of his past glories — in the Cincinnati Garden.

All-Star Team for the Era (1959-1965)

	Pos.	Pts. (ppg.)	Best Year	NPY
Jerry Lucas (Ohio St.)	C	1990 (24.3)	26.3 (So.)	1961-62
Oscar Robertson (Cin.)	F-G	2973 (33.8)	35.1 (So.)	1958-60
Jerry West (W. Virg.)	F-G	2309 (24.8)	29.3 (Sr.)	—
Art Heyman (Duke)	F	1984 (25.1)	25.3 (Jr.)	1963
Bill Bradley (Princeton)	F	2503 (30.2)	32.3 (Jr.)	1965

NPY = National Player of the Year
Honorable Mention: Gary Bradds (C, Ohio State), Walt Hazzard (G, UCLA), Rick Barry (F, Miami), Cotton Nash (F, Kentucky), Len Chappell (C, Wake Forest), Billy McGill (C, Utah), Bob Boozer (F, Kansas State), Walt Bellamy (C, Indiana), Terry Dischinger (F, Purdue)
Coach of the Era: Fred Taylor (Ohio State), NCAA Champion (1960), NCAA Runner-up (1961, 1962)

Yet for all the exploits of Oscar and Wilt in the pro arena, it was still the college game that was drawing the bulk of hoop fans' loyalties at the outset of the turbulent '60s. And in the early years of the decade there was much more to cheer than just the two crack outfits from the Midwestern basketball capital of Ohio. A new era was indeed dawning and the first signals were already being given with UCLA's strong showing during the 1962 Final Four in Louisville. Scratching their way into the Big Dance for the first time ever with a 16-9 regular season mark, John Wooden's upstart club had copped the first of a long string of crowns in the Pacific Coast Conference (which had relabeled itself the Athletic Association of Western Universities between 1960 and 1968). The upset-minded Bruins missed by an eyelash making it to the Finals against Lucas and company when they dropped a wrenching 72-70 decision to eventual champion Cincinnati in a lively semifinal game. The issue was only decided by a questionable charging call against Walt Hazzard in the closing moments, as well as by a last-second jumper from pesky Bearcat guard Tom Thacker.

The Bruins would of course have to wait a season or two before exerting their iron grip on postseason play. Cincinnati was itself not yet quite done when it captured a second straight NCAA title by making in two in a row against the Lucas-Havlicek Ohio Staters. Like the rival Buckeyes whom they had now been able to dominate both with and without a healthy Lucas, the Bearcats would themselves soon make it three trips in a row into the Finals. And their run would ultimately end in sudden and highly unexpected frustration, just as had the glory run of Ohio State's Buckeyes.

Many longtime NCAA watchers still consider the 1963 NCAA title shootout between Cincinnati and Loyola College of Chicago to be the greatest season-ending game ever played. The setting was again Louisville and the storybook matchup was created when Jucker's defending champs breezed by Texas, Colorado and Oregon State (by a laughable 80-46 count in the semis), while coach George Ireland's unheralded Ramblers surprised Illinois in the regionals and then shot down Duke, the nation's second-ranked team, despite the MVP performance of Art Heyman.

Few championship matchups have ever carried a more memorable story line than the one now on tap. Cincinnati had given every indication with a 26-1 season that it was primed to become the first team ever to pull off three straight titles. Loyola, for its part, was arguably the greatest "Cinderella Story" of NCAA tournament history. The small Jesuit school out of Chicago had put together a sterling 28-2 mark of its own and led the nation in scoring for a second year running, yet few were convinced that a program without a more honored pedigree could effectively challenge the likes of Jucker's juggernaut. And the game held another significance on the eve of the nation's decade-long civil rights movement throughout the Southland. Loyola featured four black starters and Cincinnati three, making this the first NCAA title contest to feature a majority of African-American players.

Loyola was also a most unusual NCAA title team in still another respect. George Ireland would disdain using any of his seldom-seen bench players and instead gut out the entire 45-minute overtime contest with his five starters — senior Jerry Harkness and juniors Leslie Hunter, John Egan, Vic Rouse and Ron Miller. Loyola's iron-man outfit thus became the first and last team ever to use only its starting five from start to finish during a Division I national championship game.

The game itself was exciting enough to diminish all the hype surrounding Cincinnati's mission for three titles and Loyola's mission for racial respect. The leading offensive and defensive teams in the country provided the classic on-court confrontation that everyone had expected. Early-action nervousness and poor first-half shooting (especially by Harkness) left the Ramblers behind by eight (29-21) at the intermission. Things didn't get much better in the first eight minutes of the second half for the team making its first national television appearance of the season and the Bearcats stretched the lead to 45-30 with a dozen minutes remaining.

But then the momentum shifted suddenly to the Loyola end of the court and a rash of turnovers simultaneously shifted straight to the Cincinnati end of the action. With Cincinnati misfiring at the foul line as well, the Ramblers inched closer as the clock ran down. When Les Hunter tipped in a missed Harkness shot with but 12 seconds remaining the clutch putback had trimmed the dwindling Cincinnati lead to a single point. After a free throw by Cincy's Larry Shingleton the Ramblers would hurry the ball inbounds to Harkness whose dramatic jumper sent the game into an extra session.

The overtime was as gripping as any in tournament annals. The teams traded two baskets apiece which left the count 58-58 with Loyola again playing for a final game-deciding shot. A desperate attempt at a game-winner by Harkness was partially blocked by Ron Bonham, but the embattled Loyola forward retained control of the ball and then somehow found Hunter for a second desperation jumper from the far corner. The errant shot would carom directly to the 6-6 Rouse stationed on the right side of the hoop and unaccountably left unguarded by the scrambling Bearcat defenders. Rouse simply laid the ball back into the hoop as time expired and the Cinderella miracle was complete. For the first and only time a 100-1 long shot had walked off with a national title.

There were also other interesting footnotes to the unique 1963 NCAA Final Four bonanza. Cincinnati's heart-breaking loss had left Ed Jucker with a tourney record of 11-1 which would remain the all-time best playoff winning percentage for coaches with more than 10 postseason decisions. Backcourt ace Terry Baker of Oregon State also wrote a special page in NCAA history by becoming the only football Heisman Trophy winner ever to compete in the Final Four as well. And Baker's teammate Steve Pauly provided another rare footnote for the history books by becoming the only Final Four athlete also to win an AAU national decathlon title in the very same year that his team had successfully reached Final Four competition.

But for all the great teams and exciting postseason tournament action, the early '60s was also an era of unsurpassed individual stars. One only had to watch in awe the night-in and night-out shooting, rebounding and ballhandling performances of some of these roundball luminaries to come to a quick conclusion that an unprecedented explosion of basketball interest could not be very far down the road.

The 1962 season alone seemed ample proof. While Chamberlain and Baylor were pushing individual scoring records out of sight in the NBA, a quintet of the highest scorers in collegiate history were doing the same at the amateur level. Billy McGill of Utah was at the head of the class, logging the highest season-long point-making average (38.8 points per game) since the incredible Frank Selvy eight seasons earlier. The 6-9 McGill was an agile frontcourt point-making phenomenon who accounted for 45.8 percent of the total offensive output for the sixth highest scoring team in the country. With a dozen 40-point games and four 50-point games during his remarkable senior season, "The Hill" seemed destined for true NBA greatness. (McGill was indeed the top pick of the 1962 NBA draft by the Chicago Zephyrs but only twice in a five year NBA-ABA stint did he edge into double-figure scoring.) That it didn't happen for McGill at the pro level, however, did little to diminish his impact on the collegiate game.

The same 1962 season found Jack "The Shot" Foley (33.3 points per game) burning the nets for Holy Cross, Nick Werkman (33.0) lighting up scoreboards for Seton Hall, and Terry Dischinger (despite the dominant presence of Jerry Lucas) grabbing the individual scoring honors (30.3) in the talent-laden Big Ten. A mere two years later Howie Komives would emerge as another memorable scoring phenom out of the Midwest when he racked up 844 points (36.7) for Ohio's Bowling Green State. The 6-1 guard and future NBAer would nip Werkman, the 1963 scoring champ, for the national title when he logged 50 consecutive free throws over his final five games. And along with these other prolific scorers stood the phenomenal Bill Bradley, perhaps the best all-around player of the immediate post-Oscar era, save perhaps only Jerry Lucas and Cazzie Russell.

Small school stars were much in evidence in this epoch as well. There was Gus Johnson who starred a single season (1962-63) at Idaho and later became the NBA's

In his final college game Princeton's Bill Bradley provided the greatest curtain-closer ever, a tournament record 58 points in Portland against Wichita State in the NCAA Final Four consolation game. (Princeton University photo)

first backboard smasher with the Baltimore Bullets. Paul Silas was building a reputation at Creighton and led the nation in rebounding during the 1963 campaign. The future Boston Celtics stalwart not only still holds the NCAA three-season career rebounding record but remains one of only six players in NCAA history (Walter Dukes, Bill Russell, Julius Erving, Artis Gilmore and Kermit Washington are the others) to average 20 points and 20 rebounds for an entire collegiate career. Other rebounding standouts from lesser schools during this era were Bob Pelkington of Xavier (Ohio), Toby Kimball of Connecticut and Jim Ware of Oklahoma City. Not to be outdone by either major school or small school rivals, 6-1 guard Frank Burgess of Gonzaga (32.4) also sandwiched a single national scoring title between the fabulous Oscar Robertson and the one-year-wonder Billy McGill.

But it was the big schools from the major conferences that were still providing the bulk of the entertainment and that entertainment resulted from an unprecedented collection of superstars. The 1964 national "Player of the Year" again wore the colors of the Ohio State Buckeyes. Lanky Gary Bradds now copped the honor (from both the AP and the UPI pollsters) that had been dominated by Ohio players for five of the six previous seasons (Oscar Robertson in 1958-1960 and Lucas in 1961-1962). But there was now also a player on the horizon who many considered the genuine heir apparent to both Robertson and Lucas. By the middle of the 1964 season Bill Bradley of Princeton was already demonstrating night-in and night-out that he simply could do it all, and do it all with a flare demonstrated previously only by Oscar.

Bradley had perhaps his best overall season in 1963-64, although his "Player of the Year" plaudits would wait for another year. And if the collegiate season wasn't enough, Bradley also starred on a 1964 United States Olympic team that remained somewhat in the shadow of the 1960 squad (starring Lucas, Robertson and West) but was a potent one nonetheless. Behind Bradley, Team USA bested the Soviets 73-59 to bring home another Gold Medal from Tokyo. After such a year it hardly appeared that there was anything left for an encore. But there was, as Bradley the following year raised the level of his game if not his scoring average and earned the national player of the year honors that had eluded him as a junior. It would be in 1965 that Bradley would be especially spectacular in postseason play with a record 58-point performance during his final college game — a Final Four consolation match with Wichita State. But throughout all three of his Princeton seasons Bill Bradley was at his most spectacular (33.7 points, 12 rebounds per game in nine NCAA tourney outings) when it came to March Madness tournament time.

The 1964 season would also signal the birth of a new dynasty era when the UCLA Bruins of the Pacific Coast Conference emerged at year's end in the NCAA championship seat. Of course the Bruins' curtain-closing victory was hardly recognized for what it was at the time. Instead the 1964 NCAA tournament seemed nothing more or less than another emotion-packed and thrill-charged race to the finish line. If anything, the 1964 season seemed to suggest that the collegiate sport was becoming more balanced than ever. With so many quality teams spread from East to West, perhaps it would indeed be a long time — so the thinking went — before any more Ohio States or Cincinnatis would remain quite so long on the crest of the mountain.

The 1964 NCAA Tournament came down in the end to UCLA, Duke, Kansas State and Michigan. And it was a tourney and season which again focused on an incredible collection of individual stars. Cazzie Russell had inherited the mantle from Lucas as perhaps the greatest single Big Ten talent ever. UCLA owned the potent backcourt tandem of junior Gail Goodrich and senior Walt Hazzard (the NCAA tourney MVP). Duke was now led by Jeff Mullins who had inherited the Blue Devils leadership spot from 1963 Final Four MVP Art Heyman.

UCLA walked off with the 1964 national title (its first ever) to the tune of 98-83, and it did so by besting a talented Vic Bubas-coached Duke squad that was itself visiting the Final Four for a second straight season. But that was hardly the single dominating story of either the tournament or the full season. In guard Russell and center Bill Buntin (tragically felled by a heart ailment only a few short years later) Michigan had showcased one of the great one-two punches found anywhere in the half-century annals of the sport. This spectacular Wolverine pair would make plenty of headlines of their own as the only combo in history to each average better that 23 points per game throughout both ends of a Final Four weekend. Princeton's junior All-American Bradley (32.3 points per game), a sharpshooter at unheralded Miami of Florida named Rick Barry (32.2 points per game), and Ohio State's Gary Bradds (30.6 points per game) also shared a large portion of the national headlines.

Never before had there been quite as much cage talent or quite as much competitive balance all across the land. Or so we naively assumed at the time. Events transpiring out in the Los Angeles suburb of Westwood were of course about to alter these perceptions quite radically.

8

The Sixties, Part 2

Kentuckiana, Blackball and Tobacco Road

Nowhere does basketball tradition run quite so deep as in the backwater heartlands of rural Kentucky. A loose claim of prominence can certainly be attached to the city version of the game nurtured on the playgrounds of New York and any other Eastern Seaboard metropolis like Philly, Boston or even Washington, D.C. And at least two other Midwestern hotbeds — Ohio and Indiana — boast a lengthy heritage of hotshot stars and trophy-toting teams. West Coast basketball, California-style, numbers its own fanatical boosters. But with all due respect to UCLA and the dynasty of John Wooden, no single school has maintained a record of consistent winning excellence — or a proclivity for turning out eye-popping players — that can quite match the efforts recorded down in Lexington during the half-century reign of Baron Adolph Rupp and his more recent successors Joe B. Hall, Eddie Sutton and Rick Pitino.

One trivial statistic alone perhaps speaks most eloquently about the depth of University of Kentucky cage tradition. Down through the years the Wildcats have retired so many jersey numbers — 19 at last count, honoring 26 different players — that it remains something of a small wonder there are enough digits left to supply present-day uniforms. Even the array of Boston Celtics jerseys hanging from the rafters of venerable Boston Garden (also 19 in number, but honoring only 17 players, plus one coach and one owner) fail to overwhelm when stacked up against the sheer number of white and blue uniform shirts draped atop cavernous Rupp Arena. Put differently, a full collection of honored Kentucky immortals is almost large enough to merit its own special wing at the Naismith Hall of Fame in Springfield.

This matchless Kentucky tradition dates all the way back to the arrival of Rupp at the outset of the '30s. But it was with the powerhouse teams of the late '40s that Rupp and Kentucky would first cement the Bluegrass reputation now unparalleled elsewhere in the land. Most cage historians would therefore place the "official" beginnings of Rupp's three-decade "dynasty" with the war-ending 1944-45 season.

The reason is simple: it was then that a lanky freshman named Alex Groza first arrived in Rupp's already crowded stable of unmatched thoroughbreds. It would be Groza, above all others, who would be the anchor of those first invincible Kentucky teams that owned the post-war college cage scene. The era of Alex Groza soon also became the era of "The Fabulous Five" team (Groza, Beard, Barker, Rollins, Jones)

157

which can still lay legitimate claim to the mythical honor of the best single five-man squad ever assembled. Little matter that the legend of Rupp's best-ever team would later come to depend more upon its indelible legacy as cheaters than champions.

But if the Rupp dynasty was launched in 1944-45, it must be noted in any fair history that by then the Baron had spent 15 seasons compiling credentials that could already constitute a most satisfying career for just about any other member of the coaching fraternity. The first 15 years in Lexington under Rupp had already been a full-fledged winning bonanza. The stern Kansas native who himself had played un-

der pioneering Phog Allen for the 1923 national champion Jayhawks, debuted in the coaching ranks with 15-3 and 15-2 campaigns at Lexington in 1931 and 1932. When the Southeastern Conference (a breakaway piece of the old Southern Conference) formed in time for Rupp's third Kentucky season, his Wildcats became its first champions with a season mark of 20-3 and an undefeated ledger during their eight conference games. Over the stretch of his first 15 years Rupp would post a .798 winning percentage (233-59), claim six of 11 SEC postseason tournaments and also post the best record in the league on three other occasions.

And it would of

Kentucky's Retired Jerseys	
No.	**Players (Years)**
4	Layton "Mickey" Rouse (1938-39-40)
6	Cliff Hagan (1951-52-54)*
10	Louie Dampier (1965-66-67)
11	Sean Woods (1990-91-92)
12	Ralph Beard (1946-47-48-49)†
12	Deron Feldhaus (1989-90-91-92)
15	Alex Groza (1945-47-48-49)†
16	Lou Tsioropoulos (1951-52-54)*
20	Gayle Rose (1952-54-55)*
21	Jack Givens (1975-76-77-78)
22	Cliff Barker (1947-48-49)†
22	Jerry Bird (1954-55-56)*
26	Kenny Rollins (1943-47-48)†
27	Wallace "Wah Wah" Jones (1947-48-49)†
30	Frank Ramsey (1951-52-54)*
32	Richie Farmer (1989-90-91-92)
34	John Pelphrey (1989-90-91-92)
35	Kevin Grevey (1973-74-75)
42	Billy Evans (1952-54-55)*
44	Phil Grawemeyer (1954-55-56)*
44	Cotton Nash (1962-63-64)
44	Dan Issel (1968-69-70) (Kentucky's All-Time Leading Scorer)
52	Vern Hatton (1956-57-58)

† Member of "The Fabulous Five" 1948 National Champions
* Member of 1954 Undefeated National Champions

Additional Wildcats with special retirement banners in Rupp Arena but no uniform numbers: Basil Hayden (player, 1920-22), Carey Spicer (player, 1929-31), Forest "Aggie" Sale (player, 1931-33), Adolph Rupp (coach, 1931-72), Cawood Ledford (broadcaster, 1953-92), Joe B. Hall (coach, 1973-85)

course only get better from there. In fact, it would take the incomparable Baron — famed for his drab brown suits and dour countenance — an incredible 34 seasons to finally field a team capable of losing as many as 10 games. Only once (two years later, in season No. 36) would he field a club that stood as low as .500 at season's end. When he retired after 41 campaigns the winning percentage remained an astronomical .822 (it nudged above the .800 mark in spring 1945 and never again dipped below that magic plateau), the victory total of 876 games seemed beyond the reach of any mere mortals who might follow him, and there never had been even a single losing record. Four coveted NCAA championships and two additional trips to the Final Four almost seemed nothing more than an added bonus in the face of so much relentless year-in and year-out winning.

Alex Groza had hoped to follow his famed football-playing brother to Ohio State but had to settle instead for Kentucky, a starring position on the Wildcats' "Fabulous Five" national champions and an eventual date with basketball infamy. (University of Kentucky photo)

159

There was always a lengthy list of individual stars in Rupp's program during the first decade and a half. Foremost was LeRoy "Cowboy" Edwards, a 6-foot-5 Indiana-born center who would enjoy a single All-America year at Kentucky, lead the Southeastern Conference in scoring and eventually be tabbed Helms Foundation College Player of the Year for 1935 (a retroactive award selected by a panel of basketball experts several decades later). A hefty inside scorer in an era of long-range set shooting, Edwards on several occasions outscored the opposition by himself, once registering 26 points against Chicago while the entire Maroon team was recording only 16. Edwards was something of a 1930s equivalent of Kurland and Mikan and would later also be a three-time scoring champion (1938-40) in the rag-tag Midwestern pro circuit already known as the National Basketball League.

The Baron — Adolph Rupp — survived the 1951 betting scandals to become college coaching's biggest winner and second-greatest legend. In 41 seasons at Kentucky Rupp compiled 876 wins, an .822 winning percentage, won four NCAA titles and never knew a losing season. (University of Kentucky photo)

While Cowboy Edwards provided Rupp's program with its first widespread national publicity as a bona fide All-American, he also dealt the program a severe blow by deciding to abandon college after his sophomore season in order to compete for cash (reportedly receiving a $2,400 salary which nearly equalled Rupp's) with an AAU industrial league club in his hometown of Indianapolis. But Edwards was joined by others who earned no small measure of national attention as well. Bob Brannum was a bulky center who preceded Alex Groza in the early 1940s and earned the All-American label in 1944. And the multi-talented Forest "Aggie" Sale was another Helms player of the year (1933) who twice garnered All-American commendations (1932, 1933) for his versatile performances as both a rugged rebounding forward and playmaking guard.

There were also quality role players surrounding and ably supporting Coach Rupp's stable of frontline stars. By the middle of the war years, Kentucky's honor roll of All-Americans already stood at 11: Basil Hayden (1921), Burgess Carey (1925), Carey Spicer (1929-31), Paul McBrayer (1930), Forest Sale (1932-33), Ellis Johnson (1933), John "Frenchy" DeMoisey (1934), LeRoy Edwards (1935), Bernard Opper (1939), Lee Huber (1940-41) and Bob Brannum (1944). But there were also slightly lesser lights like guards Bill Davis (1934), Warfield Donohue (1937), Bernie Opper (1938-39), Layton Rouse (1940), and Lee Huber (1941); forwards Dave Lawrence (1935), Ralph Carlisle (1936-37), Marvin Akers (1941-43), and Ermal Allen (1942); and centers James King (1941) and Melvin Brewer (1943) — all of whom were spectacular enough to earn All-Southeastern Conference honors for the talent-rich Blue and White.

The hallmark of Adolph Rupp's earliest years in the Bluegrass State was not merely a winning record and local domination of the young Southeastern Conference (formed in 1933). A still larger and more lasting contribution was his introduction of the fast-breaking style of offense which was catching on everywhere in the North, East and Midwest yet was still a stark contrast to deliberate ball-control strategies advocated by his predecessor in Lexington, Johnny Mauer. Mauer had produced competitive teams in the three seasons preceding Rupp (12-6 in 1928, 12-5 in 1929, 16-3 in 1930), but they were teams that usually plodded to low-scoring victories and then collapsed in Southern Conference postseason play.

And in addition to this change in coaching strategy Rupp also departed from his Southern colleagues by filling up his nonconference schedule with tough intersectional opponents like Notre Dame, Indiana, Ohio State, and other Big Ten and Missouri Valley teams. At the end of his first half-dozen seasons the Baron's squad was visiting hostile outposts like Philadelphia (St. Joseph's), East Lansing (Michigan State), Omaha (Creighton), Indianapolis (Butler), Chicago (University of Chicago), Cincinnati (University of Cincinnati), Detroit (University of Detroit) and Milwaukee (Marquette). He also took his teams north regularly to challenge the best New York had to offer in Madison Square Garden, even though such excursions regularly led to brutal defeats marred by hometown officiating aimed against the Southerners. Rupp was so enamored of the idea of such regional competition that by the early '30s he was already agitating for a national postseason tourney to decide a country-wide year-end champion.

One venture into hostile interregional territory by one of Rupp's better early teams resulted in a landmark 1935 matchup with NYU at Madison Square Garden. Local-leaning officials allowed NYU frontcourt brutes King Kong Klein and Slim Terjesen to push and shove and even batter LeRoy Edwards under the home team bucket while Rupp's men were repeatedly whistled for blocking fouls at the other end. A questionable last-minute infraction would also decide the slugfest in favor of the home squad and Rupp was clearly infuriated over his team's inhospitable treatment by opponents and arbiters alike. But the anger was never enough to cause the Baron to withdraw his troops from further intersectional play. Controversy surrounding the rampant roughness in this particular game did persist in the press and in coaching circles for some time to come, however, and was eventually instrumental in spurring legislation of a 3-second lane violation rule to control such rugged inside play.

Kentucky and Rupp made their first postseason appearance in 1942 when they earned a bid to the fourth NCAA tourney on the strength of another SEC title. The maiden voyage into the event Rupp had championed way back in the early '30s got off to a rousing start when the Wildcats pulled off an opening-round upset of the University of Illinois, a team with the same personnel that a year later would be known as Cinderella "Whiz Kids" and be generally acknowledged as the nation's No. 1. That rousing victory was quickly tarnished, however, by a season-ending drubbing at the hands of Dartmouth the very next night. Losers to the tune of 47-28, Rupp's club had apparently left its entire game on the floor against Illinois.

Two years later the Big Blue of Kentucky would boast an even stronger club and perhaps one that stood equal to any in the land. Losing only a single regular-season road match to Illinois (43-41 in the sixth game of the year), the SEC power-house won another league title as well as the conference postseason tourney, the latter with lopsided victories over Georgia (57-29), LSU (55-28) and Tulane (62-46). They also captured a rematch with Illinois (51-40 on the home floor in Lexington) and upended favored St. John's 44-38 in the hostile surroundings of Madison Square Garden.

Rupp then opted to take his team back into the Garden for the year-end NIT event which was at the time still the more prestigious postseason venue. In the opening round Kentucky would knock off a very tough Utah team paced by freshman scoring sensation Arnie Ferrin. An exceptionally young team destined to make waves of its own over the next couple of seasons, the Utes boasted a rotating lineup of six freshmen and a single sophomore, center and second-leading scorer Bob Sheffield. The Kentucky victory margin against Utah was nonetheless a comfortable eight points. The Cats would next lose a semifinal match with St. John's (the eventual tourney winner over George Mikan and DePaul) but rebound to outslug Oklahoma A&M with giant Bob Kurland 45-29 in the tourney consolation match. Kurland completely shut down the Kentucky pivotman, Bob Brannum, in this one; but Rupp's other players looped their shots over the goal-tending Kurland and Kentucky came home an embarrassingly easy 16-point victor.

Utah also rebounded from its eight-point loss to the Wildcats and went on to claim both the NCAA title (nudging Dartmouth 42-40 in overtime) and the popular Madison Square Garden Red Cross charity game against NIT titlest St. John's. Utah (NCAA), St. John's (NIT) and even Oklahoma A&M (with the huge sophomore Kurland) might all claim to boast the best squad in the country; yet during the course of the season Kentucky had beaten them all.

Big Blue Machine from the Bluegrass State

As World War II ground down and renewed affluence dawned on America in the mid-40s, Kentucky's Wildcats had undeniably become a fixture on the national college basketball scene, even if they had yet to claim any national titles or extend their reign of terror very far outside of the SEC (where they had already captured seven league titles in the first dozen years). It would be Rupp's Kentucky teams of those immediate post-war "boom-era" years, however, that would soon shed the role of up-and-coming contenders and don the robes of invincible champions.

As a 6-foot-4 forward-center, Wallace "Wah Wah" Jones was the third-leading scorer on the Rupp "Fabulous Five" team and the one true star of the ill-fated 1948-49 Kentucky squad to remain free of the later taint of scandal. (University of Kentucky photo)

Coach Rupp continued to wear his same colorless brown suits and flash his same colorful if ornery personality at courtside. He drilled his talented squads ceaselessly to perfect an offensive machine free of the slightest technical errors. He designed a "run-and-gun" offensive style that encouraged his charges to shoot whenever open and exploited enemy defenses to create ample opportunities for such shooting. And by the fall of 1944 he also had the talented Alex Groza on campus to provide the first cog in a team that would soon become one of the greatest single collections of starting players in all of collegiate cage history.

Groza would play only 10 games for Rupp during the 1944-45 season. As a native of Martins Ferry, Ohio, the lanky youngster had hoped to land a scholarship to Ohio State where his brother Lou (soon to earn fame as the NFL's greatest place-kicker) had already been an All-America football star. But the Buckeye coaches had shown absolutely no interest in the 6-5, 167-pound stringbean and thus he had to swallow both his pride and his disappointment and settle for Rupp and Kentucky. Once in Lexington the debut was anything but spectacular, though the Wildcats did win 11 straight after the opening bell and there was a most satisfying defeat of Ohio State in Lexington (53-48 in overtime) during which the revenge-minded freshman center played the Buckeyes' stronger and more experienced Arnie Risen to a complete draw, even outscoring him 16-14.

Kentucky basketball historian Russell Rice would years later report a perhaps apocryphal incident which reputedly transpired between Groza and Buckeye coach Harold Olsen near the shower area in the aftermath of the hard-fought game. "Son, why didn't you come to Ohio State?" inquired Olsen. "Because no one asked me," responded the still-bitter freshman, "and now it's a bit too late to ask."

Groza's rookie season was nonetheless short but sweet since by midseason he was called off for military service and would thus miss all of the coming year as well as the stretch run of 1945. The freshman debut had produced some solid results for Groza nonetheless: a 16.5 points-per-game scoring average and a perfect 10-0 record at the time of his military call-up. Without him the team did eventually drop four games (three in regular-season play, to Tennessee and Notre Dame by a single point and to Michigan State in a more one-sided affair) yet also held on for still another SEC title. When NCAA postseason play opened, however, the Cats without their freshman post man were no match for Risen and Ohio State in a spirited rematch and were quickly eliminated from the tournament by a 45-37 score.

When he finally put his war duties well behind him and returned for the 1946-47 campaign, Groza would join a refurbished squad now strengthened with a trio of sterling sophomores who had been freshman starters during his absence. Wartime depletions had resulted in a temporary frosh-eligible rule and none benefitted any more handsomely than the Ruppmen. Wah Wah (Wallace) Jones was now entrenched at the center slot but would soon move over to forward to clear the post for the returning Groza, who already had gained a couple of inches and a dozen pounds. Ralph Beard was now running the team from the guard spot and providing the bonus of double-figure scoring. Joe Holland capably filled another forward position but would spend his freshman campaign largely as a backup to junior Jack Tingle and senior Wilbur Schu.

Of the newcomers, it was Wah Wah Jones who at first seemed the biggest catch. As a local and even national high school legend out of nearby Harlan, Kentucky, Jones came into the fold toting a national scholastic record of 2,398 points and had also starred as an all-state player in both football and baseball for Harlan High. But it was as a group and not as individuals that the new recruiting class would make its splash. The trio of Jones, Beard and Groza would soon be teamed with another sophomore hotshot, forward Cliff Barker, plus junior guard Ken Rollins, to form the ballclub immortalized as Rupp's "Fabulous Five" wonder team. And it was truly a team destined for all ages.

For it was the "Fab Five" unit that would bring the Bluegrass school its first NCAA national title at the end of the 1948 season. But the 1947-48 team was not the first true national title outfit to earn bragging rights for the Wildcats. Earlier there had been the 1946 club which raced to an NIT crown during the very season that future star Alex Groza was still serving at a distant military outpost in the South Pacific. Behind the freshman trio of Jones, Beard and Holland the Wildcats would rattle off 13 victories in their first 14 contests, including a surprisingly easy conquest of St. John's and its star Harry Boykoff up in Madison Square Garden. A loss to Notre Dame on a neutral court in Louisville would then be the final defeat of the regular season as Rupp's men raced unmolested through their final seven contests, plus the four games of the SEC tournament.

With a 25-2 season record in hand and a secure No. 2 spot in the informal national rankings behind Oklahoma A&M, Rupp decided to avoid a direct confrontation with Kurland and the Cowboys in the NCAAs. He opted instead for a postseason invite to return to Madison Square Garden and a renewal of the NIT fray.

Kentucky opened up NIT festivities in a much-anticipated intersectional match with another high-scoring Wildcats team, the one representing the University of Arizona. Link Richmond led the Western team with a hefty scoring average, and future public official Stewart Udall was also in the Arizona backcourt. But the champions of the now defunct Border Conference were no match for highly rated Kentucky and the game was a one-sided 24-point affair. A much tougher battle ensued with West Virginia in the semis where the lead changed hands 14 times and the Kentucky victory came only with eight consecutive points in the final two minutes. The hard-fought 59-51 win set up a title match with Frank Keaney's fast-breaking Rhode Island team.

Keaney had long taught the running game at Rhode Island and now had his own best edition in a squad led by All-American guard Ernie Calverley. Calverley had already provided fireworks when he canned a memorable 58-foot shot in the opening round against Bowling Green which forced an overtime. But in the finals Kentucky's Beard was able to corral the Rhode Island ace and limit him to a mere eight points. When Calverley fouled Beard in the final seconds the cool freshman dropped in the game-deciding free throw. Kentucky had escaped with a 46-45 title victory and its first piece of true national postseason prominence.

The next edition of the Wildcats promised to be even better. And for most of the season they indeed were far better and then some. Groza and Brannum were now back from the service to join the returning freshman stars. Only an upset 37-31 loss to Oklahoma A&M in the Sugar Bowl tourney and a six-point spanking on the road at DePaul marred a 27-2 regular-season effort, and even those disappointments were largely nullified by a No. 1 Premo Power Poll ranking at season's end, ahead of eventual NCAA champion Holy Cross. The talent was so deep at Lexington, in fact, that many of the season's scores were downright embarrassing: 83-18 (Texas A&M), 83-46 (Georgia Tech), 96-24 (Wabash), 82-30 (Vanderbilt), 86-36 (Michigan State), 98-29 (Vanderbilt again).

Yet this was already also something of a troubled Kentucky team. With so much talent available it was inevitable that several former starters — even a couple of former All-Americans — would now be doomed to ride the bench. Two former lettermen, Brannum and Jim Jordan (a wartime All-American at North Carolina before transferring to Lexington), received a special snub when they were both left off the final traveling squad for SEC tourney and NCAA postseason play. Brannum was so disturbed by this obvious (though perhaps unavoidable) slight from Rupp and his assistant Harry Lancaster that he made immediate plans to transfer over to Michigan State. The following winter Brannum would nearly gain some small measure of revenge on Rupp by outscoring Groza in East Lansing, thus keeping his otherwise overmatched team close in a game which Kentucky only eked out 47-45 with some tough defense down the stretch.

In the SEC tournament the Wild-cats breezed to victory by scores that bordered on ridiculous. It was evident enough that Brannum and Jordan weren't at all missed, nor was starting center Groza, who sat out most of the tournament competition with a bothersome back injury. Again the Kentucky team was so dominant that the SEC all-tourney team when announced consisted of the five Wildcat starters — Jones, Beard, Rollins, Tingle and Holland.

When the Ruppmen next returned to Madison Square Garden to defend their NIT crown the road seemed to get a bit sticky for the first time all year. Rupp had finally decided to scrap Jones' role as a backup to Groza and stick the former high school and freshman phenom back into the lineup at a starting forward slot. The ploy was a masterpiece of good

Ralph Beard was the backcourt ace of Rupp's 1948-49 "Fabulous Five" two-time NCAA national champions. Unfortunately, he was also one of Kentucky's most notorious point-shavers and a future NBA star whose career was ruined in the wake of the 1951 scandals. (University of Kentucky photo)

timing as Wah Wah's clutch outside jumper provided the needed margin against a tense opening-round challenge from LIU. Then came an equally gutsy survival against annoying slowdown techniques by coach Everett Case and his North Carolina State Wolfpack. Case knew that running teams like Kentucky could be handled, if not entirely stopped, by two types of execution: deliberate ball-control offense which kept the ball out of their hands, and aggressive offensive rebounding which disrupted the launching of their running game. In the latter stages of this snail's pace contest which Case's strategies dictated, however, the Rupp Wildcats soon regained their early and midseason composure and pulled away convincingly down the stretch.

But if the deliberate style employed by Everett Case was not able to thwart Rupp's juggernaut for long, the better-executed slowdown game next attempted by Utah unfortunately was. The well-schooled Utes worked their own brand of magic in the NIT Finals when guard Wat Misaka (a Utah native of Japanese parentage) shadowed Beard so relentlessly that he never scored a single field goal. This was the same Utah team of Arnie Ferrin, Misaka and coach Vadal Peterson that had been eliminated from the 1944 NIT at the hands of Rupp and company and then surprisingly made off with an NCAA crown only a week later. Utah was thus poised for its anticipated revenge against the Cats and was now able to extract it quite successfully with another painfully slow and deliberate game plan. The final score was 49-45, Utah, and Vern Gardner of the Utes was the leading scorer (15 points) and the tournament MVP.

If Rupp took away anything from such losses he certainly learned quickly the rude lessons that they inflicted. His 1948 Kentucky team would never be thwarted in any remotely similar fashion. By the 12th game of the 1947-48 campaign the Baron had begrudgingly concluded his two-year experiment of shuffling lineups; now for the first time he patched together the playing combination that from this point forward would be known as his "Fabulous Five" contingent. It was truly a dominating quintet and one capable (quite literally, as it turned out) of running away from its opposition from the earliest weeks of the season down to the closing championship games.

The biggest test for the Fabulous Five lineup of juniors Groza, Beard, Barker, Jones and senior Rollins would wait for the second-round NCAA semifinal matchup with defending champion Holy Cross. The Doggie Julian-coached team from Worcester had its own pair of All-Americans in 6-3 center-forward George Kaftan and passing wizard Bob Cousy. A year previous, with Kaftan only a sophomore and Cousy a wet-behind-the-ears freshman, the Cinderella Crusaders (27-3) had upset Oklahoma for the national title; now they were back every bit as strong (26-4) and favored in most quarters to repeat. Ken Rollins, the elder statesman of the crack Kentucky unit, drew the assignment of guarding Cousy and was able to hold the magician guard and leading scorer to just five points. Cousy, amazingly, never did register a single field goal as long as Rollins was still in the game. Groza was equally effective in his head-to-head and toe-to-toe inside matchup with Kaftan, winning the individual shootout 23-15 and the game itself, 60-52.

The eight-point victory over Holy Cross set up a title match with Baylor (24-7 and coached by Bill Henderson) that provided an easy enough outing and also proved more than just a little anticlimactic. Groza (14) and Beard (12) shared the scoring honors in the Madison Square Garden title affair. But there was little real drama; Baylor failed to score at all in the opening five minutes, then fell well off the pace, 29-16, by halftime, and in the end mounted only a brief rally early in the second half before giving up the struggle. The 58-42 cakewalk meant that Baron Rupp — already acknowledged master of Dixie and of SEC country — now also owned the biggest postseason prize as well.

The Fabulous Five label attached by first press and then fans to the great Kentucky team at the end of the 1940s was — as any such labels often are — something of a considerable misnomer. Rupp's team was hardly an exclusive five-man unit. No fast-breaking team could afford to be without plenty of fresh substitute legs. There was indeed enough depth here for a couple of national title challengers. Holland,

Barnstable, Line and Stough all saw considerable playing time in relief of the five starters. When Holland and Rollins used up their NCAA eligibility at the end of the 1948 campaign, 6-2 forward Dale Barnstable would actually become the fifth starter for the following season.

What was perhaps the pinnacle of so many great Kentucky basketball seasons was not quite over even when the curtain rang down on the NCAA title blowout of helpless Baylor. It was an Olympic year in 1948 and the USA squad for the upcoming summer games in London was to be determined by a New York round robin tournament featuring the pro-level AAU champion, the Phillips (Oklahoma) Oilers, along with college squads from Kentucky (NCAA champs), Louisville (NAIA champs), and Baylor (NCAA runner-up, selected to replace NIT winner Saint Louis when the Billikens declined an invitation). Still-dominant Bob Kurland, two years past his college curtain call, would prove enough to lead the Oilers to a rugged 53-49 victory over Rupp's team in the final playoff match; the 7-footer canned 20 points and held Groza to only four. At the end of tourney play a final Olympic squad was chosen (by formal ballot of the Olympic Selection Committee) and consisted of only 10 men — the starting fives of both the AAU Oilers and the NCAA Kentucky Wildcats. Oiler coach Bud Browning was named pro forma as the head Olympic coach, with the embarrassed Rupp having to settle for a slot as Browning's top assistant. In the end the makeup of the team seemed to matter very little, however, as the USA Olympic squad continued its international domination by crushing France 65-21 in the gold medal finals.

The 1948 Kentucky starting five had now added even further luster to their personal and collective reputations as one half of the nation's triumphant entrant in the 1948 Olympics. And after leaving Lexington, the same unit (Groza, Beard, Jones, Barker and nonstarter Joe Holland) would also test the pro ranks together. They would sign on as players and part-owners of the aptly named Indianapolis Olympians entrant during first-year competition in the newborn National Basketball Association (an unwieldy 17-team circuit just formed by merger of the dozen-year-old NBL and three-year-old BAA). It would eventually prove to be a short-lived career in the pros for Groza and Beard, of course, one that would last only two seasons before the college point-shaving scandals broke around their heads in late '51. And of course the reasons for their early departure from the newly popular pro league would soon enough thoroughly shock the entire basketball world and grab the attention of sports fans and non-fans alike from Toledo to Timbuktu.

But it would be a while yet before the world would know anything about the treachery that had long been secretly brewing in Rupp's own private backyard. Kentucky would therefore repeat its NCAA postseason victory in 1949 as well as finishing atop the "official" national rankings in the first season of the newly instituted Associated Press sportswriters poll. None of this was at all surprising with four of the Fabulous Five back for one final fling at national glory. The powerhouse team which now featured Dale Barnstable in the starting lineup in place of Ken Rollins again swept through a regular season schedule and a postseason SEC tourney with embarrassingly little opposition. There would be only two losses all season — a heartbreaker to Saint Louis University in the December Sugar Bowl finals, and a dream-crusher to unheralded Loyola-Chicago at the outset of the year-end NIT — and both of these would later turn out to be of highly suspicious origin.

Now coach Rupp had a new challenge in mind as he set out to accomplish something no program had yet accomplished — postseason triumphs in both the NCAA and NIT playdowns. It would indeed be a fitting final jewel for the already top-heavy crown of his Fabulous Five "dream" team. But it wouldn't happen, despite the marvelous lineup, the clear path straight into both postseason events, and the seeming increased dedication of both a mastermind coach and his unparalleled players.

The plan for double national championships came to a sudden halt even before it got off the ground with the shocking loss that opened the NIT quarterfinals. In a year of huge NIT surprises, all four seeded teams were rudely bumped in their opening quarterfinal matches. Bradley stung Ohio Valley champion Western Kentucky and its hotshot Bob Lavoy; eventual winner San Francisco stunned Utah by a single point; and Bowling Green thumped a Saint Louis University team that still featured "Easy Ed" Macauley. In the biggest eye-opener of all, however, the Wildcats were also booted from the NIT field by Loyola-Chicago, when unheralded Jack Kerris dominated Groza inside and outscored the All-American 23-12. The full impact of that game would not become apparent for nearly two more years. Rupp could only be more saddened with the loss of his dual-championship dream when he eventually learned the real reasons why his talented charges had not taken home an expected NIT title.

But there was still something to be salvaged and thus the temporarily embarrassed Cats would quickly bounce back to business as usual when NCAA play opened the following week. First Villanova with Paul Arizin was dispatched as Groza canned 30 in a one-sided 85-72 win. Then Illinois, the Big Ten champion, fell as well by a lopsided 76-47 count as Groza (with a game-high 27) and Beard overwhelmed Bill Erickson and Dwight Eddleman. The title game in Seattle would thus match the Cats against Henry Iba's Oklahoma A&M Cowboys, now several seasons beyond Kurland but still the only school ever to successfully defend its NCAA title. This time there would be no stumbling and Groza did the bulk of the scoring (25 points) in his final collegiate game. The final was a 10-point victory (46-36) for the Rupp team that had been universally expected to take two titles but had now come away with only one. The consolation prize was the fact that Kentucky had joined Oklahoma A&M in the record books with only the second-ever repeat of an NCAA championship.

1950 would be the year that a genuine Cinderella — the CCNY Beavers coached by the "Original Celtic" Nat Holman — would emerge out of the East to dominate the entire national scene. But back in the fall of that year the defending NCAA champs still looked very much like the team everyone would have to beat. Despite the loss of the final 80 percent of his original Fabulous Five lineup, Rupp still had enough talent on hand to win most games almost without trying; thus the perennial SEC champions romped through another 25-4 season and remained third in the AP polls from wire to wire.

North Carolina State (at 26-5) nonetheless got the NCAA invitation from the Southeast Regional this time around, while the NIT was quick to snap up the Bluegrass team that was still one of the nation's top draws. While Rupp's Wildcats had every reason to expect further postseason success with 7-foot sophomore center Bill Spivey now showing the way, Rupp was apprehensive and with good reason. The Ruppmen sat out the opening round with a bye and then were mercilessly routed 89-50 by Nat Holman's team in the quarterfinals. It was without question the most devastating and humiliating loss of Rupp's career, and he wryly and publicly thanked his team at season's end for both earning him the Metropolitan Basketball Writers' coach of the year award and also clearly embarrassing the hell out of him at season's end.

But there would be bigger disasters for Rupp and his program before the next year and a half was out. When the point-shaving scandals broke across the face of college basketball early in 1951 it was not immediately apparent that the Baron's prestigious program was in any manner involved. The Cats with their relentless winning hardly seemed like a team that was not fully trying. But soon the taint did indeed reach all the way from New York into the heart of Bluegrass country. Kentucky players had apparently attempted to shave points during the mysterious 1949 61-56 NIT loss against Loyola (a revelation providing answers to one riddle even if it now posed others) and perhaps also in dozens of other games in New York and Lexington as well. Only weeks before any Kentucky players had been implicated the Baron had piously boasted that his own athletes were absolutely beyond the slightest hint of corruption. "Gamblers couldn't touch my boys with a 10-foot pole," the Baron had prematurely boasted to the press back in August.

But then Beard, Groza, Barnstable, Line and Hirsch were all charged with conspiring to control game scores. Beard, Groza and Barnstable for their part admitted having accepted $3,500 in payoffs to keep scores close in both the March 1949 Loyola game and the Tennessee game (a 71-56 Kentucky victory) in Lexington a month earlier. The Sugar Bowl loss to Saint Louis had apparently also been the result of a bungled effort by the same trio to maintain the presumed Kentucky victory margin within the posted spread. Before the investigation ran its course, just about every game the Ruppmen had played over the past two seasons came under serious suspicion.

As the biggest, baddest and most boastful bully on the college block the Ruppmen were a perfect target for the heaviest backlash induced by the breaking tempest. New York General Sessions Judge Saul Streit who in October 1951 handed down lengthy probations to three ex-Wildcats (Groza, Beard and Barnstable) subsequently also released a scathing 63-page report blasting the entire Kentucky athletic program. The judge assessed Kentucky athletics as being "the acme of commercialism and over-emphasis" and then detailed Rupp's own admissions that he himself had known bookmaker Ed Curd and had often inquired about point spreads on the Kentucky games. Rupp had firmly denied betting or any other wrongdoing but still failed to escape the judge's wrath. Streit concluded that both Rupp and the university "must share the full responsibility" for the plight of former players now facing ruined careers as a result of their foolhardy and illegal actions.

It was, of course, a remarkable if backhanded tribute to the less-than-honest Kentucky starters that they could maintain such dominance over the teams on their schedule and yet control game scores for profit as well. When the scandal finally did embroil his own players Rupp pleaded that his student-athletes should be treated leniently since they only fixed final scores. But this self-serving and face-saving plea rang quite hollow, since mighty Kentucky had apparently actually given the game away with their shenanigans during the botched 1949 NIT match against Loyola.

During the course of the 1950-51 season the full extent of Kentucky's involvement in the unfolding scandal was still not known, of course. Thus the team made up of juniors Spivey, Shelby Linville and Bobby Watson, and sophomores Frank Ramsey, Cliff Hagan and Lou Tsioropoulos bounced back to the top almost without skipping a beat. And they did so with a small bit of help along the way. A new rule allowed Kentucky (with the best regular-season's record) to represent the Southeastern Conference in the NCAA tourney despite a 61-57 loss in the conference tournament finals to Vanderbilt. The only other setback over the course of the long campaign had been yet another frustrating two-pointer to Saint Louis in the New Year's Sugar Bowl event.

Given new life, the Rupp team again proved unbeatable down the March home stretch. Only Illinois offered anything approaching a stern test and that came during the Eastern Regional finals at Madison Square Garden. The day was ultimately saved by Spivey who turned in a remarkable effort with 28 points and 16 rebounds, but not without large assists as well from Linville, with a clutch 14-point second half, and substitute C.M. Newton, with a crucial late-game steal.

This was still the era when Eastern and Western regional finals at separate ends of the country determined the matchup for the national championship at yet a third neutral location. A 68-44 Kansas State rout of Oklahoma A&M in Kansas City and Kentucky's 76-74 squeaker against Illinois provided the final showdown in Minneapolis. The No. 1-ranked Wildcats from Lexington were only slim pregame favorites over the fourth-ranked Wildcats from Manhattan, Kansas, and in the early going Kansas State did indeed appear to hold the edge as 6-8 Lew Hitch outplayed Spivey, and Rupp's outstanding sparkplug and sixth man Cliff Hagan appeared to be under the weather and thus considerably subpar. But things turned around in a hurry in the second half when Spivey responded to a Rupp tongue-lashing in the halftime locker room and began to dominate during the second stanza. The 7-footer corralled 21 boards and stuffed home 22 points before it was over to secure the comfortable 68-58 victory. Spivey all told had grabbed 55 rebounds in the four games of the tournament and thus won the coveted MVP honor. But more importantly, Rupp and Kentucky now owned a unique piece of NCAA history as the first three-time postseason champions.

Spivey looked for all the world by the end of the 1951 season to be next in line for true Kentucky-bred stardom. Rupp had even intimated to the press that his new towering junior sensation might well be even better than the incomparable Groza. But the big center would unfortunately follow all-too-closely in the precise footsteps of his predecessor Alex Groza. It would not be long at all before a second wave of scandal made Bill Spivey its next victim; the hero of the 1951 NCAAs was now also called to New York to face a grand jury as the investigations into wrongdoing continued to boil.

In the end Spivey was never proven guilty of accepting any bribes and he even passed a lie detector test on the issue; but he was nonetheless tried along with his former teammates on the point-shaving charges and his fate was a hung jury (which reportedly stood 9-3 for acquittal). It was clear by his own admissions that he had been approached by gamblers and that he had known of his teammates' involvements; thus his singular sin remained that he had let the matter pass unreported. For that transgression he too would pay the same terrible price of a ruined pro career. The school would drop him (its athletic board suspended his remaining eligibility more than a month before his New York trial), the NBA would quickly ban him (the Cincinnati Royals actually signed him and then withdrew the contract when other league members objected), and the curse of Alex Groza thus descended heavily on the head of Bill Spivey as well.

While Groza, Beard and Spivey (along with Barnstable, Hirsch and Line) suffered the harshest consequences from their own regrettable lapses in judgment, other teammates and the wider Kentucky basketball community as a whole suffered to somewhat lesser degrees. Kentucky's 1951 national title would thus be followed by immediate hard times in Lexington. The 1952 team would finish an impressive 29-3 behind rapidly improving juniors Cliff Hagan (21.6 ppg) and Frank Ramsey (15.9). Already the new trio of Hagan, Ramsey and Tsioropoulos were spectacular enough to wash away memories of the now disgraced Groza, Beard and Spivey. After early season losses to Minnesota and Saint Louis (the third time in four years) a winning streak began that would stretch to 23 before ending abruptly in the East Regional of the NCAA. A St. John's club which the Cats mauled by 41 earlier in the winter put a sudden cap on the season with a seven-point upset in Raleigh.

More crippling defeats for Hagan, Ramsey, Tsioropoulos and the Bluegrass fans would now transpire away from the hardwood and in courts of a far different ilk. Investigations of Rupp's program would quickly expand far beyond the point-fixing charges; Judge Streit's slap on the wrist now mushroomed into a savage blow to the midsection. Kentucky would be banned from the 1953 Southeastern Conference season and from NCAA play at large for a series of "minor transgressions" (mostly involving players' travel money and recruiting and academic irregularities) that had been uncovered when the betting scandals had spurred a full-scale investigation of Kentucky's athletic housekeeping. The biggest sin had apparently been fifty dollars or more in extra cash for meal money doled out to Wildcat players during recent December Sugar Bowl trips. Rupp clearly knew about the infractions but considered them minor stuff indeed and had shrugged them off as standard operating procedure. But Kentucky had been the glamour team of the past several seasons and now it would provide a convenient scapegoat as the college sport hurried to cover its shame and patch up some of its most glaring wounds.

In Kentucky's 1952-53 absence a new star would overnight emerge in the Deep South as junior Bob Pettit paced Louisiana State to it first-ever outright SEC league title and its first NCAA Tournament bid. LSU's perfect league record under coach Harry Rabenhorst marked the end to an eight-year Wildcat domination of the Southland's strongest conference. And on the national level veteran Phog Allen's Kansas team had now emerged out of the Big Seven as the new national powerhouse

Cliff Hagan was the linchpin of Rupp's greatest team ever which emerged in the wake of the 1951 scandals. The unit of Hagan, Frank Ramsey and Lou Tsioropoulos sat out the 1953 season on probation, then ran through the 1954 campaign undefeated only again to sit out the NCAA Tournament when the trio had used up their elgibility. (University of Kentucky photo)

and heir apparent to Rupp's recent throne. In 1952 the Jayhawks had ridden the scoring and rebounding of huge Clyde Lovellette to a national title with their 80-63 cakewalk over St. John's (the very team that had earlier ousted Kentucky) in the championship shootout. The big story of the year was not only the Kansas NCAA crown, Allen's very first in the twilight of a glorious hall of fame career, but also Lovellette's unique double. By averaging 28.4 points per game and lifting the Jayhawks past St. John's, the powerhouse 6-9 post player out of Terre Haute, Indiana, had done something that no one else has ever managed before or since — winning a national scoring title and an NCAA championship in the same season. A year later, and without Lovellette, Kansas would be back to defend its NCAA title but would fall to Indiana by a single point in another barn-burning final.

After stumbling at year's end in 1952 and sitting helpless on the sidelines in 1953, Rupp's charges would soon enough be back to take their revenge on the rest of the nation's best collegiate fives. But there would be plenty of roadblocks to avoid and challenges to surmount along the way. The 1951 national title run would not be duplicated by Rupp's program for the next half-dozen seasons. By 1958 the Wildcats would surprise even Rupp, however, as the soon-to-be legendary "Fiddlin' Five" unit would overcome the most Kentucky losses in 13 seasons (six) to roar down the stretch for Rupp's fourth NCAA title. Of course it also must be remembered that one of the greatest of all Rupp teams came along in the troubled interval that separated the 1951 and 1958 NCAA title winners. This was a 1954 powerhouse club that ran through its schedule undefeated and then sat on the sidelines while Tom Gola and La Salle (a team it had beaten soundly in December) slugged it out with Bradley for the national title. The resurrected '54 club that had emerged from the cocoon of NCAA sanctions may indeed have been — by almost any imaginable measure — the best unit Rupp ever fielded.

The most glaring and severe fallout of the 1952 betting scandal had been the cancellation of Kentucky's full 1952-53 schedule. Hagan and Ramsey and Tsioropoulos were without doubt the best threesome in the country. But they had nothing to do now but sit bitterly on the sidelines, attend to their academic affairs while informally working out behind closed gym doors in an effort to maintain competitive conditioning, and quietly prepare for a season of anticipated vengeance in 1954. When that season finally came, the uncaged Wildcats were still good enough to manhandle any and all opposition the rest of the country had to offer. Xavier stayed within six points in the eighth game of the winter but no one else all year got any closer than a dozen.

Yet one final sting of the sanctions against Rupp's team still had to be played out and would be perhaps the most bitter slap of all. When March rang down the curtain on a perfect 25-0 season the trio of Wildcat stars had now used up their final eligibility and could not take the floor for any postseason play. While they had been allowed to postpone senior-year eligibility from 1952 to 1953, the fact that they had done so meant that Hagan, Ramsey and Tsioropoulos had all accumulated more than enough academic credits for graduation and were now already enrolled in graduate school. The very best of Rupp's outfits would never now be able to demonstrate in championship play just how good they actually were.

Of course the Wildcats had already proven their point and staked their claim earlier in the year by easily handling Tom Gola and the future NCAA winner from La Salle 73-60 in the UK Invitational. The Baron and his men had little choice now but to sit out the tourney rather than taint their spectacular season by tackling tournament play with a team of untested understudies filling the lineup.

The 1958 NCAA title represented Rupp's fourth and final trip to the pinnacle. And this last championship for the Baron would come with a team destined to be remembered far more for balance and overachievement than for any individual superstars. The contingent of Vern Hatton, Johnny Cox, John Crigler, Adrian Smith and Ed Beck caught fire when the NCAA bell sounded yet didn't boast a single SEC all-conference choice anywhere in the lineup. And Rupp's final successful title chase would also be played out on a stage where Kentucky would ultimately have to share the main spotlight with several memorable performances by other teams and especially by other legendary individual players. For this was also the year of the fabulous Elgin Baylor, who carried an otherwise very average Seattle team on his broad shoulders all the way into the season's final game. It was the year as well of back-court wizard Guy Rodgers and an underdog Temple team that almost grabbed the national headlines (losing to the Ruppmen by a mere point in the NCAA semis) yet in the end settled for a third consecutive consolation prize. And above all else it was the year that Jerry West and his longtime bridesmaid West Virginia Mountaineers were somehow robbed of a deserved national title seemingly only by a strange 11th-hour twist of fate.

West Virginia had stood atop the national polls throughout the year, barely nipping Cincinnati and its great sophomore star Oscar Robertson in the final round of AP balloting. The two Midwest teams led by their sophomore aces thus seemed bound on a collision course to meet somewhere in postseason, perhaps even to decide the national title. Roberston was grabbing the bulk of the headlines as the first sophomore ever to lead the nation in scoring; the "Big O" burned the nets for better than 35 a game, a pace which allowed him to maintain a safe lead on both Seattle's Elgin Baylor (32.5) and also Wilt Chamberlain (30.1), who was struggling through a second year of battling gang defenses at Kansas. West didn't score as much as Oscar or the other big point-makers during his first varsity year (17.8 ppg), but he nonetheless anchored a balanced West Virginia team that looked for much of the season like the best in the land.

But then West Virginia ran into unexpected disaster as the season wound down. In the Southern Conference Tournament the luckless Mountaineers suffered a severe blow when captain Don Vincent broke his leg. The team that had defeated eventual NCAA champ Kentucky in Lexington by seven points earlier in the season was now no longer the same team. In a shocking upset, West and his Mountaineers were gunned down by lowly Manhattan in the very first round of the East Regional. The Jaspars for their part had lost 10 times during the regular season against far lesser competition. In their surprising victory over the nation's top club they were led by Jack Powers (today's executive director of the NIT) who drilled 29 points and also collected 15 rebounds along the way. But if the Mountaineers were done in by the absence of Don Vincent, they were also equally stymied when the sensational West was held to a mere 10 points in his initial postseason appearance.

Robertson and Chamberlain were just as quickly eliminated from the postseason contention. Cincinnati fell against Kansas State in regional semifinal action. Kansas State, by winning the Big Seven, had earlier also blocked the path for Chamberlain and his Jayhawks who were attempting to get back to the NCAA Finals where they had lost such a heartbreaker a year earlier. But while all these other teams with superstar scorers fell by the wayside, tiny Seattle and Elgin Baylor simply would not be denied. The Chieftains marched through Western rivals Wyoming, San Francisco and California on their way to joining Kansas State, Temple and Kentucky in the vaunted Final Four. And Baylor was magnificent at every turn along the way.

When he left school in 1964, Cotton Nash was Kentucky's all-time leading scorer resulting in his No. 44 joining the long list of retired Kentucky numbers. Nash's record has since been surpassed by Dan Issel, Kenny Walker, Jack Givens, Jamal Mashburn and Kevin Grevey. (University of Kentucky photo)

Seattle would have an easy time of it with Kansas State in the national semifinals (to the tune of 73-51). All-American and future NBAer Bob Boozer was no match at all for Baylor — the Chieftains' one-man gang won the individual scoring matchup 23-15 and also outdistanced the K-State All-American 22-4 on the boards. Kentucky, meanwhile, didn't have it quite so easy. The Wildcats escaped with their lives (and a simple single-point victory) against the magical Guy Rodgers and the surprising Temple Owls. This was the team that Rupp had early in the season termed his "Fiddlin' Five" for their tendency (in Rupp's own words) to keep "fiddlin' around and fiddlin' around then finally pulling it out at the end." And now more than ever they lived up once more to that caustic appraisal when they pulled off one of the most miraculous rallies of tourney lore in the final two minutes of the national semifinal game.

In the end, this 1958 Kentucky outfit featuring double-figure scorers Vern Hatton, Johnny Cox, John Crigler and Adrian Smith was perhaps as lucky as it was good. First off, the Wildcats had fate and the schedule makers on their side as they enjoyed a distinct "homecourt advantage" throughout the full tournament. They battled through a Mideast Regional on their own floor in Lexington. And in the Final Four itself they also enjoyed a friendly crowd backing on their home-state turf a few miles up the road in Louisville. If nothing else, the Kentucky-loyal crowd certainly seemed to give Baron Rupp's boys a huge lift in that strong comeback against Rodgers-led Temple during the closing moments of the semis.

Then in the finals the Wildcats seemed to get a bit lucky once again. Elgin Baylor who had been so superior throughout the tourney finally seemed to run out of gas and experienced an off-night in the finals versus Kentucky. Elgin drew three quick fouls and was thereafter ineffective on defense and on the boards; his offensive game also became tentative and he could hit only nine of 32 shots from the floor. But despite his nightmarish night the marvelous Baylor poured in 25 nonetheless and kept his team close in his individual battle with Wildcats Vern Hatton (30 points) and Johnny Cox (24 points). The final margin was only a dozen points (84-72) and Baylor and his crew had actually led at halftime. But the overall Kentucky superiority was enough to make Rupp the first-ever four-time tourney winner.

Although Rupp would not formally retire until the end of the 1972 campaign, on the heals of a fifth straight SEC title and 876 career victories, it would be the 1966 season in reality that would sound something of a glorious death-knell for the Rupp era in Lexington. The Baron would make five more trips back to the postseason fray. But never again would he advance past the second round. The 1966 title match would be the last climb all the way up the postseason ladder. And what a truly eventful swan song it would prove to be.

The 1966 Kentucky team was also Rupp's last true powerhouse outfit. And for much of the year they looked headed for another national title, running off 23 victories in a row and not tasting defeat until March, when they dropped the season's penultimate game on the road at Tennessee. This was again a relatively small Kentucky team when it came to overall height. In fact the club was so small that it earned the deserved press handle of "Rupp's Runts" with no starter over 6-5 and guard Tommy Kron the tallest man in the lineup. And it was again also a team with far more balance than superstar appeal. But it was a team that rolled through the Southeastern Conference wars nonetheless and sat atop the national polls at season's end, the first Kentucky squad to boast that honor since the stay-at-home Hagan-Ramsey-Tsioropoulos crew a dozen years earlier.

The scoring and emotional leaders were 6-0 guard Louie Dampier (21.1 ppg) and versatile Pat Riley (22.0), a 6-3 forward. Dampier would soon go on to ABA scoring fame as that short-lived circuit's all-time career leader (13,775 points) and one of only three players to complete all nine league seasons. And Riley would of course enjoy considerable NBA fame two decades later as coach of the "Showtime Lakers" of Magic Johnson and Kareem Abdul-Jabbar, and later the New York Knicks and Miami Heat. Back in 1966, however, both Dampier and Riley were hard-nosed scrappers cut in Rupp's finest tradition.

The 1966 NCAA title clash between 27-1 Kentucky and 27-1 Texas Western was one of the most surprising matchups in NCAA history. In recent years UCLA and John Wooden had grabbed hold of the national scene. And the Bruins were indeed far from done, with their string of seven straight national titles sitting just around the next corner. But the 1966 season was one in which the year-end race had been thrown wide open, with the mighty Bruins sitting out a year licking their wounds and waiting for their sensational freshman Lew Alcindor to graduate to the varsity. And an unaffiliated team of seeming unknown interlopers under coach Don Haskins (also less than a household name) took full advantage.

While Rupp's Wildcats (with five white starters) and Haskins' Miners (with an all-black lineup) were a stark contrast in color, they were indeed not all that different in numerous other respects. Texas Western was also a small and scrappy outfit with three of the Miners starters checking in at 6-1 or shorter. Scoring leader Bobby Joe Hill, at 5-10, was indeed the smallest player ever to pace an NCAA championship team in yearlong scoring. But if small in physical stature, Hill stepped up big in game action as he doubled his career scoring average during the five tournament games.

Texas Western was also a near carbon copy of Kentucky in another respect as well. This was a well-coached and highly disciplined team that totally belied the false notion that black athletes couldn't play a disciplined brand of ball and could only freelance in the loose playground style. Haskins, it turned out, was a taskmaster and stern teacher every bit the equal of Rupp. In one telling incident early in the postseason, Miners star forward-center Nevil Shed was forced to find his own transportation back to the team hotel after Haskins refused to let him board the team bus on the heels of his ejection from a close 78-76 overtime victory over Cincinnati in the second round. Haskins' Miners didn't boast a conference championship (they were an independent) and they hadn't beaten a Top 10 team during the entire season. But the fifth-year coach had them ready for any postseason challenge that might come their way.

Junior college transfer Hill turned the tide against Kentucky in the first half of the title game in Maryland's Cole Field House. Hill worked his magic with consecutive steals off befuddled Wildcat guards Kron and Dampier, and the resulting easy layups sent the Ruppmen into a tailspin from which they never fully recovered. Texas Western surprised the national television audience and shot holes in the prevailing prejudices of the day (as well as in the Kentucky defense) as they unveiled a disciplined team game down the stretch and held on for a thrilling 72-65 upset victory. An aggressive Miners defense would limit Rupp's crack team to less than 40 percent shooting for the first time all season. The game in the end was won on the free-throw line, however, where the Miners calmly sank 28 of 34 down the vital stretch run.

The storied matchup between Texas Western and Kentucky at the height of the turbulent '60s was a landmark moment in college basketball history and American sports history as well. This was the first time that an all-black team (comprised of Hill, Shed, David Lattin, Orsten Artis and Harry Flournoy) had started the NCAA tourney's prestigious final game. The significance of the moment was underscored by two factors — Kentucky's opposing five was all white, and the nation at the time was embroiled in a sea of long-latent racial tensions. The white Haskins (who had himself played for Hank Iba at Oklahoma State) soon received a flood of hate mail from fans who had witnessed and not approved of the miraculous racial transition marked by the national championship game. The hate mail stunned Haskins who had never thought for a moment of anything but playing his five best athletes, and re-cruiting the very best players of any race or creed that he could possibly locate. But there was also a positive effect of the symbolic racial clash that had been played out on national television in Cole Field House and had stirred such a regrettable fan backlash. From this point on, the Southern coaches, including Rupp, now also started recruiting black players for their own programs.

The fallout from the surprising Texas Western NCAA victory was in the long run most unpleasant on an entirely different front. It would soon become public knowledge that while blazing important athletic and social trails in one direction, Haskins and his El Paso program had also been in the forefront of another not so admirable trend regarding black athletic recruitment. Haskins' players had landed a priceless basketball championship for their school (certainly the prestigious title meant, at the very least, expanded profits from alumni contributions and future game ticket sales), but they themselves would never receive either college degrees or any other obvious career/life compensation for their valiant and valuable efforts.

Once basketball eligibility was used up, players were hustled out the door with neither sheepskin nor much classroom experience to show for their visit. Two years down the road, in one of the most famous articles ever to appear in the pages of the nation's best-known sports publication, *Sports Illustrated* staff writer Jack Olsen penned a biting expose concerning the plight of black athletes in American colleges. It was an essay that would lay bare the shame of the Texas Western recruiting pro-gram as one of the prime cases in point. And most unfortunately, the El Paso abuses — despite such public outcries from the press — were only the start of an infectious trend which would continue (and continue to raise controversy) right down to the present decade.

Birthrights of African Handball

The 1966 NCAA title game was perhaps the most symbolic in collegiate bas-ketball history. It was a contest that involved far more than turf warfare between two national powerhouse teams. It was, in reality, two distinct eras — the game's fading past and its foreboding future — that were clashing here. Also two competing styles and concepts of the game and how it might best be played. The white-dominated "country" game of the Midwest now locked horns for the first time, and on the highest levels of competition, with the black inner-city game (ironically here trans-ported all the way to Texas). And the results were indeed cataclysmic.

Texas Western was not the first black-dominated team with inner-city players to take the national title. The first inroads for this new version of "the city game" came with Bill Russell and the San Francisco Dons a full decade earlier. It was the beginning of a trend which now saw small urban colleges (especially Catholic schools) recruit inner-city black players as a regular matter of course. San Francisco had first worked the formula to a tee when Woolpert stacked his roster with Russell, K.C. Jones and Hal Perry. Next came Loyola of Chicago in the early '60s, with coach George Ireland riding a lineup of four black starters to a third-place NIT finish in 1962, and then to 29 victories and a surprise visit to the NCAA Final Four in 1963.

The Ramblers struck a major blow for both basketball and social justice when they tumbled the defending champion Cincinnati Bearcats — with their own contingent of predominately black stars — to earn a 1963 national title. Loyola traveled into the South in both 1962 and 1963, and its players had been forced into separate "black only" hotels in both New Orleans and Houston. Coach Ireland's posturing about the treatment of his players on these road trips not only stoked the fires of the integration movement then sweeping the land but focussed attention on his own rapidly improving basketball program as well.

Loyola's 1963 NCAA showdown with Mississippi State (which had boycotted the tournament only a year earlier rather than face teams with blacks) was a further signal that black teams and black players were now an accepted fixture on the college scene. The Ramblers won a hard-fought 61-51 victory over the SEC Bulldogs in the Mideast Regional and when Loyola captain Jerry Harkness and Mississippi State captain Joe Dan Gold shook hands before the game an important new milestone had been crossed. When Texas Western arrived in the winner's circle in 1966 this trend of the newly dominant black athlete was continued with a new wrinkle. The school itself was this time located far from the talent-rich playgrounds of the northern urban centers. But the roster of players clearly wasn't.

There would be many followers who would attempt to repeat the formula worked so successfully at USF, Loyola and Texas Western. Imitators would pop up around the country — at Duquesne, La Salle, Detroit, Villanova, St. John's and Boston College, among others. The nearest clone of USF or Loyola would turn up in Milwaukee in the mid- and late 1970s in the guise of Al McGuire's successful program at another Catholic urban school stocked with black players from the playgrounds of New York City. McGuire and Marquette spent most of the decade of the '70s challenging the supremacy of Wooden's UCLA juggernauts and they did so with McGuire's heavily black playground teams recruited from back East.

The collision between Rupp's still-white Kentucky team and the forces of an emerging black style was most prominent with the 1966 NCAA title game. But in reality these two antithetical versions of basketball had already stared each other down, eye to eye, eight full seasons earlier. It was then that another Rupp team had squared off against the first great proponent of the unfettered black style — Elgin Baylor of Seattle University — and the prize was the 1958 NCAA bragging rights.

Elgin Baylor certainly did not single-handedly invent the jazzy movements of ghetto basketball. Yet just as certainly no one did more to advertise them with his own virtuoso performances in front of the national sports media and legions of courtside fans. Baylor was thus the necessary popularizer if not the true founder of basketball's third dimension — space flight. In this capacity he was spiritual godfather to Julius Erving, Connie Hawkins, Joe Caldwell and the entire coming generation of high-flyers that would soon take over the college and pro courts in the late '60s and early '70s.

Oscar Robertston finished his career at Cincinnati a season before the Bearcats' three-year run to the NCAA title game. Yet the sensational play of the first-ever three-time national scoring champion would open the door on the recruitment of black athletes at colleges throughout the country. (University of Cincinnati photo)

Baylor was one of the half-dozen greatest players in collegiate history. If ever there was a player who deserved the tired cliche of "poetry in motion" it was Baylor; it was not Erving or Hawkins but rather Elgin Baylor who was first to earn the reputation of being a literal human flying machine. Here was the first "hangtime" artist who could seemingly remain endlessly suspended in flight and who could even change directions or radically alter his "moves" while still airborne around the basket.

Baylor had seemingly come out of nowhere when he arrived on the scene as the nation's third-leading scorer in 1957 and second-leading pointmaker a year later. By tournament time in '58 he was already one of the country's better-known stars despite playing for unheralded Seattle University, itself tucked far from mainstream college action. But the District of Columbia native was also an unlikely college hero. Although he drew some early notice at Washington's Spingarn High School, his shoddy academic record had blocked scholarship offers from major basketball schools. He had thus begun his collegiate career on a football scholarship at tiny College of

Idaho, transferring to Seattle when his first school suddenly dropped its athletic program. Later he would see his brilliant pro career — for all its achievements as the third 20,000-point-man in NBA annals — dogged and diminished by nagging injuries. But during several brief college seasons Baylor was as good and as colorful as anyone else ever was.

Baylor was thus one of a quartet of black stars of the late '50s (Russell, Robertson, Chamberlain were the others) who would shift the focus of college basketball dramatically. In the mid-50s the cage sport was still largely a purely white game in its racial makeup. When Don Barksdale earned All-America honors at UCLA in 1947 he was indeed a rare aberration on the American amateur sports scene. If Kurland and Mikan were deemed freaks on account of their size in the immediate post-war years, Barksdale and his famous UCLA forerunner Jackie Robinson (baseball's integrator and also the 1940 Pacific Coast Conference leading scorer) were freaks as well due to their skin tone. Only a decade later All-American teams would already be largely black, with the 1956 consensus team including Bill Russell, K.C. Jones, Willie Naulls and Sihugo Green, and the 1958 squad featuring Baylor, Chamberlain, Robertson and Guy Rodgers.

By the early 1970s basketball would already be perceived as largely a black man's game — certainly in style and ethos as well as in its player population — and this notion of basketball being as black as soul food and the blues remains the reigning view of today's fans and commentators. A most miraculous transformation had taken place between Russell and Baylor in the mid-50s and Julius Erving and an endless host of college, ABA and NBA slam dunkers of the early '70s. If basketball heroes of the '30s and '40s had been all whites like Hank Luisetti, Tony Lavelli, Bob Cousy, George Mikan, Bob Kurland and Paul Arizin, any hoops history of the late '50s already revealed a distinct black presence — the headline grabbers were now Chamberlain, Russell, Oscar and Elgin Baylor. Above all the others, however, it was Baylor whose style earliest and best brought the city playground game firmly into the national consciousness.

Black hoops grew out of freelance playing styles native to the urban school yards and the inner city playgrounds. It was a survivors' game of improvised feints and fakes, thundering self-expressive acrobatic dunks and intimidating one-on-one personal "moves" to the hoop. With these weapons inner-city youngsters battled for personal "reps" and for rare momentary feelings of individual freedom which came from soaring above or slipping around a face-to-face adversary. In this new style of playground basketball "deception" thus became a vital key to success; for youngsters battling for daily survival on ghetto streets basketball was in fact a unique escapist world in which the weapon of deception was for the first time a legitimate accepted strategy and not a guaranteed source of further trouble. Basketball — playground style — was thus also a game that was far more instinctual than it was scientific.

One astute author has captured this difference in cage playing styles with a concise definition and an instructive list of representative "white-white" and "black-black" professional ballplayers, set alongside a list of "white-black" and "black-white" pro stars also from the mid-70s era. For Jeff Greenfield, writing in 1975 in

Esquire magazine, the difference between alternative playing styles was a matter of interplay between cultural attitude and basketball's imposing spacial limitations. "Black" playing style involves utilizing superior athletic skills to adapt to and even overcome the cramped quarters of the basketball floor; "white" style is instead a matter of "pulverizing that space" with sheer practiced intensity.

Jeff Greenfield's "Black & White" Guide to Basketball Styles

Black "Black" Playing Style	White "White" Playing Style
Julius Erving, F (UMass, New York Nets)	John Havlicek, F (Ohio State, Boston Celtics)
Connie Hawkins, F (Los Angeles Lakers)	Mike Riordan, F (Providence, Washington Bullets)
Bob McAdoo, C (UNC, Buffalo Braves)	Sven Nater, C (UCLA, New York Nets)
Nate Archibald, G (Texas-El Paso, Omaha Kings)	Jerry Sloan, G (Evansville, Chicago Bulls)
Earl Monroe, G (Winston-Salem, NY Knicks)	Dave Twardzik, G (Old Dominion, Virg. Squires)

Black "White" Playing Style	White "Black" Playing Style
Paul Silas, F (Creighton, Boston Celtics)	Rick Barry, F (Miami, Golden State Warriors)
Bill Bridges, F (Kansas, Golden State Warriors)	Billy Cunningham, F (UNC, Philadelphia 76ers)
Nate Thurmond, C (Bowling Green, Chicago Bulls)	Dave Cowens, C (Florida State, Boston Celtics)
Norm Van Lier, G (St. Francis, Chicago Bulls)	Pete Maravich, G (LSU, New Orleans Jazz)
Jim McMillan, F-G (Columbia, Buffalo Braves)	Paul Westphal, G (USC, Phoenix Suns)

Instinctive body control and superb "moves" around the basket are the hallmark of the playground ballplayer, and this is the essence of a "black" playing style, whether it is adopted by an athlete of black or white skin pigment. It is a matter of rhythm and timing and the constant improvised flow of the sport and it is acquired perhaps more through instinct than training. If this "black" game is most often played by ghetto kids on glass-littered playground courts, its "white" counterpart is the Midwestern version found in farmyards and suburban driveways with backboards nailed neatly over garage doors. In Greenfield's terminology this "white" game is "ragged, sweaty, stumbling and intense" — while "black" players (we are here talking culture and not race) rely on mounting all obstacles with finesse and pure athletic grace, "white" players react by outrunning and overpowering each and every obstacle.

Greenfield provides a set of instructive hypothetical black and white teams (based on the basketball world of 1975). His lists are intended to categorize the interplay of race with athletic style, and they were also designed to demonstrate that the "black" style of play was not in the end restricted to an athlete's gene pool. There are whites who play with a distinctively "black" style (today's NBA world would offer Larry Bird or Tom Gugliotta or Rex Chapman as prime examples); there are also black ballplayers whose game is more "white" than "black" (think today of Benoit Benjamin, Maurice Cheeks, John Starks or Mark Jackson). For Greenfield, in the end, "white" basketball is the game of "patience and method" (a coach's game) that has held sway across much of the game's first half-century. "Black" basketball is more an improvised game of "electric self-expression" and as such it is the modern-era spectacle that most fans have come to expect for their entertainment dollars when now attending games at the highest levels of amateur and professional play.

But if black style would not always remain an exclusive property of black players, certainly it had found its origins in the inner-city (almost exclusively black) experience of playground basketball during the '50s and '60s. Across the national college and pro scene there had been four special events of the era that had firmly established the prominence of the black playground ballplayer. The first was clearly the mid-50s dominance of Bill Russell and the University of San Francisco Dons. A second was the individual magnetism of Elgin Baylor (the original freelancer) and Oscar Robertson (the textbook master) and the special magic of their contrasting one-on-one offensive games. Third and equally significant at the time was the national championship victory over lily-white Kentucky engineered by the black-dominated team from Texas Western. The last and perhaps most important of all in completing the transition was the short but miraculous life of the revolutionary American Basketball Association — spawning grounds for Dr. J, slam dunking flight fests, and high-soaring power forwards like Spencer Haywood and Connie Hawkins.

One huge breakthrough for the black ballplayer thus came with Oscar Robertson's debut in Madison Square Garden on January 9, 1958. Oscar would play a flawless game that night — only the 11th game of his college career — and would etch his image forever into the lengthy collective memory of basketball's greatest mecca. In a lopsided 118-54 shelling of Seton Hall, Oscar rang up a new Garden scoring mark of 56 points with his explosion of 22 field goals and 12-for-12 free-throw shooting. It would be but one of four 50-plus games for the All-American rookie. But while the "Big O" would set an eye-catching new record that night, he would also accomplish something else even more significant at the same time.

Chamberlain and Russell had already drawn considerable attention to the black hoops star. But neither played what could be considered a textbook game. Oscar, by contrast, was true master of textbook basketball as it had always been played by the best white stars. This was no freelancing and undisciplined playground leaper whose flash and flamboyance outshown his few fundamentals. As black culture historian Nelson George has so precisely phrased it, Oscar did absolutely everything the classroom coaches always loved — he dribbled with both hands, muscled inside for rebounds, passed with uncanny intelligence and accuracy and always shot unerringly from any spot within 30 feet of the hoop. The difference was he did it all much better than anyone else ever had.

While most black stars of the 1950s followed a familiar route and went to black (often Catholic) schools, Oscar had chosen to enroll at a strictly white college. In the next few winters he would put both himself and the University of Cincinnati flush at the midpoint of the college basketball map. And in his wake the University of Cincinnati would heavily recruit largely black players (Paul Hogue, Tom Thacker, Tony Yates) to finally build a championship team. Other largely white schools, especially throughout the North and along the West Coast, now quickly followed suit.

While Oscar was the first major black star, he was nonetheless a seeming exception to the emerging stereotype. Black players of the '60s who would truly revolutionize the game would be mostly leapers and dunkers and spectacular showboating freelancers. This was the playground mold of Elgin Baylor, not of the textbook mold of Oscar or Bill Russell or Wilt Chamberlain. And it was a mold that would evolve as much as anywhere from another source of black talent, the small Southern all-black college.

While black stars at large (and thus largely white) schools were beginning to grab some share of the national headlines, there was another tradition simultaneously being sustained in the backwaters of the college sport. This was the tradition of the great black college teams which often dominated NAIA small college play. Coach John McLendon, for one, had pioneered both fast-break basketball and the small college black powerhouse team during his journeyman career that took him from North Carolina Central to Hampton Institute to Tennessee State and finally on to Kentucky State. McLendon at his height would capture three consecutive NAIA titles with Tennessee State while at the same time recruiting and shaping players like Dick Barnett, Jim Barnhill and Ben Warley.

The first notable individual talent to emerge from this arena and make his lasting mark on the national hoops scene would be Sam Jones, backcourt ace with the Auerbach-coached Bill Russell Celtics of the mid and late 1960s. Jones would first carve out his reputation at North Carolina Central College under McLendon's successor Roy Brown. And he would enter the Celtics lineup as a top 1957 draft choice already sporting his later reputation as a phenomenal "carom" shooter and (in the words of Boston teammate Bob Cousy) "the fastest thing ever seen" charging up and down a 90-foot basketball floor.

With players like Jones suddenly being discovered in the backwaters of the Southland, the NAIA postseason tournament seemingly overnight emerged as the biggest and best showcase for potential pro talent. Out of this previously untapped arena would come a host of prolific scorers especially, and none would be more sensational than Travis Grant at Kentucky State. Grant — a rangy 6-8 gunner who led his team to three NAIA titles — once hammered home 75 in a single game as a sophomore. Over a four-year career (1969-72) he would build a 33.4 average and net 4,045 total points, still the Division II record a full quarter-century later. And there were others as well, like Dick Vories (2,968 points), Cecil Tuttle (2,340 points) and two-time Little All-American Charlie Grote — all from Georgetown College of Kentucky.

But the biggest find of all was a deadly jump shooter recruited off the streets of Philadelphia who first left his calling card at a tiny North Carolina college playing its games in the shadows of the neighboring big-brother ACC schools. Earl Monroe in 1966-67 unleashed what remains unquestionably the greatest one-man single-season performance of collegiate history (with 1,329 points and a 41.5 average) while simultaneously carrying Winston-Salem to a College Division national championship.

Playing under the tutelage of legendary coach Clarence "Big House" Gaines, Monroe elevated his entire team to a 31-1 record while time and again working offensive magic rarely seen on any level of college play. The smooth-as-silk ball handler with scoring moves not even invented yet would shoot better than 60 percent from the floor for an entire year; and at the same time he would fire the ball up frequently enough to log the highest season average ever posted in the small college record books. The man known simply as "The Pearl" would in the process also conveniently erase several of the Bevo Francis College Division records that had created such a storm of controversy a single decade earlier. It was during his days at

Winston-Salem that Monroe also garnered his colorful nickname. This came about when a local sportswriter penned a story referring to the star player's remarkable on-court "moves" as "Earl's pearls." The name would soon stick as permanently as the classic playground style which had inspired it.

It was at Winston-Salem that the future Baltimore Bullets and New York Knicks star would also uncover and perfect the flamboyant "shake-and-bake" one-on-one style that would soon be seen everywhere as the very paragon of "black-style" play during the coming decade and beyond. Creaky legs prevented Monroe from ever being much of a jumper, yet his feints and "jukes" kept defenders so unbalanced that he could pop shots from almost anywhere on the floor without hardly ever having to leave his feet at all.

Behind the scenes of big-time basketball "The Pearl" was quietly anticipating what "Pistol Pete" Maravich would soon be accomplishing over at LSU, and more squarely in the Division I limelight (Maravich's first season would immediately follow Monroe's last). But if there was any lingering doubt about Earl Monroe's talent against small-time competition versus Maravich's skills versus big-time opponents, this would be definitively answered (somewhat in Monroe's favor) when the two reached the professional ranks.

Many of the stars from the lesser-known (even largely unknown) black colleges would find their way onto the rosters of the ABA pro teams in the twilight of the 1960s. It was the American Basketball Association — that rebel league sporting a tri-color ball and distinct "attitude" — that brought with it the popularity of the new freelance style of play. The television and arena exposure of ABA play was indeed limited throughout much of the country, but like that second-ranking rental car company that capitalized on being "number two" this interloper pro circuit offered for all nine seasons of its history the most entertaining product in town; and it also became a bonanza to African-American athletes by featuring a new speed-based playground style of action in synch with the emerging ghetto version of the city game.

The ABA for one thing was a league dominated by forwards, not by centers and guards as had always been the NBA scenario. The new league had no Russells, Chamberlains or Wes Unselds jamming up the space around the bucket; and it also featured a popular three-point shot which opened the court by spreading guards outside the long-range circle. This league opened the driving lanes for agile forwards to strut their stuff. And it was the rim-bending forwards — largely small college blacks like Julius Erving of UMass, Spencer Haywood of Detroit, Travis Grant of Kentucky State, Darnell Hillman of San Jose State, Roger Brown of Dayton, Julius Keye of Alcorn State, Rich Jones of Memphis State, Cincy Powell of Portland, Charles Edge of LeMoyne-Owen, Gerald Govan of St. Mary's, Fly Williams of Austin Peay, Willie Wise of Drake, Larry Jones of Toledo, George Gervin of Eastern Michigan and Connie Hawkins of no college at all who soared and flew above the hoop and thus redefined the new space-aged game.

Basketball had first gone partially airborne with the jump shot in the '40s. Now it went truly vertical with the dunk shot which became the weapon of choice in the '60s and '70s. There was, of course, resistance and some of that resistance had only thinly veiled racial overtones. The dunk was banned in college for nearly a decade

186

(1967-1976, ironically the precise years that marked the ABA life span). Its practice was also shunned as "not cool" in the NBA for several decades. Even Oscar rarely dunked, though he had the other freelance moves that would distinguish a black style of play. But in the ABA the dunk took over as a league trademark alongside the red, white and blue ball and the three-point shot. And the new street-cool maneuver was soon being imitated in college play everywhere. If the dunking style was an innovation of the rebel pro league, it was soon also revolutionizing the college sport.

Foremost among the proponents of the new style would be a University of Massachusetts star off the playgrounds of suburban Long Island who left college a season early to expand his game in the ABA arenas. If Julius Erving did not become a star of first magnitude until his ABA years and a household name until moving to the NBA, he was nonetheless a college phenomenon of sorts on the local 1970 and 1971 New England scene. Erving's college game suffered from less-gifted teammates and the UMass high-flyer thus never had a chance to sparkle in the showcase of postseason play: his two appearances in the NIT (both opening-round losses, including a 90-49 thumping by North Carolina) registered only a 15-point scoring average. But pro scouts had already discovered the special talents of this soaring offensive stylist who was making his mark in Amherst as only one of six collegians ever to average more than 20 points and 20 rebounds for a career.

There were other black college players of the '60s cut in a similar mold. Perhaps the most memorable was Spencer Haywood, a 6-8 gazelle whose single junior college season (28.2 points and 22.1 rebounds at Trinidad in Colorado) and one varsity campaign (32.1 ppg and the nation's rebounding lead at Detroit) were truly the ingredients of small college legend. Haywood's first national splash would come, of course, in the 1968 Olympics. These were the games boycotted by other top black stars like Lew Alcindor, Bob Lanier of St. Bonaventure, Louisville's Wes Unseld and Houston's Elvin Hayes. But the 19-year-old junior college whiz stepped into the void, monopolized the backboards against international competition and paced an easy gold medal title defense in Mexico City.

Erving and Haywood were only the tip of the iceberg. There were others like Bob Lanier, Calvin Murphy (Niagara), Manny Leaks (Niagara), Jo Jo White (Kansas), Dave Stallworth (Wichita State), Jim McDaniels (Western Kentucky), Artis Gilmore (Jacksonville) and Ken Durrett (La Salle). Lanier was leading scorer and rebounder on a 1970 St. Bonnie's team that climbed into the NCAA semis against Gilmore and Jacksonville and might well have challenged UCLA in the finals had not Lanier himself missed the entire Final Four round with a torn ligament. The 7-2 Gilmore outdistanced the nation in rebounding in both of his two varsity seasons. McDaniels was another 7-footer who scored a shade under 30 points per game as a senior and that same season signed a secret contract with the ABA which promised his services to the league in general and not to any specified team. Most phenomenal of all was the tiny dynamo Murphy, who would eventually become the NBA's greatest free-throw marksman ever. At Niagara the spunky 5-9 playmaker and relentless scorer posted the highest point-making average on record for a sophomore outside of Maravich (38.2), then kept up the onslaught in the face of nightly gang defenses to maintain a 33.1 average over his full three-season career.

The arrival of these black stars would in the long run change the game forever. In the short run, of course, the flood of new black shooters and leapers in large part only served to hide with the glare of their performances the ongoing racial injustices darkening the world of pro and college sports. There would soon enough be the painful exposures of exploitation involving black athletes at schools like 1966 NCAA champion Texas Western. There was the sad saga of Connie Hawkins and his lifetime NBA ban (later rescinded under the threat of legal action) for alleged associations with gamblers. And there was also the strange sojourn of Spencer Haywood who became a well-compensated pawn in the bitter power struggle between a struggling ABA and retrenching NBA.

Hawkins was an incomparable playground star who had been lured by Iowa (despite questionable abilities to read or write) and then cast aside by both the college and the pro ranks only because of guilt by association in the wake of a new round of 1961 college point-shaving scandals. When Hawkins was called to testify before a grand jury regarding loans he had received from playground sharpies seeking contacts with future ghetto college stars the jittery Iowa program dropped him like unwanted baggage.

Haywood, in turn, left college as a 20-year-old sophomore and hooked on with the ABA circuit unfettered by any rules banning undergraduate signings. After an incredible first season (when he led the league in everything and was dual MVP and top rookie) Haywood decided that the NBA was both more glamorous and better paying and thus inked a new contract with the older league which as yet did not enjoy any such signing exemptions. When other NBA teams balked, the Seattle ownership announced plans for a court battle and the league quickly reversed its restrictions on undergraduate contracts.

The contract fight between the ABA's Denver Nuggets and NBA's Seattle Supersonics over Haywood's services in 1970 would lead directly to an undergraduate "hardship" early-signing provision which has since been both boon and bane to the existence of several subsequent generations of starry-eyed ghetto-bred African-American ballplayers. The newly instituted "hardship clause" (the sport's most ludicrous euphemism) more than ever made college basketball a mere stepping stone for talented black athletes seeking an elusive dream of NBA and ABA instant riches. College basketball now more than ever would become a true meat market, especially for hordes of black ghetto athletes.

March Madness on Tobacco Road

The longtime fixture known as the Southern Conference came apart at the seams at the end of the 1953 season. With the outset of the 1953-54 campaign a new enterprise was born known as the Atlantic Coast Conference. It would soon turn into a prime fixture of the college basketball wars. Several decades down the road the Carolina-Maryland-Virginia confederation could even stake legitimate claim as the best college hoops circuit of all, and by almost any available standard of measure.

The birth rites began in May of 1953 when the Southern Conference held its annual meeting at Sedgefield Inn on the outskirts of Greensboro; it was then that seven long-term members announced their joint secession and plans for a bold new affiliation. A month later the seven charter members — Clemson, Duke, Maryland, North Carolina, North Carolina State, South Carolina and Wake Forest — would meet again in Raleigh and welcome Virginia into the fold as an eighth partner. With the exception of South Carolina, the group would remain united in their venture down to the present, with Georgia Tech signing up in the late '70s and Florida State coming on board at the outset of the '90s. Few collegiate conferences have remained as stable. And when it comes to basketball, at least, none has enjoyed greater competitive successes. What was also now born was the phenomenon of Tobacco Road Basketball and with it perhaps the deepest brand of fanaticism the winter indoor sport has ever witnessed. From the very first, fans of this highly competitive new circuit and its member schools have remained the most enthusiastic to be found anywhere. They certainly had plenty of tradition to build on at schools like Duke, Wake Forest, North Carolina State, Virginia, Maryland and North Carolina. But success on the national scene would be neither automatic nor instantaneous. Although the new league was already overflowing with marquee players, legendary coaches and even powerhouse teams throughout the '50s, only North Carolina would rise to the apex of the national scene before the decade was out.

The first couple of seasons of the new league saw Duke and North Carolina State battle for supremacy. Duke had been a reigning Southern Conference power in recent seasons with Harold Bradley at the coaching helm and Dick Groat running the offense as the country's finest backcourt player. Under tutelage of the soon-legendary Everett Case, NC State had enjoyed even greater recent successes, owning seven titles during the past eight seasons in the old conference, and running up a streak over that same span in which no season featured fewer than 24 victories. Duke would grab the first regular-season title when the new circuit opened for business in 1953-54, yet Case's team would win the most overall games (26), capture the postseason playoffs (tripping Duke and then edging Wake Forest in overtime), and earn the loop's first NCAA trip (where it was a two-point loser to eventual champion La Salle in the regional semis). The next year State would again capture the conference postseason derby that was almost from the beginning the league's true showcase.

The first several ACC seasons were also noted for a handful of showcase offensive players. Buzz Wilkinson of Virginia paced the circuit in scoring in 1954 and 1955, averaging more than 30 points each year, and was only once in his career held under double figures. The latter event occurred early in the 1954 season when UNC's Frank McGuire designed a special defense to stop the hot-shooting Cavalier; three weeks later, however, Wilkinson stunned the Tar Heels with a 45-point night. But the best all-around player was forward-center Dickie Hemric of Wake Forest. Hemric would reign as the league's rebound leader (and also one of its top three scorers) in the first two seasons of conference competition; he would also complete his career as one of only a dozen players with 4,000 combined career points and rebounds, standing fourth on the all-time listing, a slot ahead of Oscar Robertson. Guard Gene Shue of Maryland also flashed brilliance that would later follow him as an NBA player and coach. And a youngster named Len Rosenbluth came on the scene in 1955 in North Carolina with a lofty 25.5 season scoring average posted as an inexperienced sophomore.

As national player of the year in 1951, future baseball star Dick Groat led Duke to the apex of the old Southern Conference immediately before the league's breakup leading to the formation of the Atlantic Coast Conference. (Duke University photo)

During the 1956 season the Wolfpack of Everett Case maintained their iron grip on both the regular season standings (tying with McGuire and Carolina) plus the league's postseason fray, winning their third straight ACC tourney in a 76-74 nail-biter over Wake Forest. NC State would again represent the league in the NCAA tourney but would unfortunately bring little in the way of glory to Tobacco Road in the process. The Wolfpack were nipped 79-78 in four overtimes by small-school Canisius in the first round. And the loss would signal the end, at least for awhile, of NC State dominance in the young conference. For Frank McGuire had now surrounded junior Len Rosenbluth with sophomores Tommy Kearns, Joe Quigg and Ken Rosemond, and the Tar Heels for the first time were a force to be reckoned with in the ACC wars.

North Carolina had matched NC State's 11-3 league record in 1956 but had tumbled to runner-up Wake Forest in the tournament semifinals. The next season there would be no stumbles, however, as the Rosenbluth-led powerhouse would post perhaps the finest single campaign in all of league history — right down to the present era of Jordan and Laettner and Stackhouse. First McGuire's Tar Heels marched unblemished through the 24-game regular campaign. Next they charged through the ACC tourney with the only close game being the semifinal 61-59 tussle with Wake Forest which was their improbable fourth straight win against the Deacons that year. Then came the dramatic NCAA run that brought a national title, only the first of several the league would own through the coming years.

The Carolina NCAA title game versus Wilt Chamberlain and the twice-beaten Kansas Jayhawks was the single event that launched both the ACC and the Tar Heel basketball program, as well as perhaps the NCAA tourney itself. No other game to date has been more dramatic or storied than the shootout between David and Goliath that turned into the longest championship game in history. None did more to turn on a national television audience to the heart-stopping drama of championship cage action. Carolina and its imported "New York City five" had earned its historic NCAA title — the first by a Southern school outside of Kentucky — by surviving back-to-back triple-overtime games on the tournament's final weekend. But this was a Carolina team that specialized in miracle survivals. Neither of the barn-burning Final Four games had been any more miraculous in its closing seconds than the ACC semifinal, where the Tar Heels again somehow survived one of the wildest games in ACC history. The 61-59 victory which kept the dream season alive came on a basket and foul shot by Lennie Rosenbluth in the closing seconds that might as easily have been called a charging foul against Rosie as he lunged in for the game-winning bucket.

Duke and North Carolina State would be back on top of the heap in the final two seasons of the decade. Duke, with a no-name lineup and no player in the league's top 10 in scoring, lost seven games in '58 and finished only 13th in the final UPI poll. Yet the 11 league victories were enough for a repeat of its inaugural-year first-place finish. But postseason events each of these two years would contain some mild surprises to keep things interesting. First fourth-place Maryland would spring an upset win in the 1958 tourney finals over defending national champion North Carolina, which itself had trailed Duke by only a single game during the regular-season conference race. A year later it would be the Tar Heels who would bounce back and again carry the ACC banner into NCAA postseason play. But this came about only on a technicality, and only after NC State had won yet another postseason ACC shootout and handed Everett Case yet another conference trophy.

The Wolfpack and Tar Heels not only tied for the ACC lead with identical 12-2 records but both also tasted a national No. 1 ranking at some point during the long season, and on one occasion they were even ranked first and third, respectively. State, with Lou Pucillo and John Richter (the league's dual scoring and rebounding leader) showing the way, was serving out the third year of a four-year probation and was thus ineligible for NCAA competition. Frank McGuire's North Carolina team, with Lee Shaffer and York Larese now in the driver's seat, thus qualified for an NCAA berth simply by making it into the conference finals alongside State. Perhaps owning a greater incentive since their season was already at an end, the Wolfpack

Lennie Rosenbluth of North Carolina guards Wilt Chamberlain of Kansas in the famed triple-overtime NCAA "David and Goliath" battle that put both the North Carolina Tar Heels and the ACC on the national basketball map. (University of North Carolina photo)

enjoyed a sterling 23-point effort from senior leader Pucillo and routed McGuire's Tar Heels in the tourney finale 80-56, thus salting away their fourth overall conference championship.

It had indeed been a most successful debut during the 1950s for the Atlantic Coast Conference, highlighted certainly by North Carolina's title run in '57 and by the new institution of the exciting ACC postseason playoffs. But when the turbulent '60s broke on the horizon the whole enterprise nearly came crashing to the ground like a feeble house of newly stacked cards. Suddenly a string of gambling and bribery scandals rocked three of the top member schools and as a result the ACC almost didn't survive the dawn of its second promising decade.

The ACC scandals first broke around North Carolina State star Don Gallagher. During the 1960 season Gallagher, a senior, became deeply involved in a scheme to aid gamblers in fixing the results of NC State games. It would be later determined that he was paid $1,000 to make certain his team lost by at least a dozen points in a February match with Duke. As it turned out, Gallagher apparently had a change of heart that night and contributed 10 points to a Wolfpack victory. As gamblers turned up the heat on the married forward he agreed to influence the outcome of other games and subsequently shaved points in at least four of his team's games. By May of 1961 warrants were issued for the arrest of three other NC State players (Stan Niewierowski, Anton Muehlbauer and Terry Litchfield) who had also been implicated in the expanding point-shaving scheme. It was the sport's second big scandal in a decade — this time one not centered in a supposed den of corruption like New York City — and the results again were disastrous for individual athletes, the schools involved and certainly the sport as a whole.

Two other league schools were also involved in the mess at a lesser level. Four players at South Carolina (a league member until 1971) were later uncovered to have been involved in point-shaving efforts between 1957 and 1961. Three players at North Carolina were also reportedly contacted by gamblers and one, Lou Brown, later himself worked to fix numerous games in other locations around the country. But it was the point-fixing at North Carolina State that almost left the league with a permanent black eye.

Fortunately there was a new batch of strong and exciting league teams and a handful of new star players to help refocus disillusioned Tobacco Road fans on legitimate basketball as the '60s unfolded. North Carolina sat atop the regular-season standings in 1960 and 1961 and boasted bona fide star players in Lee Shaffer, the 1960 league scoring champ, and stellar guard York Larese. But the Tar Heels roster during these seasons also featured an oddity — three important role players who would one day make their lasting marks in the pro ranks and especially on the NBA coaching front.

Larry Brown broke in as a sophomore guard in 1961 and was an all-ACC performer by his senior campaign. Donnie Walsh had arrived a season earlier as an important backcourt contributor off the bench and high school All-American Dog Moe a season before that. Moe was a prolific scorer who finished fourth in the league (20.4) as a senior and also tied Len Chappell for the league rebounding lead the same season. Moe would soon carry his scoring talents to the ABA where an unfortunate injury would end his playing days and launch his second successful career as a flamboyant and outspoken pro coach. All three future ABA/NBA mentors were teammates on the roster of the 1961 Carolina squad and all three were also part of the continuing Tar Heels New York recruiting connection that had been established by Gotham-native Frank McGuire during his own near-decade at the helm in Chapel Hill.

All the best Big Apple recruits were not residing at Chapel Hill, however. The surprise newcomer of the 1961 season was another New York volunteer who wore the uniform of the Duke Blue Devils. Art Heyman launched a brilliant career in 1960-61 which saw him average a league second-best 25.2 points per game. By his senior season in 1963, the Rockville Center native emerged as UPI and AP national player of the year, the first ever out of the young Atlantic Coast confederation. But for his first two campaigns he would have to play somewhat in the shadow of a 6-8 powerhouse forward at Wake Forest named Len Chappell. Wake Forest had launched a super sophomore of its own in 1959-60 when Chappell had arrived from Portage, Pennsylvania, to launch a career that would eventually make him a first-round NBA draft choice of the Syracuse Nats. After trailing North Carolina's Lee Shaffer in the league scoring race during his debut season, Chappell quickly moved to the top of the heap as the leading ACC rebounder and scorer (26.6, 30.1) during his final two college seasons.

Chappell's showing was strong enough during his junior campaign to lead Coach Bones McKinney and the Demon Deacons to a second-place regular-season finish (a game behind Carolina) and then a triumph in the postseason ACC wars. Three other fixtures on that first successful Demon Deacons team were Norm Snead (who played four games in December before dropping off the squad to participate as a starting quarterback in the Blue-Gray and Senior Bowl all-star games), Bill Hull (a burly 6-6 forward who averaged 10 points and 10 rebounds as a junior, and later starred in the

All-Star Team for the Era (1966-1971)				
	Pos.	Pts. (Ppg.)	Best Year	NPY
Lew Alcindor (UCLA)	C	2325 (26.4)	29.0 (So.)	1967, 1969
Elvin Hayes (Houston)	F	2884 (31.0)	36.8 (Sr..)	1968
Cazzie Russell (Michigan)	G	2164 (27.1)	30.8 (Sr.)	1966
Pete Maravich (LSU)	G	3667 (44.2)	44.5 (Sr.)	1970
Austin Carr (Notre Dame)	G	2560 (34.6)	38.1 (Jr.)	1971

NPY = National Player of the Year

Honorable Mention: Bob Verga (G, Duke), Sidney Wicks (F-C, UCLA), Jimmy Walker (G, Providence), Calvin Murphy (G, Niagara), Rick Mount (G, Purdue), Dave Bing (G, Syracuse), Bob Lanier (C, St. Bonaventure), Wes Unseld (C, Louisville)

Coach of the Era: John Wooden (UCLA), NCAA Champion (1967, 1968, 1969, 1970, 1971)

NFL with the Chicago Bears and the AFL with the Dallas Texans), and Billy Packer (destined for a future career as a play-by-play announcer and television commentator with a reputation as one of the foremost analysts of the college hoops game). While Hull was a role player and Snead a mere curiosity on the Wake Forest roster, Packer would prove his mettle as an all-ACC backcourt selection and the second-leading scorer on the Deacons' upcoming Final Four entry.

With Packer running the offense as a junior, Wake Forest would make it three games into the NCAA tournament, finishing the year as the Eastern Regional runner-up. The disappointing final loss would be at the hands of a St. Joseph's team that would itself enjoy a most unusual postseason run, one culminating in a record three-overtime victory over Utah in the national consolation game that would later be ruled merely a forfeit loss due to the team's earlier point-shaving activities.

Wake Forest would enjoy a still greater postseason tourney run during Chappell's and Packer's senior season. The 1962 Deacons would in fact cop their first-ever regular-season conference crown (12-2, 22-9 overall), then win a second straight ACC tourney by sinking an overachieving Clemson team that had been a surprise visitor to the finals despite a 4-10 sixth-place league record. Once NCAA play kicked off, Chappell and the Deacons quickly proved they were not only kings of the ACC hill but also a national force to be reckoned with. The ACC club would survive a pair of tense overtime victories (Yale, St. Joseph's) in the early rounds and then charge to the Final Four in Louisville, where the title run soon ended in wreckage with a semifinal loss to Ohio State and the incomparable Jerry Lucas.

Elgin Baylor of Seattle University had more "moves" than a long-distance transport company, and was truly the first great proponent of the unfettered black playground style of one-on-one offensive play. (Seattle University photo)

It was in that semifinal matchup against Wake Forest that Ohio State saw its own ship scuttled despite a convincing 84-68 drubbing of Chappell and the Deacons. Lucas was injured late in the contest and the Ohio State hopes for a revenge victory over Cincinnati in the Finals were for all practical purposes suddenly put to an end. There would still be one final game left for Chappell and the Deacons after the loss to the Buckeyes. This would be an 82-80 win over the emerging powerhouse coached by John Wooden at UCLA and the victory put a fitting cap on the best season in school history with a third-place national finish for the ACC school.

The Demon Deacons would be without Chappell in 1963, and although McKinney put together another formidable team, the loss of the league's top player could not be easily overcome. Wake captured 11 conference games which was only good enough for second place. It was now Art Heyman's turn over at Duke; in his senior season Heyman would actually score less (24.9) than his first two campaigns (25.2 and 25.3) yet would shed the runner-up spot and lead the conference scoring race with Chappell out of the way. And Heyman was not the only show at Durham, with Duke's other stellar forward, 6-4 junior Jeff Mullins, also scoring above a 20-point clip (third in the league at 20.3).

Heyman's Blue Devils would be only the second team in league history to run through the winter and early spring with an unblemished ACC ledger. Vic Bubas-coached Duke would outdistance Wake by three full games in the season standings, then prevail once more over the Deacons during the postseason. In the league tourney the championship game would fittingly match the two top clubs, and Duke, with Heyman and Mullins, would overwhelm Wake Forest 68-57 in a one-sided contest that hardly tested the nation's second-ranked team.

Having dismissed Wake Forest to earn their second-ever NCAA bid, the Duke Blue Devils would next set out to match the Deacons' postseason run of the previous season. And they would succeed by duplicating the Wake Forest successes exactly. First would come an East Regional championship, earned with a 73-59 victory over St. Joseph's, the very team that provided Wake with a similar stepping stone a year earlier. Next the Devils fell by 19 to eventual NCAA winner Loyola in a race-horse clash of two of the nation's most potent offenses. Heyman shot poorly in the disappointing semifinal game (11-for-30) yet still teamed with Mullins for an even 50 points; but it was no match for a Loyola scoring barrage that featured Jerry Harkness (20), Vic Rouse (13), Les Hunter (29), John Egan (14) and Ron Miller (18). Then in the national consolation game Duke would rebound and bring the league its second straight national third-place trophy with an 85-63 thrashing of Oregon State.

For his Final Four efforts Art Heyman would become the first ACC player ever tapped as an NCAA Tournament MVP. Jeff Mullins, about to take over as top dog at Duke, had also played a strong supporting role and would soon up his game a further notch the following season in lifting the Devils back into the national title game with Wooden's UCLA Bruins. The 1963 season was topped off, however, when Art Heyman was also singled out as the first ACC player ever selected national player of the year.

By the arrival of the mid-60s the ACC had already enjoyed one NCAA title and several visits by member schools to the Final Four in only a single decade of league play. Signs were already being sent out from Tobacco Road that the Big Ten and Pacific Coast Conferences, along with the Big Eight (which had been the Big Seven until 1958) and Southeastern Conferences were no longer able to count on regularly dividing up postseason glory exclusively among themselves. But any ACC plans for further inroads on the national championship market would next have to be put on hold for awhile. For around the corner stood John Wooden and his potent program that had now silently emerged out at UCLA.

9

The Seventies, Part 1

The Wooden Dynasty

What transpired at the Westwood Village UCLA campus on the outskirts of teeming Los Angeles between 1963 and 1975 is perhaps the most remarkable story in the entire chronology of American sports. Succinctly put, the John Wooden chronicle is unparalleled for either guts, glamour or full-blown glory. A Babe Ruth memoir or Michael Jordan biography might well rival the Wooden saga in terms of outrageous and unpredictable successes. Relentless reigns atop the American sportsworld by Red Auerbach in basketball, Casey Stengel in baseball and even Vince Lombardi in football, might nearly match it in unabashed inspirational content. But in the end, all other such Horatio Algier tales fall a good bit short of the career etched by Johnny Wooden.

It was during this dozen-year stretch that the nonpareil UCLA coach and inspirational leader pasted together — piece by continuing piece — a remarkable dynasty which totally ruled the highly competitive world of college basketball. The UCLA taskmaster would achieve his success as much by sheer willpower and a touch of pure luck as by any raw genius. The Wooden tale is thus not without its rough edges, and much of the coach's lasting image as a self-controlled and completely pacific leader would be built (by both Wooden and his chroniclers) largely after the fact.

As other respected historians of the sport have already noted, the methods which coach Wooden piously espoused once he stood atop the sportsworld were not always exactly those methods which originally had gotten him there. The carefully crafted image was always more real than the man himself. And yet that image is easily the most luminous in the entire history of a sport seemingly always built upon larger-than-life personalities.

The UCLA teams that Wooden produced indeed reflected his own image — both real and perceived. These were teams noted for great discipline and a flawless work ethic; there would be no oversized egos or selfish concentration on personal statistics; even such giants as Alcindor and Walton would mold their games within a fixed team concept. And these were also teams that won relentlessly and against all odds. Wooden's Bruins rarely if ever defeated themselves. (In this sense they provided the starkest possible contrast with that other great dynasty outfit built by Adolph Rupp in Kentucky under the shadows of World War II.) Almost as rarely were they beaten by anyone else. During the three-year reign of Alcindor and the three-year epoch of Walton it was almost never a question of whether or not Wooden's teams could repeat national championships; the issue was only if they would ever lose a single game.

The result was an unprecedented — and likely never again to be repeated — feat of 10 NCAA national championships in but 12 winters. Seven of these titles were stacked end-to-end in the most remarkable consecutive-year win streak of all time. No other team has yet won more than twice in succession. Wooden's would thus be a legacy which dwarfs all other accomplishments across the course of collegiate cage history. And it will most likely continue to do so forever.

There are indeed many other sports records that over the years have been deemed unbreakable. Some of these — Babe Ruth's baseball home run records, Gehrig's ironman streak, Cobb's standards for steals and base hits, Jim Brown's football career rushing mark — have eventually been overtaken and thus buried as historical footnotes. Others like Wilt's 100-point NBA game, DiMaggio's 56-game hit streak, Dan Marino's career passing statistics, will inevitably eventually fall by the wayside as well. Some like Connie Mack's 50-year managerial tenure, the Chicago Cub's ongoing 50-year pennant drought, Chamberlain's 50-point season's scoring average, Cy Young's 511 baseball pitching wins, today seem utterly untouchable. Yet no such record — team or individual — is likely more safe from the onslaughts of future generations than is Wooden's string of uninterrupted NCAA basketball titles.

And when it comes to comparing dynasties there seem to be only two fair challengers to the UCLA string. There is the New York Yankees' remarkable string of American League pennant victories that stretched between 1947 and 1964 — 15 flags in 18 years, including two strings of five straight and one of four in a row, plus two overlapping stretches (1949-1958 and 1955-1964) of nine out of 10. And there is the even more worthy challenge in the form of eight straight NBA titles posted by Red Auerbach and his Bill Russell-led Boston Celtics (1958-59 through 1965-66); the Celtics also ran off 11 titles in 13 season, a string which included 10 out of 11. Auerbach's NBA title string even ironically overlapped Wooden's NCAA success, making the mid- and late-60s truly the era of the basketball dynasty.

Basketball dynasties are indeed more difficult to maintain than baseball dynasties. Careers of star players last longer in the big leagues and baseballers maintain their peak of top performance longer than athletes in the cage sport. By contrast, hoop teams can put together challengers to any front-runner far more quickly and with much less financial or recruiting effort; powerhouse challengers in the cage game are built almost overnight, with but one or two key players. And injury is also a far greater factor in breaking the back of front-running basketball teams; a single star player lost can mean a winning team lost. Also in basketball — at both collegiate and professional levels — year-end championship playoffs involve far more teams and thus hold far greater potential for upsets.

But if the contrast thus comes down to Auerbach versus Wooden, there is still little room for any serious comparison. Building dynasties in collegiate basketball is a far more unlikely scenario — perhaps bordering on the near-impossible. The same group of players, however talented, is together for three seasons at most. Thus one is

Former UCLA coach John Wooden's domination of NCAA Tournament play will likely remain forever as the greatest dynasty run in the history of American sports. (UCLA photo)

always starting over in the college game, with at least some major portion of the team roster (if not the bulk of it) consisting of fresh faces and untried talents; as much or more time has to be put into recruiting next season's crop as can ever be put into perfecting the play of the current squad. If today's NBA teams face frequent roster shifting due to laxer rules on free agency, certainly this was not yet the case in Red Auerbach's era.

And there are further obstacles, especially those involving the sheer magnitude of the opposition. Regular-season and postseason challengers are far more numerous (even if the bulk of them might be patsies) and certainly less familiar and less scouted than the opposition found within the pro ranks. Home courts and home crowds are also often major factors at the collegiate level, as are game officials drawn from other often hostile conferences. In the college game, true parity — at least among the multitude of upper-echelon teams — is always much closer at hand. And the largest factor of all is the simple fact that postseason collegiate play is a matter of single-elimination playdowns. There are no best-of-five or best-of-seven encounters where a bad night or two are tolerated. Once March Madness begins for the collegiate teams a single misstep means an immediate end to the championship trail.

One can sense the difference merely by measuring the frequency of repeat NCAA cage champions compared to those in any pro sport. It is hard enough to hold sway season after season, with constantly shifting personnel, even in one's own conference. Repeat national basketball titles — especially more than a single repeat — is the toughest benchmark in all of big-time sports. It was against this challenging backdrop that Wooden built not just one dynasty team but in reality three different dynasties stretched end-to-end.

The Wooden 12-year winning skein is today so remarkable in hindsight as to border on the unfathomable. San Francisco, behind Bill Russell and coach Phil Woolpert, once maintained such a grip for nearly three seasons, way back in an era when national powerhouse teams could be counted on but two hands. But Wooden pushed the true limits of continuous winning. There were not only the 10 national titles; there was also the relentless Pac-8 conference domination for 14 straight seasons (the string ran out to 18 after Wooden's retirement); as well as the two huge winning streaks of 47 and 88 games and the half-dozen-plus (1964, 1967, 1968, 1969, 1971, 1972, 1973) unbeaten or once-beaten ballclubs.

How, then, did John Wooden actually pull it all off? There was above all else, of course, the matter of some superb recruiting. Other coaches have undeniably also stocked the coffers with seemingly endless talent — at least for short stretches — and yet have not been able to reach the top, or maintain their grip once there. Wooden did indeed have a full stable of solid team-oriented players and managed to keep the doors of that stable revolving as well. And there were also the two monster individual talents to whom the coach could anchor his back-to-back juggernauts. Also significant to a degree, of course, was the atmosphere of the times, which allowed a zealous coach like Wooden the latitude to command and receive absolute loyalty from his disciplined troops. And finally of course there was always the appropriate measure of pure unadulterated good luck — the key basket made or rebound snatched or officiating call received that could turn a crucial game in the closing seconds.

But there was another element even more vital than the mere talent font of super athletes, and it was indeed an element which held the key to Wooden's hidden genius. This was a facet particular to our culture heroes of the '70s and '80s which basketball historian Neil Isaacs best characterizes as the mold of the genuine "plastic" man. Isaacs, in one of the most insightful portraits of the Westwood Wizard, has painted coach Wooden as a man exemplifying the popular mold of the post-Vietnam epoch warrior-politician. It was the mold personified by football's coaching paragon George Allen, by Hollywood's silver screen exemplars John Wayne and Walt Disney, and by Washington politicos like Ronald Reagan, Bob Haldeman and Richard Nixon. It was also a mold perfectly in tune with the image-conscious Southern California venue where all these figures at one time or another resided. And it involved the magical properties of pure plasticity. The '70s were, after all, the ultimate "golden age" of plastics — plastic consumer products, plastic ideas, plastic people.

As writer Isaacs (*All the Moves*, 1975) has described him, the "Plastic Man" strives for results and appearances at all costs. And it is somehow all done without the slightest air of hypocrisy or cynicism. He is a leader who has absolute faith in the rightness of both his beliefs and his methods; he ruthlessly motivates all his actions with those beliefs as he strives to achieve a single and narrowly defined goal. And he bases his struggle for perfection entirely on the redeeming power of "character" — his own and of course those of his followers. In Wooden's case, of course, those followers were a dedicated band of skilled 20-year-old athletes, assembled for several brief years on the Westwood college campus for the sole purpose of winning basketball games.

Wooden would translate his vision onto the printed page in the form of his "pyramid of success" formula for winning both at sport and at life. Years later it would appear for the general public in a mildly pompous autobiography entitled *They Call Me Coach* (1972, Revised Edition 1988), a book which capsulized the Wooden philosophy as well as the Wooden on-court career. At the bottom of Wooden's pyramid are the building blocks of *industriousness, friendship, loyalty, cooperation* and *enthusiasm*; at the apex stand the twin keys to ultimate success — *patience* and *faith through prayer*. Intermediate building blocks contain such Boy Scout platitudes as *self-control, alertness, confidence, poise* and *initiative*, among others.

Critics (especially Isaacs) have been quick to point out the flaws and oversimplifications of the published Wooden doctrine. Its vital individual building blocks (qualities) are often trite, sometimes contradictory and usually overlapping. But there is even more room for cynicism or skepticism here. Wooden designed his pyramid and defined his successes and his methods largely after the fact. It was all based on how he saw himself once he had already scaled to the summit of success — a reconstruction of himself and his program in the image of what he thought he/it should be. Such elements as *patience, self-control* and *poise* were not always the elements that had gotten him there. In reality here was a coach who, as much as any other, had been impatient with the slightest lack of success and thus often cantankerous and short-tempered both on the practice court and along the sidelines. The "pyramid of success" may have captured Wooden's fantasy of the ultimate winning program, but it never explained very well quite how he got there.

There was, however, still another feature of "the plastic man" which goes much farther in uncovering the true roots of John Wooden's remarkable successes. This was the true genius and virtue of his plasticity. Success did, to a large degree, come with steadfast devotion to a program of discipline and dedication that the coach believed in unwaveringly. But if the program and especially the system of play on the floor was tightly controlled at the immediate moment, it was also remarkably flexible over the long haul. Each of the several Wooden championship teams (Goodrich-Hazzard, Alcindor-Allen, Wicks-Rowe, Walton-Wilkes, Washington-Meyers) sported a distinct personality of its own, however much each also reflected its mentor.

The key to Wooden's decade-plus span of successes was indeed his genius for flexibility. It was his ability year after year to adapt and integrate into his predefined system the diverse talents of those immensely productive players he had continually recruited. New superstar playing skills would demand redesigned offensive and defensive schemes; shifting social and political attitudes among the players would require equally large adjustments in tolerance. Methods to battle newly designed offensive and defensive schemes by the opposition were constantly called for, and so was a considerable raising of the coach's social and political consciousness. A pro-establishment mentor who at first could not tolerate even displays of shaggy facial hair among his troops was eventually accommodating both Alcindor's darkest moods and Walton's left-wing activism.

The story of Wooden's UCLA dynasty is of course not the story of a single one- or two-year team. It is indeed a story told in four episodes, each one a reflection of the degree to which the coach continually proved his remarkable abilities to shift and adjust with changing circumstances, and yet maintain a program of excellence fixed firmly in his own image.

First came a lengthy prelude covering Wooden's first 15 seasons at the helm in Westwood. Next was the convincing breakthrough in the form of a first undefeated season (30-0 in 1964) and then the successful title defense that followed a season later (28-2 in 1965). Episode three is the saga of the most successful and yet perhaps least satisfying segment of his lengthy stretch at the top. The Alcindor team was easily Wooden's best and perhaps the best in all of college cage history. But the period was nonetheless a frustrating one devoted to trying arduously to avoid defeats rather than joyously pursuing victories. It was a three-year stretch that brought recognition and endless plaudits but little joy to the UCLA mentor. And then came the second period of unmatched greatness and fourth stage of the Wooden dynasty. These were the Walton years and they fell only slightly short of the Alcindor era. After that there would be a brief fall from the top and then one final and perhaps most satisfying encore.

Donning the Wizard's Robes

Wooden's talent for adapting to changed circumstances — over the course of a long season, a single game, or even the span of a decade or a career — was seemingly there from his very earliest years in Westwood. So too was his unwavering devotion to a far-sighted plan. For John Wooden was not only a coaching pioneer but also a clear-cut product of his Midwestern athletic roots. And if these roots would sprout and blossom in Southern California in the 1960s, they indeed had been planted back in Indiana soil in the 1930s. If West Coast basketball would finally outstrip and supplant the Midwestern and Eastern varieties during the era of the Wooden dynasty, it did so only because its primary disciple had perfected a coaching plan originally born and nurtured within his own deep-seated Indiana and Big Ten heritage.

In youth John Wooden had been both an Indiana high school star (his rare athleticism early earned him the nickname of "India Rubber Man") and a Big Ten three-time All-American at Purdue. During his college years he had not only earned All-American status on a two-time league-champion Purdue team (the Boilermakers slipped to 12-5 and a second-place tie during his junior season), but he had also learned two invaluable lessons which would stay with him down through the years. One was the consistent effectiveness of the controlled fast-breaking style of play pioneered by his own coach Ward "Piggy" Lambert. Lambert had espoused a radical theory that shocked his coaching contemporaries: the team making the most mistakes would most often win a game (that is, the team that ran and gambled and turned the ball over, but also generated the most relentless offense). And the other vital lesson was a discovery of the ultimate weaknesses and limitations attached to

Known as the "India Rubber Man" for his athletic play, John Wooden was a three-time All-American guard at Purdue under coach Ward Lambert and Helms Foundation player of the year for 1932. (Purdue University photo)

the rival system, the strictly disciplined and patterned "control game" of longtime Wisconsin coach Walter "Doc" Meanwell.

After leaving Purdue, Wooden had served his 11-year apprenticeship as a high school coach in both Indiana and Kentucky. He had also moonlighted throughout this decade of schoolboy coaching as a professional player with the Indianapolis Kautsky Grocers, entrants in a rough-and-tumble industrial circuit known as the National Basketball League. Later he would eventually move up the coaching ladder for two seasons at Indiana State University in Terre Haute. Yet it was in the very first of his schoolboy seasons that the young mentor would experience his only losing campaign in a 40-year coaching career.

Two years at Indiana State brought the novice coach's first two bids for post-season play. Yet when his first ISU team was invited to participate in NAIA tournament play Wooden was quick to turn the invitation down once he was informed that the one substitute black player on his squad would not be welcomed onto the court. A year later, another bid was extended without strings and the Indiana State crew this time went all the way to the finals before losing to a Louisville team featuring future NBA star Jack Coleman. All this time Wooden was painstakingly perfecting the playing system he had learned chapter and verse from Ward Lambert.

It is now a long-forgotten footnote that the arrival at Westwood in 1948 was something of a reluctant one. Indiana's first big high school, college and barnstorming pro star never really desired to leave his Hoosier homeland, unless it was to venture out perhaps as far as Wisconsin, Iowa, Ohio or Michigan to fulfill a burning ambition to coach somewhere within the Big Ten. That very opportunity seemed to present itself overnight when the head post at Minnesota became vacant and was offered to the second-year Indiana State coach. But there was an unfortunate catch: Wooden wanted his valued assistant Eddie Powell to go along to Minneapolis with him and at first the Gopher athletic department had balked. There was also an offer from the West Coast, but UCLA was a lackluster losing program and hardly a plum job in anyone's book; and it definitely wasn't the Big Ten. Wooden clearly preferred the Minnesota position, yet he was also a man of unshakable principles and he would therefore hold out until a spot was also guaranteed for his trusted assistant.

An ultimatum was thus delivered to the Minnesota hiring committee. A time was fixed for the Minnesota response concerning Powell and if the deadline was not met then Wooden would reluctantly settle on Los Angeles. When the call didn't come in due course, John Wooden made his verbal commitment as promised, one he never went back on even though Minnesota officials called an hour later with a firm offer for both head man and assistant. A Minnesota snowstorm had been responsible for the delayed phone call and thus indirectly also for one of the most perfect marriages in college basketball history.

Such integrity would twice work to the benefit of the UCLA Bruins and seemingly to the disadvantage of the noble young coach. Two seasons after his arrival in Westwood, Wooden was suddenly offered the dream job he had hoped for back at his alma mater in West Lafayette. Yet when he informed UCLA officials of this new offer he was quickly reminded that he himself had insisted on a three-year contract that still had a full season to run. Personal advancement would never outweigh honor and integrity for Wooden and the promising Purdue job was allowed to slip away.

The first several UCLA teams put together by the man soon to be known as the Wizard of Westwood were surprisingly successful considering the state of playing quarters and practice facilities on the Los Angeles campus. Home court was the old Men's Gym with its 2,500 seats, dim lighting and colorful campus reputation as B.O. Barn. When this facility was finally ruled unsafe in 1956 the team was forced to play home games in a series of makeshift venues such as Venice High School, the Pan-Pacific Auditorium, Santa Monica City College and the Long Beach Arena.

Yet if they had no stable homecourt advantage, the UCLA teams of the early '50s were rarely patsies. The 1950 club, featuring future Wooden assistant Jerry Norman and Ralph Joeckel, earned a spot in the NCAA Western Regional where it lost by 14 to tournament runner-up Bradley (also a second-place finisher in the NIT) and its talented frontcourt All-Americans Gene Melchiorre and Paul Unruh. The two following seasons brought a conference Southern Division first-place finish in 1951 (Washington won the league playoff and an NCAA bid) and then another league championship and first round NCAA game versus Santa Clara in 1952.

Throughout the 1950s Wooden painstakingly built a respectable program. There would be six Southern Division titles and three overall Pacific Coast Conference crowns earned through 1956, as well as four 20-victory seasons and one (1956) undefeated PCC slate. And he did so without a great deal of external help from university administration, athletic department officials or even rabid alumni boosters. That support, in the form of a recruiting budget and the full weight of the Southern California sports establishment, would only come once he had brought home a proven year-in and year-out winner.

In the meantime there would only be the Wooden program of fanatic physical conditioning and relentless practicing until his fast-breaking offense and pressing defense were second nature to his well-prepared players. The first significant individual stars were Willie Naulls and Maury Taft, both of whom came on the scene in 1954, and Walt Torrence who suited up in 1957; but this was also the very era in which Bill Russell and Phil Woolpert's San Francisco team dominated the California scene while Southern Cal, Oregon State and California (first under Nibs Price and then Pete Newell) still largely ruled the PCC.

But great coaches do not ever win consistently without exceptional players. The true magic of this or any other coaching wizard lies therefore in recruiting. It would be at the start of his second full decade in Westwood that Wooden would first tap regularly into the kind of talent his run-and-gun teams desperately needed. There had already been a few isolated talents like Naulls (the first Wooden product to star in the NBA) and Torrence, but there were yet no stars of the first dimension. Not until the arrival of a speedy East Coast recruit named Walt Hazzard, snared by Naulls — now with the New York Knicks — who had seen him play in a schoolboy tourney in Philadelphia and had recommended him to Jerry Norman, Wooden's new assistant and recruiting specialist. Hazzard was a slick 6-foot-2 guard who had prepped at the same Overbrook High School which had earlier provided the basketball world with the 7-foot Goliath named Wilt Chamberlain.

If Wooden would eventually reach the twin peaks of his coaching career with two dominating centers — the first black and the second white — so too would he launch his dynasty with two talented backcourt aces. And again the first was a black man and the second a white athlete. Hazzard lit an immediate fire under the Bruins fast break. His sophomore season provided some rough spots in the early going as the fancy passing and flashy ballhandling of the East Coast import was often (quite literally) more than his teammates were prepared for. But once the new point guard and his running mates coalesced, Wooden was finally on the verge of owning a national contender. A single season later Hazzard would also be joined by the first genuine offensive star, Gail Goodrich, as well as by a steady frontcourt performer named Keith Erickson.

Hazzard first directed the UCLA offense in 1961-62, after prepping for a season at Santa Monica City College. The latest playmaking prodigy not only dished out plenty of scoring opportunities to his mates but also averaged 13.2 points per game as the club's third leading scorer. Fellow guard John Green provided the bulk of the scoring punch with a 19.3 average. Gary Cunningham at forward (13.4 ppg, 201 rebounds), Pete Blackman, also in the forecourt (11.5 ppg), and 6-5 Fred Slaughter at center (7.7 ppg, 268 rebounds) were the remaining regulars. At season's end, UCLA was back in the NCAA Tournament for the fourth time and finally fought its way out of the Western Regionals by edging Utah State and mauling conference rival Oregon State.

This was now Wooden's 14th trip to the starting gate and for the very first time he found himself participating in the season's final glamorous championship weekend. Cincinnati's defense-minded Bearcats were a huge favorite to defend the national title they had stolen from the Lucas-Havlicek Ohio State Buckeyes a year earlier, but it was Wooden's upstart Bruins that almost put a crimp in those plans during a stirring semifinal shootout that surprisingly went down to the wire. While revenge-minded Ohio State was losing its star Jerry Lucas to injury during one semifinal match with Wake Forest, Jucker's Cincinnati team had its own hands full enough with the total team effort generated by Wooden's fired-up charges. In the end the PCC team saw its bubble burst when Bearcat guard Tom Thacker beat the buzzer with his only hoop of the entire contest. It was just enough to seal a 72-70 Cincinnati heartstopper.

The near-miss '62 Bruins were perhaps still a season or two away from steamrolling all opposition. But once Gail Goodrich was on the scene alongside Hazzard the Wooden men were already a force ready to dominate their conference and seek bigger game as well. The 1963 edition showed further regular-season improvement with a 20-9 overall record and a league crown earned with a tie-breaking playoff victory over Stanford. But there were still some kinks to be worked out of the talented if erratic unit that now featured Hazzard, Slaughter, Goodrich, Erickson and 6-3 junior forward Jack Hirsch. Any expectations for a return to Final Four glory ended quickly with a subpar outing against Arizona State on the second night of the Western Regionals.

The team that truly put John Wooden on the national map was the one that found two final missing elements just in time for Hazzard's final year in Westwood. This was a team that was relatively small in physical stature and lacked a single imposing physical presence. But it was a perfectly drilled team, by way of compensation, and one that could win games in countless ways. And it was a team that now added two further dimensions that would soon spell invincibility. One was a zone press installed by Wooden to dictate the pacing of games in his own team's favor. The second was a perfect sixth man named Kenny Washington. The 6-3 sophomore out of South Carolina filled in all over the court and was equally adaptable at the guard and forward slots; he was also a sparkplug of the late-game pressing surges that often put the team over the top. The regular winning thus began in the winter of 1963-64, the junior outing for Goodrich and the senior season for Slaughter and Hirsch as well as for Walt Hazzard. And it lasted throughout the entire four-month campaign.

All the ingredients were now neatly in place with the finely drilled and cohesive 1964 team. What had for a couple of years been a serious contender was now suddenly an invincible frontrunner. Keith Erickson had added a new dimension to defense with leaping and running abilities that benefitted substantially from his background as an Olympic-caliber volleyball star. The new 2-2-1 zone press was designed to cut down taller and more physical teams and it worked to perfection largely because Erickson could roam the floor on defense and pick off court-length passes from desperate opposition guards who were pressed into errors by the trapping UCLA zone.

Clutch-shooting guard Gail Goodrich provided offensive firepower and inspirational leadership on an undefeated 1964 national championship team that launched the Wooden dynasty years. (UCLA photo)

Wooden's team went back to the NCAA this time sporting an unblemished record. And that was exactly how that record would remain after tough battles with Big Eight power Kansas State and ACC champion Duke. In the semis Tex Winter's Kansas State club aimed to prove it belonged with the likes of the undefeated Bruins, the second-ranked Michigan Wolverines and the third-ranked Duke Blue Devils. The Wildcats did just that by maintaining a five-point bulge into the final seven minutes before 11 straight UCLA points and 28-point scoring from Keith Erickson finally turned the tide. In the finals, Goodrich and Washington unleashed a devastating two-man attack that buried a stellar performance by Duke's Jeff Mullins. The final count showed a 15-point spread with the Bruins on top 98-83, with Goodrich netting 27 and Washington 26. Wooden finally had his first national title and the UCLA program had its first undefeated season as well. This was in fact only the third unbeaten championship (after San Francisco in '56 and North Carolina in '57) in NCAA tourney history.

The unbeaten skein — the first of several over the next dozen years — didn't last much longer. With a lineup that now featured Goodrich in Hazzard's slot as playmaker and newcomers Freddie Gross at the other guard and Edgar Lacey and Mike Lynn in the forecourt, the revamped national champions launched the 1964 campaign in Champaign, Illinois, and were promptly annihilated 110-83 by a sky-high Illinois quintet. This opening night blitzing in December 1964 would nonetheless have a positive impact by removing some of the intense pressure felt by a defending national champion. Now it could be back to business as usual for a second straight year. And that business included 28 victories, a perfect conference record, and only one additional loss — ironically also in December and also to a Big Ten opponent out in Iowa.

The Bruins would defend their national title in an exceptional Final Four that would include two of the great individual stars of the Golden Era '60s. Michigan owned the incredible Cazzie Russell, still only a junior with a consensus national-player-of-the-year season lying ahead of him. And Princeton boasted the even more entertaining Bill Bradley, the current season's top player who was coming off a second straight 30-plus scoring year and was virtually unstoppable anywhere within two dozen feet of the bucket. Yet in the finals it would be Gail Goodrich who would step up the biggest. Bradley had fallen in the semis where he had outpointed Russell (29-28) in the head-to-head duel but hadn't received enough support from teammates to stave off a torrid Michigan stretch drive. Russell in turn saved one of his own career-best performances for the title game with the Bruins. Cazzie rattled home 28 for the second game running in the 91-80 Bruins victory. But it was indeed Goodrich who stole the show in the championship game with a 42-point night that would remain the best all-around Final Four showing for a Bruins star until Walton broke loose against Memphis State eight years later.

The 1965 Final Four party staged in Portland did have one very important footnote. In the consolation affair involving Princeton and Wichita State, Bradley staged an incomparable showing with a record 58-point performance that nearly stole the headlines from the championship combatants. But it was now the Bruins that college hoops fanatics everywhere were talking about, to the exclusion of almost everyone and everything else. When Wooden next announced that he had grabbed the most coveted high school product since Wilt Chamberlain there was now no reason to believe that anything short of a genuine dynasty had been born.

Reaching the Mountaintop with the Big A

When it comes to selecting the greatest single team in college history few can disagree with the Alcindor-led Bruins. They lost but twice in three full seasons and furthermore avoided losing in an environment where every fan and pundit and second-guesser in the land had burdened them with an impossible and damning label of invincibility.

One of those losses came with Alcindor in a subpar physical state due to injury; the other resulted from a near meaningless game during the season-ending interlude before a final NCAA title defense. They had so much oncourt talent — Alcindor, Allen, Shackelford, Lynn, Lacey, Heitz, Sweek, Saffer, Schofield, Booker, Vallely, Patterson, Rowe, Wicks — that Wooden's greatest challenge was simply keeping revolts over playing time in check and unhappy campers contented within the fold. Lacey and Saffer eventually did quit the squad, Sweek and Wicks and Rowe fumed and often threatened a mutiny, Lynn and Allen were lost for stretches because of academic and legal troubles. And yet the machine rolled on and on against all com-

If Lew Alcindor, later Kareem Abdul-Jabbar, was not the greatest all-around player in collegiate basketball history, he was nonetheless the most dominant single force the college game has ever known. (UCLA photo)

ers. And when it came to postseason tussles with a huge reputation on the line, no team had ever been more consistently devastating in the clutch.

Against Drake in a surprisingly close NCAA semifinal during Alcindor's senior season the run of postseason perfection almost came to a crashing halt when Wooden seemed to come unglued in the face of a surprising Drake pressure defense. The normally placid coach uncharacteristically exploded at his top substitutes Sweek (who stormed to the showers when sent to the end of the bench) and Schofield (who had replaced Sweek in the closing minutes and then almost threw the game away with sloppy play). The first outburst came in full view on the bench during the closing moments of action; the second transpired out of public view in the postgame locker room. Yet all was conveniently patched up in time for a methodical drubbing of Purdue in the title game a day later.

When talented forward Edgar Lacey turned in his uniform at midyear the previous season (after Houston snapped the Bruins' 47-game win streak) because he chaffed under Wooden's disciplined system, the team only got better and romped to a second straight national title. When No. 2 scorer Lucius Allen lost all of his senior season to academic troubles and a marijuana-related arrest, all the necessary adjustments were again made to assure a third straight title defense. No other NCAA championship team ever faced quite so many potential roadblocks to continued success and yet nonetheless relentlessly accomplished every goal demanded of it.

If the late-60s Bruins are the best-ever team, the choice for the greatest-ever impact player is equally clear-cut. Lew Alcindor has almost all the arguments stacked in his favor. Here was not only the most heavily recruited high school talent ever, at least outside of Chamberlain, but the one schoolboy star who entered the big-time college scene and continued to achieve every lofty goal placed in his path. All three varsity years he led his team all the way to the promised land, pacing an undefeated squad his first season and then losing only a single game in each of his final two campaigns. A player with awesome physical tools who could undoubtedly have scored almost at will and racked up astounding numbers for points and rebounds also turned out to be the perfect team player, willing to subordinate every personal achievement and personal record to the needs of team domination. No other college cage star — again outside of Chamberlain — was ever so universally expected never to lose even a single game. And none ever came so perfectly close to accomplishing exactly that unreasonable expectation.

But this does not mean that the "Alcindor Years" were nothing but a joyride for the coach who was blessed with so much talent. Wooden was never entirely comfortable with the team he had now recruited. Alcindor was unquestionably destined to be the greatest player ever when he arrived in Westwood, and he was also likely to be the biggest challenge that this or any coach would ever face. For Alcindor carried along with his dunking and shot blocking and board sweeping his own set of monumental problems. His distinctive Afro hairstyle and his fiercely independent spirit themselves were a new and daunting challenge for a dogmatic coach who demanded absolute conformity from his tightly controlled team.

And not only was there now the threat of failure as a coach and team if every single game, league race, and tournament title wasn't won, but in order to exploit Alcindor's massive talents the coach now had to adopt an offensive style that had never before been his preference. Wooden would now have to rethink his own coaching style and reinvent his successful formula that had already brought back-to-back titles.

The speedy guard-oriented outside game and pressing defense would now have to be redesigned to accommodate a low-post game oriented toward the less-agile big man. This was the ultimate test of Wooden's plasticity and he came through with flying colors. On offense a scheme was set up to exploit the corner shooting of Shackelford and at the same time allow the bevy of talented forwards to take some of the pressure off Alcindor in the low post. Faced with an excess of talent during Lew's junior season the coach also experimented with a low-post plus high-post scheme which still left Lynn Shackelford in the corner but allowed Mike Lynn and

Edgar Lacey to log playing time alongside Alcindor. At the defensive end, an ingenious 1-3-1 trapping zone was installed to thwart the many stalling tactics applied by the Bruins' now-desperate opponents. Wooden played all the cards at his command and he played them all with consummate strategic skill.

It was perhaps the most central of all ironies surrounding John Wooden and his championship Bruins of the 1960s and 1970s that his two biggest stars would turn out to be such rebels away from the court. The irony of course lay in the uncompromising establishment views and common-good philosophy that ruled Wooden's own personal makeup and thus that of his pious program. Walton was already an antiestablishment type from his earliest UCLA days and the coach painfully ignored his star player's politics and adjusted wherever need be. Alcindor would save most of his own rebelliousness for a later professional career. At UCLA the "Big A" was a perfectly compliant and perfectly unselfish star cut squarely in the Wooden mode. At least on the surface, that is, and to all outward appearances.

But if the pressure of simply playing not to lose was always there, it was a pressure that was handled admirably. Alcindor's final record would stand at 88-2. His triple crown of NCAA titles and Final Four MVPs was the first in history. The string of NCAA titles which ran the UCLA count to five in six years allowed Wooden to overtake Adolph Rupp as the most successful coach in NCAA Tournament annals. But from the start everyone had of course expected just such victories. It would be exceedingly tough to live up to such lofty and quite unrealistic expectations. Kansas with Chamberlain had known an identical scenario a decade earlier and had miserably failed to make the grade. The Jayhawks had never won a national title behind Wilt and couldn't even make the grade in their own conference during the giant's second and final campaign. Wooden, for his own part, would never fail like Dick Harp had failed at Kansas.

But this was all still a year away. First the two-time defending champs would have to work their way through a minefield-littered season filled with potential pitfalls and worse. And the biggest trap would be their own star recruit — Alcindor. On the opening evening of the 1966-67 season the new Pauley Pavilion and the new freshman star were simultaneously unveiled in a special exhibition game that was billed as a "Salute to John Wooden Night." And in that "unofficial" season's lidlifter the sensational new post man was able almost singlehandedly to do what no team had done for the past two winters. Alcindor teamed with a remarkable freshman unit consisting of California schoolboys Lynn Shackelford and Kenny Heitz, plus Kansas recruit Lucius Allen, to ruthlessly demolish the defending national champions, 75-60. Alcindor's 31-point performance on that debut night filled Bruins faithful with dreamy visions of a string of championships down the road. But it also regrettably killed the upcoming title-defense season.

All season long — while they awaited Alcindor in the wings — the Bruins never did seem to play like defending champs. Thus the season of 1966 would belong to other teams, especially to the one from Texas Western University in El Paso. UCLA did win 18 while losing only eight. Mike Warren played respectably if somewhat tentatively as a backcourt replacement for Goodrich, and Lynn and Lacey provided frontcourt firepower. But Oregon State was the NCAA representative from the Pacific Coast Conference this time around as Wooden's team failed to win a league crown for the only time in an 18-year span stretching from 1962 through the end of the 1970s.

Everyone of course knew the lull would only be temporary. When the 1966-67 campaign opened, the worst nightmares of coaches and fans at the nation's other premier programs would be swiftly realized. It was now apparent that the best team of 1966 had indeed been found out at UCLA, but its lineup had been one that included Alcindor and company, and its coach was freshman mentor Gary Cunningham and not Wooden. The UCLA freshmen, with a 21-0 record and a 113.2 scoring average (to 56.5 for their opponents), would likely have been more than a match for varsity squads anywhere else in the land. Alcindor averaged 33, Allen 22 and Shackelford 21; the entire squad had shot the ball at a remarkable 56.8 clip from the floor.

That Alcindor as a sophomore would live up to such an advanced billing was also clear from the opening December 1966 game. Entertaining their usually tough rivals, the Southern Cal Trojans, in year-old Pauley the Bruins romped 105-90 behind the sophomore center's 56 points. The very first night of Lew Alcindor was indeed an awesome offensive show, as were so many to follow.

Wooden now built his offense and defense around a single dominant low-post fixture. But he also enjoyed other luxuries that allowed him to do this. A backcourt of cat-quick junior Mike Warren and deadeye-shooting sophomore Lucius Allen was already nearly the equal of the All-American tandem of Hazzard and Goodrich. Shackelford's superb corner shooting, combined with tenacious defense by Ken Heitz, allowed Alcindor free reign under the bucket by drawing both offenses and defenses away from collapsing entirely on the low-post position. The bench play of Sweek, who doubled at forward and guard, and Jim Neilsen, who could play both forward and center, along with Don Saffer and Gene Sutherland in the backcourt, was the equal of any in the country. When Mike Lynn (convicted of larceny) and Edgar Lacey (knee surgery) were lost for the season, this twin absence of two potential starters — something that would have wiped out almost any other team — hardly stirred notice in Westwood.

The 1967 season thus brought another record performance matching the first Wooden championship team of four years earlier. The regular season was again a perfect 30-0 ledger and a postseason romp through the NCAA tourney witnessed no victory margin of less than a comfortable 15 points. There were some early-season close calls when conference rivals Southern California and Oregon State attempted to upset the UCLA rhythm by simply holding onto the ball. At this point the new 1-3-1 zone was unveiled and quickly perfected, and there was little challenge from such opposition ploys from that point on.

The NCAA title game with overmatched Dayton and its star forward Don May was largely anticlimactic. Dayton had stunned North Carolina in one semifinal (76-62) while Wooden's boys were cruising (73-58) past a Houston team that was still a year away from serious championship caliber. May did outscore Alcindor by a single point (21-20) in the championship round, but Allen and Warren would combine for 36 in the backcourt and the Bruins pulled away from a 38-20 halftime margin to

Deadeye shooter Rick Mount of Purdue led three assaults on Lew Alcindor and Company but could never turn the tide against the invincible Bruins. (Purdue University photo)

coast down the stretch. Alcindor was an easy choice as both tourney MVP and National Player of the Year and the first year of the Big A had successfully wound to a close without any room for disappointments or doubts.

There would be some small changes for Alcindor's junior season. For one thing there was a new no dunk rule which outlawed stuffing the ball into the basket during play or even during pregame drills. It was a legislation aimed at neutralizing the new big-man sensation, just as other legislations widening the foul lanes or banning goaltending had been aimed at Mikan, Kurland, Russell and Chamberlain in the two preceding decades. Ironically, however, the rule change probably worked to heighten Alcindor's effectiveness since it now ruled out the one kind of offensive move he himself might have some trouble defending against.

And there would also be more formidable challenges on the horizon for the champion UCLA squad in the shape of a schedule full of potential pitfalls like Big Ten power Purdue and independent juggernaut Houston, now featuring an older and more developed Elvin Hayes. Purdue indeed almost pulled off a major upset in the season's opener. It was the dedication of the Boilermakers' new Mackey Arena and Rick Mount with his sensational long-range artistry brought the home team to a 71-all tie in the closing seconds. UCLA escaped only when Mount uncharacteristically botched a medium-range jumper and Bill Sweek canned a foul-line jumper of his own at the final buzzer.

The victory at Purdue allowed the victory streak to continue and it would eventually stretch to 47 games, only 13 short of the record still owned by San Francisco and Bill Russell. Then a major setback would be suffered when Alcindor was poked in the eye by a stray finger during a 44-point performance at Berkeley against the California Golden Bears. The injury couldn't have come at a worse time since this was the very eve of a January intersectional game that was already being billed as the biggest extravaganza in college basketball history.

The first Houston-UCLA battle of 1968 was indeed a landmark affair which introduced a modern television era for college basketball. A throng of 55,000 crammed the distant bleacher seats of the Houston Astrodome and millions more watched the prime-time video broadcast. Alcindor himself opted to play despite the eye abrasion which had left him with temporary double vision. The injury itself was clearly enough to neutralize Wooden's primary weapon. But the much-improved Houston team and its dynamo forward Elvin Hayes might have been too much to handle this time around even with a full-strength Alcindor. The "Big E" was at the very top of his game with 29 in the first half alone; down the stretch Hayes and backcourt ace Don Chaney kept up the pressure for a 71-69 streak-ending victory. Hayes had sealed the win with two free throws (his 38th and 39th points) with less than a half-minute left.

The January collision of giants had not only belonged to Houston but also had several residual negative effects for the Bruins. For one thing it knocked them from their No. 1 wire service ranking which Houston would now usurp and hold until the late-season rematch. And this was also the game in which Edgar Lacey heatedly left the team. The breaking point had come when Lacey was yanked from the lineup for failing to defense Hayes in the manner ordered by the coach. Yet if Houston had the upper hand in the wire service polls for the remaining weeks of January and February, a tournament-flavored rematch at season's end would soon once more prove beyond a shadow of a doubt the true dominance of both Alcindor and Wooden.

Houston and UCLA collided for a second time in 1968 during the NCAA semi-finals, this time with far more than mere bragging rights at stake. It was also the second straight year that these same two teams had squared off with a trip into the national title game squarely on the line. This time Alcindor had no troubling injuries to tip the balance in favor of Hayes. And the team that had regrouped after Lacey's mutiny was now more perfect than ever. Shackelford this time trailed Hayes all over the floor and shut down his inside game more effectively than anyone had all season. The Bruins thus romped as expected this time around and enjoyed a mind-boggling 44-point margin when Wooden finally sent his starters to the bench.

The title matchup brought a more formidable opponent than a year earlier. This time it would be North Carolina with its own long and proud tradition of postseason excellence, its stellar young coach named Dean Smith, and its own formidable lineup featuring hot-shots Larry Miller and Charlie Scott. Smith's young team (Miller was the only senior starter) featured a very disciplined four-corners offense and thus offered a controlled game of the type Wooden himself could definitely admire. But there was no beating the old master with such schemes yet, especially when he had a weapon at his disposal like Alcindor. Lew with 34 points and 16 rebounds outscored Miller and Scott combined and the Bruins coasted once again. As 78-55 winners the Bruins had handed coach Wooden another NCAA trophy that now tied him with Rupp at four.

A couple of key players were lost for Alcindor's senior season. Warren had graduated and Lucius Allen had run afoul of both the academic system (poor grades) and the legal system (an arrest for marijuana possession); this left a huge void in the Bruin backcourt. But such temporary disruptions of the seemingly inexhaustible Wooden talent pipeline only increased the pressures not to lose.

The reason was that Alcindor and Wooden now had yet another five-star supporting cast of new recruits to lean on. The key perhaps was junior John Vallely in the backcourt, an exceptional shooter and adroit pressure-situation ball handler. Vallely was a much-touted junior-college transfer who had previously been heavily recruited by Jerry Tarkanian at Long Beach State. Steve Patterson, Sidney Wicks and Curtis Rowe were also key players who had graduated from another super-talented freshman squad. At 6-9, Patterson was neither as imposing or anywhere near as talented as Alcindor; but the new backup post man was equally as team-oriented and genuinely as unselfish as the franchise player himself.

There would be a couple of dangerously close games during the early campaign. Rick Mount and Purdue challenged once again out in Los Angeles in the rematch of the two-year home-and-home series. The Boilermakers had visions of being the first club to defeat the invincible Bruins at Pauley and Mount's 17 points before intermission indeed kept it close for a half. Mount was simply brilliant with 33 and had helpless defender Ken Heitz scrambling for much of the contest, but Mount alone could keep the game no closer in the end than 94-82. Notre Dame sophomore Austin Carr also had an eye-catching offensive game in Pauley a few weeks later, but Carr was still two seasons shy of being able to single-handedly defeat a Wooden-coached team.

And then there would be a single momentary stumble just before year's end. Southern Cal coached by wily Bob Boyd was only 15-11 for the season yet provided a thorn in the side of Alcindor and company on successive nights, first falling 61-55 in overtime, then playing a perfect slow-down game to trip the Bruins 46-44.

UCLA nonetheless recovered quickly for another title defense. New Mexico State and Santa Clara offered no challenge whatsoever in the early rounds, yet when Drake threw a few new defensive wrinkles at the Bruins, specifically designed to thwart Alcindor, the unflappable coach and his charges were up to the task of midgame adjustment. Vallely took up the slack with a game-saving 29 points (before fouling out down the home stretch) in what turned out to be a surprisingly tough 85-82 triumph. Shackelford ultimately saved the day with pressure-packed foul shooting in the closing seconds. But only after Sweek stormed off the bench and into the locker room late in the second half when Wooden upbraided him for a slow response to the coach's call for a substitute, and only after Sweek's emergency replacement, sophomore Terry Schofield, floundered badly off the bench with a series of near-game-losing turnovers.

The final game with Purdue offered little of the challenge of the first two matchups with the Boilermakers. Mount, boasting a 33.3 season's average and already (as a junior) closing in on the career Big Ten career scoring record, would again pace his team in scoring with 28, but he would miss 24 of his 36 field-goal attempts and collect the bulk of his baskets only after the outcome had long since been settled. Alcindor closed out his own fabulous career with 37 points and 20 rebounds and yet had to share the spotlight with light-scoring Ken Heitz. Heitz scored nary a point yet stuck to Purdue's star like flypaper and shut down Mount completely until late in the second half. The final 92-72 score put a cap on perhaps the greatest three-year team in history. It also lifted a huge weight from the shoulders of a group of seniors whose three straight national titles were taken in most quarters as little more than what was merely expected. Shackelford for one would note in the postgame celebration that his primary emotion in the wake of another title was merely one of incredible relief.

215

The Alcindor Era had now come to an abrupt end. Wooden had done what was expected of him and perhaps even a good bit more. He had largely avoided losing with a team that most thought simply couldn't lose. He had by and large kept his individual star players satisfied and his juggernaut team motivated and bound together. And that was indeed perhaps the most praiseworthy accomplishment of all.

Second Coming of the Mountain Man

If there was any single campaign during the dozen seasons that Wooden and his teams owned the college scene in which the Bruins by all rights should have been knocked off their lofty perch, it was the 1969-70 season, the very first in the wake of Alcindor. The big man was now gone and the coach faced not only the awesome task of filling this huge void; he would also now again have to readjust his complete game plan to fit his altered circumstances. But any momentary dip in the Bruins' talent level was falsely anticipated and perhaps only a product of wishful thinking almost everywhere outside of Westwood.

With Alcindor gone, Wooden could now actually return to the team-oriented style and proven fast-breaking system with which he had always been most comfortable as well as most successful. There would be three big changes now needed to reshape the ballclub that had won so easily with Alcindor carrying the load. The high-post offense of pre-Alcindor days was revived and soon thrived behind a pair of superb forwards, Wicks and Rowe. The fast break again became a staple under the controls of sophomore point guard Henry Bibby. The zone press was also dusted off and unleashed on hapless opponents. But perhaps the biggest change of all was one of attitude — players who had remained in the shadow of Alcindor now felt for the first time that the team was theirs and that they were indeed contributing mightily to each and every victory.

It was great guard play that always made the Wooden machine run smoothly, and this was indisputably the case even with Alcindor and Walton in the fold. When the '70s first unfolded and Alcindor took his towering act off to the NBA, Wooden may well have lost the true envy of every coaching staff in the land. But the coffers were hardly now empty and the Wizard was in fact left with nothing short of one of his most balanced and talented squads ever. Sidney Wicks was a multidimensional offensive forward who would now be given the necessary freedom to unleash his free-lance driving and shooting game. Curtis Rowe was an equally talented and even more team-oriented frontcourt player. Steve Patterson was not Alcindor, but he was the perfect unselfish post player for the Wooden system, and also for his frontcourt running mates, Wicks and Rowe. In the backcourt there was an experienced shooting guard in John Vallely. And there was also an exceptionally talented sophomore ball handler named Henry Bibby.

The first post-Alcindor squad thus had the talent to win relentlessly even if many of its early-season performances were largely uninspired. There would not only be closer-than-necessary victories (one-point spreads over Minnesota, Princeton and Oregon State), but also a couple of surprise losses to Oregon and Southern Cal, the latter coming on the home floor at Pauley. And the team would also trail Rupp's Kentucky Wildcats in the weekly polls for most of the season.

Seven-footer Artis Gilmore (53) of Jacksonville was touted as the new dominant "tower of power" in the 1970 NCAA Final Four, but unheralded UCLA pivotman Steve Patterson (32) nearly matched Gilmore's offensive totals. (UCLA photo)

Yet when it came to postseason challenges, UCLA would again as always soar, while Baron Rupp's touted Kentucky team would be cut down early and in midflight. Jacksonville's 7-footer Artis Gilmore was now the new tower of strength who threatened to dominate tournament play the way Alcindor had done the previous three seasons. Jacksonville played little defense aside from the shot blocking of Gilmore and fellow 7-footer Pembrook Burrows. But in the three regional contests leading into the Final Four the offensive machine coached by Joe Williams averaged 106.3 points, and this was enough to survive against the likes of Kentucky (106-100) as well as Western Kentucky (109-96) and Iowa (104-103). The combo of Gilmore and Burrows up front was simply too much for the Wildcats to handle, even with the nation's No. 4 scorer, Dan Issel (33.9), doing yeoman service under the boards.

The Alcindor-less Bruins hardly broke a sweat in their own march toward a title showdown with Jacksonville and its original set of Twin Towers. Wins over Long Beach State (88-65), Utah State (101-79) and New Mexico State (93-77) saw the scoring load now switched unselfishly from Bibby (who killed Long Beach with his long-range bombs), to Wicks and Rowe (who combined for 52 against Utah State), to Vallely (who set the pace with 23 in the semis against New Mexico State). It was only in the title match with Gilmore and Burrows that matters got a bit sticky. The oversized Dolphins lineup would present considerable defensive problems for nearly a full half; Wooden started out with his own best shot-blocker, Wicks, assigned to front the towering Gilmore and the strategy quickly proved unworkable. But the adjustments were made in true Wooden fashion and the Jacksonville team was soon left in the dust after Wicks moved behind Gilmore and a collapsing defense was used to effectively plug up the rival big man inside. The final game tally was 80-69, with Rowe matching Gilmore at 19 apiece. But the more important tally now stood at four straight national championships and still counting.

As a new campaign opened, Vallely was the team's only serious graduation loss. And Henry Bibby was now more than ready to fill this gap as the full-time ball handler and prime engineer of the deadly Wooden fast break. And to make things rosier still out in Los Angeles, Wooden had already announced the signing of Alcindor's delayed heir, a gangly star out of San Diego named Bill Walton.

While Walton waited in the wings, the second outing for Wicks, Rowe and Bibby rolled along just as the last one had. The team was methodical in nailing down expected victories and often showed little obvious joy in winning. They did slip once in the hostile environment of the Notre Dame fieldhouse. And this particular seven-point loss would rest solely on the shoulders of an incomparable performance from one of the greatest pure scorers of all time. Austin Carr banked home 46 points and the Bruins were topped 89-82. Notably, it would be the last game they would lose anywhere until well into Walton's senior season.

It was again business as usual once the NCAA postseason rolled around. Jerry Tarkanian masterminded a near-perfect game plan for Long Beach State that almost sprung a major upset. But the Bruins escaped as usual, beating an effective zone thrown up by Tarkanian only when reserve forwards Larry Farmer and John Ecker supplied late-game bench strength to spark a 57-55 victory. And there were no further hints of upset when Final Four action moved into the cavernous Houston Astrodome for semifinal matches between UCLA and Kansas, and Villanova and Western Kentucky. In the finals, Villanova with Howard Porter (25 points) was tough enough and the Wildcats actually provided the Bruins with their closest championship match of their dozen-year reign. The outcome never seemed all that much in doubt, however, as senior center Steve Patterson enjoyed his greatest career moment with a game-high 29 and a key bucket that locked away victory in the game's waning stages. The title string had now climbed all the way to five.

The Final Four session that dropped the curtain on the 1971 season was unquestionably one of the most bizarre of all postseason history. First there was the matter of star Villanova forward Howard Porter and ace 7-footer Jim McDaniels of Western Kentucky. Both were honored on the all-tourney team and Porter even enjoyed a rare distinction of earning the tourney's outstanding player award despite his team's defeat in the finals. When it was announced, however, that ABA clubs had already signed up both Porter and McDaniels for pro contracts prior to the Final Four weekend, both players and their teams were unceremoniously stripped of all postseason honors. The 1971 tourney thus remains the only one in NCAA annals for which two of the Four Four slots as well as the MVP recipient are today posted as "vacated" in the official record books.

If Porter and McDaniels would cast an eerie shadow over the 1971 Finals, so would the behavior of coach Wooden himself. For the second time in three years the almost-always staid Wizard ironically chose the Final Four venue as a stage for displaying the less public side of his testy nature. With the semifinal match in progress against Kansas, the Bruins head man would clash openly along the sidelines over strategy matters with trusted assistant Denny Crum. Crum would depart that very spring for a prestigious head job of his own and some would later attribute Wooden's uncharacteristic flareup to the Wizard's annoyance at not having been consulted in advance on Crum's hiring by Louisville.

> ## The John Wooden File (1948-75)
>
> **NCAA National Championships:** 10 (1964, 1965, 1967, 1968, 1969, 1970, 1971, 1972, 1973, 1975). **NCAA Final Fours:** 12 (21-3 record, including 3rd-Place Consolation Games). **NCAA Tournament Appearances:** 16 (47-10 record, including Consolations). **PCC (AAWU, Pac-8) Championships:** 18 (including several division titles)
>
> **National Coach of the Year Awards:** 19 awards over 6 seasons (**1964** UPI-USBWA, **1967** AP-UPI-USBWA, **1969** AP-UPI-NABC, **1970** AP-UPI-USBWA-NABC, **1972** AP-UPI-USBWA-NABC, **1973** AP-UPI-USBWA). **Note:** AP = Associated Press, UPI = United Press International, USBWA = United States Basketball Writers Association; NABC = National Association of Basketball Coaches
>
> **Awards as Purdue University Player (1930-32):** First-Team All-American in 1930, 1931, and 1932; Helms Foundation National Player of the Year in 1932
>
> **Consensus First-Team All-American Players Coached:** 13 (Walt Hazzard, 1964; Gail Goodrich, 1965; Lew Alcindor, 1967, 1968, 1969; Sidney Wicks, 1971; Henry Bibby, 1972; Bill Walton, 1972, 1973, 1974; Keith Wilkes, 1973, 1974; David Meyers, 1975)
>
> **National Player-of-the-Year Award Winners Coached:** 7 (Walt Hazzard 1964; Lew Alcindor, 1967, 1969; Sidney Wicks, 1971; Bill Walton, 1972, 1973, 1974)

With Bill Walton moving up to the varsity in the fall of 1971 it looked for all the world like the rest of the collegiate field was again staring at three years of chasing after an invincible Wooden team built upon the same model as the one featuring Alcindor. And in large measure all who thought that way were quickly proven absolutely correct.

The Walton-led team was perhaps an even stronger one on paper than the Alcindor squad. Walton's low-post play was this time around complemented by a perfect high-post player in fellow sophomore Keith Wilkes. Wilkes was unlike any of Alcindor's running mates — a good deal better at all phases of the game than anyone surrounding the earlier low-post star. He was an uncanny soft-touch shooter, an adequate passer and smooth as "Silk" (which quickly became his nickname) at both ends of the floor. Larry Farmer and Henry Bibby provided both the necessary capable team-oriented players and experienced shooters on the wings. As a senior Bibby was now assigned his third distinctive role in three seasons, having shifted from off-guard to point guard to wingman. The point was now being handled by Greg Lee and a talented new backup named Tommy Curtis. And there was a stellar bench as well in 6-5 lefty Larry Hollyfield and backup 6-11 center Sven Nater.

Walton for his own part — and as impossible as this seemed — appeared to have even more natural tools than Alcindor. Wooden himself was quoted upon occasion as saying precisely this much. If the new star recruit's political activism left the coach quietly grumbling to himself, his game-time performances certainly never did. "If you were grading a player for every fundamental skill," observed the Wizard, "Walton would rank the highest of any center who ever played."

Such speculative comparisons aside, oncourt achievements by this latest juggernaut seemed to argue that this was indeed the best of all Wooden-coached teams, at least for the first 2½ seasons. Walton's sophomore campaign brought yet another undefeated season, Wooden's third. Postseason play seemed another mere formality, as it often had with Alcindor. In the NCAA Finals, the Florida State team of coach Hugh Durham proved to be a pesky bunch. Long-range marksmanship by FSU guard Ron King (he scored 27 on 12-of-20 shooting) kept the issue close and also kept the final score respectable at 81-76. But even though they held Walton and his mates to the smallest victory margin of the year, Durham's Seminoles could do little more than previous challengers to prevent a sixth straight UCLA national title.

The highlight of the 1973 season, Bill Walton's junior campaign, was the eventual overhauling of Bill Russell and company's untouched streak of 60 straight victories. This was one important milestone that the Alcindor group had never been able to accomplish. It was indeed perhaps the only important milestone left that Wooden's Bruins didn't already own. There was a large dose of irony attached to the pursuit, since the mark was first tied on the road against Loyola-Chicago, the same team that San Francisco had beaten for their own No. 60 back in 1956; then the record fell in another road match versus Notre Dame, the very team that had last beaten the Bruins, and had beaten them on this very same floor in South Bend. By the end of the campaign the Bruins would claim another winning distinction as well, becoming the first major college team to post back-to-back perfect seasons in the modern era of postseason tournament play.

The NCAA Tournament this time around saw Walton and his teammates best the remaining field by an average victory margin of 16 points per game. Indiana, playing only its second year for new mentor Bobby Knight, provided a few early-action surprises in the semifinal by establishing an early lead; but after closing the UCLA lead to just 51-50, the Hoosiers faded away in a 70-59 loss after losing star center Steve Downing to fouls. The championship game seemed to lose something of its luster even before it was played when a powerhouse Providence College team lead by pesky guard Ernie DiGregorio, imposing center Marvin Barnes, and versatile backcourt ace Kevin Stacom, slipped in the other semifinal against an overachieving team from Memphis State.

All this set up a title matchup that would go down in just about everyone's ledger as one of the true highlight moments from the achievement-packed UCLA legacy. It would be the finest hour for one of the game's greatest players, Bill Walton. It would also be perhaps the single greatest one-man performance in tournament finals history. Hal Lear had once had such a game, as had Bill Bradley. But both of those earlier one-man shows had come during the consolation third-place game and thus transpired out of the public view. Walton saved his own grand moment for a prime-time national television audience. The flamboyant redhead sank 21 of 22 shots from the floor (most of the layup variety) and rang up 44 points in the one-sided 87-66 victory. It would set a standard to which Walton would unfortunately never again quite measure up. And in its wake the UCLA ledger now stood at seven straight championships, nine out of the past 10.

The peak had now been reached and the denouement would now begin, gradual as it might prove to be. The story of the 1974 season would thus be largely the story of the ending of two incredible victory strings. But even before those record strings would come to an end there would also be some early-season fireworks. The Bruins would first have to slug it out toe-to-toe with two powerhouse contingents from the rugged ACC over on the other side of the country.

The Maryland game in December went down to the wire in Pauley Pavilion. Fifth-year Terps coach Lefty Driesell had his talented squad (an eventual second-place ACC finisher) primed for its season-opener and All-American center Len Elmore battled Walton even on the boards from start to finish. The scoreboard read 65-64 in favor of the home team at the buzzer when Maryland's crack guard John Lucas could not get off a potential game-winning shot as time expired.

The game against David Thompson and NC State on a neutral floor in St. Louis was, by contrast, much more one-sided than had been expected. State not only featured the best one-on-one player in the land in the guise of the spectacular Thompson, but Norm Sloan's Wolfpack were now desperate to prove their merit after posting an undefeated 1973 ledger yet sitting out the postseason due to NCAA recruiting sanctions. Even though Walton rode the bench for better than half the game in serious foul trouble, new 7-foot understudy Ralph Drollinger filled in competently and NC State could never take full advantage in the 16-point UCLA victory.

It was also in the NC State game that Keith Wilkes proved the magnitude of his growing talents. The senior forward provided the biggest offensive shooting and passing show of the night and also put a smothering blanket around Thompson, boxing out the North Carolina leaper completely near the offensive boards. Indeed, Wilkes established once and for all on this given night that he was far more than simply Bill Walton's caddy.

It would be the next extended road trip back East that would finally see the UCLA streak hit its inevitable roadblock. Walton was injured and didn't play at all versus Iowa as the string stretched to 88 games. Next up were the Notre Dame Fighting Irish, on their own dangerous home floor — in the very building in fact where Wooden had last tasted defeat two seasons earlier. Walton now played, even if not in top physical form, and throughout much of the game both the Bruins and their star center seemed indeed to be at the very peak of their fast-breaking game, as they almost always were. The score stood at 70-59 with only three minutes remaining in what appeared destined to be yet another tough road victory. Walton had canned 12 of 13 from the floor. And this time around there was seemingly to be no sensational home-team performance like the one Austin Carr had earlier unleashed in this self-same arena.

And then what had been so painstakingly built over so long a period all unraveled in a mere matter of moments. The Bruins suddenly became sloppy in their ballhandling — something highly uncharacteristic — and Shumate and Dantley hit key buckets to bring the Irish charging back into contention. Brokaw's jumper cut the lead to the slimmest possible margin. A baseline drive by Wilkes might still have saved the moment, the game and the streak. But this time the whistle went against the Bruins and while Wooden fumed at the officials, the game miraculously slipped away. Dwight Clay hit a baseline jumper to make the count 12-0 Irish over the final three minutes of play. The longest streak in college basketball annals was now finally relegated to the musty pages of history.

This time around the rare loss that had ended a lengthy UCLA winning streak would not simply be an unaccountable aberration on the roadmap of endless Bruins victories. Wooden's team now seemed for some reason to actually struggle down the stretch. There were a pair of inexplicable losses near the end of the season when Walton and his mates traveled to the state of Oregon and succumbed on consecutive nights to disciplined game plans executed by both Oregon and Oregon State. By the early weeks of March UCLA was now struggling to maintain its No. 1 spot in the polls and even to come out on top in its own conference.

Then another corner seemed to be turned. The Bruins ran over Southern Cal at the close of the regular season and appeared again more than ready to keep their lengthy NCAA victory string intact. They would not encounter another stumbling block until the national semifinals and a much-celebrated rematch with the revenge-minded North Carolina State team of coach Norm Sloan which had run its own record to 26-1. But there was a temporary scare in the opening playoff round. This came in the form of a 111-100 triple-overtime victory in which the Pacific-8 champs were barely able to squeeze by an inspired Dayton contingent.

North Carolina State had rebounded well from its own early-season drubbing at the hands of the team from Westwood. Here was truly a team on a mission and that mission was to win a national title that NCAA sanctions had denied them a short season earlier. In the ACC Tournament the Wolfpack had overcome a powerhouse Maryland team in one of the truly thrilling games of the year, squeaking by 103-100 in a game that had required an overtime session to settle the issue. Now they would have their coveted rematch with John Wooden and the Walton Gang.

The NCAA semifinal game between UCLA, with its lengthy tournament winning streak still unbroken, and NC State, with its nearly unblemished two-year regular-season record, was unquestionably a promoter's fondest dream. The game itself turned out to be quite a little less than artistic, however. But even if UCLA was not at its best on this night, neither the Bruins nor their memorable streak would succumb too easily. The record run finally and fittingly disappeared only at the hands of a double-overtime thriller.

In the end it can be said that the Walton Gang finally achieved something during the 1974 national semifinal that Wooden-coached teams had almost never done over the previous dozen or so years. They simply beat themselves. NC State seemed to own the slim advantage, going into the contest, of playing smack in its own backyard at Greensboro. And it also seemed certain that David Thompson would now be much more of a force than he had been the first time the two clubs met several months earlier in St. Louis. The first half remained a draw as David Meyers canned

Richard Washington carried the scoring load for UCLA against Kentucky in the 1975 NCAA Finals as Wooden's Bruins completed one final and extra-sweet championship campaign. (UCLA photo)

a long-range shot at the buzzer to earn the Bruins a 35-35 deadlock at intermission. Both teams missed close-range jumpers (by State's Tom Stoddard and UCLA's Greg Lee) that could have sealed victory at the end of regulation time and an overtime session was thus forced with the scored still deadlocked at 65.

A first overtime period moved at a true snail's pace as Lee's basket for the Bruins was matched by Tom Burleson's bucket for State, and then Sloan's team killed off most of the remaining time waiting for an unsuccessful final shot. The second extra session saw the Bruins open a 74-67 margin on a string of buckets by Walton and Wilkes. But then the Bruins finally came unglued and began handing both the ball and the scoring opportunities over to the resurgent Wolfpack. Clutch foul shots in the closing seconds by first David Thompson and then tiny State guard Monte Towe allowed the Wolfpack to nurse an 80-77 victory to the wire.

The long postseason victory skein was now finally at an end. It had been an unlikely ending, coming as it did in the national semifinals rather than in the show-case finals. And it also came a full year earlier than expected, in the very hour that should have been Bill Walton's crowning moment. Walton would never again, of course, reach the brilliance of his junior season at UCLA. A series of career-threatening injuries would see to that.

But there was still a last brief gasp of life left in the remarkable Wooden program which had made such a habit of spawning championship-caliber teams. This despite the fact that Bill Walton would now be gone, as would Silk Wilkes and the entire backcourt of Tommy Curtis and Greg Lee. Wooden, however, had already proven he could win with well-balanced teams long before Alcindor or Walton had ever arrived. He had once demonstrated this after the graduation loss of his first dominant big man. And he would now again demonstrate it just as emphatically in Bill Walton's absence as well.

The Bruins charged through another season at the top of the wire service polls for much of the stretch from December through March. David Meyers was now the only experienced veteran, but sophomores Marques Johnson and Richard Washington (Walton's replacement) quickly grew into their starting roles and there were only three regular-season defeats.

The season in the end turned entirely on the NCAA semifinal matchup with Louisville, now coached by ex-Wooden aid Denny Crum. There was a natural competitiveness between the mentor and his former pupil that could only have been further fueled by the Final Four blowup between the two just four seasons earlier. Washington drilled two vital free throws and Johnson put back a missed shot as the regulation game clock expired to force an overtime. In the closing seconds of the extra frame it was again Washington who drilled the off-balance jumper that spelled victory with only three ticks left on the scoreboard clock. As the din subsided on the brief locker room celebration Wooden made an announcement behind closed doors to this his final team. The championship match with Kentucky would indeed be the last outing of his glorious career.

At the time there were more than a few cynical onlookers who felt that this final Wooden trip into the NCAA Big Dance was marked more by luck than anything else. The reason behind such doubts was an easily supportable belief that the Meyers-led squad might well never have gotten past the undefeated Indiana Hoosiers, carriers of the Big Ten banner, if not for the Hoosiers' own snakebit circumstances. Knight's team suffered a morale-killing postseason injury to star forward Scott May on the heels of a perfect 28-0 record and then surprisingly fell to Kentucky (92-90 in the Southeastern Regional title game) along the road to the Finals. Instead of the top-ranked Hoosiers it would be the only slightly less formidable Wildcats who would now test Wooden one final time.

The title game with Kentucky was an emotional swansong for the coach whose reputation for so many years had been built on the complete absence of emotional demonstration. In fact it was again a display of fiery temper on the sidelines from the usually placid Bruins mentor that turned around a close came down the stretch and brought UCLA its 10th national title. The Pacific-8 Conference team still nursed a

A gifted sophomore on UCLA's 1975 national championship team, Marques Johnson was the last standout among stellar UCLA backcourt men nurtured by John Wooden. (UCLA photo)

76-75 lead midway through the second stanza when a technical foul call against David Meyers (after a questionable charging foul on a collision with Kentucky's Kevin Grevey) brought Wooden rushing onto the floor in an angry outburst that had to be restrained by his assistants. It was enough, of course, to light a flame under the entire Bruins team and a subsequent charge to the wire behind 28 points from Richard Washington and 24 from Meyers was barely enough to preserve a 92-85 victory.

This final championship of the John Wooden era had been earned with yet another gallant effort in which only six Bruins (starters Meyers, Washington, Marques Johnson, Pete Trgovich and Andre McCarter, plus backup 7-footer Ralph Drollinger) had overcome a powerhouse Kentucky squad that had dogged them in the national polls all winter long. Once again the tourney's outstanding player selection as well as the national team trophy belonged to the Bruins — and this time Richard Washington wore the MVP honor.

And despite the temporary histrionics surrounding a late-game technical call, this final Wooden championship also bore a most fitting stamp of the even-keel emotion that had always marked both the coach and his finest teams. Although Wooden's intention to retire after the tournament had now been revealed to his players and even hinted at to the media, the coach refused to exploit the moment with any emotional pregame pleas for a final triumph in his honor. Quietly addressing his team moments before the opening tip-off Wooden would only wish his charges well and quietly urge them to win the title once more — strictly for themselves.

In retrospect there are few useful yardsticks against which John Wooden's incredible dozen years at the top of the college basketball world can be fairly measured or even entirely grasped. His lead over all other challengers is so wide as to defy any such meaningful comparison. Not only had he taken his team into the Final Four in 12 of 14 seasons; not only had he at one point won 28 straight games in the single-elimination postseason dance; not only did his record for the dozen years stand at 47 victories in 52 NCAA Tournament outings. But in 10 trips to the national championship game he had come away victorious all 10 times.

Seven of those victories came by double figures and the overall victory margin in championship play (10 title games) was nearly 13½ points per game. And in the Final Four alone Wooden had walked away with 21 victories. Here, finally, lies perhaps the most impressive raw statistic of all. Wooden's 21 Final Four wins surpass the entire cumulative total logged by 26 other outstanding coaches, all of whom have also registered 500 or more career wins during a minimum of 10 seasons logged at Division I colleges since the 1939 launching of tournament play. The impressive list includes Phog Allen (four Final Four victories), Frank McGuire (3), Jerry Tarkanian (3) and Ray Meyer (1), among others. Runner-up to Wooden in Final Four game victories is Baron Adolph Rupp with but nine.

It had been a marvelous joyride stretching for an incredible dozen years. But it had not been a dynasty run without its special trials and tribulations. Nonetheless, college basketball had never seen anything like it before. And more than likely it will never see anything quite like it again.

10

The Seventies, Part 2

Hangtime and the Playground Game

While the boldface headline stories in college basketball during the 1960s and early 1970s were usually being made on the campuses of major conference schools — in the Big Ten, ACC, Pacific Coast Conference, SEC or Big Eight — there were also other minidramas played out among the second-rate powers and even among the sport's also-rans. One of the most colorful of these tales involves Providence College and its seemingly endless string of exciting backcourt stars popularly dubbed by the press and electronic media as the Friars' "Little Big Men" — Providence guards whose brilliant passing and shooting could control the action of an entire game.

The tradition of Providence College basketball had actually been launched at the dawn of the school's existence back in 1921. During that first decade the small Dominican school had already pulled off several attention-grabbing upsets against bigger New England and New York rivals, including Buck Freeman's legendary "Wonder Five" team at St. John's. Eddie Wineapple (1929) and John Krieger (1930) were the school's first cage stars, and it was Krieger who paced the upset which handed Freeman and St. John's their only 1930 defeat. In the '30s the Friars would pick up a full head of steam under their new coach, former Notre Dame player Ed Crotty, and again would count among their victories notable upsets of schools like Princeton, Villanova and Seton Hall to the South, neighbors Harvard, Yale, Dartmouth, Holy Cross, Brown and Rhode Island in New England, and Manhattan and once more St. John's among the New York City elite. The best overall season came with a 15-5 record during the war-weakened campaign of 1943 and with Coach Crotty still at the helm.

But it was not until the mid-50s and the arrival of mentor Joe Mullaney that Providence would be able to make a lasting impression on the national scene. While Crotty would win at a near 70 percent clip during his 11-year tenure that ended in 1946, Mullaney would construct a 14-year legacy that would include nine 20-win years in succession and be marred by only a single losing season in 1968 (11-14). This Mullaney tradition of excellence would mark a high point of Providence College cage history for more reasons than the regular 20-win ledgers, however. For under Mullaney, the Friars would also launch a phenomenon that would quickly become the very trademark of Providence basketball. It was the phenomenon of the stellar "little man" (that is, a guard) who always played like a big man (a star scorer or game dominator). The very first to fit the mold were the tandem of "cool" and deadly Lenny Wilkens, a sophomore in 1958, and flamboyant Johnny Egan, a Connecticut hotshot who showed up a year later.

The breakthrough came with the 1958-59 team of Wilkens' junior season. It was in his second year in the Friars' backcourt that Wilkens began building the reputation for quietly efficient and ruthlessly steady play that would soon also become the staple of a brilliant NBA career. And it was that season, as well, that the Friars debuted in the NIT in what would be the first of nine straight postseason trips.

The postseason invitation had come on the heels of Mullaney's and also the school's maiden 20-victory ledger. While Wilkens rarely called attention to himself with his smooth-as-silk backcourt style, and only scored at a 15.7 clip, nonetheless the fluid backcourt ace would nearly always pace the team in points, steals and assists, as well as igniting crucial comeback rallies and orchestrating protection of late-game leads. With Wilkens thus showing the way, the first-ever Providence postseason appearance would not wind down until a 76-55 semifinal loss to St. John's (led by Al Seiden and tourney MVP Tony Jackson) and a 71-57 consolation-game mauling at the hands of NYU (featuring tourney high-scorer Cal Ramsey).

The team was even better during Wilkens' senior season as it upped the season's win total from 20 to 24 and the NIT finish from fourth place to second. The biggest plus for the 1960 club was the emergence of junior John Egan as the perfect backcourt mate to senior All-American Wilkens. If Wilkens was a rock-steady take-charge guy, Egan was the fiery game-breaker type who ignited crowds and devastated opponents with sudden flurries of relentless scoring and brilliant playmaking. Behind this combo, and with a huge assist from rugged center Jim Hadnot, the Friars ran off 18 wins in the season's final 19 games, then strung together three straight dramatic come-from-behind Madison Square Garden tournament victories. In the NIT finals, however, they were finally outmatched by fourth-ranked Bradley and its high-scoring All-American forward Chet "The Jet" Walker. Mullaney's hard-driving Friars actually shut down the potent Walker (he had nine) in the title match, but four other Bradley sharpshooters (including unheralded Mack Herndon with 26) racked up double figures to turn the 16-point game Bradley's way. Len Wilkens, even in defeat, was tabbed the NIT's most valuable performer after his final collegiate game.

Wilkens was now gone after the 1960 season but Friar basketball had barely begun its flight toward true national prominence. John Egan carried Providence to a repeat 24 victories and straight back into the NIT finals a year later, this time with a new "little big man" as his running mate. Vinnie Ernst was only 5-foot-8 and a reluctant shooter yet he supplemented Egan's explosive offense to a tee with his own stellar playmaking, just as Wilkens had done throughout two previous seasons. Ernst didn't score much — a team-low four points — yet he unleashed his clever quarterbacking skills to control the nip-and-tuck title game against Saint Louis University that brought the Friars their first of two NIT championships. This time it was the diminutive Ernst who was tourney MVP, despite the high scoring of Jack "The Shot" Foley (with 120 points in four games) for third-place Holy Cross.

The loss of Egan seemingly signalled a more severe drop-off than the loss of Wilkens, and the 1962 Friars would be unceremoniously dumped in the very first

Jimmy Walker, 1967 national scoring leader, was only one in a long line of Providence College "Little Big Men" who provided an exciting chapter of collegiate cage history throughout the 1960s and early '70s. (Providence College photo)

round of tournament action. Temple did the honors by surprising a Providence team that had brought Mullaney his fourth consecutive 20-win season yet suddenly lacked firepower with Ernest now the primary threat in the backcourt.

But it was only a temporary slide for the Rhode Island team that was now becoming something of a New England favorite son. One year later Vinnie Ernst and company would be back for the NIT championship game — their third in four seasons — with John Thompson (the famed Georgetown coach of future decades) now installed at center and Ray Flynn now picking up the backcourt slack alongside the veteran Ernst. Just as the dynamite duo of Wilkens-Egan had given way to Egan-Ernst, now the double-barrelled "little-man attack" would be comprised of Ernst and new sidekick Flynn. Ray Flynn — himself headed for future prominence as mayor of Boston and U.S. ambassador to the Vatican — would suddenly catch fire as a senior, tying Thompson for team scoring honors (18.9) and then upping his game still another notch in time for postseason play. Flynn was the fireplug of NIT festivities as he banged home 83 points and pocketed MVP honors for his substantial efforts. The future politician canned 20 in his farewell college outing as the Friars romped over Canisius 81-66 for their second and final NIT crown.

During this glory run Providence had remained very much a minor-league player on the national scene. This fact as much as any other was the measure of how far the National Invitation Tournament had now slipped in the public estimation and how much the Madison Square Garden event had come to be seen as a regional rather than national event. Wilkens, Ernst and Flynn had all captured NIT most valuable honors and yet none had been first-team All-Americans. Furthermore Mullaney's five straight 20-win teams had never once cracked the nation's top 10 in wire service voting. And they had year after year remained outside the more prestigious NCAA postseason festival looking in.

During the next several seasons this would all change rather drastically as Providence turned the corner with three straight NCAA visits, although it never managed to escape the Eastern Regional playdowns in any of these three campaigns. The 1965 team did capture opening-round matches with West Virginia and St. Joseph's before being soundly blitzed by sensational Bill Bradley and Princeton to the tune of 109-69 in the Eastern Regional finals. If the Princeton drubbing was a year-end lowlight it was certainly not enough, however, to put much of a damper on a season which signaled bright things indeed for the immediate future.

For one thing, the '65 Friars had a new big-time little man stationed in the backcourt and this one was seemingly destined to be the best of them all. He was 6-3 guard Jimmy Walker out of Boston, and he would quickly prove the greatest offensive machine in school history. With Walker upping his scoring average from 20.5 to 24.5 as a junior and earning All-American plaudits, the Friars would barely maintain their top-10 status for 1966. Yet once again they faltered in the NCAA first round. This time old nemesis St. Joseph's provided the knockout, 65-48, to nullify an otherwise brilliant 22-5 season. As a senior, Walker would average more than 30 points per game as the nation's leading scorer, besting UCLA sophomore Lew Alcindor for the honor. Back in the NIT — despite Walker's heroics and Mullaney's ninth and final 20-win campaign — still another postseason run would peter out with a one-point quarterfinals loss to runner-up Marquette.

The Providence success run had seemingly lost steam by the end of the '60s when coach Mullaney suddenly defected to the pro ranks. But two new arrivals on the scene also offered considerable promise despite the couple of mediocre seasons that greeted their arrival. The first was an energetic young coach named Dave Gavitt who had come over from Dartmouth College where his only two seasons as head man had resulted in losing campaigns while the second was yet another "little big man" to inherit the burden of tradition in the Friars' backcourt. Ernie DiGregorio was a local Providence schoolboy sensation who already looked like a second coming of Bob Cousy grafted to an undersized version of Pete Maravich. And it wouldn't be long before the latest pint-sized floor general would indeed prove nearly the equal of Cousy as a playmaker, even if he — like absolutely everyone else — fell considerably short of Maravich as a prolific scorer.

During his sophomore season Ernie "Dee" almost singlehandedly engineered an earlier-than-expected revival in Providence cage fortunes. The reversal came in the form of another 20-victory season (the first in four winters) and a seventh trip back to the still festive if now somewhat lusterless NIT. There the Friars were dumped in the second round by eventual champion North Carolina. Unfortunately for Friars coaches, players and fans, Carolina was a revenge-minded team when Providence ran into them in the quarterfinals; the Tar Heels had nested comfortably atop the ACC all winter long only to carelessly drop out of the NCAA picture under sneak attack from South Carolina during the finals of the league tourney. But if the loss stung it didn't do much to slow the newly ignited Providence momentum, and DiGregorio's junior year found the backcourt ace pacing his team to another 21 wins and an even more prestigious NCAA Eastern Regionals berth. The postseason appearance again ended quickly, however, as they so often did for Providence teams that had such an easy time of it against lesser competition in December, January and February. This time the exit was provided with a first-round 76-60 defeat at the hands of the Ivy League champions from Pennsylvania.

The much-publicized dominance of the "little men" at Providence — from Wilkens to Ernst to Ernie "Dee" — had somewhat overshadowed some fine frontcourt play turned in over the years by a more limited lineage of "big men" that included Jim Hadnot during the era of Wilkens and Egan, and John Thompson a few seasons later. Thompson would earn the bulk of his fame only after grabbing the coaching reins for Georgetown less than a decade after his Providence graduation; before that he would serve two seasons and 74 games in the trenches as Bill Russell's infrequently used backup with Red Auerbach's dynasty Boston Celtics. Then in Hadnot's and Thompson's wake Providence would fortuitously recruit its best-ever big man, 6-8 Marvin Barnes, just in the nick of time to supplement Ernie "Dee's" final two seasons of stellar playmaking.

Dave Gavitt had his pieces in place in time for his fourth season at the Rhode Island school. Ernie "Dee" was rounding out his final season as a consensus first team All-American. Barnes had dipped some in scoring proficiency from his sophomore campaign (down to 18.3 from 21.6) but had shown marked improvement as a rebounder and defender. Kevin Stacom at 6-4 provided an important third element as a solid scorer (17.8) shoring up the backcourt alongside DiGregorio. And there were also two dependable starters at the forwards in Fran Costello (9.1 ppg) and Nehru King (8.7 ppg). This solid group compiled a 27-4 record in 1973 that was the best in school history. They also provided New England fans with their most memorable run at the major postseason prize since Holy Cross and Cousy had cracked the Final Four in the two immediate post-war seasons.

Barnes was the unsung hero. The muscular 6-8 center trailed only American University's Kermit Washington in the national rebounding chase and provided the inside strength that powered Providence to a 24-2 record. The Friars lost only to Santa Clara and UCLA on a midseason West Coast trip, took 14 straight down the stretch and had earned a No. 4 ranking (AP) heading into March tournament play.

The Providence phenomenon would thus finally peak with the tandem of DiGregorio outside and Barnes inside, and this zenith ultimately came during 1973 postseason wars when Providence finally made its long overdue mark in NCAA tourney play. St. Joseph's and Penn had often been stumbling blocks in past postseasons but not this time around. The Friars coasted past St. Joe's by 13 in the East Regional opener at Williamsburg, Virginia, largely on the strength of 31 from DiGregorio, then crushed Penn 87-65 in Charlotte to earn a date with ACC power-house Maryland in the East finals. The Friars' clubbing of Penn had featured some truly outstanding shooting: Barnes was 10-for-10 from the floor, Stacom was seven-for-nine, Nehru King chipped in with seven-for-11,and sub Charles Crawford was a perfect six-for-six as the Friars rang up a remarkable 65 percent from the field.

Behind the flashy Ernie "Dee" and the durable Marvin Barnes the Friars next charged to an Eastern Regional title with a convincing racehorse-style victory over Maryland. Maryland had been one of the nation's powerhouse teams coming into the tournament, owning a No. 9 ranking and 22 victories, with all six of its losses com-ing in highly competitive ACC league play. But even a lineup featuring juniors Len Elmore and Tom McMillen, and freshman John Lucas was not enough to slow a Providence offense powered by 30 from Ernie "Dee" and 24 from Kevin Stacom; Providence coasted 103-89 and owned a regional title in the bargain.

Providence had finally made it to the Big Dance known as the NCAA Final Four. But in the national semifinal game staged in the St. Louis Checkerdome against Memphis State the dream ended suddenly and in most unexpected fashion. The evening opened well enough as Ernie "Dee" rang up 11 early points and the Friars ran to a 24-16 lead during the first 10 minutes. Then Barnes crashed to the floor with what proved to be a dislocated right kneecap and along with the painful injury the Friars' hopes for a revenge rematch with UCLA and John Wooden came crashing earthward as well. Memphis State made up a nine-point halftime deficit in short order and rolled in the second stanza with Larry Kenon (22 rebounds, 28 points) and Ronnie Robinson (16 rebounds, 24 points) dominating the boards and the scoring in Barnes' absence. Few doubted that the 98-85 losing margin might have been quite different had a healthy Marvin Barnes been available for second-half duty. As it was, with their star rebounder now done for the year, Gavitt's depleted Friars received equally rough treatment from Indiana (97-79) in the consolation match two nights later.

The heyday era was now at an end for the Mullaney-Gavitt Friars. Yet during their partially successful run toward the top, launched with Len Wilkens back in 1959, Providence had indeed brought something of a return to glory for an Eastern basketball tradition that had seemed to wane considerably since La Salle had reached the NCAA mountaintop in the early '50s. During the 21 seasons that stretched from 1955 to 1976 and separated Loeffler's La Salle Explorers with Tom Gola from Bob Knight's Indiana Hoosiers with Scott May, five teams from New England made it into the final game of either the increasingly popular NCAAs or the decreasingly popular NIT. Four of those five teams wore the name of Providence College.

Providence as much as any team of the era represented the epitome of the play-ground style of modern basketball. It was a style once perfectly defined by historian Neil Issacs, one that obliterated all regional characteristics and all provincial play-ing styles and replaced them with five defining elements of the modern-era game. For Isaacs, these elements each had its own special prototype performer — the gunner born of Stanford's Hank Luisetti, the fancy ball handler and passer cut in the mold of Bob Cousy, the muscular inside post man patterned after George Mikan, the rebounder and defensive stopper in the shape of Bill Russell, and the all-around offensive intimidator never surpassed since Oscar Robertson (except perhaps by Air Jordan). That these elements still characterize the game at even its highest levels is attested by contemporary players like Reggie Miller (the gunner), John Stockton (the passer), Shaquille O'Neal (the inside muscleman), Dennis Rodman (the rebounder) and Michael Jordan (the offensive intimidator).

It was the meshing of these complementing elements that was the true triumph of collegiate basketball (and in its wake, also the pro version of the game) by the second decade after the world war of the mid-40s and after the disruptive betting scandals of the early '50s. Basketball had now become a national game, universally played and universally understood. Its five defining elements can always be found — in varying degrees of perfection — on any collegiate court, in any pro arena or on any schoolyard playground.

The essence of the contemporary style of basketball has thus been the merger of concrete individual moves with patterns of abstract team movement. Set plays for specific game situations and basic patterns of offense to offset an array of defensive systems are all designed with one object in mind — to free the individual player with the ball for an open shot that he has a high percentage chance of making. Ultimately the game always comes down — in the final split second of action, repeated over and over again — to the daring individual playground skills of an isolated shooter who must successfully outmaneuver one defender or multiple defenders on his way to the hoop.

At the tail end of the '60s it seemed as though individualistic "moves" of star players were taking their greatest hold upon the game. It was in the final three years of the 1960s, in particular, that some of the flashiest one-on-one artists of all time would simultaneously emerge on courts from Baltimore to Berkeley and Buffalo to Baton Rouge. Foremost among the new breed of net-fillers were Pete Maravich, who terrorized SEC opponents from his backcourt post at LSU, and midget small-school star Calvin Murphy, who nearly kept pace up at Niagara.

Maravich was a true '60s phenomenon if there ever was one. He wore floppy socks that dusted his shoe tops, featured a rock n' roller's floppy hair style and was the hardwood court's supreme individualist. He was a player who was truly the stuff of mind-stretching myth and larger-than-life legend.

In the same colorful package hoops fans here had not only the most prolific college scorer ever, but also the most flamboyant ball handler to boot. "Pistol Pete" could do things with a basketball that no one else had ever done — not even Bob Davies at Seton Hall with his behind-the-back dribbling or Bob Cousy at Holy Cross with his behind-the-back no-look passing. But most of all Pete could flat-out shoot it. If Julius Erving (whose sophomore season at Massachusetts overlapped Maravich's senior year at LSU) would by the mid-70s redefine the game played above the rim, Maravich would at the outset of the '70s already have redefined the game being played below the rim.

Pete Maravich left a scoring legacy in his wake that has never been matched. While other schools boast their select lists of career 1,000-point scorers, with Maravich LSU had a shooter who would top the four-digit figure in each of his three

Pete Maravich wore socks that often flopped on his hightops, but "Pistol Pete" so dazzled the crowds with his phenomenal shooting and passing that few ever noticed. (Louisiana State University photo)

The Scoring Legacy of "Pistol Pete" Maravich

Season-by Season Ledger

Season	G	FGM	FGA	FG%	FTM	FTA	FT%	Reb.	Pts.	Ppg.
1967-68 (So)	26	432	1022	.423	274	338	.811	195	1138	43.8
1968-69 (Jr)	26	433	976	.444	282	378	.746	169	1148	44.2
1969-70 (Sr)	31	522	1168	.447	337	437	.773	164	1381	44.5
Totals	**83**	**1387**	**3166**	**.438**	**893**	**1152**	**.775**	**528**	**3667**	**44.2**

varsity seasons. He scored more than 50 points in 28 different games and registered high games of 66 and 69. Three straight times he reigned as national scoring champ, something that only Oscar Robertson accomplished before him and no one has duplicated since. He would average a phenomenal 44.2 for an entire three-year career and do this not against phony competition, like Bevo Francis had, or inconsistent competition like Frank Selvy had, but instead against defenses from one of the premier conferences in the land. No one except Francis and Selvy had ever before scored quite like this. And neither Bevo nor Selvy ever had to face nightly opponents from conference rivals named Kentucky, Tennessee, Vanderbilt or Mississippi State, or intersectional rivals named Southern Cal (against them Pete scored 50), UCLA or St. John's (Pete outscored the entire opposing team in the second half of one Rainbow Classic matchup).

Maravich had come out of rural Aliquippa,

The Maravich NCAA Record Ledger

(Division I NCAA Records Still Held)

Most Points in Season	1,381 (1969-70)
Most Points in Career	3,667 (1968-70)
Average Per Game for Season	44.5 (1969-70)
Average Per Game for Career	44.2 (1968-70)
Games Scoring at Least 50 Points in Season	10 (1969-70)
Consecutive Games Scoring 50 Points	3 (1969-70)
Games Scoring at Least 50 Points in Career	28 (1968-70)
Field Goals Made in Season	522 (1969-70)
Field Goals Made in Career	1,387 (1968-70)
Field-Goal Attempts in Season	1,168 (1969-70)
Field-Goal Attempts in Career	3,166 (1968-70)
Free Throws Made in Game	30 (vs. Oregon State 12-22-69)
Free Throws Made in 3-Year Career	893 (1968-70)
Free-Throw Attempts in 3-Year Career	1,152 (1968-70)

Most Combined Points (Game) by Two Opposing Players: Maravich (64) and Dan Issel, Kentucky (51) on February 21, 1970

Pennsylvania, and had prepped for an extra post-high school year at Edwards Military Academy in order to polish his already unmatched talents. His college coach was his own father, the flamboyant Press Maravich, who was lured from North Carolina State in a package deal that LSU athletic officials hoped would bring their program back to the prominence enjoyed in the early '50s with Bob Pettit. The arrival of the Maraviches in Baton Rouge did indeed take some of the focus off of Rupp and Kentucky for perhaps the first time in SEC history. And together the pair added flair and color to the ever more spectacular collegiate game.

But the one thing they did not do was win any championships during the years of Pete's one-man show down at LSU. In fact they were barely an above-average team, posting two .500 campaigns before finally going 22-10 in 1970 and enjoying a third-place NIT finish. The reason was quite obvious — Maravich did nothing to make his teammates better and perhaps quite a bit to make them worse. He played over their heads, bounced spectacular passes off their legs and shoulders, gambled and freelanced himself on defense, and soloed in search of big-scoring nights rather than hard-earned team victories. It was a style that would eventually earn a seven-figure pro contract at the end of the line but few team triumphs along the way. And for all his individual brilliance, Pete Maravich was never enough of a team player to earn himself or his supporting crew even a single visit to the sport's main event, postseason NCAA play.

Calvin Murphy was every bit as phenomenal as Maravich, especially if one considers his diminutive physical stature. Here was the player everyone judged too small to play successfully in the big-time college game. Here was also a 5-9 relentless shooting machine who was as talented a pure scorer as anyone who ever rattled the rafters of a local college gym or lit up a local playground scene. Like Maravich, Murphy entertained fans with lightning-quick change-of-direction dribbles, uncanny blind passes and an array of off-balance bombs from anywhere within sight of the basket. At the same time he also devastated enemy defenses with bushels of points, including 68 against Syracuse during his junior season.

Murphy, who was tutored in long-range marksmanship by his ballplaying mother, began setting scoring marks at equally tiny New Canaan High School in rural Connecticut. He averaged 38.2 as a sophomore (second in the land to fellow second-year man Maravich) and 33.1 for his full career at Niagara University in upstate New York. And in his later pro career with the Houston Rockets the pint-sized hotshot would set new standards for free-throw shooting accuracy (95 percent for a single season and above 90 percent in five others) that long remained untouched by subsequent marksmen. Murphy's lifetime 89.2 percent from the charity stripe in NBA action trails only the 89.3 percent of Rick Barry.

Murphy would peak during 1967-68 as an unknown rookie, when he trailed only Maravich in the national scoring race. A year later as a junior he would be bested by again Maravich and Purdue standout Rick Mount. Mount was another superscorer who could hit unerringly from virtually anywhere on the floor, and his own career .483 shooting percentage (.515 as a junior) far outstrips both Maravich and Murphy (both at .438). But both Mount (6-4) and Maravich (6-5) had a hefty height advantage over Murphy that made the midget guard seem even more phenomenal to those who saw him dominate a college or even a professional game.

The tradition of Maravich and Murphy at the end of the '60s was carried on by a few additional peerless practitioners of one-on-one play in the first

By normal Wildcats standards Kentucky was quiet on the national scene between Rupp's last NCAA title in 1958 amd Joe B. Hall's single championship two decades later. But in the middle of this stretch came Kentucky's biggest all-time offensive weapon, future ABA and NBA great Dan Issel. (University of Kentucky photo)

few seasons of the '70s. Austin Carr carved out a lasting legend at Notre Dame that would be highlighted by a 41.3 scoring average in seven NCAA tourney games between 1969 and 1971. Even more brilliant in postseason play than during the rest of his remarkable record-laced career, Carr still holds NCAA tournament scoring

Pete Maravich of LSU was the talk of the college basketball world at the end of the '60s. Basketball's most relentless scorer, however, was never able to take his team into NCAA Tournament play. (Louisiana State University photo)

standards for career average, single-tournament average (52.7 in three games in 1970), and single-game points (61 versus Ohio University in 1970). And for a single winter there was also Johnny Neumann at SEC also-ran Mississippi. A 6-6 forward/guard out of Memphis, the tireless Ole Miss gunner would debut with a lofty 40.1 average to pace the country in scoring during the first campaign after Maravich's departure from LSU. Neumann would then forego the remainder of his college eligibility by inking a contract with the hometown ABA Memphis Pros. A singular spectacular sophomore year and quick departure for a disappointing pro career (he averaged 14.9 in five ABA seasons and 5.6 across two NBA years) would leave Johnny Neumann on a pedestal with Maravich alone as the only other career 40-point scorer in NCAA annals.

But it was Carr and not Neumann who would log enough playing time to rank as a legitimate runner-up to Pistol Pete in the career NCAA scoring derby. Another in the long line of Washington, D.C., playground legends that began with Elgin Baylor, Carr would be best remembered in future years for leading Notre Dame to the memorable upset win over Wooden's 1971 UCLA team in South Bend that provided the Bruins' final setback before their own remarkable 88-game win streak. Carr scored 46 against the Walton Gang in one of his typical undefensible scoring onslaughts. But the 6-3 guard with the uncanny shooting eye and the ballet-like hangtime moves around the hoop would also set other scoring standards that would leave him as the second all-time career scorer in NCAA history. Number 34 for the Irish would average better than 38 points per game during his junior and senior seasons. And his 34.6 three-year career average left him comfortably ahead of both Oscar Robertson and Calvin Murphy on the all-time list.

The end of the turbulent '60s and outset of the seditious '70s marked the greatest single era for phenomenal scorers. Maravich and Murphy and Carr stood at the head of the class. Mount and Neumann and others (Elvin Hayes at Houston, Spencer Haywood of Detroit, Dan Issel in Kentucky, and George McGinnis in Indiana) amply backed them up. It would soon be the rim-rattling slam dunk that would capture fans' emotions. But in the era of the pure shooter it was still that long-range bomb that provided the cage fan's greatest instantaneous thrills.

In the Wizard's Wake Comes a Knight in Shining Armour

If the playground style of play was the lasting legacy of the 1960s, the following decade would provide its own set of innovations and landmarks. Great scorers of the '60s a la Maravich had their parallels in the following decade, to be sure. The UCLA dynasty of the second half of the '60s would also be bookended by Wooden's continued mastery in the first half of the '70s. And when UCLA's ultimate demise at mid-decade finally did signal the end of an era, it also marked an era of new beginnings. For with the second half of the '70s would come some important new faces and some important new directions.

On the coaching front the mantle would be passed in the mid-70s from Wooden to his two most accomplished successors, Bob Knight at Indiana and Dean Smith at North Carolina. Knight came on the scene with the Hoosiers in time for the 1971-72 campaign after six moderately successful seasons as head man at Army; by the end of his second season in Bloomington he would already boast his first NCAA Final Four entrant. Smith started exactly a decade earlier in Chapel Hill and was already proud owner of nine straight postseason appearances — including an NIT title in 1971 — by the time Wooden announced his retirement.

Both Smith and Knight would earn a measure of trivial fame as the only two men ever to coach and play with an NCAA national champion. (Vic Bubas, Dick Harp and Bones McKinney were three others to both play for and then coach a Final Four team, but none ever won the title as either coach or player.) Yet both "The Dean" and "The General" would also soon enough be known for so much more than their unique Final Four double whammies. Thirty years later both would be closing in on numerous records for total victories and also have constructed legends in their own parts of the country that are second only to Rupp's in Kentucky and Wooden's everywhere else in the land.

Smith has now crossed the 800-victory plateau (a land visited by Rupp alone) and is on a safe pace to accomplish the once unthinkable, by surpassing Rupp's record total of 876 wins before the end of the 1997 campaign. Knight himself stands only a handful of victories short of the all-time top 10 list and boasts even greater successes in postseason warfare. The often controversial Hoosier mentor not only is one of but three coaches (with Smith and Pete Newell) to win titles at all three major levels (NCAA, NIT, Olympics) but also remains the single coach who has advanced a minimum of five times to the national semifinals of both the NCAA and NIT postseason parties.

The new era would also witness an unprecedented spread in popularity for the roundball sport brought on by the sudden boom of basketball as prime-time television spectacle. And the second half of the '70s would also have its set of flashy individual stars primed to take full advantage of such nightly living room exposure. There would again be scoring giants like David Thompson at NC State, Adrian Dantley of Notre Dame, Freeman Williams at Portland (1977 and 1978 national scoring leader with Maravich-like 38.8 and 35.9 averages) and Marshall Rogers at Pan American (1976 national pacesetter at 36.8). But at the end of the decade there would arise two players — as responsible as any for the new-found popularity of

Indiana's "General" Bob Knight would make his first big conquest on the national scene with an undefeated 1976 NCAA championship team that many still consider the greatest starting unit in college basketball history. (Indiana University Instructional Support Services Photo by Nick Judy)

Naismith's sport — who worked their "magic" with flair and flamboyance as well as unharnessed scoring. Earvin "Magic" Johnson at Michigan State and Larry Bird at Indiana State would provide unparalleled excitement in the final year of the decade, culminating in a ballyhooed *mano a mano* matchup that even today remains one of the true landmarks of collegiate cage history.

The years immediately following Wooden's last NCAA title were several of the most competitive in the game's modern era. Knight's Indiana team peaked with a dominating season in 1976 that provided the last undefeated national champion. But Knight and his Hoosiers could not sustain their run past a single season and didn't even make it out of their own Big Ten Conference wars the following year. The next several campaigns were marked by competitive conference races, wide-open and upset-spiced shootouts for the national title, exciting postseason play and a steady succession of top-quality teams.

Top 10 Winningest Coaches

Coach	Schools (Years)	Record (Pct.)
Adolph Rupp	Kentucky (1931-72)	876-190 (.822)
Dean Smith	North Carolina (1962-95)	830-232 (.779)
Henry Iba	Northwest Missouri, Colorado, Oklahoma State (1930-70)	767-338 (.694)
Ed Diddle	Western Kentucky (1923-64)	759-302 (.715)
Phog Allen	Baker, Kansas (1906-56)	746-264 (.739)
Ray Meyer	DePaul (1943-84)	724-354 (.672)
Ralph Miller	Wichita, Iowa, Oregon St. (1952-89)	674-370 (.646)
Don Haskins	Texas-El Paso (1962-95)	665-298 (.691)
John Wooden	**Indiana State, UCLA (1947-75)**	**664-162 (.804)**
Norm Stewart	Northern Iowa, Missouri (1962-95)	660-319 (.674)

Additional Challengers (Former Members) to All-Time Top 10

Coach	Schools (Years)	Record (Pct.)
Bobby Knight	Army, Indiana (1966-95)	659-235 (.737)
Lefty Driesell	Davidson, Maryland, James Madison (1961-95)	657-302 (.685)
Marv Harshman	Pacific Lutheran, Washington St., Washington (1946-85)	654-449 (.589)
Lou Henson	Hardin-Simmons, New Mexico State, Illinois (1963-95)	645-318 (.670)
Jerry Tarkanian	**Long Beach State, UNLV, Fresno State (1969-95)**	**631-125 (.837)**
Norm Sloan	Presbyterian, Citadel, Florida, NC State (1952-89)	627-395 (.614)

Ranked by Total Career Victories (Coaches also with .800-Plus Winning Percentage in Boldface)

One storybook team of the immediate post-Wooden era was Al McGuire's national champion 1977 Marquette Warriors. The appearance of Marquette at the top of the pack was not at all an overnight affair; with a truckload of talent which included Maurice Lucas, Bo Ellis, Earl Tatum and Lloyd Walton, the well-schooled Warriors had climbed into the Final Four in 1974 where they offered a stern challenge to David Thompson and the NC State Wolfpack in the hard-fought title game. A year earlier McGuire had his team ranked fifth entering postseason play before it stumbled against Indiana in the Mideast Regional semifinals. The '71 (2nd) and '72 (7th) McGuire teams had also finished near the top of the wire service polls but were likewise second-round NCAA victims (against Ohio State and Kentucky); and the decade had opened for Marquette with their single NIT title, earned on the strength of a 65-53 victory over local Garden favorite St. John's. The early '70s had also seen Marquette churn out a couple of consensus first-team All-Americans in 6-1 guard Dean Meminger (1971) and 6-11 center Jim Chones (1972).

Coach McGuire himself owned a storied and colorful basketball heritage. The Long Island native had performed as a fiery guard with St. John's University before logging four journeyman NBA seasons in the same New York Knicks lineup that also featured brother "Tricky" Dick as the star point guard. As a college coach McGuire would eventually serve 20 seasons, seven at tiny North Carolina-based Belmont Abbey and 13 with Marquette; he would record 405 victories, grab three national coach of the year honors (1971, 1974, 1977), visited both the NCAA and NIT final fours twice and run off 11 straight 20-win seasons to close out his brilliant career. And even in retirement Al McGuire would remain a fixture on the college basketball scene after turning to a second career as an extroverted and entertaining announcer for NBC coverage of college action.

Yet if Marquette was not a newcomer it was certainly the largest surprise during 1977 postseason play. And the Warriors did it without a marquee superstar player. The lineup was solid if not imposing, with 6-10 center Jerome Whitehead crashing

240

North Carolina mentor Dean Smith stands in his own universe as the only coach to join Baron Adolph Rupp in the exclusive circle of 800-game winners. "The Dean" now threatens to overhaul the Baron's once unapproachable standard of 876 career victories. (University of North Carolina photo)

the boards and 6-9 forward Bo Ellis still around from the '74 Final Four club. Butch Lee, a flashy 6-2 guard recruited by McGuire out of the Bronx, was a season away from becoming Marquette's third and final consensus first-team All-American. But Lee's 19.6 scoring pace in his junior season was the best of his career and he was the closest thing McGuire had to a star of the first rank. And if the Warriors had to rise above the label of anonymity they also had to overcome large first-half deficits in all four preliminary rounds (victories over Cincinnati, Kansas State, Wake Forest and UNC Charlotte in the semifinals) that earned their spot in the tournament title game.

McGuire and Marquette versus Dean Smith's North Carolina Tar Heels provided one of the most emotional title games in the modern era of tourney play. Led by a memorable guard-forward combo of Phil Ford and Walter Davis, North Carolina had captured a second straight ACC title and hovered in the AP top five all season. For the already venerable Dean Smith it was the fifth trip into the Final Four and his second to the championship affair. By contrast, it had been something of an up-and-down season for Marquette, one in which the Warriors had experienced their worst home record in years. There had been an unprecedented five losses at Milwaukee Arena, including the last three home games of the winter. And history seemed stacked against the Warriors as well: in 38 previous seasons of tourney play no team had ever risen to the title shootout with more than six regular-season defeats and Marquette already had suffered seven.

But all this only set the stage for some remarkable drama in the game's closing moments. McGuire was calling it quits after 20 years of head coaching and as his team closed in on a storybook ending for their beloved mentor the normally extroverted and always composed McGuire could no longer control his pent-up emotions. (Al McGuire was always prone to emotional outburst designed to intimidate referees; but these were calculated ploys and not genuine losses of control.) The embarrassed coach buried his face in his hands in a vain effort to conceal tears of joy at the end of the Marquette bench while the final seconds clicked off on a 67-59 championship victory. Thousands of fans in the Atlanta Omni and millions more watching on television were thus privileged to a rare display of unguarded emotion by a remarkable showman who had expended almost as much energy over two decades on building a carefully manicured public persona as he had in patching together some of the most talented basketball teams of the era. The title victory over North Carolina was certainly a fittingly ironic career-capper for a coach whose team a few seasons earlier had racked up 81 straight home victories.

Kentucky's Jack Givens put on a shooting and scoring display in the 1978 NCAA title game that nearly matched a similar feat by UCLA's Bill Walton five seasons earlier. (University of Kentucky photo)

As the decade wore down to its conclusion, a long-somnolent powerhouse would next rear its familiar head on the national scene after a full 20-year period of relative dormancy. Joe B. Hall had taken over in Kentucky after Rupp's retirement in 1972 and although the ex-player (a reserve on the 1949 title team) had brought the Wildcats into the 1975 Finals against Wooden's last team, and had also won an NIT crown in 1976, nonetheless it had been two full decades since the Ruppmen had last reigned unchallenged over the NCAA field. Hall would have many quality teams — nine won 20 or more and one captured 30 games — and produce numerous stars like Kevin Grevey, Jack Givens, Rick Robey and Kyle Macy. But only one Hall-coached ballclub would make its lasting mark on the national scene.

While Marquette would have to get by one ACC powerhouse for a 1977 national title, Kentucky would square off with another in a well-remembered 1978 national championship game. Duke boasted a young club of future pros Jim Spanarkel, Mike Gminski, Gene Banks and Kenny Dennard that was good enough to salt away 27 victories, capture the ACC postseason event, and cut a path into the title game which ran through Villanova and Notre Dame. But Kentucky owned an equal unit headed by Givens, Macy and Robey, and would boast 30 victories of its own by the time the season was played out.

When the two collided, however, the issue came down to one player and to an individual title game performance that had only one parallel in all of NCAA history. Wildcat forward Jack Givens put on a shooting display almost the equal of the one

Bill Walton had unleashed for the Bruins against Memphis State back in 1973 (44 points, 21-for-22 from the floor). The 6-4 lefty canned nine of 12 shots in the first half, scoring Kentucky's final 16 points before intermission; in the second half he remained every bit as hot and ended with 41 points on 18-for-27 marksmanship from the field. Balanced scoring for Duke (Banks, Gminski and Spanarkel all had more than 20) kept the game close until the closing moments, but Kentucky prevailed 94-88 when Rick Robey's inside game (20 points) kept the Blue Devils at bay during the final stretch drive.

But of the series of teams that succeeded UCLA into the winner's circle in the second half of the 1970s, it was the Indiana University team featuring Benson and May and a young coach named Knight that left the most lasting legacy. It was this team that would join San Francisco, North Carolina and several of Wooden's juggernauts as the only undefeated NCAA champions. And it was this team also that would introduce the college basketball world to one of its most colorful and controversial characters. The Indiana national champs of 1976 were but the first of more than two decades of stellar Indiana teams stamped with the irrepressible image of Robert Montgomery Knight, one of the half-dozen most memorable coaches in collegiate basketball history.

Knight's legacy would now seem to stand firm alongside anyone's, save perhaps those of Wooden and Rupp. He is safely ensconced as one of the winningest coaches of all time. He has left a personal stamp on his teams as great as that of any mentor — especially in the modern era when superstar players are often bigger than their coaches, their teams and even their schools. He has at times himself been bigger than his teams, and almost seemingly bigger than the collegiate game itself. And as the years wore on he became more and more immersed in endless controversy.

Knight's legacy can be best summarized with a long litany of records and milestones. He is the youngest coach to claim 600 career victories and also one of the youngest to cross the 200-, 300-, 400- and 500-victory plateaus. Three NCAA titles, five Final Four appearances and 11 Big Ten championships are enough to place Knight among the true elite of the coaching fraternity. But these milestones always fall a bit short of the legendary figure, remarkable as that may seem. Down through the years the coach that most writers and broadcasters now simply call "The General" has earned as large a reputation for his often rude treatment of the media and game officials, and his sideline tantrums with referees and his own players, as he has for his relentless winning or for the exemplary player graduation rates that have always marked his Indiana program. But above all else, Bob Knight has proven to be a huge winner, and in basketball as in life winners carry with them a certain indelible charm.

Knight's greatest championship team was his very first. But the March 1976 title run that culminated in the NCAA winner's circle had actually begun a full season earlier in 1975. A mistimed injury that year had effectively robbed Knight of his chance to end UCLA's decade-long domination a full season earlier.

Indiana by 1975 was already a team seemingly headed directly for a national championship. The Hoosiers ran through their season undefeated under their hard-driving fourth-year coach. But then the Hoosiers unexpectedly stumbled in the regional title game with Kentucky and lost by a narrow 92-90 count. This loss came despite a monster performance by Kent Benson as the 6-11 sophomore banked in 33 points and collected 23 caroms. Knight would later take complete responsibility for the defeat based on his coaching tactics. The Hoosier general had kept defensive stalwart Ted Abernethy on the bench for all but three minutes, electing to play a greater offensive threat, John Laskowski, at the big forward slot instead; later Knight rued the move as contributing mightily to his team's inability to stop the potent Kentucky shooters. But an injury to Scott May also played a key role. The club's top offensive threat had fractured his non-shooting arm four games from the end of the Big Ten season. May would be back in time for the Kentucky contest but was clearly subpar and mostly ineffective.

As it turned out, of course, the loss took on far greater proportions as the next season unfolded. When dust cleared from the Kentucky game, Indiana had missed out by a single two-point bucket not only on potential back-to-back NCAA titles, but also on possible back-to-back undefeated seasons. But it would be another year yet before such matters would come so clearly and painfully into focus.

With all the key elements returning the following winter, Indiana fans could look forward to a 1976 edition featuring a number of oversized luminaries. Benson, May, Wilkerson and Buckner would all eventually enjoy reputable NBA careers. Benson was the featured piece and a dominant collegiate player who, despite his stature as the top overall pick in the 1977 NBA draft, would never live up to the same promise within the pro ranks. May, Wilkerson and Buckner all became important NBA role players if not NBA superstars. But these four gifted players who would have been individual standouts on any other team were quickly molded by Knight into valuable pieces of a much greater whole. The whole was so great, in fact, that many still consider this to be the most perfect single college unit ever pasted together. This like all of Knight's other great teams was one on which individual ego was totally subordinated to the notion of team mission. As more than one observer has emphasized, Coach Knight has always created teams of components and not of individuals. And between 1975 and 1976 — at the very beginning of his immensely successful tenure — Knight already had found all of the perfect components.

Indiana would dominate the Big Ten in 1976, taking over precisely where it left off a season earlier and throwing together the first consecutive pair of perfect league seasons on the conference record books. This was no small feat when one remembers the Michigan team of that same year that could boast the likes of Rickey Green, Phil Hubbard and John Robinson. The Hoosiers sternest test came in the league opener with a two-point spread over the eventual basement team, Knight's alma mater at Ohio State. This would be one of 11 games all season that Indiana would take by single-digit margins, although one three-point spread in Bloomington against Michigan came in a contest actually deadlocked at the end of regulation play.

Indiana also managed to keep its unscarred record intact during the tourney. This took some last-minute heroics along the way, however, as the nation's top-rated team trailed in the second half during three of its five NCAA games. One of these was a nip-and-tuck battle with Alabama which fell Indiana's way 74-69 only when the Crimson Tide's biggest guns, Leon Douglas and Reggie King, combined for a disappointing 16 points, half of their yearlong average. Another was the 65-56 whipping of Marquette in the Mideast Regional final which found Warriors frontliners Butch Lee, Lloyd Walton and Jerome Whitehead suffering a similar slump in the face of Knight's well-drilled defenses. It was yearlong heroes Kent Benson and Scott May who would keep the Hoosiers rolling when they combined for 40 points and 16 rebounds a game during the five March Madness matchups.

Michigan had its own well-schooled outfit in 1975 and entered the postseason at 21-6 ranked in both AP and UPI top 10s. Johnny Orr's balanced team had hung close behind the unblemished Hoosiers in the conference race with only two close road losses (at Purdue and Minnesota) besides the two defeats (one in overtime) at the hands of Knight's Hoosiers. And then in tournament play they sprung the major upset that was necessary to vault them into the championship encounter. That upset came in the national semifinal game against previously unbeaten Rutgers. The Scarlet Knights featured consensus All-American forward Phil Sellers and had themselves entered the tourney with a sterling 28-0 mark. They then barely nipped Princeton (54-53) but regrouped and drubbed Connecticut (93-79) and VMI (91-75). But against the Big Ten team their big guns all misfired. Three top Rutgers scorers — Sellers plus guards Mike Dabney and Eddie Jordan — could do no better than a combined 31.4 percent (16 of 51) shooting from the floor. Meanwhile John Robinson paced Michigan with 20 points and 16 boards.

All season long Indiana and Michigan remained on an inevitable collision course. In the Final Four the pair would now provide a rarity of two teams from the same conference slugging it out for a national title. Never before had this happened and only twice in the future (1985 with Georgetown and Villanova, and 1988 with Kansas and Oklahoma) would it be destined to happen again. While Michigan had earned the matchup by upsetting the highly rated Scarlet Knights, Indiana jumped an equal hurdle by defeating the defending champion UCLA Bruins by a similar 65-51 count.

While Benson and May had been the big Hoosier guns all season, it would be Wilkerson and Buckner and a crew of unheralded reserves who would provide salvation in two Final Four shootouts. Against a feisty UCLA squad that still had Richard Washington, Marques Johnson and 7-2 Ralph Drollinger — even if Wooden was now in the grandstand — Wilkerson stepped up big with 19 rebounds and seven assists. Reserve guard Jim Crews also contributed mightily by directing Indiana's ball-control offense during the final minutes of the game. When Benson suffered early foul problems trying to defend against Washington it was Abernethy who inherited the tough defensive assignment and performed admirably. The defensive brilliance of both Wilkerson and Abernethy was enough, alongside balanced scoring from Abernethy (14), May (14) and Benson (16), to guarantee the 14-point victory and Coach Knight's first trip to the title game.

In the finals faceoff with rival Michigan it would be Buckner who would chip in the 16 points and eight rebounds that again carried Knight's team down the stretch. May and Benson once more did the heavy scoring with 26 and 25 respectively, but it was a balanced team effort that turned the tide for the title-bound Hoosiers in the second half.

When UCLA's Richard Washington joined Indiana's Scott May and Kent Benson in the 1976 NCAA semifinals it would represent the final time that more than half of the first-team consensus All-Americans would appear together during a Final Four. (UCLA photo)

But it wasn't particularly easy for the Hoosiers in the end. The 32nd and final victory of the season was indeed the toughest. Wilkerson went down with a concussion early in the game when he received an accidental elbow from Wolverine forward Wayman Britt; Knight's key defender and emotional leader was thus lost for the stretch run. Knight's charges trailed by six points at halftime but then methodically erased the deficit by scoring on almost every controlled possession across the first 10 minutes of the second stanza. With their backs to the wall the Hoosiers literally caught fire and shot a remarkable 60 percent during the game's final crucial 20 minutes. May, Benson and Buckner together canned 36 of the team's first 38 in the second half. But perhaps the biggest contributor was sophomore backup Jim Wisman who bravely stepped in for Wilkerson and competently directed the offense during the final stretch drive. In the end the Hoosiers ran away with both their coveted national title and their unlikely undefeated season to boot.

There was a strange footnote to the 1976 NCAA title game as well. It would mark the final time that more than half of the consensus first-team All-American squad would make it into the Final Four. In this case it was Benson and May from Indiana and UCLA's Richard Washington; the remaining two not on hand for the season's final weekend were John Lucas of Maryland and Adrian Dantley of Notre Dame. When Gene Bartow's Bruins were left on the sideline for the championship game it also meant that only the two Hoosier All-Americans (along with teammate Ted Abernethy, UCLA's Marques Johnson and Michigan's Rickey Green) would also enjoy a spot on the All-Tournament NCAA team.

The Arrival of Bird and Magic

If the NCAA Final Four would now become a rare stopping point for the nation's top All-American players, there would nonetheless be one March Madness final shootout just around the corner that would enjoy the bonus of the nation's top two stars actually paired head-to-head for the national title game. The 1979 season would be capped by one of the most ballyhooed title matchups of individual superstars in NCAA history. The much-hyped showdown between Michigan State's versatile Magic Johnson and Indiana State's hot-shooting Larry Bird would generate the largest basketball game rating (24.1) and market share (38 percent of sets in use at the time) in television history. And as is so rarely the case, this would be a matchup that in the end truly lived up to all the hype once the teams took the floor to do actual battle. It would in fact turn out to be a game that — perhaps more than any other — cemented the perfect marriage between television and basketball that would mark the upcoming decades of the 1980s and 1990s.

In strictly basketball terms, Earvin "Magic" Johnson was a mere baby when he led Michigan State to its first and only appearance in the NCAA national championship game. As a collegiate player Johnson was only just beginning to get his ears wet as a superb master of backcourt play. His career as one of the greatest playmakers ever would not really unfold until be took up residence in the NBA with the Los Angeles Lakers. There he would build the greatest winning record in pro cage history. Over an 11-year span with Johnson running the offense from his backcourt post the Lakers posted an unmatched 74.2 winning percentage; in postseason action during that same span the mark stood at 68.5 percent. But he would also provide considerable support for those that might want to argue that he and not Jordan or Oscar Robertson was the greatest all-around player ever. It is sometimes quickly forgotten that Johnson — at 6-9 — presented the same physical size as George Mikan or Bill Russell. At this height he rewrote the description of what the ideal basketball guard might be. Like only Mikan, Russell, Chamberlain and Robertson before him, Magic Johnson truly redefined how basketball at the highest levels was supposed to be played.

As a college player Johnson's contributions were somewhat more modest. But perhaps they only now seem modest in comparison with what came later. Few have accomplished so much by the end of a sophomore season. He was the second-leading

College basketball was turned in a bold new direction when Earvin "Magic" Johnson (with ball) of Michigan State and Larry Bird (33) of Indiana State faced off during the dramatic and much-hyped 1979 NCAA title game. It was a mano-a-mano duel that was repeated many times during the pair's successful NBA careers. (Michigan State University photo)

scorer and rebounder (trailing Greg Kelser) on a national championship team, an NCAA unanimous first-team All-American and member of the all-tourney team, the MVP of the 1979 Final Four and a mere 17 points-per-game scorer who was the first overall selection of the 1979 NBA college draft.

Consensus reigned throughout the 1978-79 season that Johnson and Bird were the finest players anywhere around. Bird's fame, however, was a bit more substantial and far more based on individual scoring feats. After a stellar junior season the Sycamores' star was favored to capture a national scoring title his senior outing. He had ranked third as a sophomore (32.8) and second as a junior (30.0), trailing Portland's Freeman Williams who had himself become the first Division I player ever to average more than 30 over a four-season career. One bad outing in mid-February, however, sabotaged Bird's title hopes. It came with a meager four-point effort against Bradley when the Braves double-teamed the Birdman, who was content to give up the ball and watch his teammates romp through the resulting four-on-three game. Nonetheless, Bird averaged 28.6 to again finish a close second.

Sophomore Johnson didn't post those kinds of numbers for the Spartans. He played on a much more balanced team that featured Kelser and Jay Vincent along the front line to carry much of the scoring load. But Johnson carried great credentials nonetheless that were also widely promoted during the season. Like the Birdman, the Magicman was also a dexterous ball handler whose pinpoint passing and uncanny playmaking matched those of the very best little men. And when the tournament rolled around Johnson was poised to demonstrate his own star quality.

Bird perfectly fit the prototype of a heartlands country ballplayer spawned in small town rural Indiana. He had developed as a high school legend in French Lick and then headed off to the campus of Indiana University to play for Knight, just as all Hoosier native sons and daughters expected. But things didn't work out in Bloomington (perhaps it was the size of the campus, or perhaps it was the size of Coach Knight's ego) and Bird was soon enrolled at Terre Haute and suited up for the Indiana State team. By his junior year Bird had embellished his own legend and also lifted Indiana State into national prominence for the first time in school history. Red Auerbach was the first to jump on the bandwagon when he drafted Bird for the Celtics at the end of his second season. Since he had already redshirted a year on the heels of his departure from Knight's program, the Sycamores star could indeed have packed it in as a junior for instant riches with the pros. But Bird smelled a national title and his decision to play at the collegiate level one final season proved in the end a wise one. So, of course, did Auerbach's gamble in drafting a player who would not join his team for yet another full year.

Bird enjoyed a stellar senior season. His scoring and all-around play was supplemented by such superb passing ability that he also averaged six assists per game. With Bird carrying the load the Sycamores remained undefeated throughout the regular season. There were skeptics, of course, who claimed that Bird provided a one-man team, that the Missouri Valley club enjoyed a soft schedule and that Indiana State would fold in March when Bird faltered against top defenses. A sometimes reluctant press seemed to have little choice, however, but to rank the unbeaten Sycamores No. 1 in the wire service polls throughout the entire 15-week season.

While Bird was the prototype farmyard player, his rival was the perfect profile of the inner-city playground star. Johnson starred for Everett High in East Lansing, then followed hometown friend Jay Vincent to the neighboring campus at Michigan State. Freshmen were once again eligible for varsity play and Johnson wasted little time emerging as a star during his first campaign in the Big Ten, scoring 17 a game and averaging nearly eight assists and an equal number of rebounds. As a sophomore he was even better as a floor leader although the numbers he posted remained the same. And Magic played on a balanced squad that also featured Kelser as an agile 6-7 forward and high school mate Jay Vincent as the rugged 6-8 post man.

But for all the firepower of Johnson, Vincent and Kelser, Michigan State experienced something of a slow start to the 1978-79 campaign. Slow, at any rate, when compared to Bird's Indiana State team that was off and running to 29 straight regular-season wins. MSU was defeated during the midwinter by four Big Ten second division teams and it was only a home floor overtime victory against Iowa that prevented Jud Heathcote's club from suffering six league defeats in one seven-game span. And MSU was even embarrassed with an 18-point road setback at the hands of struggling Northwestern, the league's perennial basement dweller and owner of a string of 25 straight losing seasons.

When March Madness rolled around, however, MSU had righted its ship completely. In each of its five tournament games the steamrolling Spartans would inflict the worst defeat of the year on their opponents. They crushed Lamar by 31, LSU by 16, Notre Dame by 12, Penn by 34, and finally Bird and company by 11. It was during the 1979 tournament that fans everywhere began understanding precisely why veteran pro scouts were already referring to the 6-9 Johnson as one of the most amazing backcourt prospects they had ever seen perform.

Postseason play was also marked by a second surprising role reversal. Indiana State, which had breezed all year, now had the slightly rougher time against intensi-fied tournament competition. But not rough enough to provide any insurmountable obstacles — at least not before the showdown with Michigan State and Magic Johnson. In the Missouri Valley playoff final ISU was able to qualify without difficulty for NCAA play and thus keep its unblemished season intact. But first-year coach

All-Star Team for the Era (1972-1979)

	Pos.	Pts. (Ppg.)	Best Yr	NPY
David Thompson (NC St)	F	2309 (26.8)	29.9 (Sr.)	1975
Bill Walton (UCLA)	C	1767 (20.3)	21.1 (So.)	1972-73-74
Larry Bird (Indiana)	F	2850 (30.3)	32.8 (So.)	1979
Scott May (Indiana)	F	1593 (17.7)	23.5 (Sr.)	1976
Phil Ford (UNC)	G	2290 (18.6)	20.8 (Sr.)	1978

NPY = National Player of the Year

Honorable Mention: Adrian Dantley (F, Notre Dame), Magic Johnson (G, Michigan State), Butch Lee (G, Marquette), Marques Johnson (F, UCLA), Kent Benson (C, Indiana), Ernie DiGregorio (G, Providence), Mike Gminski (C, Duke), Keith Wilkes (F, UCLA)

Coaches of the Era: John Wooden (UCLA), NCAA Champion (1972, 1973, 1975) and Bobby Knight (Indiana), NCAA Champion (1976)

Bill Hodges did suffer a scare when Bird broke the thumb on his non-shooting hand during the closing moments of the conference tourney. For Bird himself, of course, it was merely a brief annoyance and only a minor setback.

Even with a subpar Bird, ISU climbed some major hurdles in early NCAA action, which seemed to quiet complaints about this being a one-man team incapable of winning when the level of competition was upped a notch. A solid Oklahoma team was bested with ease when Bird canned 29 points and claimed 15 rebounds despite his heavily bandaged left hand. The Sycamores as a team enjoyed a huge 50-22 rebounding advantage over the Sooners and outscored them by almost as much, 97-73. Against fifth-rated Arkansas with All-American Sidney Moncrief, Bird poured in 25 in the first 27 minutes of play and led all scorers at game's end with 31. The Arkansas contest went right down to the wire, however, and a clutch basket by guard-forward Bob Heaton at the buzzer salvaged a tight 73-71 victory. Thus the team and Bird had again proved their mettle with a gutsy two-point win over the first top 10 club they had faced all season.

In the semifinal opener of Final Four play, Michigan State coasted against an overmatched Ivy League representative from Penn. While the Quakers had pulled off upsets of North Carolina, Syracuse and St. John's to earn regional honors, they were now a spent team and fell hopelessly behind the Spartans by an embarrassing 50-17 halftime count. Bird and ISU again met a stiffer challenge in the guise of freshman shooting sensation Mark Aguirre and the DePaul Blue Demons coached by veteran Ray Meyer. As a top 10 club, DePaul seemed a more bona fide Final Four contestant. And the Demons did indeed extend the match right down to the wire. For

Purude's All-Big Ten forward Walter Jordan looks for an opening during a 1978 league game against Michigan State. (Purdue University photo)

the second straight game the Sycamores would have to survive with some last-minute offensive heroics. Bird made key shots down the stretch and enjoyed a 16-for-19 shooting night; DePaul refused to fold, however, as Gary Garland (19), Aguirre (19), Curtis Watkins (16) and James Mitchem (12) all contributed the balanced scoring Ray Meyer's club had enjoyed all season. ISU nonetheless held on for a 76-74 heartstopper behind Bird's game-high 35 points. Now there were few left who truly doubted either the Sycamores or Larry Bird.

But Cinderella's chariot was about to turn into a full-fledged pumpkin. In the much awaited matchup in the Special Events Center at Salt Lake City, Johnson would once again rise to new heights while Bird would finally prove altogether human. Heathcote devised a trapping defense that stymied Bird from the start. The critics at long last were now proven at least partially right about ISU's shortcomings once Bird himself was effectively contained. In the face of relentless pressure the Sycamore star could make only seven of 21 shots from the floor. By contrast, Magic benefitted from stellar play by companion Kelser; the two clicked on numerous fast-breaking outlet plays. Kelser bagged 19 (matching Bird), Johnson would tally 24 points and pull down seven rebounds, and MSU coasted 75-64. When the shouting finally stopped it was Magic Johnson who walked off with both the tourney MVP trophy and the NCAA championship plaque.

Bird and Johnson would both be lost to the NBA ranks (but of course not to the nation's fans) before the opening tip-offs of the following season. Johnson was in fact an early trendsetter, anticipating the coming movements of numerous budding college stars in the '80s and '90s who would now opt for hefty pro paychecks after only two seasons of collegiate play.

In earlier epochs the loss of such stars at the midpoint of flowering college careers might have dealt a much bigger blow to the growing college sport. But so high had basketball's star now risen that most of the nation's top young athletes were selecting basketball over football or baseball as the sport of choice. As a result the talent pool had never been as great. Each loss of a young star to the lure of pro dollars only seemed to open a door or window for another equal talent to take his place. As the '70s became the '80s and then the '90s the stars flowed in an endless transition — Bird to Jordan to Sampson to Ewing to Manning to Laettner and Hurley to Grant Hill and Glenn Robinson and Jerry Stackhouse. The harvest seemed more bountiful at every turn as basketball had truly become America's front and center national game.

11

The Eighties and Nineties, Part 1

Enter the Women's Game

=======================================

College basketball — the popular spectator version played exclusively by men — caught fire as a major attraction only once the game revved up the tempo of its playmaking, picked up the pace of its scoring, and elevated the scene of its actions several feet above the net and steel rim. First the offensive side of the game took flight in the 1940s with the invention and popularization of a new ultimate weapon — the jump shot. Then defensive play soared above the rim as well with shot blockers and board sweepers like Bill Russell and Wilt Chamberlain during the mid-50s. By the 1960s the entire style of play had also elevated above the hoop with a new generation of black playground stars who brought with them today's most popular "showtime" weapons — glamorous one-on-one "moves" and spectacular "in-your-face" slam dunks. When basketball went airborne on the court it also at long last soared in the public estimation.

There were also helpful rule changes along the way that lifted basketball from a plodding curiosity to a thrilling and colorful ballet-like drama. Elimination of the center jump after each and every field goal provided the sport's most dramatic revolution and first made possible the fast-breaking action which we so strongly identify with the modern-era game. The widening of foul lanes, the addition of shot clocks to eliminate offensive stalling, the advent of three-point field goals — these and other innovations transformed an often brutal physical confrontation into an aesthetic and acrobatic art form.

Just as the more celebrated men's game needed streamlining — which came only painfully slowly during the sport's first half-century, and then at a far more rapid-fire pace over its next quarter-century — so did the women's version also demand drastic face-lifting. And since women's approximations of Naismith's indoor game were from the start even more earthbound and slow-paced than the men's version, the overhaul would of necessity be even more drastic in its scope and nature. For most of the present century, however, there was little or no overhauling at all. Despite the explosion of change and resulting popularity accompanying the men's game, women's cage play by stark contrast largely languished as a minor sport and little more than an occasional campus curiosity.

But for all its foot dragging for decades, the sport of women's basketball is hardly the recent innovation that some more casual fans might suspect. That universally recognized (that is, televised) NCAA championship play for women was a creation of the early '80s, and that formal women's collegiate competition on the national level dates back little more than a decade before that, does not mean that women were adverse to dribbling and shooting and enjoying the sport almost from the precise moment of its inception. It would only be time-worn and tiresome traditional beliefs dominating the male world of intercollegiate athletics that would soon submerge the women's game for three-quarters of a century. It would certainly not be any inherent lack of skill or interest on the part of women athletes themselves.

Women had enthusiastically adopted Naismith's game literally within weeks of its original 1891 invention. Not only did Naismith invite female students to join games at the Springfield YMCA that very first winter, but one of those pioneering women participants (Maude Sherman) soon became his wife. Collegiate women's games also date back to the same year or two when male college play was first launched, and coeds at Stanford and Cal-Berkeley are alleged to have staged a primitive contest (complete with bloomers and long black hose) as early as the winter of 1896. The earliest documented women's matches may thus actually predate (or at least approximate) the very first male campus contests.

Women's college teams are also reported at Smith College in Massachusetts in 1892 (where physical education instructor Senda Berenson gained much of the credit for sending female competition moving in the wrong direction by adapting Naismith's rules to fit Victorian notions of female daintiness) and also at nearby Mount Holyoke College (where the rule adaptations also restricted women to fixed areas of the playing floor). The same year of 1892 also found women taking up the game at Sophie Newcomb College in New Orleans (later a branch of Tulane) where dribbling was banned and 11 players were assigned to each side. Yet from the earliest weeks when women tried their hands at passing and shooting in Naismith's Springfield gym, and also elsewhere around the country, it was a very different game indeed that the women were already being coerced into playing.

Men's and women's play from the outset headed in quite different directions. Women, just like the men, started playing with nine to a side and then quickly adapted to more manageable six-player squads. Men's teams in the early going also jumped from nine or more to a side to the more workable number of six. (With larger teams of up to a couple dozen players in some physical education classes the game looked more like a free-for-all than an organized athletic competition.) Then the men's game reduced the size of its squads a step further, down to five. The first few reported college contests were played with the larger teams, but by 1896 five had been fixed as the ideal number of players for the freer-moving men's version. Six, however, remained the fixed number for the more stationary women's teams, and it remained that way into the 1970s.

But there were far more severe differences between the two games. Women's play was from the beginning, and down through much of its history to boot, an entirely "stationary" type of game. Along with six-player teams there was also a strict division for the women between offensive and defensive zones; the defenders remained frozen in their positions at one end of the floor while the shooters were locked into their own fixed areas at the opposite end of the court. The result for women's contests was indeed far closer to what its inventor probably had in mind for "Naismith Ball" in the first place. It was certainly a far cry from the type of dribbling and rapid-passing action that men's teams had already derived from the original rules in just a few short years of rapid evolution.

It was also all part and parcel, of course, of a popular decision reached in the first decade of the current century by athletic administrators (following the lead of Senda Berenson at Smith College) at both the collegiate and secondary school levels: the highly combative game of "basket-ball" (which was indeed a far more pugnacious and thus more rough-and-tumble physical affair in its early decades) was judged to be simply too strenuous to accommodate women. The "weaker sex" if they were to play at all would need a kinder, gentler type of contest.

By opting for a "safer" game the shapers of women's basketball play also cast their vote for a far duller spectacle in the process. Few women — even those who played the game seriously over the coming years — ever voiced a preference for the "stand-and-pass" version; many women athletes were outspoken in their dislike for the largely boring sport they had been handed. Not only did the rules prevent female players from running up and down the floor, but they were banned from dribbling the ball as well. The no-dribble rule would eventually be modified in the '50s to allow women a single bounce before shooting. Then by the '60s, as hang time and slam dunks took over the men's game, women's rules were further "relaxed" to allow a player three dribbles before launching a shot at the bucket. While anti-dribble legislation died a quick death in the men's sport, it lived on in one fashion or another even in modern-era women's play.

While those in charge of men's basketball allowed Naismith's original concept to evolve unfettered, until there was little left that was recognizable beyond the round ball and the elevated 10-foot goals, women's basketball remained an anachronism frozen in the image of the 1890s. Since a vast majority of women physical educators held to a belief that the proper physical training of young ladies and not the glory of competition was the issue at hand, women remained camped outside the world of competitive basketball play. For seven decades a handful played in required physical education classes, few took interest as spectators, and the stationary and watered-down "girls' game" found popular following almost nowhere but perhaps a few isolated pockets of the rural Midwest. Only in Iowa, Indiana and Kentucky did high school girls' games draw crowds and stimulate the interest of any beyond the mildly curious.

Then came some truly landmark changes at the outset of the 1970s. These were changes that revolutionized and reshaped a sport as severely as any rule changes ever have with any form of athletic endeavor. In fact, they were changes that transformed one largely uninteresting game into quite another and much more attractive game altogether. Encouraged by a steamrolling nationwide feminist movement that was now seeking equal rights for women on all social and political fronts, those in charge of women's intercollegiate and interscholastic athletic programs were finally able to seize the moment to launch a powerful revolution of their own.

Almost overnight the longstanding women's version of basketball was tossed out the window completely and the boys' game was adopted in its place as women's high school and college teams went back to playing entirely by the men's rules. Almost entirely, that is, since the women's game, so long a bystander, now actually seemed to improve upon the men's version it overnight adopted. Women's coaches not only caught up with the present but peered into the future and instituted a pro-style 30-second shot clock to force the pace of the action. All of a sudden the women were not only playing as fast a game as the men (at least in principle if not yet in athletic talent), but they were actually playing a game that by requiring shots every 30 seconds was indeed even faster in its end-to-end tempo.

The biggest official boost to the women's basketball movement indisputably arrived with long-overdue 1972 Congressional Title IX legislation prohibiting dispersement of federal funds to colleges and universities practicing any form of sex discrimination. It would only be in the late '70s, however, that serious enforcement of this legislation would be interpreted to mandate near-equal if not entirely equal funding for women's college sports teams. And that reinterpretation came largely as a result of building momentum across the nation's campuses for NCAA sponsorship of intercollegiate competition for women.

But the first tentative steps toward recognition for the women's game had already been taken several years before the first hints of Title IX, and much of the credit for those first bold efforts lies at the doorstep of pioneering women's coach Carol Eckman at West Chester (Pennsylvania) State College. Eckman set the stage for national women's competition in 1969 when she hosted the first of three invitational tournaments for women's teams, events originally staged to show off her own talented ballclub and promote the girls' game as well. It was the West Chester Invitational affair, sponsored by the loosely knit Commission on Intercollegiate Athletics for Women (CIAW), that was soon restructured into the full-fledged 1972 inaugural AIAW (Association of Intercollegiate Athletics for Women) postseason event. Eckman's team would capture the first invitational affair in 1969 and then later also appear against Immaculata College in the first official AIAW postseason tourney which was also staged at West Chester three years later.

The most visible rule adjustments had thus been the ones that transformed women's teams from six to five players on the floor and sanctioned dribbling as the standard method of play. Yet a far bigger boost, in reality, came from the 1970s NCAA legislation that also mandated equal spending on men's and women's college sports. There would now be all the trappings of a major sport as well — uniforms, full-time coaches and assistant coaches, practice facilities, games occasionally played in the larger men's arenas, even occasional tournaments and television or radio coverage. There would also be major schedules, conference standings and even athletic scholarships for talented women players who wished to use their sport as a stepping stone to achieving a college education.

Yet if revamped regulations modernized play they hardly meant instant popularity for the newly shaped and (for experienced basketball watchers) now more familiar-looking game. Women's basketball in all but a few schools would for decades to come continue to remain a minor sport, at least when compared with the men's extravaganza. American college women not only had to catch up with male counterparts who had a seven or eight decade head start, but they also had to catch up to at least a handful of other countries where men's rules had been adopted whole-sale for female players several decades earlier. When Olympic competition was opened to women in 1976 the first USA women's squad would be "manhandled" by a more experienced and more physical Russian team during the Gold Medal game. But now with the advent of recruiting and scholarships and formal intercollegiate programs there would soon be an abundance of talented players as well. And once that happened there would also be a booming audience.

The coming out party for women's college basketball took place in Madison Square Garden in 1975, just as the men's game had similarly turned the corner in an earlier version of the famed Garden half a century earlier. The landmark date of women's college play can thus be precisely fixed in mid-February of that year. The occasion was a college doubleheader that packed 12,000 fans into New York's premier downtown arena for a preliminary contest between teams from Queens College and Immaculata College and a feature attraction matching Fairfield University and the University of Massachusetts. There was little special about the Fairfield and UMass men's teams (Julius Erving had already left the UMass Redmen three seasons earlier). It was the less-publicized teams meeting in the preliminary that drew the impressive crowd, since those teams represented the two finest women's programs anywhere in the land. And appropriately enough the historic evening was launched with a stirring rendition of Helen Reddy's pop hit *I Am Woman* as the two ladies teams ran through their pregame warmups.

Immaculata had ruled the emerging women's basketball scene from the time women had first launched their own national tournament back in 1972 under the auspices of the AIAW. It was this same Immaculata squad — with a single core of players still intact — that had already won the first three AIAW national tournaments. Led by 5-foot-11 center Theresa Shank the Mighty Macs would compile an almost incredible 64-2 record across the first five seasons of the '70s. At one point coach Cathy Rush's team had run off 35 victories without tasting defeat. Rush had built her juggernaut at the tiny Philadelphia women's college around a group of talented locals, most of whom like Shank had learned the game in the city's popular female CYO league. After their triple tournament victories over West Chester State in 1972, Queens College in 1973 and Mississippi College in 1974, the Mighty Macs even began touting the perhaps deserved title of "UCLA of the East."

Theresa Shank was not the only exceptional talent on that first women's power-house team. Immaculata could also boast sharpshooting guard Mary Schraff and dependable reserves Rene Portland and Marianne Stanley. It was a team that not only won three consecutive AIAW titles but proved to be a talent font for future prominent coaches as well: Theresa Shank (Grentz) would serve admirably in later years as head coach for both Rutgers University and the 1992 U.S. Olympic team; Portland would eventually gain the head coaching position at 1990s Big Ten power-house Penn State and Stanley would have the greatest success of all by leading Old Dominion to three national titles.

The February 1975 Madison Square Garden debut of Immaculata and Queens was more than merely a showcase event for the emerging women's sport; it was also a crucial turf-protecting game for both of the excellent teams involved. It had been

Queens College that had put an end to Immaculata's 35-game unbeaten skein little more than a year earlier. In a later rematch for the 1974 AIAW title Immaculata had drawn revenge with a hard-earned 59-52 triumph, thus gaining its third national title. This was now the rubber game and the one coach Rush and her team had to have to maintain their "UCLA East" boasting rights. In the end the contest would indeed fall Immaculata's way in a bruising struggle that ended with a 65-61 count. Mary Schraff was the true star of that first women's Garden Party with 12 points and nine important rebounds. For the moment at least Immaculata had salvaged its unblemished national reputation as undisputed No. 1. But that reputation was already almost at an end.

In the afterglow of that first important Madison Square Garden shootout, the second half of the 1970s was one of pioneering stars and powerhouse teams. It was also the period which saw the first dramatic jump in public acceptance for women basketballers and for their increasingly talented intercollegiate teams. One indication that women could indeed play the game would come with the much-publicized successes of a 19-year-old Pratt Institute (New York) reserve guard named Cyndi Meserve. Meserve would blaze a somewhat different trail when she became the first woman to appear in action during a men's college game. But Meserve's short-lived career at Pratt would leave her as only a small footnote in the evolution of women's basketball. It would soon be apparent that women did not have to integrate the men's game to prove that they too could play.

While new talent seemed to appear at every turn throughout the decade of the 1970s, this sudden abundance of star-quality players did not yet guarantee anything approaching instant parity across the national scene, however. Two early powerhouse teams would instead take turns totally dominating the national women's college basketball scene. When the championship crown was finally knocked ajar from the heads of the Immaculata Mighty Macs it would immediately be placed on the

Women's National Champions

AIAW (Association of Intercollegiate Athletics for Women)

Year	Champion	Score	Runner-Up	Tournament Site
1972	Immaculata	52-48	West Chester	Normal, Illinois
1973	Immaculata	59-52	Queens (N.Y.)	Flushing, New York
1974	Immaculata	68-53	Mississippi Col.	Manhattan, Kansas
1975	Delta State	90-81	Immaculata	Harrisonburg, Va.
1976	Delta State	69-64	Immaculata	University Park, Pa.
1977	Delta State	68-55	LSU	Minneapolis, Minn.
1978	UCLA	90-74	Maryland	Los Angeles, Calif.
1979	Old Domin.	75-65	Louisiana Tech	Greensboro, N.C.
1980	Old Domin.	68-53	Tennessee	Mt. Pleasant, Mich.
1981	La. Tech	79-59	Tennessee	Eugene, Oregon
1982	Rutgers	83-77	Texas	Philadelphia, Pa.

NCAA Division I

Year	Champion	Score	Runner-Up	Tournament Site
1982	La. Tech	76-62	Cheyney	Norfolk, Virginia
1983	So. Calif.	69-67	Louisiana Tech	Norfolk, Virginia
1984	So. Calif.	72-61	Tennessee	Los Angeles, Calif.
1985	Old Domin.	70-65	Georgia	Austin, Texas
1986	Texas	97-81	Southern Cal	Lexington, Ken.
1987	Tennessee	67-44	Louisiana Tech	Austin, Texas
1988	La. Tech	56-54	Auburn	Tacoma, Wash.
1989	Tennessee	76-60	Auburn	Tacoma, Wash.
1990	Stanford	88-81	Auburn	Knoxville, Tenn.
1991	Tennessee	70-67*	Virginia	New Orleans, La.
1992	Stanford	78-62	W. Kentucky	Los Angeles, Calif.
1993	Texas Tech	84-82	Ohio State	Atlanta, Georgia
1994	N. Carolina	60-59	Louisiana Tech	Richmond, Virginia
1995	Connecticut	70-64	Tennessee	Minneapolis, Minn.

* = Overtime Game

Cheryl Miller of USC clears the boards against Old Dominion in NCAA Tournament play. Miller was the player of the decade in the 1980s when she led the Trojans to a pair of NCAA titles. She is the only USC player — male or female — with a retired uniform number. (USC photo)

brows of another set of seemingly invincible players representing the sport's new dynasty outfit — Delta State University from Cleveland, Mississippi. Delta State would first reach the AIAW finals in March 1975, a mere month after the historic Immaculata-Queens Madison Square Garden shootout. And there they would finally wrest the crown from the sport's reigning queen, Immaculata, in a high-scoring affair (90-81) which seemed to demonstrate that women could indeed run the court and fire up accurate shots at a pace every bit equal to that of their male counterparts.

Thus the 1975 AIAW Final Four which ended one early dynasty served as launching pad for yet another. Delta State was led into action by 6-3 Lusia Harris, the first truly athletic post player to emerge on the women's scene. The Harris-led Mississippi school entered the championship match with Immaculata sporting a perfect 28-0 record and had little difficulty protecting that unblemished mark when the hook-shooting and board-crashing Harris rang up 32 points and also proved an unstoppable force under the backboards. As the reign of Immaculata suddenly closed it did so in the face of an axiom that had long defined the men's game and now also entered women's play — the squad with the dominating center owned the distinct advantage among otherwise well-matched teams.

Delta State and Lusia Harris would continue their winning ways as the 1976 season unfolded and would soon stretch their unbeaten string to a record 51 games before finally falling in a late-season rematch with revenge-minded Immaculata. At season's end, however, it would again be Delta State that captured the title match — again over Immaculata and this time by a much narrower 69-64 margin.

Immaculata's string of six consecutive trips to the AIAW finals would finally run out in late March of 1977, yet Delta State's own string of consecutive championships would soon stretch out to three as the team, still led by Harris (now a senior who averaged 24.6), romped over LSU 68-53 in the season's tournament finale. This final Delta State championship would allow the Lady Statesmen to match the Immaculata record of three uninterrupted national cage titles, a record that has not been duplicated during the subsequent 18 years of AIAW and later NCAA Tournament play.

For her own part, Delta State star Lusia Harris closed out her brilliant four-year career as the first acknowledged superstar of the women's sport and also as a player whose future brilliance in the eyes of history was clouded only by the primitive record-keeping and almost nonexistent recognition system in place during her own pioneering era. There were no women's All-American teams until Harris' sophomore season (1975) and the national player of the year award would unfortunately not be instituted until the season after her own 1977 graduation.

But Harris' legacy is brilliant enough nonetheless. She would reign as MVP of the AIAW tourney for three straight seasons; would average more than 30 points per game her junior year (thus becoming the first women to crack the 30-point barrier) and 25.9 for her career; and as the top scorer on the 1972 silver-medal Olympic team she would also carve a rare piece of history by dropping in the first points ever registered by a woman player in Olympic competition. Most importantly of all, however, in 1992 Lusia Harris would also become the first female college player inducted into the Naismith Memorial Basketball Hall of Fame. Her talents were also given something of a backhanded tribute when the Delta State star was tabbed by the New Orleans Jazz in the NBA player draft. The selection was little more than a cheap publicity stunt by the fan-hungry Jazz, yet it did nonetheless speak unintentional volumes about the talent level of this first pioneering female star.

Then the corner was turned in the women's game when for the first time the big schools got fully into the act. The landmark moment came when UCLA (on the heels of Wooden's retirement from men's basketball preeminence) captured its first national women's championship. It was UCLA, fittingly, that broke the AIAW small-school stranglehold of Immaculata and Delta State by overcoming Maryland in the 1978 title game staged on the Bruins' own home floor at Pauley Pavilion. Pacing the Lady Bruins' 90-74 championship victory was a deadeye 5-8 guard, Ann Meyers, whose brother Dave Meyers had been an All-American and the leading rebounder and scorer for Wooden's final NCAA championship team.

Ann Meyers earned considerable notoriety as the first woman awarded an athletic scholarship to play basketball for the UCLA Bruins. That notoriety would accompany all four years of Meyers' collegiate career and then follow her into postcollege days as well. The brilliant passer and accomplished long-range shooter owned enough credentials and enough moves to become the first legitimate female draftee of an NBA team when her court skills earned her a preseason 1978 tryout with the Bob Leonard-coached Indiana Pacers.

While Delta State's Harris had unquestionably been seen as a profitable publicity gimmick by the NBA Jazz a season earlier, the Pacers were willing not only to invite Meyers to their preseason camp (where she was quickly cut) but also to offer a guaranteed contract that specified broadcast duties if the UCLA cager didn't make the final playing roster. This deal was soon enough nullified when Meyers decided a women's league venture was more to her liking. She would instead play two seasons with the New Jersey Gems of the short-lived WPBL (Women's Professional Basketball League) and also serve as television commentator for NCAA women's games as well as college and NBA men's games. A 1993 Naismith Hall of Fame inductee and wife of the late baseball great Don Drysdale, Meyers would thus also later earn even further distinction as half of the first married couple ever to both be elected into the halls of fame in their respective sports.

The dawn of the 1980s would next bring two developments highly significant for the history of women's play. First and foremost the NCAA would take over full administration of the women's game, a development which also wrested control from the women themselves in many cases but nonetheless meant greater overall publicity for the sport. And also on the promotional front the first NCAA-sanctioned All-American teams were announced in 1983, with squads now being named at all three levels of divisional play. And in a further development aimed at adding luster to women's competition, the Naismith Trophy was now also expanded to include a female as well as a male winner. The first women's Naismith winner would be Anne Donovan of Old Dominion, with USC's Cheryl Miller capturing the next three trophies in a row. Earlier, of course, there had already been female Kodak All-Americans, but they had received far less promotion and publicity and thus far less visibility in the public eye.

Another pioneering superstar was current NBA licensing director Carol Blazejowski, who enjoyed an outstanding four-season career of her own at Montclair State College in the late '70s and still holds "unofficial" records for career scoring average (31.7 ppg) and season's scoring average (38.6) set in 1978. Blazejowski's scoring marks remain technically "unofficial" since they preceded the beginning of NCAA-sanctioned record-keeping in the early 1980s. Nonetheless Blazejowski's 3,199 career points were enough to leave her third on the all-time overall list (behind only Lynette Woodard of Kansas with 3,649 and Tennessee's Cindy Brogdon with 3,240) and her senior-season total of 1,235 has never been bettered since the onset of NCAA-sanctioned play. Since Carol Blazejowski's Montclair State team never earned an AIAW championship, the 5-11 scoring machine was destined to fill a spot as the women's version of LSU great "Pistol Pete" Maravich. Still considered the best women's jump-shooter ever, the incomparable Blaze also once pumped home 52 points on basketball's most noteworthy stage, venerable Madison Square Garden.

Rebecca Lobo led Connecticut's drive to the 1995 national championship making the Huskies the first undefeated men's or women's team with as many as 35 victories. (University of Connecticut photo)

"Blaze" was followed immediately by a pair of stars of seemingly even greater magnitude. While Old Dominion's Nancy Lieberman didn't post the huge scoring statistics (2,430 points, 18.1 ppg) of Blazejowski or of other big gunners soon to come, she nonetheless left an indelible mark of her own upon the rapidly growing women's game. Part of that mark came from her reputation as the most outstanding ball handler and passer that AIAW play had ever witnessed. The 1980 national player of the year and captain of two national championship teams had already made her mark in high school (Far Rockaway, New York) and as a member of the 1976 U.S. Olympic squad. And Nancy Lieberman was not only a talented all-around player but also a pioneering spokeswoman for the game, even playing a major role in founding an experimental women's professional league (in which she herself briefly performed on the Dallas Diamonds team). A well-publicized post-career autobiography entitled *Lady Magic* would lend still further notice to her own court talents and to the rapidly emerging women's game she enriched.

While Nancy Lieberman was lighting up the courts with Bob Cousy-like ball-handling out on the Eastern Seaboard in 1979 and 1980, deep in the Midwest there was already another major headline-maker emerging. Lynette Woodard at Kansas University was destined to become the game's first black female superstar. The agile four-time All-American forward would hit an incredible 52.5 percent of her career shots and more importantly pace her Kansas team to a 108-32 four-season record alongside three AIAW national tournament appearances. An expert ball handler as well as a proficient shooter, Woodard would gain even greater postcollege fame as the first woman ever to play for the world-renowned Harlem Globetrotters. Before her college days were over, Woodard's all-time leading women's total of 3,649 points would fall only 18 short of the seemingly untouchable men's record posted a decade earlier by Louisiana State super gunner Pete Maravich.

There were also other great players pounding the hardwoods in the late '70s and early '80s. Old Dominion's all-time leading scorer (2,719 points, 19.9 ppg) Ann Donovan was an intimidating 6-8 center who would play for one AIAW national championship team (1980) and two gold medal Olympic squads (1984, 1988). If teammate Nancy Lieberman had been perhaps the first "flash-and-dash" style women's star of the modern era then Donovan was the first tall woman to emerge as a true impact player. Denise Curry became one of the game's half-dozen 3,000-point ca-reer scorers during her four years at UCLA (1978-81) and as a freshman starred alongside Ann Meyers on the Bruins' heralded 1978 AIAW title-winning team. Loui-siana Tech's 6-foot forward Pam Kelly captained the Lady Techsters to consecutive national titles in 1981 (AIAW) and 1982 (NCAA), and sparked a phenomenal 69-1 record over her final two seasons. And finally, Kamie Etheridge (1986) and Clarissa Davis (1989) captured a pair of national player of the year awards for Texas, allow-ing the Longhorns to join Louisiana Tech (Pam Kelly, 1982; Janice Lawrence, 1984; and Teresa Weatherspoon, 1988) as the only schools boasting multiple winners of the prestigious Margaret Ward outstanding player trophy.

The modern era — also the halcyon era — of women's play trumpeted its arrival with the 1981-82 season, the year of the first sanctioned women's NCAA tournament. The female-controlled AIAW had by now unavoidably become the pro-verbial victim of its own rather large successes of the past decade and a half. With star players and a souped-up action-packed spectacle now at its disposal, women's basketball for the first time now offered the promise of a much larger audience and even a potential television following. There was obviously money to be made and the august NCAA of course wanted a large piece of the potential action. Thus a male-dominated NCAA governing committee would hurriedly enter the arena it had so long abandoned to the female coaches and physical education instructors; and it came toting a lucrative TV contract and a full-blown women's tournament of its very own.

Thus postseason of 1982 would actually feature two separate women's cham-pionship games. While the NCAA was inaugurating its own ballyhooed event with a televised finale between Louisiana Tech and Cheyney State, Rutgers was also lining up against Texas in what would be the very last AIAW title affair. And besides the emergence of an NCAA tourney to sweeten the pot, 1982 would also be the year that marked another large step toward full legitimacy for the women's game. For the first time that season the NCAA would also begin posting official women's statistics to parallel those already long kept (since 1948) for men's action.

The 1980s would thus witness exponential gains in popularity for women's games, and largely as a direct result of the newly instituted year-end NCAA championship tournament. In actuality there would now be three NCAA Tourneys, with Division II and Division III playoffs also inaugurated the same spring. At the Division II level of competition a familiar and storied entrant — Delta State — would exploit the restructured system and reemerge with three additional national titles (1989, 1990, 1992) to

Outstanding Women's Division I Players and Coaches (1978-1995)

Year	Wade Player of the Year	Converse Coach of the Year
1978	Carol Blazejowski (Montclair St.)	Not Yet Awarded
1979	Nancy Lieberman (Old Domin.)	Not Yet Awarded
1980	Nancy Lieberman (Old Domin.)	Not Yet Awarded
1981	Lynette Woodard (Kansas)	Not Yet Awarded
1982	Pam Kelly (Louisiana Tech)	Not Yet Awarded
1983	LaTaunya Pollard (Long Beach)	Pat Summitt (Tennessee)
1984	Janice Lawrence (La. Tech)	Jody Conradt (Texas)
1985	Cheryl Miller (Southern Cal)	Jim Foster (St. Joseph's)
1986	Kamie Etheridge (Texas)	Jody Conradt (Texas)
1987	Shelly Pennefather (Villanova)	Theresa Grentz (Rutgers)
1988	Teresa Weatherspoon (La. Tech)	Vivian Stringer (Iowa)
1989	Clarissa Davis (Texas)	Tara VanDerveer (Stanford)
1990	Jennifer Azzi (Stanford)	Kay Yow (NC State)
1991	Daedra Charles (Tennessee)	Rene Portland (Penn State)
1992	Susan Robinson (Penn State)	Ferne Labati (Miami-Florida)
1993	Carol Ann Shudlick (Minnesota)	Vivian Stringer (Iowa)
1994	Charlotte Smith (North Carolina)	Marsha Sharp (Texas Tech)
1995	Rebecca Lobo (Connecticut)	Geno Auriemma (Conn.)

Wade Trophy presented by National Association for Girls and Women in Sport

add to those already captured under AIAW auspices. But just as with the men, it was Division I play that was universally assumed to crown a true national champion, and 1982 trophy-holder Louisiana Tech remained firmly in the driver's seat as the most prominent national powerhouse across the earliest years of the decade. But there were also other worthy contestants aiming for No. 1 and these included over the coming years teams from Tennessee, Stanford, Texas and Southern California. Texas, in particular, earned a special niche in 1986 when the Lady Longhorns became the very first women's NCAA national champion to duplicate the earlier AIAW feat of Delta State and complete an entire season with an unblemished record. Finishing at 34-0 under Jody Conradt, the all-time winningest coach in women's college basketball history, the Lady Longhorns clinched their title with an impressive 97-81 blowout of Southern Cal.

The decade of the 1980s also witnessed some truly spectacular individual performances, and this was especially true when it came to scoring bushels of points. Lorri Bauman at Drake blazed the trail for high-scoring women by pumping in a single-game high 58 as early as 1984. Three seasons later, on February 16, 1987, Long Beach State's Cindy Brown would raise the ceiling with a 60 point effort versus San Jose State, a mark which still stands as the national record. Kim Perrot of Southwestern Louisiana also checked in with a 58-point performance in 1990 that

Cheryl Miller of Southern Cal was arguably the greatest women's player of all time and the only three-time national player of the year. The sister of NBA superstar Reggie Miller, Cheryl Miller now holds a spot in the Naismith Basketball Hall of Fame. (USC photo)

fell only a single bucket short of Brown's milestone. And at the end of the decade would arise the greatest women's scoring phenom of them all in Patricia Hoskins of Mississippi Valley. The talented center would herself hit the 55-point mark twice during her 1989 senior season (averaging 33.6) and would continue to pour in baskets over a four-year span (1985-1989) at a rate which left her with NCAA career standards for both total points (3,122) and scoring average (28.4). Drake's Lorri Bauman (3,115) and Southern Cal's Cheryl Miller (3,018) would precede Hoskins as the only other Division I career 3,000-point scorers. (Lynette Woodard preceded NCAA record keeping.)

But by far the biggest star of the 1980s and also arguably of the entire history of women's hoop action was indisputably Southern Cal's electric and personable Cheryl Miller. Like Ann Meyers, Cheryl Miller too came from a basketball-playing family which also featured a brother, Reggie, destined for his own college (UCLA) and pro (Indiana Pacers) stardom as one of the game's most deadly three-point shooters. But for all his net-burning skills, NBA star Reggie Miller was never the biggest offensive threat in his own family; that honor clearly belonged to Cheryl from the day she knocked home a single-game record 105 points for a national high school scoring mark which has yet to be bested.

Cheryl Miller's 3,405 high school career points and 3,018 college tallies would make her one of the most productive offensive weapons in all of cage history. The only three-time Naismith Award winner and now Naismith Hall of Famer was also the only Southern Cal player, male or female, ever to have her uniform jersey number permanently retired. But this first four-time Kodak All-American was far more than just the game's most talented athlete, as great as that accomplishment might in itself be. For it was Cheryl Miller's flamboyant personal style and special flair for on-court dramatics (another feature shared with her NBA brother) that as much as anything else heaped national attention on women's basketball when the sport finally boomed during the mid-80s. It was Cheryl Miller almost single-handedly who first personified the grace of women's basketball as prime-time sporting entertainment.

Over the five seasons between 1987 and 1991 Tennessee's Lady Vols would next reign as the most consistent national power on the women's scene. The Lady Vols would capture three NCAA titles all told over this half decade. These titles would come on alternating years as the team of coach Pat Summitt defeated first Louisiana Tech (1987), then Auburn (1989) and finally Virginia in a 1991 overtime thriller which remains the only final-game overtime match in the first 14 seasons of NCAA Women's Division I tourney play. The Lady Vols would capture their titles as the result of a balanced team concept rather than through any exceptional star qualities of individual players. But they could also boast at least one superstar in Brigette Gordon, a two-time All-American who would complete her four-year career as the all-time leading scorer (388 points, 21.6 ppg) in NCAA women's tournament play.

The Lady Vols would also feature perhaps the premier coach on the women's scene during at least the past decade and perhaps more. Now on the job at Tennessee for 20 seasons, Pat (Head) Summitt remains the only female coach to win three NCAA titles and trails only Jody Conradt of Texas in total career victories (she earned her 500th win in the opening game of the 1993-94 season). Summitt would be named co-coach of the decade for the 1980s by the U.S. Basketball Writers Association and three times has been tabbed as the Naismith national coach of the year.

Stanford would briefly interrupt the Lady Vols' domination with a surprising NCAA title victory in 1990. The Pac-10 team coached by Tara VanDerveer would claw its way into the national title game against SEC powerhouse Auburn and then come away with an 88-81 victory in a game played before 20,023 fanatics at the Thompson-Boling Arena on the University of Tennessee's Knoxville campus. It would be only the second women's game ever to draw a crowd in excess of 20,000, and the huge throng was happy witness to a spirited contest in which Auburn fell in the title matchup for the third year in a row. Fans were also thrilled by the play of former local Knoxville-area high school star, Jennifer Azzi, who starred for the Cardinals in their first-ever trip to the national title game. When the Stanford team won again behind Azzi in 1992 (78-62 over Western Kentucky) the Lady Cardinals were much less of a surprise champion the second time around.

With Cheryl Miller in the driver's seat Southern Cal would have a glory run of its own in the mid-1980s. That run would lead directly to the only back-to-back national titles since the NCAA-sanctioned postseason tournament was launched in 1982. Led by the scoring of sensational freshman Miller and the bench strategy of coach Linda Sharp, the Lady Trojans slipped by Louisiana Tech in 1983 in a nip-and-tuck 69-67 title game that set new standards for dramatic and aesthetic play. The next season Sharp's Trojans would be back to knock off Tennessee on their own home grounds in Los Angeles and thus pocket a second NCAA trophy. And Southern Cal would again reach the title match two years later during Miller's fine senior season, but this time would fall to the powerful undefeated Texas team in the cavernous surroundings of Kentucky's Rupp Arena.

Few today would contest a ballot for Miller as the greatest women's player yet to come down the road. Perhaps the only serious challenge in the eyes of longtime observers of the women's game

Women's Naismith Award Winners and National Division I Scoring Leaders

Year	Player of the Year	Nat. Scoring Leader (ppg)
1982	Not Awarded	Barbara Kennedy, Clem. (29.3)
1983	Anne Donovan (Old Dom.)	L. Pollard, Long Beach (29.3)
1984	Cheryl Miller (So. Cal.)	Deborah Temple, Delta State (31.2)
1985	Cheryl Miller (So. Cal)	Anucha Browne, Northwestern (30.5)
1986	Cheryl Miller (So. Cal)	Wanda Ford, Drake (30.6)
1987	Clarissa Davis (Texas)	Tresa Spaulding, BYU (28.9)
1988	Sue Wicks (Rutgers)	LeChandra LeDay, Grambling (28.9)
1989	Clarissa Davis (Texas)	**Patricia Hoskins, Miss. Valley (33.6)**
1990	Jennifer Azzi (Stanford)	Kim Perrot, SW Louisiana (30.0)
1991	Dawn Staley (Virginia)	Jan Jensen, Drake (29.5)
1992	Dawn Staley (Virginia)	Andrea Congreaves, Mercer (33.0)
1993	Sheryl Swoopes (Texas Tech)	A. Congreaves, Mercer (31.0)
1994	Lisa Leslie (So. Cal)	Kristi Ryan, Cal-Sacramento (28.0)
1995	Rebecca Lobo (UConn)	Koko Lahanas, Cal-Fullerton (26.8)

Naismith Trophy for Women's Player of the Year Presented by the Atlanta Tip-Off Club

would come from a sensational shooter of the 1990s, Texas Tech star Sheryl Swoopes. Swoopes would of course enjoy a special stage for her own incomparable act, one that had not been available to Cheryl Miller only a few short seasons earlier. That stage was the 1993 Women's Final Four which enjoyed the event's first advance sellout in its dozen-year history. Swoopes was a 6-foot senior guard who had played only two seasons of major college basketball and yet had averaged nearly 25 points per game over that 66-game stretch (28 as a senior) and scored in double figures in all but two of her collegiate games. But Swoopes had also saved her finest hour for her career curtain call against Ohio State in the NCAA title game. An ecstatic crowd of 15,000 was treated to perhaps the finest single-game offensive display in women's cage history when the electrifying Swoopes broke loose for an incredible 47-point performance. The scoring outburst not only brought her team a national title but also smashed Bill Walton's NCAA Finals scoring record (44 versus Memphis State in 1973) in the process.

There was a special footnote to Swoopes' memorable Final Four outing on the floor of the Atlanta Omni. Attempting to satisfy the champions of Title IX legislation, NCAA executives in 1987 had demanded that a new CBS television package deal for presenting men's Final Four action also include women's Final Four coverage. The trade-off was a provision that the women's semifinals and finals be played back-to-back on Saturday and Sunday, an obvious ploy to take advantage of the men's Sunday off-day and thus boost TV ratings for the women's session. The ordeal of playing on consecutive days hardly seemed to slow the hot-shooting Swoopes, however, and it was ironically Swoopes' own dramatic performance as much as anything that gave a much-needed shot in the arm to the women's sagging TV ratings. The Texas Tech-Ohio State shootout would boost the viewer ratings a full 34 percent (5.5 rating) above those of the immediately preceding championship matches, yet would still fail to match the highest-rated women's game ever, the 1982 NCAA championship inaugural between Louisiana Tech and Cheyney State which drew a lofty 7.3 rating.

Yet, despite Swoopes' heroics in 1993, no single game of the past decade is more clearly responsible for putting women's college hoops on the map than the one that decided the 1994 national championship. The tense battle in the Richmond Coliseum had come down to the final seconds and North Carolina was trailing Louisiana Tech by a 59-57 count with 0.7 seconds showing on the scoreboard and only a desperate hope for a miracle standing between Carolina and a heart-breaking season's end.

What transpired during those last few ticks of the clock remains one of the most thrilling moments in the annals of collegiate sport. Carolina junior forward Charlotte Smith would take an inbounds pass just outside the three-point arc and

Purdue All-American guard MaChelle Joseph displays the speed and athleticism of the modern women's college basketball player. Joseph was the Big Ten's all-time career scoring leader when she completed her career at Purdue in 1992. (Darcy Chang, Lafayette Journal and Courier)

let fly an arching buzzer-beater that would send the arena into absolute pandemonium. It was a shot that could only remind hoops fans of another Carolina Final Four miracle a decade earlier, one launched in the New Orleans Superdome by no lesser star than Michael Jordan.

There was also a fitting piece of irony attaching itself to this thrilling last-second three-pointer that had brought a national championship to coach Sylvia Hatchell and her Lady Tar Heels. The author of that shot, Charlotte Smith, was the nephew of one of the greatest of all Carolina cage legends. Smith's uncle, who had painstakingly taught her the game on a homemade court in her grandparents' yard, was none other than David Thompson, hero of the 1974 North Carolina State NCAA champions and later standout ABA and NBA star. Like Ann Meyers and Cheryl Miller before her, Charlotte Smith wore a very reputable family basketball pedigree.

And the thrills have not ceased to pile up with each successive winter. The recent 1995 campaign gave birth to what was perhaps the greatest one-year women's college team found anywhere in NCAA history. Connecticut's Lady Huskies coached by Geno Auriemma had posted a sterling 30-3 record in 1994 and barely missed a Final Four trip by losing to eventual champion North Carolina in the East Regional finals. With All-American 6-4 forward Rebecca Lobo leading the way the Huskies would not be denied two seasons in a row as they charged through a perfect 35-0 campaign on their way to a coveted national title.

Lobo was everybody's "player of the year" choice, but the lanky senior was given a considerable assist from fired-up teammates in the title shootout with perennial postseason power Tennessee. Kara Wolters, a 6-7 center, and tiny guard Jennifer Rizzotti provided sufficient firepower when Lobo was benched early by foul

Women's All-Time All-Star Team (1972-95)

	Pos	Pts (ppg)	Best Year	NPY
Carol Blazejowski (Montclair)	F	3199 (31.7)	38.6 (Sr)	1978*
Nancy Lieberman (Old Domin.)	G	2430 (18.1)	20.9 (Fr)	1979-80*
Lynette Woodard (Kansas)	F	3649 (26.3)	31.0 (So)	1981*
Anne Donovan (Old Domin.)	C	2719 (19.9)	25.1 (So)	1983#
Cheryl Miller (UCLA)	F	3018 (23.6)	26.8 (Jr)	1984-86 #

Key: NPY = National Player of the Year; *= Wade Trophy; # = Naismith Trophy

Honorable Mention: Lorri Bauman (C, Drake), Patricia Hoskins (C-F, Mississippi Valley), Rebecca Lobo (F, Connecticut), Ann Meyers (G, UCLA), LaTauyna Pollard (G-F, Long Beach State), Dawn Staley (G, Virginia), Lusia Harris (C, Delta State), Sheryl Swoops (F, Texas Tech), Theresa Shank (C, Immaculata), Bridgette Gordon (F, Tennessee)

trouble and the Huskies cruised to a 70-64 victory in the Minneapolis Target Center. The 35-0 Connecticut record allowed the Huskies to join the 1986 Texas squad as the only two unbeaten NCAA women's national champions. Coach Auriemma's crew also became the first team — men's or women's — to complete a season of undefeated Division I play with as many as 35 victories.

There have been other landmarks along the way in the two-decade-plus history of big-time women's college basketball. There had earlier been Cyndi Meserve at Pratt Institute making headlines as the first woman to play on an otherwise all-male team. There were some major scoring feats like the 50-plus-point games of Cindy Brown, Kim Perrot, Lorri Bauman and Patricia Hoskins. There was even the first dunk of a basketball in game action, performed by Georgann Wells in 1984. The game's second female dunker would be Charlotte Smith of North Carolina, the same sharpshooter who had decided the 1994 national title game against Louisiana Tech with her Michael Jordan-like last-second shooting heroics.

But the women's sport for all its rapid evolution has also managed to keep much of the purity of play that has always been its hallmark. Many would now suggest that the men's version of Naismith ball has increasingly been reduced to playground-style displays of solo one-on-one showmanship and undisciplined if often spectacular star-oriented play. Fundamentals seem to have been almost entirely lost. The in-your-face slam-jam so attractive on moment-long highlight films has almost universally replaced deadeye shooting and unselfish passing as the game's artistic staple.

But in women's basketball, for all the new athleticism, the main focus is still squarely on fundamentals and on painstakingly drilled cooperative team offense and

269

defense. The women today shoot foul shots with deadly accuracy and deliver passes with pinpoint precision while some of the biggest male stars regularly display lackadaisical attitudes toward these time-honored fundamentals. While men's teams often race up and down the court for one uncontested dunk after another, their lady counterparts run effective multipass patterns that are an aesthetic delight to any "old school" fan of the passing and outside shooting game.

In the mid-1970s, at a time when John Wooden's reign had just ended at UCLA, women's hoops was still just a footnote to the history of college cage play. Two decades later the women's game stands proudly on the main stage of college athletics, even if not yet squarely at center stage. The NCAA Women's Final Four is now a major television event, staged on the Sunday afternoon sandwiched between the Saturday semifinals and Monday finals of the men's tournament and shown to the nation on a prime-

Rebecca Lobo, a 6-foot-4 center-forward from Connecticut was the 1995 women's college player of the year. Many consider her the best women's inside player ever. (University of Connecticut photo)

time broadcast. Women's teams play many games before packed arenas at some of the major institutions in the land. Stars like Connecticut's Rebecca Lobo, Carolina's Charlotte Smith, Louisiana Tech's Vicki Johnson, Ohio State's Katie Smith and Tennessee's Nikki McCray have name recognition status among a wide audience of basketball fanatics. The athletic 6-4 Rebecca Lobo even inked a major endorsement deal with Nike after her outstanding 1995 "player of the year" campaign.

Charlotte Smith's dramatic last-second shot to win a national title for North Carolina's Tar Heels in 1994 and Rebecca Lobo's truly dominant season for the undefeated champion Connecticut Huskies in 1995 were sufficient to bring legions of new and appreciative fans to the fast-growing sport of women's college basketball. No longer a minor sport, the women's version of Dr. Naismith's marvelous game now promises to be another vital chapter of the always growing college basketball story.

12

The Eighties and Nineties, Part 2

Explosions of March Madness

The '80s and '90s emerged as the gilded epoch of true competitive balance in college basketball battles. Gone was the era of the dominating superstar like Oscar Robertson or Elgin Baylor, Bill Russell or Tom Gola, Lew Alcindor or Larry Bird — the nonpareil scorer or defender who might single-handedly dominate a season or a league or even a postseason tournament.

Gone, as well, was the dynasty program or juggernaut team able to string together a handful of national titles or postseason Final Fours. In the wake of a dismantling of Wooden's legacy in 1975, the NCAA championship trophy now began to circulate as regularly as had the NBA title flag after the demise of the Auerbach Celtics at the end of the '60s. Over the 21 seasons between 1976 and 1995 only Indiana would claim three titles and only Duke, Louisville and North Carolina would carry home the NCAA banner twice. If there was a dominant team it was Duke in the late '80s and early '90s. Under Coach Mike Krzyzewski (who took the Duke reins in 1980) the Blue Devils claimed the only back-to-back championships of the last two decades and boasted six Final Four appearances within a seven-year stretch. Yet with 15 different NCAA champions in 20 postseasons the watchword had clearly now become competitive balance.

What modern-era fans had to enjoy, then, was a spectacle of constant turnover, endless new stars, fever-pitch postseason competitions and exciting parity throughout the land. The floodtide of individual star players was especially notable in the immediate wake of Larry Bird and Magic Johnson. Louisville's dynamic "Doctor Dunkenstein" — a.k.a. Darrell Griffith — first stepped into the spotlight when he teamed with fellow frontcourt talent Rodney McCray to carry Denny Crum's Louisville Cardinals to 1980 postseason glories. Quick to follow were Indiana sophomore sensation Isiah Thomas; the North Carolina powerhouse front line of Al Wood, James Worthy and Sam Perkins; DePaul's high-scoring frontcourt duo of Mark Aguirre and Terry Cummings; Utah's dazzling combo of Danny Vranes and Tom Chambers; Antoine Carr and Cliff Levingston at Wichita State; and the sweet-shooting pair of Kelly Tripucka of Notre Dame and Dale Ellis of Tennessee.

Sensational backcourt aces and agile post players were especially plentiful in the early and mid-80s, and these breeds popped up everywhere around the land. Soon leading their teams to national prominence with magic spells of ballhandling

Hoyas head man John Thompson is an imposing figure with his familiar white towel, towering frame and relentlessly successful Georgetown University cage program. A three-time national coach of the year, Thompson has won both an NCAA title and Olympic gold medal. (Georgetown University photo)

and playmaking were Michael Jordan in North Carolina, Danny Ainge at Brigham Young, Wayman Tisdale at Oklahoma and Eric "Sleepy" Floyd of Georgetown; the list of powerhouse centers consisted of Georgetown's Patrick Ewing, Virginia's Ralph Sampson, Steve Johnson at Oregon State, Sam Bowie of Kentucky, Purdue's Joe Barry Carroll and Nigerian transplant Akeem (later Hakeem) Olajuwon at Houston.

If there was suddenly far more parity among both the teams and the all-stars, this didn't necessarily mean, however, that the balance of power had shifted altogether away from the major conferences. The juggernaut teams for the past two-plus decades have continued to reside mainly in the ACC and Big Ten, along with occasional interlopers from the Northeast (Massachusetts, St. John's, Connecticut) and the Mid-Atlantic Coast (especially Georgetown and Villanova), and regular yearly visits to championship action by teams representing Kentucky, Kansas and UCLA.

Yet there were surprises. At the outset of the '80s at least one formidable new competitor also suddenly entered the scene. For it was in autumn 1979 that a new corporate enterprise formally dubbed the Big East Conference first saw the light of day. This new confederation would for the first time mix tradition-rich New England stalwarts (Providence, Boston College, Connecticut) and New York-area superpowers (St. John's, Syracuse, Seton Hall) with old standbys from Mid-Atlantic states (Georgetown, Villanova, Pittsburgh). Play opened for the 1979-80 season with seven teams and three of the five major cities of the region represented (Boston with Boston College, New York with St. John's, Washington, D.C., with Georgetown); the fourth megacenter came on board when Villanova's Wildcats (Philadelphia) signed up a year later, and Pittsburgh completed the quintet in 1983. The result was the first new conference in more than a quarter century that could honestly hope to battle toe-to-toe with more traditional powerhouse leagues when it came to annual postseason play.

The beginnings of the Big East Conference provide a miraculous if not quite surprising success story. Certainly it was an idea long waiting to happen. For several decades the power centers of the sport had resided almost exclusively among the Dixie-based ACC, Midwest corn belt Big Ten and constantly evolving Missouri Valley, along with an occasional challenge from the Metro Conference (mainly Louisville) and the SEC (Kentucky, of course, and more recently Alabama, LSU and Tennessee), plus the isolated exception of UCLA which was the singular standard bearer for West Coast honors. While New York corridor teams had once made noise in the NCAA (Holy Cross in 1947, La Salle in 1954, and especially dual-champion CCNY in 1950) and dominated the NIT in the '40s and into the '50s, that quadrant of the country had been relatively quiet since the 1951 game-fixing episodes. But now ex-Providence College coach Dave Gavitt pulled together a plan designed to change all this and thus restore Northeastern respectability.

Gavitt had been only a moderately successful bench coach, taking over for Joe Mullaney in Providence at the outset of the '70s, inheriting a solid program (as well as a genuine superstar in Ernie DiGregorio) and enjoying a single Final Four visit in only his third season on the job. Nevertheless, he never lifted the Friars past that early lofty plateau despite a cage tradition (and thus built-in recruiting appeal) in the Rhode Island capital as savory as any east of the shadows of Madison Square Garden.

Yet as an organizer he now struck instant gold. Working to exploit dormant regional pride, Gavitt pieced together a lucrative television package before the new league had ever tipped off its first game; he then also arranged a million-dollar deal that placed the conference playoffs in Madison Square Garden for three upcoming seasons (1983-85). Of course he had plenty of help along the way. John Thompson joined the mix and brought the renewed weight of Georgetown's program (with five recent postseason appearances in a row) into the fold. Colorful Lou Carnesecca carted his own mystique and that of his St. John's Redmen on board as well. Such marquee coaches and household-name institutions were a surefire formula for success. And what Gavitt, Thompson and others had hastily patched together was soon the front-page basketball story of much of the decade of the '80s.

The idea was to capture the lucrative and underexploited New England, New York and mid-Atlantic coast fan markets, and to do so by providing spirited conference competition at the highest possible level. Equally pressing was the plan for mounting a serious challenge to other sectors once NCAA postseason play rolled around each year.

The name selected for the new league would clearly broadcast these stated intentions. And the mission was almost overnight accomplished when the first several seasons of the Big East provided a clear harbinger of even better things about to unfold. The first winter witnessed a three-way tie for the conference top spot — Georgetown, St. John's, Syracuse. More importantly, all three banner carriers finished prominently positioned in the final AP national poll: Syracuse sixth, Georgetown 11th, St. John's 13th. And in only its third year of operation the infant league would also soon have one of its own teams featured in the charmed circle of the NCAA Final Four.

Georgetown (26-6) came roaring out of the Big East pack at the end of the 1982 campaign seemingly ready to charge through the 48-team tournament field as the No. 1 seed in the West Regional. A hustling and pressing style of defense keyed by a shot-blocking freshman center named Ewing and a ball-hawking senior guard named Eric "Sleepy" Floyd were enough to vault the Hoyas straight into a national title showdown with the top-ranked ACC representative from North Carolina. It was a title shootout that was destined to solidify an early reputation for two future superstars — Ewing and Jordan — both only just now learning their trade as unseasoned freshmen. One was the special project of John Thompson and the other was tutored by Carolina's Dean Smith. And it was also destined to be a Final Four encounter that would legitimately launch the national reputation of an entire novice if already quite potent new league.

Georgetown's rise to the top was hardly a mere flash in the pan. It did seem exceptionally noteworthy at the time, however, if only because Thompson was the very first African-American coach ever to lead a team into the Final Four. Under the tutelage of the ex-Providence star the Hoyas had already emerged several seasons earlier as a national powerhouse, even though now, in 1982, they were only the second-best club in their own infant conference. Villanova had taken the league race at 11-3 and Georgetown with its big freshman was still two seasons away from its own first undisputed Big East title. But Villanova, with the No. 3 East Regional seed, would fall by 10 points to Carolina in the regional finals. This left the Hoyas, with their pioneering coach and sensational freshman center, destined to carry the recently tattered banner of the entire northeast quadrant of the country on their own substantial if quite lonely shoulders. Only six teams from the region had made a Final Four appearance since the '60s, and of these only Villanova (1971) had climbed into the national finals.

Even before formation of the Big East, Thompson's teams had visited postseason play five straight times (twice in the NIT); since 1980 they had kept that string alive with a couple more NCAA bids. Nonetheless, the title match with Carolina in '82 would provide a unique stage for both school and conference. For the first time the tournament had moved into an oversized venue that seemed to be consistent with its new-found aspirations as the nation's true No. 1 sports event. Taking a clue from the ballyhooed Houston-UCLA matchup that had drawn 52,000-plus into the Astrodome back in January 1968, NCAA officials had now transported the Final Four gala into a similar venue in the spacious new Louisiana Superdome. With more than 61,000 looking on in person Georgetown was now in a position not only to make a

Just a raw freshman in 1982 and a half-dozen years away from NBA deification, North Carolina's Michael Jordan hit the game-winning shot to seal Dean Smith's long-awaited first NCAA title. (University of North Carolina photo)

loud statement about the quality of Big East play, but to make that statement on easily the most spectacular postseason stage that tournament competition had so far ever offered.

Georgetown had battled hard to climb into its roost among the nation's big boys. The Hoyas had been carried in postseason by a devastating defense, anchored by a 7-foot freshman who was already the most intimidating player on either coast or anywhere in between. At no time in the 30-6 season had that defense been more of a factor than in the three preliminary postseason wins over Wyoming (51-43), Fresno State (58-40) and Oregon State (69-45), or the 50-46 semifinals conquest of Louisville that vaulted the Hoyas into the NCAA finals. Now they would battle gamely once more, leading the ACC regular-season and tournament champs by a single point at halftime (32-31) and then clinging to the lead into the game's final minute.

During the first half it was Ewing who established the psychological edge, batting away every shot he could reach and thus registering five goaltending calls in the opening moments. It was an awesome display of defensive intimidation, even if one that would later come back to haunt the Hoyas (since the final 63-62 loss might have been avoided if any of the goaltending rejections had only missed their mark).

But in the end fate took several unaccountable turns. Michael Jordan's jumper decided the issue as the perfectly aimed missile found nothing but net with 15 seconds remaining. There would indeed be a final opportunity for the Hoyas, but it would also be lost to a traumatic blunder from an embarrassed sophomore guard named Fred Brown. As Brown brought the ball upcourt with the final seconds escaping he would launch a fateful errant pass directly into the hands of Carolina's James Worthy (the tourney MVP), robbing Georgetown of any chance for a last desperate stab at victory. A composed Georgetown coach would later stoically console his dejected player and ward off the press by claiming that Brown had already won far more games for his teammates than he had ever lost.

Naismith Award winner Patrick Ewing carried both Georgetown and the Big East Conference into the national spotlight with his intimidating defensive play á lá Bill Russell. (Georgetown University photo)

As a full decade, the 1980s would soon enough earn a much-deserved reputation for frequent last-second heroics, all played out during a string of wild NCAA Final Four encounters. Among these, no clock-beating display would be any grander to witness or to cherish than the one that Jordan provided in the championship matchup between North Carolina and Georgetown on March 29, 1982. If still a freshman waiting for the wraps to be taken off his emerging game, young "Air Jordan" had admirably demonstrated for a huge television audience that he was already laced up and down with all the stuff that true champions are made of.

It was Jordan's game-winning shot, far more than Brown's fatal lapse, that would be most recalled in later years. Many players would of course be remembered a lifetime for just such a rare moment in the sun as the one the North Carolina freshman enjoyed with his title-winning heave. But Jordan himself was soon to cast such a huge aura that such early auditions would quickly become merely the stuff of tournament trivia. What was not trivial, however, was the impact of this single memorable tournament game on the basketball histories of two tradition-rich schools. After six futile empty trips to the Final Four, Carolina's Dean Smith had finally garnered a long-expected national title. And for rival Georgetown — as well as for Thompson and Ewing — this was but the beginning. Ewing, like Jordan, had three more scheduled seasons still on tap. And for both Georgetown and the Big East they were about to turn into most memorable seasons indeed.

There was one delectable footnote to the 1981-82 season and it came early on in the year and grabbed no more than passing Page 2 headlines at the time. Just before players and fans took a brief respite for Christmas celebrations a select group of rooters in Peoria, Illinois, were privileged to witness perhaps the greatest bargain in collegiate basketball history. For their single-game admission fee those witnesses on hand for a December 21 battle between visiting Cincinnati and host Bradley were treated to a pitched battle which dragged on for nearly the length of two full games. When the final buzzer sounded on the longest game in college basketball annals the visitors owned an exhausting 75-73 victory. Four Bearcats and five Braves starters had logged at least 63 of the 75 minutes played, and none of the ticket-buying faithful likely felt cheated, even in the face of the hometown defeat.

The early successes of Georgetown were obviously built around their prize recruit Ewing, a Jamaican native lured out of Rindge-Latin High School in Boston and a player destined to become one of the greatest defensive forces since Bill Russell. Jordan had not been the only sensational freshman in the 1982 title game; beyond his shot-blocking sideshow in that contest, Ewing had also registered 23 points on 10-of-15 shooting and had hauled in a game-high 11 rebounds. Jordan for his own part would never get the Tar Heels back into the promised land. Ewing on the other hand would be far better equipped to carry a college team on his strong shoulders and to fulfill a role as franchise player with his intimidating style of inside play. Just two years later, in 1984, while Jordan's team was succumbing to Indiana in regional semifinal action (Carolina had fallen to Georgia in the regional finals during the intervening season), Ewing would be once more leading Georgetown's Hoyas all the way back to the top.

Georgetown's final confrontation of Ewing's junior season would be with the colorful Houston team (32-5) which featured a memorable nickname ("Phi Slamma Jamma" in honor of its high-flying combo of dunking frontliners during this and the previous season) and a memorable set of future NBA stars (Olajuwon, Michael Young and Greg "Cadillac" Anderson). The Cougars had been even stronger a season earlier, with Clyde Drexler and Larry Micheaux still in the lineup and boasting a 31-2 record entering the national title match with North Carolina State; nonetheless they had been a disappointing loser to the surprising charges of coach Jim Valvano. Now they were primed to take the title they had recently let slip away. In the end, however, Ewing would benefit from considerably more frontline support than his towering rival Olajuwon, and once again Houston would have to settle on its destined role as perennial bridesmaids.

In the 1983 postseason affair Houston had indeed been a Cinderella team, right down to the final moments of its shocking collapse against the equally surprising

Carolina Wolfpack. Drexler (15.9 ppg), Micheaux (13.8) and leading scorer Michael Young (17.3) had all combined with Olajuwon (13.9) to provide an impressive balanced offensive attack throughout both regular-season and tournament play.

In the season's stretch run, Guy Lewis' Cougars were joined by another Cinderella ballclub, however, and it would be the ACC contingent under Valvano that eventually would prove an even more charmed group. This would soon be evident even if State's lineup of Thurl Bailey, Dereck Whittenburg, Sidney Lowe and Lorenzo Charles didn't appear quite as imposing as the bunch Houston had to offer. Houston coasted in the first four tournament rounds: 60-50 over Maryland, 70-63 over Memphis State, 89-71 over Big East entrant Villanova in the regional title match, and 94-81 over Louisville in the national semifinals. Valvano's troops survived some far stiffer tests, climbing over stubborn Pepperdine in two overtimes in the first-round opener, next nipping UNLV by a single point in round two, and also escaping with their lives against ACC rival Virginia (63-62) in the regional title game. From the start of March Madness '83 it seemed to be NC State and not Houston that clearly owned the biggest basket full of miracles.

The showdown game in Albuquerque for the national title was one of the most thrilling ever witnessed and also one that seemed to verify the Carolina Wolfpack's apparent contract with destiny. Yet when Houston and N.C. State tipped off on April 4 it appeared to contemporary witnesses that the game would be little more than anticlimax. Houston had already strutted its stuff two nights earlier with a 58-point second-half explosion that had buried Louisville 94-81 and left viewers breathless. Olajuwon had staked his claim in this one as a power center every bit the equal of Ewing when he posted 22 rebounds and 21 points in a truly extraordinary effort. It was a contest that also caused NCAA rules committee secretary Edward Steitz to loudly sing the Cougars' praises: "I've watched every NCAA Tournament game since 1947, and that's the most exciting game and the most remarkable set of athletes I've ever seen."

But Valvano had his team more than prepared to contend with the Cougars' high-powered offense and glowing press clippings. If the dunk was the preferred weapon of Phi Slamma Jamma then this was the factor that the Wolfpack defense would concentrate on eliminating. Carolina opened with a dunk of its own by Thurl Bailey and then packed its zone defense around the basket to limit fast-break opportunities for the run-and-gun Cougars. Olajuwon provided the first Houston slam with only five minutes remaining in the half. Forced to rely on long-range jump shots, favored Houston could connect on only 31 percent and surprisingly trailed 33-25 by intermission.

Houston was further unsettled in the second stanza not only by the pesky N.C. State defensive tactics but also by the four personal fouls Drexler had accumulated during the first session. But even with Drexler and Micheaux relegated to the bench the Cougars had enough talent to storm back down the stretch. Then the unaccountable began to transpire in one of the strangest NCAA Finals stretch drives ever witnessed. Houston had powered a 17-2 comeback drive and assumed a 42-35 lead when Lewis ordered his team into an ill-advised delay game which he called his "locomotion" offense. Once more momentum shifted, and now N.C. State again took the advantage. Forced to play conservatively by their coach's tactics the Phi Slamma Jammers would connect on only four more baskets during the game's final 10 long minutes. The door had now been opened for a most memorable upset.

The fireworks came with the game's closing seconds. Long-range jump shots by Sidney Lowe (two of them) and Dereck Whittenburg (two more) knotted the score at 52 with but 1:59 to play. When Houston freshman Alvin Franklin was intentionally fouled in the closing moments and missed both charity tosses the game was suddenly Carolina's alone to win. Valvano ordered his team to hold the ball for a final shot by Whittenburg, but when the effort was almost blocked by Drexler the Wolfpack senior was left with only a final desperation off-balance heave from 30 feet away just before the buzzer. The blind shot fell far short of the rim, yet somehow Olajuwon didn't react to the errant toss and allowed Lorenzo Charles to slip into rebounding position. In a moment that will now live forever in Wolfpack lore the 6-7 sophomore forward — who had logged but a single earlier basket on the night — grabbed the missed shot in midflight and rammed home the dramatic game winner only a single tick before the buzzer. It was a shot that would live on in collective memory as the famous "bound heard round the world" and it was certainly the most memorable put-back in North Carolina State (perhaps even in ACC and NCAA) basketball history.

Houston's dramatic loss to N.C. State had been a crusher. But a year later Olajuwon and company (minus Drexler and Micheaux) would be back for another round of title play. As a junior Olajuwon was already every bit as dominating as Ewing, posting identical offensive numbers and providing the same defensive wall able to thwart any opponent's attack. (The offensive totals posted by the two were almost a perfect match for the season, with Olajuwon holding the slight edge, especially in caroms: 16.8 ppg, 500 rebounds and a .675 field-goal percentage for Akeem; 16.4 ppg, 371 rebounds and .658 shooting for Patrick.) The matchup between these two giants for a national title would itself seem to offer one of the most dramatic moments that college hoops had witnessed over the past couple of decades. It didn't quite turn out that way, of course, as neither star cracked double figures in rebounds (they each had nine) or even led his team in scoring. This time Ewing would come out the big winner, however, as the Hoyas built a 10-point halftime edge and then coasted down the stretch to an 84-75 final.

Patrick Ewing was now batting .500 in national title games; he was also two-for-three in taking his team all the way to the championship round. And his most memorable March moment — even if his most disappointing — was still another year away.

It looked like an easy enough Georgetown repeat in 1985. Even though Thompson's Hoyas were knocked off their top perch during season-long Big East wars (St. John's went 15-1 to claim the league title), nonetheless any team with Ewing in the post and an array of talented supporters on the perimeter had to be the odds-on postseason tournament favorite. A major roadblock would quickly emerge, however, and it was not surprising that it would be provided by some very familiar adversaries for Ewing and his teammates. For this was the year that the Big East would burst on the March scene with an impressive demonstration of just how far the new conference had come and how quickly it had arrived in the championship circle. When the dust had cleared the Final Four lineup would include Georgetown, Villanova, St. John's and lonely outsider Memphis State. It was the only time in a full half-century-plus of March play that three teams from the same league had somehow survived for the national semifinal contests.

With 20 points from Reggie Williams and 16 from Ewing, Georgetown would gain immediate revenge on St. John's for regular-season injuries, posting a 77-59 semifinal victory. But Villanova would refuse to abide by anything that looked like a fitting script for Ewing's collegiate curtain call. Unheralded Wildcat post player Ed Pinckney would outmaneuver Ewing most of the title game and star with 16 points (a bucket better than Patrick) and six well-placed rebounds. But the big story in the end would be Villanova's all-time record .786 field-goal shooting percentage. The final count would read 66-64 against the Hoyas. The gutsy Villanova squad of flamboyant coach Rollie Massimino had not only pulled off the championship surprise of the year but the biggest shocker of the decade as well. Perhaps most impressive of all was the fact that no team before or since had ever walked off with an NCAA title after posting 10 regular-season losses along the way to the Big Dance.

If the Big East and its inroads on March NCAA competitions was the prime story by the mid-80s, the decade had nonetheless started out with a number of very familiar faces still dominating the collegiate scene. The 1980 season, for example, was one of the most wide open in years. Three of the eventual Final Four NCAA entrants that year (UCLA, Purdue and Iowa) would be teams finishing either third or fourth in their respective leagues. By contrast, DePaul, Louisville and LSU topped the final AP weekly poll and these were hardly a set of annual visitors to the penthouse, either. But by spring, when it again came time for tournament play, the old standbys seemed to emerge as always. Two Big Ten teams would make it into the Final Four (Purdue and Iowa, who had both been there before), along with a most familiar face from UCLA. The fourth charmed team would be Louisville, itself an established power and one that had in recent years been working overtime to put the young Metro Conference squarely on the basketball map.

The most noteworthy story of the 1980 season, of course, was the re-emergence of UCLA after a brief four-year absence from participation in the final tournament weekend. Under well-traveled Larry Brown, who seemed to make a full career out of reviving college and professional cage programs and then moving quickly on to the next exciting challenge, the Bruins managed a surprising postseason run that brought them out of the West Regional as an original No. 8 seed. But in the end it was Louisville that had the strongest horses. Led by leaper Darrell Griffith, Denny Crum's balanced team walked off with the national title by outlasting the Bruins 59-54 in a low-scoring and even somewhat lackluster finale.

The next two seasons would showcase the two teams and the two coaches that shared domination in the 1980s with John Thompson at Georgetown and Denny Crum at Louisville. First to rise to the top were Bob Knight's Indiana Hoosiers. The 1981 Indiana team was a young outfit paced by a sophomore point guard destined for considerable pro celebrity after his short-lived collegiate career. In the early stretches of the season the Indiana team looked like anything but a national cham-

Isiah Thomas' stay at Indiana with coach Bob Knight was brief, yet in a brilliant and final sophomore season the flashy point guard took the Hoosiers all the way to the 1981 national championship. (Indiana University photo)

pion. There were four straight losses during the midyear holiday break, including the opening two contests of the Big Ten official league schedule. But Knight's teams usually played tough early-season opponents and often started much slower than some rivals who feasted on a regular menu of December patsies.

By the end of the season Bob Knight had his Hoosiers on a full-scale roll. Victories in the last five regular-season contests locked up a Big Ten title with a 14-4 conference mark. Lopsided victories over Maryland (99-64), Alabama-Birmingham (87-72) and St. Joseph's (78-46) sealed Coach Knight's third trip into the Final Four. In the end, the sophomore- and junior-studded team (Ray Tolbert was the only regular senior) would bring Knight his second national title. This was not a team to compare favorably with The General's 1976 undefeated outfit. But it was a championship outfit at heart nonetheless.

There was a touch of irony in the fact that Knight and his Hoosiers would return to national championship play at the very site where they had reigned supreme only five seasons earlier. The NCAA finals were returning to Philadelphia's Spectrum, and again Knight's Hoosiers would do most of the celebrating at the final lavish party. But this time around it was a party that almost didn't come off as scheduled. For the first time ever the NCAA Finals would face the serious possibility of cancellation or at least postponement, something that even World War II restrictions and post-war betting scandals had never managed to bring about. The reason had nothing to do with basketball, of course. The very evening the sports world was set for its annual showcase event the remainder of the nation was thrown into a sudden state of trauma by an assassination attempt that had gravely wounded President Ronald Reagan earlier in the day. With Reagan confined to a Washington, D.C., hospital with a gunshot wound two crucial decisions had to be quickly reached. Would the NCAA Tournament Committee now allow the prime-time event to be staged under the specter of national emergency? And if it did, would NBC cut away from news surrounding Reagan to televise the event?

Once the game did tip off it was the type of contest guaranteed to bring all eyes, at least for the moment, back to the business at hand — the business of pressure-packed championship tournament basketball. Two of the country's annual collegiate big wigs, with two of the most respected coaches, were now about to match re-sources once again for the sport's most cherished prize. And there was little disap-pointment to be found anywhere regarding the thoroughly entertaining spectacle that resulted.

If there was any difference between Knight's 26-9 Big Ten champion Hoosiers and Smith's 29-8 ACC runner-up Tar Heels it was of course the sterling 6-1 sopho-more guard who was running the offense for the Indiana club. This would be a final college game for Isiah Thomas, who would end his own stormy relationship with Knight after only two seasons by departing early for a stellar NBA career. It would be a final outing, however, that would convince most that — in ability level at least — Thomas was already a seasoned pro point guard.

With Indiana nursing a slim 27-26 margin at intermission, Thomas took total control in the opening moments of the second stanza. The outburst by the talented Chicago native included a steal and driving layup on the opening tip, several preci-sion passes leading to buckets by Landon Turner, a couple of additional steals lead-ing to further scores, and even a pair of radar-controlled jump shots. Thomas would score 10 points in the first seven minutes of the second half, push the Indiana lead to double figures and pile up a game-high 23 before it was all over. The final would read 63-50 in favor of the Hoosiers and Isiah Thomas was, of course, the runaway choice for Final Four MVP.

The 1981 NCAA Tourney carried a couple of additional noteworthy features beyond the storied matchup between Bob Knight- and Dean Smith-coached teams in the finals and the background drama surrounding the title game's delayed television start. There was for one thing now a new tournament format, or at least a new complicated and computerized scheme for assigning 48 entrants to four regions for the preliminary rounds of play. The field had jumped to 48 a year earlier, after increasing to 40 in 1979. That number itself was up from 32 between 1975 and 1978. The number of entrants had started at eight initially, doubled to 16 in 1951 and jumped to 22 in 1953; between 1954 and 1969 the field shifted back and forth be-tween 22 on the low end and 25 on the high end, depending upon the number of conferences recently losing or receiving automatic bids.

The system of first-round byes would still be in effect for 1981, but a new method of seeding would now hopefully capitalize on the ever-greater balance that clearly marked all corners of the sport. It was a format seemingly guaranteed to extend fan interest in the event even further, and the fact that more than half the 1981

Mark Price averaged 20 points per game as a sensational freshman backcourt ace for Georgia Tech in 1983. He was a consensus second-team All-American his junior season in 1985. (Georgia Tech University photo)

first-round seeds were eliminated by the second weekend seemed to put an immediate stamp of approval on the actions of the NCAA Selection Committee.

Also, 1981 would sound the death knell on the annual consolation game held as preliminary event to the title shootout. When Virginia defeated LSU, 78-74, it marked the very last time that Final Four fans would ease into their seats for the waning action of an anticlimactic playoff for third place. In a bold stroke of marketing strategy, all viewer attention was now to be focused directly on the business of determining who was truly No. 1.

The North Carolina team that fell to Indiana in 1981 was itself a team on the verge of greatness. Senior forward Al Wood carried the scoring load during his final year and would now have to be replaced. James Worthy and Sam Perkins were budding superstars; as a sophomore-and-freshman frontcourt pair both had averaged a shade under 15 points for the season. And then in 1982 veteran coach Dean Smith showcased a new freshman talent who would one day become nothing less than the greatest phenomenon the entire sport had ever known. Michael Jordan wasn't quite that extraordinary as a college freshman, of course, averaging just 13.5 points per game as the club's No. 3 offensive threat behind Worthy and Perkins. But as a pure leaper, agile defender and backcourt ball handler he was already nonetheless extraordinary enough.

The second half of the '80s would provide the stage for continued dominance on the national scene by the same set of all-too-familiar powers. First Denny Crum and his Louisville Cardinals returned to national prominence, again cracking the NCAA Final Four in both 1982 and 1983, plus the NIT final weekend the very next year. Louisville had its own freshman sensation by 1986 and he was just what was needed to carry the crucial rebounding load on a team that already had Billy Thompson (14.9) and Milt Wagner (14.8) up front to do the bulk of the scoring. Crum's secret weapon was a 6-9 underclassman center named Pervis Ellison who was already good enough as a rookie to pace the Cardinals down the stretch toward their second national banner of the decade. He was perhaps almost too good, in fact. For Pervis Ellison's career would never again yield quite such plentiful bounty after his sensational debut season.

But as a freshman Ellison owned the tournament's final weekend just as he had owned much of the season that had made championship play possible. His game-high 13 rebounds played a major role in scuttling LSU 88-77 in the national semifinals. And then in the Finals it was also Ellison running amuck at both ends of the floor against helpless Duke. Three seasons earlier another Louisville squad, also on its way to the Final Four, had manhandled Duke on its own home floor 91-76 even without Ellison to man the basket regions; this time around it would be closer. But with Pervis earning his nickname of "Never Nervous" by slamming home a game-high 25 points and grabbing 11 caroms, the Cardinals hung on 72-69 for the year's biggest prize. When Ellison was named tourney MVP it would mark the first time a freshman had won that honor since Utah's Arnie Ferrin more than 40 years earlier.

The following season was a time for the Hurryin' Hoosiers and flamboyant and inflammable Bob Knight to climb back onto the zenith perch. The Big East contingent had maintained its power position across its own first half-dozen seasons almost without any serious interruption, and the Big Ten was still its usual healthy self. The latter conference boasted four clubs within the nation's top 11 in the year's final AP weekly rankings. This was quite a contrast to a season earlier, which had been something of an off-year for both the Big Ten and the Big East, with neither league able to claim one of its own among the NCAA final eight teams during postseason wars. Meanwhile, out in the Far West, a new independent powerhouse was about to emerge in the guise of UNLV's "Runnin' Rebels" — a team designed and directed by towel-chewing self-promoter Jerry Tarkanian.

But the most significant thing about the 1986-87 season was the introduction of a new three-point field goal rule. The new "bonus basket" would now be awarded for all successful goals made from outside an arc measured at 19 feet 9 inches from the center of the basket. Scoring marks around the country immediately underwent new onslaughts and Indiana was as successful as anyone with the newly legislated "trey" or "home run" shot, hitting more than half (50.8 percent) of its season's long-range attempts. By NCAA tournament time it would be this new offensive weapon, especially in the hands of Indiana's Steve Alford, that would already be playing a significant role in determining a new national champion.

Another headline story during the turning point 1987 season was a surprising player-of-the-year selection. For all the talk of long-range shooting it was yet another big man that stood center stage for much of the campaign. David Robinson, Navy's 7-1 tower of strength, was not only one of the most dominating big men to come on the scene in years, but he was also one of the rarest success stories in the long annals of college basketball lore. Robinson (28.2 ppg) trailed two undersized sharpshooters, Kevin Houston (32.9) of Army and Dennis Hopson (29.0) of Ohio State, in the national scoring race; he also ranked only fourth in the land in rebounding (11.8). But there was little question that David Robinson could do it all — score, rebound, block shots (he led the nation at 4.5 per game) and run the floor — with a grace and agility rarely if ever before seen in any 7-footer.

What was unique about Robinson's stature was the fact that he dominated the college basketball scene from a most unusual stage — a Naval Academy team that had never before made even the slightest ripple on the country's cage landscape. Service academy height regulations had always worked against outstanding basketball teams in Annapolis; Robinson himself exceeded those limits when an unexpected growth spurt took him over the 6-10 standard during his sophomore year. But what had really expanded to unanticipated proportions during Robinson's four-year undergraduate career were the basketball talents that had been totally latent when he left high school. As a sophomore the surprise phenom would carry the Midshipmen to their first NCAA appearance in a quarter-century, and as a junior he would lift them all the way to an East Regional championship showdown with Duke. By his senior season the future pro all-star provided enough firepower to pace Navy to its third NCAA appearance in succession.

If the emergence of the Big East had been the No. 1 story of the first half of the decade, it was the spectacular growth of the NCAA Tournament that was the headline material for collegiate basketball in the latter part of the decade. Each year the tourney seemed to stir even more frenzy — more fans, more office pools, bigger television advertising revenues, a more vice-like grip on the attention of the nation's sports fans. Tournament time was clearly now the nation's No. 1 sporting spectator attraction by almost any informal (sports talk show air time) or formal (TV market shares) measure. The mail-in ticket quest for Final Four ducats was now the nation's biggest lottery event, and the annual half-hour CBS *Selection Sunday* broadcast of the year's tournament pairings now seized the attention of sports followers with a ferocity once reserved for baseball's Opening Day or football's New Year's Day bowl game extravaganzas. And if the pro hoops game had reached high tide popularity in the mid- and late '80s with Magic and Bird and Air Jordan, edging ahead of the college game for at least some fans, even the NBA Finals never quite matched the two weeks of March Madness for raw fan energy and universal appeal.

It was a most fortunate run of dramatic championship games as much as anything else that had kick-started the NCAA prime-time event in the '80s. There was Michael Jordan's deciding shot, of course, made against Georgetown on a huge stage that for the first time reflected college basketball's new inflated aspirations. Then there was Valvano's Wolfpack with their magnificent upset of Drexler, Olajuwon and the Phi Slamma Jamma crew in Albuquerque. Next came three consecutive title games that went straight to the wire. Villanova shocked Georgetown in 1985 on the strength of record-setting field-goal accuracy and a truly clutch performance against Ewing by unheralded senior Ed Pinckney. Louisville edged Duke on the strength of a freshman named Ellison who proved in the biggest game of the year to be one of the most memorable "secret weapons" of NCAA history. And finally Bobby Knight's Hoosiers completed the cycle by nipping Syracuse with some clutch shooting of their own down the stretch and with some last-minute heroics that paralleled exactly the earlier North Carolina-Georgetown climax.

Keith Smart would can the game winner in the 1987 final played back in New Orleans, on the very floor where Jordan had started this latest NCAA glory run with his similar clutch bucket five seasons earlier. But it was Indiana's Steve Alford who led the way for the Hoosiers when it counted most and who also demonstrated in only the first season of its use the true impact of the new three-point shot. Alford registered eight-for-15 from the floor during the 74-73 Indiana victory, but he was seven of 10 from three-point range. Those seven shots meant seven extra points which in the end spelled the difference between an easy Syracuse win and a dramatic Indiana victory.

But nothing was any more dramatic than Michigan's March title chase in the final campaign of the decade. The entire Michigan season of 1988-89 seemed an unlikely story from opening tap in November to final whistle in April. Bill Frieder's team was solid all season long at 24-7 overall and 12-6 (third place) in Big Ten competition; but it was certainly not a dominant outfit, even in its own league where the Wolverines lost twice to Illinois and twice to Indiana. Then as postseason action was about to get underway a strange set of events would suddenly surround the Michigan team. Bill Frieder announced on the eve of NCAA action that he would depart for the head job at Arizona State as soon as the year's last game had been played. Dismayed Michigan officials were not about to let their team enter the NCAAs under a lame duck coaching staff and immediately issued a stunning announcement of their own. Frieder was out and assistant Steve Fisher would now steer the club for whatever games remained.

Under interim coach Fisher the Wolverines overnight became an inspired outfit. Never before had the college postseason known such a script — a coach beginning his career on the opening night of the year-end championship tourney and then turning a team reeling in confusion into one that was suddenly invincible. The solid lineup featuring Glen Rice (25.6 ppg) in the frontcourt and Rumeal Robinson (14.9 ppg) at the point guard slot now played like a team with a mission; the Maize and Blue averaged more than 94.3 points during the next four contests while climbing over Xavier (Ohio), South Alabama, North Carolina and Virginia on their way to a Final Four showdown with Illinois, Duke and Seton Hall. Before it was over the Wolverines' unlikely run to the title would provide one of the most fairy-tale-like scenarios in the half-century history of NCAA play.

Seton Hall was simultaneously constructing a fairy tale of its own. No Big East school offered a better example of the sudden and unlikely ascendancy enjoyed by that newcomer conference. The Hall had once been a power on the East Coast with pioneering ball handler Bob Davies in the early '40s, and then towering All-American Walter Dukes in the early '50s. John "Honey" Russell had once built a coaching legend of considerable proportions at the urban New Jersey campus. But in those years the school had preferred to compete annually in the locally more glamorous NIT and had even won the Madison Square Garden event back in 1953. The Seton Hall Pirates had then waned and had in fact never before been entered in the NCAA postseason festival. Davies and Dukes remained the school's only two All-Americans right down to the present decade. But starting in 1988 the charter member of the Big East would put together a long string of tourney appearances under coach William Raftery that would include six visits over the next seven years. And none was more successful than the second visit in 1989 which took them all the way to a finals showdown with the equally surprising outfit from Michigan.

Nothing could have been any more fitting than to have the 50th-anniversary NCAA title game turn out as one of the most dramatic lid-cappers ever. Michigan and Seton Hall found themselves in the first overtime final in a full quarter-century. Seton Hall was well prepared and keyed on tourney MVP Glen Rice in the first half, forcing Rumeal Robinson to carry the Michigan scoring load. But Rice came alive in the opening minutes of the second stanza and Michigan quickly built a 51-39 margin mainly on the strength of deadly outside shooting. Yet Seton Hall refused to die under the double-barreled offensive pressure from Rice and Robinson as Pirate guard John Morton poured in 17 points over the final eight minutes of regulation play. Morton's game-high 35 points would in fact be the highest total ever for a player on the losing team in the NCAA title game. But the final heroics would be reserved for Michigan backcourt leader Rumeal Robinson.

A pair of free throws by Sean Higgins had provided Michigan with a 71-68 margin in the final minute of regulation. Morton still had the hot hand, however, and tied the contest once more with a three-pointer 24 seconds from the end. Another "trey" by Morton put the Pirates on top with less than three minutes remaining during the extra session. Terry Mills brought the Wolverines back to within one in the closing minute before Robinson grabbed control of both the ball and the game as the final seconds expired. A missed shot by Morton in the final seven seconds with Seton Hall still on top 79-78 was the break Michigan needed. Robinson drove the length of the floor and lunged toward both the basket and Seton Hall defender Gerald Greene in a desperate effort at a final score. The referee's whistle and the final buzzer sounded almost simultaneously as Greene was called for the blocking foul and Robinson was put on the charity stripe with time expired and a chance to finally determine the issue one way or the other. The confident junior calmly sank both free throws for the 80-79 victory and the national title.

In the aftermath of Rumeal Robinson's clutch overtime free-throw shooting performance Michigan had not only won the final game in dramatic fashion but had also survived as perhaps the biggest "clutch" team in tourney history. Sean Higgins' last-second rebound put-back had preserved the Wolverines' heart-stopping 83-81 semifinal victory over conference rival Illinois. Thus no other team before or since has matched Michigan's feat of capturing its two Final Four games by a hairs-breadth margin of but three total points.

It was perhaps inevitable that the drama of the 1989 season could hardly be matched during the next couple of years. And if there was to be a temporary lull in the excitement it was probably due in large part to the fact that the 1990 campaign would be a total runaway from beginning to end. The competitive balance of recent seasons that marked both a constant flux in weekly wire service rankings and also upset-filled postseason competitions now fell to the wayside in the face of the jugger-naut team that Jerry Tarkanian had brought together for Nevada-Las Vegas. Tarkanian's 1990 UNLV team was the most dominating from one end of the season to the other since the Wooden teams of the early and mid-70s. A lineup of Larry Johnson and Stacey Augmon at the forwards and Anderson Hunt and Greg Anthony in the backcourt provided the seemingly perfect blend of deadly shooting, power rebounding, aggressive shotblocking and athletic racehorse-style offense. The Runnin'

Rebels compiled 35 victories in winning their national title, one of the highest totals ever. In the NCAAs they ran up three 100-point games, including the most lopsided finals victory to date with a 103-73 crushing of Duke. For one short season (and much of the next as it would soon turn out) this was one of the best teams yet.

College basketball, like the rest of life, has never been entirely free from the realm of painful tragedy — especially violent death's premature sting. Ironically each decade has seemingly had its single defining tragic event, each guaranteed to focus attention back upon the important flesh and blood issues of life too often lost amidst the staged emotion of athletic competition. In the 1960s, for example, there was the shocking accidental and needless death of Utah State star Wayne Estes. And in the '70s the nation was stunned by the loss of an entire Evansville University team. Evansville — both school and community — was cast into deep mourning when the team plane crashed in December 1977 en route to the squad's fifth game of the season, instantly killing coach Bobby Watson and all his players less than a month into the school's first year of Division I play.

Estes' story was especially tragic, if any one such cruel twist of fate can be somehow more humbling than another. Late in the 1965 campaign the Utah State scoring phenom had trailed only Miami's Rick Barry in the race for a national scoring title. Estes had in fact just become the school's first 2,000-point scorer and was averaging 33.7 as the season opened its penultimate month. Then fate harshly stepped in, and in the cruelest imaginable way. Barely three hours after a 48-point performance versus Denver that had vaulted him over the 2,000-point mark, the Aggies' cage hero was crossing campus on foot with several teammates when they stopped to inspect the scene of a recent fatal auto accident. Estes somehow brushed against an unnoticed dangling "live" high tension wire and the 2,700 volts of electricity that surged through his body were more than enough to kill him instantly.

There have also been postcareer tragedies played out away from media glare and thus often ignored by the general fandom. Bill Buntin, Cazzie Russell's talented teammate who averaged more than 20 points per game in each of his three seasons (1963-65), would suffer a fatal heart attack during a playground pickup game shortly after leaving the Wolverines for a promising career with the NBA Pistons. The same fate would of course await LSU's legendary Pete Maravich in January 1988, though Maravich's early death came at the end and not the beginning of a lucrative pro career. Another Michigan school would also be marked for such sorrow when ex-Michigan Stater Terry Furlow was killed prematurely (at the end of his fourth NBA season) in a violent automobile crash. And still another Big Ten headliner of the '60s would also succumb far too early when Ohio State national player of the year Gary Bradds fell as an early victim to prostate cancer.

But no single institution owned any larger black mark against its former stars than did North Carolina State. No fewer than four of the Wolfpack's top performers from the Everett Case era of the mid-50s all met with equally tragic circumstances. Ron Shavlik, 1956 ACC player of the year, was also felled by cancer shortly after witnessing the dramatic 1983 Wolfpack national title run. Surrounding Shavlik's tragedy were a trio of others: Cliff Dwyer suffered a fatal heart attack in 1975, John Richter committed suicide in 1985, and Bob Seitz died of a rare gland disease in

1967, at age 33. Ironically, all four had played center on Everett Case-coached teams within a brief span of three short years.

But in the end it was the '80s and '90s that provided the two most shocking and most publicized basketball tragedies. The first came at Maryland in the spring of 1986 and involved all the imaginable intrigue of outright scandal. Len Bias — an athletic 6-8 forward of almost unlimited potential — had emerged by his senior season as one of the great players of ACC history. Bias seemed to have the world by the throat when pro basketball's royalty, the Boston Celtics, tabbed him as second overall pick during the June NBA draft. Auerbach's rebuilding Celtics were apparently looking forward to a true glory era with Bias who hopefully would be Boston's next Dave Cowens or perhaps even the next Larry Bird. But it was not meant to be. Two days after the June draft that had brought him instant riches Bias died suddenly of a cocaine overdose in his College Park dormitory room.

The death of Len Bias, just like the basketball betting scandals of an earlier decade, seemed to redirect attention for the short term squarely onto the darkest side of double dealings that seemed somehow always to shadow the big-time college game. There were even several overnight pot-boiler books soon on the newsstands which focused on the case and in doing so exposed bent rules and the hidden semipro status of Terp ballplayers. These were indiscretions that appeared to define basketball at Maryland, and likely also elsewhere around the ACC and at most other major institutions. Bias' death itself had apparently been entirely accidental, yet the tragedy of the moment now seemed to be only the visible tip of a very ugly iceberg.

There were some other significant events involving "passages" that also filled up the 1986 season and gave it a rather heavy air of ominous transition. At Maryland, for starters, 26-year veteran mentor Lefty Driesell tumbled into disgrace in the wake of the Len Bias affair. Lefty had racked up 348 wins and two conference crowns in 17 seasons at the ACC's northern-most outpost; he had also maintained a controversial program long suspected of questionable if not underhanded recruiting tactics. With the Bias scandal now front page news, the man who had guided the first ACC NIT champion way back in 1972 was finally more of a liability than an asset to the beleaguered ACC school. Driesell was forced to resign and Maryland Athletic Director Dick Dull was pressured to step down at the same time. Lengthy internal and external investigations of the school's entire athletic program also ensued, and when it was revealed that after four years of classes Len Bias was still 21 credits short of graduation, so did stricter guidelines aimed at governing academic responsibilities for Maryland's student-athletes.

While Driesell's sudden dismissal torpedoed one success story on the East Coast, another was winding down out West, where UCLA finally saw its streak of 32 straight winning conference records also snapped. And while one California winning tradition finally crumbled another was nipped in the bud when UCLA's rival, Southern Cal, saw its first potentially great team in years sacked before it ever got off the ground or out of the starting blocks. In 1986 the surprising Trojans boasted three truly outstanding freshmen in Hank Gathers, Bo Kimble and Tom Lewis. But all three would be gone within a year and would thus enjoy their considerable individual successes elsewhere. Lewis moved on to Pepperdine while Gathers and Kimble departed together via the transfer route, bound for Loyola Marymount. Yet for all this activity, nothing quite matched the soap opera story of unfulfilled potential and shady dealings tragically played out around Maryland's Len Bias.

Four years later, in the spring of 1990, the American sports world was again stunned by tragedy of an eerily similar nature. This time the shocking event was seemingly freer from the taint of vicious scandal, though not altogether so. On March 4, 1990, Loyola Marymount All-American Hank Gathers (the same Gathers who flashed promise as a Southern Cal rookie during Len Bias' senior season) slumped to the floor in the closing moments of a conference tournament game with Portland. Two hours later the All-American and outstanding pro prospect was pronounced dead, victim of apparent heart failure. The Atlas-like 6-7 center had been the nation's dual scoring and rebounding leader only a season earlier. His ailment had been known to university officials (he was taking medication for an accelerated heartbeat) yet he had nonetheless been cleared by both coaches and team doctors to play. Conference championships and future pro careers seemed once more to outweigh any threats to life and personal health. Questions would once more be raised about the medical ethics involved in such a case, as well as about the "win-at-all-costs" mentality which seemed to be so universally accepted as the game's bottom line. Like Bias, Gathers and his tragedy were rallying points for those wishing to challenge the absent amateur spirit of collegiate sport.

Meanwhile, Gathers' shocked yet now inspired Loyola teammates would carry on by dedicating remaining postseason action to their fallen comrade. The Western Conference playoffs had been suspended in the wake of Gathers' death, but with a regular season conference crown already in hand the 20-5 Loyola Marymount Lions were off to the NCAA Western Regionals anyway. Paced by the nation's top scorer, Bo Kimble, the nation's top scoring team rode its high-octane offense and a wave of adrenaline-feeding emotion straight to the regional finals, ringing up typical point totals of 111 (versus New Mexico State) and 145 (versus Michigan) along the way. But emotion and racehorse offense were not enough to get a one-dimensional team like Loyola past a well-rounded team like title-bound UNLV. Paul Westhead's shot-crazy Lions were fresh off a new national scoring record of 122.4 points per game, but without Gathers and without much defense Loyola would be soundly clubbed 131-101 by a UNLV squad that could boast the likes of Larry Johnson, Stacey Augmon, Greg Anthony and Anderson Hunt. By Final Four weekend Loyola Marymount would no longer be front page news; yet for a few weeks in early March Hank Gathers had provided one of collegiate basketball's saddest tales of storybook inspiration.

If familiar faces and names had filled the 1980s, still there was nothing anywhere in sight that looked anything like a true dynasty team. Villanova and Michigan had unarguably been the charming Cinderella candidates of the decade. But no single coach or team was able to dominate the weekly polls or postseason title.chases for even as long as two full seasons without interruption. Houston almost made it twice, but the Cougars fell a bit short on both occasions. Despite one of the nation's two most celebrated centers in Akeem Olajuwon, plus strong supporting casts in Drexler and Micheaux one year and Michael Young and Alvin Franklin the other, nonetheless Guy Lewis' running and dunking Cougars came up a few minutes and a few points short during the season's final game twice running. Each time Knight's Indiana Hoosiers, Crum's Louisville Cardinals, Dean Smith's North Carolina Tar Heels or John Thompson's Georgetown Hoyas clawed their way onto the top of the heap, there would be only a single season as king of the hill before some new resurgent bully had wrested away the fleeting No. 1 honors.

But with the coming of the 1990s that was about to change. It would change first with the incredible success run of the Duke Blue Devils under a coach who owned an unpronounceable name, an impressive pedigree, and a seemingly inexplicable knack for dodging every trap and minefield along the way to the charmed Final Four. Mike Krzyzewski played and coached under Knight at Army and now his Duke team dominated the early '90s just like Wooden had dominated the '70s, even if their reign would not be quite as extensive nor their championships anywhere near as numerous. Duke would begin its own string in 1991 and 1992 with the first repeat championships since UCLA's. And the Devils would also enjoy an even more miraculous run at the Final Four in the process, one which lasted for five straight seasons, eventually stretched to seven Final Fours within nine years, and thus boasted truly UCLA-like proportions. When Coach "K" brought his club back to the title tilt in 1994 after only a one-season hiatus it was the fourth time he had played in the title game in five consecutive seasons, something that only Wooden before him could claim. In the end it was the best seven-year string ever manufactured anywhere outside of Westwood.

The Blue Devils emerged as a national power in 1991 with a star-studded lineup that featured 6-11 junior center Christian Laettner as the hefty scorer (19.8 ppg), sophomore point guard Bobby Hurley as the efficient playmaker, and multitalented freshman forward Grant Hill (son of former NFL running back sensation Calvin Hill) along with sophomore guard Billy McCaffrey as the offensive and defensive catalysts. Throughout the long winter season, however, few thought of Duke as the best team in the country, or even the best in the ACC. North Carolina seemed to own the latter distinction with a 29-6 season's mark, the conference tournament title and a solid fourth slot in the final AP weekly polls. Defending NCAA champion UNLV, with Larry Johnson and Stacey Augmon still only juniors, rode atop the season-long wire service rankings, followed by Arkansas and the Big Ten co-champs from Indiana.

Tarkanian's Runnin' Rebels were indeed fortunate to be around for a title defense at all in 1991, despite their stellar returning lineup and a 27-0 blitzing of all regular-season opposition. Earlier recruiting violations had brought a stiff NCAA sanction on the heels of the 1990 championship and UNLV had been ruled ineligible for any postseason title defense in '91. But then a sudden softening of heart among NCAA officials (likely not entirely unrelated to pressuring from network television sponsors for the postseason event) reversed the earlier stance and postponed any penalties until after the upcoming title defense.

But if UNLV had been thrown back into the postseason fray and seemed an insurmountable obstacle for all challengers, and if traditional big-conference standard bearers like North Carolina, Indiana and SEC-entrant Arkansas seemed as formidable as ever, nonetheless once postseason play opened the mighty would unaccountably fall in a series of shocking upsets that were now becoming standard fare on the thrilling NCAA March Madness scene. In the tourney semifinals Duke itself would author perhaps the biggest shocker by gunning down the unbeaten UNLV Rebels in certainly the most memorable upset in years. Most fans and pundits alike had assumed the Rebels would find little challenge in making their run at back-to-back titles. But then Duke turned up the heat in a performance that still has to rank as one of the finest in rich Blue Devils history.

Duke certainly had something to prove in the wake of its crushing defeat at the hands of the same Las Vegas team a season earlier. Hurley in particular had vanished under pressure against the Rebels as a freshman. But now the seasoned sophomore would completely reverse the odds. Duke took a quick lead when no one inside or outside for UNLV could contain Laettner's accurate jumpers in the early going. At the same time the Devils' defense threw wraps around player-of-the-year Larry Johnson. But the huge supply of UNLV talent eventually brought Tarkanian's men back into the game down the stretch. The tide turned against the Rebels one final time, however, when playmaker Greg Anthony fouled out with nearly four minutes still remaining. Three-pointers by Hurley and Thomas Hill put the Blue Devils in a position to win with a 77-77 tie; and then two foul shots by Laettner sealed victory. Conference rival North Carolina had also made it into the Final Four, but the Tar Heels fell to Kansas in another upset nearly as surprising. Now the pathway was absolutely clear for Coach K and his "upset kids" to finally grab that grand prize which had eluded so many great Duke teams in the past.

It was the ninth visit to the Final Four for the persistent Blue Devils, and the ninth time would finally prove to be the elusive charm. Laettner enjoyed a marvelous tournament, leading all scorers with 28 (on nine of 14 from the field and nine of 11 from the line) during the upset of UNLV, then also posting a record for free-throw shooting when he was a perfect 12-for-12 in the title matchup with Kansas. No player had ever before reached double figures in free-throw attempts during an NCAA championship match without missing a single charity toss.

In the final game Duke would coast to its first title without breaking much of a sweat. Coach K's formula for victory combined a relentless outside shooting attack with a quick and hustling defense that prevented Roy Williams' Jayhawks from ever finding easy layups or other high-percentage shots. Kansas also boasted a proud tradition over the years and came into this year's championship game in Indianapolis with an impressive string of NCAA victories against Indiana, Arkansas and North Carolina, three straight conference champions. But this time around the Jayhawks were no match for the destiny-favored Blue Devils.

If there was anywhere a team destined to share glory and headlines with the Duke Blue Devils in the early '90s it would have to be the Michigan club that Steve Fisher had suddenly inherited from Bill Frieder on the eve of the 1989 NCAA festivities. What Fisher had inherited was far more than a solid program with winning ways and tons of tradition; it was also more than an immediate NCAA championship in the two weeks following his unexpected takeover. For Fisher was also recipient of an exceptional incoming freshman class in 1992, one he himself had signed up and

Michigan's "Fab Five" began their college careers with great expectations, and although they reached the NCAA title game in both their freshman and sophomore seasons, they never earned championship laurels.From left are Ray Jackson, Chris Webber, Juwan Howard, Jalen Rose and Jimmy King. (University of Michigan photo)

delivered, and also one that was considered in many quarters to be perhaps the best total contingent ever landed by the same school in the same year.

It was certainly the most hyped quintet of new recruits ever — Chris Webber (6-10 forward), Juwan Howard (6-9 forward), Jalen Rose (6-8 guard), Ray Jackson (6-6 forward) and Jimmy King (6-5 guard). Two were local Detroit schoolboy products (Webber and Jalen Rose, who happened to be a son of former NBA and Providence College great Jimmy Walker), two were out of Texas (Jackson from Austin and King from Plano), and Howard had been plucked off the playgrounds of Chicago. The "Fab Five" lineup (all five started from the outset) was universally tabbed a surefire guaranteed winner from their first day in Ann Arbor. And it was a curse guaranteed to make their legacy one of disappointing "near misses" over the next several seasons of Big Ten and tournament action.

Michigan started somewhat slowly with its touted freshman bunch. There were three losses in the first five Big Ten games and a final 11-7 conference record that was only good enough for third place and a sixth seed in NCAA Southeast Regional parings. But once back in postseason play Fisher seemed once again to have the magic touch as his talented if inexperience group jelled under tournament pressures.

Temple, East Tennessee State and Oklahoma State all fell by the wayside en route to a regional championship match in Lexington with conference rival Ohio State. The pitched Big Ten battle for a ticket to the Final Four came down to Michigan's sensational freshman contingent against outstanding Buckeye All-American Jim Jackson, and Michigan's superior numbers turned the tide in the overtime period as Webber (23 points) and Rose (20) overmatched Jackson (20) in the closing stretches of the extra session.

The national title game was one guaranteed to tickle the promoters as well as the TV advertisers. It matched veteran Duke trying for the first NCAA repeat in two decades and novice Michigan trying to pull off the impossible with an all-freshman lineup and no established All-Americans to rival "Mr. Inside" Laettner and "Mr. Outside" Hurley. But the final shootout didn't contain all that much drama once it was underway. Michigan seemed to be brimming with confidence when a brash Chris Webber affirmed that "Tomorrow's not promised and we want it all now" in referring to a national title that he and his teammates might have at least a couple more cracks at winning. Duke in turn seemed at a disadvantage with senior co-captain Brian Davis sidelined by a severe ankle sprain suffered in the semifinal victory over Indiana. And Duke seemed to be reeling even further when Laettner suffered through a first half shooting slump and Michigan surprisingly maintained a 31-30 halftime edge.

The final 20-minute session of the season was anything but artistic as the two heavyweight teams stood toe-to-toe and slugged it out with far more energy than either artistry or efficiency. Duke's shooting woes continued until late in the contest yet Michigan could gain little offensive momentum, either. Hurley seemed to lose his legs down the stretch, but the clutch Laettner had now regrouped with several key buckets and sophomore Grant Hill took over the offensive load during the game's closing minutes. With the Blue Devils finding their offensive touch and outscoring the Wolverines 23-6 across the final seven minutes the game had become a full-scale rout by the time the clock touched zero. The final was 71-51 and Duke, despite its early sluggishness, had indeed put a resounding exclamation point upon its trend-breaking national title defense.

Easily the most dramatic moment of this particular edition of the NCAA Tourney — indeed the highlight moment of this and many previous seasons — was found not in the Final Four frays but in the exhausting regional finals matchup a weekend earlier in Philadelphia. It was one of the greatest postseason shootouts ever, a 104-103 Duke overtime victory over Kentucky that left both a lively Spectrum throng and a national television audience limp with enjoyment.

The finish came down to sensational overtime heroics after the two teams deadlocked at 93 in regulation, and the extra session began with Kentucky star Jamal Mashburn already dismissed to the bench with five personal fouls. Duke held the slim advantage 102-101 with only seconds to play when Wildcat guard Sean Woods cashed in on a driving off-balance shot that seemed to seal the issue with 2.1 ticks remaining. But on the game's final play, Laettner caught Grant Hill's long inbounds pass in the free-throw circle, turned and shot, the ball drawing only net as the inaudible buzzer sounded. For older fans the last-second desperation shot by Laettner recalled the one by Jerry Harkeness of Loyola decades earlier. For those without such historical perspective it was nonetheless still the kind of moment that had seemingly sustained the fervor of March Madness across most of the recent decade.

Christian Laettner single-handedly rescued Duke twice along the road to the 1992 national championship. With Laettner graduated to the pros, Duke's magical run would end in surprising fashion one spring later. The Blue Devil string of five straight trips into the Final Four came to a crashing halt during a major upset at the hands of California in the tourney's second round. Bobby Hurley would thus be thwarted in his unique bid to become the first player ever to start in four straight NCAA Finals (a feat earlier denied a flock of UCLA players since freshman eligibility had not been on the books during Wooden's dynasty years). But Hurley would nonetheless continue to rack up assists at a record-setting rate. By the time he had logged his final NCAA game the extraordinary Duke playmaker had recorded 145 assists in 20 outings, thus becoming the only player ever to top the 125 mark for career tournament play.

Michigan's "Fab Five" for their own part would not fall victim to any such shocking derailment, at least not until the title game itself. For the second straight year the youthful Wolverines would hang around in postseason competition long enough to earn a second crack at the national title for which they somehow seemed almost destined. If Webber and his crew had been denied their wish to "have it all" the first time around, perhaps now they would not be so easily denied during a second stab at the sport's biggest prize.

This time the opponent in the NCAA Finals would be that other perennial ACC title challenger, the one coached by Dean Smith. North Carolina had picked up the gauntlet in NCAA play at the very point where Duke had finally faltered. An overtime victory against Cincinnati had pulled the Tar Heels into the New Orleans Superdome — site of their 1982 triumph — and a hard-fought 10-point win (78-68) over Kansas meant Dean Smith's fifth trip back to the championship round. If Dean Smith had stolen a championship banner from Georgetown 11 seasons earlier, this return visit would soon bring a title pilfering of even grander scale. For in the final-game matchup the Michigan Wolverines would once again prove to be an unaccountably snakebit team prone to snatching defeat from the very jaws of victory. And this time the Michigan championship loss would seem even more frustrating than the one that had already capped the Fab Five's debut season.

Michigan had a golden opportunity to win down the stretch. Carolina's ace rebounder George Lynch had provided late-game heroics for the Tar Heels with several key defensive stops and a clutch jumper during the final three minutes. But a late Michigan rally had trimmed the Carolina lead to 73-71 with less than 20 seconds remaining and Michigan owned the basketball. Then came one of the most memorable moments in collegiate cage history. Chris Webber — the consensus player of the year — called a final desperation time-out that the luckless Wolverines simply didn't have. Webber had been double-teamed along the sideline by Lynch and Derrick Phelps and his fatal error in judgment provided technical foul shots by Carolina's Donald Williams from which the Wolverines never recovered. In a few seconds of indecision the Michigan title hopes had again come crashing in.

The Naismith Award winner in 1994, Purdue's Glenn Robinson joined the elite collection of players who have topped 1,000 points in a single season. (Purdue University photo)

As quickly as it had all started, just as quickly an end to championship contention had already arrived for Steve Fisher's Fab Five. The dream was over after only two short seasons together in Ann Arbor. Webber would now turn his talents over to the pros rather than return for a third stab at collegiate glories. And Michigan would succumb to Arkansas in the regional finals a season later with only four of the Fab Five still wearing the Maize and Blue Michigan uniform.

If Michigan would not be back in the limelight of postseason play in 1994, Duke nevertheless would be. Hurley (seventh overall pick of Sacramento in 1993) and Laettner (third overall choice by Minnesota in 1992) were now both gone to the NBA. But future NBA rookie of the year Grant Hill had emerged as the senior leader and was the team's leading scorer (17.4) and second-leading rebounder (6.9), as well as perhaps the finest all-around player in the land next to Purdue's Glenn Robinson. Duke clawed its way back into the charmed Final Four by besting Purdue of the Big Ten in the Eastern Regional, 69-60, when Hill outplayed Robinson defensively in the ballyhooed face-to-face matchup. Robinson would later be tabbed as national player of the year and was also the first Big Ten national scoring champ in three decades with his 30.3 season's average. But in the East Regional finals Robinson had neither the balanced game nor the necessary help from teammates to carry the Big Ten Boilermakers against a multidimensional team or two-way offensive-defensive threat like Duke and Grant Hill. In the Final Four Duke then snuck by upstart Florida to reach yet another title game.

But this time the Duke effort would come up somewhat short. There was a new powerhouse on the scene out of the Southeastern Conference, one that would finally end that league's dry spell stretching back to Kentucky's last national title in 1978. Led by a pair of sophomore forwards named Corliss Williamson and Scotty Thurman the Arkansas Razorbacks had built a 26-3 record and stood near the top of the polls all season long. In the national title game the Arkansas team coached by Nolan Richardson would ride the stellar play of Williamson straight to the championship. And in the process they would make Richardson the first coach ever to post year-end titles at the junior college (Western Texas in 1980), NIT (Tulsa in 1981) and NCAA levels. Williamson indeed had a spectacular final week of the season and at one point had passed Bill Walton's playoff field-goal shooting standard of 68.6 percent. Misses on his first five shots of the title contest would rob Williamson of the tourney record, but these early misfirings would not slow his eventual title-game effort as he poured in 23 for game-high honors and the Final Four MVP trophy as well. It was a performance, however, that the hefty 6-7 power forward would not come anywhere close to duplicating a single season later.

Like Duke and UNLV before it, a young sophomore-led Arkansas club seemed destined for a long-term run at the top of the heap. But it would soon be the fate of the Razorbacks to demonstrate once again just how difficult repeating was. Juniors Corliss Williamson and Scotty Thurman who had carried the club in the 1994 victory over Duke would a year later prove completely ineffectual in the face of ingenious defense tactics employed by upstart UCLA. So lackluster was the play of both Williamson and Thurman in the title game, in fact, that both would see their once luminous stars tumble out of the heavens altogether during June's NBA college draft day.

Arkansas would stand near the top of the pack during much of the regular season, maintaining a top 10 ranking and posting a 28-6 mark through the long season preceding another NCAA playdown. It wasn't as smooth this time around, as Kentucky captured the regular-season SEC crown and then nipped the defending national champions 95-93 in overtime to take the league tournament as well. And when March Madness began it seemed like the reeling Razorbacks were indeed a marked team. Several times Nolan Richardson's beleaguered but experienced club barely survived in the tournament's early rounds, and these survivals seemed to come as much through luck as anything. Unheralded Texas Southern was nudged by only two points in a 96-94 shooting match; Syracuse was dispatched in overtime

Future NBA slam-dunk champion Harold Miner was already performing his aerial act as a 2,000-point career scorer for the University of Southern California in the early 1990s. (USC photo)

only after Orangeman star Lawrence Moten committed a fatal ballhandling error in the closing seconds of regulation time; and Memphis (68-61) and Virginia (75-68) both came close to sabotaging the final steps to a repeat Final Four visit.

Then luck ran out in the title game against a surprising UCLA squad which was back in the big dance for the first time in over a decade. Jim Harrick's Pac-10 team was a sentimental favorite to recapture past Wooden-era glories. And in a sterling year-end performance it did just that. The Bruins excelled at the transition game, mainly due to quick-handed defenders like 5-10 guard Tyus Edney (74 steals) and 6-8 All-American forward Ed O'Bannon (64 steals). O'Bannon was the NCAA MVP, but it was 6-5 swingman guard Toby Bailey who provided the stretch-run spark with two 26-point tournament games after cracking the late-season starting lineup. For all their vaunted predecessors in Westwood this was the first Bruins team (at 31-2) ever to win more than 30 games in a campaign. Coach Jim Harrick's brilliant ploy of switching to a zone defense for the second half of the championship game, despite Arkansas' potent long-range gunners, was sufficient to keep the Bruins on top 89-78. Finally the series of Wooden successors that had included Gene Bartow and Larry Brown before Harrick had climbed out from under a huge shadow that had dogged every Bruins team since the Wizard's retirement exactly two decades earlier.

The 15-year span between 1980 and 1995 had seen all doubt removed that the showcase of college basketball was the NCAA men's tournament. It was a period that also established March Madness firmly on the top of the heap as the nation's best annual sporting spectacle. The NCAA event of the '80s and '90s had offered just about every thrill imaginable. There were memorable championship games featuring last-second heroics (like those of Jordan, Lorenzo Charles, Worthy, Keith Smart and

All-Star Team for the Era (1980-1995)				
	Pos.	Pts. (Ppg.)	Best Year	NPY
Christian Laettner (Duke)	F	2460 (16.6)	21.5 (Sr.)	1992
David Robinson (Navy)	C	2669 (21.0)	28.2 (Sr.)	1987
Ralph Sampson (Virginia)	C	2228 (16.9)	19.1 (Sr.)	1981-83
Patrick Ewing (Georgetown)	C	2184 (15.3)	17.7 (So.)	1985
Michael Jordan (UNC)	G-F	1788 (17.7)	20.0 (Jr.)	1984

NPY = National Player of the Year
Honorable Mention: Hersey Hawkins (G, Bradley), Johnny Dawkins (G, Duke), Chris Mullin (G, St. John's), Danny Manning (C, Kansas), Bobby Hurley (G, Duke), Glenn Robinson (F, Purdue), Lionel Simmons (F, La Salle), Jim Jackson (G, Ohio State), Akeem Olajuwon (C, Houston)
Coach of the Era: Mike Krzyzewski (Duke), NCAA Champion (1991, 1992)

Christian Laettner) as well as last-minute self-destructions (Fred Brown, Chris Webber and the entire Michigan team in 1993). The tourney had once more been expanded to include more teams and provide still more national interest and excitement. And never had there been a greater array of individual star players either. Jordan and Olajuwon and Ewing and Laettner and numerous others had made their reputations in the month of March. Neither the sport nor its stars had ever been any bigger.

There were some ominous danger signs on the horizon. The rush of stars to sign with the pros as underclassmen had subtly changed the nature of the game. Dynasties were seemingly no longer possible — teams could now be built for only two years duration and talent turnover was constant. And the huge revenues at stake seemed to raise the threat of age-old problems. In the past money had on several occasions corrupted and nearly ruined the game — players were dehumanized objects, utilized to assure victories and then cast aside when injury or loss of eligibility rendered them useless; some were pawns of unscrupulous gamblers and nearly as unscrupulous coaches and school administrators. Would not game-fixing, for one thing, again become an issue sooner or later when so much money was being wagered on game outcomes? Or were today's stars all facing such attractive promises of wealth around the corner in the form of professional contracts that undergraduate offers from gamblers would now no longer seem to turn any heads or even gain any recruits? Didn't a player, for the first time in history, suddenly have more to lose (in pure dollar and cents terms) from loss of legal payoffs than he had to gain from potential illegal ones?

There were indeed dangers requiring constant vigilance. But these seemed to pale alongside the huge strides the sport had now made. And as collegiate basketball

Indiana's Calbert Cheaney was the national player of the year in 1993. When he completed his four-year career he was also the all-time Big Ten scoring leader with 2,613 points. (Indiana University photo)

reached its centennial year there was also a fitting sense of closure at hand. UCLA had emerged back on top as national champion in 1995 and with the Bruins' return came echoes of the sport's greatest modern-day era. Television and basketball had finally come into full harmony in recent years and millions of spectators were now viewing hundreds of games in an almost nightly festival of non-stop colorful action. The individual superstar was again the main focus of the game and the floodtide of such stars seemed at its greatest crest, at least in terms of pure numbers. But most importantly, the college game had never before seemed to feature such true competitive balance — from north to south, independent urban schools to perennial conference powerhouses. College basketball was now at its hour of greatest triumph. And all signs pointed to a future even brighter still.

College Basketball Chronology

Summarized on the following pages are major events that have marked the first 100 years of collegiate basketball competition. Each year has brought something of significance to the historical evolution of our most popular team spectator sport. Here are college basketball's highlight moments in brief capsule form.

1894-95 **(February 9)** — First intercollegiate game is played between Hamline College (St. Paul, Minnesota) and the Minnesota State School of Agriculture, with the Hamline team falling, 9 goals to 3. Nine contestants play for each side. One month later Haverford College defeats Temple University 6-4 in another nine-to-a-side game. California and Stanford are believed to have played first women's intercollegiate game (in April) but no score is recorded. Original free-throw line at 20 feet from basket is now experimentally placed at only 15 feet.

1895-96 **(January 16)** — Football pioneer Amos Alonzo Stagg (an associate of James Naismith at Springfield College in 1891) coaches University of Chicago club team to 15-12 victory over YMCA team representing University of Iowa. This is the first five-on-a-side college game on record. Backboards (10 feet above the floor) used for the first time, with open nets allowed on the baskets.

1896-97 **(March 20)** — Yale University defeats Pennsylvania University 32-10 in the first official "conference" game between Ivy League schools. Yale was the first team to employ the "dribble" as an offensive strategy. Beginning with this season a field goal is changed from one to two points and a free throw from three points to one point. Five-man teams also become the standard.

1897-98 — Rules are adopted banning "overhead" dribbles (tapping balls in the air volleyball style), and also outlawing the "double dribbles" (discontinued dribbles) or two-handed dribbles. Also the free-throw line is now standardized at 15 feet from the hoop.

1898-99 — James Naismith, fresh from earning medical degree in Colorado, is appointed head of physical education department and also coach of basketball team at University of Kansas. Jayhawks play their first official game February 3, against Kansas City YMCA.

1899-1900 — Yale team barnstorms across country during Christmas holidays in what is advertised as "longest trip ever taken by a United States college team." Nebraska's Cornhuskers become college basketball's first recognized unbeaten team, remaining undefeated over 19 games and three full seasons (1898-1900). Dartmouth embarrasses Boston College by 44-0 count in an exhibition match featured at annual New England Sportsman's Show in Boston's Mechanics Hall. This is largest recorded shutout of the game's first decade.

1900-01 — Yale University, Trinity College (Hartford, Conn.) and Wesleyan College (Middletown, Conn.) form the first formal college basketball conference called the Triangle League. Later the same winter a second confederation, the New England League, is formed by Dartmouth, Holy Cross, Amherst College, Williams College and Trinity College. Also Columbia, Cornell, Harvard, Princeton and Yale band together to form a confederation called the Eastern League and Yale claims the first league title.

301

During the 1951-52 season, Seattle's diminuitive Johnny O'Brien became the first player to top the 1,000-point mark for a single season. Only 5 feet 9 inches tall, he gained national attention with a 43-point game from the pivot post in this charity exhibition contest against the Harlem Globetrotters.

1901-02 — University of Minnesota team compiles a 15-0 record in Western Conference (Big Ten) play, and will eventually extend its winning streak to 34 games, not losing again until 1904. Pennsylvania University, which dropped the sport four years earlier due to inadequate facilities, returns to competition.

1902-03 — A new rule is adopted (it will remain in effect through 1908) which prohibits the dribbler from shooting the basketball. Cadet "Vinegar Joe" Stillwell (who earned later World War II fame as a general) organizes the first basketball team for the United States Military Academy at West Point. Bucknell University defeats Philadelphia College of Pharmacy 159-5 with Bucknell player John Anderson scoring 80 points.

1903-04 (July 13-14) — The Olympic Games in St. Louis are host to a national college basketball tournament billed as the Olympic World's College Basketball Championship. This is an outdoor event featuring only three schools (Hiram College, Wheaton College, Latter Day Saints College which is today Brigham Young University). Hiram defeats Wheaton 25-20 and Latter Day Saints 25-18 to win the title. First "suction-sole" shoes are advertised by Spalding, marking the birth of basketball sneakers.

1904-05 — Potsdam Normal College (Pennsylvania) humiliates Plattsburgh Normal by 123-0 score, the most lopsided game recorded in the first decade of college play. In April, representatives of 15 colleges meet in Philadelphia (and later New York) to standardize rules, gain control of the collegiate game from the AAU and form their own governing body that would eventually become known as the National Collegiate Athletic Association (NCAA). Christian Steinmetz of Wisconsin becomes first collegian to surpass 1,000 career points.

1905-06 — Western Athletic Conference (later the Big Ten) launches its first formal winter of conference competition, with Minnesota (6-1) edging Wisconsin (6-2) for the league title. Spalding publishes its first *Official Collegiate Basketball Guide*, focusing on six Eastern (Ivy) League teams (Yale, Harvard, Princeton, Columbia, Cornell, Pennsylvania) and a single Western Athletic Conference school (Minnesota).

1906-07 — Dr. James Naismith gives up his job as basketball coach at Kansas (turning reins over to Forrest "Phog" Allen) yet remains on school's faculty as physical education instructor until 1937. University of Chicago coached by Joseph Raycroft launches four-year period of dominance in Western Athletic Conference with a 22-2 overall record and 6-2 conference mark.

1907-08 — Western Athletic Conference power Chicago (after besting Wisconsin on "miracle" last-second shot by Pat Page) defeats Eastern champion Penn in home-and-home playoff series and is declared winner of "unofficial" national championship. Player committing five fouls (including traveling or other such violations) is now disqualified from game.

1908-09 — The rule is adopted which disqualifies a player once he commits five personal fouls. National concern about roughness in college sports reaches its height when President Theodore Roosevelt expresses his own concern about increasing serious injuries in college football competition. Harvard president Charles Eliot recommends colleges ban basketball since it is even more brutal than football. Missouri Valley Conference is formed with two divisions.

1909-10 — Glass backboards (invented by Chicago's 1909 player-of-the-year John Schommer) are employed for first time in bold experiment designed to make it easier for spectators to view games. University of Chicago, with national player-of-the-year Harlan "Pat" Page, establishes itself as one of early dynasty teams by winning fourth-straight Western Athletic Conference (Big Ten) title. Schommer and Page combine to lead Chicago to 78-12 decade-long record.

1910-11 — Second referee is optionally added to college games to cut down on violent play and players are now disqualified after four personal fouls. Future barnstorming pro star and Hall of Famer Barney Sedran at 5 feet, 4 inches leads City College of New York in scoring from 1909 to 1911 and becomes cage sport's first noteworthy long-range shooting little man.

1911-12 — Wisconsin (12-0) and Purdue (10-0) both complete undefeated seasons in the Western Athletic Conference (Big Ten) and share the title on the basis of winning percentage.

1912-13 — Open-bottom nets, already in use for several years, are officially sanctioned for use in all amateur championship contests. (Cylindrical wire baskets were first produced in 1893 by Lew Allen in Hartford, Connecticut, and braided cord nets appeared the following year. Before 1912 referees pulled a chain attached to the bottom of the net to release the ball from the basket.)

1913-14 — New rule awards out-of-bounds balls to the team not touching the ball last. Before this, players were allowed to "scramble" over the line for out-of-bounds balls with the first player over the line gaining possession.

1914-15 — AAU officials agree to meet with representatives of the YMCA and the International Athletic Association (early name for NCAA) to standardize rules for amateur play everywhere in the country. Standing zone defenses are introduced to combat a patterned offensive style introduced by Doc Meanwell at Wisconsin and remain a popular defensive style for a full decade.

1915-16 — University of Texas team finishes its third straight undefeated season with a 12-0 record to extend unbeaten string to 40 games. Rules governing act of "dribbling" are standardized.

1916-17 — Texas runs its record unbeaten streak to 44 before finally losing to Rice University 24-18. National rules committee governing amateur play outlaws glass backboards by legislating that all backboards must be painted white. This attempt at uniformity would be dropped after several seasons.

1917-18 (**February 9**) — First tie in college basketball history occurs when an official scorer's error leaves Kentucky and Kentucky Wesleyan knotted at 21 apiece. Baskets are moved two feet inside the playing court, thus allowing shots to be taken from anywhere within the playing area. Michigan becomes the 10th team in the Western Athletic Conference and sportswriters begin referring to the league as the Big Ten.

1918-19 — Newspaper reports on college games begin referring regularly to cage sport as "basketball" (one word) rather than "basket ball" (two words) as in previous years. Nat Holman, star professional player with the New York Whirlwinds and famous Original Celtics, takes over as paid head coach at City College of New York.

1919-20 (**March**) — NYU defeats CCNY 39-21 in a game staged in the 168th Street Regiment Armory before an overflow crowd of more than 10,000. It was this landmark game which first revealed the enormous financial potential of college basketball games.

1920-21 — New college rule allows a player removed from the game to reenter play one time only. Michigan, Wisconsin and Purdue share the Big Ten title with identical 8-4 records.

1921-22 — Backboards are moved 2 feet from the end walls, thus preventing the practice of players jumping on walls to shoot layups. University of Kansas begins back-to-back seasons atop the college basketball world with 16-2 (1922) and 17-1 (1923) records. This Jayhawks team would be remembered for its cast of coaching celebrities: head coach Forrest ("Phog") Allen, assistant James Naismith and little-used reserve Adolph Rupp.

1922-23 — Ott Romney begins a highly successful coaching stint at Montana State which will see him post a 144-31 record over the next five seasons. The United States Military Academy decides to improve its basketball program after several embarrassing defeats by Navy and hires successful coach Harry Fisher away from Columbia College.

1923-24 — New rule ends practice of awarding free-throw shots for violations such as traveling (running with ball) and double-dribbling. Rejuvenated U.S. Military Academy team under coach Harry Fisher compiles a two-year winning streak that finally ends at 31 games.

Frank Selvy of Furman set the college basketball world on its ear when he poured in 100 points during a game against Newberry College on Feb. 13, 1954. It was a scoring feat that has never been duplicated or even approached in the four decades to follow. (Furman University photo)

1924-25 — New rule specifies that player fouled must take free throws awarded. Previously "designated free-throwers" were regularly used. Practice of each player shooting his own free throws is first pioneered in the 1910s by a pro barnstorming team (also inventors of bounce passes), the Troy (N.Y.) Trojans.

1925-26 — Kansas Jayhawks under coach Phog Allen win their fourth of six Missouri Valley crowns in a row, posting a 16-2 record. Purdue, Michigan, Indiana and Iowa finish in rare four-way tie in Big Ten Conference. Player of the year Victor Hanson, three-time All-American, leads Syracuse to mythical national championship as well as 48-7 record over three-year career.

1926-27 — Dartmouth wins its first Eastern (Ivy) League title in 15 seasons with 26-24 thriller over Princeton as Tigers miss tying basket with only 10 seconds left. Michigan wins its first-ever Big Ten Conference championship. Phog Allen and James Naismith at Kansas lead successful fight to overturn new proposal outlawing dribbling by restricting players to single bounce of the ball (this antidribble legislation being introduced by Wisconsin's Doc Meanwell).

1927-28 — Record crowd of 10,000 in Penn's new Palestra gym (opened January 1, 1927) watches Pennsylvania defeat Princeton 24-22 for the Ivy League title. Victory comes on 30-foot basket with two minutes remaining by reserve forward Donald Noble. Oklahoma posts 18-0 record to win Missouri Valley title and end Kansas reign of six straight conference crowns.

305

1928-29 — George Gregory, All-Eastern Conference center for Columbia, earns notoriety as first noteworthy black player at an East Coast college. Sporting goods manufacturers first introduce concealed-lace basketball, an innovation that eliminates irregular bounces plaguing dribblers and passers during earlier games. Oklahoma enjoys second straight undefeated season (10-0) in Missouri Valley Conference and St. John's "Wonder Five" team posts 18-game win streak and 23-2 record. New rule defines "charging fouls" as new type of violation.

1929-30 — All uses of rope or chicken wire around the edges of the court are eliminated. But players will continue to be known as "cagers" as a result of the earlier practice. With two All-Americans in Charles "Stretch" Murphy and John Wooden, Purdue finishes an unbeaten Big Ten season at 10-0. Two officials rather than one becomes standard for college games.

1930-31 (January 21) — First Madison Square Garden tripleheader is staged by sportswriter Dan Daniel and draws more than 16,000. The three games involve Columbia, Fordham, Manhattan, NYU, St. John's and CCNY, and launch the popularity of MSG college basketball events. St. John's "Wonder Five" team builds a 27-game win streak and a four-year 86-8 record as the best collegiate team of the day.

1931-32 — Three-time All-American guard John Wooden leads Purdue to its second Big Ten title in three seasons and paces Piggy Lambert's fast-breaking team in scoring with 154 points.

1932-33 — Rule is introduced requiring teams to advance the ball over the half-court line in 10 seconds. This rule results from 1932 games between USC-UCLA and Kansas-Missouri in which stalling teams attempted to hold the ball under their own basket. Also, no player *with the ball* is allowed to stand in the free-throw lane more than three seconds.

1933-34 — Ned Irish plans to promote a game between NYU and CCNY in Madison Square Garden but the plot falls through when a conflict with a boxing match kills the deal. In his third year at Long Island University (LIU) coach Clair Bee leads his team to a 27-1 mark, losing only to St. John's. The first basketball stamp is issued in the Philippines.

1934-35 (December 29) — First intersectional college basketball doubleheader at Madison Square Garden is staged by sportswriter Ned Irish and draws a throng of 16,180 to see NYU beat Notre Dame and Westminster defeat St. John's. The circumference of the ball is officially reduced from 32 inches to between 29½ and 30¼ inches.

1935-36 — United States team (comprised largely of college players) wins the first Olympic basketball gold medal by defeating Canada on an outdoor dirt court during a driving rainstorm in Berlin, Germany. James Naismith tosses up the first ball of the tournament. Hank Luisetti of Stanford revolutionizes offensive play by shooting the ball one-handed and averaging 20 points per game for the season.

1936-37 (December 30) — Memorable intersectional battle in Madison Square Garden sees Stanford with Hank Luisetti defeat Clair Bee's unbeaten LIU team by a 45-31 score. This landmark game ended LIU's 43-game victory string and established the legitimacy of Luisetti's one-hand shooting style and of the West Coast style of wide-open play. NAIA (small college) launches the first postseason tournament in which Central Missouri earns the title by besting Morningside (Iowa) 35-24.

1937-38 — Temple University captures first National Invitation Tournament title at Madison Square Garden with a 60-36 victory over Colorado. On New Year's Day Stanford's Hank Luisetti scores a then-phenomenal 50 points versus Duquesne, becoming the first modern-era college player to top the half-century total. Rule requiring center jump taken after each field goal is eliminated.

1938-39 — Oregon's "Tall Firs" win the first postseason NCAA Tournament with a 46-33 victory over Ohio State in Evanston, Illinois. This championship game is played in Northwestern's Patten Gym before 5,500 fans.

1939-40 (February 28) — Basketball appears on television for the first time as station W2XBS in New York airs college doubleheader action from Madison Square Garden to an estimated audience of not more than several hundred viewers. The sparse audience saw Pittsburgh defeat Fordham 57-37 and NYU defeat Georgetown 50-37. Backboards are moved from 2 feet to 4 feet away from the end line. James Naismith dies (November 28) at age 78 in Lawrence, Kansas.

1940-41 — Basketball celebrates its first half-century as Wisconsin's Badgers defeat Washington State 39-34 to capture the third NCAA postseason tournament. Wisconsin becomes one of the biggest surprises in NCAA history since the school had finished ninth in the Big Ten race a season earlier. Naismith's posthumous book is published under the title of *Basketball, Its Origins and Development*. Fan-shaped backboards are legalized.

1941-42 — Stan "Stutz" Modzelewski of Rhode Island State College breaks Hank Luisetti's career national scoring record with 1,730 points. Luisetti's alma mater, Stanford, takes the NCAA title, however, besting Dartmouth 53-38 despite the absence of star Jim Pollard who is bedridden with the flu.

1942-43 — Wartime player shortages cause numerous schools to allow freshmen in varsity competition and lead others to cancel their season's schedules. Illinois' "Whiz Kids" team is undefeated in Big Ten play and probably the best team in the country, but the Illini decline to compete in either postseason tourney so that its players can enlist in the military. First Red Cross Benefit Game is staged by Ned Irish in Madison Square Garden, matching NCAA champ Wyoming and NIT champ St. John's.

1943-44 — New rules include a five-foul limit on individual players regardless of the number of overtimes, plus a ban on defensive players touching the ball on its downward flight toward the basket (goaltending). Latter restriction was aimed at giants George Mikan (De Paul) and Bob Kurland (Oklahoma A&M). Unlimited substitution is permitted for the first time. St. John's becomes the first back-to-back winner in the NIT by nipping DePaul 47-39 behind coach Joe Lapchick.

1944-45 — Bob Kurland leads Oklahoma A&M and coach Hank Iba to the first of two NCAA tourney wins, a 49-45 triumph over NYU. George Mikan enjoys his finest hour in college while leading DePaul to the NIT title in a 71-54 victory over Bowling Green. Two giants then meet in a much-heralded Red Cross war relief benefit game at Madison Square Garden, but the match fizzles when Mikan fouls out after 14 minutes and Oklahoma A&M wins easily. Number of time-outs allowed is increased from four to five.

1945-46 — Wyoming's Kenny Sailors is credited with inventing the jump shot. Oklahoma A&M, behind giant Bob Kurland, becomes the first school to win back-to-back NCAA tourney titles, nipping North Carolina 43-40. Kurland is also the first NCAA tourney repeat MVP. One of the highlights of the year, however, is a spectacular 55-foot shot by Rhode Island State's Ernie Calverley in the NIT semifinals. Ohio State and Northwestern set a Big Ten single-game attendance record (22,822) at Chicago Stadium.

1946-47 — Holy Cross College with freshman Bob Cousy and senior George Kaftan becomes first New England team to win national cage championship, edging Oklahoma 58-47 in spirited NCAA title game.

1947-48 — Murray Wier of Iowa wins first "official" NCAA scoring title with average of 21 points per game. Kentucky's "Fabulous Five" outfit featuring Alex Groza and Ralph Beard paces United States Olympic team to 65-21 gold medal victory over France at the 1948 Summer Games in London.

1948-49 (January 18) — Associated Press announces results of its first-ever weekly basketball poll, with St. Louis University ranked first. Behind Groza and Beard, Kentucky equals Oklahoma A&M's earlier accomplishment of repeat NCAA tournament victories. The second straight title for Adolph Rupp is ironically a 46-36 victory over none other than Oklahoma A&M. New rule allows coaches to speak with players during time-outs. Rectangular glass backboards become official for college games.

1949-50 — For the only time in history one school wins both the NCAA and NIT tourneys in the same postseason. CCNY, loser of five regular-season games, closes fast and defeats Bradley twice for the two trophies. First two black players (Chuck Cooper of Duquesne and Earl Lloyd of West Virginia State) are drafted out of the college ranks by the NBA.

1950-51 (January) — Shocking college basketball betting scandal begins to unravel when Manhattan College star Junius Kellogg reports to his coach that he has been offered a $1,000 bribe. Most affected are teams at CCNY, LIU, Manhattan, Bradley, Toledo and Kentucky; former Kentucky stars Alex Groza and Ralph Beard are banned for life from NBA play as direct result of their involvement in point shaving. Ernie Beck of Pennsylvania becomes first "official" NCAA rebounding champion.

1951-52 — Former Oklahoma A&M star Bob Kurland, who bypassed a pro career, paces the 1952 U.S. Olympic team to another gold medal triumph with a 36-25 victory over the Soviet Union in Helsinki. Seattle's pint-sized guard Johnny O'Brien becomes first-ever college player to reach 1,000 points for a single season, then finishes up with a career-record 2,537 points the following year.

1952-53 — Bevo Francis becomes a national celebrity overnight when he scores 116 points in a small college game for tiny Rio Grande of Ohio. Francis also averages 50.1 points per game but his marks are thrown out by the NCAA records committee since many of his team's 39 games were against opponents that were not four-year colleges.

1953-54 — Bevo Francis repeats his 100-point performance with 113 against Hillsdale (Michigan), but Francis is overshadowed by Frank Selvy (Furman) who also cracks the century mark in a major college game against Newberry. Selvy in the process also becomes the first player ever to post a 40-point scoring average. But the big story is small school La Salle which earns an NCAA title behind junior rebounding phenomenon Tom Gola.

1954-55 — Unheralded San Francisco University becomes king of the basketball world behind its defensive whiz Bill Russell. Although his team loses to Russell's 77-63 in the NCAA finals, La Salle's Tom Gola ends his own career with a record lifetime rebounding total that has still never been topped. In a *Sport* magazine poll of 123 coaches, George Mikan of DePaul University and the Minneapolis Lakers is named the greatest basketball player of all time.

1955-56 — Yale coach Howard Hobson leads a successful drive to have the foul lanes for college and high school play expanded from 6 feet to 12 feet. San Francisco, under coach Phil Woolpert, runs its win streak to a remarkable 55 games and defends its national title in Bill Russell's final game with an easy 83-71 victory over Iowa.

1956-57 — Most thrilling NCAA final game ever finds North Carolina upsetting Kansas and Wilt Chamberlain in a three-overtime thriller. Early in the season the record University of San Francisco winning streak finally ends at 60 games. Another ending also comes when Kansas coach Forrest "Phog" Allen retires after 46 seasons and 771 victories.

1957-58 — Offensive goaltending is banned. Cincinnati sophomore Oscar "Big O" Robertson becomes first rookie ever to win national scoring title (35.1 ppg) and "Big O" is also first athlete ever to be named national player of the year in his debut campaign. New rule allows team to shoot a bonus free throw once opponent commits seven fouls in a half.

1958-59 — Brilliant shooter Jerry West narrowly misses out on NCAA title when his West Virginia University team is nipped 71-70 by California club coached by defensive wizard Pete Newell. Cincinnati's Oscar Robertson wins second straight national scoring title.

1959-60 — Ohio State wins national title with one of strongest teams in history, a mostly sophomore club featuring Jerry Lucas and John Havlicek. Oscar Robertson closes his brilliant career with NCAA scoring record but still no trip to NCAA championship game. Robertson and West Virginia's Jerry West pace strongest U.S. Olympic team ever assembled to still another gold medal in Rome Summer Olympics.

1960-61 — Ohio State fails to defend its national title when Buckeyes are upset in NCAA Finals by instate rival Cincinnati. Bearcats ironically become champs a year after losing star Oscar Robertson, and this overtime championship victory makes new coach Ed Jucker first mentor ever to win a national title in his rookie season as head coach at a Division I school.

1961-62 — Cincinnati's Bearcats make it two in a row by repeating NCAA Finals triumph over Jerry Lucas and company. Lucas' injury in semifinal play against Wake Forest prevents Buckeyes' three-time NCAA finalists from bowing out as champs, but Lucas does end his career as first player ever to win five national statistical titles (two for rebounding and three for field-goal percentage). St. Bonaventure loses its 99-game home winning streak and Ohio State also sees its regular-season winning streak stopped at 47 games. Duke is first team to feature uniforms with players' names on the back.

1962-63 — Loyola (Chicago) pulls off one of biggest upsets in NCAA history by defeating two-time champion Cincinnati in overtime title game matching nation's top offensive team (91.8 ppg) versus its top defensive club (52.9 points allowed per game). One-eyed guard Tom Boyer of Arkansas becomes first player to win back-to-back national free-throw shooting titles. SEC champion Mississippi State ends school's racially motivated three-season boycott of NCAA tourney and loses to eventual champion Loyola (with four black starters) in Mideast Regional semifinal game.

1963-64 — UCLA under John Wooden wins first national title and posts its first unbeaten season while fielding a small but defensively solid team of Walt Hazzard, Gail Goodrich, Fred Slaughter and Kenny Washington. Cincinnati's 86-game homecourt winning streak begun in 1957 is snapped by Kansas. Bowling Green's Howie Komives hits 50 consecutive free throws in season's last five games to edge defending champ Nick Werkman of Seton Hall for national scoring title.

309

Fabulous Oscar "The Big O" Robertson became the first player ever to win a national scoring title and be named national Player of the Year when he averaged 35.1 points per game for Cincinnati in 1958. (Naismith Basketball Hall of Fame photo)

1964-65 — UCLA wins second straight national title on the strength of balanced offense and defense from Gail Goodrich and Kenny Washington. Princeton's Bill Bradley steals the NCAA tournament spotlight with a record 58-point performance in Final Four consolation game. In May, New York schoolboy standout Lew Alcindor (later known as Kareem Abdul-Jabbar) decides he will attend UCLA in the fall and play for coach John Wooden. The now almost ignored NIT postseason event expands its field from 12 to 14 teams.

1965-66 — UCLA falters after a preseason loss to its own freshman team led by newcomers Alcindor and Lucius Allen. Purdue's Dave Schellhase edges Idaho State's Dave Wagnon by four hundredths of a point to become the last national scoring champ from the Big Ten until the 1990s. In the NCAA tourney, surprising Texas Western squares off with Kentucky and beats Rupp's team 72-65 in a classic confrontation between black-style playground ball and white-style disciplined pattern offense.

1966-67 — UCLA sophomore sensation Lew Alcindor records highest field-goal percentage to date in college history and leads Bruins to both NCAA title and undefeated (30-0) season. Texas Christian University center James Cash is first African-American to play varsity basketball in Southwestern Conference. Kentucky (13-13) suffers only non-winning season during Adolph Rupp's 41-year coaching tenure.

1967-68 (**January 20**) -- Crowd of 52,693, largest ever to see a college basketball game, jams Houston Astrodome to watch the Houston Cougars and Elvin Hayes end UCLA's win streak at 47 games. At season's end UCLA makes it two in a row in postseason play with 78-55 thrashing of North Carolina that represents biggest victory margin to date in NCAA Finals. When Alcindor and other top stars decline tryouts with Olympic team, unknown junior college star Spencer Haywood of Detroit paces USA to still another gold medal victory. Dunk shots (primarily as a result of Alcindor) are made illegal for both NCAA games and pregame warm-ups.

1968-69 — Pete Maravich (LSU) scores 50 or better in nine different games for second straight year. UCLA runs string of NCAA titles to three, becoming first school ever to accomplish this feat. Lew Alcindor also becomes only player named NCAA tourney MVP for three straight seasons.

1969-70 — UCLA wins fourth NCAA title in a row, knocking off Jacksonville with 7-footer Artis Gilmore in the finals. Pete Maravich sets single-season scoring record (44.5) which still stands and also finishes with career scoring mark (3,667 points) that is yet to be challenged. Maravich (with 64) and Kentucky's Dan Issel (51) each score more than 50 points in same game. Purdue's Rick Mount sets Big Ten single-game mark with 61, but his team loses game (108-107) against Iowa.

1970-71 — UCLA loses but once, to Notre Dame when Austin Carr scores 46 for Irish. It will be final Bruin loss before record 88-game win streak. UCLA's postseason win streak also reaches 28 when Bruins defeat Villanova 68-62 for their fifth-straight national championship banner. Julius Erving leaves Massachusetts after junior season for pro career without ever having played in an NCAA Tournament game. Carr averages 38 points per game for second consecutive year and also finishes second in national scoring race for second straight time, thus becoming most prolific non-scoring leader in NCAA history.

1971-72 (**March 20**) — Immaculata defeats West Chester 52-48 to win first AIAW (Association of Intercollegiate Athletics for Women) tournament. UCLA retools under stellar sophomore center Bill Walton, finishes with perfect 30-0 record and sixth straight NCAA title, and also runs its unbeaten string to 45 games. Walton becomes only player besides Oscar Robertson (1958) ever to be named national player of the year in his first season of competition. Adolph "Baron" Rupp retires after 41 full seasons at Kentucky with unmatched 875-190 career record.

1972-73 — UCLA wins its seventh NCAA title and extends its unbeaten string to 75 games. Bill Walton captures his second tourney MVP and puts on perhaps the greatest single-man show in NCAA Finals history, making 21 of 22 field goals for 44 points in title-game slaughter of Memphis State. Freshmen again allowed to play major-college varsity basketball.

1973-74 (**January 19**) — UCLA's win streak is stopped at 88 by Notre Dame with 71-70 upset victory in South Bend. North Carolina State becomes year's biggest story as it recovers from an early-season loss to UCLA's Bruins to win the national title, upsetting the Bruins 80-77 in double overtime during NCAA semifinals.

1974-75 — NCAA tournament field expands to 32 teams; UCLA returns to the top and claims one final title before closing out Wooden era. Indiana (31-1) might have ended Bruins' hopes for a rebound victory, but Bob Knight's Hoosiers lose their only game of the season in NCAA regionals to runner-up Kentucky when star scorer Scott May is out of action with broken hand. Wooden retires after NCAA Finals with 664-162 29-year record.

1975-76 — Indiana replaces UCLA at the top with undefeated 33-0 season and easy 86-68 NCAA Finals victory over conference rival Michigan. Knight's Hoosier thus finish their glorious two-year run with only a single defeat alongside 64 victories and Hoosier forward Scott May is consensus national college player of the year.

1976-77 — Slam dunk is reinstituted in college basketball after nine-year absence. Postseason play is filled with plenty of drama and emotion as Marquette captures an NCAA title, 67-59, over often-frustrated Dean Smith and North Carolina Tar Heels. Veteran Marquette coach Al McGuire had announced his retirement when his team floundered in midseason, then watched in tears as his Warriors wrapped up an upset NCAA title.

1977-78 — Gunner Freeman Williams of Portland State wins his second straight national scoring title (35.9) and finishes second on the all-time career scoring list behind Pete Maravich. But year's most sensational clutch game is turned in by Kentucky's Jack "Goose" Givens who hits 18 baskets for 41 points to lead the Wildcats to a 94-88 victory over Duke in national title game.

1978-79 — Most memorable single one-on-one shootout in NCAA Finals history matches future NBA greats Larry Bird of Indiana State and Earvin "Magic" Johnson of Michigan State. MSU Spartans come out on top and hand Bird and his Sycamores their only defeat of the season. Bird finishes his brilliant college career fifth on NCAA all-time scoring list. UCLA sets NCAA record with its 13th consecutive conference (Pac-8, Pac-10) championship.

1979-80 — Ann Meyers, four-time All-American at UCLA, is first woman to sign an NBA contract (with Indiana Pacers) but Old Dominion University senior Nancy Lieberman is named year's most outstanding women's player. In season's most sensational moment, guard Les Henson of Virginia Tech cans longest basket (89 feet, 3 inches) on record to stun Florida State at the buzzer. NCAA tourney field grows to 48 entrants; Louisville captures its first NCAA title behind sensational all-around play of slam-dunk wizard Darrell Griffith.

1980-81 (**November 29**) — Ronnie Carr of Western Carolina University scores first-ever collegiate three-point goal as new scoring rule goes into effect on an experimental basis in Southern Conference. Bob Knight captures second national title with Indiana Hoosiers, defeating Dean Smith's North Carolina 63-50. Indiana's star performer is sophomore guard, Isiah Thomas, who soon departs college ranks for promising pro career.

1981-82 — NCAA conducts first women's postseason tourney with Louisiana State defeating Cheyney State 76-62 for the title. Veteran coach Dean Smith finally wins a national title for North Carolina. Victory comes when frosh Michael Jordan — future all-time NBA great — cans a last-second jumper before a record crowd of 61,612 in the New Orleans Superdome. Harry Kelly of Texas Southern wins the first of his two straight national scoring titles and Louisiana Tech sets a new record in women's play with 54 straight victories. Jump balls are now used only to start games and overtime periods, with alternating-possession arrows replacing other jump-ball situations.

1982-83 — Akeem Olajuwon, Clyde Drexler and a Houston team known as "Phi Slamma Jamma" make headlines during most of the regular season with a 31-3 record and the nation's top ranking. But Cougars are upset in a dramatic NCAA title game by North Carolina State. Jim Valvano-coached Wolfpack are first team ever to win the national title after losing 10 or more regular-season games.

312

1983-84 — North Carolina is ranked No. 1 for the second time in three years and Michael Jordan is the Tar Heels' top scorer for the third year in a row. But the big story in postseason play is Houston's second NCAA finals defeat in a row. This comes when Patrick Ewing and Georgetown top Olajuwon and his Cougars in a celebrated year-end battle of the nation's two top big men.

1984-85 **(December 21)** — Georgeann Wells of West Virginia is the first woman to slam dunk a ball during NCAA game action. Two Big East powerhouses, Villanova and Georgetown, square off in the NCAA title game and the Wildcats surprise the defending champion Hoyas 66-64. NCAA Tournament field has now been expanded to include 64 teams. Xavier McDaniel of Wichita State becomes the first player to lead the nation in both scoring (27.2) and rebounding (14.8).

1985-86 — 45-second shot clock is instituted for all men's games. Led by All-American guard Johnny Dawkins, Duke (37-3) finishes atop the wire service polls for the first time since the rankings began. Blue Devils are upset in the NCAA title game, however, by Louisville and its sensational freshman Pervis Ellison. UCLA's streak of 32 consecutive winning seasons in conference play finally ends.

1986-87 — New rule allows three points for field goals beyond a line 19 feet, 9 inches from the basket. Nevada-Las Vegas (UNLV) dominates regular-season play with one loss and a yearlong No. 1 ranking, but is tumbled in NCAA tourney play by eventual champion Indiana. Bob Knight's Hoosiers are NCAA champs for the fifth time. Maryland's Ben Wade becomes first-ever African-American coach in prestigious ACC Conference.

1987-88 — Hersey Hawkins of Bradley leads the nation in scoring (36.3) and Kansas, led by All-American center Danny Manning, wins the NCAA tournament despite not finishing in the regular-season Top 10 rankings. Center Steve Scheffler completes his career at Purdue with a new NCAA career record (68.5) for field-goal percentage.

1988-89 — Michigan pulls a surprise at the end of the season when Steve Fisher takes over the team during the NCAA tournament and guides it to its first national title ever. During regular-season play Loyola Marymount (Calif.) displays its high-powered fast-breaking offense with a 181-150 victory over U.S. International in which several NCAA records are set, including total points, points by one team and points by a losing team.

1989-90 — West Coast Conference Tourney finals are marred by tragedy when Loyola Marymount star Hank Gathers collapses on court and dies later that day of a previously treated heart ailment. UNLV under coach Jerry Tarkanian enjoys a phenomenal regular season (35-5) and also rolls to a 30-point trouncing of Duke in the NCAA finals. La Salle's Lionel Simmons ends his career with a record 115 consecutive games scoring in double figures.

1990-91 — Defending national champion UNLV is ousted by eventual champ Duke in national semifinals. Runnin' Rebels nonetheless go down in history as one of most potent teams ever, the only team ever with at least four teammates (Stacey Augmon, Greg Anthony, Anderson Hunt and Larry Johnson) to finish with more than 1,500 career points.

1991-92 — Duke (35-2) becomes first NCAA back-to-back titlist since UCLA dynasty ended 18 seasons earlier. Lopsided 71-51 victory in NCAA Finals comes against Michigan's heralded "Fab Five" all-freshman team. Duke's Bobby Hurley is shortest Final Four MVP winner since Temple's Hal Lear in 1956, but true NCAA tourney star is Blue Devils' Christian Laettner who finishes career as all-time tournament scoring leader and also hits a dramatic last-second game-winner in East Regional finals versus Kentucky.

1992-93 — Michigan's Fab Five again fails in NCAA final game as Chris Webber calls a time-out that Michigan doesn't have in game's closing seconds to seal a victory for North Carolina, 77-71. Duke's Bobby Hurley completes his career with new NCAA record of 1,076 assists, while Mississippi Valley shooting guard Alphonso Ford becomes only Division I player to score more than 700 points and average more than 25 points per game in each of four college seasons.

1993-94 — Shot clock is reduced from 45 to 35 seconds. Purdue's Glenn Robinson is national collegiate player of the year after he becomes first Big Ten player to lead nation in scoring in more than three decades as well as first Big Ten scorer to top 1,000 points in a single season. Ricky Nedd of Appalachian State establishes a new career mark (69.0) for field-goal percentage.

1994-95 — UCLA returns to winner's circle with surprising NCAA Tournament championship under coach Jim Harrick. Jerry Stackhouse, brilliant North Carolina sophomore forward, is consensus collegiate player of the year. Kurt Thomas of Texas Christian University accomplishes rare feat of pacing nation in both scoring and rebounding.

1995-96 — Rebecca Lobo of University of Connecticut's 1995 NCAA Women's championship team makes history by signing contract with men's pro United States Basketball League and landing contract to promote Nike athletic shoes.

College Basketball's Most
Memorable Players and Coaches

The top dozen, two dozen, even 100 of the greatest college players of all time is a matter of endless speculation and delightful debate. A small handful of players seem automatic on any such list, no matter how selective or biased. Others are perhaps more a matter of the era, the regional orientation, or the aesthetics of the selector himself. Yet no history of the game seems quite complete without some attempt at an honor roll of the game's true immortals.

Below are career capsules for this author's own all-time top 10 players, 100 additional all-time greats and 30 most memorable or influential coaches from the game's first full century. While some readers are certain to be dismayed by the absence of a personal favorite or two, it should be recalled that the emphasis here is strictly on collegiate careers and not on subsequent NBA successes or failures.

Ten Greatest College Players of All Time

Lew Alcindor — UCLA, C (7-2), National Player of the Year (1967, 1969)

Only three-time winner of the NCAA Tournament MVP award. Later changed his name to Kareem Abdul-Jabbar. Led team to 88-2 record and three straight NCAA titles. Considered by many as the most dominating center and perhaps the greatest all-around player ever.

Seasons	Games	Points	FG	FT	Rebounds	PPG Average
3 (1967-69)	88	2325	934	439	1367 (15.5)	26.4

Elgin Baylor — Seattle (College of Idaho), F (6-6), All-American (1957, 1958)

Nation's leading rebounder in 1957 and NCAA Final Four MVP in 1958. Missed by three-tenths of a point (junior year) averaging above 30 ppg all three seasons. Renowned for incomparable "hangtime" offensive moves.

Seasons	Games	Points	FG	FT	Rebounds	PPG Average
3 (1955-58)	80	2500	956	588	1559 (20.0)	31.3

Bill Bradley — Princeton, F (6-5), National Player of the Year (1965)

Two-time unanimous All-American (1964-65), nation's free-throw accuracy leader in 1965, and Final Four Most Outstanding Player in 1965. Closed career with 58-point effort versus Wichita State in 1965 NCAA Consolation game.

Seasons	Games	Points	FG	FT	Rebounds	PPG Average
3 (1963-65)	83	2503	856	791	1008 (12.1)	30.2

Tom Gola — La Salle, F-C (6-6), National Player of the Year (1955)

Still career leader in total rebounds and total combined points and rebounds (4663). Three-time All-American (consensus twice, 1954-55) and only player ever to be named both NIT (1952) and NCAA (1954) Final Four MVP. Perhaps inch-for-inch the most competitive and even the greatest player of all time.

Seasons	Games	Points	FG	FT	Rebounds	PPG Average
4 (1952-55)	118	2462	904	654	2201 (18.7)	20.9

Jerry Lucas — Ohio State , C (6-8), National Player of the Year (1961, 1962)

Ranks with Alcindor, Gola and Oscar Robertson as perhaps the greatest ever. Three-time unanimous All-American and three-time national leader in field goal accuracy. Twice national rebounding leader (1961-62). Twice NCAA Final Four MVP. One of the few to play in NCAA title game all three of his seasons.

Seasons	Games	Points	FG	FT	Rebounds	PPG Average
3 (1960-62)	82	1990	776	438	1411 (17.2)	24.3

"Pistol Pete" Maravich — LSU, G-F (6-5), National Player of the Year (1970)

Three-time unanimous All-American. All-time greatest scorer and holder of numerous national records including: highest career average, highest single-season average, total career points, total field goals and free-throws. Never played in NCAA tournament. Also perhaps the flashiest ball handler ever.

Seasons	Games	Points	FG	FT	Rebounds	PPG Average
3 (1968-70)	83	3667	1387	893	528 (6.4)	44.2

Oscar Robertson — Cincinnati, F (6-5), National Player of the Year (1958-60)

Choice of many as the greatest total-package player ever. First and only three-time national scoring champion and national player of the year. Still ranks third all-time in career scoring average and sixth in total career points scored.

Seasons	Games	Points	FG	FT	Rebounds	PPG Average
3 (1958-60)	88	2973	1052	869	1338 (15.2)	33.8

Bill Russell — San Francisco, C (6-9), National Player of the Year (1956)

One of six players to average more than 20 points and 20 rebounds per game for full career. Leading scorer and rebounder for two NCAA championship teams (1955-1956) and Final Four Most Outstanding Player in 1955. Leading scorer for 1956 US Olympic team and two-time All-American (1955 and 1956).

Seasons	Games	Points	FG	FT	Rebounds	PPG Average
3 (1954-56)	79	1636	625	386	1606 (20.3)	20.7

Cazzie Russell — Michigan, G (6-5), National Player of the Year (1966)

Two-time unanimous All-American and the nation's third-leading scorer as a senior. Member of NCAA All-Tourney team in 1965 and leading scorer for NCAA third-place team in 1964 and national runner-up in 1965 (as a junior). One of the most productive shooting guards in collegiate basketball history.

Seasons	Games	Points	FG	FT	Rebounds	PPG Average
3 (1964-66)	80	2164	839	486	676 (8.5)	27.1

Bill Walton — UCLA, C (6-11), National Player of the Year (1972-74)

Three-time unanimous All-American and second of John Wooden's two incomparable franchise centers. Led team to record 88-game winning streak. Twice named NCAA Final Four Most Outstanding Player. Enjoyed perhaps the single greatest performance in tournament history with 21 for 22 shooting from the field in 44-point effort versus Memphis State in 1973 NCAA Finals.

Seasons	Games	Points	FG	FT	Rebounds	PPG Average
3 (1972-74)	87	1767	747	273	1370 (15.7)	20.3

College Basketball's Additional Top 100 All-Time Stars

Mark Aguirre — DePaul, F (6-6), National Player of the Year (1980)

Naismith Outstanding Player Award winner (1980) and two-time unanimous All-American. Member of NCAA All-Tournament team and leading scorer for 1979 national third-place finishers. Averaged 20.6 in seven NCAA games.

Seasons	Games	Points	FG	FT	Rebounds	PPG Average
3 (1979-81)	89	2182	863	456	706 (7.9)	24.5

Paul Arizin — Villanova, F (6-4), Helms National Player of the Year (1950)

Pioneer one-handed jump shooter and national scoring leader in 1949-50. Consensus All-American as senior and averaged 26 points in two NCAA games. First in series of local greats playing for Philadelphia schools in '50s.

Seasons	Games	Points	FG	FT	Rebounds	PPG Average
3 (1948-50)	80	1596	571	454	NA	20.0

Rick Barry — Miami (Florida), F (6-7), All-American (1965)

One of the greatest pure shooters and most adept free-throw shooters of all-time. Averaged 34.7 ppg over final two seasons. Never appeared in NCAAs but averaged 19.3 in 3 NIT games in 1963 and 1964. Naismith Hall of Fame. Nation's leading scorer and fourth-best rebounder during senior year (1965).

Seasons	Games	Points	FG	FT	Rebounds	PPG Average
3 (1963-65)	77	2298	816	666	1274 (16.5)	29.8

Dave Bing — Syracuse, G (6-3), All-American (1966)

Supreme shooting guard of the '60s and one of the best rebounders among backcourt men in college hoops history (12.0 rpg as a junior). Nation's fifth leading scorer as a senior (1966). Collected 31 points in single NIT appearance.

Seasons	Games	Points	FG	FT	Rebounds	PPG Average
3 (1964-66)	76	1883	729	425	786 (10.3)	24.8

Larry Bird — Indiana State, F (6-9), National Player of the Year (1979)

Won all the major individual player awards in 1979 while leading team to NCAA runner-up spot and earning place on NCAA All-Tournament team. Averaged 27.2 ppg and 13.4 rpg in five NCAA games. One of only 12 (he stands 10th) to top 4,000-plateau in combined career points and rebounds.

Seasons	Games	Points	FG	FT	Rebounds	PPG Average
3 (1977-79)	94	2850	1154	542	1247 (13.3)	30.3

Gary Bradds — Ohio State, C (6-8), National Player of the Year (1964)

Replaced Jerry Lucas at center for Buckeyes in 1963 and averaged almost 30 ppg over next two seasons. Unanimous All-American, nation's sixth leading scorer, and country's top player as senior. Averaged above 30 ppg in Big Ten play while leading league in scoring during two final seasons (30.9 and 33.9).

Seasons	Games	Points	FG	FT	Rebounds	PPG Average
3 (1962-64)	74	1530	563	404	706 (9.5)	20.7

Michael Brooks — La Salle, F (6-7), National Player of the Year (1980)

One of the dozen players with combined career totals of 4,000 points and rebounds. Averaged 32 points and 13 rebounds in two NCAA Tourney games. Top scorer (13.2) for 1980 Olympic team. Career field-goal percentage of .538.

Seasons	Games	Points	FG	FT	Rebounds	PPG Average
4 (1977-80)	114	2628	1064	500	1372 (12.0)	23.1

Austin Carr — Notre Dame, G (6-3), National Player of the Year (1971)

One of greatest scorers in cage history. Averaged 38 ppg in each of final two seasons but finished second nationally both times (to Pete Maravich and Johnny Neumann). Averaged 41.3 ppg in 7 NCAA Tourney games (career record) overall and 52.7 ppg in 3 1970 NCAA games (single tourney record).

Seasons	Games	Points	FG	FT	Rebounds	PPG Average
3 (1969-71)	74	2560	1017	526	538 (7.3)	34.6

317

Wilt "The Stilt" Chamberlain — Kansas, C (7-1), All-American (1957, 1958)

NCAA Final Four most outstanding player in 1957 despite loss in Finals to North Carolina. First truly agile college giant whose appearance inevitably caused several rule changes. Averaged 30.3 ppg and 15.5 rebounds in 4 NCAA games in 1957. Harassed by gang defenses and left Kansas after only 2 seasons.

Seasons	Games	Points	FG	FT	Rebounds	PPG Average
2 (1957-58)	48	1433	503	427	877 (18.3)	29.9

Len Chappell — Wake Forest, F-C (6-8), All-American (1962)

Leading scorer and rebounder for 1962 NCAA 3rd-place team and member of NCAA All-Tournament team. Averaged 27.6 ppg and 17.1 rebounds in eight NCAA games over two seasons. Two-time ACC scoring and rebound leader.

Seasons	Games	Points	FG	FT	Rebounds	PPG Average
3 (1960-62)	87	2165	764	637	1213 (13.9)	24.9

Bob Cousy — Holy Cross, G (6-1), All-American (1950)

Famed ball handler and passing wizard who popularized the behind-the-back pass and began his dribbling magic as a freshman starter on 1947 Holy Cross NCAA championship team. Averaged 10.6 points in eight NCAA Tourney games (1947-1950). Also a proficient shooter who averaged 19.4 ppg as senior.

Seasons	Games	Points	FG	FT	Rebounds	PPG Average
4 (1947-50)	117	1775	709	357	NA	15.2

Bob Davies — Seton Hall, G (6-1), All-American (1942)

Pioneering ball handler who invented the behind-the-back dribble during college career at Seton Hall. Averaged 11.3 ppg in three games for 1941 NIT 3rd-place finisher. Later performed incredible "double" when he earned NBL (National Basketball League) MVP honors with the Rochester Royals in 1947 while at same time coaching his alma mater to 24-3 record.

Seasons	Games	Points	FG	FT	Rebounds	PPG Average
3 (1940-42)	59	661	250	161	NA	11.2

Ernie DiGregorio — Providence, G (6-0), All-American (1973)

Last in the line of great '60s-era "little men" at Providence that began with Lenny Wilkens, John Egan and Vinnie Ernst. Leading scorer for 1973 NCAA 4th-place team. Averaged 24.2 in six NCAA games and 21.5 in two NIT games.

Seasons	Games	Points	FG	FT	Rebounds	PPG Average
3 (1971-73)	86	1760	757	246	292 (3.4)	20.5

Terry Dischinger — Purdue, F (6-7), All-American (1961, 1962)

Three-time Big Ten scoring champ who played in the shadows of Jerry Lucas and Oscar Robertson. Finished seventh once (sophomore) and fourth twice in the national scoring race. Did not play in postseason but was member of the outstanding 1960 US Olympic team considered best amateur team in history.

Seasons	Games	Points	FG	FT	Rebounds	PPG Average
3 (1960-62)	70	1979	633	713	958 (13.7)	28.3

Walter Dukes — Seton Hall, C (7-0), All-American (1953)

One of six players with career averages above 20 in both points and rebounds. Dominant college center during period between Mikan and Kurland in mid-40s and Chamberlain in mid-50s. NIT most outstanding player in 1953 for tournament championship team. Averaged 22.5 ppg during four NIT games.

Seasons	Games	Points	FG	FT	Rebounds	PPG Average
2 (1952-53)	59	1385	441	503	1247 (21.1)	23.5

Sean Elliott — Arizona, F (6-8), National Player of the Year (1989)

Wooden Outstanding Player Award winner in 1989 and two-time unanimous first-team All-American. Leading scorer and rebounder for 1988 Final Four team and averaged 23.6 ppg and 6.8 rebounds in 10 NCAA games (1986-1989).

Seasons	Games	Points	FG	FT	Rebounds	PPG Average
4 (1986-89)	133	2555	896	623	808 (6.1)	19.2

Julius Erving — Massachusetts, F (6-6)

One of only six players to average more than 20 points and 20 rebounds per game for full career. Left after two seasons to sign as undergraduate free agent with ABA Virginia Squires. One of earliest practitioners of new high-flying "above-the-rim" playground style which revolutionized cage play in 1970s.

Seasons	Games	Points	FG	FT	Rebounds	PPG Average
2 (1970-71)	52	1370	524	322	1049 (20.2)	26.3

Patrick Ewing — Georgetown, C (7-0), National Player of the Year (1985)

Naismith Award winner (1985) and three-time All-American (unanimous twice). NCAA Final Four MVP in 1984 and three-time All-Tournament team selection (1982, 1984, 1985). Leading rebounder and scorer for 1984 national champion and 1985 runner-up. Played in 18 NCAA Tournament games (14.2 ppg scoring average) and on two Gold Medal US Olympic teams (1984, 1992).

Seasons	Games	Points	FG	FT	Rebounds	PPG Average
4 (1982-85)	143	2184	857	470	1316 (9.2)	15.3

Arnie Ferrin — Utah, F (6-4), All-American (1945, 1947, 1948)

Most outstanding player of 1944 NCAA Tournament as freshman star and leading scorer for national champion Utah. Only freshman to win Final Four MVP honors. Played on NIT winner in 1947 and averaged 13.5 in four games.

Seasons	Games	Points	FG	FT	Rebounds	PPG Average
4 (1944-48)	82	1125	NA	NA	NA	13.7

Danny Ferry — Duke, F-C (6-10), National Player of the Year (1989)

Naismith Award winner, unanimous All-American, and member of NCAA All-Tournament team in 1989. Leading scorer and rebounder for NCAA Final Four teams in 1988 and 1989. Freshman starter on national runner-up team in 1986. Averaged 14.2 points and 6.9 rebounds in 19 NCAA Tourney games.

Seasons	Games	Points	FG	FT	Rebounds	PPG Average
4 (1986-89)	143	2155	810	427	1003 (7.0)	15.1

Darrell Floyd — Furman, G-F (6-1), All-American (1956)

Led nation in scoring as junior and senior to give Furman four straight national scoring titles (first two by Frank Selvy). Also teamed with Selvy as sophomore to give Furman highest-scoring backcourt pair in history (41.7 ppg for Selvy and 24.3 for Floyd). Averaged 34.8 ppg over final two seasons.

Seasons	Games	Points	FG	FT	Rebounds	PPG Average
3 (1954-56)	71	2281	868	545	611 (8.6)	32.1

Phil Ford — North Carolina, G (6-2), National Player of the Year (1978)

Wooden Award winner (1978) and twice a first-team All-American choice. Leading scorer for 1977 NCAA runner-up and averaged 14.7 points and 4.9 assists over ten tournament games (1975-78). Member of 1976 Olympic team.

Seasons	Games	Points	FG	FT	Rebounds	PPG Average
4 (1975-78)	123	2290	865	560	261 (2.1)	18.6

Clarence "Bevo" Francis — Rio Grande, C-F (6-9), All-American (1954)

The greatest scoring machine in college basketball history. Averaged 50.1 ppg in 39-game freshman season (all but 12 games versus non-four-year schools). Twice scored 100 points in a single game, including 113 versus Hillsdale which now stands as recognized Division II record. Deadly jump shooter from around the key and exceptional free-throw shooter. Played only two seasons.

Seasons	Games	Points	FG	FT	Rebounds	PPG Average
2 (1953-54)	67	3270	NA	NA	NA	48.8

Robin Freeman — Ohio State, G (5-11), All-American (1955, 1956)

One of the most exciting little men ever to appear in Big Ten action. Still owns highest single-season scoring average in Ohio State history. Nation's 2nd leading scorer in 1956. First 30 ppg scorer in Big Ten Conference history.

Seasons	Games	Points	FG	FT	Rebounds	PPG Average
3 (1954-56)	57	1597	593	411	NA	28.0

Richie Fuqua — Oral Roberts, G (6-4), All-American (1972)

Hot-shooting guard who averaged 33.9 ppg across his sophomore and junior seasons. Second in the nation in scoring in 1972 but not ranked on the all-time career scoring list (his 3004 points would be sixth) since Oral Roberts was in Division II his first two seasons. Averaged 30.7 points in three NIT games.

Seasons	Games	Points	FG	FT	Rebounds	PPG Average
4 (1970-73)	111	3004	1273	458	523 (4.7)	27.1

Hank Gathers — Loyola Marymount, F-C (6-7), All-American (1990)

Prolific scorer and rebounder and outstanding pro prospect whose life was cut short by heart attack suffered in 1990 postseason play. One of three players (with Xavier McDaniel and Kurt Thomas) to lead nation in both scoring and rebounding during same season. Averaged 21.3 points in three NCAA games.

Seasons	Games	Points	FG	FT	Rebounds	PPG Average
4 (1986-90)	117	2723	1127	469	1128 (9.6)	23.3

Artis Gilmore — Jacksonville, C (7-2), All-American (1971)

Two-time national rebounding leader (1970, 1971) and only player to average more than 22 points and 22 rebounds for his career. Leading scorer and rebounder for 1970 NCAA runner-up. Averaged 24 ppg and 19.2 rebounds in six NCAA games (1970, 1971) and named to NCAA All-Tourney team in 1970.

Seasons	Games	Points	FG	FT	Rebounds	PPG Average
2 (1970-71)	54	1312	536	240	1224 (22.7)	24.3

Gail Goodrich — UCLA, G (6-1), All-American (1965)

Twice named to NCAA All-Tournament team (1964, 1965) and backcourt ace of John Wooden's first two UCLA national champions. Leading scorer on 1964 undefeated Bruins. Also star of 1965 NCAA title victory over Michigan (his final career game) with 42 points. Averaged 23.5 ppg in 10 NCAA games.

Seasons	Games	Points	FG	FT	Rebounds	PPG Average
3 (1963-65)	89	1690	637	416	415 (4.7)	19.0

Travis "Machine Gun" Grant — Kentucky State, C (6-8)

College basketball's only 4,000-point man and Division II career scoring record holder. Also holds career (1760) and single-season (539) small school records for field goals, and Division II mark for career scoring average (33.4 ppg). Averaged 39.5 ppg as senior and logged 75-point game versus Norwood College in 1970. Led Kentucky State to three straight NAIA Tournament titles.

Seasons	Games	Points	FG	FT	Rebounds	PPG Average
4 (1969-72)	121	4045	1760	525	1138 (9.4)	33.4

Sihugo Green — Duquesne, G (6-3), All-American (1955, 1956)

Lightning-quick guard with equal scoring, rebounding and playmaking skills. Averaged 21.3 ppg in eight NIT games and played in the NIT championship final twice (1954, 1955). Paced Duquesne with 33 points in 1955 NIT title victory over Dayton. Number one pick (Rochester Royals) in 1956 NBA Draft, the year Bill Russell was picked third by the Boston Celtics.

Seasons	Games	Points	FG	FT	Rebounds	PPG Average
3 (1954-56)	81	1603	598	407	936 (11.6)	19.8

Hal Greer — Marshall, G (6-2)

One of earliest black college stars and first to play for a major college in West Virginia. Exceptional outside shooter; completed career with .545 field-goal percentage. Exceptional rebounder for guard (career average above 10); adroit playmaker who advanced to Hall of Fame pro career.

Seasons	Games	Points	FG	FT	Rebounds	PPG Average
3 (1956-58)	71	1377	531	315	765 (10.8)	19.4

Darrell Griffith — Louisville, G (6-4), National Player of the Year (1980)

"Dr. Dunkenstein" was famed for his slam dunks but equally effective with long-range shooting. Wooden Award winner; NCAA Final Four most outstanding player in 1980, when he led Louisville to NCAA title. Averaged 20.3 ppg and 4.6 rebounds in ten NCAA Tourney games (1977-80).

Seasons	Games	Points	FG	FT	Rebounds	PPG Average
4 (1977-80)	126	2333	981	371	585 (4.6)	18.5

Dick Groat — Duke, G (6-0), Helms National Player of the Year (1951)

Future major league baseball star (1960 National League MVP) was second in nation in both scoring (26.0) and assists (7.6) as senior. Didn't appear in postseason, but played in baseball College World Series in 1952. Two-time All-American. Finished fourth in country in scoring as sophomore (25.2) but set new single-season points record (with 831) and free-throw record (261 of 388).

Seasons	Games	Points	FG	FT	Rebounds	PPG Average
3 (1950-52)	82	1886	682	522	NA	23.0

Alex Groza — Kentucky, C (6-7), All-American (1947, 1949)

Leading star of Baron Rupp's great two-time national championship team known as the "Fabulous Five" (1947-49). NCAA Tourney most outstanding player in 1948 and 1949, averaging 22.7 points in six tourney games. Leading scorer (11.1 ppg) on 1948 US Olympic team. Career ended in disgrace when banned for life from NBA as result of 1951 college point-shaving scandals.

Seasons	Games	Points	FG	FT	Rebounds	PPG Average
4 (1945-49)	120	1744	667	410	NA	14.5

Cliff Hagan — Kentucky, F-C (6-4), All-American (1952, 1954)

One of all-time Kentucky greats despite missing junior season while Rupp's Wildcats served yearlong suspension. Leading scorer for undefeated 1954 team that chose to bypass NCAA play. Freshman starter for 1951 national championship team. Averaged 12 points in six NCAA Tournament games. Earned pro fame as only player ranked in top 10 in all categories for a season.

Seasons	Games	Points	FG	FT	Rebounds	PPG Average
3 (1951-54)	77	1475	567	341	1035 (13.4)	19.2

Hersey Hawkins — Bradley, G (6-3), National Player of the Year (1988)

Fifth on all-time career scoring list with 3008 points. National scoring leader, unanimous first-team All-American as senior. Averaged 29 points, 7.3 rebounds in three NCAA contests. Member of 1988 US Olympic team. Recorded seventh highest season scoring total ever (1,125 points in 1988).

Seasons	Games	Points	FG	FT	Rebounds	PPG Average
4 (1985-88)	125	3008	1100	690	818 (6.5)	24.1

Elvin Hayes — Houston, F (6-9), National Player of the Year (1968)

One of highest scoring forwards and most prolific rebounders in collegiate history. Nation's third-highest scorer as senior (behind Maravich and Calvin Murphy) but actual leader in total points. Second highest single-season point total in Division I history (1214 in 1968). Third all time in total career points and rebounds (4486, behind Tom Gola and Lionel Simmons). Leading scorer and rebounder for Final Four teams in 1967 (3rd place) and 1968 (4th place).

Seasons	Games	Points	FG	FT	Rebounds	PPG Average
3 (1966-68)	93	2884	1215	454	1602 (17.2)	31.0

Spencer Haywood — Detroit, F-C (6-8), All-American (1969)

One of greatest one-season players ever with 32.1 ppg scoring average and nation's-best 22.1 rebound average. Did not play in postseason. Averaged 28.2 ppg and 22.1 rebounds in one junior college season (Trinidad State, Colorado) and leading scorer (16.1 ppg) for 1968 US Olympic team. Signed with ABA Denver Rockets after sophomore year at Detroit and became instant pro star.

Seasons	Games	Points	FG	FT	Rebounds	PPG Average
1 (1969)	24	771	288	195	530 (22.1)	32.1

Walt Hazzard — UCLA, G (6-2), National Player of the Year (1964)

Player most responsible for launching Wooden UCLA dynasty in 1964. Playmaker and second-leading scorer (18.6 ppg) for undefeated 1964 national champions. Final Four most outstanding player, NCAA All-Tournament team pick. Averaged 16.2 points, 5.7 rebounds in 10 NCAA games.

Seasons	Games	Points	FG	FT	Rebounds	PPG Average
3 (1962-64)	87	1401	508	385	475 (5.5)	16.1

Tom Heinsohn — Holy Cross, F (6-7), All-American (1956)

Relentless shooter (nicknamed "Ack-Ack" for machine gun approach) and rebounder at both college and pro levels. Excellent collegiate career largely overshadowed by Hall of Fame pro tenure with Boston Celtics (only NBAer to be both rookie of the year and coach of the year during his career). Ranked in nation's top 10 in scoring (27.4, 4th) and rebounding (21.1, 8th) as senior.

Seasons	Games	Points	FG	FT	Rebounds	PPG Average
3 (1954-56)	81	1789	661	467	1254 (15.4)	22.1

Dickie Hemric — Wake Forest, F-C (6-6), All-American (1955)

First great ACC star and conference player-of-the-year during first two ACC seasons (1954-55). Consistent scorer who ranked in nation's top 10 in three of four years and averaged between 22 and 28 each season. Among nation's top 10 rebounders (18.6 rpg.) as freshman. Averaged 29 points and 17.5 rebounds in two NCAA games.

Seasons	Games	Points	FG	FT	Rebounds	PPG Average
4 (1952-55)	104	2587	841	905	1802 (17.3)	24.9

Art Heyman — Duke, F (6-5), National Player of the Year (1963)

ACC scoring leader (1963) and all-around offensive star of first Duke team to earn national prominence. Two-time All-American (unanimous in 1963). NCAA Final Four MVP in 1963 with 22.3 ppg and 10.5 rpg. (4 games). Leading scorer and rebounder for 1963 national third-place team. Among nation's top 10 scorers as sophomore and senior and ACC Player of the Year (1963).

Seasons	Games	Points	FG	FT	Rebounds	PPG Average
3 (1961-63)	79	1984	713	558	865 (10.9)	25.1

Joe Holup — George Washington, C (6-6)

Sensational rebounder and also efficient inside scorer who twice led nation in field-goal percentage (1954, 1956). One of dozen players with career combined scoring and rebounding total above 4000, and also national rebounding leader in 1956. Ranks second in total career rebounds and only player outside of Tom Gola to garner above 2000 career rebounds.

Seasons	Games	Points	FG	FT	Rebounds	PPG Average
4 (1953-56)	104	2226	756	714	2030 (19.5)	21.4

Bob Houbregs — Washington, F-C (6-7), National Player of the Year (1953)

Popularizer of the hook shot as a major offensive weapon and one of most memorable performers in first decade and a half of NCAA Tournament. Two-time All-American and leading scorer and rebounder for 1953 NCAA third-place team. Averaged 27.4 ppg over seven NCAA Tournament games. What Joe Fulks did for the jumper, Jordan and Dr. J for the slam dunk, and Russell and Mark Eaton for the blocked shot, Houbregs did for the hook shot.

Seasons	Games	Points	FG	FT	Rebounds	PPG Average
3 (1951-53)	91	1774	NA	NA	971 (10.7)	19.5

Bailey Howell — Mississippi State, F (6-7), All-American (1958, 1959)

Remarkable scorer; probably best non-Kentucky player (along with LSU's Pettit) in SEC history. All-around rugged performer who led nation in field-goal percentage as sophomore while averaging 25.9 points, 19.7 rebounds. Fourth in country in scoring as junior (27.8 ppg) and senior (27.5).

Seasons	Games	Points	FG	FT	Rebounds	PPG Average
3 (1963-65)	75	2030	674	682	1277 (17.0)	27.1

"Hot Rod" Hundley — West Virginia, G-F (6-4), All-American (1957)

Earned lasting famed for clowning as both college and pro star, but also one of finest offensive guards of '50s. Nation's seventh leading scorer as junior. Sensational ball handler and dribbler who always entertained even when he didn't shoot (which he often refused to do in one-sided games). Amazing array of trick shots and serious shots displayed in every outing. Led West Virginia to 25-5 record and Southern Conference championship a year before Jerry West arrived.

Seasons	Games	Points	FG	FT	Rebounds	PPG Average
3 (1955-57)	89	2180	785	610	941 (10.6)	24.5

Bobby Hurley — Duke, G (6-0), All-American (1993)

All-time career assists leader and also one of most successful playmakers in NCAA Tournament history. Holds NCAA Tournament career records for three-point field goals and assists. Final Four MVP in 1992 and floor leader and playmaker for two-time national champions (1991, 1992). Averaged 12 ppg and 8.1 assists in 20 NCAA games in which his team posted 18-2 record.

Seasons	Games	Points	FG	FT	Rebounds	PPG Average
4 (1990-93)	140	1731	513	441	306 (2.2)	12.4

Dan Issel — Kentucky, F-C (6-9), All-American (1970)

All-time leading scorer for tradition-rich Kentucky and one of top frontcourt players in SEC history. Fourth in nation in scoring in 1970. Averaged 29.3 ppg and 11.3 rebounds in six NCAA games (1968-1970). Naismith Hall of Famer.

Seasons	Games	Points	FG	FT	Rebounds	PPG Average
3 (1968-70)	83	2138	825	488	1078 (13.0)	25.8

Earvin "Magic" Johnson — Michigan State, G (6-9), All-American (1979)

Short college career was spectacular yet doomed to be nearly forgotten in afterglow of Hall of Fame NBA performance. Final Four most outstanding player for 1979 national champs. Averaged 17.8 points, 8 rebounds, 9.5 assists in eight NCAA games.

Seasons	Games	Points	FG	FT	Rebounds	PPG Average
2 (1978-79)	62	1059	348	363	471 (7.6)	17.1

Larry Johnson — UNLV, F (6-7), National Player of the Year (1991)

Perfect prototype of modern power forward and one of most bruising inside players in collegiate history. Naismith and Wooden Award winner and two-time All-American. Leading scorer and rebounder for 1990 NCAA champion and averaged 20.2 ppg and 11.5 rebounds in eleven NCAA games. Averaged 26 ppg and 11.6 rebounds during two junior college seasons (Odessa, Texas).

Seasons	Games	Points	FG	FT	Rebounds	PPG Average
2 (1990-91)	75	1617	612	363	837 (11.2)	21.6

323

Superb leaper George Kaftan paced Holy Cross to the NCAA national championship in 1947. A sophomore, Kaftan was named the outstanding player in the tournament. The knee pads and rope netting indicate a far different era for the sport. (Holy Cross University photo)

Michael Jordan — N. Carolina, G (6-6), National Player of the Year (1984)

College heroics overshadowed by perhaps greatest NBA career ever, but still phenomenal all-around college star famed for clutch game-winning shot as freshman in 1982 NCAA title contest. ACC leading scorer and player of the year during final (junior) season. Naismith and Wooden Award winner in 1984 and NCAA All-Tournament team member in 1982. Averaged 16.5 ppg and 4.2 rebounds in ten NCAA games and member of two US Olympic teams.

Seasons	Games	Points	FG	FT	Rebounds	PPG Average
3 (1982-84)	101	1788	720	314	509 (5.0)	17.7

George Kaftan — Holy Cross, F (6-3), All-American (1948)

Leading scorer and all-around star for 1947 NCAA champion Holy Cross team also featuring freshman Bob Cousy. Renowned for leaping ability in era of pattern offenses and long-range set-shooting. Final Four most outstanding player in 1947 for national champions. Second-leading scorer for 1948 NCAA third-place finisher. Averaged 17.3 ppg in six NCAA games (1947 and 1948).

Seasons	Games	Points	FG	FT	Rebounds	PPG Average
4 (1946-49)	87	1177	464	249	NA	13.5

Harry Kelly — Texas Southern, F (6-7)

Two-time scoring leader (1982, 1983), fourth in career scoring (behind Maravich, Freeman Williams, Lionel Simmons). One of rare dozen players with combined career totals above 4000 points, rebounds. One of seven players with 1200 career field goals. Did not play in postseason.

Seasons	Games	Points	FG	FT	Rebounds	PPG Average
4 (1980-83)	110	3066	1234	598	1085 (9.9)	27.9

Bernard King — Tennessee, F (6-7), All-American (1977)

One of most artistic and efficient scorers in SEC league history. Led nation in field-goal percentage in 1975 and finished in nation's top fifteen scorers all three seasons. Registered 23 points and 12 rebounds in single NCAA game. Exceptional collegiate career dimmed by even more sensational NBA tenure.

Seasons	Games	Points	FG	FT	Rebounds	PPG Average
3 (1975-77)	76	1962	811	340	1004 (13.2)	25.8

Bob Kurland — Oklahoma A&M, C (7-0), National Player of the Year (1946)

Mikan's rival (and perhaps superior) as game's first great giant of World War II era. Twice NCAA Tournament most valuable player for first repeat NCAA Tournament winner in 1945, 1946. Averaged 13.7 ppg in three NIT games for 1944 fourth-place finisher. Three-time consensus All-American and leader of two Gold Medal US Olympic teams (1948, 1952). Naismith Hall of Famer.

Seasons	Games	Points	FG	FT	Rebounds	PPG Average
4 (1943-46)	118	1669	675	319	NA	14.1

Christian Laettner — Duke, C-F (6-11), National Player of the Year (1992)

Arguably most effective and successful performer in NCAA Tournament history; holder of several individual NCAA Tourney records (career points, career free throws made and attempted, single-year field-goal percentage). Final Four MVP in 1991; member of NCAA All-Tourney team in 1991, 1992. Leading scorer, rebounder for back-to-back national champs. Averaged 17.7 ppg, 7.3 rebounds in 23 NCAA games. Played in Final Four four years and in title game final three seasons.

Seasons	Games	Points	FG	FT	Rebounds	PPG Average
4 (1989-92)	148	2460	834	713	1149 (7.8)	16.6

Dwight "Bo" Lamar — SW Louisiana, G (6-1), All-American (1972, 1973)

One of greatest scorers in history whose 3493 career points are surpassed only by Maravich (doesn't rank on all-time top 10 list, since first two seasons were at Division II level). Led nation in scoring as junior and ranked sixth as senior. Averaged 29.2 ppg in six Division I NCAA Tournament games and 33.2 ppg in five Division II Tourney games for 1971 national third-place team.

Seasons	Games	Points	FG	FT	Rebounds	PPG Average
4 (1970-73)	112	3493	1445	603	406 (3.6)	31.2

Bob Lanier — St. Bonaventure, C (6-11), All-American (1970)

Last player of national prominence produced by onetime powerhouse St. Bonaventure and one of great rebounders of late '60s. Leading scorer and rebounder for 1970 NCAA Tournament 4th-place team. Averaged 25.2 points and 14.2 rebounds in six NCAA contests (1968, 1970). Among nation's top 10 rebounders as senior and also ranked in top 10 in field goal accuracy twice.

Seasons	Games	Points	FG	FT	Rebounds	PPG Average
3 (1968-70)	75	2067	850	367	1180 (15.7)	27.6

Tony Lavelli — Yale, G (6-3), Helms National Player of the Year (1949)

One of game's first regular 20 ppg scorers; national scoring champ in 1949. Second in country in scoring to Iowa's Murray Wier during first season of official NCAA stats (1948). Barely missed (by 36 points) being first collegian to top 2000 career points. Three-time consensus All-American.

Seasons	Games	Points	FG	FT	Rebounds	PPG Average
4 (1946-49)	97	1964	700	564	NA	20.2

Butch Lee — Marquette, G (6-2), National Player of the Year (1978)

Star playmaker for memorable Marquette team that captured NCAA championship in Al McGuire's final season as coach. Final Four MVP, NCAA All-Tournament choice in 1977. Averaged 16 points in ten NCAA games. Naismith Award winner (1978) and two-time All-American.

Seasons	Games	Points	FG	FT	Rebounds	PPG Average
4 (1975-78)	115	1735	666	403	375 (3.3)	15.1

Clyde Lovellette — Kansas, C (6-9), Helms National Player of the Year (1952)

Only player ever to lead nation in scoring and play on NCAA winner in same season. Final Four MVP (1952), averaging 35.3 ppg in four games. Two-time consensus All-American (1951-52). Leading scorer for 1952 US Olympic team.

Seasons	Games	Points	FG	FT	Rebounds	PPG Average
3 (1950-52)	77	1888	774	340	786 (10.2)	24.5

Hank Luisetti — Stanford, F (6-2), National Player of the Year (1937, 1938)

Greatest player of the prewar decades and inventor and popularizer of one-handed shooting style that revolutionized basketball. Three-time consensus All-American and the country's top scorer twice (1936 and 1937, before NCAA began official statistics). Posted 50-point game versus Duquesne in era when full teams rarely hit that level, since there were center jumps after every basket.

Seasons	Games	Points	FG	FT	Rebounds	PPG Average
3 (1936-38)	80	1291	NA	NA	NA	16.1

"Easy Ed" Macauley — St. Louis, C-F (6-8), National Player of Year (1948)

Graceful big man of post-war era who specialized in smooth moves and uncanny shooting rather than rugged inside play. Two-time All-American (unanimous in 1949) and 1949 national leader in field goal accuracy. NIT most outstanding player in 1948 as top scorer for tournament champion. Outplayed Dolph Schayes (outpointing NYU star 24-8) in 1948 NIT championship game.

Seasons	Games	Points	FG	FT	Rebounds	PPG Average
4 (1946-49)	104	1417	511	395	NA	13.6

Danny Manning — Kansas, F-C (6-10), National Player of the Year (1988)

One of dozen double-threat players to top combined total of 4000 career points and rebounds. Two-time unanimous All-American (1987-1988) and Naismith and Wooden Award winner. Final Four most outstanding player for 1988 national champion and also leading scorer and second-leading rebounder for 1986 Final Four team. Posted 20.5 ppg and 7.3 rpg. in 16 NCAA games.

Seasons	Games	Points	FG	FT	Rebounds	PPG Average
4 (1985-88)	147	2951	1216	509	1187 (8.1)	20.1

Scott May — Indiana, F (6-7), National Player of the Year (1976)

Star of undefeated national champion Indiana team which many consider the best starting five in collegiate history. Two-time All-American and Naismith Award winner. Leading scorer (23.5 ppg) and second leading rebounder for last undefeated NCAA champions. Leading rebounder and second leading scorer on 1976 US Olympic team. Averaged 14.4 points in eight NCAA games.

Seasons	Games	Points	FG	FT	Rebounds	PPG Average
4 (1973-76)	90	1593	666	261	594 (6.6)	17.7

Gene Melchiorre — Bradley, G (5-8), All-American (1951)

Brilliant playmaking and shooting guard of post-war period whose many accomplishments unfortunately dimmed by involvement in 1951 collegiate point-shaving scandals. Averaged 15.3 points in three games for 1950 NCAA runner-up and 16.7 points in six games for NIT Final Four team of 1949, 1950.

Seasons	Games	Points	FG	FT	Rebounds	PPG Average
4 (1948-51)	137	1581	544	493	NA	11.5

Xavier McDaniel — Wichita State, C (6-7), All-American (1985)

First player in NCAA history (and one of only three, with Hank Gathers and Kurt Thomas) to lead nation in both scoring and rebounding in same season. Two-time national rebounding leader (1983 and 1985) and also third as junior.

Seasons	Games	Points	FG	FT	Rebounds	PPG Average
4 (1982-85)	117	2152	893	366	1359 (11.6)	18.4

Billy "The Hill" McGill — Utah, C (6-9), All-American (1961, 1962)

Posted highest-scoring single season ever for college center. Averaged 38.8 as senior to lead nation and also logged single-game 60-point outburst. During sensational senior year finished in top 10 nationally in field-goal percentage while scoring nearly 40 ppg. Led team to Final Four as a junior and averaged 23.7 points and 10.7 rebounds in seven (1960, 1961) NCAA Tournament games.

Seasons	Games	Points	FG	FT	Rebounds	PPG Average
3 (1960-62)	86	2321	916	489	1106 (12.9)	27.0

George Mikan — DePaul, C (6-10), National Player of the Year (1944, 1945)

Three-time consensus first-team All-American, two-time national scoring leader (1945, 1946, before official NCAA statistics), and NIT Final Four most outstanding player in 1945. Leading scorer as freshman for 1943 NCAA Final Four team. Shared spotlight with Bob Kurland in World War II era as game's first two marquee big men. Leading scorer in NIT (28.2 ppg) in 1944 and 1945.

Seasons	Games	Points	FG	FT	Rebounds	PPG Average
4 (1943-46)	96	1870	709	452	NA	19.1

Bill Mlkvy — Temple, F (6-4), All-American (1951)

One-season wonder who led nation in scoring (29.2) as a junior and earned one of the sport's most memorable nicknames ("The Owl Without a Vowel") because of his unusual name. Also a national runner-up in rebounds in 1951.

Seasons	Games	Points	FG	FT	Rebounds	PPG Average
3 (1950-52)	73	1539	624	291	NA	21.1

Earl "The Pearl" Monroe — Winston-Salem State, G (6-4)

True paragon of offensive moves who led nation's small-school scorers with remarkable 41.5 average (third highest ever) and a record 1329 points in 1967. Perhaps possessed the greatest below-the-rim one-on-one moves in history. Enjoyed one of greatest single season efforts in college history in 1967, leading Winston-Salem to Division II title (31-1) and shooting 60 percent from field.

Seasons	Games	Points	FG	FT	Rebounds	PPG Average
4 (1964-67)	88	2772	1087	598	596 (6.7)	31.5

Rick Mount — Purdue, G (6-4), All-American (1969, 1970)

One of game's most deadly and exciting long-range shooters. All-time Big Ten scoring leader (per game average) with seventh highest Division I career mark (32.3). Averaged 30.5 ppg in four NCAA Tournament appearances for

Purdue's 1969 national runner-up. Member of 1969 All-Tourney team and only one among great scorers of late-'60s (including Maravich, Murphy, Carr, Dwight Lamar, Bird Averitt, Travis Grant) to play for a top 10 ranked team.

Seasons	Games	Points	FG	FT	Rebounds	PPG Average
3 (1968-70)	72	2323	910	503	211 (2.9)	32.2

Calvin Murphy — Niagara, G (5-9), All-American (1969, 1970)

Shares honors with Johnny O'Brien as college basketball's greatest all-time sub-six-foot offensive wizard. Displayed incomparable shooting, dribbling and passing skills and uncanny free-throw shooting abilities. Second in nation (to Maravich) in scoring (38.2 ppg) as sophomore, third as junior (32.4), and eighth as senior. Hit for 68 points in single 1969 game versus Syracuse and averaged 29.3 points and 6.3 rebounds in three NCAA Tournament games. Owns fourth- highest career scoring average (after Maravich, Carr, Robertson).

Seasons	Games	Points	FG	FT	Rebounds	PPG Average
3 (1968-70)	77	2548	947	654	308 (4.0)	33.1

Johnny Neumann — Mississippi, F-G (6-6), All-American (1971)

Greatest "single-season wonder" in collegiate history and only 40 points-per-game career scorer (Division I) besides Pete Maravich. Also only sophomore besides Maravich to average 40 ppg. National scoring leader for single 1971 season.

Seasons	Games	Points	FG	FT	Rebounds	PPG Average
1 (1971)	23	923	366	191	152 (6.6)	40.1

Johnny O'Brien — Seattle, G (5-8), All-American (1953)

Diminutive pure shooter and unstoppable scorer who put equally tiny Seattle University on basketball map before Elgin Baylor. Earned lasting fame with 43-point exhibition game versus Harlem Globetrotters when he played pivot position against Goose Tatum. First collegian to score 1000 points in single season (1051 in 1952). Third leading scorer as senior (would have led nation as junior but Seattle still Division II). Graduated as career scoring record holder (later passed by Oscar Robertson). Played big league baseball with Pittsburgh.

Seasons	Games	Points	FG	FT	Rebounds	PPG Average
3 (1951-53)	106	2733	904	925	NA	25.8

Akeem (Hakeem) Olajuwon — Houston, C (7-0), All-American (1984)

Powerful inside rebounding and defensive force for two-time NCAA runner-up in 1983 and 1984. One of handful of players to appear in NCAA Final Four all three seasons and Final Four most outstanding player in 1983 (as junior). Led nation in rebounding (13.5), blocked shots (5.6), and field-goal percentage (.675) as senior in 1984. Twice member of NCAA All-Tournament team and one of the most dominant Final Four players in NCAA Tournament history.

Seasons	Games	Points	FG	FT	Rebounds	PPG Average
4 (1981-84)	100	1332	532	268	1067 (10.7)	13.3

Shaquille O'Neal — LSU, C (7-1), National Player of the Year (1991)

Two-time unanimous first-team All-American who lead nation in rebounds (14.7) in 1991 and blocked shots (5.2) in 1992. Most intimidating big man on both offense and defense in SEC history. Averaged 24 ppg and 13.2 rebounds in five NCAA contests (1990-1992). Left LSU as the top NBA draft pick of 1992.

Seasons	Games	Points	FG	FT	Rebounds	PPG Average
3 (1990-92)	90	1941	786	369	1217 (13.5)	21.6

Bob Pettit — Louisiana State, F-C (6-9), All-American (1954)

One of greatest big men in SEC history and biggest Dixie attraction during the early 1950s outside of Adolph Rupp's Kentucky teams. Leading scorer, rebounder for 1953 Final Four team while averaging 30.5 points in six NCAA games (1953, 1954). Second to Frank Selvy in 1954 national scoring race.

Seasons	Games	Points	FG	FT	Rebounds	PPG Average
3 (1952-54)	69	1893	711	471	1010 (14.6)	27.4

David Robinson — Navy, C (7-0), National Player of the Year (1987)

Naismith and Wooden Award winner as senior; nation's rebounding leader (13.0) as junior. Top shot-blocker in country during final two seasons. Averaged 28.6 ppg, 12.3 rebounds in seven NCAA Tournament games. Star of two Olympic teams (1988, 1992) and one Pan-Am Games team (1987).

Seasons	Games	Points	FG	FT	Rebounds	PPG Average
4 (1984-87)	127	2669	1032	604	1314 (10.3)	21.0

Glenn Robinson — Purdue, F (6-8), National Player of the Year (1994)

Nation's scoring leader (30.3) in 1994 and first player in Big Ten to score 1000 points (all games) in a single season. Set Big Ten season's record of 560 points (conference games) and averaged 31.4 ppg and 9.8 rebounds in five NCAA contests. One of greatest single-season stars in collegiate basketball history.

Seasons	Games	Points	FG	FT	Rebounds	PPG Average
2 (1993-94)	62	1706	614	367	602 (9.7)	27.5

Guy Rodgers — Temple, G (6-0), All-American (1957, 1958)

Flashiest and fastest backcourt star in Philadelphia collegiate history; paced Temple to three consecutive national third-place finishes (twice in NCAA, once in NIT). Leading scorer (20.1) and All-Tourney selection with 1958 NCAA Final Four team. Averaged 23.3 points in three NIT games.

Seasons	Games	Points	FG	FT	Rebounds	PPG Average
3 (1956-58)	90	1767	708	351	587 (6.5)	19.6

Lenny Rosenbluth — North Carolina, F (6-5), All-American (1957)

Leading scorer (28 ppg), second leading rebounder for undefeated 1957 NCAA champions. Member of NCAA All-Tournament team in 1957; averaged 28 points, 9.2 rebounds in five NCAA games. Ranked in top 10 in country in scoring final two seasons and led ACC in scoring as junior.

Seasons	Games	Points	FG	FT	Rebounds	PPG Average
3 (1955-57)	76	2045	721	603	790 (10.4)	26.9

Ralph Sampson — Virginia, C (7-4), National Player of the Year (1981-83)

Most celebrated big man in collegiate history with three national-player-of-the-year awards, three Naismith Awards and two Wooden Awards, and three-time unanimous All-American selection. Led ACC in rebounding three seasons (second once) and paced Virginia to ACC title as sophomore. Leading rebounder and second-leading scorer on 1981 NCAA third-place team. NIT MVP for 1980 championship team and averaged 19.2 ppg in five NIT games.

Seasons	Games	Points	FG	FT	Rebounds	PPG Average
4 (1980-83)	132	2228	899	427	1511 (11.4)	16.9

Frank Selvy — Furman, F (6-3), All-American (1954)

College basketball's first 40 ppg scorer for a full season and two-time national scoring champion. Only Division I player to score 100 points in a single game. Sixth best all-time career scoring average. Did not play in NCAAs or NIT.

Seasons	Games	Points	FG	FT	Rebounds	PPG Average
3 (1952-54)	78	2538	922	694	NA	32.5

Bill Sharman — Southern California, G (6-1), All-American (1950)

Dual sports star who later made Brooklyn Dodgers big league roster and also enjoyed Hall of Fame NBA career with Cousy-era Boston Celtics. Exceptional free-throw shooter with collegiate career average above 80%. Did not play in postseason. Last USC consensus All-American until Harold Miner in 1992.

Seasons	Games	Points	FG	FT	Rebounds	PPG Average
4 (1947-50)	82	1107	429	249	NA	13.5

329

Paul Silas — Creighton, F-C (6-7), All-Time College Rebounding Leader

Holds career three-year record for total rebounds and stands sixth on the all-time rebound list. One of the game's supreme post players and also one of six averaging over 20 points and rebounds for entire career. National rebounding leader in 1963 (own lowest single-season total of 20.6) and second other two years (trailing Jerry Lucas in 1960). Averaged 17.5 ppg in six NCAA games.

Seasons	Games	Points	FG	FT	Rebounds	PPG Average
3 (1962-64)	81	1661	643	375	1751 (21.6)	20.5

Lionel Simmons — La Salle, F (6-7), National Player of the Year (1990)

Trails only Tom Gola with career total of 4646 combined points and rebounds. Naismith and Wooden Award winner in 1990 and two-time All-American. Averaged 26.5 points and 12 rebounds in four NCAA games (1988-90) and 23.4 points and 10.4 rebounds in five NIT games for 1987 second-place finisher. Third behind Maravich and Freeman Williams on all-time career scoring list.

Seasons	Games	Points	FG	FT	Rebounds	PPG Average
4 (1987-90)	131	3217	1244	673	1429 (10.9)	24.6

Bill Spivey — Kentucky, C (7-0), All-American (1951)

Towering center Baron Rupp thought was even better than earlier "Fabulous Five" All-American Alex Groza. Leading scorer (19.2) and rebounder on 1951 NCAA championship team. Dropped from university after two seasons and banned from NBA for alleged involvement with 1951 point-shaving scandal.

Seasons	Games	Points	FG	FT	Rebounds	PPG Average
2 (1950-51)	63	1213	477	259	NA	19.3

Dave Stallworth — Wichita State, F (6-7), All-American (1967, 1969)

Among select group of players averaging 20 ppg or better in four different seasons. Averaged 29.5 ppg, 19.5 rebounds in two NCAA games; 17 ppg in two NIT contests. Poured in 46 to lead Wichita State to upset victory ending defending NCAA champion Cincinnati's 37-game win streak.

Seasons	Games	Points	FG	FT	Rebounds	PPG Average
4 (1962-65)	79	1918	714	490	827 (10.5)	24.3

Tom Stith — St. Bonaventure, F (6-5), All-American (1960, 1961)

Runner-up to Oscar Robertson in national scoring race as junior and third in nation as senior. Averaged 29 ppg in three NCAA Tournament games and 24.8 in five NIT contests. Leading scorer (35.4 ppg in four games) in 1960 NIT and paced team to record 99 straight home court victories through 1961.

Seasons	Games	Points	FG	FT	Rebounds	PPG Average
3 (1959-61)	76	2052	807	438	711 (9.4)	27.0

David Thompson — NC State, F (6-4), National Player of the Year (1974, 1975)

Sensational high-flying dunker; the original "Air Jordan" of collegiate basketball. Two-time player of the year, Final Four MVP for 1974 NCAA national champions. Among nation's top five in scoring final two seasons. Averaged 24.3 points and 7.3 rebounds in four NCAA Tournament games.

Seasons	Games	Points	FG	FT	Rebounds	PPG Average
3 (1973-75)	86	2309	939	431	694 (8.1)	26.8

Wayman Tisdale — Oklahoma, F (6-8), All-American (1983, 1984, 1985)

Ranked among nation's top 10 scorers all three seasons and rare three-time first-team All-American. Leading rebounder (6.4) for 1984 US Olympic team. Averaged 22.6 points and 9.6 rebounds in seven NCAA Tournament games.

Seasons	Games	Points	FG	FT	Rebounds	PPG Average
3 (1983-85)	104	2661	1077	507	1048 (10.1)	25.6

Wes Unseld — Louisville, C (6-7), All-American (1967, 1968)

Collected 35 points and 26 rebounds in one NIT game in 1966. Averaged 20.5 points and 17.5 rebounds during four NCAA Tournament games (1967, 1968). Finished second (1966), third (1967) and fourth (1968) in the nation in rebounds during three-year career. A superb collegiate rebounder who would also become one of the best boards men in NBA history. One of only two players (with Chamberlain) to be NBA's MVP and top rookie in same season.

Seasons	Games	Points	FG	FT	Rebounds	PPG Average
3 (1966-68)	82	1686	630	426	1551 (18.9)	20.6

Chet "The Jet" Walker — Bradley, F (6-6), All-American (1961, 1962)

A freewheeling lane driver and nearly unstoppable offensive threat who finished among the nation's top 10 scorers as both a junior and senior. Did not play in NCAAs but averaged 23.5 points in four NIT games. Leading scorer (21.8 ppg) as a sophomore for NIT champions, and also fourth in country in field-goal percentage (.560) that same year.

Seasons	Games	Points	FG	FT	Rebounds	PPG Average
3 (1960-62)	81	1975	750	475	1036 (12.8)	24.4

Jimmy Walker — Providence, G (6-3), All-American (1966, 1967)

Country's top scorer (30.4) in 1967. Averaged 20 ppg in four NCAA games, 36.5 ppg in two NIT games. Most prolific offensive threat among great lineage of star Providence guards during '60s and early '70s which included Lenny Wilkens, Johnny Egan, Vinnie Ernst, Ray Flynn, Ernie DiGregorio.

Seasons	Games	Points	FG	FT	Rebounds	PPG Average
3 (1965-67)	81	2045	782	481	509 (6.3)	25.2

Nick Werkman — Seton Hall, F (6-3)

Ninth highest career scoring average of all-time and national scoring leader in 1963 (during only season under 30 ppg). Third in national scoring race as sophomore and second as senior. Never played in postseason NCAA or NIT.

Seasons	Games	Points	FG	FT	Rebounds	PPG Average
3 (1962-64)	71	2273	812	649	1036 (14.6)	32.0

Jerry West — West Virginia, G-F (6-3), All-American (1959, 1960)

Fabulous pure shooter and all-around offensive talent who remained in the shadows of Oscar Robertson yet took his team to NCAA championship game as junior (1959). Fifth in nation in scoring as junior (26.6) and fourth as senior (29.3). Leading scorer and rebounder on 1959 NCAA runner-up and Tourney MVP winner. Averaged 30.6 ppg and 13.8 rebounds in nine NCAA games.

Seasons	Games	Points	FG	FT	Rebounds	PPG Average
3 (1958-60)	93	2309	843	623	1240 (13.3)	24.8

Sidney Wicks — UCLA, F-C (6-8), National Player of the Year (1971)

Leading scorer and rebounder for national champions in 1970 and 1971 and also starter on 1969 NCAA championship team. Final Four most outstanding player in 1970 and member of All-Tournament team in both 1970 and 1971. Averaged 13.3 points and 9.3 rebounds in 12 NCAA games. Also averaged 26 ppg and 19.5 rebounds in one season at Santa Monica Community College.

Seasons	Games	Points	FG	FT	Rebounds	PPG Average
3 (1969-71)	90	1423	549	325	894 (9.9)	15.8

Freeman Williams — Portland State, G (6-4), All-American (1978)

National scoring leader for 1977 and 1978 and runner-up in 1976. Second behind Maravich on all-time Division I career scoring list (total points). Also second (by 15) to Maravich in career field goals. Did not play in postseason.

Seasons	Games	Points	FG	FT	Rebounds	PPG Average
4 (1975-78)	106	3249	1369	511	458 (4.3)	30.7

Three-time national player of the year Ralph Sampson of Virginia was one of the most celebrated performers in collegiate basketball history. (University of Virginia photo)

James Worthy — North Carolina, F (6-9), All-American (1982)

NCAA Final Four most outstanding player of 1982 as leading scorer and second-leading rebounder on national champion. Started on 1981 Final Four team and averaged 15.3 points and 5.5 rebounds in 10 NCAA Tourney games.

Seasons	Games	Points	FG	FT	Rebounds	PPG Average
3 (1980-82)	84	1219	485	249	620 (7.4)	14.5

Thirty Most Memorable College Coaches of All Time

Forrest "Phog" Allen (Baker, Haskell, Central Missouri State, Kansas)

Legendary mentor of two Helms Foundation national champions (1922, 1923) and one NCAA tournament winner (1952). Holds the record for most years coached (48). His 1953 team lost to Indiana in the NCAA title game. Was an assistant to James Naismith at beginning of his career, then coached Adolph Rupp in his middle years and Dean Smith at the end of his tenure. Recruited Wilt Chamberlain for Kansas but forced to retire before Wilt's 1957 debut.

Years	Games	Wins-Losses	Pct.	National (Tournament) Championships
48 (1908-56)	1010	746-264	.739	1922, 1923 (Helms), 1952 (NCAA)

Clair Bee (Rider, Long Island University)

Today remembered for his series of juvenile sports novels but also one of the top coaches during the '30s-'40s heyday-era of New York City basketball. Won two NIT championships (1939, 1941) and owns second-highest career winning percentage. Retired during the embarrassment of 1951 point-shaving scandals.

Years	Games	Wins-Losses	Pct.	National (Tournament) Championships
21 (1929-51)	499	412-87	.826	1939 (Helms), 1939, 1941 (NIT)

Lou Carnesecca (St. John's)

Greatest modern-era New York City coach with sixteen 20-victory seasons and two 30-win campaigns. Twice named National Coach of the Year (1983 and 1985). Won NIT in 1989 and guided 1985 team to NCAA Final Four (which featured three Big East Conference teams). Three-year coach of ABA New York Nets.

Years	Games	Wins-Losses	Pct.	National (Tournament) Championships
24 (1966-70, 74-92)	726	526-200	.725	1989 (NIT)

Everett Case (North Carolina State)

Coached six Southern Conference Tournament champions (1947-51, 1953) and four Atlantic Coast Conference Tourney winners (1954-56, 1959). Twenty or more victories in each of his first ten seasons. Reached NCAA Final Four (third) in 1950 and NIT Final Four (third) in 1947. Naismith Hall of Famer.

Years	Games	Wins-Losses	Pct.	National (Tournament) Championships
18 (1947-64)	511	377-134	.738	None

Everett Dean (Carleton, Indiana, Stanford)

Led Stanford to 1942 NCAA championship. Won three Midwest Conference titles with Carleton College, three Big Ten (Western Conference) crowns at Indiana, and two Pacific Coast Conference championships at Stanford. Took Stanford baseball team to 1953 College World Series. Only coach to capture NCAA Tourney in single appearance (thus only undefeated coach in NCAA postseason play).

Years	Games	Wins-Losses	Pct.	National (Tournament) Championships
28 (1922-51)	591	374-217	.633	1942 (NCAA)

Ed Diddle (Western Kentucky)

Shares record with Ray Meyer of De Paul for most seasons (42) coached at one school. Coached four Ohio Valley Conference Tournament champions (1949, 1952-54). Took team to NIT Final Four three times (second in 1942, third in 1948, fourth in 1954). Eighteen seasons with 20 victories or more and five seasons with 28 wins or better. Fourth on all-time victory list, and only Baron Rupp and Dean Smith have more wins with single school. Naismith Hall of Famer.

Years	Games	Wins-Losses	Pct.	National (Tournament) Championships
42 (1923-64)	1061	759-302	.715	None

Howard Hobson (South Oregon, Oregon, Yale)

Coached the first NCAA Tourney winner at Oregon in 1939. Early advocate of the fast-break style of offense and later influential member of US Olympic rules committee. Won 100-plus games, one Ivy League title (1949) at Yale.

Years	Games	Wins-Losses	Pct.	National (Tournament) Championships
24 (1933-56)	658	431-270	.615	1939 (NCAA)

Nat Holman (CCNY)

Star player for the '20s-era Original Celtics who earned greatest fame as only coach to win NCAA and NIT tournaments in the same season. Saw double-champion Cinderella CCNY team dismantled and disgraced by the 1951 point-fixing scandals. Suffered no losing seasons during first 23 years at CCNY. Also coached teams to NCAA Final Four in 1947 (4th) and NIT Final Four in 1941.

Years	Games	Wins-Losses	Pct.	National (Tournament) Championships
37 (1920-60)	658	423-190	.690	1950 (NIT), 1950 (NCAA)

Hank Iba (Northwest Missouri State, Colorado, Oklahoma State)

Three-time US Olympic team mentor (1964, 1968, 1972) and holder of NCAA career record for most total games coached (1105). Reached NCAA Final Four 4 times (1945, 1946, 1949, 1951) and NIT Final Four 3 times (1938, 1940, 1944). Coached first back-to-back NCAA Tournament champions in 1945 and 1946.

Years	Games	Wins-Losses	Pct.	National (Tournament) Championships
41 (1930-70)	1105	767-338	.694	1945, 1946 (NCAA)

Ed Jucker (King's Point, Rensselaer, Cincinnati, Rollins)

Inherited Cincinnati program year after Oscar Robertson's departure and took team to NCAA championship game next three straight seasons. National Coach of the Year in 1963. Owns NCAA Tournament record for highest winning percentage (11-1, .917) among coaches appearing in at least 10 games.

Years	Games	Wins-Losses	Pct.	National (Tournament) Championships
17 (1946-77)	375	266-109	.709	1961, 1962 (NCAA)

Frank Keaney (Rhode Island)

Pioneered in the '30s with the fast-breaking style of running offense that would eventually become the preferred method of play. Had only one losing season (his first) in 27 years at Rhode Island and won seven straight New England Conference titles. Best teams featured sharpshooter Ernie Calverley in the war era and finished 4th (1945) and 2nd (1946, to Kentucky) in the NIT.

Years	Games	Wins-Losses	Pct.	National (Tournament) Championships
27 (1922-48)	504	387-117	.768	None

Bobby Knight (Army, Indiana)

One of the most successful and also controversial coaches in collegiate history. As well known for tempestuous and haughty behavior with players, fans and media as for his three NCAA titles (1976, 1981, 1987) and one NIT championship (1979). Has reached NCAA Final Four five times and coached undefeated 1976 Indiana NCAA championship team many consider the best ever. Olympic team coach in 1984 and winningest coach in Big Ten history.

Years	Games	Wins-Losses	Pct.	National (Tournament) Championships
30 (1966-95)	894	659-235	.737	1976, 1981, 1987 (NCAA), 1979 (NIT)

Mike Krzyzewski (Army, Duke)

Three-time National Coach of the Year (1986, 1989, 1991) and winner of two NCAA titles (1991, 1992). Reached Final Four seven times in nine-year stretch (1986-1994) including five times in a row. Served as a player (Army) and an assistant coach (Indiana) under Bob Knight. Olympic team assistant in 1992.

Years	Games	Wins-Losses	Pct.	National (Tournament) Championships
20 (1976-95)	636	435-201	.684	1991, 1992 (NCAA)

Ward "Piggy" Lambert (Purdue)

Perfected fast-breaking style of play with All-Americans John Wooden and Charles "Stretch" Murphy at Purdue in early '30s. Won or shared 11 Big Ten championships during 29-year career with Boilermakers. Coach of the 1932 Helms National Championship team and suffered only three losing seasons.

Years	Games	Wins-Losses	Pct.	National (Tournament) Championships
29 (1917-46)	523	371-152	.709	1932 (Helms)

Joe Lapchick (St. John's)

Legendary player with 1920s-era Original Celtics and, at 6-5, reputed to be basketball's first genuine "big man" post player. Coached St. John's to four NIT titles (1943, 1944, 1959, 1965) during 20-year career there and posted 326-247 pro record with New York Knicks (1948-1956), reaching NBA finals twice.

Years	Games	Wins-Losses	Pct.	National (Tournament) Championships
20 (1937-47, 57-65)	464	335-129	.722	1943, 1944, 1959, 1965 (NIT)

All-time Michigan great Cazzie Russell (33) scores in a 1965 Big Ten game against Ohio State. (University of Michigan photo)

Guy Lewis (Houston)

Two-time National Coach of the Year (1968, 1983) and also coach of four Southwest Conference Tournament champions (1978, 1981, 1983, 1984). Never won NCAAs but reached Final Four five times, including three in a row and two losses in the finals (1983, 1984). Coach of famed "Phi Slamma Jamma" 1984 Houston team with Akeem Olajuwon and Clyde "The Glyde" Drexler, and also of 1967 NCAA third-place team with scoring champion Elvin Hayes.

Years	Games	Wins-Losses	Pct.	National (Tournament) Championships
30 (1957-86)	871	592-279	.680	None

Ken Loeffler (Geneva, Yale, La Salle, Texas A&M)

Forever associated with great La Salle team that spanned the career of Tom Gola (1952-55). Claimed one NIT title (1952) and one NCAA crown (1954) and lost in NCAA title game to San Francisco in 1955. Successful pro coach during early NBA (BAA) years with Providence Steamrollers and St. Louis Bombers.

Years	Games	Wins-Losses	Pct.	National (Tournament) Championships
22 (1929-57)	508	310-198	.610	1952 (NIT), 1954 (NCAA)

Al McGuire (Belmont Abbey, Marquette)

Twice named National Coach of the year (1971, 1974). Winner of one NIT title (1970) and one NCAA title (1977), the latter in his final season. Had two other teams in the national championship game (1967 in NIT and 1974 in NCAA). His Marquette teams won more than 20 games in each of his final 11 seasons.

Years	Games	Wins-Losses	Pct.	National (Tournament) Championships
20 (1958-77)	548	405-143	.739	1970 (NIT), 1977 (NCAA)

Phil Woolpert brought early West Coast basketball to its zenith when his San Francisco Dons claimed back-to-back NCAA titles in 1955-56. (San Francisco University photo)

Frank McGuire (St. John's, North Carolina, South Carolina)

Only coach to win more than 100 games at three different schools (103 with St. John's, 164 with North Carolina, 283 with South Carolina). Directed North Carolina to their 1957 undefeated NCAA championship season. Also took St. John's to College World Series as baseball coach and coached Philadelphia Warriors when Wilt Chamberlain averaged 50 ppg. Naismith Hall of Famer.

Years	Games	Wins-Losses	Pct.	National (Tournament) Championships
30 (1948-52, 53-61, 65-80)	785	550-235	.701	1957 (NCAA)

Walter "Doc" Meanwell (Wisconsin, Missouri)

Famed for carefully choreographed offensive patterns that established the disciplined style of play popular in the '20s and early '30s. Coached nine Big Ten champions in first dozen seasons of 22-year career. Coach of three Helms National Championship teams (1912, 1914 and 1916). Charter member of the National Association of Basketball Coaches and leader of movement in late '20s to eliminate the dribble as a legal strategy.

Years	Games	Wins-Losses	Pct.	National (Tournament) Championships
22 (1912-34)	381	280-101	.735	1912, 1914, 1916 (Helms)

Ray Meyer (DePaul)

Won 1945 NIT championship and coached two other teams (1944, 1983) in NIT title game. Twice appeared in NCAA Final Four. Sixth on the all-time career winning list. Coached two national players of the year (Mikan in 1944 and 1945, and Aguirre in 1980) almost four decades apart. Shares the longest coaching tenure at one school (42 years) with Ed Diddle of Western Kentucky.

Years	Games	Wins-Losses	Pct.	National (Tournament) Championships
42 (1943-84)	1078	724-354	.672	1945 (NIT)

Ralph Miller (Wichita State, Iowa, Oregon State)

Earned 33 winning seasons during 38-year tenure at three different schools. Eight 20-win seasons near the end of his career in 1980s. Seventh on all-time winning list among Division I coaches. Twice named National Coach of the Year (1981, 1982). Played under legendary Phog Allen at Kansas in early 1940s.

Years	Games	Wins-Losses	Pct.	National (Tournament) Championships
38 (1952-89)	1044	674-370	.646	None

Pete Newell (San Francisco, Michigan State, California)

Brought San Francisco to prominence with NIT title in 1949, then coached California to back-to-back Final Four appearances, including NCAA title in 1959. Both UPI National Coach of the Year and Olympic head coach in 1960. Proponent of disciplined, patterned offensive schemes who learned his trade with Phil Woolpert under mentor James Needles at Loyola of Los Angeles.

Years	Games	Wins-Losses	Pct.	National (Tournament) Championships
14 (1947-60)	357	234-123	.655	1949 (NIT), 1959 (NCAA)

Adolph "Baron" Rupp (Kentucky)

College basketball's all-time winningest coach and leader of four NCAA national champions (1948, 1949, 1951, 1958) and one NIT champion (1946). Served 41 seasons at Kentucky without a single losing season. Won three national titles with his greatest teams even though star players were shaving points. Won 24 SEC championships and also 13 league tournaments. Leading candidate with John Wooden for the mythical title of all-time greatest coach.

Years	Games	Wins-Losses	Pct.	National (Tournament) Championships
41 (1931-72)	1066	876-190	.822	1946 (NIT), 1948, 1949, 1951, 1958 (NCAA)

Dean Smith (North Carolina)

Scheduled to become college basketball's winningest coach before the end of the 1997 season. Only Division I 800-game winner outside of Adolph Rupp. Twice National Coach of the Year (1977, 1979), twice NCAA Tournament winner (1982, 1993), US Olympic team head coach in 1976. Has won more NCAA tournament games (60) than anyone and has been in more Final Fours (10) than anyone but John Wooden. One of only two men (along with Indiana's Bobby Knight) to win the NCAA title as both a player and a coach.

Years	Games	Wins-Losses	Pct.	National (Tournament) Championships
34 (1962-95)	1066	830-236	.778	1971 (NIT), 1982, 1993 (NCAA)

Jerry Tarkanian (Long Beach State, UNLV, Fresno State)

Joins Adolph Rupp (.822) and John Wooden (.804) as only major college coaches with lifetime winning percentages above .800. His UNLV team of mid-80s and early '90s is only one to compile 300 or more victories in single 10-year span. Fifth on the all-time list with 37 NCAA tournament victories.

Years	Games	Wins-Losses	Pct.	National (Tournament) Championships
24 (1969-92)	756	631-125	.837	1990 (NCAA)

Fred Taylor (Ohio State)

Guided Jerry Lucas-John Havlicek Ohio State team to three straight national title games and the 1960 NCAA crown. Only Big Ten coach ever to win five consecutive league titles. Two-time national Coach of the Year (1961, 1962). Was one of the youngest coaches (35) ever to claim an NCAA championship.

Years	Games	Wins-Losses	Pct.	National (Tournament) Championships
18 (1959-76)	455	297-158	.7653	1960 (NCAA)

John Thompson (Georgetown)

Three-time National Coach of the Year (USBWA, 1982; NABC, 1985; UPI, 1987) and coach of 1984 NCAA title winners. Reached Final Four three times (1982, 1984, 1985). Coach of six Big East Conference Tournament champions at Georgetown and also 1988 Olympic head coach. Produced three of the best recent big men in Patrick Ewing, Dikembe Mutombo and Alonzo Mourning.

Years	Games	Wins-Losses	Pct.	National (Tournament) Championships
23 (1973-95)	724	524-200	.724	1984 (NCAA)

John Wooden (Indiana State, UCLA)

Builder of the greatest "dynasty" in American sports history with seven straight NCAA titles and ten in twelve years. Won record 39 straight NCAA tournament games. Elected National Coach of the Year a record six times and also a Naismith Hall of Famer. Recruited and trained perhaps the two greatest college centers ever in Lew Alcindor (Kareem Abdul-Jabbar) and Bill Walton. Also three-time All-American player and Helms National Player of the Year.

Years	Games	Wins-Losses	Pct.	National (Tournament) Championships
29 (1947-75)	826	664-162	.804	1964, 1965, 1967, 1968, 1969, 1970, 1971, 1972, 1973, 1975 (NCAA)

Phil Woolpert (San Francisco, San Diego)

Directed San Francisco team of Bill Russell and K.C. Jones to back-to-back NCAA titles (1955 and 1956) and also to record 60-game unbeaten streak. Took Dons back to Final Four without Russell in 1957 and finished third. Twice UPI National Coach of the Year (1955, 1956) and a Naismith Hall of Famer.

Years	Games	Wins-Losses	Pct.	National (Tournament) Championships
16 (1951-69)	403	239-164	.593	1955, 1956 (NCAA)

Statistical Appendices

Year-by-Year NCAA Tournament Results

Year	Champion (Coach)	Score	Runner-Up	Third Place	MVP	Site
1939	Oregon (Howard Hobson)	46-33	Ohio State	Okla/Vill.#	None Selected	Evanston
1940	Indiana (Branch McCracken)	60-42	Kansas	Duq./So. Cal#	Marv Huffman (Indiana)	Kansas City
1941	Wisconsin (Harold Foster)	39-34	Wash. St.	Pitt./Ark.#	John Kotz (Wisconsin)	Kansas City
1942	Stanford (Everett Dean)	53-38	Dartmouth	Colo./Ken.#	Howie Dallmar (Stanford)	Kansas City
1943	Wyoming (Everett Shelton)	46-43	Georgetown	Tex./DePaul#	Kenny Sailors (Wyoming)	New York
1944	Utah (Vadal Peterson)	42-40*	Dartmouth	Ia. St./Ohio St.#	Arnie Ferrin (Utah)	New York
1945	Oklahoma A&M (Henry Iba)	49-45	NYU	Ark./Ohio St.#	Bob Kurland (Okla. A&M)	New York
1946	Oklahoma A&M (Henry Iba)	43-40	N. Carolina	Ohio State	Bob Kurland (Okla. A&M)	New York
1947	Holy Cross (Alvin Julian)	58-47	Oklahoma	Texas	George Kaftan (Holy Cross)	New York
1948	Kentucky (Adolph Rupp)	58-42	Baylor	Holy Cross	Alex Groza (Kentucky)	New York
1949	Kentucky (Adolph Rupp)	46-36	Okla. A&M	Illinois	Alex Groza (Kentucky)	Seattle
1950	CCNY (Nat Holman)	71-68	Bradley	N.C. State	Irwin Dambrot (CCNY)	New York
1951	Kentucky (Adolph Rupp)	68-58	Kansas State	Illinois	None Selected	Minneapolis
1952	Kansas (Phog Allen)	80-63	St. John's	Illinois	Clyde Lovellette (Kansas)	Seattle
1953	Indiana (Branch McCracken)	69-68	Kansas	Washington	B. H. Born (Kansas)	Kansas City
1954	La Salle (Ken Loeffler)	92-76	Bradley	Penn State	Tom Gola (La Salle)	Kansas City
1955	S. Francisco (Phil Woolpert)	77-63	La Salle	Colorado	Bill Russell (S. Francisco)	Kansas City
1956	S. Francisco (Phil Woolpert)	83-71	Iowa	Temple	Hal Lear (Temple)	Evanston
1957	N. Carolina (Frank McGuire)	54-53+	Kansas	S. Francisco	Wilt Chamberlain (Kansas)	Kansas City
1958	Kentucky (Adolph Rupp)	84-72	Seattle	Temple	Elgin Baylor (Seattle)	Louisville
1959	California (Pete Newell)	71-70	W. Virginia	Cincinnati	Jerry West (W. Virginia)	Louisville
1960	Ohio State (Fred Taylor)	75-55	California	Cincinnati	Jerry Lucas (Ohio State)	S. Francisco
1961	Cincinnati (Ed Jucker)	70-65*	Ohio State	St. Joseph's##	Jerry Lucas (Ohio State)	Kansas City
1962	Cincinnati (Ed Jucker)	71-59	Ohio State	Wake Forest	Paul Hogue (Cincinnati)	Louisville
1963	Loyola (George Ireland)	60-58*	Cincinnati	Duke	Art Heyman (Duke)	Louisville
1964	UCLA (John Wooden)	98-83	Duke	Michigan	Walt Hazzard (UCLA)	Kansas City
1965	UCLA (John Wooden)	91-80	Michigan	Princeton	Bill Bradley (Princeton)	Portland
1966	Texas Western (Don Haskins)	72-65	Kentucky	Duke	Jerry Chambers (Utah)	College Park
1967	UCLA (John Wooden)	79-64	Dayton	Houston	Lew Alcindor (UCLA)	Louisville
1968	UCLA (John Wooden)	78-55	N. Carolina	Ohio State	Lew Alcindor (UCLA)	Los Angeles
1969	UCLA (John Wooden)	92-72	Purdue	Drake	Lew Alcindor (UCLA)	Louisville
1970	UCLA (John Wooden)	80-69	Jacksonville	New Mexico St.	Sidney Wicks (UCLA)	College Park
1971	UCLA (John Wooden)	68-62	Villanova##	W. Kentucky##	Howard Porter (Vill)++	Houston
1972	UCLA (John Wooden)	81-76	Florida St.	N. Carolina	Bill Walton (UCLA)	Los Angeles
1973	UCLA (John Wooden)	87-66	Memphis State	Indiana	Bill Walton (UCLA)	St. Louis
1974	N.C. State (Norm Sloan)	76-64	Marquette	UCLA	David Thompson (NC St.)	Greensboro
1975	UCLA (John Wooden)	92-85	Kentucky	Louisville	Rich Washington (UCLA)	San Diego
1976	Indiana (Bobby Knight)	86-68	Michigan	UCLA	Kent Benson (Indiana)	Philadelphia
1977	Marquette (Al McGuire)	67-59	N. Carolina	UNLV	Butch Lee (Marquette)	Atlanta
1978	Kentucky (Joe Hall)	94-88	Duke	Arkansas	Jack Givens (Kentucky)	St. Louis
1979	Michigan St. (Jud Heathcote)	75-64	Indiana State	DePaul	Magic Johnson (Mich.St.)	Salt Lake City
1980	Louisville (Denny Crum)	59-54	UCLA	Purdue	Darrell Griffith (Louisville)	Indianapolis
1981	Indiana (Bobby Knight)	63-50	N. Carolina	Virginia	Isiah Thomas (Indiana)	Philadelphia
1982	N. Carolina (Dean Smith)	63-62	Georgetown	Houst./Louisville#	James Worthy (N.Caro.)	New Orleans
1983	N.C. State (Jim Valvano)	54-52	Houston	Louisville/Geo.#	Akeem Olajuwon (Hou)	Albuquerque
1984	Georgetown (John Thompson)	84-75	Houston	Kentucky/Virgina#	Patrick Ewing (Georgetown)	Seattle
1985	Villanova (Rollie Massimino)	66-64	Georgetown	St. John's/Mem.St.#	Ed Pinckney (Villanova)	Lexington
1986	Louisville (Denny Crum)	72-69	Duke	Kansas/LSU#	Pervis Ellison (Louisville)	Dallas
1987	Indiana (Bobby Knight)	74-73	Syracuse	UNLV/Providence#	Keith Smart (Indiana)	New Orleans
1988	Kansas (Larry Brown)	83-79	Oklahoma	Arizona/Duke#	Danny Manning (Kansas)	Kansas City
1989	Michigan (Steve Fisher)	80-79*	Seton Hall	Illinois/Duke#	Glen Rice (Michigan)	Seattle
1990	UNLV (Jerry Tarkanian)	103-73	Duke	Ga. Tech/Ark.#	Anderson Hunt (UNLV)	Denver
1991	Duke (Mike Krzyzewski)	72-65	Kansas	UNLV/N.Car#	Christian Laettner (Duke)	Indianapolis
1992	Duke (Mike Krzyzewski)	71-51	Michigan	Cin./Indiana#	Bobby Hurley (Duke)	Minneapolis
1993	N. Carolina (Dean Smith)	77-71	Michigan	Kansas/Kentucky#	Donald Williams (N.Car.)	New Orleans
1994	Arkansas (Nolan Richardson)	76-72	Duke	Arizona/Florida#	Corliss Williamson (Ark.)	Charlotte
1995	UCLA (Jim Harrick)	89-78	Arkansas	Ok. State/N.Car.#	Ed O'Bannon (UCLA)	Seattle

KEY — * = Overtime Game; + = Triple Overtime Game; # = Tied for 3rd place, no consolation game; ## = Vacated position because players were declared ineligible after tournament; ++ = Vacated when Howard Porter declared ineligible for competition.

Multiple Championships: UCLA (11), Kentucky (5), Indiana (5), North Carolina (3), Oklahoma A&M (2), Kansas (2), Cincinnati (2), San Francisco (2), North Carolina State (2), Duke (2), Louisville (2). **Coaches with Most NCAA Championships:** John Wooden (10), Adolph Rupp (4), Bobby Knight (3). **Coaches with Most Final Four Appearances:** John Wooden (12), Dean Smith (9), Mike Krzyzewski (7), Denny Crum (6), Adolph Rupp (6). **Most NCAA Appearances:** Kentucky (36), UCLA (30), North Carolina (29), Louisville (25), Notre Dame (24), Indiana (24), Kansas (24). **Most Tournament Career Points Scored:** Christian Laettner (Duke) 407 (1989-92); **Most Tournament Career Rebounds:** Elvin Hayes (Houston) 222 (1966-68); **Most Tournament Career Assists:** Bobby Hurley (Duke) 145 (1990-93); **Most Tournament Career Steals:** Grant Hill (Duke) 39 (1991-94); **Most Tournament Career Games Played:** Christian Laettner (Duke) 23 (1989-92); **Most Tournament Career Blocked Shots:** Alonzo Mourning (Georgetown) 37 (1989-92).

Year-by-Year National Invitation Tournament Results

Annual Site: Madison Square Garden, New York

(Finals and Semifinals only after 1977)

Year	Champion	Score	Runner-Up	Third Place	Fourth Place	Tournament MVP
1938	Temple	60-36	Colorado	Oklahoma A&M	NYU	Don Shields (Temple)
1939	L.I.U.	44-32	Loyola (Chi)	Bradley	St. John's	Bill Lloyd (St. John's)
1940	Colorado	51-40	Duquesne	Oklahoma A&M	DePaul	Bob Doll (Colorado)
1941	L.I.U.	56-42	Ohio U	CCNY	Seton Hall	Frank Baumholtz (Ohio)
1942	W. Virginia	47-45	W. Kentucky	Creighton	Toledo	Rudy Baric (W. Virginia)
1943	St. John's	48-27	Toledo	Wash. & Jeff.	Fordham	Harry Boykoff (St. John's)
1944	St. John's	47-39	DePaul	Kentucky	Okla. A&M	Bill Kotsores (St. John's)
1945	DePaul	71-54	Bowling Green	St. John's	Rhode Island	George Mikan (DePaul)
1946	Kentucky	46-45	Rhode Island	W. Virginia	Muhlenberg	Ernie Calverley (RIU)
1947	Utah	49-45	Kentucky	N. Carolina St.	W. Virginia	Vern Gardner (Utah)
1948	St. Louis	65-52	NYU	W. Kentucky	DePaul	Ed Macauley (St. Louis)
1949	San Fran.	48-47	Loyola (Chi)	Bowling Green	Bradley	Don Lofgran (San Fran.)
1950	CCNY**	69-61	Bradley**	St. John's	Duquesne	Ed Warner (CCNY)
1951	BYU	62-43	Dayton	St. John's	Seton Hall	Roland Minson (BYU)
1952	La Salle	75-64	Dayton	St. Bonaventure	Duquesne	Tom Gola (La Salle)
1953	Seton Hall	58-46	St. John's	Duquesne	Manhattan	Walter Dukes (Seton Hall)
1954	Holy Cross	71-62	Duquesne	Niagara	W. Kentucky	Togo Palazzi (Holy Cross)
1955	Duquesne	70-58	Dayton	Cincinnati	St. Francis (Pa.)	Maurice Stokes (St. Francis)
1956	Louisville	93-80	Dayton	St. Joseph's	St. Francis (NY)	Charlie Tyra (Louisville)
1957	Bradley	84-83	Memphis St.	Temple	St. Bonaventure	Win Wilfong (Memphis St.)
1958	Xavier (Oh)	78-74	Dayton	St. Bonaventure	St. John's	Hank Stein (Xavier)
1959	St. John's	76-71*	Bradley	NYU	Providence	Tony Jackson (St. John's)
1960	Bradley	88-72	Providence	Utah State	St. Bonaventure	Len Wilkens (Providence)
1961	Providence	62-59	St. Louis	Holy Cross	Dayton	Vinnie Ernst (Providence)
1962	Dayton	73-67	St. John's	Loyola (Chicago)	Duquesne	Bill Chmielewski (Dayton)
1963	Providence	81-66	Canisius	Marquette	Villanova	Ray Flynn (Providence)
1964	Bradley	86-54	New Mexico	Army	NYU	Lavern Tart (Bradley)
1965	St. John's	55-51	Villanova	Army	NYU	Ken McIntyre (St. John's)
1966	BYU	97-84	NYU	Villanova	Army	Bill Melchionni (Villanova)
1967	So. Illinois	71-56	Marquette	Rutgers	Marshall	Walt Frazier (So. Illinois)
1968	Dayton	61-48	Kansas	Notre Dame	St. Peter's (NJ)	Don May (Dayton)
1969	Temple	89-76	Boston College	Tennessee	Army	Terry Driscoll (BC)
1970	Marquette	65-53	St. John's	Army	LSU	Dean Meminger (Marquette)
1971	N. Carolina	84-66	Ga. Tech	St. Bonaventure	Duke	Bill Chamberlain (UNC)
1972	Maryland	100-69	Niagara	Jacksonville	St. John's	Tom McMillen (Maryland)
1973	Va. Tech	92-91	Notre Dame	N. Carolina	Alabama	John Shumate (Notre Dame)
1974	Purdue	87-81	Utah	Boston Col.	Jacksonville	Mike Sojourner (Utah)
1975	Princeton	80-69	Providence	Oregon	St. John's	Ron Lee (Oregon)
1976	Kentucky	81-76	UNC-Char.	N. Carolina St.	Providence	Cedric Maxwell (UNCC)

Modern-Era National Invitational Tournament

(All Rounds Before Finals and Semifinals Now Played at Campus Sites)

Year	Champion	Score	Runner-Up	Third Place	Fourth Place	Tournament MVP
1977	St. Bonnies	94-91	Houston	Villanova	Alabama	Greg Sanders (St. Bonnies)
1978	Texas	101-93	N. Carolina St.	Rutgers	Georgetown	Jim Krivacs (Texas) Ron Baxter (Texas)
1979	Indiana	53-52	Purdue	Alabama	Ohio State	Butch Carter (Indiana) Ray Tolbert (Indiana)
1980	Virginia	58-55	Minnesota	Illinois	UNLV	Ralph Sampson (Virginia)
1981	Tulsa	86-84*	Syracuse	Purdue	W. Virginia	Greg Stewart (Tulsa)
1982	Bradley	67-58	Purdue	Georgia-Oklahoma (No Game)		Mitch Anderson (Bradley)
1983	Fresno State	69-60	DePaul	Nebraska-Wake Forest (No Game)		Ron Anderson (Fresno St.)
1984	Michigan	83-63	Notre Dame	Virginia Tech	SW Louisiana	Tim McCormick (Michigan)

341

1985	**UCLA**	65-62	Indiana	Tennessee	Louisville	Reggie Miller (UCLA)
1986	**Ohio State**	73-63	Wyoming	Louisiana Tech	Florida	Brad Sellers (Ohio State)
1987	**So. Miss.**	84-80	La Salle	Nebraska	Arkansas-LR	Randolph Keys (So. Miss.)
1988	**Connecticut**	72-67	Ohio State	Colorado State	Boston College	Phil Gamble (Connecticut)
1989	**St. John's**	73-65	St. Louis	Alabama-Birm.	Michigan State	Jayson Williams (St. John's)
1990	**Vanderbilt**	74-72	St. Louis	Penn State	New Mexico	Scott Draud (Vanderbilt)
1991	**Stanford**	78-72	Oklahoma	Colorado	Massachusetts	Adam Keefe (Stanford)
1992	**Virginia**	81-76	Notre Dame	Utah	Florida	Bryant Stith (Virginia)
1993	**Minnesota**	62-61	Georgetown	Alabama-Birm.	Providence	Voshon Lenard (Minnesota)
1994	**Villanova**	80-73	Vanderbilt	Siena	Kansas State	Doremus Bennerman (Siena)
1995	**Virginia Tech**	65-64*	Marquette	Penn State	Canisius	Shawn Smith (Va. Tech)

KEY** = CCNY also won the NCAA Tournament in 1950, again defeating Bradley in the Finals (71-68); * = Overtime Game.

Multiple Championships: St. John's (5), Bradley (4), Providence (2), LIU (2), BYU (2), Kentucky (2), Dayton (2).
NIT Tournament Apperances: St. John's (25), Dayton (17), Bradley (16), Duquesne (16), Fordham (16), St. Louis (15), Manhattan (15); **Conferences Winning Most NIT Titles:** Big Ten (5), ACC (4), Big East (3), Southeastern Conference (3).

Year-by-Year National Invitation Tournament Leading Scorers

Year	Full Tournament High Scorer	Single Game High Scorer (Opponent)
1938	Ed Boyle (Temple), 39 (3 Games)	Carl Schunk (Bradley), 18 vs. Temple
1939	Bill Lloyd (St. John's), 50 (3 Games)	Bill Lloyd (St. John's), 31 vs. Roanoke
1940	Paul Widowitz (Duquesne), 35 (3 Games)	Bob Doll (Colorado), 16 vs. DePaul
1941	Frank Baumholtz (Ohio), 53 (3 Games)	Frank Baumholtz (Ohio), 22 vs. Duquesne
1942	Bob Gerber (Toledo), 65 (3 Games)	Bob Gerber (Toledo), 37 vs. Rhode Island
1943	Harry Boykoff (St. John's), 56 (3 Games)	Harry Boykoff (St. John's), 22 vs. Fordham
1944	George Mikan (DePaul), 49 (3 Games)	George Mikan (DePaul), 27 vs. Muhlenberg
1945	George Mikan (DePaul), 120 (3 Games)	George Mikan (DePaul), 53 vs. Rhode Island
1946	Ernie Calverley (Rhode Island), 51 (3 Games)	Don Otten (Bowling Green), 31 vs. Rhode Island
1947	Vern Gardner (Utah), 51 (3 Games)	Bob Negley (NC State), 22 vs. W. Virginia
1948	Ed Mikan (DePaul), 64 (3 Games)	Ray Lumpp (NYU), 29 vs. DePaul
1949	Paul Unruh (Bradley), 80 (4 Games)	Gene Melchiorre (Bradley), 28 vs. W. Kentucky
		Paul Unruh (Bradley), 28 vs. W. Kentucky
1950	Ed Warner (CCNY), 87 (4 Games)	Bob Lavoy (W. Kentucky), 32 vs. Niagara
1951	Don Meineke (Dayton), 85 (4 Games)	Don Meineke (Dayton), 37 vs. Arizona
1952	Don Meineke (Dayton), 84 (4 Games)	Don Meineke (Dayton), 30 vs. NYU
		Tom Gola (La Salle), 30 vs. Seton Hall
1953	Walter Dukes (Seton Hall), 70 (3 Games)	Dick Ricketts (Duquesne), 26 vs. Tulsa
		Walter Dukes (Seton Hall), 26 vs. Niagara
1954	Tom Marshall (W. Kentucky), 82 (3 Games)	Jim Gerber (Bowling Green), 39 vs. W. Kentucky
1955	Maurice Stokes (St. Francis-PA), 124 (4 Games)	Maurice Stokes (St. Francis-PA), 43 vs. Dayton
1956	Charlie Tyra (Louisville), 73 (3 Games)	Charlie Tyra (Louisville), 29 vs. St. Joseph's
		Terry Rand (Marquette), 29 vs. Seton Hall
1957	Win Wilfong (Memphis State), 89 (4 Games)	Win Wilfong (Memphis State), 31 vs. Bradley
1958	Hank Stein (Xavier-Ohio), 90 (4 Games)	Alex Ellis (Niagara), 41 vs. Xavier-Ohio
1959	Cal Ramsey (NYU), 82 (4 Games)	Joe Dougherty (Manhattan), 34 vs. Providence
1960	Tom Stith (St. Bonaventure), 114 (4 Games)	Tom Stith (St. Bonaventure), 37 vs. St. John's
1961	John Foley (Holy Cross), 120 (4 Games)	John Foley (Holy Cross), 35 vs. Dayton
1962	Bill Chmielewski (Dayton), 107 (4 Games)	Bill Green (Colorado), 37 vs. Holy Cross
1963	Ray Flynn (Providence), 83 (3 Games)	Ray Flynn (Providence), 38 vs. Miami-Ohio
1964	Happy Hairston (NYU), 91 (4 Games)	Rick Barry (Miami-Florida), 35 vs. St. Joseph's
1965	Ken McIntyre (St. John's), 101 (4 Games)	Ken McIntyre (St. John's), 42 vs. Boston College
1966	Bill Melchionni (Villanova), 109 (4 Games)	Jim Williams (Temple), 38 vs. BYU
1967	Bob Lloyd (Rutgers), 129 (4 Games)	George Stone (Marshall), 46 vs. Nebraska
1968	Don May (Dayton), 106 (4 Games)	Elnardo Webster (St. Peter's), 51 vs. Marshall
1969	Terry Driscoll (Boston College), 96 (4 Games)	Bill Justus (Tennessee), 34 vs. Ohio University
1970	Dan Hester (LSU), 95 (4 Games)	Pete Maravich (LSU), 30 vs. Oklahoma

1971	Bill Chamberlain (North Carolina), 87 (4 Games) ...... Bill Chamberlain (North Carolina), 34 vs. Ga. Tech

1971   Bill Chamberlain (North Carolina), 87 (4 Games) ...... Bill Chamberlain (North Carolina), 34 vs. Ga. Tech
1972   Marshall Wingate (Niagara), 92 (4 Games) .... Rich Fuqua (Oral Roberts), 42 vs. Memphis State
1973   John Shumate (Notre Dame), 95 (4 Games) .... Allen Murphy (Louisville), 36 vs. American University
1974   Ticky Burden (Utah), 118 (4 Games) .... Ticky Burden (Utah), 34 vs. Rutgers
1975   Ron Lee (Oregon), 87 (4 Games) .... Ron Lee (Oregon), 31 vs. St. John's
1976   Cedric Maxwell (UNCC), 109 (4 Games) .... Cedric Maxwell (UNCC), 30 vs. Oregon State
1977   Otis Birdsong (Houston), 116 (4 Games) .... Tony Roberts (Oral Roberts), 65 vs. Oregon
1978   Jim Krivacs (Texas), 99 (4 Games) .... Jim Krivacs (Texas), 33 vs. NC State
1979   Reggie King (Alabama), 132 (5 Games) .... Reggie King (Alabama), 43 vs. Virginia
1980   Ralph Sampson (Virginia), 96 (5 Games) .... Michael Johnson (UNLV), 31 vs. Illinois
1981   Erich Santifer (Syracuse), 106 (5 Games) .... Trent Tucker (Minnesota), 35 vs. Connecticut
1982   Keith Edmonson (Purdue), 116 (5 Games) .... David Little (Oklahoma), 33 vs. Oral Roberts
1983   Bernard Thompson (Fresno St.), 101 (5 Games) .... Charles Bradley (South Florida), 34 vs. Fordham
1984   Tom Sluby (Notre Dame), 102 (5 Games) .... Tom Sewell (Lamar), 32 vs. Santa Clara
1985   Steve Alford (Indiana), 102 (5 Games) .... Johnny Newman (Richmond), 35 vs. Fordham
1986   Fennis Dembo (Wyoming), 116 (5 Games) .... Horace Grant (Clemson), 33 vs. Middle Tennessee
1987   Lionel Simmons (La Salle), 117 (5 Games) .... Richard Morton (Cal-Fullerton), 35 vs. California
1988   Dana Barros (Boston College), 110 (5 Games) .... Todd Lichti (Stanford), 34 vs. Long Beach St.
                                                                                                                              (3 others also)

1989   Jayson Williams (St. John's), 118 (5 Games) .... Steve Smith (Michigan State), 34 vs. Villanova
1990   Anthony Bonner (St. Louis), 102 (4 Games) .... Adam Keefe (Stanford), 31 vs. Hawaii)
                                                                                                                              (3 others also)

1991   Adam Keefe (Stanford), 115 (5 Games) .... Shaun Vandiver (Colorado), 34 vs. Massachusetts
1992   Bryant Stith (Virginia), 123 (5 Games) .... Elmer Bennett (Notre Dame), 39 vs. Virginia
1993   Voshon Leonard (Minnesota), 99 (5 Games) .... Lyndsey Hunter (Jackson State), 39 vs. Connecticut
1994   Doremus Bennerman (Siena), 174 (5 Games) .... Askia Jones (Kansas State), 62 vs. Fresno State

NIT Individual Player Records (1938-1995)

Points, One Game	65	Anthony Roberts, Oral Roberts, 1977
Points, Five Games	174	Doremus Bennerman, Siena, 1994
Field Goals, One Game	25	Anthony Roberts, Oral Roberts, 1977
Field-Goal Attempts, One Game	38	George Stone, Marshall, 1967
Field Goals, Five Games	50	Keith Edmundson, Purdue, 1982
Free Throws, One Game	27	Doremus Bennerman, Siena, 1994
Free-Throw Attempts, One Game	30	Doremus Bennerman, Siena, 1994
Free Throws, Five Games	78	Doremus Bennerman, Siena, 1994
Rebounds, One Game	37	Al Inniss, St. Francis (NY), 1956
Assists, One Game	14	Jere Nolan, Boston College, 1974;
		also Stew Robinson, Indiana, 1985
Blocked Shots, One Game	9	Ralph Sampson, Virginia, 1980;
		also Brad Sellers, Ohio State, 1986
Consecutive Free Throws (One Game)	18	Bill Justus, Tennessee, 1969

Scoring, Rebounding and Assists Leaders

Year-by-Year NCAA National Scoring Leaders (1948-1995)

Year	Player (Team)	Ht.	Class	G	FG	FT	Pts.	PPG
1948	Murray Wier (Iowa)	5-9	Sr.	19	152	95	399	21.0
1949	Tony Lavelli (Yale)	6-3	Sr.	30	228	215	671	22.4
1950	Paul Arizin (Villanova)	6-3	Sr.	29	260	215	735	25.3
1951	Bill Mlkvy (Temple)	6-4	Sr.	25	303	125	731	29.2
1952	Clyde Lovellette (Kansas)	6-9	Sr.	28	315	165	795	28.4
1953	Frank Selvy (Furman)	6-3	Jr.	25	272	194	738	29.5
1954	**Frank Selvy (Furman)**	6-3	Sr.	**29**	427	**355°**	**1,209**	**41.7**
1955	Darrell Floyd (Furman)	6-1	Jr.	25	344	209	897	35.9
1956	Darrell Floyd (Furman)	6-1	Sr.	28	339	268	946	33.8
1957	Grady Wallace (S. Carolina)	6-4	Sr.	29	336	234	906	31.2
1958	Oscar Robertson (Cincinnati)	6-5	So.	28	352	280	984	35.1

1959	Oscar Robertson (Cincinnati)	6-5	Jr.	30	331	316	978	32.6
1960	Oscar Robertson (Cincinnati)	6-5	Sr.	30	369	273	1011	33.7
1961	Frank Burgess (Gonzaga)	6-1	Sr.	26	304	234	842	32.4
1962	Billy McGill (Utah)	6-9	Sr.	26	394	221	1009	38.8
1963	Nick Werkman (Seton Hall)	6-3	Jr.	22	221	208	650	29.5
1964	Howie Komives (Bowling Green)	6-1	Sr.	23	292	260	844	36.7
1965	Rick Barry (Miami-Fla.)	6-7	Sr.	26	340	293	973	37.4
1966	Dave Schellhase (Purdue)	6-4	Sr.	24	284	213	781	32.5
1967	Jimmy Walker (Providence)	6-3	Sr.	28	323	205	851	30.4
1968	**Pete Maravich (LSU)**	6-5	So.	26	432	274	**1138**	**43.8**
1969	**Pete Maravich (LSU)**	6-5	Jr.	26	433	282	**1148**	**44.2**
1970	**Pete Maravich (LSU)**	6-5	Sr.	31	**522°**	337	**1381°**	**44.5°**
1971	**Johnny Neumann (Mississippi)**	6-6	Soph.	23	366	191	923	**40.1**
1972	Dwight Lamar (SW Louisiana)	6-1	Jr.	29	429	196	1054	36.3
1973	William (Bird) Averitt (Pepperdine)	6-1	Sr.	25	352	144	848	33.9
1974	Larry Fogle (Canisius)	6-5	Soph.	25	326	183	835	33.4
1975	Bob McCurdy (Richmond)	6-7	Sr.	26	321	213	855	32.9
1976	Marshall Rodgers (Pan American)	6-2	Sr.	25	361	197	919	36.8
1977	Freeman Williams (Portland State)	6-4	Jr.	26	417	176	1010	38.8
1978	Freeman Williams (Portland State)	6-4	Sr.	27	410	149	969	35.9
1979	Lawrence Butler (Idaho State)	6-3	Sr.	27	310	192	812	30.1
1980	Tony Murphy (Southern)	6-3	Sr.	29	377	178	932	32.1
1981	Zam Fredrick (South Carolina)	6-2	Sr.	27	300	181	781	28.9
1982	Harry Kelly (Texas Southern)	6-7	Jr.	29	336	190	862	29.7
1983	Harry Kelly (Texas Southern)	6-7	Sr.	29	333	169	835	28.8
1984	Joe Jakubick (Akron)	6-5	Sr.	27	304	206	814	30.1
1985	Xavier McDaniel (Wichita St.)	6-8	Sr.	31	351	142	844	27.2
1986	Terrance Bailey (Wagner)	6-2	Jr.	29	321	212	854	29.4

(After Adoption of 3-Point Field Goal)

Year	Player (Team)	Ht.	Class	G	FG	3FG	FT	Pts.	PPG
1987	Kevin Houston (Army)	5-11	Sr.	29	311	63	268	953	32.9
1988	Hersey Hawkins (Bradley)	6-3	Sr.	31	377	87	284	1125	36.3
1989	Hank Gathers (Loyola-LA)*	6-7	Jr.	31	419	0	177	1015	32.7
1990	Bo Kimble (Loyola-LA)	6-7	Sr.	32	404	92	231	1131	35.3
1991	Kevin Bradshaw (U.S. Intern'l)**	6-6	Sr.	28	358	60	278	1054	37.6
1992	Brett Roberts (Morehead St.)	6-8	Sr.	29	278	22	193	815	28.1
1993	Isaiah Rider (UNLV)	6-5	Sr.	28	282	55	195	814	29.1
1994	Glenn Robinson (Purdue)	6-7	Jr.	34	368	79	215	1030	30.3
1995	Kurt Thomas (Texas Christian)	6-9	Sr.	27	288	3	202	871	28.9

° National Record (40+ PPG Scorers in Boldface)
** Kevin Bradshaw played at U.S. International and Bethune-Cookman
* Hank Gathers played at Loyola-Marymount and Southern California

Most Career NCAA Total Points (1948-1995)

Player (Team)	Ht.	Last Year	G	FG	3FG	FT	Points
Pete Maravich (LSU)	6-5	1970 (3 years)	83	1387	NA	893	**3667**
Freeman Williams (Portland St.)	6-4	1978 (4)	106	1369	NA	511	**3249**
Lionel Simmons (La Salle)	6-7	1990 (4)	131	1244	56	673	**3217**
Harry Kelly (Texas Southern)	6-7	1983 (4)	110	1234	NA	598	**3066**
Hersey Hawkins (Bradley)	6-3	1988 (4)	125	1100	118	690	**3008**
Oscar Robertson (Cincinnati)	6-5	1960 (3)	88	1052	NA	869	2973
Danny Manning (Kansas)	6-10	1988 (4)	147	1216	10	509	2951
Alfredrick Hughes (Loyola-Chicago)	6-5	1985 (4)	120	1226	NA	462	2914
Elvin Hayes (Houston)	6-8	1968 (3)	93	1215	NA	454	2884
Larry Bird (Indiana State)	6-9	1979 (3)	94	1154	NA	542	2850
Otis Birdsong (Houston)	6-4	1977 (4)	116	1176	NA	480	2832
Kevin Bradshaw (US International)**	6-6	1991 (4)	111	1027	132	618	2804
Hank Gathers (Loyola-Marymount)*	6-7	1990 (4)	117	1127	0	469	2723

Reggie Lewis (Northeastern)	6-7	1987 (4)	122	1043	30	592	2708
Daren Queenan (Lehigh)	6-5	1988 (4)	118	1024	29	626	2703
Byron Larkin (Xavier-Ohio)	6-3	1988 (4)	121	1022	51	601	2696
David Robinson (Navy)	7-1	1987 (4)	127	1032	1	604	2669
Wayman Tisdale (Oklahoma)	6-9	1985 (3)	104	1077	NA	507	2661
Michael Brooks (La Salle)	6-7	1980 (4)	114	1064	NA	500	2628
Calbert Cheaney (Indiana)	6-7	1993 (4)	132	1018	148	429	2613
Mark Macon (Temple)	6-5	1991 (4)	126	980	246	403	2609
Don MacLean (UCLA)	6-10	1992 (4)	127	943	11	711	2608
Joe Dumars (McNeese State)	6-3	1985 (4)	116	941	NA	723	2605
Terrance Bailey (Wagner)	6-2	1987 (4)	110	985	42	579	2591
Dickie Hemric (Wake Forest)	6-6	1955 (4)	104	841	NA	905	2587
Calvin Natt (Northeast Louisiana)	6-5	1979 (4)	108	1017	NA	547	2581
Derrick Chievous (Missouri)	6-7	1988 (4)	130	893	30	764	2580

Best Career NCAA Scoring Averages
(1948-1995, Minimum of 2 Seasons Played)

Player (Team)	Last Year	Years	G	FG	FT	Points	PPG
Pete Maravich (LSU)	1968	3	83	1387	893	3667	**44.2**
Austin Carr (Notre Dame)	1971	3	74	1017	526	2560	34.6
Oscar Robertson (Cincinnati)	1960	3	88	1052	869	2973	33.8
Calvin Murphy (Niagara)	1970	3	77	947	654	2548	33.1
Dwight Lamar (Southwest Louisiana)	1973	2	57	768	326	1862	32.7
Frank Selvy (Furman)	1954	3	78	922	694	2538	32.5
Rick Mount (Purdue)	1970	3	72	910	503	2323	32.3
Darrell Floyd (Furman)	1956	3	71	868	545	2281	32.1
Nick Werkman (Seton Hall)	1964	3	71	812	649	2273	32.0
Willie Humes (Idaho State)	1971	2	48	565	380	1510	31.5
William (Bird) Averitt (Pepperdine)	1973	2	49	615	311	1541	31.4
Elgin Baylor (Seattle/College of Idaho)	1958	3	80	956	588	2500	31.3
Elvin Hayes (Houston)	1968	3	93	1215	454	2884	31.0
Freeman Williams (Portland State)	1978	4	106	1369	511	3249	30.7
Larry Bird (Indiana State)	1979	3	94	1154	542	2850	30.3
Bill Bradley (Princeton)	1965	3	83	856	791	2503	30.2
Rich Fuqua (Oral Roberts)	1973	2	54	692	233	1617	29.9
Wilt Chamberlain (Kansas)	1958	2	48	503	427	1433	29.9
Rick Barry (Miami-Florida)	1965	3	77	816	666	2298	29.8
Doug Collins (Illinois State)	1973	3	77	894	452	2240	29.1

National Rebounding Leaders (1951-1995)

Year	Player (Team)	Ht.	Class	G	Rebounds	Average (RPG)
1951	Ernie Beck (Pennsylvania)	6-4	So.	27	556	20.6
1952	Bill Hannon (Army)	6-3	So.	17	355	20.9
1953	Ed Conlin (Fordham)	6-5	So.	26	612°	23.5
1954	Art Quimby (Connecticut)	6-5	Jr.	26	588	22.6
1955	**Charlie Slack (Marshall)**	6-5	Jr.	21	538	**25.6°**
1956	Joe Holup (George Washington)	6-6	Sr.	26	604	.256# (23.2)
1957	Elgin Baylor (Seattle)	6-6	Jr.	25	508	.235# (20.3)
1958	Alex Ellis (Niagara)	6-5	Sr.	25	536	.262# (21.4)
1959	**Leroy Wright (Pacific)**	6-8	Jr.	26	652	.238# (**25.1**)
1960	Leroy Wright (Pacific)	6-8	Sr.	17	380	.234# (22.4)
1961	Jerry Lucas (Ohio State)	6-8	Jr.	27	470	.198# (17.4)
1962	Jerry Lucas (Ohio State)	6-8	Sr.	28	499	.211# (17.8)
1963	Paul Silas (Creighton)	6-7	Sr.	27	557	20.6
1964	Bob Pelkington (Xavier-Ohio)	6-7	Sr.	26	567	21.8
1965	Toby Kimball (Connecticut)	6-8	Sr.	23	483	21.0
1966	Jim Ware (Oklahoma City)	6-8	Sr.	29	607	20.9
1967	Dick Cunningham (Murray St.)	6-10	Jr.	22	479	21.8

345

1968	Neal Walk (Florida)	6-10	Jr.	25	494	19.8
1969	Spencer Haywood (Detroit)	6-8	So.	22	472	21.5
1970	Artis Gilmore (Jacksonville)	7-2	Jr.	28	621	22.2
1971	Artis Gilmore (Jacksonville)	7-2	Sr.	26	603	23.2
1972	Kermit Washington (American)	6-8	Jr.	23	455	19.8
1973	Kermit Washington (American)	6-8	Sr.	22	439	20.0
1974	Marvin Barnes (Providence)	6-9	Sr.	32	597	18.7
1975	John Irving (Hofstra)	6-9	So.	21	323	15.4
1976	Sam Pellom (Buffalo)	6-8	So.	26	420	16.2
1977	Glenn Mosley (Seton Hall)	6-8	Sr.	29	473	16.3
1978	Ken Williams (North Texas)	6-7	Sr.	28	411	14.7
1979	Monti Davis (Tennessee St.)	6-7	Jr.	26	421	16.2
1980	Larry Smith (Alcorn State)	6-8	Sr.	26	392	15.1
1981	Darryl Watson (Mississippi Valley)	6-7	Sr.	27	397	14.0
1982	LaSalle Thompson (Texas)	6-10	Jr.	27	365	13.5
1983	Xavier McDaniel (Wichita St.)	6-8	So.	28	403	14.4
1984	Akeem Olajuwon (Houston)	7-0	Jr.	37	500	13.5
1985	Xavier McDaniel (Wichita St.)	6-8	Sr.	31	460	14.8
1986	David Robinson (Navy)	6-11	Jr.	35	455	13.0
1987	Jerome Lane (Pittsburgh)	6-6	So.	33	444	13.5
1988	Kenny Miller (Loyola-Chicago)	6-9	Fr.	29	395	13.6
1989	Hank Gathers (Loyola-Marymount)*	6-7	Jr.	31	426	13.7
1990	Anthony Bonner (St. Louis)	6-8	Sr.	33	456	13.8
1991	Shaquille O'Neal (LSU)	7-1	So.	28	411	14.7
1992	Popeye Jones (Murray State)	6-8	Sr.	30	431	14.4
1993	Jervaughn Scales (Southern)	6-7	Sr.	31	393	12.7
1994	Jerome Lambert (Baylor)	6-9	Jr.	24	335	14.8
1995	Kurt Thomas (Texas Christian)	6-9	Sr.	27	393	14.6

° National Record (Walter Dukes set record of 734 but finished second in average at 22.2)

1956 to 1962, leader determined by highest individual recoveries from total by both teams in all games

* Hank Gathers played at Loyola-Marymount and Southern California

Most Career NCAA Rebounds (1948-1995)

Player (Team)	Ht.	Last Year	Years	G	Rebounds	RPG
Tom Gola (La Salle)	6-6	1955	4	118	**2201**	18.7
Joe Holup (George Washington)	6-6	1956	4	104	**2030**	19.5
Charlie Slack (Marshall)	6-5	1956	4	88	1916	**21.77**
Ed Conlin (Fordham)	6-5	1955	4	102	1884	18.4
Dickie Hemric (Wake Forest)	6-6	1955	4	104	1802	17.3
Paul Silas (Creighton)	6-7	1964	3	81	1751	**21.62**
Art Quimby (Connecticut)	6-5	1955	4	80	1716	**21.45**
Jerry Harper (Alabama)	6-8	1956	4	93	1688	18.1
Jeff Cohen (William & Mary)	6-7	1961	4	103	1679	16.3
Steve Hamilton (Morehead State)	6-7	1958	4	102	1675	16.4
Charlie Tyra (Louisville)	6-8	1957	4	95	1617	17.0
Bill Russell (San Francisco)	6-9	1956	3	79	1606	**20.3**
Elvin Hayes (Houston)	6-8	1968	3	93	1602	17.2

(For Careers Beginning After 1973)

Derrick Coleman (Syracuse)	6-11	1990	4	143	1537	10.7
Ralph Sampson (Virginia)	7-4	1983	4	132	1511	11.4
Pete Padgett (Nevada-Reno)	6-8	1976	4	104	1464	14.1
Lionel Simmons (La Salle)	6-7	1990	4	131	1429	10.9
Anthony Bonner (St. Louis)	6-7	1990	4	133	1424	10.7
Tyron Hill (Xavier-Ohio)	6-9	1990	4	126	1380	10.9
Popeye Jones (Murray State)	6-8	1992	4	123	1374	11.2
Michael Brooks (La Salle)	6-7	1980	4	114	1372	12.0
Xavier McDaniel (Wichita State)	6-7	1985	4	117	1359	11.6
John Irving (Arizona/Hofstra)	6-9	1977	4	103	1348	13.1
Sam Clancy (Pittsburgh)	6-6	1981	4	116	1342	11.6

Giant Walter Dukes of Seton Hall (20) still holds the NCAA record for single season rebounds (734 in 1953). He is also one of only six major college players to average more than 20 points and 20 rebounds throughout his college career. (Seton Hall University photo)

347

Keith Lee (Memphis State)	6-10	1985	4	128	1336	10.4
Larry Smith (Alcorn State)	6-8	1980	4	111	1334	12.0
Clarence Weatherspoon (So. Miss.)	6-7	1992	4	117	1320	11.3
Michael Cage (San Diego State)	6-9	1984	4	112	1317	11.8
Bob Stephens (Drexel)	6-7	1979	4	99	1316	13.3

Most Career NCAA Assists (1985-1995)

Player (Team)	Ht.	Last Year	Years	G	Assists	APG
Bobby Hurley (Duke)	6-0	1993	4	140	**1076**	7.7
Chris Corchiani (NC State)	6-1	1991	4	124	**1038**	8.4
Keith Jennings (E. Tenn. State)	5-7	1991	4	127	983	7.7
Sherman Douglas (Syracuse)	6-0	1989	4	138	960	6.9
Greg Anthony (Portland/UNLV)	6-1	1991	4	138	950	6.9
Gary Payton (Oregon State)	6-2	1990	4	120	939	7.8
Andre La Fleur (Northeastern)	6-3	1987	4	128	894	6.9
Jim Les (Bradley)	5-11	1986	4	118	884	7.5
Frank Smith (Old Dominion)	6-0	1988	4	120	883	7.4
Taurence Chislom (Delaware)	5-7	1988	4	110	877	7.9
Grayson Marshall (Clemson)	6-2	1988	4	122	857	7.0
Anthony Manuel (Bradley)	5-11	1989	4	108	855	7.9
Avery Johnson (Cameron/Southern)	5-11	1988	3	94	838	**8.9**
Pooh Richardson (UCLA)	6-1	1989	4	122	833	6.8
Butch Moore (SMU)	5-10	1986	4	125	828	6.6
Drafton Davis (Marist)	6-0	1988	4	115	804	6.9
Marc Brown (Siena)	5-11	1991	4	123	796	6.5
Tyrone Bogues (Wake Forest)	5-3	1987	4	119	781	6.6
Jeff Timberlake (Boston University)	6-2	1989	4	121	778	6.4
Kenny Smith (N. Carolina)	6-3	1987	4	127	768	6.0
Bruce Douglas (Illinois)	6-3	1986	4	130	765	5.9
Andre Turner (Memphis State)	5-10	1986	4	132	763	5.8

Single-Season Individual 40 PPG Scoring Averages

Player (Team)	Season	G	FG	FT	Points	PPG
Pete Maravich (LSU)	1970	31	522	337	1381	44.5
Pete Maravich (LSU)	1969	26	433	282	1148	44.2
Pete Maravich (LSU)	1968	26	432	274	1138	43.8
Frank Selvy (Furman)	1954	29	427	355	1209	41.7
Johnny Neumann (Mississippi)	1971	23	366	191	923	40.1

1,100 or More Points Scored in Single Season

Player (Team)	Season	G	FG	3FG	FT	Points
Pete Maravich (LSU)	1970	31	522	NA	337	1381
Elvin Hayes (Houston)	1968	33	519	NA	176	1214
Frank Selvy (Furman)	1954	29	427	NA	355	1209
Pete Maravich (LSU)	1969	26	433	NA	282	1148
Pete Maravich (LSU)	1968	26	432	NA	274	1138
Bo Kimble (Loyola-LA)	1990	32	404	92	231	1131
Hersey Hawkins (Bradley)	1988	31	377	87	284	1125
Austin Carr (Notre Dame)	1970	29	444	NA	218	1106
Austin Carr (Notre Dame)	1971	29	430	NA	241	1101

Murray Wier of Iowa was the very first NCAA national scoring leader (21.0 ppg) at the end of the 1948 season. He was also the only player shorter than 6 feet to turn the trick until Kevin Houston of Army did it in 1987. (University of Iowa photo)

NCAA Consensus First-Team All-Americans
Boldface indicates National Player of the Year (Helms, 1938-1954)

Player	Pos.	Year	School
1937-38			
Meyer "Mike" Bloom	C	Sr	Temple
Hank Luisetti	F	Sr	Stanford
John Moir	F	Sr	Notre Dame
Paul Nowak	C	Sr	Notre Dame
Fred Pralle	G	Sr	Kansas
Jewell Young	F	Sr	Purdue
1938-39			
Ernie Andres	G	Sr	Indiana
Jimmy Hull	F	Sr	Ohio State
Chester "Chet" Jaworski	G	Sr	Rhode Island
Irving Torgoff	F	Sr	Long Island
Urgel "Slim" Wintermute	C	Sr	Oregon
1939-40			
Gus Broberg	G-F	Jr	Dartmouth
John Dick	F	Sr	Oregon
George Glamack	C	Jr	North Carolina
Bill Hapac	F	Sr	Illinois
Ralph Vaughn	F	Sr	So. California
1940-41			
John Adams	F	Sr	Arkansas
Gus Broberg	G-F	Sr	Dartmouth
George Glamack	C	Sr	North Carolina
Howard Engleman	F	Sr	Kansas
Gene Englund	C	Sr	Wisconsin
1941-42			
Price Brookfield	C	Sr	W. Texas State
Bob Davies	G	Sr	Seton Hall
Bob Kinney	C	Sr	Rice
John Kotz	F	Jr	Wisconsin
Andy Phillip	F	So	Illinois
Stan "Stutz" Modzelewski	F	Sr	Rhode Island
1942-43			
Ed Beisser	C	Sr	Creighton
Charles Black	F	So	Kansas
Harry Boykoff	C	So	St. John's
Bill Closs	C	Sr	Rice
Andy Phillip	F	Jr	Illinois
George Senesky	F	Sr	St. Joseph's
1943-44			
Bob Brannum	C	Fr	Kentucky
Audley Brindley	C	Jr	Dartmouth
Otto Graham	F	Sr	Northwestern
Leo Klier	F	Jr	Notre Dame
Bob Kurland	C	So	Okla. A&M
George Mikan	C	So	DePaul
Allie Paine	G	Jr	Oklahoma
1944-45			
Arnie Ferrin	F	So	Utah
Wynold Gray	F	So	Bowling Green
Walt Kirk	G	Jr	Illinois
Bob Kurland	C	Jr	Okla. A&M
George Mikan	C	Jr	DePaul
1945-46			
Leo Klier	F	Sr	Notre Dame
Bob Kurland	C	Sr	Okla. A&M
George Mikan	C	Sr	DePaul

Player	Pos.	Year	School
Max Morris	F-C	Sr	Northwestern
Sid Tannenbaum	G	Jr	NYU
1946-47			
Ralph Beard	G	So	Kentucky
Alex Groza	C	So	Kentucky
Ralph Hamilton	F	Sr	Indiana
Sid Tannenbaum	G	Sr	NYU
Gerry Tucker	C	Sr	Oklahoma
1947-48			
Ralph Beard	G	Jr	Kentucky
Ed Macauley	C-F	Jr	St. Louis
Jim McIntyre	C	Jr	Minnesota
Kevin O'Shea	G	So	Notre Dame
Murray Wier	G	Sr	Iowa
1948-49			
Ralph Beard	G	Sr	Kentucky
Vince Boryla	F	Sr	Denver
Alex Groza	C	Sr	Kentucky
Tony Lavelli	G	Sr	Yale
Ed Macauley	C-F	Sr	St. Louis
1949-50			
Paul Arizin	F	Sr	Villanova
Bob Cousy	G	Sr	Holy Cross
Dick Schnittker	F	Sr	Ohio State
Bill Sharman	G	Sr	So. California
Paul Unruh	F	Sr	Bradley
1950-51			
Clyde Lovellette	C	Jr	Kansas
Gene Melchiorre	G	Sr	Bradley
Bill Mlkvy	F	Jr	Temple
Sam Ranzino	F	Sr	North Carolina
Bill Spivey	C	Jr	Kentucky
Dick Groat	G	Jr	Duke
1951-52			
Chuck Darling	C	Sr	Iowa
Rod Fletcher	G	Sr	Illinois
Dick Groat	G	Sr	Duke
Cliff Hagan	F	Jr	Kentucky
Clyde Lovellette	C	Sr	Kansas
1952-53			
Ernie Beck	F	Sr	Pennsylvania
Walter Dukes	C	Jr	Seton Hall
Tom Gola	C-F	So	La Salle
Bob Houbregs	C	Sr	Washington
Johnny O'Brien	G	Sr	Seattle
1953-54			
Tom Gola	C-F	Jr	La Salle
Cliff Hagan	F	Sr	Kentucky
Bob Pettit	C	Sr	LSU
Don Schlundt	C	Jr	Indiana
Frank Selvy	F	Sr	Furman
1954-55			
Dick Garmaker	F	Sr	Minnesota
Tom Gola	C-F	Sr	La Salle
Sihugo Green	G	Jr	Duquesne
Dick Ricketts	F-C	Sr	Duquesne
Bill Russell	C	Jr	San Francisco

350

Player	Pos.	Year	School	Player	Pos.	Year	School
1955-56				**1965-66**			
Robin Freeman	G	Sr	Ohio State	Dave Bing	G	Sr	Syracuse
Sihugo Green	G	Sr	Duquesne	Clyde Lee	C	Sr	Vanderbilt
Tom Heinsohn	F	Sr	Holy Cross	**Cazzie Russell**	G	Sr	Michigan
Bill Russell	C	Sr	San Francisco	Dave Schellhase	F	Sr	Purdue
Ron Shavlik	C	Sr	N. Carolina St.	Jimmy Walker	G	Jr	Providence
1956-57				**1966-67**			
Wilt Chamberlain	C	So	Kansas	**Lew Alcindor**	C	So	UCLA
Chet Forte	G	Sr	Columbia	Clem Haskins	G-F	Sr	W. Kentucky
Rod Hundley	G-F	Sr	West Virginia	Elvin Hayes	F-C	Jr	Houston
Lennie Rosenbluth	F	Sr	North Carolina	Bob Verga	G	Sr	Duke
Charlie Tyra	C	Sr	Louisville	Bob Lloyd	G	Sr	Rutgers
1957-58				**1967-68**			
Elgin Baylor	F-C	Jr	Seattle	Lew Alcindor	C	Jr	UCLA
Bob Boozer	F	Jr	Kansas State	**Elvin Hayes**	F-C	Sr	Houston
Wilt Chamberlain	C	Jr	Kansas	Pete Maravich	G	So	LSU
Oscar Robertson	F	So	Cincinnati	Larry Miller	F	Sr	North Carolina
Guy Rodgers	G	Sr	Temple	Wes Unseld	C	Sr	Louisville
1958-59				**1968-69**			
Bob Boozer	F	Sr	Kansas State	**Lew Alcindor**	C	Sr	UCLA
Johnny Cox	F	Sr	Kentucky	Spencer Haywood	F-C	Jr	Detroit
Bailey Howell	F	Sr	Mississippi St.	Pete Maravich	G	Jr	LSU
Oscar Robertson	F	Jr	Cincinnati	Rick Mount	G	Jr	Purdue
Jerry West	F	Jr	West Virginia	Calvin Murphy	G	Jr	Niagara
1959-60				**1969-70**			
Darrell Imhoff	C	Sr	California	Dan Issel	F-C	Sr	Kentucky
Jerry Lucas	C	So	Ohio State	Bob Lanier	C	Sr	St. Bonaventure
Oscar Robertson	F	Sr	Cincinnati	**Pete Maravich**	G	Sr	LSU
Tom Stith	F	Jr	St. Bonaventure	Rick Mount	G	Sr	Purdue
Jerry West	F	Sr	West Virginia	Calvin Murphy	G	Sr	Niagara
1960-61				**1970-71**			
Terry Dischinger	F	Jr	Purdue	**Austin Carr**	G	Sr	Notre Dame
Roger Kaiser	G	Sr	Georgia Tech	Artis Gilmore	C	Sr	Jacksonville
Jerry Lucas	C	Jr	Ohio State	Jim McDaniels	C	Sr	W. Kentucky
Tom Stith	F	Sr	St. Bonaventure	Dean Meminger	G	Sr	Marquette
Chet Walker	F	Jr	Bradley	Sidney Wicks	F	Sr	UCLA
1961-62				**1971-72**			
Len Chappell	C	Sr	Wake Forest	Henry Bibby	G	Sr	UCLA
Terry Dischinger	F	Sr	Purdue	Jim Chones	C	Jr	Marquette
Jerry Lucas	C	Sr	Ohio State	Bob McAdoo	C	Jr	North Carolina
Billy McGill	C	Sr	Utah	Tom Riker	C	Sr	South Carolina
Chet Walker	F	Sr	Bradley	**Bill Walton**	C	So	UCLA
1962-63				**1972-73**			
Ron Bohnam	F	Jr	Cincinnati	Doug Collins	G	Sr	Illinois State
Jerry Harkness	F	Sr	Loyola-Chi.	Ernie DiGregorio	G	Sr	Providence
Art Heyman	F	Sr	Duke	David Thompson	F	So	N. Carolina St.
Barry Kramer	F	Jr	NYU	**Bill Walton**	C	Jr	UCLA
Tom Thacker	F-G	Sr	Cincinnati	Ed Ratleff	F-G	Sr	Long Beach St.
1963-64				**1973-74**			
Gary Bradds	C	Sr	Ohio State	Marvin Barnes	C	Sr	Providence
Bill Bradley	F	Jr	Princeton	John Shumate	C-F	So	Notre Dame
Walt Hazzard	G	Sr	UCLA	David Thompson	F	Jr	N. Carolina St.
Cotton Nash	F	Sr	Kentucky	**Bill Walton**	C	Sr	UCLA
Dave Stallworth	F	Jr	Wichita State	Keith Wilkes	G	Sr	UCLA
1964-65				**1974-75**			
Rick Barry	F	Sr	Miami (Fla.)	Adrian Dantley	F	So	Notre Dame
Bill Bradley	F	Sr	Princeton	John Lucas	G	Jr	Maryland
Gail Goodrich	G	Sr	UCLA	Scott May	F	Jr	Indiana
Fred Hetzel	F-G	Sr	Davidson	Dave Meyers	F	Sr	UCLA
Cazzie Russell	G	Jr	Michigan	**David Thompson**	F	Sr	N. Carolina St.

Player	Pos.	Year	School	Player	Pos.	Year	School
1975-76				**1985-86**			
Kent Benson	C	Jr	Indiana	Steve Alford	G	Jr	Indiana
Adrian Dantley	F	Jr	Notre Dame	**Walter Berry**	F	Jr	St. John's
John Lucas	G	Sr	Maryland	Len Bias	F	Sr	Maryland
Scott May	F	Sr	Indiana	Johnny Dawkins	G	Sr	Duke
Richard Washington	C-F	Jr	UCLA	Kenny Walker	F	Sr	Kentucky
1976-77				**1986-87**			
Kent Benson	C	Sr	Indiana	Steve Alford	G	Sr	Indiana
Otis Birdsong	G	Sr	Houston	Danny Manning	F-C	Jr	Kansas
Phil Ford	G	Jr	North Carolina	**David Robinson**	C	Sr	Navy
Rickey Green	G	Sr	Michigan	Kenny Smith	G	Sr	North Carolina
Marques Johnson	F	Sr	UCLA	Reggie Williams	F-G	Sr	Georgetown
1977-78				**1987-88**			
Larry Bird	F-C	Jr	Indiana State	Sean Elliott	F	Jr	Arizona
Phil Ford	G	Sr	North Carolina	Gary Grant	G	Sr	Michigan
David Greenwood	F	Jr	UCLA	**Hersey Hawkins**	G	Sr	Bradley
Butch Lee	G	Sr	Marquette	Danny Manning	F-C	Sr	Kansas
Mychal Thompson	C	Sr	Minnesota	J.R. Reid	C	So	North Carolina
1978-79				**1988-89**			
Larry Bird	F-C	Sr	Indiana State	Sean Elliott	F	Sr	Arizona
Mike Gminski	C	Jr	Duke	Pervis Ellison	C	Sr	Louisville
David Greenwood	F	Sr	UCLA	**Danny Ferry**	F-C	Sr	Duke
Earvin "Magic" Johnson	G	So	Michigan State	Chris Jackson	G	Fr	LSU
Sidney Moncrief	G-F	Sr	Arkansas	Stacey King	C	Sr	Oklahoma
1979-80				**1989-90**			
Mark Aguirre	F	So	DePaul	Derrick Coleman	F	Sr	Syracuse
Michael Brooks	F	Sr	La Salle	Chris Jackson	G	So	LSU
Joe Barry Carroll	C	Sr	Purdue	Larry Johnson	F	Jr	UNLV
Darrell Griffith	G	Sr	Louisville	Gary Payton	G	Sr	Oregon
Kyle Macy	G	Sr	Kentucky	**Lionel Simmons**	F	Sr	La Salle
1980-81				**1990-91**			
Mark Aguirre	F	Jr	DePaul	Kenny Anderson	G	So	Georgia Tech
Danny Ainge	G	Sr	Brigham Young	Jim Jackson	G-F	So	Ohio State
Steve Johnson	C	Sr	Oregon State	**Larry Johnson**	F	Sr	UNLV
Ralph Sampson	C	So	Virginia	Shaquille O'Neal	C	So	LSU
Isiah Thomas	G	So	Indiana	Billy Owens	F	Jr	Syracuse
1981-82				**1991-92**			
Terry Cummings	F-C	Jr	DePaul	Jim Jackson	G-F	Jr	Ohio State
Quintin Dailey	G	Jr	San Francisco	**Christian Laettner**	F-C	Sr	Duke
Eric "Sleepy" Floyd	G	Sr	Georgetown	Harold Miner	G	Jr	So. California
Ralph Sampson	C	Jr	Virginia	Alonzo Mourning	C	Sr	Georgetown
James Worthy	F	Jr	North Carolina	Shaquille O'Neal	C	Jr	LSU
1982-83				**1992-93**			
Dale Ellis	F	Sr	Tennessee	**Calbert Cheaney**	F	Sr	Indiana
Patrick Ewing	C	So	Georgetown	Anfernee Hardaway	G	Jr	Memphis State
Michael Jordan	G	So	North Carolina	Bobby Hurley	G	Sr	Duke
Sam Perkins	C	Jr	North Carolina	Jamal Mashburn	F	Jr	Kentucky
Ralph Sampson	C	Sr	Virginia	Chris Webber	F	So	Michigan
1983-84				**1993-94**			
Patrick Ewing	C	Jr	Georgetown	Grant Hill	F-G	Sr	Duke
Michael Jordan	G	Jr	North Carolina	Jason Kidd	G	So	California
Akeem Olajuwon	C	Jr	Houston	Donyell Marshall	F	Jr	Connecticut
Sam Perkins	C	Sr	North Carolina	**Glenn Robinson**	F	Jr	Purdue
Wayman Tisdale	C-F	So	Oklahoma	Clifford Rozier	C-F	Jr	Louisville
1984-85				**1994-95**			
Johnny Dawkins	G	Jr	Duke	**Jerry Stackhouse**	F	So	North Carolina
Patrick Ewing	C	Sr	Georgetown	Michael Finley	F	Sr	Wisconsin
Xavier McDaniel	F	Sr	Wichita State	Shawn Respert	G	Sr	Michigan State
Chris Mullin	G-F	Sr	St. John's	Ed O'Bannon	F	Sr	UCLA
Wayman Tisdale	F-C	Jr	Oklahoma	Bryant Reeves	C	Sr	Oklahoma State
				Randolph Childress	G	Sr	Wake Forest

National College Players of the Year

Key: **UPI** = United Press International, **AP** = Associated Press, **USBWA** = United States Basketball Writers' Association, **NABC** = National Association of Basketball Coaches, **Naismith** = James Naismith Award, **Wooden** = John Wooden Award, **Helms Foundation** = Helms Foundation Retroactive Award. **National Scoring Champions in Boldface.**

Year	Player (School)	Award
1905	Christian Steinmetz (Wisconsin)	Helms Foundation
1906	George Grebenstein (Dartmouth)	Helms Foundation
1907	Gilmore Kinney (Yale)	Helms Foundation
1908	Charles Keinath (Pennsylvania)	Helms Foundation
1909	John Schommer (Chicago)	Helms Foundation
1910	Harland "Pat" Page (Chicago)	Helms Foundation
1911	Theodore Kiendl (Columbia)	Helms Foundation
1912	Otto Stangel (Wisconsin)	Helms Foundation
1913	Eddie Calder (St. Lawrence)	Helms Foundation
1914	Gil Halstead (Cornell)	Helms Foundation
1915	Ernest Houghton (Union)	Helms Foundation
1916	George Levis (Wisconsin)	Helms Foundation
1917	Ray Woods (Illinois)	Helms Foundation
1918	William Chandler (Wisconsin)	Helms Foundation
1919	Erling Platou (Minnesota)	Helms Foundation
1920	Howard Cann (NYU)	Helms Foundation
1921	George Williams (Missouri)	Helms Foundation
1922	Charles Carney (Illinois)	Helms Foundation
1923	Paul Endacott (Kansas)	Helms Foundation
1924	Charles Black (Kansas)	Helms Foundation
1925	Ed Mueller (Colorado College)	Helms Foundation
1926	John Cobb (North Carolina)	Helms Foundation
1927	Victor Hanson (Syracuse)	Helms Foundation
1928	Victor Holt (Oklahoma)	Helms Foundation
1929	John Thompson (Montana State)	Helms Foundation
1930	Chuck Hyatt (Pittsburgh)	Helms Foundation
1931	Bart Carlton (E. Central Oklahoma)	Helms Foundation
1932	John Wooden (Purdue)	Helms Foundation
1933	Forest "Aggie" Sale (Kentucky)	Helms Foundation
1934	Wesley Bennett (Westminster)	Helms Foundation
1935	Leroy Edwards (Kentucky)	Helms Foundation
1936	John Moir (Notre Dame)	Helms Foundation
1937	Hank Luisetti (Stanford)	Helms Foundation
1938	Hank Luisetti (Stanford)	Helms Foundation
1939	Chester Jaworski (Rhode Island)	Helms Foundation
1940	George Clamack (North Carolina)	Helms Foundation
1941	George Clamack (North Carolina)	Helms Foundation
1942	Stan Modzelewski (Rhode Island)	Helms Foundation
1943	George Senesky (St. Joseph's)	Helms Foundation
1944	George Mikan (DePaul)	Helms Foundation
1945	George Mikan (DePaul)	Helms Foundation
1946	Bob Kurland (Oklahoma A&M)	Helms Foundation
1947	Gerald Tucker (Oklahoma)	Helms Foundation
1948	Ed Macauley (St. Louis)	Helms Foundation

With two 100-point single-game explosions in 1953-54, Clarence "Bevo" Francis rescued both tiny Rio Grande College and the scandal-plagued game of college basketball. Shown here against Adelphi College in Madison Square Garden, Francis still holds the all-time single-game scoring mark. (Rio Grande College photo)

1949 .... **Tony Lavelli (Yale)** .... **Helms Foundation**
1950 .... **Paul Arizin (Villanova)** .... **Helms Foundation**
1951 .... Dick Groat (Duke) .... Helms Foundation
1952 .... **Clyde Lovellette (Kansas)** .... **Helms Foundation**
1953 .... Bob Houbregs (Washington) .... Helms Foundation
1954 .... Tom Gola (La Salle) .... Helms Foundation

Year	Player (School)	Ht	Yr	Scoring Average (PPG)	Award(s)
1955	Tom Gola (La Salle)	6-6	Sr.	24.2	UPI
	Bill Russell (San Francisco)	6-6	Jr	21.4	Helms
1956	Bill Russell (San Francisco)	6-9	Sr	20.6	Helms, UPI
1957	Chet Forte (Columbia)	5-9	Sr	28.9	UPI
	Lenny Rosenbluth (N. Carolina)	6-5	Sr	28.0	Helms
1958	**Oscar Robertson (Cincinnati)**	**6-5**	**So**	**35.1**	**UPI**
	Elgin Baylor (Seattle)	6-6	Sr	32.5	Helms
1959	**Oscar Robertson (Cincinnati)**	**6-5**	**Jr**	**32.6**	**Helms, UPI, USBWA**
1960	**Oscar Robertson (Cincinnati)**	**6-5**	**Sr**	**33.7**	**Helms, UPI, USBWA**
1961	Jerry Lucas (Ohio State)	6-8	Jr	24.9	Helms, AP, UPI, USBWA
1962	Jerry Lucas (Ohio State)	6-8	Sr	21.8	AP, UPI, USBWA
	Paul Hogue (Cincinnati)	6-9	Sr	16.8	Helms
1963	Art Heyman (Duke)	6-5	Sr	24.9	Helms, AP, UPI, USBWA
1964	Gary Bradds (Ohio State)	6-8	Sr	30.6	AP, UPI
	Walt Hazzard (UCLA)	6-2	Sr	18.6	Helms, USBWA
1965	Bill Bradley (Princeton)	6-5	Sr	30.5	Helms, AP, UPI, USBWA
	Gail Goodrich (UCLA)	6-1	Sr	24.8	Helms
1966	Cazzie Russell (Michigan)	6-5	Sr	30.8	Helms, AP, UPI, USBWA
1967	Lew Alcindor (UCLA)	7-2	So	29.0	Helms, AP, UPI, USBWA
1968	Elvin Hayes (Houston)	6-8	Sr	36.8	AP, UPI, USBWA
	Lew Alcindor (UCLA)	7.2	Jr	26.2	Helms
1969	Lew Alcindor (UCLA)	7-2	Sr	24.0	Helms, AP, UPI, USBWA, Naismith
1970	**Pete Maravich (LSU)**	**6-5**	**Sr**	**44.5**	**Helms, AP, UPI, USBWA, Naismith**
	Sidney Wicks (UCLA)	6-8	Jr.	18.6	Helms
1971	Austin Carr (Notre Dame)	6-9	Sr.	20.6	AP, UPI, Naismith
	Sidney Wicks (UCLA)	6-8	Sr	21.3	USBWA
1972	Bill Walton (UCLA)	6-11	So	21.1	AP, UPI, USBWA, Naismith
1973	Bill Walton (UCLA)	6-11	Jr	20.4	AP, UPI, USBWA, Naismith
1974	Bill Walton (UCLA)	6-11	Sr	19.3	UPI, USBWA, Naismith
	David Thompson (N. Caro. St)	6-4	Jr	26.0	AP
1975	David Thompson (N. Caro. St)	6-4	Sr	29.9	AP, UPI, NABC, USBWA, Naismith
1976	Scott May (Indiana)	6-7	Sr	23.5	AP, UPI, NABC, Naismith
	Adrian Dantley (Notre Dame)	6-5	Jr	28.6	USBWA
1977	Marques Johnson (UCLA)	6-7	Sr	21.4	AP, UPI, NABC, USBWA, Naismith, Wooden
1978	Phil Ford (North Carolina)	6-2	Sr	20.8	NABC, USBWA, Wooden
	Butch Lee (Marquette)	6-2	Sr	17.7	AP, UPI, Naismith
1979	Larry Bird (Indiana State)	6-9	Sr	28.6	AP, UPI, NABC, USBWA, Naismith, Wooden
1980	Mark Aguirre (DePaul)	6-7	So	26.8	AP, UPI, USBWA, Naismith
	Michael Brooks (La Salle)	6-7	Sr	24.1	NABC
	Darrell Griffith (Louisville)	6-4	Sr	22.9	Wooden
1981	Ralph Sampson (Virginia)	7-4	So	17.7	AP, UPI, USBWA, Naismith
	Danny Ainge (Brigham Young)	6-5	Sr	24.4	NABC, Wooden
1982	Ralph Sampson (Virginia)	7-4	Jr	15.8	AP, UPI, NABC, USBWA, Naismith, Wooden
1983	Ralph Sampson (Virginia)	7-4	Sr	19.0	AP, UPI, NABC, USBWA, Naismith, Wooden
1984	Michael Jordan (North Carolina)	6-6	Jr	19.6	AP, UPI, NABC, USBWA, Naismith, Wooden
1985	Chris Mullin (St. John's)	6-6	Sr	19.8	UPI, USBWA, Wooden
	Patrick Ewing (Georgetown)	7-0	Sr	14.6	AP, NABC, Naismith
1986	Walter Berry (St. John's)	6-8	Sr	23.0	AP, UPI, NABC, USBWA, Wooden
	Johnny Dawkins (Duke)	6-2	Sr	20.2	Naismith
1987	David Robinson (Navy)	6-11	Sr	28.2	AP, UPI, NABC, USBWA, Naismith, Wooden

1988	Hersey Hawkins (Bradley)	6-3	Sr	36.3	AP, UPI, USBWA
	Danny Manning (Kansas)	6-10	Sr	24.8	NABC, Naismith, Wooden
1989	Danny Ferry (Duke)	6-10	Sr	22.6	UPI, USBWA, Naismith
	Sean Elliott (Arizona)	6-8	Sr	22.3	AP, NABC, Wooden
1990	Lionel Simmons (La Salle)	6-7	Sr	26.5	AP, UPI, NABC, USBWA, Naismith, Wooden
1991	Larry Johnson (UNLV)	6-7	Sr	22.7	NABC, USBWA, Naismith, Wooden
	Shaquille O'Neal (LSU)	7-1	So	27.6	AP, UPI
1992	Christian Laettner (Duke)	6-11	Sr	21.5	AP, NABC, USBWA, Naismith, Wooden
	Jim Jackson (Ohio State)	6-6	Jr	22.4	UPI
1993	Calbert Cheaney (Indiana)	6-7	Sr	22.4	AP, UPI, NABC, USBWA, Naismith, Wooden
1994	**Glenn Robinson (Purdue)**	**6-8**	**Jr**	**30.3**	**AP, UPI, NABC, USBWA, Naismith, Wooden**

National College Coaches of the Year

Key: (NCAA) after won-lost record indicates coach of NCAA Tournament winner, **UPI** = United Press International, **AP** = Associated Press, **USBWA** = United States Basketball Writers' Association, **NABC** = National Association of Basketball Coaches, **Naismith** = James Naismith Award.

Year	Coach (School)	Season Record Overall	Conference	Award(s)
1955	Phil Woolpert (San Francisco)	28-1	12-0 (NCAA)	UPI
1956	Phil Woolpert (San Francisco)	29-0	14-0 (NCAA)	UPI
1957	Frank McGuire (North Carolina)	27-0	14-0 (NCAA)	UPI
1958	Tex Winter (Kansas State)	22-5	10-2	UPI
1959	Eddie Hickey (Marquette)	23-6	NA	USBWA
	Adolph Rupp (Kentucky)	24-3	12-2	UPI
1960	Pete Newell (California)	28-2	11-1	UPI, USBWA
1961	Fred Taylor (Ohio State)	27-1	14-0	UPI, USBWA
1962	Fred Taylor (Ohio State)	26-2	13-1	UPI, USBWA
1963	Ed Jucker (Cincinnati)	26-2	11-1	UPI, USBWA
1964	John Wooden (UCLA)	30-0	15-0 (NCAA)	UPI, USBWA
1965	Dave Strack (Michigan)	24-4	13-1	UPI
	Butch van Breda Kolff (Princeton)	23-6	13-1	USBWA
1966	Adolph Rupp (Kentucky)	27-2	15-1	UPI, USBWA
1967	John Wooden (UCLA)	30-0	14-0 (NCAA)	AP, UPI, USBWA
1968	Guy Lewis (Houston)	31-2	NA	AP, UPI, NABC, USBWA
1969	John Wooden (UCLA)	29-1	13-1 (NCAA)	AP, UPI, NABC
	Maury John (Drake)	26-5	13-3	USBWA
1970	John Wooden (UCLA)	28-2	12-2 (NCAA)	AP, UPI, NABC, USBWA
1971	Al McGuire (Marquette)	28-1	NA	AP, UPI, USBWA
	Jack Kraft (Villanova)	23-6	NA	NABC
1972	John Wooden (UCLA)	30-0	14-0 (NCAA)	AP, UPI, NABC, USBWA
1973	John Wooden (UCLA)	30-0	14-0 (NCAA)	AP, UPI, USBWA
	Gene Bartow (Memphis State)	24-6	12-2	NABC
1974	Al McGuire (Marquette)	26-5	NA	NABC
	Digger Phelps (Notre Dame)	26-3	NA	UPI
	Norm Sloan (North Carolina State)	30-1	12-0 (NCAA)	AP, USBWA
1975	Bob Knight (Indiana)	31-1	18-0	AP, UPI, NABC, USBWA
1976	Bob Knight (Indiana)	32-0	18-0 (NCAA)	AP, USBWA
	Johnny Orr (Michigan)	25-7	14-4	NABC
	Tom Young (Rutgers)	31-2	NA	UPI
1977	Bob Gaillard (San Francisco)	29-2	14-0	AP, UPI
	Dean Smith (North Carolina)	28-5	9-3	NABC
	Eddie Sutton (Arkansas)	26-2	16-0	USBWA
1978	Eddie Sutton (Arkansas)	32-4	14-2	AP, UPI
	Ray Meyer (DePaul)	27-3	NA	USBWA
	Bill Foster (Duke)	27-7	8-4	NABC (Tie)
	Abe Lemons (Texas)	26-5	14-2	NABC (Tie)
1979	Bill Hodges (Indiana State)	33-1	16-0	AP, UPI
	Ray Meyer (DePaul)	26-6	NA	NABC
	Dean Smith (North Carolina)	23-6	9-3	USBWA

1980	Ray Meyer (DePaul)	26-2	NA	AP, UPI, USBWA
	Lute Olson (Iowa)	23-10	10-8	NABC
1981	Ralph Miller (Oregon State)	26-2	17-1	AP, UPI, USBWA, NABC (Tie)
	Jack Hartman (Kansas State)	24-9	9-5	NABC (Tie)
1982	Ralph Miller (Oregon State)	25-5	16-2	AP
	Don Monson (Idaho)	27-3	13-1	NABC
	Norm Stewart (Missouri)	27-4	12-2	UPI
	John Thompson (Georgetown)	30-7	10-4	USBWA
1983	Lou Carnesecca (St. John's)	28-5	12-4	USBWA, NABC
	Guy Lewis (Houston)	31-3	16-0	AP
	Jerry Tarkanian (UNLV)	28-3	15-1	UPI
1984	Ray Meyer (DePaul)	27-3	NA	AP, UPI
	Marv Harshman (Washington)	24-7	15-3	NABC
	Gene Keady (Purdue)	22-7	15-3	USBWA
1985	Lou Carnesecca (St. John's)	31-4	15-1	UPI, USBWA
	Bill Frieder (Michigan)	26-4	16-2	AP
	John Thompson (Georgetown)	35-3	14-2	NABC
1986	Eddie Sutton (Kentucky)	32-4	17-1	AP, NABC
	Mike Krzyzewski (Duke)	37-3	12-2	UPI
	Dick Versace (Bradley)	32-3	16-0	USBWA
1987	John Chaney (Temple)	32-4	17-1	USBWA
	Tom Davis (Iowa)	30-5	14-4	AP
	Bob Knight (Indiana)	30-4	15-3 (NCAA)	Naismith
	Pick Pitino (Providence)	25-9	10-6	NABC
	John Thompson (Georgetown)	29-5	12-4	UPI
1988	John Chaney (Temple)	32-2	18-0	AP, UPI, NABC, USBWA
	Larry Brown (Kansas)	27-11	9-5 (NCAA)	Naismith
1989	Bob Knight (Indiana)	27-8	15-3	AP, UPI, USBWA
	P.J. Carlesimo (Seton Hall)	31-7	11-5	NABC
	Mike Krzyzewski (Duke)	28-8	9-5	Naismith
1990	Jim Calhoun (Connecticut)	31-6	12-4	AP, UPI
	Bobby Cremins (Georgia Tech)	28-7	8-6	Naismith
	Jud Heathcote (Michigan State)	28-6	15-3	NABC
	Roy Williams (Kansas)	30-5	11-3	USBWA
1991	Randy Ayers (Ohio State)	27-4	15-3	AP, Naismith, USBWA
	Mike Krzyzewski (Duke)	32-7	11-3 (NCAA)	NABC
	Rick Majerus (Utah)	30-4	15-1	UPI
1992	Perry Clark (Tulane)	21-8	8-4	UPI, USBWA
	Mike Krzyzewski (Duke)	34-2	14-2 (NCAA)	Naismith
	George Ravling (So. California)	24-6	15-3	NABC
	Roy Williams (Kansas)	27-5	11-3	AP
1993	Eddie Fogler (Vanderbilt)	28-6	14-2	AP, UPI, NABC, USBWA
	Dean Smith (North Carolina)	28-1	12-0	UPI
1994	Norm Stewart (Missouri)	28-4	14-0	AP, UPI
	Nolan Richardson (Arkansas)	31-3	14-2 (NCAA)	Naismith
	Charlie Spoonhour (St. Louis)	23-6	8-4	USBWA
	Gene Keady (Purdue)	29-5	14-4	NABC

NCAA Individual Player Records

Chronology of College Basketball Records

Modern-era records begin with 1937-38 season, first without center jump after each field goal.

National scoring and shooting statistics compiled beginning with 1947-48 season.

Individual rebounding statistics compiled beginning with 1950-51 season.

Assists records compiled beginning with 1983-84 season.

Blocked shots records compiled beginning with 1985-86 season.

Three-point field goal added in 1986-87 season.

Freshmen became eligible for varsity competition beginning with 1973-74 season.

Women's statistics compiled beginning with 1981-82 season.

Men's Individual Records, Division I (1938-1994)

Points Scored, Game .... Frank Selvy (Furman), **100** (vs. Newberry, 2-13-1954)
(Against Division I Schools) .... Kevin Bradshaw (US International), **72** (vs. Loyola Marymount, 1-5-1991)
Points Scored, Season .... Pete Maravich (LSU), **1381** (1970)
Points Scored, Career .... Pete Maravich (LSU), **3667** (1968-70)
Scoring Average, Season .... Pete Maravich (LSU), **44.5** (1970)
Scoring Average, Career .... Pete Maravich (LSU), **44.2** (1968-70)
Most Games Scoring Double Figures .... Danny Manning (Kansas), **132** (1985-88)
Most Field Goals, Game .... Frank Selvy (Furman), **41** (vs. Newberry, 2-13-1954)
Most Field Goals, Season .... Pete Maravich (LSU), **522** (1970)
Most Field Goals, Career .... Pete Maravich (LSU), **1387** (1968-70)
Most Field Goal Attempts, Game .... Jay Handlan (Washington & Lee), **71** (vs. Furman, 2-17-1951)
Most Field-Goal Attempts, Season .... Pete Maravich (LSU), **1168** (1970)
Most Field-Goal Attempts, Career .... Pete Maravich (LSU), **3166** (1968-70)
Field-Goal Percentage, Season .... Steve Johnson (Oregon State), **.746** (1981)
Field-Goal Percentage, Career .... Ricky Nedd (Appalachian State), **.690** (1991-94)
Three-Point Field Goals, Game .... Dave Jamerson (Ohio), **14** (vs. Charleston, 12-21-1989)
Askia Jones (Kansas State), **14** (vs. Fresno State, 3-24-1994)

Three-Point Field Goals, Season .... Darrin Fitzgerald (Butler), **158** (1986-87)
Three-Point Field Goals, Career .... Doug Day (Radford), **401** (1990-93)
Free Throws Made, Game .... Pete Maravich (LSU), **30** (vs. Oregon State, 12-22-1969)
Free Throws Made, Season .... Frank Selvy (Furman), **355** (1953-54)
Free Throws Made, Career .... Dickie Hemric (Wake Forest), **905** (1952-55, 4 seasons)
Pete Maravich (LSU), **893** (1968-70, 3 seasons)

Consecutive Free Throws, Game .... Arlen Clark (Oklahoma State), **24** (vs. Colorado, 3-7-1959)
Consecutive Free Throws, Season .... Joe Dykstra (Western Illinois), **64** (1981-82)
Free-Throw Attempts, Game .... Ed Tooley (Brown), **36** (vs. Amherst, 12-4-1954)
Free-Throw Attempts, Season .... Frank Selvy (Furman), **444** (1953-54)
Free-Throw Attempts, Career .... Dickie Hemric (Wake Forest), **1359** (1952-55, 4 seasons)
Pete Maravich (LSU), **1152** (1968-70, 3 seasons)

Free-Throw Percentage, Season .... Craig Collins (Penn State), **.959** (1984-85)
Free-Throw Percentage, Career .... Greg Starrick (Kentucky and So. Illinois), **.909** (1969, 1970-72)
Rebounds, Game ....Bill Chambers (William & Mary), **51** (vs. Virginia, 2-14-1953)
Rebounds, Season .... Walter Dukes (Seton Hall), **734** (1952-53)
Rebounds, Career .... Tom Gola (La Salle), **2201** (1952-55)
Rebounding Average, Season .... Charlie Slack (Marshall), **25.6** (1954-55)
Rebounding Average, Career .... Artis Gilmore (Jacksonville), **22.7** (1970-71)
Assists, Game .... Tony Fairley (Charleston Southern), **22** (vs. Armstrong St., 2-9-1987)
Avery Johnson (Southern), **22** (vs. Texas Southern, 1-25-1988)
Sherman Douglas (Syracuse), **22** (vs. Providence, 1-28-1989)

Assists, Season .... Mark Wade (UNLV), **406** (1986-87)
Assists, Career .... Bobby Hurley (Duke), **1076** (1990-93)
Assists Average, Season .... Avery Johnson (Southern), **13.3** (1987-88)
Assists Average, Career .... Avery Johnson (Cameron and Southern), **8.9** (1985, 1987-88)
Blocked Shots, Game ....David Robinson (Navy), **14** (vs. NC-Wilmington, 1-4-1986)
Shawn Bradley (BYU), **14** (vs. Eastern Kentucky, 12-7-1990)

Blocked Shots, Season .... David Robinson (Navy), **207** (1985-86)
Blocked Shots, Career .... Alonzo Mourning (Georgetown), **453** (1989-92)
Blocked Shots per Game, Season .... David Robinson (Navy), **5.9** (1985-86)
Blocked Shots per Game, Career .... David Robinson (Navy), **5.2** (1985-87)
Steals, Game .... Mookie Blaylock (Oklahoma), **13** (vs. Centenary, 12-12-1987)
Mookie Blaylock (Okla), **13** (vs. Loyola Marymount, 12-17-1988)

Steals, Season ....Mookie Blaylock (Oklahoma), **150** (1987-88)
Steals, Career .... Eric Murdock (Providence), **376** (1988-91)
Steals per Game, Season .... Darron Brittman (Chicago State), **5.0** (1985-86)
Steals per Game, Career ....Mookie Blaylock (Oklahoma), **3.8** (1987-89)
Games Played, Career .... Christian Laettner (Duke), **148** (1989-92)

College Basketball's 20-20 Men
20 Points Per Game and 20 Rebounds Per Game for College Career

Name (School)	Years Played	Points Per Game	Rebounds Per Game
Walter Dukes (Seton Hall)	1952-1953	23.5	21.1
Bill Russell (San Francisco)	1954-1956	20.7	20.3
Paul Silas (Creighton)	1962-1964	20.5	21.6
Julius Erving (Massachusetts)	1970-1971	26.3	20.2
Artis Gilmore (Jacksonville)	1970-1971	24.3	22.7
Kermit Washington (American)	1971-1973	20.1	20.2

Men's Individual Records, Division II (1938-1994)

Points Scored, Game .... Clarence (Bevo) Francis (Rio Grande), **113** (vs. Hillsdale, 2-2-1954)
Points Scored, Season .... Earl Monroe (Winston-Salem), **1329** (1966-67)
Points Scored, Career .... Travis Grant (Kentucky State), **4045** (1969-72)
Scoring Average, Season .... Clarence (Bevo) Francis (Rio Grande), **46.5** (1953-54)
Scoring Average, Career .... Travis Grant (Kentucky State), **33.4** (1969-72)
Most Field Goals, Game .... Clarence (Bevo) Francis (Rio Grande), **38** (vs. Alliance, 1-16-1954)
Clarence (Bevo) Francis (Rio Grande), **38** (vs. Hillsdale, 2-2-1954)

Most Field Goals, Season .... Travis Grant (Kentucky State), **539** (1971-72)
Most Field Goals, Career .... Travis Grant (Kentucky State), **1760** (1969-72)
Most Field Goal Attempts, Game .... Clarence (Bevo) Francis (Rio Grande), **71** (vs. Alliance, 1-16-1954)
Most Field Goal Attempts, Season .... Jim Toombs (Stillman), **925** (1964-65)
Most Field Goal Attempts, Career .... Bob Hopkins (Grambling), **3309** (1953-56)
Field Goal Percentage, Season .... Todd Linder (Tampa), **.752** (1986-87)
Field Goal Percentage, Career .... Todd Linder (Tampa), **.708** (1984-87)
Three-Point Field Goals, Game .... Andy Schmidtmann (Wisc-Parkside), **14** (vs. Lakeland, 2-14-1989)
Three-Point Field Goals, Season .... Alex Williams (California State-Sacramento), **167** (1987-88)
Three-Point Field Goals, Career .... Tony Smith (Pfeiffer), **431** (1989-92)
Free Throws Made, Game .... Clarence (Bevo) Francis (Rio Grande), **37** (vs. Hillsdale, 2-2-1954)
Free Throws Made, Season .... Joe Miller (Alderson-Broaddus), **401** (1956-57)
Free Throws Made, Career .... Joe Miller (Alderson-Broaddus), **1130** (1954-57)
Consecutive Free Throws, Game .... Carl Hartman (Alderson-Broaddus), **23** (vs. Salem, 12-6-1954)
Consecutive Free Throws, Season .... Mike Hall (Adams State), **74** (1991-92)
Free-Throw Attempts, Game .... Clarence (Bevo) Francis (Rio Grande), **45** (vs. Hillsdale, 2-2-1954)
Free-Throw Attempts, Season .... Clarence (Bevo) Francis (Rio Grande), **510** (1953-54)
Free-Throw Attempts, Career .... Joe Miller (Alderson-Broaddus), **1460** (1954-57)
Free-Throw Percentage, Season .... Kent Andrews (McNeese State), **.944** (1967-68)
Billy Newton (Morgan State), **.944** (1975-76)

Free-Throw Percentage, Career .... Kent Andres (McNeese State), **.916** (1967-69)
Rebounds, Game .... Tom Hart (Middlebury), **46** (vs. Trinity-Hartford, 2-5-1955)
Tom Hart (Middlebury), **46** (vs. Clarkson, 2-12-1955)

Rebounds, Season .... Elmore Smith (Kentucky State), **799** (1970-71)
Rebounds, Career .... Jim Smith (Steubenville), **2334** (1955-58)
Rebounding Average, Season .... Tom Hart (Middlebury), **29.5** (1955-56)
Rebounding Average, Career .... Tom Hart (Middlebury), **27.6** (1953, 1955-56)
Assists, Game .... Ali Baaqar (Morris Brown), **25** (vs. Albany State, 1-26-1991)
Adrian Hutt (Metropolitan St.), **25** (vs. Cal-Sacramento, 2-9-1991)

Assists, Season .... Steve Ray (Bridgeport), **400** (1988-89)
Assists, Career .... Demetri Beekman (Assumption), **1044** (1990-93)
Assists Average, Season .... Steve Ray (Bridgeport), **12.5** (1988-89)
Assists Average, Career .... Steve Ray (Bridgeport), **12.1** (1988-90)
Blocked Shots, Game .... Mark Hensel (Pitt-Johnstown), **15** (vs. Slippery Rock, 1-22-1994)
Blocked Shots, Season .... Antonio Harvey (Pfeiffer), **155** (1992-93)
Blocked Shots per Game, Season .... Antonio Harvey (Pfeiffer), **5.3** (1992-93)
Steals, Game .... Ken Francis (Molloy), **11** (vs. Concordia, 1-29-1994)
Aaron Johnson (C.W. Post), **11** (vs. Concordia, 1-22-1994)
Steve Maryin (Bowie State), **11** (vs. Shaw, 11-29-1993)

Steals, Season .... Ken Francis (Molloy), **116** (1993-94)
Tyronne McDaniel (Lenoir-Rhyne), **116** (1992-93)
Steals per Game, Season .... Ken Francis (Molloy), **4.3** (1993-94)
Games Played, Career .... Pat Morris (Bridgeport), **133** (1989-92)

Women's Individual Records, Division I (1982-1994)

Points Scored, Game .... Cindy Brown (Long Beach State), **60** (vs. San Jose St., 2-16-1987)
Points Scored, Season .... Cindy Brown (Long Beach State), **974** (1986-87)
Points Scored, Career .... Patricia Hoskins (Mississippi Valley), **3122** (1985-89)
Scoring Average, Season .... Patricia Hoskins (Mississippi Valley), **33.6** (1988-89)
Scoring Average, Career .... Patricia Hoskins (Mississippi Valley), **28.4** (1985-89)
Most Field Goals, Game .... Lorri Bauman (Drake), **27** (vs. Southwest Missouri St., 1-6-1984)
Most Field Goals, Season .... Barbara Kennedy (Clemson), **392** (1981-82)
Most Field Goals, Career .... Joyce Walker (LSU), **1259** (1981-84)
Field Goal Percentage, Season .... Renay Adams (Tennessee Tech), **.717** (1990-91)
Field Goal Percentage, Career .... Regina Days (Georgia Southern), **.651** (1984-88)
Three-Point Field Goals, Season .... Lisa McMullen (Alabama State), **126** (1990-91)
Three-Point Field Goals, Career .... Karen Middleton (South Carolina), **317** (1987-91)
Free Throws Made, Game .... Shaunda Green (Washington), **23** (vs. No. Illinois, 11-30-1991)
Free Throws Made, Season .... Lorri Bauman (Drake), **275** (1981-82)
Free Throws Made, Career .... Lorri Bauman (Drake), **907** (1981-84)
Consecutive Free Throws, Season .... Ginny Doyle (Richmond), **60** (1991-92)
Free-Throw Attempts, Game .... Renee Daniels (Southeastern La.), **31** (vs. New Orleans, 1-23-1985)
Free-Throw Attempts, Season .... Kristy Ryan (Cal-State, Sacramento), **353** (1993-94)
Free-Throw Attempts, Career .... Valorie Whiteside (Appalachian State), **1173** (1984-88)
Free-Throw Percentage, Season .... Ginny Doyle (Richmond), **.950** (1991-92)
Free-Throw Percentage, Career .... Karen Murray (Washington), **.876** (1981-84)
Rebounds, Game .... Deborah Temple (Delta State), **40** (vs. UAB, 2-14-1983)
Rebounds, Season .... Wanda Ford (Drake), **534** (1984-85)
Rebounds, Career .... Wanda Ford (Drake), **1887** (1983-86)
Rebounding Average, Season .... Rosina Pearson (Bethune-Cookman), **18.5** (1984-85)
Rebounding Average, Career .... Wanda Ford (Drake), **16.1** (1983-86)
Assists, Game .... Michelle Burden (Kent State), **23** (vs. Ball State, 2-6-1991)
Assists, Season .... Suzie McConnell (Penn State), **355** (1986-87)
Assists, Career .... Suzie McConnell (Penn State), **1307** (1984-88)
Assists Average, Season .... Suzie McConnell (Penn State), **11.8** (1986-87)
Assists Average, Career .... Neacole Hall (Alabama State), **10.3** (1986-89)
Blocked Shots, Season .... Michelle Wilson (Texas Southern), **151** (1988-89)
Blocked Shots, Career .... Genia Miller (Cal-State, Fullerton), **428** (1987-91)
Steals, Season .... Natalie White (Florida A&M), **172** (1993-94)
Steals, Career .... Heidi Caruso (Lafayette), **532** (1990-94)
Steals per Game, Season .... Natalie White (Florida A&M), **6.1** (1993-94)
Steals per Game, Career .... Neacole Hall (Alabama State), **4.9** (1987-89)

Women's All-Americans (Division I after 1983)
(Naismith Trophy Winner in Boldface)

1975 - Carolyn Bush (Wayland Baptist), Marianne Crawford (Immaculata), Nancy Dunkle (Cal-State, Fullerton), Lusia Harris (Delta State), Jan Irby (William Penn), Ann Meyers (UCLA), Brenda Moeller (Wayland Baptist), Debbie Oing (Indiana), Sue Rojcewicz (Southern Connecticut), Susan Yow (Elon)

1976 - Carol Blazejowski (Montclair State), Cindy Brogdon (Mercer), Nancy Dunkle (Cal-State, Fullerton), Doris Felderhoff (Stephen Austin), Lusia Harris (Delta State), Ann Meyers (UCLA), Maryann Crawford Stanley (Immaculata), Pearl Worrell (Wayland Baptist), Susan Yow (North Carolina State), Susie Kudrna (William Penn)

1977 - Carol Blazejowski (Montclair State), Nancy Dunkle (Cal-State, Fullerton), Rita Easterling (Mississippi College), Susie Snider Eppers (Baylor), Doris Felderhoff (Stephen Austin), Lusia Harris (Delta State), Charlotte Lewis (Illinois State), Ann Meyers (UCLA), Patricia Roberts (Tennessee), Mary Scharff (Immaculata)

1978 - Genia Beasley (North Carolina State), Carol Blazejowski (Montclair State), Debbie Brock (Delta State), Cindy Brogdon (Tennessee), Julie Gross (LSU), Althea Gwyn (Queens), Kathy Harston (Wayland Baptist), Nancy Lieberman (Old Dominion), Ann Meyers (UCLA), Lynette Woodard (Kansas)

1979 - Cindy Brogson (Tennessee), Carol Chason (Valdosta State), Pat Colasardo (Montclair State), Denise Curry (UCLA), Nancy Lieberman (Old Dominion), Jill Rankin (Wayland Baptist), Susan Taylor (Valdosta State), Rosie Walker (Stephen Austin), Franci Washington (Ohio State), Lynette Woodard (Kansas)

1980 - Denise Curry (UCLA), Tina Gunn (BYU), Pam Kelly (Louisiana Tech), Nancy Lieberman (Old Dominion), Inge Nissen (Old Dominion), Jill Rankin (Tennessee), Susan Taylor (Valdosta State), Rosie Walker (Stephen Austin), Holly Warlick (Tennessee State), Lynette Woodard (Kansas)

1981 - Denise Curry (UCLA), Anne Donovan (Old Dominion), Pam Kelly (Louisiana Tech), Kris Kirchner (Rutgers), Carol Menken (Oregon State), Cindy Noble (Tennessee), LaTaunya Pollard (Long Beach State), Bev Smith (Oregon), Valerie Walker (Cheyney State), Lynette Woodard (Kansas)

1982 - Pam Kelly (Louisiana Tech), Angela Turner (Louisiana Tech), Valerie Walker (Cheyney State), Bev Smith (Oregon), Jerilynn Harper (Tennessee Tech), Janet Harris (Georgia), Barbara Kennedy (Clemson), June Olkowski (Rutgers), Mary Ostrowski (Tennessee), Valerie Still (Kentucky)

1983 - **Anne Donovan (Old Dominion)**, Valerie Still (Kentucky), LaTaunya Pollard (Long Beach State), Paula McGee (Southern Cal), Cheryl Miller (Southern Cal), Janice Lawrence (Louisiana Tech), Tanya Haave (Tennessee), Joyce Walker (LSU), Jasmina Perazic (Maryland), Priscilla Gary (Kansas State)

1984 - Pam McGee (Southern Cal), **Cheryl Miller (Southern Cal)**, Janice Lawrence (Louisiana Tech), Yolanda Laney (Cheyney State), Tresa Brown (North Carolina), Janet Harris (Georgia), Becky Jackson (Auburn), Annette Smith (Texas), Marilyn Stephens (Temple), Joyce Walker (LSU)

1985 - Anucha Browne (Northwestern), Sheila Collins (Tennessee), Kristen Cummings (Long Beach State), Medina Dixon (Old Dominion), Teresa Edwards (Georgia), Kamie Ethridge (Texas), Janet Harris (Georgia), Eun Jung Lee (Northeast Louisiana), Pam Grant (Louisiana Tech), **Cheryl Miller (Southern Cal)**

1986 - **Cheryl Miller (Southern Cal)**, Kamie Ethridge (Texas), Lillie Mason (Western Kentucky), Teresa Edwards (Georgia), Cindy Brown (Long Beach State), Wanda Ford (Drake), Jennifor Gillom (Mississippi), Pam Leake (North Carolina), Katrina McLain (Georgia), Sue Wicks (Rutgers)

1987 - Cindy Brown (Long Beach State), **Clarissa Davis (Texas)**, Tracey Hall (Ohio State University), Donna Holt (Virginia), Andrea Lloyd (Texas), Katrina McLain (Georgia), Vickie Orr (Auburn), Shelly Pennefather (Villanova), Teresa Weatherspoon (Louisiana Tech), Sue Wicks (Rutgers)

1988 - Michelle Edward (Iowa), Bridgette Gordon (Tennessee), Tracey Hall (Ohio State), Donna Holt (Virginia), Suzie McConnell (Penn State), Vickie Orr (Auburn), Penny Toler (Long Beach State), Teresa Weatherspoon (Louisiana Tech), Beverly Williams (Texas), **Sue Wicks (Rutgers)**

1989 - Jennifer Azzi (Stanford), Vicky Bullett (Maryland), **Clarissa Davis (Texas)**, Bridgette Gordon (Tennessee), Nora Lewis (Louisiana Tech), Nikita Lowry (Ohio State), Vickie Orr (Auburn), Chana Perry (San Diego State), Deanna Tate (Maryland), Penny Toler (Long Beach State)

1990 - Venus Lacey (Louisiana Tech), **Jennifer Azzi (Stanford)**, Dawn Staley (Virginia), Carolyn Jones (Auburn), Andrea Stinson (North Carolina State), Franthea Price (Iowa), Daedra Charles (Tennessee), Dale Hodges (St. Joseph's), Portia Hill (Stephen Austin), Wendy Scholtens (Vanderbilt)

1991 - Daedra Charles (Tennessee), Sonja Henning (Stanford), Kerry Bascom (Connecticut), Joy Holmes (Purdue), Andrea Stinson (North Carolina State), **Dawn Staley (Virginia)**, Genia Miller (Cal-State, Fullerton), Delmonica DeHorney (Arkansas), Carolyn Jones (Auburn), Dana Chatman (LSU)

1992 - Shannon Cate (Montana), Dena Head (Tennessee), MaChelle Joseph (Purdue), Rosemary Kosiorek (West Virginia), Tammi Reiss (Virginia), Susan Robinson (Penn State), Frances Savage (Miami-Florida), **Dawn Staley (Virginia)**, Sheryl Swoopes (Texas Tech), Val Whiting (Stanford)

1993 - Andrea Congreaves (Mercer), Toni Foster (Iowa), Lauretta Freeman (Auburn), Heidi Gillingham (Vanderbilt), Lisa Harrison (Tennessee), Katie Smith (Ohio State), Karen Jennings (Nebraska), **Sheryl Swoopes (Texas Tech)**, Milica Vukadinovic (California), Val Whiting (Stanford)

1994 - Jessica Barr (Clemson), Janice Felder (Southern Mississippi), Niesa Johnson (Alabama), **Lisa Leslie (Southern Cal)**, Rebecca Lobo (Connecticut), Nikki McCray (Tennessee), Andrea Nagy (Florida International), Tonya Sampson (North Carolina), Carol Ann Shudlick (Minnesota), Natalie Williams (UCLA)

College Basketball Reading List

Albom, Mitch. *Fab Five — Basketball, Trash Talk and the American Dream.* New York: Warner Books, 1993.

Ashe Jr., Arthur R. *A Hard Road to Glory: Basketball — The African-American Athlete in Basketball.* New York: Amistad (Penguin), 1993.

Beall Barns, Rebecca (Editor). *At the Rim: A Celebration of Women's Collegiate Basketball.* Charlottesville, Virginia: Eastman Kodak and Thomasson-Grant Company, 1991.

Bell, Marty. *The Legend of Dr. J. — The Story of Julius Erving.* New York: Coward, McCann & Geoghegan, 1975.

Benagh, Jim. *Basketball: Startling Stories Behind the Records.* New York: Sterling Publishing, 1991.

Bjarkman, Peter C. *ACC Basketball.* Indianapolis: Masters Press (Howard W. Sams), 1996.

Bjarkman, Peter C. *Big Ten Basketball.* 2nd Edition. Indianapolis: Masters Press (Howard W. Sams), 1994.

Bollig, Laura E. (Editor). *NCAA Basketball's Finest: All-Time Great Men's Collegiate Players and Coaches.* Overland Park, Kansas: NCAA (National Collegiate Athletic Association), 1991.

Brill, Bill and Mike Krzyzewski. *A Season is a Lifetime: The Inside Story of the Duke Blue Devils and Their Championship Season.* New York: Simon and Schuster, 1993.

Brill, Bill. *Duke Basketball: An Illustrated History, 1906-1986.* Dallas, Texas: Taylor Publishing Company, 1986.

Brown, Gene (Editor). *The Complete Book of Basketball — The New York Times Scrapbook Encyclopedia.* Indianapolis: Bobbs-Merrill, 1980.

Clary, Jack. *Basketball's Greatest Moments.* New York: McGraw-Hill Book Company, 1988.

Cole, Lewis. *Never Too Young to Die: The Death of Len Bias.* New York: Pantheon Books, 1989.

Cole, Lewis. *A Loose Game: The Sport and Business of Basketball.* Indianapolis: The Bobbs-Merrill Company, 1978.

Devaney, John. *The Story of Basketball.* New York and Toronto: Random House, 1976.

Douchant, Mike. *Encyclopedia of College Basketball.* Washington, D. C. and Detroit: Visible Ink, 1994.

Feinstein, John. *A Season on the Brink: A Year with Bob Knight and the Indiana Hoosiers.* New York: Macmillan Company, 1986.

Fox, Larry. *The Illustrated History of Basketball.* New York: Grosset and Dunlap, 1974.

Garber, Angus. *Hoops! Highlights, History, and Superstars of Professional and Collegiate Basketball.* New York: Mallard Press, 1992.

George, Nelson. *Elevating the Game: Black Men and Basketball.* New York: HarperCollins, 1992.

Gergen, Joe. *The Final Four — An Illustrated History of College Basketball's Showcase Event.* St. Louis, Missouri: The Sporting News, 1987.

Gutman, Bill. *The History of NCAA Basketball.* New York: Crescent Books (Random House), 1992.

Gutman, Bill. *The Pictorial History of College Basketball.* New York: Gallery Books (W. H. Smith), 1989.

Gutman, Bill. *Pistol Pete Maravich: The Making of a Basketball Superstar.* New York: Grosset and Dunlap, 1974 (1972).

Hill, Bob and Randall Baron. *The Amazing Basketball Book: The First 100 Years.* Louisville, Kentucky: Devyn Press, 1987.

Hollander, Zander (Editor). *The Modern Encyclopedia of Basketball.* Revised Edition. New York: Four Winds Press, 1973 (1969).

Isaacs, Neil. *All the Moves — A History of College Basketball.* Philadelphia: J. B. Lippincott, 1975.

Jacobs, Barry. *Three Paths to Glory: A Season on the Hardwood with Duke, N.C. State and North Carolina.* New York: Macmillan Company, 1993.

Jares, Joe. *Basketball — The American Game.* Chicago: Rutledge-Follett, 1971. (Chapter 2: "The Colleges — Phog, Baron and the India Rubber Man")

Jarrett, William S. *Timetables of Sports History: Basketball.* New York: Facts on File, 1990.

Kimble, Bo. *For You, Hank — The Story of Hank Gathers and Bo Kimble.* New York: Dell (Bantam), 1992.

Maravich, Pete and Darrel Campbell. *Pistol Pete: Heir to a Dream.* Nashville: Thomas Nelson Publishers, 1987.

Mellen, Joan. *Bob Knight: His Own Man.* New York: Donald I. Fine, 1988 (New York: Avon Books, 1989).

Montieth, Mark. *Passion Play: A Season with the Purdue Boilermakers and Coach Gene Keady.* Chicago: Bonus Books, 1988.

Morris, Ron (Editor). *ACC Basketball: An Illustrated History.* Chapel Hill, North Carolina: Four Corners Press, 1988.

Neely, Tim. *Hooping it Up: The Complete History of Notre Dame Basketball.* Notre Dame, Indiana: Diamond Communications, 1985.

Pace, Lee (Editor). *Return to the Top — The Inside Story of Carolina's 1993 NCAA Championship.* Chapel Hill, North Carolina: Village Sports Publishing, 1993.

Packer, Billy and Roland Lazenby. *The Golden Game — The Hot Shots, Great Moments and Classic Stories from Basketball's First 100 Years.* Dallas, Texas: Jefferson Street Press, 1991.

Packer, Billy and Roland Lazenby. *College Basketball's 25 Greatest Teams.* St. Louis, Missouri: The Sporting News, 1989.

Phil Pepe. *Stand Tall: The Lew Alcindor Story.* New York: Grosset & Dunlap, 1970.

Pettit, Bob (with Bob Wolff). *Bob Pettit: The Drive Within Me.* Englewood Cliffs, New Jersey: Prentice-Hall, 1966.

Reynolds, Bill. *Big Hoops: A Season in the Big East Conference.* New York: New American Library, 1989.

Rice, Russell. *Kentucky Basketball's Big Blue Machine.* Huntsville, Alabama: Strode Publishers, 1976.

Savage, Jim. *The Encyclopedia of the NCAA Basketball Tournament.* New York: Dell Publishing, 1990.

Smith, C. Fraser. *Lenny, Lefty, and the Chancellor — The Len Bias Tragedy and the Search for Reform in Big-Time College Basketball.* Baltimore, Maryland: Bancroft Press, 1992.

Stern, Robert. *They Were Number One: A History of the NCAA Basketball Tournament.* New York: Leisure Press, 1983.

Telander, Rick. *Heaven is a Playground.* New York: Simon and Schuster, 1988 (1976).

Valenti, John (with Ron Naclerio). *Swee' Pea and Other Playground Legends: Tales of Drugs, Violence and Basketball.* New York: Michael Kesend Publishing, 1990.

Vitale, Dick (with Mike Douchant). *Tourney Time.* Indianapolis: Masters Press (Howard W. Sams), 1993.

West, Jerry (with Bill Libby). *Mr. Clutch: The Jerry West Story.* New York: Grosset and Dunlap, 1969.

Wolf, David. *Foul! The Connie Hawkins Story.* New York: Holt, Rinehart and Winston, 1972.

Wolff, Alexander. *100 Years of Hoops — A Fond Look Back at the Sport of Basketball.* New York: Oxmoor House, 1991.

Wooden, John (with Jack Tobin). *They Call Me Coach.* Revised, Expanded and Updated Edition. Chicago: Contemporary Books, 1988 (1972).